Lecture Notes in Computer Science 1752

Edited by G. Goos, J. Hartmanis and J. van Leeuwen

Springer
Berlin
Heidelberg
New York
Barcelona
Hong Kong
London
Milan
Paris
Singapore
Tokyo

Sacha Krakowiak   Santosh Shrivastava (Eds.)

Advances in Distributed Systems

Advanced Distributed Computing:
From Algorithms to Systems

Springer

Series Editors

Gerhard Goos, Karlsruhe University, Germany
Juris Hartmanis, Cornell University, NY, USA
Jan van Leeuwen, Utrecht University, The Netherlands

Volume Editors

Sacha Krakowiak
Université Joseph Fourier, Grenoble
Laboratoire SIRAC, INRIA Rhône-Alpes
655 avenue de l'Europe, 38330 Monbonnot Saint-Martin, France
E-mail: Sacha.Krakowiak@inrialpes.fr

Santosh Shrivastava
University of Newcastle upon Tyne
Department of Computing Science
Newcastle upon Tyne NE1 7RU, UK
E-mail: Santosh.Shrivastava@ncl.ac.uk

Cataloging-in-Publication Data applied for

Die Deutsche Bibliothek -CIP-Einheitsaufnahme

Advances in distributed systems : advanced distributed computing
from algorithms to systems / Sacha Krakowiak ; Santosh Shrivastava
(ed.). - Berlin ; Heidelberg ; New York ; Barcelona ; Hong Kong ;
London ; Milan ; Paris ; Singapore ; Tokyo : Springer, 2000
(Lecture notes in computer science ; 1752)
ISBN 3-540-67196-X

CR Subject Classification (1991): C.2.4, D.1.3, C.2, D.4, F.1.2, F.2

ISSN 0302-9743
ISBN 3-540-67196-X Springer-Verlag Berlin Heidelberg New York

Springer-Verlag is a company in the BertelsmannSpringer publishing group.
© Springer-Verlag Berlin Heidelberg 2000

Typesetting: Camera-ready by author, data conversion by Boller Mediendesign
Printed on acid-free paper   SPIN 10719562   06/3142   5 4 3 2 1 0

Preface

In 1992 we initiated a research project on large scale distributed computing systems (LSDCS). It was a collaborative project involving research institutes and universities in Bologna, Grenoble, Lausanne, Lisbon, Rennes, Rocquencourt, Newcastle, and Twente. The World Wide Web had recently been developed at CERN, but its use was not yet as common place as it is today and graphical browsers had yet to be developed. It was clear to us (and to just about everyone else) that LSDCS comprising several thousands to millions of individual computer systems (nodes) would be coming into existence as a consequence both of technological advances and the demands placed by applications. We were excited about the problems of building large distributed systems, and felt that serious rethinking of many of the existing computational paradigms, algorithms, and structuring principles for distributed computing was called for. In our research proposal, we summarized the problem domain as follows: *"We expect LSDCS to exhibit great diversity of node and communications capability. Nodes will range from (mobile) laptop computers, workstations to supercomputers. Whereas mobile computers may well have unreliable, low bandwidth communications to the rest of the system, other parts of the system may well possess high bandwidth communications capability. To appreciate the problems posed by the sheer scale of a system comprising thousands of nodes, we observe that such systems will be rarely functioning in their entirety. The potential for unintentional unavailability of system services will result not only from failed hardware and software modules, but also from congested gateways and communications channels. The system is expected to change continually: nodes will be mobile, new components and services will be added, existing services will be modified, some components will be taken out of service and so forth."*

The project, named BROADCAST (standing for: Basic Research On Advanced Distributed Computing: from Algorithms to SysTems), was funded by the European Union from 1992 to 1995 under the ESPRIT Basic Research Scheme. The project continued as a working group funded by the Union from 1996 to 1999, and incorporating two industrial partners (ANSA/APM, now part of Citrix, and Chorus systems, now part of Sun Microsystems).

The papers in this volume represent some of the key research results produced by the BROADCAST partners. We have structured this volume in four parts. Part one, *Distributed Algorithms*, chapters 1-6, contains papers on topics that address fundamental issues, such as time, clocks, and ordering of events, consensus in distributed systems, group communication, and garbage collection. Part two, *Systems Architecture*, chapters 7-12, addresses system structuring issues that range from treatment of network partitions to dependable distributed objects and Web services. A number of application support environments are described in the third part, *Application Support*, chapters 13-17; these include support for Web caching, transactional workflow system, component based programming environment and support for mobile Java applications. The fourth and final part of the volume, *Case Studies*, chapters 18-21, describes a number of working systems built by the partners.

We are confident that the papers in this volume will prove rewarding to all computer scientists working in the area of distributed systems. As already stated, the work reported here, spanning from 1992 to 1999, has been funded in part by the ESPRIT Project BROADCAST (project No. 6366) and the ESPRIT Working Group BROADCAST (project no. 22455). We thank Nick Cook, who acted as the administrative coordinator during this period, for overseeing the smooth running of our research activities.

November 1999   Sacha Krakowiak
                                                       Santosh Shrivastava

Table of Contents

Part 1 Distributed Algorithms

Part 2 Systems Architecture

Part 3 Applications Support

Part 4 Case Studies

Author Index

Time in Distributed System Models and Algorithms

Paulo Veríssimo[1] and Michel Raynal[2]

[1] Univ. of Lisboa, Faculty of Sciences, Lisboa - Portugal,
pjv@di.fc.ul.pt, http://www.navigators.di.fc.ul.pt
[2] IRISA, Campus de Beaulieu, Rennes - France
raynal@irisa.fr, http://www.irisa.fr

Abstract. This chapter gives an account of recent advances with regard to both the analysis and the use of time in distributed systems models and algorithms. We discuss timed models for distributed systems, timing failures and their detection, clock synchronisation and time services for large-scale settings, real-time causal delivery and temporal order, and protocols that in one way or the other take advantage from time.

1 Introduction

This chapter gives an account of recent advances with regard to both the analysis and the use of time in distributed systems models and algorithms. We start with models for distributed systems, where we discuss timed models, in contrast with classical time-free or fully asynchronous models. This section reports work based on [23], together with some recent results [21]. Then we discuss timing failures as a consequence of the introduction of timed models, and timing failure detection, as a need for ensuring the correct operation of systems. As special case of timing failure detectors, quality-of-service failure detectors are explained. This section is based on [2, 13]. Next, we present advances on clock synchronisation and time services for large-scale (worldwide) settings. We show that despite the poor communication determinism and quality of global networks, it is possible to achieve excellent degrees of synchronisation, by resorting to hybrid algorithm structure and communication infrastructures. This section is based on [22]. We discuss real-time causal delivery and temporal order, in contrast to the classical approaches of time-free causal ordering [5], such as logical clocks, vectors or matrices [8]. We present advances that allow treating the problem of timestamp based ordering and real-time causal communication in an effective way. This section is based on [24, 25]. We finalise by giving a few examples of protocols that in one way or the other take advantage from time. This section is based on [2, 6, 7].

2 Timed System Models

The explosive growth of networked and distributed systems in several application domains has changed the way we reason about distributed systems in many ways.

S. Krakowiak, S.K. Shrivastava (Eds.): Distributed Systems, LNCS 1752, pp. 1–32, 2000.

One issue of definitive importance is the following: what model to use for large-scale interactive or mission-critical applications?

A traditional trend when large-scale, unpredictable and unreliable infrastructures are at stake (e.g. Internet) has been to use asynchronous models.

However, a large part of the emerging services has interactivity or mission-criticality requirements. That is, service must be provided on time, either because of dependability constraints (e.g. air traffic control, telecommunication intelligent network architectures), or because of user-dictated quality-of-service requirements (e.g. network transaction servers, multimedia rendering, synchronised groupware). This behaviour is materialised by *timeliness* specifications, which in essence call for synchronous system models.

2.1   Canonical Models

This status quo leaves us with a problem, since neither of the canonical models serve our purpose: fully asynchronous models do not satisfy our needs, because they do not allow timeliness specifications; on the other hand, correct operation under fully synchronous models is very difficult to achieve (if at all possible) in the large-scale infrastructures we are aiming at, since they have poor baseline timeliness properties. Given the everlasting controversy synchrony versus asynchrony, we spend some time analysing the question.

The Asynchronous Model Perspective Looking at the problem from an asynchronous model perspective, the question is that in such a model, we cannot guarantee that an execution completes by the time we would like it to complete. If faults occur, it has been shown that it is impossible to guarantee the deterministic solution of basic problems such as consensus, a statement which became known as the FLP impossibility result[16]. Moreover, from the fault-tolerance viewpoint, for example when managing replicas, we cannot even reconfigure the system deterministically to another stable state under such generic consistency models such as primary partition[9]. Fully asynchronous distributed systems are defined by the following properties:

Pa 1 *Unbounded or unknown processing delays*

Pa 2 *Unbounded or unknown message delivery delays*

Pa 3 *Unbounded or unknown local clock rate of drift*

Pa 4 *Unbounded or unknown difference of local clocks*

Failure detection has been used to assist the correct execution of distributed system protocols when failures occur. Chandra and Toueg have proposed a taxonomy and specification of failure detectors[10], which we assume the reader to be at least familiar with. They have shown that with increasingly strong failure detectors, increasingly complex problems can be solved. However, they also showed that the weakest detector that solves two of the interesting problems, consensus and atomic broadcast (they are equivalent) cannot be implemented in fully asynchronous systems. The best that can be achieved is the assurance that nothing wrong happens and that consensus is **possibly** solvable if the system remains stable for long enough and less than half the processes fail[10].

The Synchronous Model Perspective An asynchronous model expects very little from the environment. It may wait an undefined amount of time for the completion of a problem, but nothing bad happens during that period. From that sense, it is a very safe model, but not live. Indeed, from a system's builder and user perspective, availability and continuity of service provision are mandatory requirements. It we need to solve problems in bounded time, the alternative approach seems to be a synchronous model. A synchronous model is one where known bounds exist for execution duration, message delivery delay, etc.

Ps 1 *There exists a known bound* $T_{D_{max}}^1$ *on processing delays*

Ps 2 *There exists a known bound* $T_{D_{max}}^2$ *on message delivery delay*

Ps 3 *There exists a known bound* $T_{D_{max}}^3$ *on local clock rate drifts*

Ps 4 *There exists a known bound* $T_{D_{max}}^4$ *on the difference among local clocks*

Property **Ps 1** refers to the determinism in the execution time of code elements. Property **Ps 2** refers to the determinism in the time to exchange messages among participantes. It is the hardest to ensure. Property **Ps 3** refers to the existence of local clocks whose individual drift is known. Property **Ps 4** which, without loss of generality, is secured by any adequate clock synchronisation tooling, yields a *global notion of time*, i.e. local clocks are synchronised. For more detail about clock synchronisation, *see* Section 4.

In such a system, it is possible to implement a Perfect Failure Detector (pFD), and all hard problems are solvable (e.g. consensus, atomic broadcast, clock synchronisation) [10]. However, because we want to target applications and environments that have a dynamic behavior, it becomes very difficult to evaluate a worst-case scenario in such conditions.

2.2 Partial Synchrony Models

Given the above discussion, the fundamental problem is how to run distributed algorithms in bounded time, and its hardness boils down to achieving reliable and timely communication in a distributed system over an infrastructure with uncertain timeliness, i.e. one that is neither fully synchronous, nor fully asynchronous.

Quasi-Synchronous Model Perspective The power of the quasi-synchronous (QS) model[23] lies in its resiliency to failure of timing assumptions. The approach is based on the observation of two aspects of real-life environments:

- the worst-case delays are much larger than the normal-case ones;
- the degree of synchronism is not the same everywhere in the system.

The first fact is illustrated in Figure 1. In fact, in real environments, the distribution function for the time it takes for an activity to complete, rather than being a step, has a shape similar to the one represented in the figure. The worst-case delivery time $(T_{D_{max}})$ if it exists, is much higher than the normal case, such that it becomes useless. The assumption of shorter, artificial bounds $(T_{D'_{max}}$ or $T_{D''_{max}})$ renders the environment useful, but increases the probability of timing failures, as illustrated in the figure: it is easy to see that T'_{Dmax} has a non-negligible probability of not holding. However, if we might detect these timing failures, we would be able to react accordingly and preserve system correctness. Timing failure detectors are a new class of detectors that will be discussed in Section 3. As for the second fact, it opens the door for assuming a channel with *better* characteristics. Enough networks and network protocols have a notion of privileged, high priority channels, where synchronous behaviour can be reasonably assumed (e.g., FDDI, ATM, RTP, ISO-Ethernet, GSM, LEO-Iridium).

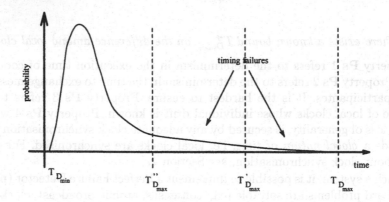

Fig. 1. Distribution function of message delivery times

We just described the rationale for a model between asynchrony and synchrony, that we call the *quasi-synchronous model*, and a framework for correct execution of problems with timeliness specifications. In this model, it is only necessary that a part of the system be synchronous. The rest can exhibit a more uncertain behaviour.

The Timed-Asynchronous Model Perspective There is another work that has some similarities to the quasi-synchronous work from the point of view of goals. It is based on a model called *Timed-Asynchronous*[14] which in contrast assumes that local clocks are not synchronised, though having a bounded rate of drift. There is not a bound for process execution and for message delivery delays. The fault model assumes that processes may crash or experience timing failures and messages can have omissions or timing failures. On top of this model a datagram service is built that has knowledge about failures (*fail-aware*).

The TA model covers a spectrum of application classes smaller than the QS model, but on the other hand, the latter requires stronger assumptions and in consequence, the adequate structure to enforce them. For example, since the TA model does not have bounds for execution or delivery delays, any assumption on timeliness of execution is merely indicative. The non-existence of bounds also means that trustworthy crash failure detection is impossible[14]. On the other hand, the quasi-synchronous model requires the existence of a control channel, even if virtual, that is synchronous.

2.3   The Quasi-Synchronous Model

The properties of a fully synchronous system model are assumed to hold without limitations: there are no timing failures, omission failures can be masked, and crash failures detected by a pFD. However, the problem is that the resilience to uncoverage of timeliness assumptions is doubtful, as we have discussed earlier.

A quasi-synchronous system is modelled as if it were a synchronous system, in the sense that it is defined in terms of synchronism properties **Ps** 1 through **Ps** 4. However, some or all of those bounds are not precisely known, or have values that are too far from the normal case. So, in order to meet the system requirements, we stipulate artificial, shorter bounds, that have a non-negligible probability of being violated. Any timeliness property i is defined in terms of a pair $\langle T^i_{D_{max}}; P^i \rangle$, where $T^i_{D_{max}}$ is the **assumed** upper timeliness bound and $P^i \leq 1$ is the **assumed** coverage[1] [4].

The violation of timeliness properties entails the possibly unreliable behavior of the system. In order to avoid it, we need a detector more elaborate than a crash failure detector, of a new class that we call **timing failure detector**. Informally, this detector must be: timely, detecting failures immediately they occur; complete, providing knowledge of that detection to all interested processes; accurate, not giving false indications of failure. *See* Section 3 for more detail on timing failure detectors.

To exemplify the quasi-synchronous model, we address a specific instance of the model where only the communication delay property is relaxed, that is, it has coverage lower than one. From the point-of-view of the communication protocols, the system is composed of a set P of participants noted *p, q, r, ...* We use participant and process interchangeably. We assume the system to follow an omissive failure model, that is, components *only do timing failures*— and of course, omission and crash, since they are subsets of timing failures— and no

---

[1] Probability of that bound holding.

value failures occur. More precisely, they only do *late* timing failures. This means that timeliness properties can, under certain circumstances, by violated.

The properties of the quasi-synchronous model in this instance are presented below. From now on, superscripts will be omitted when there is not risk of ambiguity.

Pqs 1 *There exists a known bound* $T_{D_{max}}^1$ *on processing delays with an assumed coverage* $P^1 = 1$

Pqs 2 *There exists a known bound* $T_{D_{ctl}}^2$ *on* **control** *message delivery delay with an assumed coverage* $P^2 = 1$

Pqs 3 *There exists a known bound* $T_{D_{max}}^3$ *on local clock rate drifts with an assumed coverage* $P^3 = 1$

Pqs 4 *There exists a known bound* $T_{D_{max}}^4$ *on the difference among local clocks with an assumed coverage* $P^4 = 1$

Pqs 2' *There exists an assumed upper bound* $T_{D_{max}}^2$ *on* **payload** *message delivery delay with an assumed coverage* $P^2 < 1$

Note the meaning of the assumed coverage less than one for property **Pqs 2'**: by assuming artificial and deliberately shorter bounds, we relax in part the synchrony of the system. Moreover, we do so for all the general traffic, that we call *payload*, but we assume as synchronous a small bandwidth communication channel for high priority messages, that we designate by *control* traffic. The idea is to use this small synchronous part of the system to build components able to control and validate the other parts of the system, thus making it possible to achieve safety in a timely fashion. This can be a dedicated network, as it is sometimes used for clock synchronisation, or can be a virtual channel over a more traditional real-time network. Additionally, we assume the existence of a global clock (for example, *see* Section 4 on CESIUMSPRAY).

3   Timing Failures and Detectors

We have seen in the previous section that failure detectors are useful building blocks for reliable distributed systems. The majority of detectors known are *crash* failure detectors. Its utility has been discussed in several works both in the asynchronous and synchronous worlds. More recently, a paper by Chandra & Toueg has established a hierarchy of crash failure detectors, and the problems they can solve. The most powerful is a **perfect crash failure detector**, which has the **CFD** properties. Then, in the measure that synchronism decreases, we have decreasing failthfulness of failure detection, and less and less accurate detectors, with weaker properties.

CFD 1 Strong Completeness: *There is a time after which any crashed process is permanently suspected by all other correct process*

CFD 2 Strong Accuracy: *A correct process is never suspected by any other correct process*

Crash failures are particular cases of timing failures, where the process responsible for executing a specification produces infinitely many timing failures with infinite lateness degree. In consequence, a detector capable of detecting timing failures is more generic, since besides its obvious utility in timed models, it is also capable of detecting crash failures. In fact, there is a transformation from the TFD we define in this section to a Crash Failure Detector that we do not introduce here, due to lack of space.

3.1   Timing Failure Detection

Let us try to understand what a timing failure is. When we want a system to do timely executions in bounded time, there are a number of informal ways of specifying such a behaviour: "task T must execute with a period of Tp"; "any message is delivered within a delay Td"; "any transaction must complete within Tt from the start". All the properties above can be reduced to the form of a predicate that holds at a certain real time instant at the latest, infinitely many times. An appropriate *time operator* to define timeliness properties in this context is based on durations: *within T from* ⟨ time of initial condition ⟩.

In order to be able to detect timing failures, we need to follow the runtime (real-time) behaviour that derives from the implementation of such properties. To that purpose, we introduce *timed action*, which we define as the execution of some operation within a known bounded time T_A from its start t_A. T_A is the allowed maximum duration of the action. Examples of timed actions are the release of tasks with deadlines, the send of messages with delivery delay bounds, and so forth. For example, timeliness property "any message delivered to any process is delivered within T from the time of the send request" must be implemented by a protocol that turns each request send_request (p, M_i) *of message M_i addressed to p*, issued at real time t_s, into a timed action: *execute the delivery of M_i at p within T from t_s.* Generalizing, a timed action can be defined as follows:

Timed Action - *Given process p, a reference real time instant t_A, interval T_A, and a termination event e, a timed action $X(p, e, T_A, t_A)$ is the execution of some operation, such that its termination event e should take place at p, within T_A from t_A*

The time-domain correctness of the execution of a timed action may be observed if e is observable. If a timed action does not incur in a timing failure, the action is *timely*, otherwise, a timing failure occurs:

Timing Failure - *given the execution of a timed action X specified to terminate until real time instant t_e, there is a timing failure at p, iff the termination event takes place at a real time instant t'_e, $t_e < t'_e \leq \infty$. The amount of delay, $Ld = t'_e - t_e$, is the lateness degree*

Now we can understand timing failure detection as being the detection of the occurrence of a timing failure in an observable termination event e as defined above. A *Perfect Timing Failure Detector (pTFD)*, using an adaptation of the terminology of Chandra[10], has the following properties:

TFD 1 Timed Strong Completeness: *There exists $T_{TFD_{max}}$ such that given a timing failure at p in any timed action $X(p, e, T_A, t_A)$, it is detected within $T_{TFD_{max}}$ from t_e*

TFD 2 Timed Strong Accuracy: *There exists $T_{TFD_{min}}$ such that any timed action $X(p, e, T_A, t_A)$ that terminates at p before $t_e - T_{TFD_{min}}$ is considered timely*

Timed Strong Completeness can be understood as follows: "strong" specifies that any timing failure is perceived by all correct processes; "timed" specifies that the failure is perceived at most within $T_{TFD_{max}}$ of its occurrence. In essence, it specifies the detection latency of the pTFD.

Timed Strong Accuracy can also be understood under the same perspective: "strong" means that no timely event is wrongly detected as a timing failure; but "timed" qualifies 'timely', by introducing a minimum separation $T_{TFD_{min}}$ between the event and the detection threshold (the bound). In essence, it specifies the detection accuracy of the pTFD.

3.2   A Timing Failure Detector

The main function of the TFD is to disseminate, in a timely fashion, vital information among nodes. There will be more than one way to implement the TFD. We chose a periodic, time-triggered protocol approach. Each TFD module (there is one in each node) broadcasts periodic messages to all participants, using the control channel.

There are known implementations of time-triggered, clock-driven protocols in synchronous systems that exhibit properties **Pqs1**, **Pqs2**, **Pqs3** and **Pqs4**. The interested reader may look in [27] for a survey. In consequence, we focus our attention on how to correctly use such a protocol, with the help of Figure 2 where, in background with a communication protocol execution, the TFD is exchanging information among all participants. Namely, all participants must send information about messages sent and received. Message m timestamped with T_m is supposed to be disseminated and delivered to all group participants (p, q and r) by the low level communication protocol by $T_m + T_{Dis_{max}}$ on the recipients' local clocks. When that does not happen, there is a timing failure. In the case represented in Figure 2, as early as at time T_i (before $T_m + T_{Dis_{max}}$) participant r obtains information about the existence of a message m, with timestamp T_m, sent by participant p. This way, participant r knows that it is supposed to receive message m by $T_m + T_{Dis_{max}}$. Since that will not happen in the example, there is a timing failure, *promptly* detected by r.

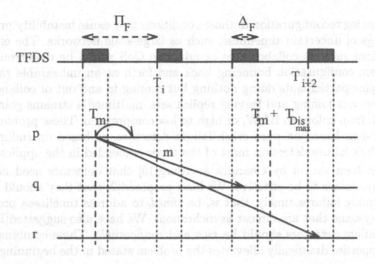

Fig. 2. Relation between communication protocol messages and TFD messages

Π_F and Δ_F are respectively the period and the latency of the timing failure detection service (periodic messages) (see Figure 2). Note that if a periodic message is not received in time, it means that there is a failure (because it is periodic). The general latency of detection depends on the information needed by the communication protocol, which in turn depends on the properties it wants to provide (order, agreement, timeliness). That is, the TFD may provide answers to questions such as those listed in Table 1, within the delays listed. A complete discussion on these timing variables can be found in [2].

Control information timings	
any other message sent before and not yet delivered?	$T_m + \Pi_F + \Delta_F$
message received by anyone?	$T_m + T_{Dis_{max}} + \Pi_F + \Delta_F$
failure as soon as possible	$\max(T_m + T_{Dis_{max}}; T_m + \Pi_F + \Delta_F; T_m + T_{Dis})$

Table 1. Timings associated with control information related to failures

3.3 Quality-of-Service Failure Detection

Usually, the output of failure detectors serves the purpose of system reconfiguration, for example, a new view in the membership of a group- oriented system. However, when: (a) the criterion for a detector to declare crash of a process or node is static; (b) the semantics of such detection is poor, then chances are that the system: (a') will not be able to adapt to the changing environment; (b') will suffer from the many mistakes of the detector.

Triggering reconfiguration in those conditions may cause instability problems in settings of uncertain timeliness, such as large-scale networks. The effect on applications such as collaborative or adaptive QoS would be disastrous, with the system configuration bouncing back and forth at an unbearable rate. We can imagine participants doing nothing but coming in and out of collaboration groups, servers joining and leaving replica sets, multimedia streams going back and forth from colour to B&W, or high to low compression. These problems still affect designs based on pure crash failure detectors, or based on rudimentary and implicit failure detection most of the times embedded in the application.

It has been shown by Chandra & Toueg[10] that detectors need *accuracy* and *completeness* to be effective. We have proposed[2] that they should further detect timing failures timely, that is, be *timed*, to address timeliness problems, even in systems that are almost asynchronous. We have also suggested[13] that timing failure detectors should be *rich* and *configurable*. These combination of these properties drastically alleviates the problem stated in the beginning of this section.

We recall that timing and omission failures can be reduced to crash failures. Together these three form what we call the omissive failure class. Secondly we point out that the quantitative measures we include in the notion of quality of service (QoS) or level of service (LoS) (*see* Chapter 13), such as bandwidth, latency, omission degree or rate, are specifiable in terms of the omissive failure class. Now we are ready to understand what is a performability or *quality-of-service* failure detector.

A QoS-FD is designed to evaluate a number of relevant operational parameters (that is, a rich semantics). The detector we designed for NAVTECH, for example, was oriented to assess connectivity, and thus measured[13]: roundtrip delay, throughput and omission error rate. The application can configure the failure detector, by issuing a **QoS specification**. A QoS specification indicates the conditions, the goals and the importance of each parameter P:

Sampling Period (TS)- the interval over which the value of the parameter is acquired. If $TS = \infty$, it means continuous sampling. For any positive integer TS, it means the interval over which samples of P, or of variables leading to the computation of P, are collected. For example, if P is a round-trip time, a distribution function is computed with the samples. If P is a bandwidth, it is computed with the amount of bits exchanged during TS, divided by TS. If P is an omission rate, it means that we are interested in the number of omissions over interval TS.

Threshold (TH)- the upper or lower acceptable bound on P. A typical upper bound is for a round-trip duration. A typical lower bound is for a bandwidth. A plus or minus signal is used to denote whether it is lower or upper, respectively. For example, $TH = 10^-$ means the parameter is valid for 10 and below (upper bound).

Weight (WT)- a measure of the relative importance of parameter P. A value of 0 would mean that the parameter would not taken into account.

A test is invoked by an application, by issuing a QoS specification and a set of target resources to the failure detector. We are interested in the distribution facet of the problem, that of the QoS offered to a distributed computation through a set $\mathcal{N} = \{p_1, p_2, ..., p_n\}$ of processes in different nodes that is, the end-to-end QoS seen from each p_i to every other $p_{j \neq i}$. For simplicity, in the ensuing discussion we consider one process in each node and use node and process interchangeably. Each parameter of the QoS specification is evaluated by the QoS-FD at each node p_i, for every other node of the set. We note the variable V associated with parameter P kept at local node i about some remote node j as $V_i^j(P)$. For instance, $V_i^j(roundtrip)$ denotes the roundtrip delay between nodes i and j as measured at i. A test epoch is defined by the following global parameters:

QoS Spec - the specification containing the definitions for each parameter P
    (TS, TH, WT)
Target - the set of nodes $p_i \in \mathcal{N}$ involved
QoS Sampling Period - the interval of observation for a QoS specification.
Value (V)- the parameter's value in the last sampling period.
Threshold Exceeded (TE)- percentage of the sampling periods of P where
    it fell beyond the bound TH during TS (or since the start, for continuous
    sampling), for each p_j as seen from p_i. For example, $TE = 10$ for bandwidth
    means that in 10% of the sampling periods, the bandwidth was below the
    threshold TH. For example, $TE = 2$ for round-trip time in continuous sam-
    pling means that in 2% of the samples since the start the round-trip time
    threshold was exceeded. In other words, over time, TE gives a measure of
    the coverage of the TH assumption for P. In this last example, the round-
    trip time assumption holds with a probability of 98%.
QoS Disturbance Index - a weighted average of the TE of all parameters P,
    for each p_j as seen from p_i. That is:

$$DI_i^j = \sum_P WT(P) * TE_i^j(P) / \sum_P WT(P)$$

DI Threshold - the global acceptable upper bound on the Disturbance Index.
Local Suspicion Vector (LSV) - a vector of booleans with $\mathcal{N}$ positions, for
    each local node p_i, where position $LSV_i[j] = 1$ iff the QoS Disturbance
    Index DI seen from p_i to p_j at that position exceeded (was worse than) the
    DI Threshold.

DI is computed periodically for each process p_i in $\mathcal{N}$, as specified by the QoS sampling period. After the computation of the DI, TE variables are reset, and incremented from zero until the next computation of DI. A very low DI value means that the QoS in the current set is within satisfactory thresholds. A value of DI_i^j exceeding the DI threshold means a QoS failure of p_j, in the opinion of p_i. At the end of each epoch, each process p_i has thorough information provided by the QoS-FD about the QoS of its connectivity with other processes, namely the $V_i^j(P)$ and DI_i^j for all j and all P. This information allows the application to fine-tune parameters, for example by choosing which ones to relax when DI

shows insufficient QoS. Likewise, when a parameter P holds with 100% coverage, the application may tighten the specification. This game of tightening some and loosening others aims at the final end-to-end goal, that of obtaining the best possible QoS.

At this point, the reader will also note that each local QoS-FD instance has a *Local Suspicion Vector*, or LSV_i, a vector of Booleans. Now it is necessary to test each other's opinions, to assess the symmetry and transitivity of the node's connections. Failure Detectors exchange their LCV's to build a *Global Suspicion Matrix*, or GSM, where each row $GSM[i,-]$ is LSV_i. If node i has 'bad' connectivity to j then $GSM[i,j]$ is true, and false otherwise.

Another refinement we introduced in failure detection is the possibility of placing more trustworthiness on the decision of some local FDs than on others'. An integer value, called the *Suspicion Weight* (SW_i) is associated with every p_i. Another integer, called the *Global Suspicion Quorum* (GSQ), is the global suspicion threshold to declare a p_j faulty. Consider $GSM[i,j]$ as a matrix of integers 1 and 0, in place of logical 'true' and 'false'. Then, p_j is more precisely faulty when the weighted sum of column j (the opinion of each p_i with regard to p_j) equals or exceeds GS:

$$\sum_i \text{GSM}[i,j] \times \text{SW}_i \geq \text{GSQ}$$

The values of Suspicion Weights and of the Global Suspicion Quorum can be set by the application to define different failure detection triggering conditions. Suspicion weights solve a number of problems that are encountered in QoS-oriented applications, where it sometimes is important that the opinion of one node about the QoS to all the others supersedes all other opinions. In cooperative applications, weights may reflect the 'social role', or a measure of the relative importance of each user: for example, a meeting can lose members but should not lose the moderator. More sophisticated triggering conditions are reported in [12].

There is another very important issue concerning the generality of QoS-FDs, and their complementarity to crash failure detectors. Let us forget for a moment that the QoS failure detector is fine-tuneable, and consider a QoS specification addressed solely at measuring the general QoS of the connectivity between nodes. Up to now, we have not said anything about the feasibility of reaching agreement on a Global Suspicion Matrix GSM, or about the allowed contents of GSM. Consider that all LSV exist, that nodes want to exchange them so as to build a GSM and that $SW_i = 0$. Substitute *crash* for *QoS* failure. Then, for the construction of the GSM we have exactly the same constraints as for Chandra's hierarchy of failure detectors. That is, crash failure detectors are reducible to Qos failure detectors. We do not give the proof here, but it is easy to see that the transformation of a QoS failure detector into a crash failure detector is the transformation from the discrete DI's into the LSV's that we have already described. Moreover, Chandra's algorithms can be used to build the GSM. In consequence, the QoS failure detector concept is coherent with the crash failure detector concept. There is a hierarchy of QoS failure detectors depending on the synchrony of the environment (weak, strong, etc.). For example, a strong QoS failure detector can build a matrix GSM such that: for every QoS-failed p_j, $GSM[i,j] = 1$ for all i and there exists at least one p_k such that $GSM[i,k] = 0$ for all i. A QoS specification oriented to connectivity and an example test epoch are illustrated in Table 2.

QoS Specification				Test Results									
				$node_1$		$node_2$		...	$node_i$		...	$node_n$	
Parameter	TS	TH	WT	TE	V_i^1	TE	V_i^2	...	TE	V_i^i	...	TE	V_i^n
roundtrip (ms)	0	100^-	2	5	120	30	250	...	-	-	...	0	30
throughput (Kb/s)	100m	50^+	1	0	90	20	5	...	-	-	...	0	70
omission rate (/s)	10m	1^-	1	0	0	0	0	...	-	-	...	0	0
...								...	-	-	...		
Disturbance Index (DI)	10s	5^-	-	2.5		20		...	-		...	0	
Local Suspicion Vector LCV_i →				0		1		...	-		...	0	

Table 2. QoS Specification for a Test and Example Results at Node p_i

There is a final innovative characteristic of our failure detectors. In all previously known systems, the failure detector, besides being a crash-only detector, was directly hooked to the reconfiguration module (a group membership protocol, in group-oriented systems). We introduced **program-controlled failure notification**, whereby the notification of the failure of p_i may be prevented or produced by the application upon the analysis and integration of QoS tests. In modern systems, this should be produced by a high-level middleware toolbox, for example what are called Activity Services in NavTech (*see* Chapter 6). Note that the mistakes that the FD does on account of environment instability are significantly higher with a Boolean decision criterion (crashed or alive) than they are with an analog decision criterion (QoS DIs). In consequence, we would already be better off with QoS failure detectors. However, we can go even further, by leaving the ultimate decision to the application. This crucial architectural feature was used by applications built on top of NavTech, to improve the accuracy of failure detection and avoid premature group exclusions[12]: we did an on-line comparison of the decisions of our QoS failure detector with those of a classical crash failure detector, in a test-bed where the environment was degraded sporadically, and indeed the QoS FD showed significantly more stable operation.

In conclusion, we have shown the benefits of rich semantics and configurable detection:

- specifying QoS: analog instead of binary failure specifications;
- specifying levels of importance: suspicion weights and quorums

– specifying triggering decisions: having control over what and when to report from the failure detector in order to initiate reconfiguration.

4   Clock Synchronisation and Time Services

A global timebase is a requirement of growing importance in distributed systems, enabling decentralised agreement on the time to trigger actions, or on the time at which events occurred. It is also a very useful block for building fault-tolerant distributed algorithms.

Previous works have largely ignored the potential that may arise from the combination of different algorithmic approaches, and of different network structures. A large-scale distributed system can reasonably be modelled by a WAN-of-LANs. It is easy to enforce synchronism of the local networking part, in contrast with what happens for the global part. Likewise, different clock synchronisation algorithms have different behaviour, depending on whether they run in local or global area networks. In the system we present, we take advantage of the remarks made above: we use a hybrid clock synchronisation algorithm; and we take advantage of the hybrid structure of large-scale networks.

The global time service we present here is called CESIUMSPRAY [22], and it is suitable for large-scale (world-wide) systems. The service exhibits high precision and accuracy, and is virtually indefinitely scalable. The global synchronisation scheme is *hierarchical*, as depicted in Figure 3. As the figure suggests, the root of the hierarchy is the source of absolute time— the set of cesium TAI clocks in the NavStar GPS[19] (Global Positioning System) satellites— which "spray" their unique reference time over a set of nodes provided with GPS receivers (GPS-nodes). This forms the first level of the hierarchy, where wireless synchronisation maintains the GPS-nodes highly accurate and precise. Local networks form the second level of the hierarchy of the system, with the condition that each be provided with at least one GPS-node. Fault-tolerance is achieved by replicating the GPS-nodes. In this level, synchronisation is performed in a way such that the external time resident in the GPS-node is further "sprayed" inside the local network, i.e. used as the reference for the internal synchronisation rounds.

Not all synchronisation algorithms are suitable for this latter objective, and for preserving the high precision and accuracy obtained in the first step. The underlying synchronisation algorithm is inspired by the *a posteriori agreement* algorithm, which uses properties of broadcast networks to significantly reduce the impact of message delivery delay variance on the obtained precision. However, the algorithm is innovative in that it introduces a new class of *hybrid* internal/external synchronisation algorithms. Unlike previously known algorithms, it is not a round-trip clock synchronisation algorithm. In short, it is an internal synchronisation algorithm which runs symmetrically among all processors. However, some of these processors are the external time references, which also cooperate in the protocol execution.

Fault-tolerance of the external synchronisation scheme is achieved by replicating GPS-nodes in the desired local networks. Fault-tolerance of the internal synchronisation scheme is achieved by having enough nodes to mask the assumed failures. If external synchronisation fails, the internal global time is preserved by the internal synchronisation algorithm, which exhibits quasi-optimal accuracy preservation[22].

The time service described here can readily be materialised for large-scale systems over global WAN-of-LAN networks, such as the wide-area point-to-point Internet, with real-time LAN technologies in the edges. The merit of the scheme is also related to the fact that it is not technically viable to provide every other node with a GPS receiver.

4.1   Time Service Architecture

We assume the reader to be familiar with the clock synchronisation problem. A discussion is detailed in [22]. A physical clock *ticks*, which corresponds to a discrete amount of time g, the *granularity* of the clock. Precision says informally that any two correct clocks are never separated by more than a quantity π_v. Accuracy says that any correct clock is never separated from real time by more than α_v. An interesting consequence is that in a set of clocks with accuracy α_v, precision is at least as good as $\pi_v = 2.\alpha_v$. Due to the imperfection of physical clocks (normally quartz crystal), precision and accuracy can only be assured through periodic clock re- synchronisation. Internal synchronisation is sufficient for the former, external is necessary for the latter. In CESIUMSPRAY , external time is injected by GPS-nodes, which have *GPS- clocks*, synchronised by the NavStar system, satisfying the GPS-clock accuracy condition, saying that all correct GPS-clocks are never apart from real time more than α_g.

Assumptions In the architecture presented, we assume that each network *node* holds a clock *processor*, so we will use both words interchangeably. We assume further that: **clocks** may have arbitrary failures (eg. provide erroneous or conflicting values when read); clock server **processors** (the ones running the synchronisation protocol) may have from crash to uncontrolled (or general) omission or timing failures. **Network components** are *weak-fail-silent*, with omission degree f_o (they behave correctly or crash if they do more than f_o omissions). Additionally, we assume that it is possible to put a bound on the time to send a message, to process a received message and read a clock value, etc. The power of this *hybrid* fault assumption is detailed in [22].

Broadcast Local Network Model Broadcast local area networks have a number of properties on which clock synchronisation may be built, namely the ability to deterministically generate a "simultaneous" event at all correct processors in the system. The precision budget of an algorithm boils down to the error in reading from a remote clock. We identify two terms of the error, the propagation and receive errors, respectively the variance of the physical propagation time on the medium, and of the time to process the message at the receiver. Let us call this quantity $\Delta\Gamma_{tight} = \Delta\Gamma_{prp} + \Delta\Gamma_{rec}$. Next we identify an abstract network property that applies to all LANs in general, and is the crux of the synchronisation effectiveness of our algorithm:

BNP 1 (Tightness) *Nodes receiving an uncorrupted message transmission, receive it at real time values that differ, at most, by a known small constant $\Delta\Gamma_{tight}$.*

That is, $\Delta\Gamma_{tight}$ is given by two terms whose sum can be made much smaller than the message delivery delay variance, $\Delta\Gamma$.

Generating and Detecting a Tight Broadcast If we devised a synchronisation protocol that would depend on the network tightness $\Delta\Gamma_{tight}$, it would likely exhibit excellent precision. The network primitives that make this conjecture come true, transferring the tightness assumption into a protocol execution, are:

Tight Broadcast (TB) - a single broadcast transmission, that is received by all correct nodes within $\Delta\Gamma_{tight}$.
Detected Tight Broadcast (dTB) - a tight broadcast known to be such by at least one node.

We save the details for [22], but at this point it is important to understand that more important than having a tight broadcast, is knowing we have one. This is because failures can occur, preventing TB from always being achieved. Achieving **TB** is ensured in the first place by detecting failed nodes, and removing them from the set of recipients. Then, based on the *bounded omission degree* property of the network, the protocol must guarantee that an error-free broadcast occurs. Achieving **dTB** additionally requires that the sender know that its message got through to all. In conclusion, achieving and detecting a tight broadcast is equivalent to guaranteeing that there is at least one round (of send-replies) where a message is delivered to all correct nodes and all replies to *that* message come back. Suppose that message is a command for all nodes to: read their clocks; start a timer; and send the values back. Then, not only have we an extremely *precise* measure of the clocks' mutual deviations (read within $\Delta\Gamma_{tight}$), but also we have a very *accurate* measure of their absolute value (the time marker initiated at the same time they were read).

The Hybrid Synchronisation Approach The architecture of CESIUMSPRAY is shown in Figure 3. As said in the introduction, the clock synchronisation scheme is hierarchical, and a hybrid of external and internal synchronisation. From the accuracy viewpoint, all GPS-clocks are α_g accurate to real time. The internal synchronisation algorithm is such that it imposes the GPS-node time on the other nodes, and guarantees a precision of the local set of clocks of π_l. That is, accuracy of the latter to the GPS-node absolute reference is bounded by π_l. In consequence, the global accuracy of CESIUMSPRAY becomes: $\alpha_{CS} = \alpha_g + \pi_l$.

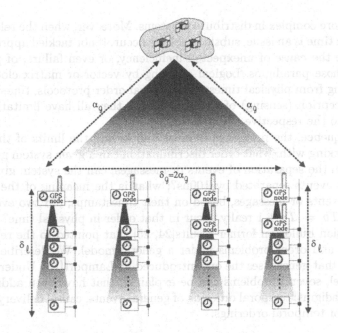

Fig. 3. The architecture of CESIUMSPRAY

On the other hand, it is easy to see that the worst-case precision of CESIUM-SPRAY world-wide, between any two nodes, is just influenced by three terms: precision of GPS-clocks amongst themselves, which is twice their accuracy; two times the internal precision in a local network. The contribution of these terms is illustrated in Figure 3. Precision of CESIUMSPRAY can thus be easily derived: $\pi_{CS} = 2(\alpha_g + \pi_l)$.

A posteriori agreement allies the time marker principle of non-averaging protocols to the clock reading and agreement principle of averaging ones. In that sense it is a hybrid of the two techniques. It combines them, in an interesting way, with the enhancement of precision and preservation of accuracy. These are achieved in different phases of the protocol, and thus in an orthogonal way.

We made experimental measurements of CESIUMSPRAY. They are detailed in [22]. The most relevant figure is the initial precision after resynchronisation, which is as good as $\delta_{ap} = 12.2\mu s$, which is a significant improvement w.r.t. software-based algorithms.

5   Real-Time Causal Delivery and Temporal Order

A crucial problem in a distributed system is to capture its state consistently, or else make it evolve consistently with a specification. The order of events is the fundamental paradigm behind that objective. The problem of ordering is very simple in centralised systems, since it can be reduced to the physical order of occurrence of events on a local imaginary timeline. Not surprisingly, it becomes somewhat more complex in distributed systems. Moreover, when the relationship of order with time is an issue, subtle problems occur. If not tackled appropriately, they may be the cause of unexpected inefficiency, or even failure, of programs relying on those paradigms. Logical ordering by vector or matrix clocks, temporal ordering from physical timestamps, causal order protocols, time-triggered lattices, perception (sensing) of external events, they all have limitations, and boundaries to the respective effectiveness.

In consequence, the programmer must understand the limits of the system he/she is working with: what order discrimination can a given system guarantee, depending on the separation of events or messages; can the system give me the order of two events separated by 100ns?; what is the meaning of the ordering of any two events or messages, based on their timestamps; did two events with timestamps $Tb = Ta + 1$ really occur in that order in physical time?

This section builds on former results[24, 25] that pointed to the representation of time and order problems under a generic model. We describe a causal order model that generalises the one introduced by Lamport[18]. Under the light of that model, several problems can be explained that have been addressed by different paradigms: temporal ordering of general events; causal delivery; anomalous logical or temporal orderings.

5.1   Causal Order

We assume the reader to be familiar with the (potential) causal order problem: given two events a and b, a can only be causally related to b, in the measure where an information departing from a site where a occurred, arrives at the site of b before b occurs.

For example, a widely known form of causally ordering messages sent by a protocol is through a *logical* ordering on the messages exchanged [3, 5]:

> **Logical Order:** A message $m1$ is said to logically precede, $(\xrightarrow{l})$, $m2$ if: $m1$ *is sent before* $m2$, *by the same participant* **or** $m1$ *is delivered to the sender of* $m2$ *before it sends* $m2$ **or** *there exists* $m3$ *s.t.* $m1 \xrightarrow{l} m3$ *and* $m3 \xrightarrow{l} m2$.

However, if participants do not exchange messages, or exchange them in a way that does not reveal causal relations correctly, we have to devise an alternative solution. At this point, we might ask: if participants do not exchange messages, how do they create causal interactions?

5.2   Anomalous Behaviour

Logical order is based on a simple observation: if participants only exchange information by sending and receiving messages, they can only define causality relations through those messages. However, participants can still interact without necessarily exchanging messages through a given logical order protocol:

 – by exchanging messages via a protocol other than the ordering protocol;
 – by interacting via the outside world.

In both cases there are *hidden* channels, that is, information flowing between participants which is not controlled by the ordering discipline, so to speak, taking place in a *clandestine* manner. The first anomaly was first identified by Lamport[18], and reported in [11] as a limitation of causal ordering, which it is not: in fact it is a limitation of 'logical implementations of causal ordering' as we will see ahead. A less known situation, first pointed out in [28], is concerned with the interaction between the computer system and the outside world, when the hidden channels develop by means of feedback paths through the controlled process. *There is no way that logical order implementations know about these paths.*

These examples have shown that the problem has a generic nature that supersedes either of them. In fact, they suggested that the problem had to do with the existence of hidden channels, regardless of their form. In consequence, they inspired the development of a general model for causal ordering, extending Lamport's model to arbitrary systems with hidden channels[25]. We discuss it in the next sections.

5.3 General Precedence Model

We consider a system defined by a set P of participants noted p, q, r, ... A participant can be a computing process, a sensor or actuator controller, but also some component of an external physical system under control. The system is synchronous, in the sense that there are known bounds on: processing speed; message transmission delay; local clock rate drift.

We model the history of the participants as a sequence of events: e_p^i is the ith event of participant $p \in P$. Event e_p^i can be a local event or an external event. For the sake of representing their place in a (Newtonian) time-line, whenever necessary, we associate physical timestamps to events: $t(e_p^i)$ is the timestamp of e_p^i, as defined by an omniscient external observer. We consider two types of external events, action, ACT, and observation, OBS:

 – $ACT_p(a)$ is an event by which the participant p takes some external action a, be it an action on the environment (e.g. an I/O actuation) or a message send;
 – $OBS_p(a)$ is an event by which the participant p observes some external action a, be it an observation of the environment (e.g. a sensor reading) or the delivery of a message sent by a participant q.

An event *precedes* another event if it could have caused the latter, that is, if it is causally related to it. This model, presented in [25], introduces the precedence relation $\xrightarrow{p}$ between events, a generalisation of the "happened before" relation first introduced by Lamport for message-based systems [18], to arbitrary events, including those taking place in the environment (external networks, external subsystems, physical processes, etc.):

Definition 1 Precedence. *An event precedes (* $\overset{p}{\rightarrow}$ *) another event if one of the following conditions hold: for* $j > i$, e_p^i $\overset{p}{\rightarrow}$ e_p^j; *for* $p \neq q$, e_p^i $\overset{p}{\rightarrow}$ e_q^j *if* e_p^i *is an external event* $ACT_p(a)$ *and* e_q^j *an external event* $OBS_q(a)$; *for* $p \neq q$, e_p^i $\overset{p}{\rightarrow}$ e_q^j *if there exists an event* e *such that* e_p^i $\overset{p}{\rightarrow}$ e *and* e $\overset{p}{\rightarrow}$ e_q^j.

At this point, it is clear that a logical order is insufficient to represent all instances of this model. An obvious alternative artefact is 'time'. Given that for an event to cause another it must happen before the latter, a protocol ordering events by their order of physical occurrence will return their precedence order.

5.4 Temporal Order

It is impossible to have a discrimination of this physical order for two events separated by an infinitely small interval. Besides, it is not even necessary. Similarly to logical order, where participants only generate causal relations through interactions, in a distributed computer system or in a physical process, it takes a finite amount of time for an input event (OBS, eg. deliver) to *cause* an output event (ACT, eg. send). For example, the time for an information to travel from one site to the other; the execution time of a computer process; the feedback time of a control loop in a physical process. Supposing there is a known such minimum time δ_t for a given system, we define temporal delivery order:

Temporal Order: A message m_1 is said to temporally precede ($\overset{\delta_t}{\rightarrow}$) m_2 if: *the* send *event of* m_1 *occurs before that of* m_2 *by more than* δ_t, *i.e.* $t(send(m_2)) - t(send(m_1)) > \delta_t$.

5.5 Constraints to Ordering: The μ Parameters

Real systems have definable constraints to the magnitude of $\overset{\delta_t}{\rightarrow}$. Let us exemplify what it means for an application supported by temporal order to execute correctly.

Consider the example of two participants P_A and P_B at different sites, competing for a resource controlled by P_C at a third site. They both try to grab it approximately at the same time, by sending messages m_A and m_B through a temporal order protocol. Suppose P_A sends first, but P_B would get the resource, because the protocol ordered m_B before m_A. The fact is that this would only be anomalous if P_A could know it had requested it first. This might only happen if m_A $\overset{p}{\rightarrow}$ m_B, according to the definition of precedence (Def. 1). In other words, if there would be time for an information, departing from A when $send(m_A)$ occurs, to reach B, and be processed before $send(m_B)$ occurs.

This example shows that not all messages have to be ordered by the physical order of the *send* requests. That is only required when two *send* events are time-like separated, by more than the time it takes to overcome their space-like separation[2].

---

[2] "Time-like" is measured in the time coordinate, "space-like" concerns the space coordinates, in Relativity jargon.

Since in our model we make no assumptions about the way information is propagated— it can even travel through the physical process— a conservative figure to represent the above-mentioned space-like separation, is the absolute minimum **propagation delay** between any two participants in the system. As noted before, this delay is not necessarily related to network message passing, it can be concerned with propagation through a physical process under control— for example, from a computer controlling an actuator, to another computer reading from a sensor in that process loop.

Suppose now that the request from P_A, if received at P_B, should cause P_B *not* to request, after being interpreted by a processing step with a duration of $5ms$. If the participants were separated by, say, 100 meter, their space-like separation would thus be $\simeq 300ns$ at the speed of light (the minimum propagation delay). In consequence, P_A would have to request, in real time, more than $300ns + 5ms$ before P_B, to *cause* the inhibition of P_B. Otherwise, the message-passing subsystem could order m_B before m_A— against their physical order— and the system would still behave correctly, since no participant has means to confirm or infirm such an ordering.

In fact, this second example shows that it is of no use to have a protocol order two messages because they are just separated by more than the space-like separation— that is, $300ns$ in this case— since a process needs time to generate the causal relation between them— that is, $5ms$ in this case— and we may add that time to the causal chain. So, it is also useful to represent the time-like separation between processing steps made by the same participant, that we introduce as **local granularity**, the minimum interval between any two *related* consecutive events in the time-line of a participant.

The examples above served to exemplify what happens with distributed real-time programs in general: they perform execution steps within bounded delays and exchange messages and/or perform input/outputs in result of those computations; they have a limited capability (in the time domain) of acquiring information and producing responses, formalised below.

Definition 2 Local granularity, μ_t, *of a system, is the minimum delay between two related consecutive events in any participant p,* e_p^i *and* e_p^{i+1}:
$$\forall p, \ \forall i \quad t(e_p^{i+1}) - t(e_p^i) \geq \mu_t$$

For example, Definition 2 defines that two related consecutive message sends from the same participant are separated by at least μ_t. It defines as well the minimum time for an input to cause a response in any reactive process of the system, that is, the minimum duration of a computation.

Definition 3 Propagation delay, μ_s, *of a system, is the minimum delay between an* $ACT_p(a)$ *event and the corresponding* $OBS_q(a)$ *event:*
$$\forall p, q, p \neq q \ t(OBS_q(a)) - t(ACT_p(a)) \geq \mu_s$$

At this point, we have: a general causal precedence model; definitions for temporal event and message delivery ordering; system-level constraints to the production of order relations. We will spend the rest of this section equating conditions for securing the causal precedence order (as defined in Definition 1) in: (i) event sets; (ii) message delivery.

5.6   Event Ordering

We refer the reader to the detailed development of this material in [24]. The main method for extracting event orderings in arbitrary systems (where there may or may not be communication between sites) is through physical timestamps from a global time-base. Global time-bases have been discussed in Section 4 of this Chapter. A fundamental result in this context is that given two events a and b in different sites, timestamped from a global virtual clock of precision π, and granularity $g_v \geq \pi$, their temporal order is guaranteed to be asserted from the respective timestamps only if $|t_b - t_a| \geq \pi + g_v$. This theory has been contributed by Lamport, Cristian and Kopetz. Under our model, we could further say that it is a sufficient condition for the implementation above to guarantee temporal order for any two events a and b anywhere in the system, that the events be $\stackrel{\pi+g_v}{\rightarrow}$ precedent.

Figure 4 illustrates this remark by depicting the limit situation: the clocks $C1$ and $C2$ of two sites are separated by π; a occurs immediately after *tick* 1 in $C1$. For b to be ordered after a, it must receive a timestamp in *tick* 2. In consequence, the figure displays the minimum separation between events so that they are ordered, when clocks are worst-case separated by π.

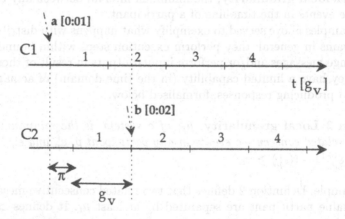

Fig. 4. Limit situation for temporal ordering from timestamps

We have generalised this result under the general precedence model with μ parameters. The execution granularity of computer processes is normally much coarser than clock granularity. In consequence, one can use a new virtual clock whose granularity may be relaxed to g'_v, improving the concurrency of the system, and that leads to:

Remark 1 *Given any two related events a and b in a system[3] with μ_t and μ_s parameters, timestamped from a global clock of granularity g'_v and precision π, if a $\;p\!\!\rightarrow\;$ b, then it is always $T(a) < T(b)$, iff $g'_v \leq \min(\mu_s - \pi, \mu_t)$.*

Parameters μ_t and μ_s define the time-like and space-like separation for causality to develop between any two events. It is easy to see that the Remark holds for events in the same site: for $g'_v \leq \mu_t$ any two causally related local events receive different timestamps. Figure 5 illustrates the more subtle situation of events in different sites: the clocks $C1$ and $C2$ at two sites are separated by π; a occurs immediately after *tick* 1 in $C1$; the causality path (through the communication system or through the environment) is the shortest possible, that is, equal to μ_s, which implies that the earliest event that may be causally related to a occurs at t_b. Now notice that all events occurring at or after t_b are ordered with regard to a: virtual clock granularity is chosen in order that $\mu_s \geq g'_v + \pi$, so that event b is indeed timestamped with the tick after the one of a.

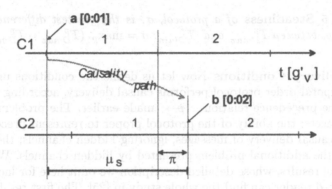

Fig. 5. Limit situation for Remark 1

5.7 Causal Delivery

However, another very important use of temporal order in distributed real-time applications is to determine causal precedence relations among a particular type of events: messages exchanged by the participants in a distributed computation. These are also called causal delivery guarantees. There are several ways of implementing *causal delivery*, i.e. guaranteeing that messages are delivered in their precedence order [4] in a distributed system. Given the system model of the previous section, we note $send_p(m)$ the event corresponding to the transmission of m by p, and $deliver_q(m)$ the delivery of m to q. For simplicity of notation, we may omit the subscript, when there is no risk of ambiguity. The $send(m)$ and $deliver(m)$ events are, respectively, *ACT* and *OBS* events.

---

[3] For example, message **sends** and **receives**.

[4] Or *potential causal* order, sometimes only called causal, for simplicity.

Definition 4 Causal delivery. *Consider two messages* m_1, m_2 *sent by p, resp q, to the same destination participant r. Causal delivery ensures that if* $send_p(m_1)$ $\ p\!\!\rightarrow\ $ $send_q(m_2)$ *then* $deliver_r(m_1)$ $\ p\!\!\rightarrow\ $ $deliver_r(m_2)$, *i.e.* m_1 *is delivered to r before* m_2.

We have discussed ordering anomalies, so we are concerned with implementations that secure causal precedence in message delivery, despite the existence of hidden channels. Formally, these hidden channels are represented in our model by the existence of ACT and OBS events inside a causality chain which do not correspond to sends and deliveries of the causal order protocol. Given any μ parameters, it should be possible to define what are the conditions for a protocol to ensure causal delivery. The reason is that in a distributed computer system or in a physical process, it takes a finite amount of time for an input event (OBS, eg. deliver) to *cause* an output event (ACT, eg. send), as we have already seen.

Before we proceed, we define the *steadiness* σ of a communication protocol, which is a synchronism property:

Definition 5 Steadiness *of a protocol,* σ, *is the greatest difference, for any participant p, between* T_{Dmax}^p *and* T_{Dmin}^p: $\sigma = \max_p (T_{Dmax}^p - T_{Dmin}^p)$

Causal Delivery Conditions Now let us define the conditions under which a given temporal order protocol performs causal delivery, according to the definition of the precedence relation $\ p\!\!\rightarrow\ $ made earlier. The problem as we see it has two facets: the ability of the protocol proper to represent precedence, i.e. implement causal delivery of messages, ignoring hidden channels; the ability to do so with the additional problem presented by hidden channels. We have derived a set of results, whose detailed description we omit here for lack of space. The interested reader can find the whole study in [25]. The first result considers the existence of hidden channels:

Remark 2 *Given a system with local granularity* μ_t *and propagation delay* μ_s, *a protocol such that* $\mu_t > \max_u (T_{Dmax}^u) - \mu_s$, *ensures causal delivery order.*

The correctness of Remark 2 is made evident by Figure 6, both for different senders (left) and the same sender. If we rule hidden channels out, the result of Remark 2 can be improved by the introduction of condition $\mu_s = \min_u (T_{Dmin}^u)$. That is, channels external to the protocol are slower than or as fast as the latter, or do not exist at all. This is beneficial since it lowers the allowed minimum value of μ_t, that becomes a function of the protocol steadiness.

Remark 3 *Given a system with local granularity* μ_t *and propagation delay* μ_s, *a protocol such that* $\min_u (T_{Dmin}^u) = \mu_s$ *and* $\sigma < \mu_t$ *ensures causal delivery order.*

The correctness of Remark 3 is also made evident by Figure 6, with the new values for the parameters. A complete proof of these results can be found in [25].

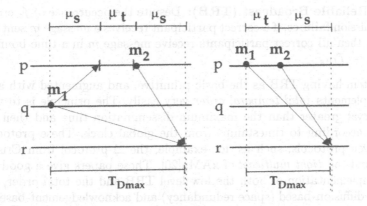

Fig. 6. Correctness of temporal order implemented by protocols with σ steadiness (T_{Dmax} stands for $\max_u (T^u_{Dmax})$)

For environments where interactions through external subsystems or the environment itself coexist with message exchanges, these message exchanges secure causal delivery in the model we have described. In order to duly appreciate the general result of Remarks 2 and 3, and just for the sake of example, consider a system exhibiting a propagation delay of $\mu_s = 100\mu s$, and a distributed real-time control program with a granularity of $\mu_t = 100ms$, requiring temporal order to be secured. A protocol with a steadiness as coarse as $\sigma = 100ms$ and $T^i_{Dmin} \leq 100\mu s$ would do. This could be ensured by simple timer-driven protocols, instead of more complex clock-driven ones[25].

6   Communication

In this section we discuss two protocols using time in large-scale systems: an early-delivery causal total order protocol using a timing failure detector[1]; and a Δ-causal order protocol [6, 7].

6.1   Early-Delivery Causal Total Order Protocol

We devote our attention to the timeliness and contamination problems of the protocol, in order to illustrate the utility of timing failure detection. We begin by describing the situation in the absence of timing failures, and then we address the problem of contamination, and its avoidance with the timing failure detector.

We consider that an underlying *timely reliable broadcast* [5] primitive exists and we describe it concisely:

---

[5] A real system should perform multicast rather than broadcast, but that distinction is not made here for the sake of simplicity, since it is not relevant to our timeliness discussions.

Timely Reliable Broadcast (TRB): Despite the occurrence of f_c crash and f_o omission failures, if a correct participant receives a message m sent at time t_{send}, then all correct participants receive message m in a time bounded by $t_{send} + T_{Dis_{max}}$

A system having TRB as the basic primitive, and augmented with a global clock, implements *total temporal order* very easily. The principle is to wait for a Δ interval greater than the maximum dissemination time and then deliver messages according to timestamps from the global clock. These protocols are clock-driven protocols, such as, for example, the Δ-protocol from Cristian *et al.* [15], and the *tight multicast* of xAMp[20]. These papers give a good insight on the implementation of both the low level TRB and the total order, respectively for diffusion-based (space redundancy) and acknowledgement-based (time redundancy) approaches.

The latency of those protocols is greater than the worst-case message delay, since message delivery is only done at time $T_m + \Delta$ on the recipient's clock, where T_m is the timestamp of the message. This is a high cost to pay, so it makes sense to try and provide early-delivery when possible.

Early-Delivery Atomic Broadcast Causal atomic broadcast means that the total order secured by the protocol obeys causal delivery. Moreover, it obeys real-time causal delivery, which is crucial to ensure correctness of real-time applications relying on the causality model (*see* Section 5).

A protocol providing early-delivery, tries to deliver with a latency lower than Δ [17]. These protocols assume a diffusion primitive with a latency Δ, try to obtain early-delivery by the use of acknowledgements, and provide a total order based on timestamps obtained from synchronised clocks. When the sender has received an acknowledgement from all recipients, it can early-deliver because it knows that they all have received the message, and they will deliver it at most by the time their local clocks show the value $T_m + T_{Dis_{max}}$. The sender informs all participants of the fact, so that they can also early-deliver.

Preserving Causal Total Order The way the protocol is presented above, it secures agreement but not order. In order to make sure that the order of delivery is correct (total temporal order), the protocol always sends the acknowledgement message. In case that an acknowledgement message is lost or arrives too late at some recipients, early-delivery will not be possible. In consequence, message delivery will be done at time $T_m + T_{Dis_{max}}$ on the clocks of the recipients concerned, and the order will be based on the timestamp.

Timing Failures and Contamination The major problem with the protocol just described is that it relies on the maximum message dissemination time to achieve order, in the situations where it is not possible to provide early-delivery. The coverage of Δ protocols to the violation of the maximum dissemination time assumption is minimal. Under the quasi-synchronous perspective, where the value $T_{Dis_{max}}$ is an *assumed bound*, with an assumed risk of uncoverage. The problem, we remind the reader, is that it is sometimes possible for a message dissemination time to be greater than the assumed value. If nothing is done, a situation may occur where there is contamination, that is, where the violation of timeliness properties implies violation of other safety properties, such as order or agreement, for example.

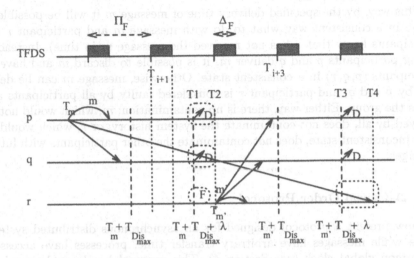

Fig. 7. Use of TFD to handle the contamination problem

Using the Timing Failure Detector Given a timing failure detector (TFD) such as defined in Section 3, all situations of timeliness violation are detected, timely enough to avoid contamination. As explained in that section, TFD uses periodic messages to disseminate control information to all participants. These messages are sent using a synchronous channel, and they have a period of Π_F and a latency of Δ_F.

The situation is shown in Figure 7: we have the control information from TFD, and we need to increase the latency of the communication protocol so as to be able to use the information provided by TFD. This latency increment is $\lambda = \Pi_F + \Delta_F$. This way, instead of having $T_m + T_{Dis_{max}}$ as the maximum time to deliver a message m, we will have $T_m + T_{Dis_{max}} + \lambda$. However, message m is still supposed to be *received* until $T_m + T_{Dis_{max}}$ that is, the maximum message dissemination time. If that does not happen, this situation is considered a timing failure (as before).

From the Figure 7, it can be seen that with the help of TFD, a given participant is able to make a correct decision in a timely fashion. For example, at time $T1$ ($T_m + T_{Dis_{max}} + \lambda$ - message delivery time for message m) participants must decide whether they deliver message m, or discard it. That depends on the status of the other participants. Have they all received the message in time, or was there a timing failure (message not received until $T_m + T_{Dis_{max}}$)?

With TFD they have the answer to that question: the control information disseminated by TFD at time T_{i+1} ($T_{i+1} > T_m + T_{Dis_{max}}$ as in Figure 7) will contain, for each participant, the information of whether the message m was received until $T_m + T_{Dis_{max}}$. All participants will have this control information at time $T_{i+1} + \Delta_F$. Since $T_{i+1} \le T_m + T_{Dis_{max}} + \Pi_F$, it means that the control information will be available at least by the delivery time ($T_m + T_{Dis_{max}} + \lambda$), because $\lambda = \Pi_F + \Delta_F$.

This way, by the specified delivery time of message m it will be possible to decide in a consistent way what to do with message m and participant r (all participants know that r has not received the message m in time). Instead of having participants p and q deliver m, it is possible to discard m and have all participants (p, q, r) in a consistent state. Otherwise, message m can be delivered by p and q, and participant r is considered faulty by all participants and leaves the group. Either way, there is no contamination: m, which would not be received by all, does not contaminate the system history; or r, which would be in an inconsistent state, does not contaminate the other participants with future messages.

6.2 Δ-Causal Order Protocol

We now present a protocol designed for an asynchronous distributed systems where while messages have arbitrary transfer time, processes have access to a common global clock (*see* Section 4). This protocol has been designed for multimedia-like applications. Those are characterized by the following two points. First, all data have a lifetime Δ. This means that if a piece of data is created and sent at some time t, it is meaningful only until $t + \Delta$. After this time, the value of the data is obsolete (this means that the content of the message that carries the data has to be discarded if the message arrives too late). The second point concerns the quality of service provided by the underlying communication channels: messages can be lost (as long as some messages arrive). These two points are typically met in real-time image processing applications: (1) each image has a lifetime, after which it is meaningless; (2) some images can be lost without degrading the service offered to end users.

The protocols introduced in [6] and [7] solve this problem in the context of point-to-point communication and broadcast communication respectively. Let us first note that, to be consistent, data have to be processed according to their creation order, so these protocols implement the so-called Δ-causal order.

Δ-**Causal Order**   If a message is sent at t, its deadline is $t + \Delta$. Let M be the set of messages that arrive at their destination before their deadline. Δ-causal order is defined by the two following properties:

- Liveness Property. $\forall m \in M$: m is delivered to its destination process before its deadline. $\forall m \notin M$: m is never delivered to its destination process.
- Safety Property. All message deliveries respect causal order.

So, if $\Delta = +\infty$, Δ-causal order tends to causal order. There is a strong distinction between the arrival of a message at a process and its delivery. As it has been seen in previous sections, this distinction is necessary when one has to ensure any delivery order, since the physical arrival order may not be the correct delivery order.

Figure 8 illustrates Δ-causal order in the context of broadcast communications. The right side of the figure shows that the messages m_1 and m_2 are delivered by p_i and p_j by their deadlines and according to causal order. Process p_k delivers only m_2, it never delivers m_1 because this message arrived at p_k after its deadline. As it will be shown in the protocol, the delivery of m_2 at p_k can be delayed until p_k knows that for sure m_1 will bypass its deadline. The left side of the figure shows the case where all messages, namely m_3 and m_4, are received, and consequently are delivered, by their deadlines.

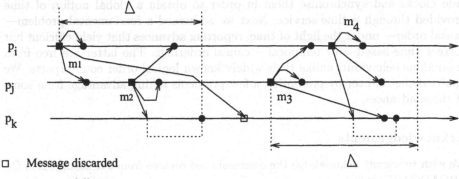

□   Message discarded

●   Message delivery

■   Message sent

Fig. 8. Deliveries of broadcast communications respecting Δ-causal order

Principle of the Protocols The protocols presented in [6, 7] follow similar principles. First they discard a message m, when it arrives after its deadline. This only requires that a message piggybacks its sending date.

The difficult part lies in ensuring messages arrived by their deadlines are delivered without violating causal order. This is done in the following way. Every message m carries control information indicating the sending time of each message that causally precedes m. A simple examination shows that it is sufficient to carry n sending times (one for each possible sender process, n being the number of processes in the application) [7].

So, when a message arrives, a delivery condition is evaluated. If the message has bypassed its deadline, it is immediately discarded. Otherwise, the message delivery is delayed until each message that has been sent (causally) before it either: has been delivered; or will inevitably miss its deadline. Due to the control information piggybacked in each message, the condition associated with the delay can be locally evaluated. The proof shows that all messages arrived by their deadline are actually delivered.

7 Summary

In this chapter, we have addressed a few advances with regard to the role and the use of time and distributed systems. We started by equating the fundamental problem: 'what model to use in distributed systems?'. We discussed the emerging partial synchrony models, by motivating the statement that one cannot do without a notion of time in current distributed systems models. Two sections followed that are direct implications of this approach to modelling distributed systems, showing how to: (i) define, detect and process timing failures; (ii) provide clocks and synchronise them in order to obtain a global notion of time provided through a time service. Next we addressed a fundamental problem— causal order— under the light of time, reporting advances that yield efficient but correct time-based— or temporal— causal orderings. The latter are free from anomalous behaviour, unlike their widely known logical order counterparts. We finalised the chapter by presenting a few protocols taking advantage from some of these advances.

Acknowledgements

We wish to warmly acknowledge the comments and reviews from our colleagues in the BROADCAST project.

References

[1] Carlos Almeida and Paulo Veríssimo. An adaptive real-time group communication protocol. In *Proceedings of the First IEEE Workshop on Factory Communication Systems*, Leysin, Switzerland, October 1995.

[2] Carlos Almeida and Paulo Veríssimo. Timing failure detection and real-time group communication in *quasi-synchronous* systems. In *Proceedings of the 8th Euromicro Workshop on Real-Time Systems*, L' Aquila, Italy, June 1996. (also available as INESC technical report RT/20-95).

[3] K. Birman and T. Joseph. Reliable Communication in the Presence of Failures. *ACM, Transactions on Computer Systems*, 5(1), February 1987.

[4] Powell D., Failure Modes Assumptions and Assumption Coverage. *Proc. 22th IEEE Symposium on Fault-Tolerant Computing (FTC'92)*, Boston, MA, 1992, pp. 386-392.

[5] Raynal M., Schiper A. and Toueg S., The Causal Ordering Abstraction and a Simple Way to Implement it. *Information procesing Letters*, 39:342-350, 1991.

[6] Baldoni R., Mostefaoui A. and Raynal M., Causal Delivery of Messages with Realtime Data in Unreliable Networks. *Realtime Systems Journal*, 10:245-262, 1996.

[7] Baldoni R., Prakash R., Raynal M. and Singhal M., Efficient Δ-Causal Broadcasting. *Computer Systems Science and Engineering*, 13(5):125-131, 1998.

[8] Raynal M. and Singhal M., Logical Time: Capturing Causality in Distributed Systems. *Computer*, 29(2):49-56, February 1996.

[9] Tushar Chandra, Vassos Hadzilacos, Sam Toueg, and Bernadette Charron-Bost. On the impossibility of group membership. In *Proceedings of the 15th ACM Symposium on Principles of Distributed Computing*, pages 322-330, Philadelphia, USA, May 1996. ACM.

[10] Tushar Chandra and Sam Toueg. Unreliable failure detectors for reliable distributed systems. *Journal of the ACM*, 43(2):225-267, March 1996.

[11] D. Cheriton and D. Skeen. Understanding the limitations of causally and totally ordered communication. In *Proceedings of the 14th Symposium on Operating Systems Principles*, Asheville, NC, USA, December 1993.

[12] François J.N. Cosquer, Pedro Antunes, and Paulo Veríssimo. Enhancing dependability of cooperative applications in partitionable environments. In *Dependable Computing - EDCC-2*, volume 1150 of *Lecture Notes in Computer Science*, chapter 6, pages 335-352. Springer-Verlag, October 1996.

[13] François J.N. Cosquer, Luís Rodrigues, and Paulo Veríssimo. Using Tailored Failure Suspectors to Support Distributed Cooperative Applications. In *Proceedings of the 7th International Conference on Parallel and Distributed Computing and Systems*, pages 352-356. IASTED, October 1995.

[14] Flaviu Cristian and Christof Fetzer. The timed asynchronous system model. In *Proceedings of the 28th Annual International Symposium on Fault-Tolerant Computing*, pages 140-149, Munich, Germany, June 1998. IEEE Computer Society Press.

[15] Flaviu Cristian. Synchronous atomic broadcast for redundant broadcast channels. *The Journal of Real-Time Systems*, 2(1):195-212, 1990.

[16] M. J. Fischer, N. A. Lynch, and M. S. Paterson. Impossibility of distributed consensus with one faulty process. *Journal of the Association for Computing Machinery*, 32(2):374-382, April 1985.

[17] A. Gopal, R. Strong, S. Toueg, and F. Cristian. Early-delivery atomic broadcast (extended abstract). In *Proceedings of the 9th ACM Annual Symposium on Principles of Distributed Computing*, pages 297-309, Quebec City, Canada, 1990.

[18] Leslie Lamport. Time, Clocks and the Ordering of Events in a Distributed System. *CACM*, 21(7):558-565, July 1978.

[19] B. Parkinson and S. Gilbert. Navstar: Global positioning system— ten years later. *Proceedings of the IEEE*, 71(10):1177-1186, October 1983.

[20] L. Rodrigues and P. Veríssimo. xAMp: a Multi-primitive Group Communications Service. In *Proceedings of the 11th Symposium on Reliable Distributed Systems*, pages 112-121, Houston, Texas, October 1992. IEEE. INESC AR/66-92.

[21] P. Veríssimo and A. Casimiro. The timely computing base. In *Digest of Fast Abstracts, The 29th International Symposium on Fault-Tolerant Computing*, Madison, USA, June 1999. IEEE. Extended version in DI/FCUL TR 99-2, Department of Informatics, University of Lisboa, April 1999.

[22] P. Veríssimo, L. Rodrigues, and A. Casimiro. Cesiumspray: a precise and accurate global clock service for large-scale systems. *Journal of Real-Time Systems*, 12(3):243-294, 1997.

[23] Paulo Veríssimo and Carlos Almeida. Quasi-synchronism: a step away from the traditional fault-tolerant real-time system models. *Bulletin of the Technical Committee on Operating Systems and Application Environments (TCOS)*, 7(4):35-39, Winter 1995.

[24] P. Veríssimo. Ordering and Timeliness Requirements of Dependable Real-Time Programs. *Journal of Real-Time Systems, Kluwer Eds.*, 7(2):105–128, September 1994. Also as INESC AR/14-94.

[25] P. Veríssimo. Causal Delivery Protocols in Real-time Systems: a Generic Model. *Journal of Real-Time Systems*, 10(1):45–73, January 1996.

[26] P. Veríssimo and L. Rodrigues. A posteriori Agreement for Fault-tolerant Clock Synchronization on Broadcast Networks. In *Digest of Papers, The 22nd International Symposium on Fault-Tolerant Computing*, Boston - USA, July 1992. IEEE. INESC AR/65-92.

[27] Paulo Veríssimo. Real-time Communication. In S.J. Mullender, editor, *Distributed Systems, 2nd Edition*, ACM-Press, chapter 17, pages 447–490. Addison-Wesley, 1993.

[28] Paulo Veríssimo, P. Barrett, P. Bond, A. Hilborne, L. Rodrigues, and D. Seaton. The Extra Performance Architecture (XPA). In D. Powell, editor, *Delta-4 - A Generic Architecture for Dependable Distributed Computing*, ESPRIT Research Reports, pages 211–266. Springer Verlag, November 1991.

[29] Paulo Veríssimo, L. Rodrigues, and J. Rufino. The Atomic Multicast protocol (AMp). In D. Powell, editor, *Delta-4 - A Generic Architecture for Dependable Distributed Computing*, ESPRIT Research Reports, pages 267–294. Springer Verlag, November 1991.

Consensus in Asynchronous Distributed Systems: A Concise Guided Tour

Rachid Guerraoui[1], Michel Hurfin[2], Achour Mostefaoui[2], Riucarlos Oliveira[1], Michel Raynal[2], and Andre Schiper[1]

[1] EPFL, Département d'Informatique, 1015 Lausanne, Suisse
[2] IRISA, Campus de Beaulieu, 35042 Rennes Cedex, France

Abstract. It is now recognized that the Consensus problem is a fundamental problem when one has to design and implement reliable asynchronous distributed systems. This chapter is on the Consensus problem. It studies Consensus in two failure models, namely, the Crash/no Recovery model and the Crash/Recovery model. The assumptions related to the detection of failures that are required to solve Consensus in a given model are particularly emphasized.

Keywords: Asynchronous Distributed Systems, Atomic Broadcast, Atomic Commitment, Consensus, Crash/no Recovery, Crash/Recovery.

1 Introduction

Distributed applications are pervading many aspects of everyday life. Booking-reservations, banking, electronic and point-of-sale commerce are noticeable examples of such applications. Those applications are built on top of distributed systems. When building such systems, system designers have to cope with two main issues: asynchrony and failure occurrence. *Asynchrony* means that it is impossible to define an upper bound on process scheduling delays and on message transfer delays. This is due to the fact that neither the input load from users nor the precise load of the underlying network can be accurately predicted. This means that whatever is the value used by a process to set a timer, this value cannot be trusted by the process when it has to take a system-wide consistent decision. Similarly, *failure occurrences* cannot be predicted. The net effect of asynchrony and failure occurrences actually create an *uncertainty* on the state of the application (as perceived by a process) that can make very difficult or even impossible to determine a system view that can be validly shared by all non-faulty processes. The mastering of such an uncertainty is one of the main problems that designers of asynchronous systems have to solve.

As a particular example, let us consider the case of a service whose state has been distributed on several nodes. To maintain a consistent copy of the service state, each node must apply to its copy the same sequence of the updates that have been issued to modify the service state. So, there are two problems to solve. (1) Disseminate the updates to the nodes that have a copy of the service state.

S. Krakowiak, S.K. Shrivastava (Eds.): Distributed Systems, LNCS 1752, pp. 33–47, 2000.
© Springer-Verlag Berlin Heidelberg 2000

And (2), apply the updates in the same order to each copy. The first problem can be solved by using a *reliable multicast* primitive [21]. The second problem is more difficult to solve. The nodes have to agree on a common value, namely, the order in which they will apply the updates. This well known problem (namely, the *Atomic Broadcast* problem) is actually a classical *Agreement problem*.

It appears that any agreement problem can be seen as a particular instance of a more general problem, namely, the *Consensus* problem. In the Consensus problem, each process proposes a value, and all non-faulty processes have to agree on a single decision which has to be one of the proposed values. This chapter presents a few results associated with the Consensus problem. It is composed of seven sections. Section 2 defines the Consensus problem. Section 3 studies Consensus in the Crash/no Recovery model. Section 4 discusses issues related to the communication channel semantics. Section 5 introduces the differences between two main distributed computing models: (1) the Crash/no Recovery model, and (2) the Crash/Recovery model. Section 6 studies Consensus in the Crash/Recovery model, and Section 7 concludes the chapter.

2   The Consensus Problem

2.1   General Model

A *distributed system* is composed of a finite set of n sites interconnected through a communication network. Each site has a local memory (and possibly a stable storage according to the needs of applications) and executes one or more processes. To simplify and without loss of generality, we assume that there is only one process per site. Processes synchronize and communicate by exchanging messages through channels of the underlying network.

We consider *asynchronous* distributed systems: there are bounds neither on communication delays, nor on process speeds. The interest of the asynchronous model comes from its practicability. Open distributed systems such as systems covering large geographic areas, or systems subject to unpredictable loads that may be imposed by their users, are basically asynchronous due to the unpredictability of message transfer delays and process scheduling delays in those systems [2]. This makes the asynchronous model a very general model.

A process is either a *good* process or a *bad* process. What determines a process as being good or bad depends on the failure model. Section 3 and Section 6 provide instantiations of what is a good/bad process, in the Crash/no Recovery model and in the Crash/Recovery model, respectively. Roughly speaking, a *good* process is a process that behaves as expected. A *bad* process is a process that is not good. In both cases, a process is fail-silent: (1) until it crashes, a process behaves according to its specification, and (2) when crashed, it does nothing.

2.2   What Is the Consensus Problem?

In the *Consensus* problem, defined over a set $\{p_1, p_2, \ldots, p_n\}$ of processes, each process p_i proposes initially a value v_i, and all good processes have to decide on some common value v that is equal to one of the proposed values v_i [3].

Formally, the *Consensus* problem is defined in terms of two primitives: propose and decide. When a process p_i invokes propose(v_i), where v_i is its proposal to the Consensus problem, we say that p_i "proposes" v_i. When p_i invokes decide() and gets v as a result, we say that p_i "decides" v. The semantics of propose() and decide() is defined by the following properties:

- C-Termination. *Every good process eventually decides.*
- C-Agreement. *No two good processes decide differently.*
- C-Validity. *If a process decides v, then v was proposed by some process.*

While C-Termination defines the liveness property associated with the *Consensus* problem, C-Agreement and C-Validity define its safety properties.

The C-Agreement property allows bad processes to decide differently from good processes. This fact can be sometimes undesirable as it does not prevent a bad process to propagate a different decision throughout the system before crashing. In the *Uniform Consensus* problem, agreement is defined by the following property, which enforces the same decision on any process that decides:

- C-Uniform-Agreement. *No two processes (good or bad) decide differently.*

Actually, all Consensus algorithms discussed in this chapter solve the Uniform Consensus algorithm.

2.3   From an Agreement Problem to Consensus

When practical agreement problems have to be solved in real systems, a transformation is needed to bring them to the Consensus problem specified in the previous section. We illustrate below such a transformation on the Atomic Commitment problem. Transformation of other agreement problems to Consensus (*e.g.*, Group Membership to Consensus, View Synchronous Communication to Consensus, Atomic Broadcast to Consensus, Atomic Multicast to Consensus, Clock Management to Consensus) can be found in [3,5,10,18,20,24,25,29]. So Consensus can be viewed as the common denominator of the different agreement problems. This explains the importance of Consensus, and justifies the large interest in the literature for this problem.

The Atomic Commitment Problem As an example of agreement problem let us consider the *Non-Blocking Atomic Commitment* Problem. At the end of a computation, processes are required to enter a commitment protocol in order to commit their local computations (when things went well) or to abort them (when things went wrong). So, when it terminates its local computation each process has to vote YES or NO. If for any reason (deadlock, storage problem, concurrency control conflict, local failure, etc.) a process cannot locally commit its local computation, it votes NO. Otherwise a vote YES means that the process commits locally to make its updates permanent if it is required to do so. Based on these votes, the decision to commit or to abort is taken. The decision must be COMMIT if things went well (all process are good and voted YES). It must be ABORT if things went wrong [12]. We consider here that a good process is a process that does not crash.

More formally, NBAC in an asynchronous distributed system can be defined by the following properties:

- NBAC-Termination. *Every good process eventually decides.*
- NBAC-Agreement. *No two processes decide differently.*
- NBAC-Validity. This property gives its meaning to the decided value. It is composed of three parts.
  - Decision Domain. *The decision value is* COMMIT *or* ABORT.
  - Justification. *If a process decides* COMMIT, *then all processes have voted* YES.
  - Obligation. *If all participants vote* YES *and none of them is perceived as bad, then the decision value must be* COMMIT.

The justification property states that the "positive" outcome, namely COMMIT, has to be justified: if the result is COMMIT, it is because, for sure, things went well (*i.e.*, all processes voted YES). Finally, the obligation property eliminates the trivial solution where the decision value would be ABORT even when the situation is satisfactory to commit.

Reducing Atomic Commit to Consensus Actually the NBAC is a particular instance of the Consensus problem. Figure 1 describes a simple protocol that reduces NBAC to Consensus.

```
(1)      ∀ p_j  do send(vote) to p_j end do;
(2.1)    wait (   (delivery of a vote NO)
(2.2)        or (∃ p_j: p_i perceives p_j as a bad process)
(2.3)        or (from each p_j: delivery of a vote YES from p_j)
(2.4)    );
(3.1)    case
(3.2)        a vote NO has been delivered    → v_i := ABORT
(3.3)        a process is perceived as bad   → v_i := ABORT
(3.4)        all votes are YES               → v_i := COMMIT
(3.5)    end case;
(4)      propose(v_i); decision:=decide(); % Consensus execution %
```

Fig. 1. From Consensus to NBAC in Asynchronous Systems (code of process p_i)

The behavior of every process p_i is made of 4 steps. First (line 1), p_i disseminates its vote to all processes. Then (lines 2.*), p_i waits until either it has received a NO vote (line 2.1), or it has received a YES vote from each process (line 2.3), or it perceives a process as being (crashed) bad (line 2.2). Then (lines

3.*), p_i builds its own view v_i of the global state: v_i is COMMIT if from its point of view everything went well (line 3.4), and ABORT if from its point of view something went wrong (lines 3.2 and 3.3). Finally (line 4), p_i participates in a Consensus. After having proposed v_i, process p_i waits for the result of the Consensus (invocation of *decide*) and saves it in the local variable *decision*. It can be easily shown that this reduction protocol satisfies the NBAC-Termination, the NBAC-Agreement and the NBAC-Validity properties. More information on the relations between the NBAC problem and the Consensus problem can be found in [13,14,16,17,30,31].

3   The Crash/no Recovery Model

3.1   Good and Bad Processes

We consider here the Crash/no Recovery model. This model is characterized by the following process behavior: when a process crashes, it permanently stops working, and a process that does not crash always follows its specification. So, in this model, a *good* process is a process that never crashes, and (as in any model) a *bad* process is a process that is not good. From a practical point of view, this means that a good process does not crash during the execution of the Consensus algorithm. A process that crashes is a *bad* process. Moreover, this section assumes that each pair of processes is connected by a reliable channel. Roughly speaking, a reliable channel ensures that no message is created, corrupted or duplicated by the channel, and that any good process eventually receives every message sent to it. Readers interested by a theoretical classification of problems in the Crash/Recovery model can consult [11,21].

3.2   A Fundamental Impossibility Result

A fundamental result on the Consensus problem has been proved by Fischer, Lynch and Paterson [9]. This result states that it is impossible to design a deterministic Consensus algorithm in an asynchronous distributed system subject to even a single process crash failure.

The intuition that underlies this impossibility result lies in the impossibility, in an asynchronous distributed system, to safely distinguish between a crashed process, a very slow process, and a process with which communications are very slow.

This impossibility result has been misunderstood by a large community of system implementors [19], but has challenged other researchers to find a set of minimal assumptions that, when satisfied by an asynchronous distributed system, makes the Consensus problem solvable in this system. Minimal synchronism [6], partial synchrony [8] and unreliable failure detectors [3] constitute answers to this challenge. In this chapter, we consider the unreliable failure detectors formalism.

3.3 Unreliable Failure Detectors

The unreliable failure detectors formalism, introduced by Chandra and Toueg in [3], is a powerful abstraction for designing and building reliable distributed applications. Conceptually, a failure detector is a distributed oracle which provides processes with an approximate view of the process crashes occurring during the execution of the system. With respect to its structure, a failure detector is usually seen and used as a set of n, one per process, failure detector modules. These modules are responsible for providing their associated processes with the set of processes they currently *suspect* to have crashed. When the failure detector module of process p_i suspects p_j to have crashed, we say that p_i *suspects* p_j.

Due to asynchrony, and consistently with the impossibility result of Section 3.2, it is natural to expect the failure detector to make mistakes: a failure detector may not suspect a bad (crashed) process or, erroneously suspect a good one. However, to be useful, failure detectors have to eventually provide some correct information about process crashes during the execution and thus, their mistakes are typically bounded by a *completeness* and an *accuracy* properties. The completeness property requires bad processes to be eventually suspected, and accuracy restricts the erroneous suspicions of good processes. Combining different definitions for the completeness and accuracy properties, several classes of failure detectors can be defined [3]. In the following we consider the class of *Eventual Strong* failure detectors, which is denoted by $\Diamond S$ and defined by:

- **Strong completeness:** Eventually every bad process is permanently suspected by every good process.
- **Eventual weak accuracy:** Eventually some good process is never suspected by any good process.

Note that, in practice, strong completeness can be easily satisfied using "I am alive" messages and timeouts. On the other hand, even if eventual weak accuracy might be satisfied by some executions, it cannot be ensured that it will be satisfied by all executions. This observation shows the limit of asynchronous systems, as far as crash detection is concerned: there is no mean to ensure accurate process crash detection.

3.4 Consensus Algorithms Based on Unreliable Failure Detectors

The first Consensus algorithm designed to work with a failure detector belonging to the class $\Diamond S$ was proposed by Chandra and Toueg [3]. Since then, other algorithms based on $\Diamond S$ have been proposed: one of them has been proposed by Schiper [32], another one by Hurfin and Raynal [22]. All these algorithms share the following design principles:

- The algorithm is based on the *rotating coordinator* paradigm and proceeds in consecutive asynchronous rounds. Each round is coordinated by a process. The coordinator of round r, process p_c, is a predetermined process (*e.g.*, $c = (r \bmod n) + 1$).

- Each process p_i manages a local variable est_i that represents p_i's current estimate of the decision value (initially, est_i is the value v_i proposed by p_i). This value is updated as the algorithm progresses and converges to the decision value.
- During a round r, the coordinator proposes its estimate est_c as the decision value. To this end processes have to cooperate:

  • Processes that do not suspect p_c to have crashed, eventually receive its proposal and *champion* it, adopting est_c as their own estimate of the decision. The proposal of the coordinator becomes the decision value as soon as a majority of processes champion it. The termination of the algorithm directly depends on the *accuracy* property of $\diamond S$ which ensures that, eventually, there is a round during which the coordinator is not suspected by any good process.

  • The crash of the coordinator is dealt by moving to the next round (and coordinator). By the *completeness* property of $\diamond S$, if the coordinator crashes, every good process eventually suspects the coordinator. When this happens, processes *detract* the coordinator's proposal and proceed to the next round.

It is possible that not all processes decide in the same round, depending on the pattern of process crashes and on the pattern of failure suspicions that occur during the execution. One important point which differentiates the algorithms is the way they solve this issue, while ensuring that there is a single decision value (*i.e.*, without violating the agreement property of Consensus).

Other differences between these Consensus algorithms lie in the message exchange pattern they generate and in the way they use the information provided by the failure detector. Chandra-Toueg's algorithm is based on a centralized scheme: during a round all messages are from (to) the current round coordinator to (from) the other processes. In Schiper's and Hurfin-Raynal's algorithms, the message exchange pattern is decentralized: the current coordinator broadcasts its current estimate to all processes, and then those cooperate in a decentralized way to establish a decision value. An important difference between Schiper's algorithm and Hurfin-Raynal's algorithm is the way each algorithm behaves with respect to failure suspicions. Basically, a design principle of Schiper's algorithm is not to trust the failure detector: a majority of processes must suspect the current coordinator to allow a process to proceed to the next round, and to consider another coordinator. Differently, a basic design principle of Hurfin-Raynal's algorithm is to trust the failure detector. Consequently, Hurfin-Raynal's algorithm is particularly efficient when the failure detector is reliable. Schiper's algorithm resists in a better way to failure detector mistakes.

What makes these algorithms far from being trivial is the fact that they can tolerate an unbounded number of incorrect failure suspicions, while ensuring the agreement property of the Consensus problem. This is particularly important from a practical point of view, as it allows to define aggressive time-out values, that might be met only whenever the system is stable, without having the risk of violating the agreement property during unstable periods of the system.

Finally, the algorithms satisfy the validity and agreement properties of Consensus despite the number of bad processes in the system, and satisfy termination whenever a majority of processes are good and the failure detector is of class $\Diamond S$.

The S class includes all failure detectors that satisfy strong completeness and *perpetual* weak accuracy (this means that, from the beginning of the system excution, there is a correct process that is never suspected). A generic Consensus algorithm that works with S (whatever the number of crashes is) and with $\Diamond S$ (when a majority of processes is correct) has been proposed by Mostefaoui and Raynal [26]. This surprisingly simple generic algorithm is based on the use of quorums. Its respective instantiations in systems equipped with S and with $\Diamond S$ require only to modify the quorum definition.

3.5   Other Fundamental Results

Three important results are associated with the class $\Diamond S$ of failure detectors:

- Chandra, Hadzilacos and Toueg [4] showed that the $\Diamond S$ class is the weakest class of failure detectors allowing to solve Consensus. This indicates that, as far as the detection of process crashes is concerned, the properties defined by $\Diamond S$ constitute the borderline beyond which the Consensus problem cannot be solved.
- Chandra and Toueg [3] proved that a majority of processes must be good (*i.e.*, must not crash) to solve Consensus using failure detectors of the $\Diamond S$ class.
- Guerraoui [13] proved that any algorithm that solves Consensus using failure detectors of the class $\Diamond S$, also solves Uniform Consensus.

4   On Channel Semantics

The algorithms mentioned in Section 3 assume reliable channels [3,22,32]. However, a reliable channel is an abstraction whose implementation is problematic. Consider for example a reliable channel between processes p_i and p_j. If p_i sends message m to p_j, and crashes immediately after having executed the send primitive, then p_j eventually receives m if p_j is good (*i.e.*, does not crash). This means that the channel is not allowed to lose m because retransmission of m is not possible since p_i has crashed. Indeed, the reliable channel abstraction assumes that the underlying communication medium does not lose a single message, which is an unreasonable assumption given the *lossy* communication channels offered by existing network layers.

It turns out that the algorithms in [3,22,32] are correct with a weaker channel semantics, which is sometimes called *eventual* reliable channel[1]. An eventual reliable channel is *reliable* only if both the sender and the receiver of a message

---

[1] Also *quasi-reliable* channel, or *correct-restricted* reliable channel.

are good processes. Implementation of eventual reliable channels is straightforward. Messages are buffered by the sender, and retransmitted until they are acknowledged by the receiver. However, what happens if the destination process crashes? If the system is equipped with a perfect failure detector (a failure detector that does not make mistakes), then the sender stops retransmitting messages once it learns that the receiver has crashed. If the failure detector is unreliable, the sender has to retransmit messages forever, which might require unbounded buffer space!

Fortunately, a weaker channel semantics, called *stubborn channels*, is sufficient for solving Consensus [15]. Roughly speaking, a k-stubborn channel retransmits only the k most recent messages sent through it. Contrary to reliable channels or eventual reliable channels, a stubborn channel may lose messages if the sender is a good process. It is shown in [15] that Consensus can be solved with 1-stubborn channels and $\Diamond S$ failure detectors, and that the required buffer space is logarithmically bounded by the number of rounds of the algorithm.

Being able to solve Consensus in the Crash/no Recovery model with lossy channels is a first step towards solving Consensus in the Crash/Recovery model (Section 6). Indeed, solving Consensus in the Crash/Recovery model, among other difficulties requires to cope with the loss of messages. To illustrate the problem consider a message m sent by p_i to p_j and assume that p_j crashes and afterwards recover from the crash. If m arrives at p_j while p_j is crashed, then p_j cannot receive m, i.e., m is lost. If p_j never recovers then the loss of m is not a problem. This is no more the case if p_j eventually recovers. Notice that in this case the loss of m is not the fault of the channel. However, the reason for the loss of the message does not make any difference for the Consensus algorithm.

5   Crash/no Recovery Model *vs* Crash/Recovery Model

While in Section 2 we have defined *one* instance of the Consensus problem, in a real system Consensus is a problem that has to be solved multiple times. Solving multiple instances of the Consensus problem is called *Repeated Consensus*. Repeated Consensus allows us to clarify the difference between the Crash/no Recovery model and the Crash/Recovery model.

In the context of Repeated Consensus, let us consider instance #k of the Consensus problem. In the Crash/no Recovery model a process p_i that crashes while solving Consensus #k is excluded forever from Consensus #k, even if p_i recovers before Consensus #k is solved[2]. Notice that this does not prevent process p_i from learning the decision of Consensus #k, neither does this prevent p_i from taking part in Consensus #$(k + 1)$. In contrast, in the Crash/Recovery model a process p_i that crashes while solving Consensus #k remains allowed to take part in Consensus #k after its recovery. Of course, this helps only if Consensus #k is not yet solved when p_i recovers. This is typically the case

---

[2] This can easily been achieved making p_i to exclude itself from actively participating in the algorithm upon recovery.

whenever the crash of p_i prevents the other processes from solving Consensus #k.

As an example, consider a Consensus algorithm that requires a majority of processes to take part in the algorithm (let us call such an algorithm *Maj-C-Algorithm*), and the case in which three processes ($n = 3$) have to solve Consensus #k. If we assume that no more than one single process crashes during the execution of Consensus #k, a Maj-C-Algorithm based on the Crash/no Recovery model is perfectly adequate. However, if we admit now that *more* than one process crashes, Consensus #k is not solvable with a Maj-C-Algorithm based on the Crash/no Recovery model. Such an algorithm leads the whole system to block whenever a majority of processes crash: (1) the surviving process cannot solve Consensus alone, (2) waiting for the recovery of the crashed processes would not help, and (3) if Consensus #k cannot be solved, none of the subsequent instances of Consensus #(k + 1), #(k + 2), etc., will ever be launched.

To overcome the above situation, an algorithm based on the Crash/Recovery model is required. With such an algorithm, the assumption of failure free processes can be released and processes that recover are allowed to actively participate in the instance of Consensus being currently solved. These advantages have certainly a price: apart from the issue of message loss (Section 4), appropriate failure detectors have to be defined, and stable storage becomes necessary.

6   The Crash/Recovery Model

6.1   Good and Bad Processes

In this model, a process can recover after a crash. So, this new particularity of a process behavior has to be taken into account to define what is a *good/bad* process. Actually, according to its crash pattern, a process belongs to one of the following four categories:

- *AU*: the set of processes that never crash (*AU* stands for "Always Up").
- *EAU*: the set of processes that eventually recover and no longer crash (*EAU* stands for "Eventually Always Up").
- *AO*: the set of processes that crash and recover infinitely often (*AO* stands for "Always Oscillating").
- *EAD*: the set of processes that (maybe after a finite number of oscillations) eventually crash and no longer recover (*EAD* stands for "Eventually Always Down").

Let us observe that processes that (after several possible recoveries) remain permanently crashed, can be detected. So, the set *EAD* can eventually be detected. More difficult to manage is the set of processes that forever oscillate between up and down. Actually, it is possible that those processes be never up "long enough" to contribute to the computation of a decision value. Moreover, on one side, it is possible that their "oscillations" perturb the computation of correct processes. On the other side, it is also possible that, due to the unpredictability of the crash and communication patterns occurring during an execution, an AO process is always down whenever a message is delivered to it. In this scenario the process is is unable to contribute to the progress of the algorithm.

The previous discussion provides us with an insight sufficient to define which processes have to be considered as *good* (resp. *bad*) in the Crash/Recovery model. *Good* processes are those that are eventually up during a period of time "long enough" to allow Consensus to be solved. So, *good* processes are those of the set $AU \cup EAU$. Consequently, the set of *bad* processes is the set $AO \cup EAD$. Let us finally note that, as in the Crash/no Recovery model, the relevant period during which process crashes are observed spans only the execution of the Consensus algorithm (this gives its practical meaning to the words "long enough period" used previously).

6.2   Failure Detection

Solving Consensus in the Crash/Recovery model requires the definition of appropriate failure detectors. From a practical point of view, it is unreasonable to assume failure detectors satisfying *strong completeness* (such as those in the $\Diamond S$ class) in the presence of processes that crash and recover infinitely often (processes in the AO set)[3]. Recall that *strong completeness* requires good processes to eventually suspect bad processes *permanently* which would imply to safely[4] eventually distinguish between EAU and AO processes. Since there is no bound for the number of times a process may crash and recover, this distinction would mean predicting the crash pattern of the process.

We present here the $\Diamond S_r$ class of failure detectors [28]. $\Diamond S_r$ differs from $\Diamond S$ in the completeness property. Any failure detector of the class $\Diamond S_r$ satisfies *Eventual weak accuracy* and the following completeness property:

- Recurrent strong completeness: Every bad process is infinitely often suspected by every good process[5].

As with $\Diamond S$ failure detectors, completeness can be realized by using "I am alive" messages and timeouts for detecting EAD processes. Detecting AO processes however requires a different scheme. It can be accomplished by having each process to broadcast a "I recovered" message each time the process recovers from a crash. It is worth to notice that those control messages are handled by each process failure detector module which is part of the process and thus subject to its crash pattern.

---

[3] In [7], the defined Crash/Recovery model does not consider AO processes which allows the adoption of $\Diamond S$ failure detectors.

[4] Without compromising the accuracy property of the failure detector.

[5] Let us note that this property is weaker than reclaiming eventual "permanent suspicion".

6.3   Stable Storage

In practice, processes have their state on local volatile memory whose contents is lost in the event of a crash. To overcome this loss and to be able to restore their state when recovering from crashes, processes need to be provided with some sort of stable storage.

Access to stable storage is usually a source of inefficiency and should be avoided as much as possible. Therefore, a pertinent question is whether Consensus can be solved in the Crash/Recovery model without using stable storage at all? This question has been answered by Aguilera, Chen and Toueg [1]. Let $x = |AU|$ (number of processes that never crash) and $y = |AO \cup EAD|$ (number of bad processes). They have shown that Consensus can be solved without using stable storage if and only if $x > y$. Intuitively, this means that the number of processes that (with the help of their volatile memory) can simulate a "stable storage for the whole system" (this number is x) has to exceed some threshold (defined by y) for a physical stable storage be useless.

This result shows that, even without resorting to stable storage, it is possible (when $x > y$) to solve Consensus in the presence of transient process crashes (with complete loss of state) which otherwise would not be possible with algorithms designed for the Crash/no Recovery model. On the other hand, allowing any good process to crash and recover at least once, requires processes to periodically log critical data. When and what data needs to be logged obviously depends on each particular algorithm. Critical process data that has invariably to be persistent to crashes is data contributing to the decision, that is, data which reflects a championed or detracted proposed estimate of the decision.

6.4   Algorithms

An algorithm for solving Consensus in the Crash/Recovery model without requiring stable storage has been proposed in [1]. This algorithm is bound to the requirement of stable storage (Section 6.3) and thus, to terminate, requires that the number of processes that never crash be greater than the number of bad processes ($|AU| > |AO \cup EAD|$).

Several Consensus algorithms suited to Crash/Recovery distributed systems equipped with a stable storage have been proposed [1,23,27]. They tolerate the crash and recovery of any process, and allow recovering process to take part in the computation.

These algorithms borrow their design principles from the Consensus algorithms for the Crash/no Recovery model [3,22,32]. All algorithms require a majority of good processes and rely on the semantics of stubborn communication channels. Apart from their structure, their major differences lie in the failure detectors they assume and on the use processes make of stable storage. The algorithms of Oliveira, Guerraoui and Schiper [27] and Hurfin, Mostefaoui and Raynal [23] were designed using failure detectors satisfying *strong completeness* and can be proved correct with failure detectors satisfying *Recurrent strong completeness* [28]. The algorithm of Aguilera, Chen and Toueg [1] uses a hybrid failure detector which satisfies *strong completeness* regarding EAD processes and handles the detection of AO processes by providing an estimate count of the number of recoveries of all processes.

With regards to stable storage, the algorithms described in [1,27] require each process to log critical data in every round. The algorithm in [23] is particularly efficient since each process accesses its stable storage at most once during a round.

7   Conclusion

The Consensus problem is a fundamental problem one has to solve when building reliable asynchronous distributed systems. This chapter has focused on the definition of Consensus and its solution in two models: the Crash/no Recovery model and the more realistic Crash/Recovery model. Theoretical results associated with Consensus have also been presented. A fundamental point in the study of the Consensus problem lies in the *Non-Blocking* property. An algorithm is non-blocking if the good (non-faulty) processes are able to terminate the algorithm execution despite bad (faulty) processes. The termination property of the Consensus problem is a non-blocking property. From a theoretical point of view, there are two main results associated with the Consensus problem. The first is due to Fischer, Lynch and Paterson who proved that there is no deterministic non-blocking Consensus algorithm in a fully asynchronous distributed system. The second one is due to to Chandra, Hadzilacos and Toueg who have exhibited the minimal failure detector properties (namely, $\Diamond S$) for solving the non-blocking Consensus problem with a deterministic algorithm. From a practical point of view, it is important to understand the central role played by the Consensus problem when building reliable distributed systems.

References

1. Aguilera M.K., Chen W. and Toueg S., Failure Detection and Consensus in the Crash-Recovery Model. In *Proc. 11th Int. Symposium on Distributed Computing (DISC'98, formerly WDAG)*, Springer-Verlag, LNCS 1499, pp. 231-245, Andros, Greece, September 1998.
2. Bollo R., Le Narzul J.-P., Raynal M. and Tronel F., Probabilistic Analysis of a Group Failure Detection Protocol. *Proc. 4th Workshop on Object-oriented Realtime Distributed Systems (WORDS'99)*, Santa-Barbara, January 1999.
3. Chandra T. and Toueg S., Unreliable Failure Detectors for Reliable Distributed Systems. *Journal of the ACM*, 43(1):225-267, March 1996 (A preliminary version appeared in *Proc. of the 10th ACM Symposium on Principles of Distributed Computing*, pp. 325-340, 1991).
4. Chandra T., Hadzilacos V. and Toueg S., The Weakest Failure Detector for Solving Consensus. *Journal of the ACM*, 43(4):685-722, July 1996 (A preliminary version appeared in *Proc. of the 11th ACM Symposium on Principles of Distributed Computing*, pp. 147-158, 1992).

5. Défago X, Schiper A., Sergent N., Semi-Passive Replication. *Proc. 17th IEEE Symp. on Reliable Distributed Systems*, West Lafayette, Indiana, USA, October 1997, pp. 43-50.
6. Dolev D., Dwork C. and Stockmeyer L., On the Minimal Synchronism Needed for Distributed Consensus. *Journal of the ACM*, 34(1):77–97, January 1987.
7. Dolev D., Friedman R., Keidar I. and Malkhi D., Failure Detectors in Omission Failure Environments. *Technical Report 96-1608*, Department of Computer Science, Cornell University, Ithaca, NY, September 1996.
8. Dwork C., Lynch N. and Stockmeyer L., Consensus in the Presence of Partial Synchrony. *Journal of the ACM*, 35(2):288–323, April 1988.
9. Fischer M.J., Lynch N. and Paterson M.S., Impossibility of Distributed Consensus with One Faulty Process. *Journal of the ACM*, 32(2):374–382, April 1985.
10. Fritzke U., Ingels Ph., Mostefaoui A. and Raynal M., Fault-Tolerant Total Order Multicast to Asynchronous Groups. *Proc. 17th IEEE Symposium on Reliable Distributed Systems*, Purdue University (IN), pp.228-234, October 1998.
11. Fromentin E., Raynal M. and Tronel F., On Classes of Problems in Asynchronous Distributed Systems with Process Crashes. *Proc. 19th IEEE Int. Conf. on Distibuted Computing Systems (ICDCS-19)*, Austin, TX, pp. 470-477, June 1999.
12. Gray J.N. and Reuter A., *Transaction Processing: Concepts and Techniques*, Morgan Kaufmann, 1070 pages, 1993.
13. Guerraoui R., Revisiting the Relationship between Non-Blocking Atomic Commitment and Consensus. *Proc. 9th Int. Workshop on Distributed Algorithms* (WDAG95), Springer-Verlag LNCS 972 (J.M. Hélary and M. Raynal Eds), Sept. 1995, pp. 87-100.
14. Guerraoui R., Larrea M. and Schiper A., Reducing the Cost for Non-Blocking in Atomic Commitment. *Proc. IEEE 16th Intl. Conf. Distributed Computing Systems*, Hong-Kong, May 1996, pp. 692-697.
15. Guerraoui R., Oliveira R. and Schiper A., Stubborn Communication Channels. *Research Report*, Département d'informatique, EPFL, Lausanne, Switzerland, July 1997.
16. Guerraoui R., Raynal M. and Schiper A., Atomic Commit And Consensus: a Unified View. (In French) *Technique et Science Informatiques*, 17(3):279-298, 1998.
17. Guerraoui R. and Schiper A., The Decentralized Non-Blocking Atomic Commitment Protocol. *Proc. of the 7th IEEE Symposium on Parallel and Distributed Systems*, San Antonio, TX, 1995, pp. 2-9.
18. Guerraoui R. and Schiper A., Total Order Multicast to Multiple Groups. *Proc. 17th IEEE Int. Conf. on Distributed Computing Systems (ICDCS-17)*, Baltimore, MD, 1997, pp. 578-585.
19. Guerraoui R. and Schiper A., Consensus: the Big Misunderstanding. *Proc of the Sixth IEEE Workshop on Future Trends of Distributed Computing Systems*, Tunis, 1997, pp. 183-186.
20. Guerraoui R. and Schiper A., The Generic Consensus Service. *Research Report 98-282*, EPFL, Lausanne, Suisse, 1998. A previous version appeared in *Proc. IEEE 26th Int Symp on Fault-Tolerant Computing (FTCS-26)*, June 1996, pp. 168-177.
21. Hadzilacos V. and Toueg S., Reliable Broadcast and Related Problems. In *Distributed Systems (Second Edition)*, ACM Press (S. Mullender Ed.), New-York, 1993, pp. 97-145.
22. Hurfin M. and Raynal M., A Simple and Fast Asynchronous Consensus Protocol Based on a Weak Failure Detector. *Distributed Computing*, 12(4):209-223, 1999.

23. Hurfin M., Mostefaoui A. and Raynal M., Consensus in Asynchronous Systems Where Processes Can Crash and Recover. *Proc. 17th IEEE Symposium on Reliable Distributed Systems*, Purdue University (IN), pp. 280-286, October 1998.
24. Hurfin M., Macedo R., Raynal M. and Tronel F., A General Framework to Solve Agreement Problems. *Proc. 18th IEEE Symposium on Reliable Distributed Systems*, Lausanne, October 1999.
25. Mostefaoui A., Raynal M. and Takizawa M., Consistent Lamport's Clocks for Asynchronous Groups with Process Crashes. *Proc. 5th Int. Conference on Parallel Computing Technologies (PACT'99)*, St-Petersburg, Springer Verlag LNCS 1662, pp. 98-107, 1999.
26. Mostefaoui A. and Raynal M., Solving Consensus Using Chandra-Toueg's Unreliable Failure Detectors: a General Quorum-Based Approach. *Proc. 13th Int. Symposium on Distributed Computing (DICS'99, formerly WDAG)*, Springer-Verlag LNCS 1693, pp. 49-63, Bratislava (Slovakia), September 1999.
27. Oliveira R., Guerraoui R. and Schiper A., Consensus in the Crash/Recovery Model. *Research Report 97-239*, EPFL, Lausanne, Suisse, 1997.
28. Oliveira R., Solving Asynchronous Consensus with the Crash and Recovery of Processes. *PhD Thesis, EPFL Département d'Informatique, 1999* (to appear).
29. Pedone F. and Schiper A., Generic Broadcast. *Proc. 13th Int. Symposium on Distributed Computing (DICS'99, formerly WDAG)*, Springer-Verlag LNCS 1693, pp. 94-108, Bratislava (Slovakia), September 1999.
30. Raynal M., Consensus-Based Management of Distributed and Replicated Data. *IEEE Bulletin of the TC on Data Engineering*, 21(4):31-37, December 1998.
31. Raynal M., Non-Blocking Atomic Commitment in Distributed Systems: A Tutorial Based on a Generic Protocol. *Journal of Computer Systems Science and Engineering*, Vol.14, 1999.
32. Schiper A., Early Consensus in an Asynchronous System with a Weak Failure Detector. *Distributed Computing*, 10:149-157, 1997.

Group Communication in Partitionable Distributed Systems[*]

Özalp Babaoğlu, Renzo Davoli, and Alberto Montresor

Università di Bologna, Mura Anteo Zamboni 7, I-40127 Bologna (Italy)
{babaoglu,davoli,montresor}@cs.unibo.it,
http://www.cs.unibo.it/projects/jgroup

Abstract. We give a formal specification and an implementation for a partitionable group communication service in asynchronous distributed systems. Our specification is motivated by the requirements for building "partition-aware" applications that can continue operating without blocking in multiple concurrent partitions and reconfigure themselves dynamically when partitions merge. The specified service guarantees liveness and excludes trivial solutions; it constitutes a useful basis for building realistic partition-aware applications; and it is implementable in practical asynchronous distributed systems where certain stability conditions hold.

1 Introduction

Functional requirements, which define how output values are related to input values, are usually sufficient for specifying traditional applications. For modern network applications, however, non-functional requirements can be just as important as their functional counterparts: the services that these applications provide must not only be correct with respect to input-output relations, they must also be delivered with acceptable "quality" levels. Reliability, timeliness and configurability are examples of non-functional requirements that are of particular interest to network applications.

A correct application satisfies its functional requirements in all possible operating environments: it just may take more or less time to do so depending on the characteristics of the environment. On the other hand, there may be operating environments in which it is impossible to achieve non-functional properties beyond certain levels. For this reason, non-functional requirements of network applications define acceptable quality *intervals* rather than exact values. In order to deliver quality levels that are both feasible and acceptable, network applications need to be *environment aware* such that they can dynamically modify their behavior depending on the properties of their operating environment.

By their nature, network applications for mobile computing, data sharing or collaborative work involve cooperation among multiple sites. For these applications, which are characterized by reliability and configurability requirements,

---

[*] Portions reprinted, with permission, from *IEEE Trans. on Software Engineering*.

S. Krakowiak, S.K. Shrivastava (Eds.): Distributed Systems, LNCS 1752, pp. 48–78, 2000.
© Springer-Verlag Berlin Heidelberg 2000

possible partitionings of the communication network is an extremely important aspect of the environment. In addition to accidental partitionings caused by failures, mobile computing systems typically support "disconnected operation" which is nothing more than a voluntary partitioning caused by deliberately unplugging units from the network. The nature of a partitioning will determine the quality for the application in terms of which of its services are available where, and at what performance levels. In other words, partitionings may result in service *reduction* or service *degradation* but need not necessarily render application services completely unavailable. Informally, we define the class of *partition-aware* applications as those that are able to make progress in multiple concurrent partitions without blocking.

Service reduction and degradation that are unavoidable during partitionings depend heavily on the application semantics and establishing them for arbitrary applications is beyond the scope of this chapter. For certain application classes with strong consistency requirements, it may be the case that all services have to be suspended completely in all but one partition. This situation corresponds to the so-called *primary-partition* model [32, 22] that has traditionally characterized partitioned operation of network applications. In this chapter we focus on the specification and implementation of system services for supporting partition awareness such that continued operation of network applications is not restricted to a single partition but may span multiple concurrent partitions. Our goal is for the system to provide only the necessary mechanisms without imposing any policies that govern partitioned operation. In this manner, each application itself can decide which of its services will be available in each partition and at what quality levels.

Our methodology for partition-aware application development is based on the *process group* paradigm [22, 8] suitably extended to partitionable systems. In this methodology, processes that cooperate in order to implement a given network application join a named group as members. All events that are relevant for partition awareness (process crashes and recoveries, network partitionings and merges) are unified in a single abstraction: the group's current membership. At each process, a *partitionable group membership service* installs *views* that correspond to the process's local perception of the group's current membership. Partition-aware applications are programmed so as to reconfigure themselves and adjust their behavior based on the composition of installed views. In a partitionable system, a group membership service has to guarantee that processes within the same partition install identical views and that their composition corresponds to the partition itself. Otherwise, inconsistencies may compromise functional correctness or may result in quality levels that are lower than what is feasible.

Specifying properties for fault-tolerant distributed services in asynchronous systems requires a delicate balance between two conflicting goals. The specification must be strong enough to exclude degenerate or trivial solutions, yet it must be weak enough to be implementable [3]. Formal specification of a partitionable group membership service in an asynchronous system has proven to be elusive and numerous prior attempts have been unsatisfactory [29, 1, 14, 15, 16, 17, 5,

33]. Anceaume *et al.* discuss at length the shortcomings of previous attempts [3]. In summary, existing specifications admit solutions that suffer from one or all of the following problems: (i) they are informal or ambiguous [33, 5, 16], (ii) they cease to install new views even in cases where the group membership continues to change [17], (iii) they capriciously split the group into several concurrent views, possibly down to singleton sets [29, 1, 14, 15, 17], (iv) they capriciously install views without any justification from the operating environment [14, 15]. The lack of a satisfactory formal specification also makes it impossible to argue the correctness of various partitionable group membership service implementations that have been proposed.

In this chapter we give a formal specification for partitionable group membership services that has the following desirable properties: (i) it does not suffer from any of the problems that have been observed for previous solutions, (ii) it is implementable in asynchronous distributed systems that exhibit certain stability conditions which we formally characterize, (iii) it is useful in that it constitutes the basis for system abstractions that can significantly simplify the task of developing realistic partition-aware applications. To "prove" the usefulness of a collection of new system abstractions, one would need to program the same set of applications twice: once using the proposed abstractions and a second time without them, and compare their relative difficulty and complexity. In another paper, we have pursued this exercise by programming a set of practical partition-aware applications on top of a *group communication service* based on our group membership specification extended with a reliable multicast service with *view synchrony* semantics [7]. For this reason, the current chapter is limited to the specification of these services and their implementability.

The rest of the chapter is organized as follows. In the next section, we introduce the system model and define basic properties of communication in the presence of partitions. In Sect. 3 we give a formal specification for partitionable group membership services that guarantees liveness and excludes useless solutions. In Sect. 4 we extend the *failure detector* abstraction of Chandra and Toueg [11] to partitionable systems and show how it can be implemented in practical asynchronous systems where certain stability conditions hold. In Sect. 5 we prove that our specification is implementable on top of an unreliable datagram communication service in systems that admit failure detectors. In Section 6 we briefly illustrate how our partitionable group membership service may be extended to a group communication service based on view synchrony. Section 7 relates our specification to numerous other proposals for group communication and Sect. 8 concludes the work.

2   System Model

We adopt notation and terminology similar to that of Chandra and Toueg [11]. The system comprises a set Π of processes that can communicate by exchanging messages through a network. Processes are associated unique names that they maintain throughout their life. The communication network implements channels connecting pairs of processes and the primitives *send*() and *recv*() for sending and receiving messages over them. The system is asynchronous in the sense that neither communication delays nor relative process speeds can be bounded. Practical distributed systems often have to be considered as being asynchronous since transient failures, unknown scheduling strategies and variable loads on the computing and communication resources make it impossible to bound delays.

To simplify the presentation, we make reference to a discrete global clock whose ticks coincide with the natural numbers in some unbounded range $\mathcal{T}$. This simplification is not in conflict with the asynchrony assumption since processes are never allowed to access the global clock.

2.1   Global Histories

The execution of a distributed program results in each process performing an event (possibly null), chosen from a set $\mathcal{S}$, at each clock tick. Set $\mathcal{S}$ includes at least the events *send*() and *recv*() corresponding to their respective communication primitives. In Sect. 3 we extend this set with other events related to group membership. The *global history* of an execution is a function σ from $\Pi \times \mathcal{T}$ to $\mathcal{S} \cup \{\epsilon\}$, where ϵ denotes the null event. If process p executes an event $e \in \mathcal{S}$ at time t, then $\sigma(p,t) = e$. Otherwise, $\sigma(p,t) = \epsilon$ indicating that process p performs no event at time t. Given some interval $\mathcal{I}$ of $\mathcal{T}$, we write $e \in \sigma(p, \mathcal{I})$ if p executes event e sometime during interval $\mathcal{I}$ of global history σ (i.e, $\exists t \in \mathcal{I} : \sigma(p,t) = e$).

2.2   Communication Model

In the absence of failures, the network is logically connected and each process can communicate with every other process. A process p sends a message m to a process q by executing $send(m, q)$, and receives a message m that has been sent to it by executing $recv(m)$. Communication is unreliable (as described below) and sequencing among multiple messages sent to the same destination need not be preserved (i.e., channels are not FIFO). Without loss of generality, we assume that (i) all messages sent are globally unique, and (ii) a message is received only if it has been previously sent. Note that this communication model is extremely faithful to practical distributed systems built on top of typical unreliable datagram transport services such as IP and UDP.

2.3   Failure Model

Processes may fail by *crashing* whereby they halt prematurely. For simplicity, we do not consider process recovery after a crash. The evolution of process failures during an execution is captured through the *crash pattern* function C from $\mathcal{T}$ to 2^{Π} where $C(t)$ denotes the set of processes that have crashed by time t. Since crashed processes do not recover, we have $C(t) \subseteq C(t+1)$. With $Correct(C) = \{p \mid \forall t : p \notin C(t)\}$ we denote those processes that never crash, and thus, are correct in C.

A variety of events, including link crashes, buffer overflows, incorrect or inconsistent routing tables, may disable communication between processes. We refer to them generically as *communication failures*. Unlike process crashes, which are permanent, communication failures may be temporary due to subsequent repairs. The evolution of communication failures and repairs during an execution is captured through the *unreachability pattern* function U from $\Pi \times T$ to 2^{Π} where $U(p, t)$ denotes the set of processes with which p cannot communicate at time t. If $q \in U(p, t)$, we say that process q is *unreachable* from p at time t, and write $p \not\leadsto_t q$ as a shorthand; otherwise we say that process q is *reachable* from p at time t, and write $p \leadsto_t q$. As noted above, communication failures are not necessarily permanent but may appear and disappear dynamically. This is reflected by the fact that the sets $U(p, t)$ and $U(p, t + 1)$ may differ arbitrarily.

Note that the unreachability pattern is an abstract characterization of the communication state of a system, just as the crash pattern is an abstract characterization of its computational state. Only an omnipotent external observer can construct the unreachability and crash patterns that occur during an execution and neither can be inferred from within an asynchronous system. Nevertheless, they are useful in stating desired properties for a group membership service. Any implementation of the specified service in an asynchronous system will have to be based on approximations of unreachability and crashes provided by *failure detectors* [11] as we discuss in Sect. 4.

Reachable/unreachable are attributes of individual communication channels (identified as ordered process pairs), just as correct/crashed are attributes of individual processes. In the rest of the chapter, we also refer to communication failure scenarios called *partitionings* that involve multiple sets of processes. A partitioning disables communication among different *partitions*, each containing a set of processes. Processes within a given partition can communicate among themselves, but cannot communicate with processes outside the partition. When communication between several partitions is reestablished, we say that they *merge*.

Process and communication failures that occur during an execution are not totally independent, but must satisfy certain constraints that are captured through the notion of a *failure history*:

Definition 1 (Failure History). *A failure history F is a pair (C, U), where C is a crash pattern and U is an unreachability pattern, such that (i) a process that has crashed by time t is unreachable from every other process at time t, and (ii) a process that has not crashed by time t is reachable from itself at time t. Formally,[1]*

$$(i) \ p \in C(t) \ \Rightarrow \ q \not\leadsto_t p$$
$$(ii) \ p \notin C(t) \ \Rightarrow \ p \leadsto_t p \ .$$

---

[1] In these formulas and all others that follow, free variables are assumed to be universally quantified over their respective domains (process events, time, messages, views, etc.), which can be inferred from context.

By definition, the unreachability pattern subsumes the crash pattern in every failure history. We nevertheless choose to model crash and unreachability patterns separately so that specifications can be made in terms of properties that need to hold for *correct* processes only.

Finally, we need to relate crash and unreachability patterns to the events of the execution itself. In other words, we need to formalize notions such as "crashed processes halt prematurely" and "unreachable processes cannot communicate directly". We do this by requiring that the global and failure histories of the same execution conform to constraints defining a *run*.

Definition 2 (Run). *A run R is a pair (σ, F), where σ is a global history and $F = (C, U)$ is the corresponding failure history, such that (i) a crashed process stops executing events, and (ii) a message that is sent will be received if and only if its destination is reachable from the sender at the time of sending. Formally,*

$$(i) \ p \in C(t) \ \Rightarrow \ \forall t' \geq t : \sigma(p, t') = \epsilon$$
$$(ii) \ \sigma(p, t) = send(m, q) \ \Rightarrow \ (\ recv(m) \in \sigma(q, T) \Leftrightarrow p \leadsto_t q \ ) \ .$$

Note that by Definition 1(ii), the reachable relation for correct processes is *perpetually* reflexive — a correct process is always reachable from itself. Transitivity of reachability, on the other hand, need not hold in general. We make this choice so as to render our model realistic by admitting scenarios that are common in wide-area networks, including the Internet, where a site B may be reachable from site A, and site C reachable from B, at a time when C is unreachable from A directly. Yet the three sites A, B and C should be considered as belonging to the same partition since they *can* communicate with each other (perhaps indirectly) using communication services more sophisticated than the send/receive primitives offered by the network. As we shall see in Sect. 5.1, such services can indeed be built in our system model so that two processes will be able to communicate with each other whenever it is possible. And our notion of a partition as the set of processes that can mutually communicate will be based on these services.

We do not assume perpetual symmetry for the reachable relation. In other words, at a given time, it is possible that some process p be reachable from process q but not vice versa. This is again motivated by observed behavior in real wide-area networks. Yet, to make the model tractable, we require a form *eventual* symmetry as stated below:

Property 1 (Eventual Symmetry). If, after some initial period, process q becomes and remains reachable (unreachable) from p, then eventually p will become and remain reachable (unreachable) from q as well. Formally,

$$\exists t_0, \forall t \geq t_0 : p \leadsto_t q \ \Rightarrow \ \exists t_1, \forall t \geq t_1 : q \leadsto_t p$$
$$\exists t_0, \forall t \geq t_0 : p \not\leadsto_t q \ \Rightarrow \ \exists t_1, \forall t \geq t_1 : q \not\leadsto_t p \ .$$

This is a reasonable behavior to expect of practical asynchronous distributed systems. Typically, communication channels are bidirectional and rely on the same physical and logical resources in both directions. As a result, the ability or inability to communicate in one direction usually implies that a similar property will eventually be observed also in the other direction.

To conclude the system model, we impose a fairness condition on the communication network so as to exclude degenerate scenarios where two processes are unable to communicate despite the fact that they become reachable infinitely often. In other words, the communication system cannot behave maliciously such that two processes that are normally reachable become unreachable precisely at those times when they attempt to communicate.

Property 2 (Fair Channels). Let p and q be two processes that are not permanently unreachable from each other. If p sends an unbounded number of messages to q, then q will receive an unbounded number of these messages. Formally,

$$(\forall t, \exists t_1 \geq t : p \leadsto_{t_1} q) \wedge (\forall t, \exists t_2 \geq t : \sigma(p, t_2) = send(m, q)) \Rightarrow$$
$$(\forall t, \exists t_3 \geq t : \sigma(q, t_3) = recv(m') \wedge send(m', q) \in \sigma(p, \mathcal{T})) .$$

3 Partitionable Group Membership Service: Specification

Our methodology for partition-aware application development is based on the *process group* paradigm with suitable extensions to partitionable systems. In this methodology, processes cooperate towards a given network application by *joining* a group as members. Later on, a process may decide to terminate its collaboration by explicitly *leaving* the group. In the absence of failures, the *membership* of a group comprises those processes that have joined but have not left the group. In addition to these voluntary events, membership of a group may also change due to involuntary events corresponding to process and communication failures or repairs.

At each process, a *partitionable group membership service* (PGMS) tracks the changes in the group's membership and installs them as *views* through $vchg()$ events. Installed views correspond to the process's local perception of the group's current membership. Partition-aware applications are programmed so as to reconfigure themselves and adjust their behavior based on the composition of installed views. In the absence of partitionings, every correct process should install the same view, and this view should include exactly those members that have not crashed. This goal is clearly not feasible in a partitionable system, where processes in different partitions will have different perceptions of the membership for a given group. For these reasons, a partitionable group membership service should guarantee that under certain stability conditions, correct processes within the same partition install identical views and that their composition correspond to the composition of the partition itself.

In the next section, we translate these informal ideas in a formal specification for our partitionable group membership service. The specification is given as a set of properties on view compositions and view installations, stated in terms of the unreachability pattern that occurs during an execution. The specification we give below has benefited from extensive reflection based on actual experience with programming realistic applications and has gone through numerous refinements over the last several years. We believe that it represents a minimal set of properties for a service that is both useful and implementable.

3.1 Formal Specification

For sake of brevity, we assume a single process group and do not consider changes to its membership due to voluntary join and leave events. Thus, the group's membership will vary only due to failures and repairs. We start out by defining some terms and introducing notation. Views are labeled in order to be globally unique. Given a view v, we write $\bar{v}$ to denote its composition as a set of process names. The set of possible events for an execution, S, is augmented to include $vchg(v)$ denoting a view change that installs view v. The *current view* of process p at time t is v, denoted $view(p, t) = v$, if v is the last view to have been installed at p before time t. Events are said to occur *in the view* that is current. View w is called *immediate successor of v at p*, denoted $v \prec_p w$, if p installs w in view v. View w is called *immediate successor* of v, denoted $v \prec w$, if there exists some process p such that $v \prec_p w$. The *successor* relation $\prec^*$ denotes the transitive closure of $\prec$. Two views that are not related through $\prec^*$ are called *concurrent*. Given two immediate successor views $v \prec w$, we say that a process *survives* the view change if it belongs to both v and w.

The composition of installed views cannot be arbitrary but should reflect reality through the unreachability pattern that occurs during an execution. In other words, processes should be aware of other processes with which they can and cannot communicate directly in order to adapt their behaviors consistently. Informally, each process should install views that include all processes reachable from it and exclude those that are unreachable from it. Requiring that the current view of a process perpetually reflect the actual unreachability pattern would be impossible to achieve in an asynchronous system. Thus, we state the requirement as two eventual properties that must hold in stable conditions where reachability and unreachability relations are persistent.

GM1 (View Accuracy). *If there is a time after which process q remains reachable from some correct process p, then eventually the current view of p will always include q. Formally,*

$$\exists t_0, \forall t \geq t_0 : p \in Correct(C) \wedge p \leadsto_t q \implies \exists t_1, \forall t \geq t_1 : q \in \overline{view(p, t)} \ .$$

GM2 (View Completeness). *If there is a time after which all processes in some partition Θ remain unreachable from the rest of the group, then eventually the current view of every correct process not in Θ will never include any process in Θ. Formally,*

$$\exists t_0, \forall t \geq t_0, \forall q \in \Theta, \forall p \notin \Theta : p \not\leadsto_t q \implies$$
$$\exists t_1, \forall t \geq t_1, \forall r \in Correct(C) - \Theta : \overline{view(r, t)} \cap \Theta = \emptyset \ .$$

View Accuracy and View Completeness are of fundamental importance for every PGMS. They state that the composition of installed views cannot be arbitrary but must be a function of the actual unreachability pattern occurring during a run. Any specification that lacked a property similar to View Accuracy could be trivially satisfied by installing at every process either an empty view or a singleton view consisting of the process itself. The resulting service would exhibit what has been called *capricious view splitting* [3] and would not be very useful. View Accuracy prevents capricious view splitting by requiring that eventually, all views installed by two permanently-reachable processes contain each other. On the other hand, the absence of View Completeness would admit implementations in which processes always install views containing the entire group, again rendering the service not very useful.

Note that View Accuracy and View Completeness are stated slightly differently. This is because the reachable relation between processes is not transitive. While q being reachable directly from p is justification for requiring p to include q in its view, the converse is not necessarily true. The fact that a process p cannot communicate directly with another process q does not imply that p cannot communicate indirectly with q through a sequence of pairwise-reachable intermediate processes. For this reason, View Completeness has to be stated in terms of complementary sets of processes rather than process pairs. Doing so assures that a process is excluded from a view only if communication is impossible because there exists no path, directly or indirectly, for reaching it.

View Accuracy and View Completeness state requirements for views installed by individual processes. A group membership service that is to be useful must also place constraints on views installed by different processes. Without such coherency guarantees for views, two processes could behave differently even though they belong to the same partition but have different perceptions of its composition. For example, consider a system with two processes p and q that are permanently reachable from each other. By View Accuracy, after some time t, both p and q will install the same view v containing themselves. Now suppose that at some time after t, a third process r becomes and remains reachable from q alone. Again by View Accuracy, q will eventually install a new view w that includes r in addition to itself and p. Presence of process r is unknown to p since they are not directly reachable. Thus, p continues believing that it shares the same view with q since its current view v continues to include q, when in fact process q has gone on to install view w different from v. The resulting differences in perception of the environment could lead processes p and q to behave differently even though they belong to the same partition. The following property has been formulated to avoid such undesirable scenarios.

GM3 (View Coherency).
(i) If a correct process p installs view v, then either all processes in $\bar{v}$ also install v, or p eventually installs an immediate successor to v. Formally,

$$p \in Correct(C) \wedge vchg(v) \in \sigma(p, T) \wedge q \in \bar{v} \Rightarrow$$
$$(vchg(v) \in \sigma(q, T)) \vee (\exists w : v \prec_p w) .$$

(ii) If two processes p and q initially install the same view v and p later on installs an immediate successor to v, then eventually either q also installs an immediate successor to v, or q crashes. Formally,

$$vchg(v) \in \sigma(p, T) \wedge vchg(v) \in \sigma(q, T) \wedge v \prec_p w_1 \wedge q \in Correct(C) \implies$$
$$\exists w_2 : v \prec_q w_2 .$$

(iii) When process p installs a view w as the immediate successor to view v, all processes that survive from view v to w along with p have previously installed v. Formally,

$$\sigma(p, t_0) = vchg(w) \wedge v \prec_p w \wedge q \in \overline{v} \cap \overline{w} \wedge q \neq p \implies vchg(v) \in \sigma(q, [0, t_0[) .$$

Returning to the above example, the current view of process p cannot remain v indefinitely as GM3(ii) requires p to eventually install a new view. By assumption, q never installs another view after w. Thus, by GM3(i), the new installed by p must be w as well and include r. As a result, processes p and q that belong to the same partition return to sharing the same view. In fact, we can generalize the above example to argue that View Coherency together with View Accuracy guarantee that every view installed by a correct process is also installed by all other processes that are permanently reachable from it. Note that the composition of the final view installed by p and q includes process r as belonging to their partition. This is reasonable since p and r can communicate (using q as a relay) even though they are not reachable directly.

View Coherency is important even when reachability and unreachability relations are not persistent. In these situations where View Accuracy and View Completeness are not applicable, View Coherency serves to inform a process that it no longer shares the same view with another process. Consider two processes p and q that are initially mutually reachable. Suppose that p has installed a view v containing the two of them by some time t. The current view of process q could be different from v at time t either because it never installs v (e.g., it crashes) or because it installs another view after having installed v (e.g., there is a network partitioning or merge). In both cases, GM3(i) and GM3(ii), respectively, ensure that process p will eventually become aware of this fact because it will install a new view after v.

When a process installs a new view, it cannot be sure which other processes have also installed the same view. This is an inherent limitation due to asynchrony and possibility of failures. GM3(iii) allows a process to reason *a posteriori* about other processes: At the time when process p installs view w as the immediate successor of view v, it can deduced which other processes have also installed view v. And if some process q belonging to view v never installs it, we can be sure that q cannot belong to view w. Note that these conclusions are based entirely on *local* information (successive pairs of installed views) yet they allow a process to reason globally about the actions of other processes.

The next property for group membership places restrictions on the order in which views are installed. In systems where partitionings are impossible, it is reasonable to require that all correct processes install views according to some total order. In a partitionable system, this is not feasible due to the possibility of concurrent partitions. Yet, for a partitionable group membership service to be useful, the set of views must be consistently ordered by those processes that do install them. In other words, if two views are installed by a process in a given order, the same two views cannot be installed in the opposite order by some other process.

GM4 (View Order).   *The order in which processes install views is such that the successor relation is a partial order. Formally, $v \prec^* w \Rightarrow w \nprec^* v$.*

When combined with View Accuracy and View Coherency, View Order allows us to conclude that there is a time after which permanently reachable processes not only install the same set of views, they install them in the same order.

The final property of our specification places a simple integrity restriction on the composition of the views installed by a process. By Definition 1(ii), every correct process is always reachable from itself. Thus, Property GM1 ensures that eventually, all views installed by a process will include itself. However, it is desirable that self-inclusion be a perpetual, and not only eventual, property of installed views.

GM5 (View Integrity).   *Every view installed by a process includes the process itself. Formally,*

$$vchg(v) \in \sigma(p, \mathcal{T}) \Rightarrow p \in \bar{v} .$$

Properties GM1–GM5 taken together define a *partitionable group membership service* (PGMS).

3.2   Discussion

Recall that Properties GM1 and GM2 are stated in terms of runs where reachability and unreachability relations are persistent. They are, however, sufficient to exclude trivial solutions to PGMS also in runs where reachability and unreachability among processes are continually changing due to transient failures. As an example, consider a system composed of two processes p and q and a run R_0 where they are permanently mutually reachable. By View Accuracy and View Coherency, we know there is a time t_0 by which both p and q will have installed a view composed of themselves alone. Now, consider run R_1 identical to R_0 up to time $t_1 > t_0$ when p and q become unreachable. The behavior of processes p and q under runs R_0 and R_1 must be identical up to time t_1 since they cannot distinguish between the two runs. Thus, if they install views composed of p and q by time t_0 under run R_0, they must install the same views also under run R_1 where reachability relations are not persistent but transient. This example can be generalized to conclude that any implementation satisfying our specification cannot delay arbitrarily installation of a new view including processes that remain reachable for sufficiently long periods. Nor can it delay arbitrarily installation of a new view excluding processes that remain unreachable for sufficiently long periods.

Asynchronous distributed systems present fundamental limitations for the solvability of certain problems in the presence of failures. Consensus [19] and primary-partition group membership [10] are among them. Partitionable group membership service, as we have defined it, happens to be not solvable in an asynchronous system as well. A proof sketch of this impossibility results can be found in the extended version of the paper [6]. The impossibility result for PGMS can be circumvented by requiring certain stability conditions to hold in an asynchronous system. In the next section we formulate these conditions as abstract properties of an unreliable failure detector [11]. Then in Sect. 5 we show how the specified PGMS can be implemented in systems that admit the necessary failure detector.

4 Failure Detectors for Partitionable Systems

In this section, we formalize the stability conditions that are necessary for solving our specification of partitionable group membership in asynchronous systems. We do so indirectly by stating a set of abstract properties that need to hold for failure detectors that have been suitably extended to partitionable systems. Similar failure detector definitions extended for partitionable systems have appeared in other contexts [25, 12]. The failure detector abstraction originally proposed by Chandra and Toueg [11] is for systems with perfectly-reliable communication. In partitionable systems, specification of failure detector properties has to be based on reachability between pairs of processes rather than individual processes being correct or crashed. For example, it will be acceptable (and desirable) for the failure detector of p to suspect q that happens to be correct but is unreachable from p.

Informally, a failure detector is a distributed oracle that tries to estimate the unreachability pattern U that occurs in an execution. Each process has access to a local module of the failure detector that monitors a subset of the processes and outputs those that it currently suspects as being unreachable from itself. A *failure detector history* H is a function from $\Pi \times T$ to 2^Π that describes the outputs of the local modules at each process. If $q \in H(p, t)$, we say that p suspects q at time t in H. Formally, a *failure detector* $\mathcal{D}$ is a function that associates with each failure history $F = (C, U)$ a set $\mathcal{D}(F)$ denoting failure detector histories that could occur in executions with failure history F.

In asynchronous systems, failure detectors are inherently unreliable in that the information they provide may be incorrect. Despite this limitation, failure detectors satisfying certain *completeness* and *accuracy* properties have proven to be useful abstractions for solving practical problems in such systems [11]. Informally, completeness and accuracy state, respectively, the conditions under which a process should and should not be suspected for $H(p, t)$ to be a meaningful estimate of $U(p, t)$. We consider the following adaptations of completeness and accuracy to partitionable systems, maintaining the same names used by Chandra and Toueg for compatibility reasons [11]:

FD1 (Strong Completeness).   *If some process q remains unreachable from correct process p, then eventually p will always suspect q. Formally, given a failure history $F = (C, U)$, a failure detector $\mathcal{D}$ satisfies Strong Completeness if all failure detector histories $H \in \mathcal{D}(F)$ are such that:*

$$\exists t_0, \forall t \geq t_0 : p \in Correct(C) \wedge p \not\leadsto_t q \; \Rightarrow \; \exists t_1, \forall t \geq t_1 : q \in H(p, t) .$$

FD2 (Eventual Strong Accuracy).   *If some process q remains reachable from correct process p, then eventually p will no longer suspect q. Formally, given a failure history $F = (C, U)$, a failure detector $\mathcal{D}$ satisfies Eventual Strong Accuracy if all failure detector histories $H \in \mathcal{D}(F)$ are such that:*

$$\exists t_0, \forall t \geq t_0 : p \in Correct(C) \wedge p \leadsto_t q \; \Rightarrow \; \exists t_1, \forall t \geq t_1 : q \notin H(p, t) .$$

Borrowing from Chandra and Toueg [11], failure detectors satisfying Strong Completeness and Eventual Strong Accuracy are called *eventually perfect*, and their class denoted $\diamond\tilde{\mathcal{P}}$. In addition to the properties stated above, we can also formulate their weak and perpetual counterparts, thus generating a hierarchy of failure detector classes similar to those of Chandra and Toueg [11]. Informally, *weak* completeness and accuracy require the corresponding property to hold only for *some* pair of processes (rather than all pairs), while their *perpetual* versions require the corresponding property to hold from the very beginning (rather than eventually).

While a detailed discussion of failure detector hierarchy for partitionable systems and reductions between them is beyond the scope of this chapter, we make a few brief observations. In absence of partitionings, failure detector classes with the weak version of Completeness happen to be equivalent to those with the strong version. [2] In such systems, it suffices for *one* correct process to suspect a crashed process since it can (reliably) communicate this information to *all* other correct processes. In partitionable systems, this is not possible and failure detector classes with weak completeness are strictly weaker than those with strong completeness.

In principle, it is impossible to implement a failure detector $\mathcal{D} \in \diamond\tilde{\mathcal{P}}$ in partitionable asynchronous systems, just as it is impossible to implement a failure detector belonging to any of the classes $\diamond\mathcal{P}$, $\diamond\mathcal{Q}$, $\diamond\mathcal{S}$ and $\diamond\mathcal{W}$ in asynchronous systems with perfectly-reliable communication [11]. In practice, however, asynchronous systems are expected to exhibit reasonable behavior and failure detectors for $\diamond\tilde{\mathcal{P}}$ can indeed be implemented. For example, consider the following algorithm, which is similar to that of Chandra and Toueg [11], but is based on *round-trip* rather than *one-way* message time-outs. Each process p periodically sends a p-ping message to every other process in Π. When a process q receives a p-ping, it sends back to p a q-ack message. If process p does not receive a q-ack within $\Delta_p(q)$ local time units, p adds q to its list of suspects. If p receives a

---

[2] These are the $\mathcal{P} \cong \mathcal{Q}$, $\mathcal{S} \cong \mathcal{W}$, $\diamond\mathcal{P} \cong \diamond\mathcal{Q}$ and $\diamond\mathcal{S} \cong \diamond\mathcal{W}$ results of Chandra and Toueg [11].

q-ack message from some process q that it already suspects, p removes q from the suspect list and increments its time-out period $\Delta_p(q)$ for the channel (p, q).

Note that since processes send *ack* messages only in response to *ping* messages, a process p will continually time-out on every other process q that is unreachable from it. Thus, the above algorithm trivially satisfies the Strong Completeness property of $\diamond\tilde{\mathcal{P}}$ in partitionable asynchronous systems. On the other hand, in an asynchronous system, it is possible for some process p to observe an unbounded number of premature time-outs for some other process q even though q remains reachable from p. In this case, p would repeatedly add and remove q from its list of suspects, thus violating the Eventual Strong Accuracy property of $\diamond\tilde{\mathcal{P}}$. In many practical systems, increasing the time-out period for each communication channel after each mistake will ensure that eventually there are no premature time-outs on any of the communication channels, thus ensuring Eventual Strong Accuracy.

The only other scenario in which the algorithm could fail to achieve Eventual Strong Accuracy occurs when process q is reachable from process p and continues to receive p-ping messages but its q-ack messages sent to p are systematically lost. In a system satisfying Eventual Symmetry, this scenario cannot last forever and eventually p will start receiving q-ack messages, causing it to permanently remove q from its suspect list and thus satisfy Eventual Strong Accuracy.

Given that perfectly reliable failure detectors are impossible to implement in asynchronous systems, it is reasonable to ask: what are the consequences of mistakenly suspecting a process that is actually reachable? As we shall see in the next section, our use of failure detectors in solving PGMS is such that incorrect suspicions may cause installation of views smaller than what are actually feasible. In other words, they may compromise View Accuracy but cannot invalidate any of the other properties. As a consequence, processes that are either very slow or have very slow communication links may be temporarily excluded from the current view of other processes to be merged back in when their delays become smaller. This type of "view splitting" is reasonable since including such processes in views would only force the entire computation to slow down to their pace. Obviously, the notion of "slow" is completely application dependent and can only be established on a per-group basis.

5 Partitionable Group Membership Service: Implementation

In this section we present an algorithm that implements the service specified in Sect. 3 in partitionable asynchronous systems augmented with a failure detector of class $\diamond\tilde{\mathcal{P}}$. Our goal is to show the implementability of the proposed specification for PGMS; consequently, the algorithm is designed for simplicity rather than efficiency. The overall structure of our solution is shown in Fig. 1 and consists of two components called the *Multi-Send Layer* (MSL) and *View Management Layer* (VML) at each process. In the figure, FD denotes any failure detector module satisfying the abstract properties for class $\diamond\tilde{\mathcal{P}}$ as defined in Sect. 4.

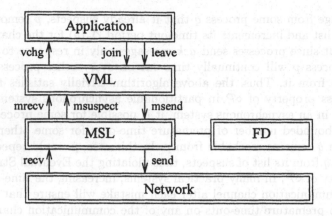

Fig. 1. Overall structure of the partitionable group membership service.

All interactions with the communication network and the failure detector are limited to MSL which uses the unreliable, unsequenced datagram transport service of the network through the primitives *send*() and *recv*(). Each MSL can also read the suspect list of the corresponding failure detector module FD. MSL implements the primitives *msend*(), *mrecv*() and *msuspect*() as described below, which in turn are used by VML. Recall that we consider group membership changes due to failures and repairs only. Thus, the implementation we give includes only the view change notification event *vchg*() but not the primitives *join*() and *leave*() for voluntarily joining and leaving the group.

In order to distinguish between the various layers in our discussion, we say that a process *m-sends* and *m-receives* messages when it communicates through the MSL primitives *msend*() and *mrecv*(), respectively. We reserve *send* and *receive* to denote communication directly through the network services without going through MSL. Similarly, we say that a process *m-suspects* those processes that are notified through a *msuspect*() event while *suspect* is reserved for describing the failure detector itself.

The following notation is used in the presentation of our algorithms. We use *italic* font for variable and procedure names. Tags denoting message types are written in SMALLCAPS. The **wait-for** construct is used to block a process until a *mrecv*() or a *msuspect*() event is generated by MSL. The **generate** construct produces an upcall of the specified type to the next layer in the architecture.

5.1   The Multi-send Layer

Implementing a group membership service directly on top of a point-to-point unreliable, unsequenced datagram transport service provided by the network would be difficult. The difficulty is aggravated by the lack of transitivity of the reachability relation as provided by the failure detector. The task of MSL is to hide this complexity by transforming the unreliable, point-to-point network communication primitives to their best-effort, one-to-many counterparts. Informally, MSL tries to deliver m-sent messages to all processes in some destination set. MSL also "filters" the raw failure detector suspect list by eliminating from it those processes that can be reached indirectly. In other words, the notion of reachability above the MSL corresponds to the transitive closure of reachability at the failure detector layer. What distinguishes MSL from a typical network routing or reliable multicast service is the integration of message delivery semantics with the reachability information. In that sense, MSL is much closer to the *dynamic routing layer* of Phoenix [24] and the MUTS layer of Horus [34].

Informally, properties that MSL must satisfy are:

Property 3. (a) if a process q is continuously unreachable from p, then eventually p will continuously m-suspect q; (b) if a process q is continuously reachable from p, then eventually every process that m-suspects q also m-suspects p; (c) each process m-receives a message at most once and only if some process actually m-sent it earlier; (d) messages from the same sender are m-received in FIFO order; (e) a message that is m-sent by a correct process is eventually m-received by all processes in the destination set that are not m-suspected; (f) a process never m-suspects itself; (g) the reachability relation defined by the *msuspect()* events is eventually symmetric.

Properties (a) and (b) are the non-triviality conditions of our communication service. Properties (c) and (d) place simple integrity and order requirements on m-receiving messages. Property (e) defines a liveness condition on the m-sending of messages. Finally, property (f) prevents processes from m-suspecting themselves, while property (g) requires that if a correct process p stops m-suspecting another correct process q, then eventually q will stop m-suspecting p. It is important to note that from the combination of properties (b) and (f) we conclude that if q is continuously reachable from p, then p eventually stops m-suspecting q. Moreover, from properties (b) and (e) we conclude that if q is continuously reachable from p, then every message m-sent by q to p is eventually m-received.

A formal description of these properties, along with an algorithm to achieve them can be found in the extended version of this work [6]. The proposed algorithm is based on the integration of a routing algorithm and a failure detector of class $\diamond\tilde{\mathcal{P}}$.

5.2   The View Management Layer

VML uses the services provided by MSL in order to construct and install views as defined by the PGMS specification. At each process, let the *reachable set* correspond to those processes that are not currently m-suspected. These reachable sets form a good basis for constructing views since part of the PGMS specification follows immediately from the properties of MSL that produce them. In particular, Property GM2 is satisfied by Property 3(a) requiring that if a process q is continuously unreachable from p, then eventually p will continuously m-suspect q. Property GM1 is satisfied by Properties 3(b) and 3(f), as discussed above. Finally, Property GM5 is satisfied by Property 3(f).

The main difference between reachable sets as constructed by MSL and views as defined by PGMS is with respect to coherency. While reachable sets are completely individualistic and lack any coordination, views of different processes need to be coherent among themselves as defined by Property GM3. VML achieves this property by using reachable sets as initial estimates for new views but installs them only after having reached agreement on their composition among mutually-reachable processes. To guarantee liveness of our solution, each execution of the agreement algorithm must terminate by actually installing a new view. Yet the composition of installed views cannot invalidate any of the properties that are inherited from MSL as described above.

The main algorithm for VML, illustrated in Fig. 2, alternates between an *idle phase* and an *agreement phase*. A process remains idle until either it is informed by MSL that there is a change in its perception of the reachable set (through a *msuspect()* event), or it m-receives a message from another process that has observed such a change. Both of these events cause the process to enter agreement phase. The agreement protocol, illustrated in Fig. 3, is organized as two sub-phases called *synchronization phase* and *estimate exchange phase* (for short, s-phase and ee-phase, respectively).

At the beginning of s-phase, each process m-sends a synchronization message containing a version number to those processes it perceives as being reachable, and then waits for responses. This message acts to "wake-up" processes that have not yet entered s-phase. Furthermore, version numbers exchanged in the s-phase are used in subsequent ee-phases to distinguish between messages of different agreement protocol invocations. A process leaves s-phase to enter ee-phase either when it m-receives a response to its synchronization message from every process that has not been m-suspected during the s-phase, or when it m-receives a message from a process that has already entered ee-phase.

Each process enters ee-phase (Fig. 4 and 5) with its own estimate for the composition of the next view. During this phase, a process can modify its estimate to reflect changes in the approximation for reachability that is being reported to it by MSL. In order to guarantee liveness, the algorithm constructs estimate sets that are always monotone decreasing so that the agreement condition is certain to hold eventually. Whenever the estimate changes, the process m-sends a message containing the new estimate to every process belonging to the estimate itself. When a process m-receives estimate messages, it removes from its own estimate those processes that are excluded from the estimate of the sender. At the same time, each change in the estimate causes a process to m-send an agreement proposal to a process selected among the current estimate to act as a *coordinator*. Note that while estimates are evolving, different processes may select different coordinators. Or, the coordinator may crash or become unreachable before the agreement condition has been verified. In all these situations, the current agreement attempt will fail and new estimates will evolve causing a new coordinator to be selected.

When the coordinator eventually observes that proposals m-received from some set S of processes are all equal to S, agreement is achieved and the coordi-

```
1    thread ViewManagement
2        reachable ← {p}              % Set of unsuspected processes
3        version ← (0, ..., 0)        % Vector clock
4        symset ← ({p}, ..., {p})     % Symmetry set
5        view ← ( UniqueID(), {p} )   % Current view id and composition
6        cview ← view                 % Corresponding complete view
7        generate vchg(view))
8
9        while true do
10           wait-for event           % Remain idle until some event occurs
11           case event of
12
13               msuspect(P):
14                   foreach r ∈ (Π − P) − reachable do symset[r] ← reachable
15                   msend(⟨SYMMETRY, version, reachable⟩, (Π − P) − reachable)
16                   reachable ← Π − P
17                   AgreementPhase()
18
19               mrecv(⟨SYNCHRONIZE, V_p, V_q, P⟩, q):
20                   if (version[q] < V[q]) then
21                       version[q] ← V[q]
22                       if (q ∈ reachable) then
23                           AgreementPhase()
24                   fi
25
26           esac
27       od
```

Fig. 2. The main algorithm for process p.

nator m-sends to the members of S a message containing a new view identifier and composition equal to S. When a process m-receives such a message, there are two possibilities: it can either install a *complete* view, containing all processes indicated in the message, or it can install a *partial* view, containing a subset of the processes indicated in the message. Partial views are necessary whenever the installation of a complete view would violate Property GM3(iii). This condition is checked by verifying whether the current views of processes composing the new view intersect[3]. If they do, this could mean that a process in the intersection has never installed one of the intersecting views, thus violating Property GM3(iii). For this reason, the m-received view is broken in to a set of non-intersecting partial views, each of them satisfying Property GM3(iii). If, on the other hand, current views do not intersect, each process can install the new complete view as m-received from the coordinator. Note that classification of views as being complete or partial is completely internal to the implementation. An application

---

[3] This condition can be checked locally since current views of processes composing the new view are included in the message from the coordinator.

```
1    procedure AgreementPhase()
2      repeat
3        estimate ← reachable              % Next view estimation
4        version[p] ← version[p] + 1        % Generate new version number
5        SynchronizationPhase()
6        EstimateExchangePhase()
7      until stable                         % Exit when the view is stable
8
9    procedure SynchronizationPhase()
10     synchronized ← {p}                   % Processes syncronized with p
11     foreach r ∈ estimate − {p} do
12       msend(⟨SYNCHRONIZE, version[r], version[p], symset[r]⟩, {r})
13     while (estimate ⊈ synchronized) do
14       wait-for event                     % Remain idle until some event occurs
15       case event of
16
17           msuspect(P):
18             foreach r ∈ (Π − P) − reachable) do symset[r] ← reachable
19             msend(⟨SYMMETRY, version, reachable⟩, (Π − P) − reachable)
20             reachable ← Π − P
21             estimate ← estimate ∩ reachable
22
23           mrecv(⟨SYMMETRY, V, P⟩, q):
24             if (version[p] = V[p]) and (q ∈ estimate) then
25               estimate ← estimate − P
26
27           mrecv(⟨SYNCHRONIZE, Vp, Vq, P⟩, q):
28             if (version[p] = Vp) then
29               synchronized ← synchronized ∪ {q}
30             if (version[q] < Vq) then
31               version[q] ← Vq
32               agreed[q] ← Vq
33               msend(⟨SYNCHRONIZE, version[q], version[p], symset[q]⟩, {q})
34             fi
35
36           mrecv(⟨ESTIMATE, V, P⟩, q)
37             version[q] = V[q]
38             if (q ∉ estimate) then
39               msend(⟨SYMMETRY, version, estimate⟩, {q})
40             elseif (version[p] = V[p]) and (p ∈ P) then
41               estimate ← estimate ∩ P
42               synchronized ← P
43               agreed ← V
44             fi
45
46       esac
47     od
```

Fig. 3. Agreement and synchronization phases for process p.

programmer using the provided service in unaware of the distinction and deals with a single notion of view. Although each invocation of the agreement protocol terminates with the installation of a new view, it is possible that the new view does not correspond to the current set of processes perceived as being reachable, or that a new synchronization message has been m-received during the previous ee-phase. In both cases a new agreement phase is started.

In the extended version of this work [6], we give a proof that our algorithm satisfies the properties of PGMS. Here, we discuss in high-level terms the techniques used by the algorithm in order to satisfy the specification. Leaving out the more trivial properties such as View Completeness, View Integrity and View Order, we focus our attention on View Coherency, View Accuracy and liveness of the solution. Property GM3 consists of three parts. GM3(iii) is satisfied through the installation of partial views, as explained above. As for GM3(i) and GM3(ii), each process is eventually informed if another process belonging to its current view has not installed it, or if it has changed views after having installed it, respectively. The process is kept informed either through a message, or through an m-suspect event. In both cases, it reenters the agreement phase. As for liveness, each invocation of the agreement protocol terminates with the installation of a new view, even in situations where the reachability relation is highly unstable. This is guaranteed by the fact that successive estimates of each process for the composition of the next view are monotone decreasing sets. This is achieved through two actions. First, new m-suspect lists reported by MSL never result in a process being added to the initial estimate. Second, processes exchange their estimates with each other and remove those that have been removed by others. In this manner, each process continues to reduce its estimate until it coincides exactly with those processes that agree on the composition of the next view. In the limit, the estimate set will eventually reduce to the process itself and a singleton view will be installed. This approach may seem in conflict with View Accuracy: if process p m-receives from process r a message inviting it to remove a process q, it cannot refuse it. But if p and q are permanently reachable, non-triviality properties of MSL guarantee that after some time, r cannot remove q from its view estimate without removing p as well. So, after some time, r cannot m-send a message to p inviting it to exclude q, because p cannot belong to the current estimate of r. Moreover, s-phase of view agreement constitutes a "barrier" against the propagation of old "remove q" messages. In this way, it is possible to show that there is a time after which all views installed by p contain q.

A more detailed description of the VML algorithm can be found in the extended version of this work [6].

6   Reliable Multicast Service: Specification

The class of partition-aware applications that can be programmed using group membership alone is limited [7]. In general, network applications require closer cooperation that is facilitated through communication among group members.

```
1    procedure EstimateExchangePhase()
2        installed ← false              % True when a new view is installed
3        InitializeEstimatePhase()
4    repeat
5        wait-for event                 % Remain idle until some event occurs
6        case event of
7
8            msuspect(P):
9                foreach r ∈ (Π − P) − reachable do symset[r] ← reachable
10               msend(⟨SYMMETRY, version, reachable⟩, (Π − P) − reachable)
11               msend(⟨ESTIMATE, agreed, estimate⟩, (Π − P) − reachable)
12               reachable ← Π − P
13               if (estimate ∩ P ≠ ∅) then
14                   SendEstimate(estimate ∩ P)
15
16           mrecv(⟨SYMMETRY, V, P⟩, q):
17               if (agreed[p] = V[p] or agreed[q] ≤ V[q]) and (q ∈ estimate) then
18                   SendEstimate(estimate ∩ P)
19
20           mrecv(⟨SYNCHRONIZE, V_p, V_q, P⟩, q):
21               version[q] ← V_q
22               if (agreed[q] < V_q) and (q ∈ estimate) then
23                   SendEstimate(estimate ∩ P)
24
25           mrecv(⟨ESTIMATE, V, P⟩, q):
26               if (q ∈ estimate) then
27                   if (p ∉ P) and (agreed[p] = V[p] or agreed[q] ≤ V[q]) then
28                       SendEstimate(estimate ∩ P)
29                   elseif (p ∈ P) and (∀r ∈ estimate ∩ P : agreed[r] = V[r]) then
30                       SendEstimate(estimate − P)
31                   fi
32
33           mrecv(⟨PROPOSE, S⟩, q):
34               ctbl[q] ← S
35               if (q ∈ estimate) and CheckAgreement(ctbl) then
36                   InstallView(UniqueID(), ctbl)
37                   installed ← true
38               fi
39
40           mrecv(⟨VIEW, w, C⟩, q):
41               if (C[p].cview.id = cview.id) and (q ∈ estimate)) then
42                   InstallView(w, C)
43                   installed ← true
44               fi
45
46       esac
47   until installed
```

Fig. 4. Estimate exchange phase for process p: Part (a).

```
1     procedure InitializeEstimatePhase()
2         SendEstimate(∅)
3
4     procedure SendEstimate(P)
5         estimate ← estimate − P
6         msend(⟨ESTIMATE, agreed, estimate⟩, reachable − {p})
7         msend(⟨PROPOSE, (cview, agreed, estimate)⟩, Min(estimate))
8
9     function CheckAgreement(C)
10        return  (∀q ∈ C[p].estimate : C[p].estimate = C[q].estimate)
11              and (∀q, r ∈ C[p].estimate : C[p].agreed[r] = C[q].agreed[r])
12
13    procedure InstallView(w, C)
14        msend(⟨VIEW, w, C⟩, C[p].estimate − {p})
15        if (∃q, r ∈ C[p].estimate :
16              q ∈ C[r].cview.comp ∧ C[q].cview.id ≠ C[r].cview.id) then
17            view ← ( (w, view.id), {r|r ∈ C[p].estimate ∧ C[r].cview.id = cview.id})
18        else
19            view ← ((w, ⊥), C[p].estimate)
20        generate vchg(view)
21        cview ← (w, C[p].estimate)
22        stable ← (view.comp = reachable) and
23              (∀q, r ∈ C[p].estimate : C[p].agreed[r] = agreed[r])
```

Fig. 5. Estimate exchange phase for process p: Part (b).

In this section, we briefly illustrate how the group membership service of Sect. 3 may constitute the basis of more complex group communication services. The proposed extension is based on a reliable multicast service with *view synchrony* semantics that governs the delivery of multicast messages with respect to installation of views. After having introduced the reliable multicast specification, we illustrate how our solution for PGMS may be easily extended in order to implement view synchrony.

Group members communicate through reliable multicasts by invoking the primitive $mcast(m)$ that attempts to deliver message m to each of the processes in the current view through a $dlvr()$ upcall. Multicast messages are labeled in order to be globally unique. To simplify the presentation, we use M_p^v to denote the set of messages that have been delivered by process p in view v.

Ideally, all correct processes belonging to a given view should deliver the same set of messages in that view. In partitionable systems, this requirement could result in the multicast to block until communication failures are repaired so that those processes that have become unreachable since the view was installed can deliver the message. Thus, we relax this condition on the delivery of messages as follows: a process q may be exempt from delivering the same set of messages as some other correct process p in a view v if q crashes or if it becomes unreachable from p. In other words, agreement on the set of delivered messages in a view v

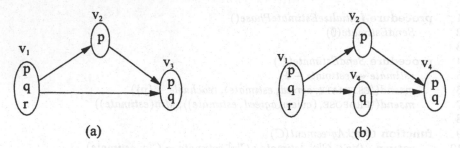

(a)   (b)

Fig. 6. Merging scenarios. Ovals depict view compositions as sets of process names. Directed edges depict *immediate successor* relations between views.

is limited to those processes that survive a view change from view v to the same next view.

RM1 (Message Agreement). *Given two views v and w such that w is an immediate successor of v, all processes belonging to both views deliver the same set of multicast messages in view v. Formally,*

$$v \prec_p w \wedge q \in \overline{v} \cap \overline{w} \;\Rightarrow\; M_p^v = M_q^v \;.$$

The importance of Message Agreement can be better understood when considered together the properties offered by the group membership service specified in Sect. 3. Given two permanently reachable processes, there is a time after which they install the same sequence of views and deliver the same set of messages between every pair of successive views.

Note that Property RM1 places no restrictions on the set of messages delivered by a process q that belonged to view v along with p but that subsequently ends up in a different partition and is excluded from w. In this case, process q may or may not deliver some message m that was delivered by p in view v. If, however, q indeed delivers message m, it must do it in the same view v as p. This observation leads to the next property.

RM2 (Uniqueness). *Each multicast message, if delivered at all, is delivered in exactly one view. Formally,*

$$(m \in M_p^v) \wedge (m \in M_q^w) \;\Rightarrow\; v = w \;.$$

Properties RM1 and RM2 together define what has been called *view synchrony* in group communication systems. In distributed application development, view synchrony is extremely valuable since it admits global reasoning using local information only: Process p knows that all other processes surviving a view change along with it have delivered the same set of messages in the same view as p itself. And if two processes share some global state in a view and this state depends only on the set of delivered messages regardless of their order, then they will continue to share the same state in the next view if they both survive the view change[4].

Unfortunately, the group communication service specified so far does not allow global reasoning based on local information in partitionable systems. Consider the scenario depicted in Fig. 6(a) where three processes p, q, r have all installed view v_1. At some point process r crashes and p becomes temporarily unreachable from q. Process p reacts to both events by installing view v_2 containing only itself before merging back with q and installing view v_3. Process q, on other hand, reacts only to the crash of r and installs view v_3 excluding r. Suppose that p and q share the same state in view v_1 and that p modifies its state during v_2. When p and q install v_3, p knows immediately that their states may have diverged, while q cannot infer this fact based on local information alone. Therefore, q could behave inconsistently with respect to p. In an effort to avoid this situation, p could collaborate by sending q a warning message as soon as it installs view v_3, but q could perform inconsistent operations before receiving such a message. The problem stems from the fact that views v_1 and v_2, that merge to form view v_3, have at least one common member (p). The scenario of the above example can be easily generalized to any run where two overlapping views merge to form a common view. We rule out these runs with the following property.

RM3 (Merging Rule). *Two views merging into a common view must have disjoint compositions. Formally,*

$$(v \prec u) \wedge (w \prec u) \wedge (v \neq w) \;\Rightarrow\; \overline{v} \cap \overline{w} = \emptyset \ .$$

The sequence of view installations in a run respecting this property is shown in Fig. 6(b): Before installing v_3, process q has to first install view v_4. Thus the two views that merge to form v_3 have empty intersection. As a result, when p and q install view v_3, they both knows immediately that their states could have diverged during the partitioning. Note that Property RM3 may appear to be part of the group membership specification since it is concerned with view installations alone. Nevertheless, we choose to include it as part of the reliable multicast service specification since RM3 becomes relevant only in the context of multicast message deliveries. In other words, applications that need no guarantees for multicast messages but rely on PGMS alone would not be interested in RM3.

The next property places simple integrity requirements on delivery of messages to prevent the same message from being delivered multiple times by the same process or a message from being delivered "out of thin air" without first being multicast.

RM4 (Message Integrity). *Each process delivers a message at most once and only if some process actually multicast it earlier. Formally,*

---

[4] For applications where the shared state is sensitive to the order in which messages are delivered, specific order properties can be enforced by additional system layers.

$$\sigma(p,t) = dlvr(m) \Rightarrow$$
$$(dlvr(m) \notin \sigma(p, \mathcal{T} - \{t\})) \wedge (\exists q, \exists t' < t : \sigma(q,t') = mcast(m)) .$$

Note that a specification consisting of Properties RM1–RM4 alone can be trivially satisfied by not delivering any messages at all. We exclude such useless solutions by including the following property.

RM5 (Liveness).
(i) A correct process always delivers its own multicast messages. Formally,

$$p \in Correct(C) \wedge \sigma(p,t) = mcast(m) \Rightarrow (\exists t' > t : \sigma(p,t') = dlvr(m)) .$$

(ii) Let p be a correct process that delivers message m in view v that includes some other process q. If q never delivers m, then p will eventually install a new view w as the immediate successor to v. Formally,

$$p \in Correct(C) \wedge \sigma(p,t) = dlvr(m) \wedge q \in \overline{v} \wedge$$
$$view(p,t) = v \wedge dlvr(m) \notin \sigma(q, \mathcal{T}) \Rightarrow$$
$$\exists t' > t : \sigma(p,t') = vchg(w) .$$

The second part of Property RM5 is the liveness counterpart of Property RM1: If a process p delivers a message m in view v containing some other process q, then either q also delivers m, or p eventually excludes q from its current view.

Properties RM1–RM5 that define our Reliable Multicast Service can be combined with Properties GM1–GM5 of group membership to obtain what we call a *Partitionable Group Communication Service* with *view synchrony* semantics. In the extended version of this work [6] we show how our solution to PGMS can be extended to satisfy this specification.

7 Related Work and Discussion

The process group paradigm has been the focus of extensive experimental work in recent years and group communication services are gradually finding their way into systems for supporting fault-tolerant distributed applications. Examples of experimental group communication services include Isis [9], Transis [13], Totem [28], Newtop [17], Horus [35], Ensemble [21], Spread [2], Moshe [4] and Jgroup [27]. There have also been several specifications for group membership and group communication not related to any specific experimental system [30, 18, 31].

Despite this intense activity, the distributed systems community has yet to agree on a formal definition of the group membership problem, especially for partitionable systems. The fact that many attempts have been show to either admit trivial solutions or to exhibit undesirable behavior is partially responsible for this situation [3]. Since the work of Anceaume *et al.*, several other group membership specifications have appeared [20, 18, 4].

Friedman and Van Renesse [20] give a specification for the Horus group communication system that has many similarities to our proposal, particularly with respect to safety properties such as View Coherency and Message Agreement. There are, however, important differences with respect to non-triviality properties: The Horus specification is conditional on the outputs produced by a failure detector present in the system. This approach is also suggested by Anceaume et al. [3] and adopted in the work of Neiger [30]. We feel that a specification for group membership should be formulated based on properties of *runs* characterizing actual executions and not in terms of suspicions that a failure detector produces. Otherwise, the validity of the specification itself would be conditional on the properties of the failure detector producing the suspicions. For example, referring to a failure that never suspects anyone or one that always suspects everyone would lead to specifications that are useless. Thus, it is reasonable for the correctness of a group membership service *implementation*, but not its *specification*, to rely on the properties of the failure detector that it is based on.

Congress and Moshe [4] are two membership protocols that have been designed by the Transis group. Congress provides a simple group membership protocol, while Moshe extends Congress to provide a full group communication service. The specification of Moshe has many similarities with our proposal and includes properties such as *View Identifier Local Monotony, Self Inclusion* and *View Synchrony*, that can be compared to GM4, GM5 and RM1 of our proposal. Property RM5 is implied by Properties *Self Delivery* and *Termination of Delivery* of Moshe. On the other hand, the specification of Moshe does not guarantee Properties RM3 and RM4, thus undesirable scenarios similar to those described in Sect. 6 are possible. The main differences between Moshe and our proposal are with respect to non-triviality requirements. Moshe includes a property called *Agreement on Views* that may be compared to our Properties GM1, GM2 and GM3. The *Agreement on Views* property forces a set of processes, say S, to install the same sequence of views only if there is a time after which every process in S (i) is correct, (ii) is mutually reachable from all other processes in S, (iii) is mutually unreachable from all processes not in S, and (iv) is not suspected by any process in S. As in our proposal, this requirement may be relaxed by requiring that the condition hold only for a sufficiently long period of time, and not forever. Despite these similarities, the non-triviality requirements of Moshe and our proposal have rather different implications. For example, Moshe does not guarantee that two processes will install a common sequence of views even if they are mutually and permanently reachable but there are other processes in the system that become alternately reachable and unreachable from them. In our proposal, however, processes that are mutually and permanently reachable always install the same sequence of views, regardless of the state of the rest of the system. And this is desirable since a common sequence of installed views which is the basis for consistent collaboration in our partition-aware application development methodology.

Fekete et al. present a formal specification for a partitionable group communication service [18]. In the same work, the service is used to construct an ordered broadcast application and, in a subsequent work, to construct replicated data services [23]. The specification separates safety requirements from performance and fault-tolerance requirements, which are shown to hold in executions that stabilize to a situation where the failure status stops changing. The basic premise of Fekete *et al.* is that existing specifications for partitionable group communication services are too complex, thus, unusable by application programmers. And they set out to devise a much simpler formal specification, crafted to support the specific application they have in mind.

Simple specifications for partitionable group communication are possible only if services based on them are to support simple applications. Unfortunately, system services that are indeed useful for a wide range of applications are inherently more complex and do not admit simple specifications. Our experience in developing actual realistic partition-aware applications supports this claim [7].

The specification and implementation presented in this work form the basis of Jgroup [27], a group-enhanced extension to the Java RMI distributed object model. Jgroup enables the creation of object groups that collaborate using the facilities offered by our partitionable group communication service. Clients access an object group using the standard Java remote method invocation semantics and remotely invoking its methods as if it were a single, non-replicated remote object. The Jgroup system includes a *dependable registry service*, which itself is a partition-aware application built using Jgroup services [26]. The dependable registry is a distributed object repository used by object groups to advertise their services under a symbolic name (*register* operation), and by clients to locate object groups by name (*lookup* operation). Each registry replica maintains a database of bindings from symbolic group names to group object composition. Replicas are kept consistent using group communication primitives offered by Jgroup. During a partitioning, different replicas of the dependable registry may diverge. Register operations from within a partition can be serviced as long as at least one replica is included inside the partition. A lookup, on the other hand, will not be able to retrieve bindings that have been registered outside the current partition. Nevertheless, all replicas contained within a given partition are kept consistent in the sense that they maintain the same set of bindings and behave as a non-replicated object. When partitions merge, a reconciliation protocol is executed to bring replicas that may have been updated in different partitions back to a consistent state. This behavior of the dependable registry is perfectly reasonable in a partitionable system where clients asking for remote services would be interested only in servers running in the same partition as themselves.

8   Conclusions

Partition-aware applications are characterized by their ability to continue operating in multiple concurrent partitions as long as they can reconfigure themselves consistently [7]. A group membership service provides the necessary properties so that this reconfiguration is possible and applications can dynamically establish which services and at what performance levels they can offer in each of the partitions. The *primary partition* version of group membership is not suitable for supporting partition-aware applications since progress would be limited to at most one network partition. In this chapter we have given a formal specification for a partitionable group communication service that is suitable for supporting partition-aware applications. Our specification excludes trivial solutions and is free from undesirable behaviors exhibited by previous attempts. Moreover, it requires services based on it to be live in the sense that view installations and message deliveries cannot be delayed arbitrarily when conditions require them.

We have shown that our specification can be implemented in any asynchronous distributed system that admits a failure detector satisfying *Strong Completeness* and *Eventual Strong Accuracy* properties. The correctness of the implementation depends solely on these abstract properties of the failure detector and not on the operating characteristics of the system. Any practical failure detector implementation presents a trade-off between accuracy and responsiveness to failures. By increasing acceptable message delays after each false suspicion, accuracy can be improved but responsiveness will suffer. In practice, to guarantee reasonable responsiveness, finite bounds will have to be placed on acceptable message delays, perhaps established dynamically on a per channel or per application basis. Doing so will guarantee that new views will be installed within bounded delays after failures. This in turn may cause some reachable processes to be excluded from installed views. Such processes, however, have to be either very slow themselves or have very slow communication links, and thus, it is reasonable to exclude them from views until their delays return to acceptable levels.

Each property included in our specification has been carefully studied and its contribution evaluated. We have argued that excluding any one of the properties makes the resulting service either trivial, or subject to undesirable behaviors, or less useful as a basis for developing large classes of partition-aware applications. Specification of new system services is mostly a social process and "proving" the usefulness of any of the included properties is impossible. The best one can do is program a wide range of applications twice: once using a service with the proposed property, and a second time without it, and compare their relative difficulty and complexity. We have pursued this exercise for our specification by programming a set of practical partition-aware applications [7]. In fact, the specification was developed by iterating the exercise after modifying properties based on feedback from the development step. As additional empirical evidence in support of our specification, we point to the Jgroup system based entirely on the specification and implementation given in this chapter. As discussed in Sect. 7, the dependable registry service that is an integral part of Jgroup has been programmed using services offered by Jgroup itself. Work is currently underway in using Jgroup to develop other partition-aware financial applications and a partitionable distributed version of the Sun tuple space system called Javaspaces.

References

[1] Y. Amir, L.E. Moser, P.M. Melliar-Smith, D.A. Agarwal, and P. Ciarfella. The Totem Single-Ring Ordering and Membership Protocol. *ACM Transactions on Computer Systems*, 13(4):311–342, November 1995.

[2] Y. Amir and J. Stanton. The Spread Wide-Aread Group Communication System. Technical report, Center of Networking and Distributed Systems, Johns Hopkins University, Baltimore, Mariland, April 1998.

[3] E. Anceaume, B. Charron-Bost, P. Minet, and S. Toueg. On the Formal Specification of Group Membership Services. Technical Report TR95-1534, Department of Computer Science, Cornell University, August 1995.

[4] T. Anker, G. Chockler, D. Dolev, and I. Keidar. Scalable Group Membership Services for Novel Applications. In *Proceedings of the DIMACS Workshop on Networks in Distributed Computing*, pages 23–42. American Mathematical Society, 1998.

[5] Ö. Babaoğlu, R. Davoli, L.A. Giachini, and M.G. Baker. RELACS: A Communications Infrastructure for Constructing Reliable Applications in Large-Scale Distributed Systems. In *Proceedings of the 28th Hawaii International Conference on System Sciences (HICS)*, pages 612–621, Maui, Hawaii, January 1995.

[6] Ö. Babaoğlu, R. Davoli, and A. Montresor. Group Communication in Partitionable Systems: Specification and Algorithms. Technical Report UBLCS-98-1, Department of Computer Science, University of Bologna, April 1998.

[7] Ö. Babaoğlu, R. Davoli, A. Montresor, and R. Segala. System Support for Partition-Aware Network Applications. In *Proceedings of the 18th International Conference on Distributed Computing Systems (ICDCS)*, pages 184–191, Amsterdam, The Netherlands, May 1998.

[8] K. Birman. The Process Group Approach to Reliable Distributed Computing. *Communications of the ACM*, 36(12):36–53, December 1993.

[9] K. Birman and R. van Renesse. *Reliable Distributed Computing with the ISIS Toolkit*. IEEE Computer Society Press, 1994.

[10] T. Chandra, V. Hadzilacos, S. Toueg, and B. Charron-Bost. On the Impossibility of Group Membership. In *Proceedings of the 15th ACM Symposium on Principles of Distributed Computing (PODC)*, pages 322–330, May 1996. Also available as technical report TR95-1533, Department of Computer Science, Cornell University.

[11] T.D. Chandra and S. Toueg. Unreliable Failure Detectors for Reliable Distributed Systems. *Journal of the ACM*, 43(1):225–267, March 1996.

[12] D. Dolev, R. Friedman, I. Keidar, and D. Malki. Failure Detectors in Omission Failure Environments. In *Proceedings of the 16th ACM Symposium on Principles of Distributed Computing (PODC)*, Santa Barbara, California, August 1997. Also available as Technical Report TR96-1608.

[13] D. Dolev and D. Malki. The Transis Approach to High Availability Cluster Communication. *Communications of the ACM*, 39(4), April 1996.

[14] D. Dolev, D. Malki, and R. Strong. An Asynchronous Membership Protocol that Tolerates Partitions. Technical Report CS94-6, Institute of Computer Science, The Hebrew University of Jerusalem, 1994.

[15] D. Dolev, D. Malki, and R. Strong. A Framework for Partitionable Membership Service. Technical Report CS95-4, Institute of Computer Science, The Hebrew University of Jerusalem, 1995.

[16] D. Dolev, D. Malki, and R. Strong. A Framework for Partitionable Membership Service. In *Proceedings of the 15th ACM Symposium on Principles of Distributed Computing (PODC)*, May 1996.

[17] P.E. Ezhilchelvan, R.A. Macêdo, and S.K. Shrivastava. Newtop: A Fault-Tolerant Group Communication Protocol. In *Proceedings of the 15th International Conference on Distributed Computing Systems (ICDCS)*, Vancouver, BC, Canada, June 1995.

[18] A. Fekete, N. Lynch, and A. Shvartsman. Specifying and Using a Partitionable Group Communication Service. In *Proceedings of the 16th ACM Symposium on Principles of Distributed Computing (PODC)*, Santa Barbara, California, August 1997.

[19] M.J. Fischer, N.A. Lynch, and M.S. Patterson. Impossibility of Distributed Consensus with one Faulty Process. *Journal of the ACM*, 32(2):374–382, April 1985.

[20] R. Friedman and R. Van Renesse. Strong and Weak Virtual Synchrony in Horus. Technical Report TR95-1537, Department of Computer Science, Cornell University, March 1995.

[21] M. Hayden. *The Ensenble System*. PhD thesis, Department of Computer Science, Cornell University, January 1998.

[22] F. Kaashoek and A. Tanenbaum. Group Communication in the Amoeba Distributed Operating System. In *Proceedings of the 12th IEEE Symp. on Reliable Distributed Systems*, pages 222–230, Arlington, TX, May 1991.

[23] R. Khazan, A. Fekete, and N. Lynch. Multicast Group Communication as a Base for a Load-Balancing Replicated Data Service. In *Proceedings of the 12th Symposium on Distributed Computing*, August 1998.

[24] C. Malloth. *Conception and Implementation of a Toolkit for Building Fault-Tolerant Distributed Applications in Large-Scale Networks*. PhD thesis, Ecole Polytechnique Fédérale de Lausanne, 1996.

[25] C. Malloth and A. Schiper. View Synchronous Communication in Large Scale Networks. In *Proceedings of the 2nd Open Workshop of the ESPRIT Project Broadcast*, Grenoble, France, July 1995.

[26] A. Montresor. A Dependable Registry Service for the Jgroup Distributed Object Model. In *Proceedings of the 3rd European Reasearch Seminar on Advances in Distributed Systems (ERSADS)*, Madeira, Portugal, April 1999.

[27] A. Montresor. The Jgroup Reliable Distributed Object Model. In *Proceedings of the 2nd IFIP International Working Conference on Distributed Applications and Systems (DAIS)*, Helsinki, Finland, June 1999.

[28] L. Moser, P. Melliar-Smith, D. Agarwal, R. Budhia, and C. Lingley-Papadopoulos. Totem: A Fault-Tolerant Group Communication System. *Communications of the ACM*, 39(4), April 1996.

[29] L.E. Moser, Y. Amir, P.M. Melliar-Smith, and D.A. Agarwal. Extended Virtual Synchrony. In *Proceedings of the 14th International Conference on Distributed Computing Systems (ICDCS)*, Poznan, Poland, June 1994.

[30] G. Neiger. A New Look at Membership Services. In *Proceedings of the 15th ACM Symposium on Principles of Distributed Computing (PODC)*, May 1996.

[31] R. De Prisco, A. Fekete, N. Lynch, and A. Shvartsman. A Dynamic View-Oriented Group Communication Service. In *Proceedings of the 17th ACM Symposium on Principles of Distributed Computing (PODC)*, June 1998.

[32] A. Ricciardi and K. Birman. Using Process Groups to Implement Failure Detection in Asynchronous Environments. In *Proceedings of the 10th ACM Symposium on Principles of Distributed Computing (PODC)*, pages 341–352, August 1991.

[33] A. Schiper and A. Ricciardi. Virtually-synchronous Communication Based on a Weak Failure Suspector. In *Proceedings of the 23rd International Symposium on Fault-Tolerant Computing (FTCS)*, pages 534–543, June 1993.

[34] R. van Renesse, K. Birman, R. Cooper, B. Glade, and P. Stephenson. The Horus System. In K. Birman and R. van Renesse, editors, *Reliable Distributed Computing with the Isis Toolkit*, pages 133–147. IEEE Computer Society Press, 1993.

[35] R. van Renesse, K.P. Birman, and S. Maffeis. Horus: A Flexible Group Communication System. *Communications of the ACM*, 39(4):76–83, April 1996.

Enhancing Replica Management Services to Cope with Group Failures

Paul D Ezhilchelvan and Santosh K Shrivastava

Department of Computing Science
University of Newcastle upon Tyne
Newcastle upon Tyne, NE1 7RU, UK

Abstract. In a distributed system, replication of components, such as objects, is a well known way of achieving availability. For increased availability, crashed and disconnected components must be replaced by new components on available spare nodes. This replacement results in the membership of the replicated group 'walking' over a number of machines during system operation. In this context, we address the problem of reconfiguring a group after the group as an entity has failed. Such a failure is termed a group failure which, for example, can be the crash of every component in the group or the group being partitioned into minority islands. The solution assumes crash-proof storage, and eventual recovery of crashed nodes and healing of partitions. It guarantees that (i) the number of groups reconfigured after a group failure is never more than one, and (ii) the reconfigured group contains a majority of the components which were members of the group just before the group failure occurred, so that the loss of state information due to a group failure is minimal. Though the protocol is subject to blocking, it remains efficient in terms of communication rounds and use of stable store, during both normal operations and reconfiguration after a group failure.

1. Introduction

In a distributed system, component replication (where a component is taken to mean a computational entity such as a process, module) is a well known way of achieving high availability. Equally well-known are the techniques for building a replica group using services such as membership and message ordering services. In this paper, we will consider the issue of enhancing the availability of a replica group in the presence of failures, while preserving the *strong consistency* property which requires that the states of all replicas that are regarded as available be mutually consistent. *Dynamic voting paradigm* is an efficient way of achieving this end [12]: when, say, network failures partition the replica group into disjoint subgroups, availability is maintained only in the partition (if any) that contains a majority of the replicas (called the *master subgroup*), with the replicas in all other partitions becoming unavailable. That is, the majority partition (if any) forms the master sub-group and offers the services previously provided by the group; if a partition further disconnects a majority of the current master subgroup from the rest, then this connected majority becomes the new master subgroup. Thus, each newly formed master sub-group contains a majority of

S. Krakowiak, S.K. Shrivastava (Eds.): Distributed Systems, LNCS 1752, pp. 79–103, 2000.

the previously existed master sub-group. Replica management with dynamic voting offers a better way of maintaining system availability than *static voting* that requires a majority of all the members that initially formed the group to remain connected. The following example illustrates dynamic voting:

Stage 0: Let the group configuration be initially $G_0 = \{C1, C2, C3, C4, C5, C6, C7\}$, where Ci is the ith component.

Stage 1: Say, a network partition splits G_0 into $G_1 = \{C1, C2, C3, C4, C5\}$ and $G'_1 = \{C6, C7\}$; G_1 now becomes the master subgroup and thereby the new, second group configuration.

Stage 2: Say, G_1 splits into $G_2 = \{C1, C2, C3\}$ and $G'_2 = \{C4, C5\}$; G_2 now becomes the master subgroup and thereby the third group configuration.

The above example indicates how the dynamic voting can preserve the availability of group services even though the original group G_0 got split into islands with each island having less than half the members of G_0. Availability can be however maitained only if the master subgroup exists after a failure. Suppose that after stage 2, each member of G_2 detaches from other members. Now, no master subgroup exists and hence the normal services can no longer be provided. We call this a *group failure* (*g-failure* for short). Note that many combinations of failures can lead to a g-failure. For example, a g-failure after stage 2 can be caused by simultaneous crashing of each member of G_2, crashing of C3 and detachment of C2 and C1, and so on. When the bound on communication delays between components is not known with certainty, a g-failure can occur even in the absence of any physical failure in the system: when a sudden burst of network traffic, for instance, increases the communication delay between two connected components beyond what was considered to be likely, each component can falsely conclude that the other is not responding and hence must have crashed or got disconnected. Therefore, g-failures should not be regarded as rare events when bound on message delays cannot be estimated accurately.

Let us assume that the components have stable states which do not get destroyed by node crashes. Given that the component state survives node crash, it would be preferable to have the replica management service enhanced to cope with g-failures, instead of relying only on cold-start to resume the group services after a g-failure. To achieve this, we propose a *configuration protocol* that enables the members of the last master subgroup prior to a g-failure, to reconstruct the group once sufficient number of those members have recovered and got reconnected. Of course, the protocol must ensure that only one such group is formed. The protocol objectives cannot be met solely by the services used to build a replica group, in particular the membership service. To illustrate this, let us continue on the above example into stage 3 described below:

Stage 3: C3 crashes before it could record in its stable store the fact that the new master subgroup $G_2 = \{C1, C2, C3\}$ has been formed; the remaining members of G_2, C1 and C2, record in their stable store that G_2 is the latest master subgroup and then disconnect from each other.

No master-subgroup now exists and a g-failure has occurred. Next, suppose that C3 recovers and reconnects with C4 and C5, and C2 reconnects to C1. The set $\{C3, C4, C5\}$ forms the 'master subgroup' on the basis that its members form a majority of the last group configuration G_1 that is known to all of them, while $\{C1, C2\}$ also forms the 'master subgroup' on the same basis that its members are a majority in the last known configuration G_2. Now, we have two live master subgroups. To prevent this from happening, we require that (i) a new master subgroup be considered to have been formed only after a majority of the previous master subgroup have recorded in the stable store the composition of the new master subgroup (*req1*); and, (ii) the master subgroup constructed after a g-failure include at least a majority of the members of the latest master subgroup formed prior to the g-failure (*req2*). Requirement *req1* ensures that there can be only one group configuration that qualifies to be the latest master subgroup formed before a g-failure (and, in general, at any given time). In the above example, a majority of G_1 did not record G_2 before the occurrence of the g-failure of stage 3; so, only G_1 is the latest master subgroup formed before a g-failure. Requirement *req2* permits no more than one master subgroup to emerge after a g-failure.

We assume that the construction of the replica management system (with dynamic voting) can avail the use of a group membership service which provides each operational component with an agreed set of components that are currently believed to be functioning and connected. For such a replica management system, we develop a *configuration management* subsystem - the main contribution of the paper - that provides (i) a group view installation service to enable members of the master subgroup to record group membership information on stable store; and (ii) a group configuration service that makes use of these stable views to enable group formation after a g-failure as soon as enough number of the components of the last configuration have recovered and reconnected. A prototype version of the configuration management service described here has been implemented [5] on an existing replica management system called Somersault [19]. Our service enhances Somersault by providing recovery from group failures.

The paper is the extended version of [8] and is structured as follows: section two introduces the system architecture, some definitions and notations; it also specifies the two services provided by the configuration management subsytem, namely the view installation and the group configuration services. The next two sections describe in detail how these services are provided. Section five compares and contrasts our work with the approaches taken in the published papers in this area, and Section six concludes the chapter.

2. System Overview and Requirements

2.1. Assumptions and System Structure

It is assumed that a component's host node can crash but contains a stable store whose contents survive node crashes. Components communicate with each other by passing messages over a network which is subject to transient or long-lived partitions. We assume that a partition eventually heals and a crashed node eventually recovers; the bound on repair/recovery time is finite but not known with certainty. For increased availability, we permit new components created on spare nodes to join the group, with no restriction on the number of such joining nodes and on the time of their joining. Our system leaves to the administrator to decide how many among the available spare nodes should be instructed to join the group, and when. Given that the spares instructed by the administrator are attempting to join the group, our system enables them to join with a guarantee that they could compute the most uptodate component state from the existing members. For simplicity, we assume that members of a group do not voluntarily leave the group, but are only forced out because of crashes or partitions.

2.1.1. View Maker (VM) Subsystem

We assume that our replica management system has been constructed by making use of the services provided by a group membership subsystem. This subsystem resident in the host node of an active component, say p, constructs membership *views* for p, where a view is the set of components currently believed to be functioning and connected to p. We call this subsytem the *View Maker*, or VM for short, and denote the VM of p as VM_p. In delivering the uptodate views constructed, VM_p is required to provide the abstraction of *view synchrony* or *virtual synchrony* if primary-partition model is assumed for the underlying communication subsystem. We refer the reader to [2, 3] and [21] for a complete list of the properties of view synchronous and virtual synchronous abstractions, respectively. Below, we highlight some of these properties that are considered important for our discussions.

vs1: p is present in any view constructed by VM_p. (*self-inclusion.*)

vs2: a message *m* from another component q is delivered to p only when the view constructed by VM_p prior to the delivery of *m* contains q. (*view-message integrity.*)

vs3: the delivery of constructed views is synchronised with the delivery of messages such that components receive identical set of messages between consecutive views that are identical. (*view-message synchrony.*)

vs4: If VM_p delivers a view *v*, then for every component q in *v*, either VM_q delivers *v* or VM_p constructs consecutive view *w* that excludes q. (*view agreement.*)

There are many protocols in the literature which can be used to implement the assumed VM subsystem; e.g., [4, 17, 20] for an asynchronous system with the primary-partition assumption, [1, 2, 7, 16, 18] for partitionable asynchronous systems. These protocols are not designed to cope with g-failures. The subsystem described below deals with g-failures using the services of the VM subsystem.

2.1.2. Configuration Management (CM) Subsystem

On top of the VM service exists a configuration management (CM) subsystem (see Figure 2). CM of component p, denoted as CM_p, carefully records the view information provided by VM_p in the local stable store. In a traditional replica management system, a new view decided by VM_p is usually delivered straight to p. In our system, it reaches p via CM_p. VM_p regards CM_p as an application and delivers every new view it decides.

CM_p of member p essentially provides the following three functionalities.

(i) it considers each view delivered by VM_p and decides whether a g-failure may have occurred. If g-failure occurrence is ruled out, CM_p passes on that view to p, provided certain conditions are met which ensure strong consistency.

(ii) if a new view delivered to p contains a spare node attempting to join the group, CM_p facilitates the spare node (in co-operation with CM of other members in the new view) to compute the most recent component state.

(iii) if a view constructed by VM_p indicates that a g-failure may have occurred, CM_p executes a *configuration protocol* with CM of connected components. This execution ensures that if the group is reconfigured, it is the master subgroup of the configuration that existed just before the g-failure was suspected to have occurred.

It must be emphasized here that CM_p can only suspect, not accurately diagnose, the occurrence of a g-failure when it inspects a new view from VM_p. To illustrate this consider the disconnected component C3 in figure 1. With the recent group membership being {C1, C2, C3}, when CM of C3, CM_3, is delivered a singleton view {C3}, it cannot know whether the partition has split the group in three ways causing a g-failure (as in Fig. 1(a)), or in two ways (as in Fig. 1(b)) permitting C1 and C2 to form the next master sub-group. So, in both cases, CM_3 would suspect a g-failure and execute the configuration protocol. In case of 3-way partition, C3 will form the post-g-failure master subgroup with, say, C1, if it re-connects to C1 while CM_1 is also executing the protocol. In the second case, when the partition heals, C3 will learn that it has been 'walked over': C1 and C2 have formed the new master subgroup without it; C3 will then join the pool of spares. Note that it is also possible for C3 to be walked over in the first case: if the isolation of C3 lasts so long that C1 and C2 reconnect in the mean time and form the next master group. Thus, the outcome of the reconfiguration attempts by components is decided by the pattern and timing of components recovery and reconnection.

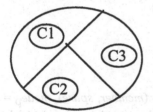   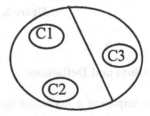

Figure 1. (a) 3-way partitioning   (b) 2-way partitioning.

2.2. View Names within the System

Our replica management system (above the communication layer) is structured in two layers as shown in fig. 2. Recall that CM_p delivers to p a view constructed by VM_p, only if certain conditions are met. That is, a view becomes more significant as it moves up within the system. To reflect this, we call a view differently at different levels. The views constructed by VM_p are called the *membership views* or simply Mviews. VM_p delivers Mviews to CM_p via a queue called $ViewQ_p$ where Mviews are placed in the order of delivery. CM_p deals with one Mview at a time, and only when an Mview reaches the head of $ViewQ_p$, which is denoted as $head_p$. CM_p stores the head$_p$ in the stable store as the new component view, provided a set of conditions are met. The component view of p is called Cview$_p$. Only Cview$_p$ is made visible to component p and provides p with the current membership view. For reasons discussed earlier (see *req1* of Section 1), making head$_p$ as Cview$_p$ is done in two stages; head$_p$ is first *recorded* in stable store as the *stabilised* view of p called Sview$_p$, and then *installed* as Cview$_p$. CM uses a view numbering scheme for sequentially numbering the view contents of Sview$_p$ and Cview$_p$.

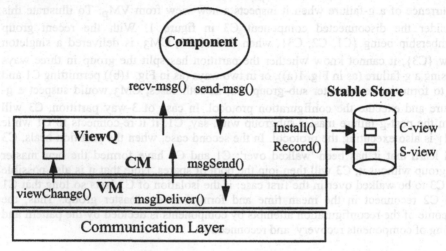

Figure 2. The system Architecture.

2.3. Notations and Definitions

Each component p maintains three variables *status$_p$* = (*member, spare*), *mode$_p$* = (*normal, reconfiguration, waiting, joining*), and *view-number$_p$* (an integer variable) in its stable store. In addition, it also maintains two view variables, Cview$_p$ and Sview$_p$, initialised to null set, if p is spare. Sview$_p$ has a view number associated with it, and the view number of Cview$_p$ is indicated by *view-number$_p$*. *status$_p$* is set to *member* when p considers itself to be a member of the group, or to *spare* otherwise. When a member p (with *status$_p$* = *member*) observes a g-failure and subsequently has to execute the configuration protocol, it sets its *mode$_p$* to *reconfiguration*. The *mode$_p$* changes to *normal* if p succeeds in becoming a member of the re-formed group; otherwise p becomes a spare setting *status$_p$* = *spare* and *mode$_p$* = *waiting*. The *mode$_p$* of a spare component p can be either *waiting* or *joining*; the former is when p is waiting to be informed by its VM$_p$ that it has been connected to members of the group; once connected, p attempts to join the group by setting its *mode$_p$* to *joining*. If the join attempt by p succeeds, *status$_p$* is set to *member* and *mode$_p$* is set to *normal*. The variable *view-number$_p$* is intialised to -1 at system start time (before the group is formed) and whenever p becomes a spare; it is incremented every time CM_p installs a new Cview.

We define the terms *survivors* and *joiners* for a pair of Mviews constructed by VM_p of a component p. Let vu_i, vu_{i+1}, ... vu_j, $j \geq i+1$, be a sequence of Mviews constructed by VM_p in that order. The set *survivors*(vu_i, vu_j) is the set of all components that survive from vu_i into every Mview constructed upto vu_j: *survivors*(vu_i, vu_j) = vu_i $\cap vu_{i+1} \cap ... \cap vu_j$. The term *joiners*($vu_i$, vu_j) will refer to the set of components in vu_j which are not in *survivors*(vu_i, vu_j): *joiners*(vu_i, vu_j) = vu_j - *survivors*(vu_i, vu_j). Finally, we define M_SETS(g) for a set g of components as the set of all majority subsets s of g: M_SETS(g) = $\{s \mid s \subseteq g \wedge |s| > (|g|)/2\}$.

2.4. View Maintenance

When viewQ$_p$ is non-empty, CM_p of member p checks for the occurrence of a g-failure by inspecting the contents of head$_p$, and by evaluating the condition: *survivors*(Cview$_p$, head$_p$) $\in$M_SETS(Cview$_p$). If this condition is not satisfied, a g-failure is assumed to have occurred. CM_p first sends an *Abort* message to all components in *joiners*(Cview$_p$, head$_p$), informing the CM of any joiner not to attempt at recording/installing head$_p$. We will denote this *Abort* message of CM_p (which contains head$_p$) as $AMsg_p$(head$_p$). CM_p then sets its variable *mode$_p$* to *reconfiguration* and executes the configuration protocol to reconfigure the group. If the above condition is met, a copy of head$_p$ is atomically recorded in the local stable store as the new Sview$_p$ with the view number = (*view-number$_p$+1*), *provided recording conditions are satisfied*. This Sview$_p$ represents the potential next Cview$_p$. If the recording conditions are not met, the CM_p either concludes that a g-failure has occurred and proceeds to execute the configuration protocol setting *mode$_p$* to *reconfiguration,* or dequeues head$_p$ and proceeds to work with the next head$_p$ (if any). The recording conditions, the need for them, and how they are verified will be discussed in the next section.

The newly recorded Sview$_p$ is regarded ready for becoming the next Cview$_p$ if *an installation condition* is satisfied (again, the need for this condition and how it is verified will be discussed in the next section). In which case, CM_p installs the new component view by replacing the current Cview$_p$ by Sview$_p$, and dequeues and discards head$_p$. The local stable store update operations are indicated here within curly braces and are carried out atomically: {Cview$_p$:= Sview$_p$; *view-number$_p$* := *view-number$_p$* + 1;} If the installation condition is not met, a g-failure is considered to have occurred and the configuration protocol is executed.

The view number of Cview$_p$ is indicated in *view-number$_p$*. Since Cview$_p$ and Sview$_p$ are modified along with their view number as an atomic operation, there will be exactly one Cview$_p$ and one Sview$_p$ associated with a given view number, provided the view numbers increase monotonically. Further, CM_p installing the Sview$_p$ (as the next $Cview_p$) can be interrupted only by its suspecting a g-failure; in particular, when no g-failure is suspected, CM_p will not record a new $Sview_p$ until the existing one is installed. Thus, in the absence of g-failure suspicions, either the view number of $Sview_p$ = the view number of $Cview_p$, or the view number of $Sview_p$ = view number of $Cview_p+1$, the latter being true while the installation condition is being waited upon to be satisfied. Let $Vu_p(k)$ be the Sview or the Cview that CM_p handled with view number k; similarly, let $Vu_{p'}(k')$ be an Sview or a Cview that $CM_{p'}$ handled with view number k', where p and p' may be the same component or distinct ones. We will say $Vu_{p'}(k')$ *is later than* $Vu_p(k)$, denoted as $Vu_{p'}(k')$ » $Vu_p(k)$, if and only if k' > k.

2.5. Requirements of the CM Subsystem

We now state the two requirements the CM subsystem must meet. The first one is concerned with the "normal service" period during which no g-failure occurs, whereas the second one is concerned with group formation after a g-failure.

Existence of at most one master subgroup at any time is achieved by ensuring that any two components that install Cviews with identical view number, install identical views. Let $Cview_p(k)$ denote the Cview that p installs with view number k, $k \geq 0$. The predicate $installed_p(k)$ is true if p has installed $Cview_p(k)$, and the predicate $!Cview_p(k)$ is true if $Cview_p(k)$ is unique, i.e., no component q can install $Cview_q(k)$ that is different from $Cview_p(k)$:

$!Cview_p(k) \Rightarrow \forall q: \neg installed_q(k) \vee Cview_q(k) = Cview_p(k)$.

Note that any view installed by a component must contain the installing component. So, if $Cview_p(k)$ is unique, then no component outside $Cview_p(k)$ installs a Cview with view number k; so, there can be only one kth membership set for the group, hence only one kth master subgroup.

During normal service period, the CM modules of components ensure that the Cviews installed are sequentially numbered, and that the kth Cview installed by p is unique, provided that (k-1)th Cview installed is unique.

Formally, CM subsystem ensures:

Requirement 1:

$\forall k > 0, installed_p(k) \Rightarrow \exists p': installed_{p'}(k-1)$; and,

$\forall k > 0, installed_p(k) \wedge !Cview_{p'}(k-1) \Rightarrow !Cview_p(k)$.

Section 3 discusses how this requirement is met.

If we assume that Cview(0) is unique when the group is initially formed and that the above requirement is met, then there will exist a unique latest Cview at any time. We define this latest view as the *last Cview*, or simply the *last*.

Requirement 2: following a g-failure, a set Σ of functioning and connected components with identical Cview, *restart-view*, should be formed as soon as possible, with the following properties:

Uniqueness: $\Sigma \cap last \in M\_SETS(last)$. If *last* is unique before g-failure, there can be only one Σ that can contain a majority of the *last*.

Continuity: *restart-view* ≠ *last* ⇒ view-number(*restart-view*) =view-number(*last*)+1. The sequentiality of CView numbering is preserved across g-failures. Thus, coping with g-failures is transformed into a view installation of different kind which nevertheless preserves the uniqueness and numbering of Cviews during the normal service period. Section 4 discusses how requirement 2 is met.

3. Maintaining Unique Component Views

We describe the recording and installation conditions mentioned earlier and discuss how they help meet Requirement 1. We will first define a predicate $recd_p(m_q)$ which becomes true when CM_p of component p receives a message m_q from CM_q of another component q, and becomes false if CM_p believes that q had crashed or got disconnected before m_q is sent. We later present a non-blocking algorithm for CM_p to evaluate this predicate.

3.1. Recording Conditions for a Member Component

Let us assume (as induction hypothesis) that any two members have identical Cview with identical view number. That is, for members p and q, $Cview_p = Cview_q$ and $view\text{-}number_p = view\text{-}number_q = k$ (say). Let $head_p$, the Mview at the head of $viewQ_p$, become non-empty for member p. *survivors*($Cview_p$, $head_p$) and *joiners*($Cview_p$, $head_p$) follow different procedures for recording Sviews. Let us consider the *survivor* or *member* p first and let *survivors*($Cview_p$, $head_p$) ∈ M_SETS($Cview_p$). As discussed in subsection 2.4, CM_p can record a copy of $head_p$ as $Sview_p$ only if recording conditions are satisfied. These recording conditions essentially ensure that all *joiners*($Cview_p$, $head_p$) have obtained view information as well as replica states from *survivors*($Cview_p$, $head_p$) and made it stable. This is necessary, as a *joiner* component j has no replica state and other view related information. (It will only have $view\text{-}number_j = -1$, $Sview_j = Cview_j = null$, $mode_j = waiting$ and $status_j = spare$.) So, the recording conditions need to be satisfied only if there are *joiners* in $head_p$, i.e., *joiners*($Cview_p$, $head_p$) ≠ { }.

Suppose that there are *joiners* in $head_p$. CM_p multicasts a *State* message to every component in $head_p$ (including itself). This message contains a copy of $head_p$, $Cview_p$, *survivors*($Cview_p$, $head_p$), $view\text{-}number_p$, and p's state. We will denote this message of CM_p as $SMsg_p(head_p)$. CM_p then waits to see whether (i) enough number of *survivors* in $head_p$ have sent their *State* messages, and (ii) all *joiners* have computed and recorded the component state and also the view information in their stable store.

We will suppose that a *joiner* j in $head_p$ can compute the component state only by receiving *State* messages from some minimum number of distinct components in $Cview_p$ which is the group membership when $head_p$ is being dealt with. We will assume that this number is proportional to the size of $Cview_p$ and is some function of $|Cview_p|$, denoted as $\Phi(Cview_p)$. (If it is a fixed one and not proportional to the size of $Cview_p$, then $\Phi(Cview_p)$ will be a constant function.) Since at most less than $(|Cview_p|/2)$components need not survive into $head_p$ without causing a g-failure, $\Phi(Cview_p)$ cannot exceed $(|Cview_p|/2)+1$. So, $1 \leq \Phi(Cview_p) \leq (|Cview_p|/2)+1$.

Recording Condition 1 (rc1): It is to verify that at least $\Phi(Cview_p)$ survivors in $head_p$ have sent their *State* messages. Formally,

$$|\{q \in survivors(Cview_p, head_p): recd_p(SMsg_q(head_p))\}| \geq \Phi(Cview_p).$$

Recording Condition 2 (rc2): It is to ensure that all *joiners* in $head_p$ have computed and stored the component state and also recorded Sview which is the same as $head_p$. We will suppose that after CM_j of joiner j has stored the component state and recorded an Mview, say *vu*, as $Sview_j$, it multicasts a *Recorded* message to every component in *vu*. This message contains the recorded view *vu* and is denoted as $RMsg_j(vu)$. So, the second condition is that CM_p receive an $RMsg_j(head_p)$ from every joiner j in $head_p$. Formally, $\forall j \in joiners(Cview_p, head_p): recd_p(RMsg_j(head_p))$.

If *rc1* and *rc2* are met, CM_p atomically records a copy of $head_p$ as its next $Sview_p$ with view number = $view\text{-}number_p+1$. It then multicasts an $RMsg_p(head_p)$ to all components (including itself) in $head_p$. If *rc1* is met but not *rc2*, CM_p dequeues $head_p$ from $ViewQ_p$ but retains a copy to evaluate $survivors(Cview_p, head_p)$ for the next $head_p$. If *rc1* is not met, CM_p proceeds to execute the reconfiguration protocol after setting $mode_p$ to *reconfiguration*. Since no joiner can send $RMsg(head_p)$ without first receiving at least $\Phi(Cview_p)$ *State* messages, it is not possible for *rc2* to be met without *rc1*.

3.2. Recording Condition for a Joining Component

The recording condition is verified by CM_j of joiner j (with $mode_j$ = *waiting*) as soon as its $head_j$ - the first Mview in $ViewQ_j$ - is constructed by VM_j. It should be designed to become false if it is not possible for CM_j to receive the minimum number of *State* messages from members in $head_j$. The design is made somewhat difficult by the fact that when VM_j delivers an Mview it cannot indicate who in that Mview are members and who else (except j itself) are joiners. VM_j can obtain such information only from VMs of member components. Recall that, as far as VM modules of member components are concerned, the local Cview is transparent and is merely an internal variable used by a local application called CM (see figure 2). Moreover, when *rc1* is met but not *rc2*, CM_p of member p dequeues $head_p$, and proceeds to work with the next Mview in $ViewQ_p$; therefore, VM_p cannot even assume that when a given Mview reaches the $head_p$, the Mview it delivered immediately before $head_p$ would have been installed as $Cview_p$. So, CM_j cannot rely on VM_j to indicate the Cview of members in $head_j$.

When CM_j does not know $Cview_p$ of member p in $head_j$, its attempt to record $head_j$ can result in a deadlock if $head_j$ contains more than one joiner. For example, if every member p in $head_j$ crashes before sending the *State* or the *Abort* message, then each joiner will wait for ever to receive *State* messages from other joiners. Therefore, it is essential that CM_j first constructs a *reference Cview* which can be effectively used in place of $Cview_p$ of member p in $head_j$ until an $SMsg_p(head_j)$ is received from p which will contain a copy of $Cview_p$. This reference Cview constructed for working with $head_j$ is denoted as $RefCview_j(head_j)$ and is initially set to $head_j$ itself. (Since the discussions are for a given $head_j$, we will refer to $RefCview_j(head_j)$ as simply $RefCview_j$.) CM_j then sends a *Join* message to every component in $head_j$, announcing that it is a joiner. We denote this message as $JMsg_j(head_j)$. Whenever CM_j receives $JMsg_{j'}(head_j)$, it removes the sender j' of that message from $RefCview_j$. However, if it receives an $SMsg(head_j)$, it irreversibly sets $RefCview_j$ to the Cview contained in that message. No $JMsg(head_j)$ that is received after receiving the first $SMsg(head_j)$ modifies $RefCview_j$. The *survivors* and *view-number* contained in the received $SMsg(head_j)$ are noted in variables $members_j$ and $RefCviewNo_j$, respectively.

Once $RefCview_j$ is initialised to $head_j$, the recording condition stated below is waited upon to become true or false. (Verifying the recording connddition is done concurrently to modifying or irreversibly setting $RefCview_j$.) This condition is similar to *rc1* stated above for a member:

Recording Condition for joiner (rc_joiner): It verifies whether at least $\Phi(RefCview_j)$ distinct components sent their *State* messages. Formally,
$$|\{q \in RefCview_j: recd_j(SMsg_q(head_j))\}| \geq \Phi(RefCview_j).$$

If *rc_joiner* is met, CM_j atomically records a copy of $head_p$ as its next $Sview_j$ with view number = $RefCviewNo_j+1$ and sets $mode_j = joining$. It then multicasts an $RMsg_j(head_j)$ to all components (including itself) in $head_j$. If *rc_joiner* is not met or if an *Abort* message $AMsg(head_j)$ is received, CM_j dequeues $head_j$ from $ViewQ_j$ and discards it.

Recall that CM_p multicasts $AMsg_p(head_p)$ only if $survivors(Cview_p, head_p)$ M_SETS($Cview_p$) when it starts to deal with $head_p$. So, it sends either $SMsg_p(head_p)$ or $AMsg_p(head_p)$, not both, for a given $head_p$; hence CM_j will not receive an $AMsg_q(head_j)$ once *rc_joiner* is met. Otherwise, this would mean that CM_p sent $SMsg_p(head_j)$ without suspecting a g-failure at the start, while CM_q of member q has $head_q = head_j$ and $survivors(Cview_q, head_q)$ M_SETS($Cview_q$). This would in turn mean that $Cview_p$ and $Cview_q$ are not identical which is a violation of the induction hypothesis.

To illustrate how certain failure cases that could lead to deadlock are handled, consider the group {p,q,r} with unique $Cview_p$; i.e., $Cview_p = Cview_q = Cview_r = \{p,q,r\}$. Let the VM modules deliver an enhanced Mview such that $head_p = head_q = head_r = \{p,q,r,j,j1,j2,j3\} = head_j$, where j, j1, j2, and j3 are joiners. Say, p, q, and r crash before multicasting their *State* messages; if {j, j1, j2, j3} remain connected,

$RefCview_j$ eventually changes to $\{p, q, r\}$ from its initial value of $head_j$. By its definition, $recd_j(SMsg_c(head_j))$ will become false for crashed $c = p$, q, and r and CM_j will deduce that rc_joiner cannot be met.

3.3. Installation Conditions

Having recorded $head_p$ as $Sview_p$, CM_p installs the $Sview_p$ as the new $Cview_p$ only after verifying that a majority of the existing $Cview_p$ have recorded the $head_p$.

Installation condition (ic): $\{q \in survivors(Cview_p, head_p): recd_p(RMsg_q(head_p))\}$
$\in M\_SETS(Cview_p)$.

The CM_j of a *joiner* j has two installation conditions. The first one verifies whether all joiners of $head_j$ have recorded $head_j$; the second one is the same as the *ic* stated above for member p. Note that CM_j has recorded $head_j$ means that it has received *State* messages from some member p in $head_j$; so, $RefCview_j = Cview_p$ and $members_j$ = $survivors(Cview_p, head_p)$.

Installation condition 1 for joiner (ic1_joiner):
$$\forall c \in head_j - members_j: recd_j(RMsg_c(head_j)).$$
Installation condition 2 for joiner (ic2_joiner):
$$\{p \in members_j: recd_j(RMsg_p(head_j))\} \in M\_SETS(RefCview_j).$$
If both conditions are met CM_j makes component j a member by atomically executing: $\{Cview_j := Sview_j; view\text{-}number_j := RefCviewNo_j + 1; status_j = member; mode_j = normal; \}$. The $head_j$ is then dequeued and discarded. If the first condition is not met, no member p in $head_j$ would have recorded $head_j$; so, CM_j's recording of $head_j$ is undone by atomically executing: $\{Sview_j = null; mode_j = waiting; \}$. The $head_j$ is then dequeued and discarded. If only the second condition is not met, CM_j sets its $mode_j$ to *reconfiguration* and executes the reconfiguration protocol. Observe that when CM_j sets $mode_j$ to *reconfiguration*, $Cview_j$ and $view\text{-}number_j$ remain unchanged at their initial values which are *null* and -1 respectively.

3.4. Correctness and Liveness

Correctness: Suppose that CM_p installs $head_p$ as the new $Cview_p$ with view number $(k+1)$. The majority requirement in the installation condition (ic) implies that a majority of $Cview_p(k)$ have recorded $head_p$ as their $Sview$ with view-number $(k+1)$. The recording condition $(rc2)$ ensures that every CM of $joiners(Cview_p(k), Cview_p(k+1))$ has also recorded $head_p$ as its $Sview$ with view-number $(k+1)$. No CM records a new $Sview$ before the existing one is installed. Therefore, given that $Cview_p(k)$ is unique, if CM_q of a *survivor* or *joiner* q installs $Cview_q(k+1)$, then $Cview_q(k+1) = Cview_p(k+1)$. This means that $Cview_p(k+1)$ is also unique.

Liveness: CM_p verifying the recording/installation condition requires the evaluation of the predicate $recd_p(m_q)$ which in turn involves checking whether an expected message m_q has been/can be received from CM_q. Since the node of q can crash before m_q can be sent, the evaluation of $recd_p(m_q)$ must involve checking whether q continues to be present in the subsequent Mviews constructed by VM_p. With this in mind, we present an algorithm for evaluating $recd_p(m_q)$ which does not block indefinitely.

Figure 3 shows the ViewQ's of CM_p and CM_q which, for simplicity, are taken to be identical. We will also assume that $Cview_p = Cview_q = \{p, q, r1, r2, r3\}$ and view-number$_p$ = view-number$_q$ = k (say). That is, $Cview_p(k)$ is unique. Let us denote the Mviews of $ViewQ_p$ and $ViewQ_q$ as: $vu1 = \{p, q, r1, r2, j\}$, $vu2 = \{p, q, r1, j\}$ and $vu3 = \{p, q, j\}$. $vu1$ indicates the disconnection of member r3 (from p and q) and the inclusion of a new component j, $vu2$ the disconnection of r2, and $vu3$ the disconnection of r1.

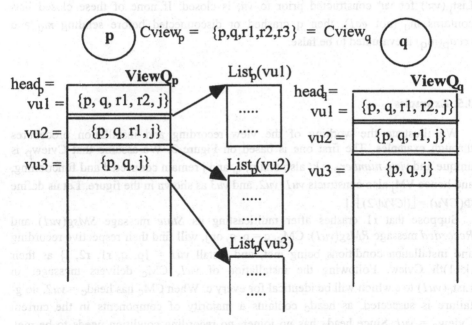

Figure 3. Closed and Open lists of messages delivered by VM after a given Mview.

We define $List_p(Mview)$ as the set of messages which VM_p intends to deliver between the delivery of Mview and the delivery of the immediate successor view to Mview. $List_p(vu3)$ is shown to be open and will remain so until a successor view to $vu3$ is constructed. $List_p(vu1)$ and $List_p(vu2)$, on the other hand, are shown 'closed' to indicate that no received message can enter these lists any longer. By the view-message synchrony property of the VM subsystem (see §2.1.1), $List_p(vu1) = List_q(vu1)$, and $List_p(vu2) = List_q(vu2)$.

The algorithm for evaluating $recd_p(m_q)$ is as follows: CMp waits for one of the following two comditions to become true.

Evaluation condition 1 (ec1): $\exists\ vu \in ViewQ_p$: $m_q \in List_p(vu) \wedge (vu \neq head_p \Rightarrow q \in survivors(head_p, vu))$.

Evaluation condition 2 (ec2): $\exists\ vu \in ViewQ_p$: $q \notin vu$.

The condition *ec1* is true when m_q is present in $List_p(vu)$ for some Mview vu in $ViewQ_p$ and q is present in all the views VM_p constructed from $head_p$ through to this vu; *ec2* becomes true when VM_p constructs an Mview without q.

$boolean\ recd_p(m_q)$

    {wait until *ec1* $\vee$ *ec2*; *if ec1 then* return *true else* return *false*;}

Recall that CM_p evaluates $recd_p(m_q)$ only for such $q \in head_p$. Suppose that VM_p constructs an Mview vu that does not contain q (*ec2*). By message-view integrity property of VM, the expected message from q cannot be in $List_p(vu)$. Every $List_p(vu')$ for vu' constructed prior to vu, is closed. If none of these closed lists contains m_q (not *ec1*), then q crashed or disconnected before sending m_q and $recd_p(m_q)$ is evaluated to be false.

3.5. Examples

We illustrate the working of the view recording and installation procedures through examples. The first one is based on Figure 3. We assume that $Cview_p$ is unique and $view\text{-}number_p = k$; also that p, q, and j remain connected and functioning, and hence VM_j also constructs $vu1$, $vu2$, and $vu3$ as shown in the figure. Let us define $\Phi(CVu) = \lfloor(|CVu|/2)\rfloor + 1$.

Suppose that r1 crashes after multicasting its *State* message $SMsg(vu1)$ and *Recorded* message $RMsg(vu1)$. CM_c, c = p, q, or j, will find their respective recording and installation conditions being met, and install $vu1$ = {p, q, r1, r2, j} as their (k+1)th Cview. Following the installation of $vu1$, CM_c delivers messages in $List_c(vu1)$ to c which will be identical for every c. When CM_c has $head_c = vu2$, no g-failure is suspected, as $head_c$ contains a majority of components in the current $Cview_c = vu1$. Since $head_c$ has no joiner, no recording condition needs to be met. Since p, q, and j remain connected and functioning, CM_c will find the installation condition being met, install $vu2$ as the (k+1)th Cview, and deliver messages in $List_c(vu2)$ to c. Then, CM_c will install $vu3$ as the (k+3)th Cview and deliver messages in $List_c(vu3)$. This example shows that when VM_c and $VM_{c'}$ construct an identical sequence of Mviews, CM_c and $CM_{c'}$ behave identically; they also deliver an identical set of messages between two consecutive Cviews they install.

Suppose that r1 and r2 crash before multicasting their *State* message $SMsg(vu1)$, then CM_c, c = p, q, or j, will find the recording conditions not being met for $head_c = vu1$. CM_p and CM_q will proceed to execute the configuration protocol, while CM_j remains with no change in its *status* (= *spare*) and *mode* (= *waiting*).

Example with Concurrent Mviews

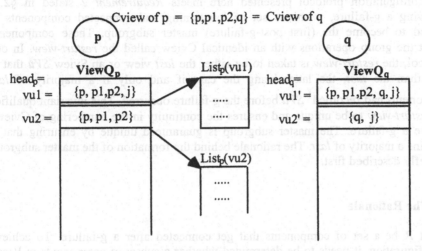

Figure 4. Concurrent and overlapping head views.

The second example is based on Figure 4 and illustrates scenarios that lead CM_p of a member p to dequeue $head_p$ without recording it, and CM_j of joiner j to execute the configuration protocol with $Cview_j = null$. As in the previous example, we will assume that $Cview_p$ is unique and $view\text{-}number_p = k$. The figure shows component j attempting to join the group {p, p1, p2, q}, and VM_p and VM_q reaching different view agreement due to the subsequent detachment of {p, p1, p2} from {q, j}. Let us suppose that p, p1, and p2 remain connected to each other, and so do q and j. Let c denote p, p1, or p2, and c' denote q or j. Every VM_c constructs $vu1$ and $vu2$ shown for p in the figure, and every $VM_{c'}$ constructs $vu1'$ and $vu2'$ shown for q. Given that VM_c and $VM_{c'}$ have constructed non-identical, overlapping $vu1$ and $vu1'$, they must subsequently construct $vu2$ and $vu2'$ respectively, due to the view agreement property (see subsection 2.1.1). Let $\Phi(CVu)$ be defined to be 1, that is, a joiner can compute the component state by receiving a single *State* message.

When CM_c has $head_c = vu1$, it will find $rc1$ met; but it will not receive $RMsg_j(head_c)$ from CM_j and will find $rc2$ not being met. Hence, it dequeues $head_c$, and delivers messages in $List_c(vu1)$ when $Cview_c$ is still {p, p1, p2, q}. Note that $List_c(vu1)$ will not contain any application message from j as j does not yet consider itself as a member. Thus, the view-message integrity property (of subsection 2.1.1) is preserved by CM_c. Since $\Phi(CVu) = 1$, both CM_q and CM_j will find for $head_{c'} = vu1'$

the recording conditions being met, but not the installation conditions. They will proceed to execute the reconfiguration protocol, with $Cview_q$ unchanged, $Sview_q = vul'$ = $Sview_j$, and $Cview_j = null$.

4. Reconfiguration after a g-Failure

The configuration protocol presented here meets *Requirement 2* stated in §2.5: following a g-failure, a unique set of functioning and connected components is formed to become the (first post-g-failure) master subgroup. These components restart the group operations with an identical Cview called the *restart-view*. In our protocol, the *restart-view* is taken to be either the *last* view or an Sview SVu that is later than the *last*, the latter being the case if and only if a majority of *last* components had recorded[1] SVu before the g-failure occurred. This invariant qualifies the *restart-view* to be unique and ensures the continuity in the numbering of Cviews despite a g-failure. The master subgroup is guaranteed unique by ensuring that it contains a majority of *last*. The rationale behind the formation of the master subgroup is briefly described first.

4.1. The Rationale

Let R be a set of components that get connected after a g-failure. To achieve reconfiguration, it needs to be determined whether a subset of components in R can become the master subgroup. Let $Sview_r$ and $Cview_r$ denote the Sview and the Cview of a component r in R, respectively. (If r is recovering from a crash it obtains $Cview_r$ and $Sview_r$ from its stable store.) Let *presumed_last* be the latest Cview among the $Cview_r$ of all r in R: for every r in R, either *presumed_last* = $Cview_r$ or *presumed_last* » $Cview_r$. By definition, *presumed_last* is either the *last* Cview or some Cview installed prior to the *last*.

Let us consider the Sviews recorded by the components of *presumed_last* (not just those in *presumed_last* ∩ R). One of the following three (mutually exclusive) situations must exist:

(i) A majority of *presumed_last* components recorded (at some time in the past) an identical Sview that is later than the *presumed_last*.

(ii) A majority of *presumed_last* components never recorded an Sview that is later than the *presumed_last*.

(iii) Neither 1 nor 2. That is, the number of *presumed_last* components that recorded an Sview that is later than the *presumed_last*, is at most $|presumed\_last|/2$; similarly, the number of *presumed_last* components that never recorded an Sview that is later than the *presumed_last*, is at most $|presumed\_last|/2$.

Let us first consider situation (1). Suppose that R contains (a) more than $|presumed\_last|/2$ components with Sview = *presumed_last*+ and Cview =

---

[1] No *last* component could have installed SVu; otherwise the installed version of SVu would be the *last* which, by definition, is the latest Cview installed by a component.

presumed_last, and (b) a majority subset of *presumed_last+*. We claim that if (a) and (b) are met, *restart-view = presumed_last+*. The (simple) proof is by contradiction.

Proof: Suppose that (a) and (b) are met but *presumed_last+ ≠ restart-view*. Meeting of (a) implies that a majority of components in *presumed_last* have recorded *presumed_last+*. By the definition of *restart-view*, if *restart-view ≠ presumed_last+*, then *restart-view » presumed_last+*. For this to be true, a majority of components in *presumed_last+* must have installed *presumed_last+* as their Cview and then must have proceeded to record an Sview *presumed_last++* (say), *presumed_last++ »* *presumed_last+*. None of these components that installed *presumed_last+* as their Cview, can be in R, as per the way *presumed_last* is computed. This means that (b) cannot be true - a contradiction.

Thus, when (a) and (b) are met, *presumed_last+* becomes the *restart-view* and R∩*presumed_last+* consider themselves to be the master subgroup.

In both situations (2) and (3), a majority of *presumed_last* have not recorded a progressive Sview that is later than *presumed_last*; therefore *presumed_last* must be the *last*, and also the *restart-view*. To deduce the existence of (2), R must contain more than |*presumed_last*|/2 components with Sview not later than *presumed_last*; and for (3) R must contain all *presumed_last* components.

Observe that deducing which one of the three situations exists, requires R to contain at least a majority of *presumed_last* components with appropriate Sviews, or all of them in the third situation. So, it is possible that a given R does not meet this requirement. In that case, the attempt to form the master subgroup with R is given up, and the recovery and reconnection of more number of components need to be awaited.

4.2. The Protocol

The protocol is made up of five steps:

Step 0. CM_p sets $mode_p$ to *reconfiguration* and waits for p to be connected with other components, i.e., for $viewQ_p$ to become non-empty. Say, $ViewQ_p$ becomes non-empty and R = $head_p$. (Note: the first Mview in $ViewQ_p$ is only copied into R, not dequeued.) The remaining four steps are done using R.

Step 1. Send {$Sview_p$, $Cview_p$} to every r in R (including itself);
             Receive {$SviewRecd_r$, $CviewRecd_r$} from every r in R;

Step 2. Determine the *presumed_last* to be the latest $CviewRecd_r$;

Step 3. Determine the *restart-view* if possible; if not possible dequeue R from
             $viewQ_p$, discard R and go to step 0.

Step 4. components of R ∩*restart-view*:
             install *restart-view* and resume group services;
      components of R - *restart-view*:
             become *spares;*
Each step is described in detail in the subsections below.

4.2.1. Step 1: View Exchange

CM_p multicasts a message msg(Sview$_p$, Cview$_p$, mode$_p$) containing Sview$_p$, Cview$_p$ and mode$_p$. It then evaluates the predicate $recd_p(msg_r$(SviewRecd$_r$, CviewRecd$_r$, mode$_r$)) for every r ∈ R. If this predicate is true for a given r, CM_p then checks whether CviewRecd$_r$ » Cview$_p$ and mode$_r$ = *normal*. If this condition is true, an exception *Walked-Over* is raised indicating that p has been slow in recovery, during which time the group is reconfigured without p. This exception is handled by making p a spare and exiting the execution of the protocol. If the predicate is false for some r, then working with R is given up: terminate the execution with R, dequeue R from viewQ$_p$, and go to step 0. The pseudo-code for step 1 is given below:

> multicast msg(Sview$_p$, Cview$_p$, mode$_p$) to all r in R;
> evaluate $recd_p(msg_r$(SviewRecd$_r$, CviewRecd$_r$, mode$_r$)) for every r in R;}
> catch (*Walked-Over*): { write atomically: {Sview$_p$:= *null*; status$_p$:= *spare*;
> mode$_p$:= *waiting*;}
> exit; }
> if (∃r ∈ R: ¬$recd_p(msg_r$(SviewRecd$_r$, CviewRecd$_r$, mode$_r$)))
> then {give up on R;}

4.2.2. Step 2: Determine Presumed_Last

presumed_last is computed to be the latest non-null view among the received Cviews. If a majority of *presumed_last* is not in R, then the execution with current R is given up.

> { *presumed_last* := CviewRecd$_r$ of some r ∈ R: (*presumed_last* ≠ *null*) ∧
> (∀ r' ∈ R: *presumed_last* = CviewRecd$_{r'}$ ∨ *presumed_last* »CviewRecd$_{r'}$);
> if (| *presumed_last* ∩ R| ≤ (| *presumed_last* |/2) then { give up on R;}
> }

Note that by requiring that *presumed-last* be non-null, an R of only spare components with *mode = waiting* are prohibited from forming the *master subgroup*.

4.2.3. Step 3: Attempt to Determine Restart-View

CM_p divides the components in *presumed_last* ∩R into non-overlapping subsets, called candidate sets and denoted as CS_v, v ≥ 0, based on the components' Sview. Let *presumed_last*+$_i$, i ≥1, be an Sview[2] that is later than *presumed_last*. Each CS_v, v ≥

---

[2] *presumed_last*+ need not be unique after a g-failure; different *presumed_last* components could have recorded different progressive Sviews, due to their VM modules concluding view agreement at different points. Let, for example, *last* = {1,2,3,4,5}. Let C5 crash and VM of C4 reach agreement on, and deliver {1,2,3,4}. If VMs of C1, C2, and C3 suspect C4 before they reach agreement on {1,2,3,4}, they will reach agreement straightaway on {1,2,3}. If a

1, contains the components in *presumed_last* $\cap$ R whose SviewRecd$_r$ = *presumed_last*$+_v$; CS$_0$ contains those components in *presumed_last* $\cap$ R whose SviewRecd$_r$ is not later than *presumed_last*. The code for this third step is given below.

(1)   if ($\exists$ CS$_v$: $v \geq 1 \wedge$ CS$_v \in$ M_SETS(*presumed_last*)

$\wedge$ *presumed_last*$+_v \cap$ R $\in$ M_SETS(*presumed_last*$+_v$)) then

{*restart-view* := *presumed_last*$+_v$;}

// *existence of situation (1) is deduced*

(2)   else if (CS$_0 \in$ M_SETS(*presumed_last*) then

{*restart-view* := *presumed_last*;}

// *existence of situation (2) is deduced*

(3)   else if (*presumed_last* $\subseteq$ R) then

{*restart-view* := *presumed_last*;}

// *existence of situation (3) is deduced*

else {give up on R;}

4.2.4. Step 4: Commencing Group Operations

Any p that is not in the *restart-view* becomes a spare, otherwise CM$_p$ updates view information in its stable store. The pseudo code is as follows:

{   if (p $\notin$ *restart-view*) then { write atomically:

{*Sview*$_p$, *Cview*$_p$:= *null*; *status*$_p$:= *spare*;

mode$_p$:= *waiting*; *view-number*$_p$:= -1;}

exit; }

write atomically:

{*view-number*$_p$:= view-number(*restart-view*);

Sview$_p$, *Cview*$_p$:= *restart-view*; *status*$_p$:= *member*;

mode$_p$:= *normal*; }

}

4.3   Examples

We explain the working of the protocol with the help of examples and by referring to the evolution of Sviews depicted in Table 1. For simplicity, assume that all g-failures considered in this discussion are caused by node crashes only, and partitions may occur only when the group is being reconfigured after a g-failure.

Table 1 depicts a possible sequence of membership changes for a group of size 5 and adopts the following style to represent the state of the view installation: an Sview$_p$ in normal font indicates that it has been installed as the Cview$_p$; an Sview$_p$ that is yet to be installed is written in mixed fonts: survivors (from the current Cview$_p$ into this

---

g-failure occurs after CMs have recorded the delivered views, Sview$_4$ = {1,2,3,4} (say, *presumed_last*$+_1$), and Sview$_1$ = Sview$_2$ = Sview$_3$ = {1,2,3} (say, *presumed_last*$+_2$).

Sview$_p$) in normal font, joiners in italics and excluded components (i.e., the ones that are in the current Cview$_p$ but not in the Sview$_p$) in bold. The superscript of an Sview$_p$ indicates its view-number.

Stage No	Sview of C1, C2	Sview of C3	Sview of C4, C5	Sview of C6, C7	Description
1	$\{1,2,3,4,5\}^0$	$\{1,2,3,4,5\}^0$	$\{1,2,3,4,5\}^0$	---	group initialised, n=5; C6 and C7 are spares
2	$\{1,2,\mathbf{3,4,5}\}^1$	$\{1,2,3,4,5\}^0$	$\{1,2,3,4,5\}^0$	---	C4 and C5 crash; CM1 and CM2 record their exclusion first
3	$\{1,2,\mathbf{3,4,5}\}^1$	$\{1,2,\mathbf{3,4,5}\}^1$	$\{1,2,3,4,5\}^0$	---	Slow CM3 records Sview(1)
4	$\{1,2,3\}^1$	$\{1,2,\mathbf{3,4,5}\}^1$	$\{1,2,3,4,5\}^0$	---	CM1 and CM2 install Sview(1)
5	$\{1,2,3\}^1$	$\{1,2,3\}^1$	$\{1,2,3,4,5\}^0$	---	CM3 installs its Sview(1)
6	$\{1,2,3,\mathit{6,7}\}^2$	$\{1,2,3,\mathit{6,7}\}^2$	$\{1,2,3,4,5\}^0$	$\{1,2,3,6,7\}^2$	C6 and C7 join; all active CM record Sview(2) = $\{1,2,3,6,7\}$
7	$\{1,2,3,\mathit{6,7}\}^2$	$\{1,2,3,\mathit{6,7}\}^2$	$\{1,2,3,4,5\}^0$	$\{1,2,3,6,7\}^2$	CM3, CM6 and CM7 install Sview(2)
8	$\{1,2,3,6,7\}^2$	$\{3,6,7\}^3$	$\{1,2,3,4,5\}^0$	$\{3,6,7\}^3$	C1, C2 crash before installing Mview(2); CM3, CM6, CM7 record and then install $\{3,6,7\}$

Table 1. An evolution of Sviews.

The group is initially formed with $\{C1, C2, C3, C4, C5\}$. At the end of stage 1, each member has $\{1,2,3,4,5\}^0$ as its (initial) Sview in stable store; this is also the Cview. At the end of stage 2, CM$_1$ and CM$_2$ have recorded Sview(1) which cannot be installed now as $\{1,2\} \notin$ M_SETS(Sview(0)). The situation changes after stage 3, and CM$_1$ and CM$_2$ install Sview(1) in stage 4. In stage 6, the spares C6 and C7 join the group: CM1, CM2, CM3, CM6, and CM7 record the Sview $\{1,2,3,6,7\}$. In the next stage, C3, C6, and C7 install the Sview, since all components in the old view $\{1,2,3\}$ are known to have recorded $\{1,2,3,6,7\}$. But C1 and C2 crash before they could install the recorded view. In stage 8, C3, C6, and C7 install the Cview without C1 and C2. According to Table 1, $\{1,2,3,6,7\} \gg \{1,2,3\}$ and $\{1,2,3,6,7\} \gg \{1,2,3,4,5\}$. Further, *last* is $\{1,2,3,4,5\}^0$ until stage 3, $\{1,2,3\}^1$ in stages 4, 5, and 6, $\{1,2,3,6,7\}^2$ in stage 7, and $\{3,6,7\}^3$ in stage 8.

Example 0:   This example shows that the protocol is safe in not allowing more than one master subgroup to be formed after a g-failure. Let C1 and C2 recover and get connected after stage 8 but remain partitioned from other components. So, R = {C1, C2}. Both C1 and C2 will estimate *presumed_last* to be $\{1,2,3\}^1$. Since {C3, C6, C7} is already functioning as the group, another master subgroup should not be allowed to emerge from R even though R contains a majority subset of *presumed_last*. Components of R will find that they have an identical (progressive) Sview $\{1,2,3,6,7\}^2$ » *presumed_last*, and R does not contain a majority subset of $\{1,2,3,6,7\}^2$. So, none of the conditions in Step 3 of the protocol is satisfied and R will be given up.

Example 1:   This exemplifies the behaviour of the protocol under the situation 1 mentioned in section 4.1. Suppose that a g-failure occurs immediately after stage 6. Here, *last* is $\{1,2,3\}^1$ and all of the *last* components have recorded $\{1,2,3,6,7\}^2$. So, *restart-view* is $\{1,2,3,6,7\}^2$. Say, R = {C1, C2, C4, C6}. By step 3.1 of the protocol, each component r in R determines *restart-view* to be $\{1,2,3,6,7\}^2$. Finding itself not in *restart-view*, C4 will exit the protocol and join the pool of spares. The others in (R ∩ *restart-view*) install *restart-view* as their Cview and resume normal group services. Note that the view R is still the at head of every ViewQ$_r$, r ∈ R. Upon detecting ViewQ not empty, CMs of (R ∩ *restart-view*) will execute the view installation protocol as members and CM of C4 as a joiner. Assuming no further failures or disconnections, C1, C2, C4, and C6 will get install R as the Cview.

Example 2 considers situation 2 where a majority of *presumed-last* have not recorded an Sview that is later than *presumed-last*. Say, a g-failure occurs at the end of stage 1. *last* = $\{1,2,3,4,5\}^0$. Since no *last* component has recorded a later Sview, *restart-view* is also $\{1,2,3,4,5\}^0$; further, since all *last* components have identical Sview, an R that contains *any* three (majority subset) of the *last* members will lead to the master subgroup. Say, R = {C3, C4, C5}. Assuming that R remains connected for long, each CM of R computes *presumed-last* to be $\{1,2,3,4,5\}^0$, i.e., *last* itself. Next, each CM of R forms CS$_0$ = R and decides in step 3.2 of the protocol the *restart-view* to be *presumed-last* = $\{1,2,3,4,5\}^0$. After (re-)installing *restart-view* as their Cview, CMs of C3, C4, and C5 subsequently install R as their next Cview = $\{3,4,5\}^1$.

Say, after CMs of C3, C4, and C5 have installed $\{3, 4, 5\}^1$ in the above scenario, let C1 and C2 recover and reconnect with C3, C4, and C5. While CMs of C1 and C2 execute the reconfiguration protocol with R = {1,2,3,4,5}, CMs of C3, C4, and C5 will execute view installation protocol for the delivered view $\{1, 2, 3, 4, 5\}^2$ in which C1 and C2 are regarded as joiners. This conflict gets resolved very easily: CMs of C3, C4, and C5 expect CMs of C1 and C2 to send *recorded* messages but instead find messages of configuration protocol. They would then respond by sending its *mode* and Cview to CM$_1$ and CM$_2$ which would get *Walked_Over* exception, become *spares*, and then start executing the view installation protocol as joiners, with the head of their ViewQ (still) having R = {1,2,3,4,5}.

In **Example 3**, we illustrate the need for R to contain *all* the *last* members in certain circumstances. Let a g-failure occur at the end of stage 2. The *last* view here is

$\{1,2,3,4,5\}^0$ which is also the Cview of every member component. We will assume R $= \{C1, C2, C4, C5\}$. The *presumed_last* is the same as *last* $= \{1,2,3,4,5\}^0$. Each component of R knows that a minority of *presumed_last* (i.e. two) have not recorded an Sview that is later than *presumed_last*; and also that only a minority of *presumed_last* (i.e. two again) are known to have recorded an Sview $\{1,2,3,4,5\}^1$ that is later than *presumed_last*. When Sview of C3 is $\{1,2,3,4,5\}^0$ (as it is now), then *restart-view* becomes $\{1,2,3,4,5\}^0$. If Sview of C3 had been $\{1,2,3,4,5\}^1$ (as it is at the end of Stage 3), then *restart-view* becomes $\{1,2,3\}^1$. Hence determining the *restart-view* requires that the components of R know the Sview of C3. Here, R is given up in step 3.3 of the protocol which requires R to contain *presumed_last* when neither the situation 1 nor 2 is known to prevail.

5. Related Work

Using the traditional, 2-Phase Commit (2PC) protocol [10] for atomically updating membership-related information, [12] maintains at most one distinguished partition in a replicated database system. Our CM subsystem also uses a variation of this traditional 2PC for Cview installation and the variations are inspired by our requirements and efficiency. In the traditional 2PC way of installing Cviews, the coordinator - a deterministically chosen member in the new Cview - would initiate the second (view-installation) phase after learning during the first phase that *every* component of the new Cview has recorded the view. Note that while view installation is in progress, delivery of application messages is put on hold to maintain view-synchrony. Since we only require that at least a majority subset, not necessarily all, of the current Cview install the next Cview, we can speed up the view-installation by having the coordinator initiate the second phase as soon as a *majority* of the current Cview and all joiners (if any) in the new Cview have recorded the new view i.e. as soon as the installation conditions of section 3.3 are met. Further, the coordinator based execution of traditional 2PC are susceptible to co-ordinator crashes. We eliminate this weakness by executing our version of 2PC in a decentralised manner where every component checks installation conditions.

Since we use a 2PC protocol for view installations, the configuration protocol cannot be non-blocking. This blocking can be removed by using a 3PC protocol [22]. The protocol of [14] employs the principles of an extended 3PC protocol [13] and builds a unique master subgroup after a g-failure. Not surprisingly, our architecture is remarkably similar to theirs. They differ from our protocol in one other major aspect: a component can simultaneously have, and may have to exchange, more than one Sview; so more stable information needs to be maintained and message size is increased. Obviously these features of [14] increase the overhead of the protocol. The advantage, on the other hand, is that a reconnected set need only contain a particular majority subset of *last*, never all *last* components as we would require in certain cases when a g-failure occurs during view update (see example 3 of section 4.2).

The primary partition membership service in [4, 17, 20] make the assumption that a majority of components in the Cview do not suspect each other and that a functioning component is rarely detected as failed. This assumption may not hold true during periods of network instability caused for example by bursty traffic or network congestion. This instability can lead to incorrect failure detections which in turn can lead to g-failures. In these circumstances, our CM subsystem (also [14]) can provide recovery from g-failures once the network traffic stabilises.

The weakest failure detector (denoted as $\Diamond S/\Diamond W$) for solving the consensus problem is derived in [6]. Using a $\Diamond S$-based consensus protocol, a (primary-partition) membership service is designed [15] and implemented [9]. This membership service can construct a totally ordered sequence of views, with a majority of each view surviving into the next view. It blocks from delivering a new view during the periods of g-failures (i.e., when a connected majority does not exist) and the blocking is released as soon as the requirements of $\Diamond S$ are realised. Does this mean a $\Diamond S$ based membership service provides recovery from g-failures for the weakest system requirements of $\Diamond S$? The answer appears to be no. The first view which the $\Diamond S$ based membership service constructs after a g-failure, is what we call the *restart-view* (see requirement 2 in §2.5). Determining the *restart-view* does not necessarily mean that the new master subgroup exists to restart the group services. To see this, consider the following example. Let the current view be {p, q, r, s, t} with view-number = k, and s and t crash before a g-failure occurs. With the $\Diamond S$ based membership service, it is possible for R = {r, s, t} to reconnect and decide that the (k+1)th view is {p, q, r}. Though the *restart-view* is now known, the group operations cannot be resumed as R does not contain a majority subset of the *restart-view*. (Permitting any subset of R to form the master subgroup will lead to two concurrent master subgroups if {p, q} is operating in a seperate partition.) Group re-configuration with R must therefore wait for either p or q to recover/reconnect. Our approach is different in that the *restart-view* cannot be determined until the reconnected set (R) contains at least a majority of the *restart view* itself (see section 4.1); in other words, determining the *restart-view* straight leads to the re-formation of the group (barring the occurrence of further g-failures). As a future work, we intend to compare these two approaches further in a more detailed manner.

6. Conclusions

Group failures can occur even in the absence of any physical failures, and be caused by sudden bursts in message traffic with potentials to lead to virtual partitions. We have designed and implemented a configuration management subsystem which can provide automatic recovery from group failures, once the real/virtual partitions disappear and components recover. Our system employs a variation of two-phase commit protocol for view updates. Consequently, the recovery provided is subject to blocking. On the other hand, it is efficient in terms of message size, message rounds and use of stable store, during both normal operations and reconfiguration after a group failure; it costs only one extra message round to update views in the normal, failure-free periods. This low, failure-free overhead makes our system particularly suited to soft real-time systems where it can be incorporated in the manner proposed in [11].

Acknowledgements

The work described here has been supported in part by Hewlett-Packard Laboratories, Bristol. Roger Flemming and Paul Harry from Hewlett-Packard Laboratories provided facilities and resources for implementing our reconfiguration system over Somersault. Discussions with Andre Schiper over ◊S-based consensus protocol were useful in clarifying many subtle issues.

References

1. Y. Amir, Dolev, D., Kramer, S., and Malki, D., "Membership Algorithm for Multicast Communication Groups", Proc. of 6th Intl. Workshop on Dist. Algorithms, pp 292-312, November 1992.
2. O.Babaoglu, R. Davoli, and A Montresor, "Group Membership and View Synchrony in Partitionable Asynchronous Distributed Systems: Specifications", Technical Report UBLCS-95-18, Dept. of Computer Science, University of Bologna, Italy, Nov 1995.
3. O.Babaoglu, A. Bartoli, and G Dini, "Enriched View Synchrony: A Programming Paradigm for Partitionable Asynchronous Distributed Systems", IEEE ToCS, 46(6), June 1997, pp.642-658.
4. K.Birman and T. Joseph, "Exploiting virtual synchrony in distributed systems", Proc. of 11th ACM Symposium on Operating System Principles, Austin, November 1987, pp. 123-138.
5. D. Black, P. Ezhilchelvan and S.K. Shrivastava, "Determining the Last Membership of a Process Group after a Total Failure", Tech. Report No. 602, Dept. of Computing Science, University of Newcastle upon Tyne.
6. T. D. Chandra, V. Hadzilacos, and S. Toueg, "The weakest Failure Detector for Solving Consensus", JACM, 43(4), pp. 685 - 722, July 1996.
7. P. Ezhilchelvan, R. Macedo and S. K. Shrivastava, "Newtop: a fault-tolerant group communication protocol", 15th IEEE Intl. Conf. on Distributed Computing Systems, Vancouver, May 1995, pp. 296-306.
8. P D Ezhilchelvan and S K Shrivastava, "Enhancing Replica Management Services to Tolerate Group Failures", Proceedings of the second International Symposium on Object oriented Real-time Computing (ISORC), May 1999, St Malo, France.
9. P Felber, R Guerraoui and A Schiper, "The implementation of CORBA Object service", Theory and Prctice of Object Systems, Vol. 4, No. 2, 1998, pp. 93-105.
10. J N Gray, "Notes on Database Operating Systems", In *Operating Systems: An Advanced Course*, Lecture Notes In Computer Science, Vol 60, pp. 393-481. Springer Verlag, Berlin, 1978.
11. M. Hurfin and M. Raynal, "Asynchronous Protocols to Meet Real-Time Constraints: Is It Really Sensible? How to Proceed?", Proc. of 1st Int. Symp. on Object-Oriented Real-Time Distributed Computing, (ISORC98) pp. 290-297, April 98.
12. S Jajodia and D Mutchler, "Dynamic Voting Algorithms for Maintaining the Consistency of a Replicated Database", *ACM Transactions on Database Systems*, Vol 15, No 2, June 1990, pp. 230-280
13. I Keidar and D Dolev, "Increasing the Resilience of Distributed and Replicated Database Systems", *Journal of Computer and System Sciences* (JCSS). 1995.
14. E Y Lotem, I Keidar and D Dolev, "Dynamic Voting for Consistent Primary Components", Proceedings of ACM Symposium on Principles of Distributed Computing (PODC), pp. 63-71, 1997.

15. C Malloth and A Schiper, "Virtually Synchronous Communication in Large Scale Networks", BROADCAST Third Year Report, Vol 3, Chapter 2, July 1995. (Anonymous ftp from broadcast.esprit.ec.org in directory projects/broadcast/reports)
16. P. M. Melliar-Smith, Moser L.E., and Agarwala, V., "Membership Algorithms for Asynchronous Distributed Systems", Proc. of 12th Intl. Conf. on Distributed Comp. Systems, pp. 480-488, May 1991.
17. S. Mishra, L. Peterson and R. Schlichting, "A membership Protocol Based on Partial Order", Proc. IFIP Conf. on Dependable Computing For Critical Applications, Tuscon, Feb. 1991, pp 137-145.
18. L.E. Moser, P.M. Melliar-Smith et al, "Totem: a Fault-tolerant multicast group communication system", CACM, 39 (4), April 1996, pp. 54-63.
19. P. Murray, R. Flemming, P. Harry and P. Vickers, "Somersault software fault-tolerance", Hewlett-Packard Technical Report, 1997.
20. A. Ricciardi and K P Birman, "Using Process Groups to Implement Failure Detection in Asynchronous Environments", In Proceedings of ACM symposium on PoDC, pp. 480-488, May 91.
21. A Schiper and A Sandoz, "Primary-Partition Virtually Synchronous Communication is Harder Than Consensus", Proc. of the 8th International Workshop on Distributed Algorithms (WDAG-94), Sept. 94, LNCS 857, Springer Verlag. (Also in BROADCAST Second Year Report, Vol 2, October 1994).
22. D. Skeen, "Non-Blocking Commit Protocols", ACM SIGMOD, pp.133 - 142, 1981.

Recent Advances in Distributed Garbage Collection

Marc Shapiro[1,3], Fabrice Le Fessant[1*], and Paulo Ferreira[2]

[1] INRIA Projet SOR, Rocquencourt, France,
http://www-sor.inria.fr/
[2] INESC, Lisboa, Portugal
[3] Microsoft Research Ltd., Cambridge, United Kingdom

1 Why Distributed Garbage Collection

Dynamically-allocated memory must eventually be reclaimed. But manual reclamation is error-prone, and if an object is de-allocated prematurely, a program that later follows a pointer to it might behave incorrectly. In contrast, *garbage collection* (GC) automatically reclaims objects that can no longer be reached by any path of pointers.

In a distributed system, an object might not only be referenced from one program, but also from other programs and other computers. This makes manual reclamation quite intractable. We consider here the problem of *distributed garbage collection* (DGC). DGC is particularly important in a large-scale distributed system, since a de-allocation error might cause a completely unrelated program to fail, possibly far away and an arbitrarily long time later.

DGC has been a subject of academic research since at least 1977 [4]. With the growth of the Internet, DGC is now receiving its share of commercial attention. For instance, both Java RMI [28] and DCOM [23] come with some form of DGC.

The next section contains a quick review of DGC techniques; for a more indepth treatment, we refer to published surveys [1, 21]. Then we detail two recent advances in DGC, both developed in the context of the Broadcast project. One is an algorithm for collecting distributed cycles of garbage in a message-passing system; the other is an algorithm for DGC in a system with caching and/or replication. Both have been implemented in real systems and are in actual use.

This article assumes some familiarity with centralised GC, now a mature area [11, 27]. We use the following vocabulary. Objects connected by references form a graph; a remote reference may point into another process. An application or mutator enters the graph via roots, allocates objects, and performs assignment of reference variables. The system or collector reclaims garbage, i.e., objects that are reachable by no path from any root.

2 Distributed Garbage Collection Approaches

Distributed algorithms should be scalable, which implies local execution, absence of remote synchronisation, low complexity and costs, and fault tolerance.

---

* Ph.D. student at École Polytechnique. Also with INRIA projet PARA.

S. Krakowiak, S.K. Shrivastava (Eds.): Distributed Systems, LNCS 1752, pp. 104–126, 2000.

Scalability in DGC is often achieved at the cost of incompletness, i.e., only re-claiming a safe subset of actual garbage. Scalability excludes the apparently straightforward approach of running one of the existing centralised algorithms over a consistent view of the object graph, e.g., over a snapshot [5] or in a trans-action. Our approach instead is to use the unique properties of DGC that enable specific, efficient solutions.

2.1   Two Models of Distributed Systems

Before going into more detail, it is appropriate to explain our two models of distributed system. Classically, a distributed system is defined as a set of disjoint processes, sharing no memory, and communicating by *message passing*; this is our first model. We do not assume any upper bound on message delivery time. An object exists at a single process at any time.

In the alternative *shared-memory model*, processes interact by sharing mem-ory. The system simulates a shared memory by sending (in a message) the value of a chunk of memory to a remote site, where it is cached and mapped into application space. We call the different copies of a given chunk of memory its replicas. The system keeps replicas consistent, detecting updates and sending messages invalidating or updating out-of-date replicas. Messages are not visi-ble to applications. This model includes Distributed Shared Memories (DSMs) such as Ivy [18], distributed shared object systems such as Orca [3], and cached distributed file systems or databases.

We use the word *bunch* for the smallest subdivision of the shared memory that can be replicated, often a page or segment. An object resides in a single bunch, but at any point in time the bunch (and the objects it contains) might be replicated to multiple processes.

2.2   Basic DGC Techniques

The simplest DGC algorithm uses time-outs, as was first proposed in the Bullet file system [26]. Time-outs are simple and effective but unsafe, since a transient error can cause a reachable object to disappear.

Other DGC algorithms derive from the two well-known families of GC algo-rithms, namely *counting* and *tracing*. A counting algorithm maintains a count of references to every object. Counting is a local operation, hence the algorithm scales well. It has the disadvantage that it does not collect cycles of garbage. *Ref-erence listing* generalises couting to maintain the list (and not just the number) of pointers to an object; this allows a reference originating from a site declared crashed to be reclaimed.

A tracing algorithm determines garbage by direct examination of the graph. A tracing collector collects all garbage, including cycles. However distributed tracing is not scalable, because it is a global algorithm, and because it runs globally synchronised phases.

Some authors advocate *back-tracing* [20]: if a backwards graph walk returns to the start object and does not encounter a root, then that object is part of a garbage cycle. The backwards walk is expensive; therefore we do not consider back-tracing any further.

2.3   Hybrid Collection Algorithms

Practical DGC algorithms are a hybrid of tracing, counting, and time-out. For instance a hybrid DGC is used in the commercial remote-object system Java RMI [28]. Two systems that we developed, SSP Chains [24] and PerDiS [9], are also based on hybrid DGC; they will be examined in more detail in the later sections.

A distributed system is typically partitioned for locality. In the DGC context, we call each part a *space*. DGC algorithms typically focus on collecting references that cross the boundaries between spaces. Such remote references are managed with reference lists.

Each space independently takes care of its local garbage with a tracing algorithm.[1] An incoming remote reference is (conservatively) considered part of the local root set. When a local collector determines that an outgoing remote reference has become unreachable, the DGC sends a message to the target space, causing it to decrement its reference count. Time-outs are used to detect that a space has crashed; reference listing allows to selectively ignore references from a crashed space.

A hybrid DGC combines the best of all worlds. Within a space, the local collector will reclaim all garbage, including cycles, without imposing a global algorithm. Across spaces, listing provides scalability.

However, a hybrid algorithm does not collect cycles of garbage that span spaces. Furthermore, time-outs must be used with utmost care.

Hybrid Collection in the Message-Passing Model. In the message-passing model, each process (or processor) is a space. It is easy to detect reference mutations, because assigning a remote pointer requires a message, containing the reference, between processes. Then, sending or receiving the message causes the incrementation of the corresponding count.

This algorithm model is well understood; remaining open questions have to do with fault tolerance and with collecting distributed cycles of garbage. Section 3 presents a new algorithm for collecting distributed cycles in a large-scale distributed system.

Hybrid Collection in the Shared-Memory Model. In the shared-memory model, each bunch replica constitutes a separate space. At some arbitrary point in time, replicas of a same bunch may be mutually inconsistent. Multiple spaces may coexist in a single process. A pointer to an object designates any of its replicas, independent of process. Pointer assignments occur directly in memory.

---

[1]   Local tracing is not an obligation; local counting or even manual collection is possible too.

The collector must somehow be notified when the application assigns a pointer across a bunch boundary. This all makes it hard to determine which objects are reachable. The advance described in Section 4 is the Larchant algorithm, an efficient, scalable DGC algorithm for a distributed shared memory, which takes these issues into account.

3   Collecting Distributed Garbage Cycles in the Message-Passing Model

In this section, we present our recent work on collecting distributed cycles of garbage in message-passing systems. This work is mainly inspired from Hughes' algorithm, but our detector [15] extends Hughes to asynchronous distributed systems.

After introducing the main properties of our detector, we will present the algorithm and argue for its scalability and fault-tolerance. More detail can be found elsewhere [15].

3.1   Introduction

Terminology. In this paper, we use the terminology of the Stub-Scion Pair Chains system (SSPC) [24].

Stubs and Scions. Each remote reference R from object A in space X to object B in space Y is represented by a local pointer in X from object A to a special object $stub_X(R)$, called a *stub* and used as a proxy in X for object B, and a local pointer in Y from another special object $scion_Y(R)$, called a *scion* and used as a local root in Y, to the object B. For the reference R, X is the *upstream* space, and Y the *downstream* space.

Stubs and scions come in pairs: each stub has exactly one *matching* scion, and each scion has at most one matching stub. A remote reference R is created by first creating the scion, then sending the reference (in fact, the scion identifier, called the *locator*) in a message, and finally by creating the associated stub in the remote space.

Timestamps and Dates. In the SSPC acyclic garbage collector, all messages are stamped to prevent race conditions. In our algorithm, we use both the original SSPC timestamps, and other timestamps (starting times of global traces, generated by a distributed Lamport clock) on stubs and scions to distinguish multiple concurrent traces. To avoid confusion, the former are called *timestamps*, while the latter ones are called *dates*.

Overview. Like Hughes' algorithm [10], our detector is based on multiple global traces progressing concurrently in the system. Each global trace starts as some space's local garbage collection. It uses as its marker the current date from the

Lamport clock at its starting space, and propagates that date from local roots to stubs reachable from those roots. Dates on stubs are then propagated along chains of remote pointers, from stubs to scions by messages and from scions to reachable stubs by local garbage collections. A stub is always marked with the highest date of all scions or local roots it is known to be reachable from.

As a consequence, reachable stubs are marked with increasing dates, remotely-propagated from their original roots. On the contrary, unreachable stubs eventually stabilise at the starting date of the latest global trace when they were found to be reachable.

A global trace is *terminated* when its starting date no longer appears on reachable stubs and scions. Using an analysis of increasing dates on its stubs, a space computes the date (noted localmin) of the oldest global trace which has not yet terminated at this space. All localmins are gathered on a central location, called the *detection server*, in order to compute the oldest date (noted globalmin) among traces which have not terminated in one or more spaces. Any scion that is marked with a date earlier than globalmin is removed from the roots, since it is marked with the date of a terminated trace.

Main Properties. This algorithm presents interesting properties for distributed systems:

- *It is centralised:* centralisation is often seen as a drawback in distributed systems. However, for this problem, it enables a simpler, lightweight and fault-tolerant solution. We will show that the central server is not a performance or fault-tolerance bottleneck.
- *It is topology-aware:* A network is often organised as a closely-coupled LAN, loosely connected to the rest of the world through a WAN. In our model, there would one server per LAN, and only intra-LAN cycles are detected. Inter-LAN cycles are not detected.
- *It is optional:* SSPCs constitute the basic reference and communication mechanism. The new algorithm presented here detects detects cycles of garbage spanning participating spaces. A process may decline to participate while still using SSPCs normally. A cycle of garbage that goes through a non-participating space is not collected, but there is no further overhead for the non-participant.
- *It is asynchronous:* messages are sent asynchronously. Neither a mutator nor a collector is ever blocked by the DGC.
- *It consumes few resources:* our algorithm relies on small local data structures, it sends few messages, only to spaces in the immediate vicinity, and its computation overhead is negligeable.
- *It has a low implementation cost:* our algorithm has been implemented for the Objective-CAML [17] platform of Stub-Scion Pair Chains [13]. Only minor modifications of the runtime were necessary to propagate timestamps as a side-effect of local garbage collection. Other parts of the algorithm were implemented over the runtime as an optional library.

– *It is fault-tolerant:* the algorithm is safe in the presence of unreliable communications (messages can be lost, re-ordered or duplicated) and crashes.

Comparison with Hughes' Algorithm. Hughes' assumptions are quite stronger than ours: his algorithm relies on a global clock, on instantaneous and reliable communication, and does not tolerate space crashes. Thus, important aspects of large-scale distributed systems, such as messages in transit or failures, are not addressed. These strong assumptions enable to detect termination using Rana's algorithm [22], based on a snapshot of local states.

Our algorithm replaces Rana's algorithm by the centralised computation of the minimum of an integer vector. Our assumptions are more realistic: communications are assumed asynchronous and unreliable, and the detection process is not broken by space crashes. Hughes' global clock is replaced by a Lamport logical clock [12]. Moreover, most computation is delayed until local garbage collection time, leading to a more conservative but cheaper algorithm.

3.2   The Algorithm: Propagation of Dates

Local Propagation. At the beginning of each local garbage collection, local roots are marked with the current date of the local Lamport clock. Local roots and scions are then sorted,[2] and traced in decreasing order of their dates. A reachable stub is marked with the date of the root being traced. Since an object is only marked once during a local collection, a stub ends up marked with the greatest date of all roots from which it is reachable.

Remote Propagation. After a local collection, a marked stub whose date has increased, propagates its date to its downstream scion, using a **Stubdates** message. A stub whose date has remained constant or has decreased does not propagate anything.

SSPC timestamps are used to check if a scion locator has been sent, and not received before the **Stubdates** message was sent, in which case the scion date[3] must not be updated, since the new reference was not taken into account in the propagated dates.

Characterising a Cycle of Garbage. At each local garbage collection, local roots propagate a new larger date. Thus, the date of any reachable stub will eventually increase. In contrast, dates belonging to unreachable cycles evolve in two phases: the greatest date is first propagated to all stubs and scions in the cycle. Then, since there is no local root leading to the cycle, no new date can enter the cycle, and the dates remain constant forever (see figure 1).

---

[2]   Scions are marked with the date received from their associated stub. Initially, they are marked with a special date, called *top*, which is always replaced by the current date in computations.

[3]   The scion date is always set to *top* when its locator is sent.

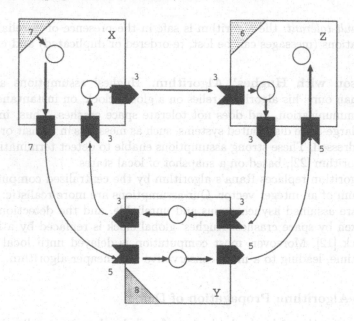

Fig. 1. As a consequence of date propagation, unreachable stubs in a cycle are eventually marked with the date of a terminated trace (date 3), whereas dates on reachable stubs continue to increase with successive global traces (dates 5 and 7).

The system is recurringly traversed by concurrent traces originating at the different local roots. Each one is characterised by its marker, the date at which it started. A reachable stub is recurringly marked by a new trace, i.e., with a greater marker. An unreachable stub, in contrast, remains marked with the the starting date of the last trace that found it to be reachable.

The goal of our algorithm is therefore to compute an increasing threshold, called globalmin, which is a minimum on dates found on stubs marked by successive global traces. Globalmin is a conservative approximation of the date of the oldest concurrent trace that has not yet terminated somewhere.

3.3   The Algorithm: Computation of globalmin

Computation of globalmin by the Detection Server. The computation of globalmin requires a consensus involving all participating spaces. A fully distributed and fault-tolerant consensus would be extremely complex. However, for our particular case, the use of a centralised computation will be shown to be scalable and fault-tolerant.

In our system, globalmin is computed by a dedicated process, called the *detection server*. Each participating space computes a value (called localmin), representing the date of oldest trace that has not yet terminated at this space. The space then sends localmin to the detection server in a Localmin message. Since a trace that is locally terminated can be revived by receiving the marker of that date from another space, the value of localmin varies non-monotonically.

However, globalmin, the conservative minimum of all localmins, is monotonically increasing, since a trace is terminated only when terminated for all spaces. An unreachable stub or scion is marked with the date of a terminated trace, which eventually becomes smaller than globalmin.

The value of globalmin on the server does not need to be always up-to-date. Keeping an old value of globalmin means that the termination of some traces has not been detected by the detection server yet, and therefore that the reclamation of cycles with those dates is simply delayed. To reduce the load on the detection server, globalmin can be computed unfrequently, with a period depending only on the actual need of memory space in the participating spaces.

The only information maintained by the detection server is the list of participating spaces and, for each participating space, the last value of localmin received. This information is simple to recover in the case of a crash of the detection server. A new detection server can be started promptly in the same computation state, without aborting any global trace.

Computation of localmin by a Participating Space. For any participating space, localmin is a conservative approximation of the oldest date of the traces that have not terminated yet for that space. We say that a space *protects* a date, preventing any stub or scion marked with that date from being reclaimed, when its computed localmin is smaller than, or equal to, that date.

The value localmin is computed according to the following *protection* rule:

- When the local garbage collector of some space increases the date of a stub, that stub's previous date must remain protected by the space until the collector of the downstream space has itself propagated the new date from the stub's downstream scion, and the resulting localmin (computed by the downstream space) has been received by the detection server (see Figure 2).

Indeed, if the local garbage collector increases the date of a stub, that stub is probably reachable. Since the stub's downstream scion is still marked with the previous date of the stub, the global trace for that date is not terminated yet.

However, the downstream space will not protect that date until it has itself detected that the associated global trace has not terminated yet. This detection will occur when the increased date has been propagated to the downstream space by a message, and to possibly reachable stubs by a local garbage collection. Finally, for the protection to be effective, the detection server must have received the associated localmin message from the downstream space.

This rule can be implemented by the following protocol: The local garbage collector computes, for each downstream space, the minimum date which must be protected, called ProtectNow, by comparing the new and old dates on stubs. ProtectNow entries are ensered into the ProtectedSet of all dates protected on

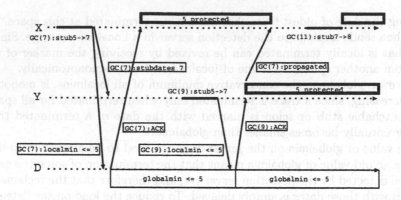

Fig. 2. Our protection rule is safe: space X stops protecting date 5 when Y has started protecting it.

the space. Localmin is then computed as the minimum of all entries in the ProtectedSet.

Localmin is sent to the detection server, which returns an Ack message, containing the current value of globalmin. When the Ack is received, the space knows that all new dates received before the local garbage collection have been propagated and that the new localmin has been received by the server. According to the protection rule, upstream spaces may stop protecting old dates associated with the stubs and local garbage collection whose new dates have just been propagated.

Moreover, when a space receives a Stubdates message, it stores the associated upstream local garbage collection date in a set, called the PropagatedSet. When a Ack message is received, the space sends a Propagated message to each upstream space mentioned in PropagatedSet. This message contains the entries of the PropagatedSet entered before the acknowledged local garbage collection. When an upstream space receives Propagated, it may remove the entries in its ProtectedSet for the sending space for all local collections up to the propagated one.

Coping with Mutator Activity. The mutator may send remote references (thus creating stub-scion pairs or using existing ones), or invoke reference targets, while the distributed collector runs.

When a new stub-scion pair is created, the scion date is initialized to *top* and the stub date to the current date of its space. When re-using an existing stub-scion pair, the scion owner does not know if the stub associated with its scion is still live. Thus, it must behave as if a new pair were created: the scion date is set to *top*. The *top* date on a scion is only replaced when a new date is propagated from its matching stub. However, to avoid race conditions, the

Stubdates message propagating the new date must have been sent after the last message containing the scion locator has been received by the sender space. Observe that this simple mechanism also handles non-participating spaces, since scions reachable from them remain marked with *top*, and thus are never collected.

When the mutator invokes an object through a stub-scion pair, this is sufficient proof that the stub is reachable. Therefore, an invocation increases the stub's date to the current date. As a consequence of the protection rule, its previous date must therefore be protected by subsequent localmin values.

3.4   Complexity

We can now examine the complexity of our algorithm, in memory, computation time and communication requirements.

Participating Spaces

Memory Consumption. Compared to the basic SSPC, each stub contains two extra dates and each scion one. Our algorithm needs two new data structures at each participating space. ProtectedSet contains the dates to be protected for each remote space by the value of localmin. PropagatedSet contains the dates of Stubdates messages received before a local garbage collection for which Localmin message is awaiting acknowledgement. Both can be implemented as FIFO queues, one for each remote participating space.

One entry is put in each queue of ProtectedSet at each local garbage collection. Therefore size of a queue depends on the frequency of local garbage collections with respect to remote ones. If the frequencies are similar across spaces, each queue should contain a small number of entries. However, if a space collects more frequently, causing its set to become too large, date propagation and computation of localmin should be avoided until sufficient entries have been removed from its ProtectedSet.[4]

The size of the PropagatedSet depends on the delay between transmitting a Localmin message and receiving the Ack. Thus, it should be small unless communication is very unreliable.

Computation Time. The major computation load on a space occurs during local garbage collection. The local trace requires that scions are sorted by decreasing order of their dates. This sort can be done from scratch (cost $O(N.log(N))$) in the number of scions) at each local garbage collection, or by inserting a scion into a sorted table each time its scion date is modified. If there are fewer dates than scions, another approach is to group scions by date, and sort the groups.

Localmin is computed as the minimum of the old dates of increasing stubs, and of all the entries in the ProtectedSet. Thus, there is one comparison for

---

[4] Notice than one remote garbage collection can remove several entries at once, i.e., all the entries for local garbage collections whose Stubdates messages were received before the date of the remote garbage collection.

each stub, to compute the current date to be protected for the current local garbage collection for each remote space, and one comparison for each entry in the ProtectedSet, i.e., $O(n_{stubs}) + O(n_{spaces})$.

Detection Server. The detection server, although centralised, is not a bottleneck. Indeed, the computation and memory requirements are low, and linear in the number of participating spaces:

Memory consumption: The detection server maintains a vector containing the last localmin received from each participating space.

Computation time: Globalmin is computed periodically as the minimum of the localmins of the participating spaces. To trigger this computation, a good stimulus is that all participating spaces whose previous localmins were equal to globalmin have increased their localmin. The number of such spaces can easily be computed during the computation of globalmin.

Messages. For each local garbage collection, two messages are sent to each remote space in the vicinity: Stubdates and Propagated. There are also two messages exchanged with the detection server: Localmin and Ack. Whereas Propagated, Localmin and Ack are small messages (containing at most three values), Stubdates contains one date per live stub. However, this message can be merged with the Live message of basic SSPC, which also contains one date per live stub.

3.5   Fault-Tolerance

This algorithm is tolerant both to unreliable communication and to space failures. Although building reliable communication above unreliable communication is often not a problem, space failures cannot be avoided in a real distributed system.

Unreliable communication is tolerated because of the conservative approach taken in the communication of globalmin and localmin. Localmins are computed not only from the protected dates of the current garbage collection, but also for some previous garbage collections (Protected Set). Globalmin is computed from the last localmins received, and its value is always safe, even if not up-to-date.

The detection server can crash. Any other processor can then become the new detection server, without aborting either the current detection process nor the current global traces.

A participating space can also crash. In such a case, the detection server must first propagate the new list of participants to all remaining ones. If the upstream space of a scion is not know to be one of the participants, its date is set to the special value *top*. Then, the detection server waits for the new localmin value computed after this update, before computing the next value of globalmin.

3.6 Scalability

Our algorithm imposes few requirements on participating spaces. The computational and memory overhead is low, and few messages are sent for each local garbage collection. However, it has two major drawbacks: the computation is centralised, and a slow space will slow down the detection of distributed cycles of garbage (but not the detection of non-cyclic garbage, which is down by the base SSPC system).

However, we consider this algorithm interesting in large scale networks. Indeed, the limitation introduced by these two drawbacks is on the *number* of participating spaces, and not the *distance* between them. Since cycle detection is most useful between long-lived (and/or persistent) servers, these limitations are not problematic. A short-lived client does not need to participate in cyclic collection, since any garbage cycles through it will be collected when it dies. Only long-lived processes should participate.

3.7 Conclusion

We have described a detector of distributed cycles of garbage. Our cycle detector presents some interesting properties for large-scale systems: asynchrony between participating spaces, optional participation, tolerance to communication faults and space crashes, low resource requirements, and ease of implementation (no modifications to local objects, only a few to the local garbage collector). Moreover, this algorithm has already been implemented in a distributed system, and the implementation details can be found in le Fessant [15].

We are now working on a new version of this cycle detector using both propagation of marks and back-tracing. This new algorithm will have the same properties as the one described here, plus the ability to detect cycles spanning any spaces in the whole system. This new algorithm is currently being implemented for our mobile agents platform [14].

4 The Larchant DGC Algorithm for Distributed Shared Stores

4.1 Introduction

Modern distributed systems rely on caching and replication to speed up access to remote objects. A reference can then be resolved directly in the local memory. The purest example is provided by a Distributed Shared Memory (DSM) [18], which enables processes on different computers to share data simply by using pointers, just like in a centralised program. Distributed file systems and object-oriented databases provide similar facilities. In what follows we will refer to all such cached or replicated memories as DSMs.

DGC in a distributed shared memory is a harder problem than DGC in the message-passing model studied in Section 3 because:

- Applications modify the graph concurrently and by pointer assignment, not by sending messages. This is a very frequent operation, which should not be slowed down; for instance reference counting at each pointer assignment would not be acceptable.
- Replicas are not instantly coherent. Observing a consistent image of the graph is difficult and costly.
- The pointer graph may be very large and distributed. Much of it resides on disk. Tracing the whole graph in one go is unfeasible.
- A single assigment can affect vast and remote portions of the graph. This has consequences on the global ordering of operations.
- GC should not compete with applications. For instance, it should not take locks, cause coherence operations, nor cause I/O.

We consider previous results on collecting a DSM [2, 16, 19, 29] inapplicable because it does not take the above issues into account. We describe now work done in the context of Larchant, a distributed and persistent shared store, intended for interactive cooperative tasks. Larchant consists essentially of a large-scale DSM; only objects reachable from a *persistent root* (e.g., a name server) persist.

The main goals of our distributed GC algorithm are correctness, scalability, low overhead, and independence from any particular coherence algorithm. Secondary goals are avoiding source code and compiler changes.

Our approach divides the global GC into small, local, independent pieces, that run asynchronously, hence can be deferred and run in the background:

- The store is partitioned into "bunches;" a bunch may be replicated. GC is a hybrid of tracing within a bunch and counting across bunches.
- Each site runs a collector with a standard tracing algorithm [27] that works in one or more bunch replicas (on that site) at the same time.
- The cooperation protocol between collectors does not entail mutual synchronisation.
- A collector examines only the local portion of the graph, without causing any I/O or taking locks.
- A collector may run even when local replicas are not known to be coherent.

We exhibit five simple rules for the correctness of collection in a DSM, which Larchant satisfies. The algorithm is safe (no reachable data is reclaimed) and live (garbage is eventually reclaimed). Sadly, but unavoidably, it is not complete.

The underlying theoretical model and a proof of correctness can be found in Ferreira and Shapiro [8]. More information about the Larchant algorithm can be found in previous publications [6, 7, 25].

4.2   GC Algorithm and Safety Rules

The Larchant memory, as shown in Figure 3, is subdivided into coarse-grain *bunches* (typically, a set of contiguous pages) in which objects are allocated. A bunch can be replicated (e.g., cached) in multiple processes. An object can

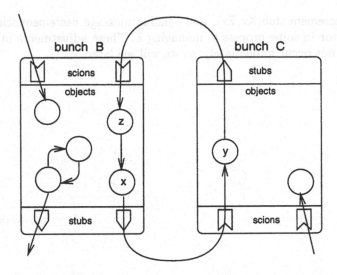

Fig. 3. *Two bunches containing objects, stubs, and scions.*

point to another object, either in the same bunch or across bunches. In both cases the reference is a raw pointer. In the second case only, the collector maintains additional data structures, a *stub* for an outgoing pointer and a *scion* for an incoming one.[5] A typical execution example is shown in Figure 4.

Larchant uses a hybrid DGC, as defined in Section 2.3. Each replica of each bunch forms a space.[6] A reference within a bunch is subject to tracing collection, whereas references that cross bunch boundaries are counted. To avoid interfering with the application, we assume that the collector discovers pointer assignments after the fact, as it traces a bunch. Tracing a bunch causes stubs to be created or deleted; the counting algorithm adjusts scions accordingly.

We now outline the basic algorithm and define some notation. When a mutator performs the assignment noted $<x := y>_i$ (i.e., copy the value of pointer y into pointer x in process i), up to three processes are involved in the corresponding counting. Say objects x, y, z and t are located in bunches X, Y, Z and T respectively; prior to the assignment, x pointed to z and y pointed to t. As a consequence of the assignment, the collector of process i increments the reference count for t by performing the local operation $<increment.stub(Xx, Tt)>_i$ and sending message increment.scion(Xx, Tt) to the collector in some process j managing T. It also decrements the reference count for z by performing the local

---

[5] Despite the similar vocabulary and role, these stubs and scions are somewhat different from those in SSPC used in Section 3. Larchant's stubs and scions are auxiliary data structures of the distributed collector; the mutator does not see them in any way; increments and decrements occur in the background.

[6] To the first approximation only, because Larchant changes space boundaries dynamically by grouping together a number of bunches [25]. However this is beyond the scope of the current discussion.

operation decrement.stub(Xx, Zz), and sending message decrement.scion(Xx, Zz) to the collector in some process k, managing Z. These adjustments ot reference counts need not occur immediately, as we will see later.

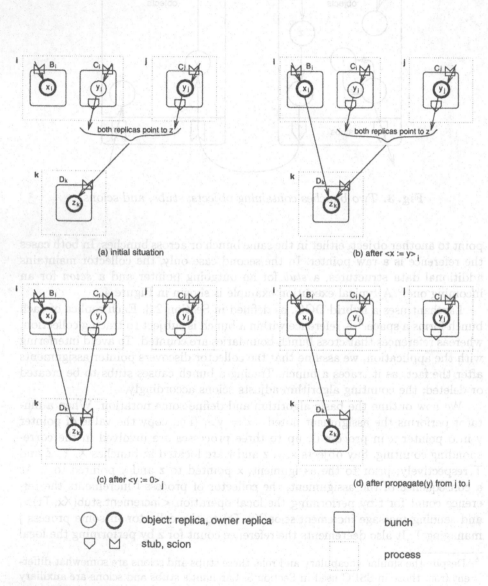

Fig. 4. *Prototypical example of mutator execution. Note that the stubs and scions become temporarily inconsistent with the pointers. However, as described in the paper, this does not compromise safety.*

Tracing in the Presence of Replicas: The Union Rule. Each process runs a standard centralised tracing collector. The issue we raise now is how collectors cooperate, in order to take replication into account. It is desirable that a collector remain independent, both of remote collectors, and of the coherence algorithm. Thus, a collector may scan a local replica, even if it is not known to be coherent, and independently of the actions of remote collectors.

The collector at process i might observe x_i to be pointing to z, whereas collector at process j concurrently observes x_j to be pointing to t. The coherence protocol will eventually make both replicas equal, but the collector cannot tell which value of x is correct. In the absence of better information, the collector must accept all replicas as equally valid, and never reclaim an object until it is observed unreachable in the union of all replicas. This is captured by the following rule.

Safety Condition I: Union Rule. *If some replica x_i points to z, and some replica x_j is reachable, then z is reachable.*

The above says that if some object z is referenced only by an unreachable replica x_i, it is reachable nonetheless if some other replica x_j, $i \neq j$, of x is reachable. This very conservative formulation is necessary in the absence of knowledge of the coherence algorithm.

An efficient implementation of the Union Rule applies to single-owner coherence protocols such as entry consistency. In such protocols, a single "owner" process centralizes the information about a given object.[7] The collectors centralise the information about pointers from x at the owner of x, using what we call **union messages**. In other words, a process holding replica x_j sends a union message, to x's owner, after detecting a change in the pointers from x_j. (Note that this detection is achieved by tracing x_j's enclosing bunch.)

Now, suppose that x points to z, and x is assigned a new value (for instance the null pointer). It is only when all the replicas of x have the new value, and the corresponding collectors have informed x's owner (by sending it a union message) that there are no pointers from x to z, that the owner of x sends a message to the owner of z, to decrement the corresponding scion's reference count. This technique moves some of the responsibility for reference counting to the owner of the objects where references originate.

Cross-Bunch Counting and More Safety Rules. The standard approach to reference counting is to instrument assignments in order to immediately increment/decrement the corresponding counts. This approach requires compiler modification, and is expensive when assignments are frequent and counting is a remote operation, as is the case in Larchant.

Our solution consists of deferring the counting to a later tracing. In fact, the counts need not be adjusted immediately. Consider an assignment $\langle x := y \rangle_i$, where y points to z. At the time of the assignment, z is reachable by definition,

---

[7] The owner of an object may change over time.

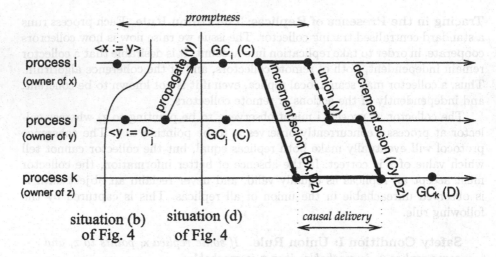

Fig. 5. *Timeline showing the effect of some of the safety rules for the example of Figure 4. On site* i, *the sending of* increment.scion(Bx, Dz) *may be delayed at most until sending* union(y). *Note the causal dependence (indicated by the thick lines) between the* increment.scion *and* decrement.scion *messages, carried by the* union *message.*

and is guaranteed to remain reachable as long as y_i is not modified and remains reachable. It is not necessary for (a process managing) x to increment z's reference count, as long as (some process managing) y does not decrement it.

Let us return to the example of Figure 4. At the time of $<x := y>_i$, object z is reachable (from both replicas of y) and is protected by some scion, say scion(Tt,-Zz); presumably, but not necessarily, T = Y and t = y. As long as z's scion has a non-zero count, it is safe to delay the increment of scion(Bx, Dz). (Recall that it is the trace of bunch X which updates X's set of stubs, which in turn causes the corresponding scion count to be adjusted.)

However, a problem remains with this approach. In the example, once situation (d) has been reached, it is possible that decrement.scion(Cy, Dz) reaches site k before increment.scion(Bx, Dz); then z could be incorrectly reclaimed. To avoid this unsafe situation, it suffices to give precedence to increment.scion over decrement.scion and union messages. This is illustrated in Figure 5: the interval labeled *promptness*, shows how much the message increment.scion(Bx, Dz) can be delayed with respect to the moment when the corresponding assignment operation ($<x := y>_i$) has been performed.

A set of further safety rules determine how late counting can be deferred, while still receiving messages in a safe order. We now state these rules, which will be justified in the following section.

Safety Condition II: Increment Before Decrement Rule. *Scanning an object causes the corresponding* increment.scion *messages to be sent immediately.*

Safety Condition III: Comprehensive Tracing Rule. *When process i sends a* union *or* decrement.scion *message, all replicas at i must have been scanned since most recently assigned.*

Safety Condition IV: Clean Propagation Rule. *When process i sends* propagate(x)*, x_i has been scanned since it was most recently assigned.*

Safety Condition V: Causal Delivery Rule. *Garbage-collection messages (*increment.scion, union *and* decrement.scion*) are delivered in causal order.*

Rule II allows an object replica to be scanned at any time; scanning an object that contains a new pointer immediately sends an increment.scion message to the referent. It's important to mention that messages are asynchronous, so its actual transmission might take place later, provided messages are delivered in order, which is ensured by Rule V.[8]

Rule III ensures that union and decrement.scion messages are sent after increment.scion messages. In conjunction with Rule II, it ensures that, if an increment.scion message depends on a union or a decrement.scion, the latter will be sent before the former.

Rule IV ensures that when a process receives a new object via a propagate operation, any increment.scions corresponding to its new value have already been sent.

If delivery order is no better than FIFO, races can appear between increment.scion and decrement.scion messages. Rule V solves this problem. Note that coherence messages do not need causal delivery, thus limiting the cost.

Rules I through V are sufficient for the safe coexistence of replicated data and a hybrid garbage collector. They are independent of the coherence and tracing algorithms, and impose very few interactions between collection and coherence.

Justification of the Safety Rules. We now explain the preceding rules in more detail, by example.

Comprehensive Tracing Rule. This section justifies the Comprehensive Tracing Rule with an example of what happens if it is not enforced.

Consider Figures 4 and 5 in situation (d) , i.e., after mutators have executed $<x := y>_i$, $<y := 0>_j$, and y has propagated to site i. (Note that scion(Bx, Dz) has not been created yet.) Suppose that trace$_i$(C) runs and the Comprehensive Tracing Rule is not followed. The collector could send a union message to j (owner of y) indicating that stub(Cy, Dz) has disappeared in process i, but not perform scan$_i$(x) and increment.scion(Bx, Dz) not sent. When j applies the Union Rule, it executes $<$send.decrement.scion(Cy, Dz)$>_j$, causing scion(Cy, Dz) to be deleted by k. Then, if trace$_k$(D) runs, object z is reclaimed incorrectly.

---

[8] In other words, sending a message only puts it on an ordered send queue.

The Comprehensive Tracing Rule prevents the above scenario because it forces x_i to be scanned before i sends the union message to j. Then, according to the Increment Before Decrement Rule, $<$send.increment.scion$(Bx, Dz)>_i$ is performed before the union message is sent (and j applies the Union Rule and executes $<$send.decrement.scion$(Cy, Dz)>_j)$. Since we assumed causal delivery (Rule V) scion(Bx, Dz) is created before scion(Cy, Dz) is deleted. Consequently, z is not reclaimed by trace$_k(D)$.

Clean Propagation Rule. This section provides an example of what can happen when the Clean Propagation Rule is not enforced.

Consider Figures 4 and 5 after the mutator has executed $<x := y>_i$ and before $<y := 0>_j$, i.e., in situation (b). Now, suppose that the coherence algorithm propagates the new value of x_i to some process w without first performing scan$_i(x)$. Then, the mutator executes $<x := 0>_i$. At this point, x no longer points to z, and the only scion that protects z is scion(Cy, Dz). Suppose that both replicas of y are assigned in processes i and j to longer point to z either. By the collection algorithm, scion(Cy, Dz) is deleted. Thus, z may be incorrectly reclaimed by trace$_k(D)$ (x_w still points to z).

The Clean Propagation Rule prevents the above scenario as it forces x_i to be scanned. Thus, by Rule II, $<$send.increment.scion$(Bx, Dz)>_i$ is performed immediately, i.e., before x_i is propagated to site w.

Causal Delivery Rule. This section justifies the Causal Delivery Rule by yet another counter-example.

Consider Figure 4 in situation (d), i.e., after mutators have executed $<x := y>_i$, $<y := 0>_j$, and y propagated to site i. (Note that scion(Bx, Dz) has not been created yet.) Then, the collectors on sites i and j perform as follows: i executes $<$send.increment.scion$(Bx, Dz)>_i$, whereas j executes $<$send.decrement.-scion$(Cy, Dz)>_j$. In an asynchronous system, the former could be delivered after the latter, causing z to be incorrectly reclaimed. In fact, there is a hidden causality relation through the shared variable y. In our algorithm, this causal relation is captured by the union message, as apparent in Figure 5. Thus, given the Causal Delivery Rule, there is at all times at least a scion protecting z from incorrect reclamation.

4.3 Discussion: A DGC Algorithm for Replicated Memory

What precedes focused on the interactions between garbage collection and replication (or caching), applied to a replicated (or cached) shared memory. We showed that both the tracing and the distributed counting garbage collector can execute independently of coherence. Garbage collection does not need coherent data, never causes coherence messages nor input/output, and it does not compete with applications' locks or working sets. However, coherence messages must at times be scanned before sending.

Our GC is a hybrid algorithm for a DSM. It combines tracing within a partition, with reference-counting across partition boundaries. Each process may trace its own replicas, independently of other replicas. Counting (adjusting stubs and scions) at some process happens concurrently to other processes, and in the background with respect to the local mutator. In addition, counting is deferred and batched.

We presented five safety rules that guarantee the correctness of the distributed reference-counting algorithm. These safety rules are minimal and generally applicable:

– Union Rule: an object may be reclaimed only if it is unreachable from the union of all replicas (of the pointing objects);
– Increment before Decrement Rule: when an object is scanned, the corresponding increment.scion messages must be sent immediately;
– Comprehensive Tracing Rule: when a union or a decrement.scion message is sent, all replicas (on the sending site) must be have been scanned since they were most recently assigned;
– Clean Propagation Rule: an object must be scanned before being propagated; and
– Causal Delivery Rule: GC messages must be delivered in causal order.

Measurements of our first (non-optimized) implementation [6] show that the cost of tracing is independent of the number of replicas, and that there is a clear performance benefit in delaying the counting.

Causal delivery, imposed by Rule V, is non-scalable in the general case; however, we do not consider this to be a serious problem in real implementations because causality can be ensured by taking advantage of the specific coherence protocols. For example, in our current implementation (supporting entry consistency) causal delivery is ensured by a mixture of piggy-backing and acknowledgments.

The Larchant algorithm is in use by the Esprit Project PerDiS [9], where it supports a large-scale cooperative engineering CAD application. This will enable us to measure and characterize the behaviour of real persistent applications, to fully study the performance of the distributed GC algorithm and to evaluate its completeness in a real-world environment. The PerDiS implementation is freely available at http://www.perdis.esprit.ec.org/.

5   Conclusion

We presented two recent advances in Distributed Garbage Collection in large-scale distributed computing systems. The first one is an algorithm for collecting cycles of garbage in a partitioned message-passing system. It is applicable in a clustered system (e.g., a network of LANs) communicating by RPC, as in Corba, Java RMI or DCOM. This algorithm has been implemented and proved correct. It is used in a prototype extension to ML supporting mobile objects, the JoCAML system [14].

Our second advance is an algorithm to collect garbage in a replicated or cached memory. It is applicable to distributed shared memories, object-oriented databases, and persistent distributed stores. It has been proven safe and live, although by design for scalability, it is not complete. The algorithm provides the basis for the PerDiS platform developed in Esprit project 22.533 and used for cooperative engineering applications.

Acknowledgments

The research for both these algorithms was conducted within the Broadcast, Broadcast-WG, and PerDiS projects. We are grateful to Xavier Blondel for his improvements of Larchant and his research and implementation of DGC for the PerDiS platform. Many thanks to Steve Caughey and Ian Piumarta for their constructive comments.

References

[1] Saleh E. Abdullahi and Graem A. Ringwood. Garbage collecting the internet: a survey of distributed garbage collection. *ACM Computing Surveys*, 30(3):330–373, September 1998. http://www.acm.org/pubs/articles/journals/surveys/1998-30-3/p330-abdullahi/p330-abdullahi.pdf.

[2] Laurent Amsaleg, Olivier Gruber, and Michael Franklin. Efficient incremental garbage collection for workstation-server database systems. In *Proc. 21st Very Large Data Bases (VLDB) Int. Conf.*, Zürich (Switzerland), September 1995.

[3] Henri E. Bal, Raoul Bhoedjang, Rutgwe Hofman, Ceriel Jacobs, Koen Langendoen, Tim Rühl, and M. Frans Kaashoek. Performance evaluation of the Orca shared-object system. *ACM Transactions on Computer Systems*, 16(1):1–40, feb 1998.

[4] P.B. Bishop. Computer systems with a very large address space and garbage collection. Technical Report MIT/LCS/TR-178, Mass. Insitute of Technology, Cambridge MA (USA), 1977.

[5] K. Mani Chandy and Leslie Lamport. Distributed snapshots: determining global states of distributed systems. *ACM Transactions on Computer Systems*, 3(1):63–75, February 1985.

[6] Paulo Ferreira. *Larchant: ramasse-miettes dans une mémoire partagée répartie avec persistance par atteignabilité*. Thèse de doctorat, Université Paris 6, Pierre et Marie Curie, Paris (France), May 1996. http://www-sor.inria.fr/publi/ferreira_thesis96.html.

[7] Paulo Ferreira and Marc Shapiro. Garbage collection and DSM consistency. In *Proc. of the First Symposium on Operating Systems Design and Implementation (OSDI)*, pages 229–241, Monterey CA (USA), November 1994. ACM. http://www-sor.inria.fr/publi/GC-DSM-CONSIS_OSDI94.html.

[8] Paulo Ferreira and Marc Shapiro. Modelling a distributed cached store for garbage collection. In *12th Euro. Conf. on Object-Oriented Prog. (ECOOP)*, Brussels (Belgium), July 1998. http://www-sor.inria.fr/publi/MDCSGC_ecoop98.html.

[9] Paulo Ferreira, Marc Shapiro, Xavier Blondel, Olivier Fambon, João Garcia, Sytse Kloosterman, Nicolas Richer, Marcus Roberts, Fadi Sandakly, George Coulouris, Jean Dollimore, Paulo Guedes, Daniel Hagimont, and Sacha Krakowiak. PerDiS: design, implementation, and use of a PERsistent DIstributed Store. Technical

Report QMW TR 752, CSTB ILC/98-1392, INRIA RR 3525, INESC RT/5/98, QMW, CSTB, INRIA and INESC, October 1998. http://www-sor.inria.fr/publi/PDIUPDS_rr3525.html.

[10] John Hughes. A distributed garbage collection algorithm. In Jean-Pierre Jouannaud, editor, *Functional Languages and Computer Architectures*, number 201 in Lecture Notes in Computer Science, pages 256–272, Nancy (France), September 1985. Springer-Verlag.

[11] Richard Jones and Rafael Lins. *Garbage Collection, Algorithms for Automatic Dynamic Memory Management*. Wiley, Chichester (GB), 1996. ISBN 0-471-94148-4.

[12] Leslie Lamport. Time, clocks, and the ordering of events in a distributed system. *Communications of the ACM*, 21(7):558–565, July 1978.

[13] Fabrice Le Fessant. The camlsspc system. http://www-sor.inria.fr/projects/sspc/, 1997.

[14] Fabrice Le Fessant. The jocaml system. Technical report, INRIA, 1998. http://pauillac.inria.fr/join.

[15] Fabrice Le Fessant, Ian Piumarta, and Marc Shapiro. An implementation for complete asynchronous distributed garbage collection. In *Proceedings of SIGPLAN'98 Conference on Programming Languages Design and Implementation*, ACM SIGPLAN Notices, Montreal, June 1998. ACM Press.

[16] T. Le Sergent and B. Berthomieu. Incremental multi-threaded garbage collection on virtually shared memory architectures. In *Proc. Int. Workshop on Memory Management*, number 637 in Lecture Notes in Computer Science, pages 179–199, Saint-Malo (France), September 1992. Springer-Verlag.

[17] Xavier Leroy. The objective-caml system software. Technical report, INRIA, 1996. http://pauillac.inria.fr/ocaml.

[18] Kai Li and Paul Hudak. Memory coherence in shared virtual memory systems. *ACM Transactions on Computer Systems*, 7(4):321–359, November 1989.

[19] Barbara Liskov, Mark Day, and Liuba Shrira. Distributed object management in Thor. In *Proc. Int. Workshop on Distributed Object Management*, pages 1–15, Edmonton (Canada), August 1992.

[20] U. Maheshwari and B. Liskov. Collecting distributed garbage cycles by back tracing. In *Principles of Distributed Computing*, Santa Barbara CA (USA), aug 1997. ACM.

[21] David Plainfossé and Marc Shapiro. A survey of distributed garbage collection techniques. In *Proc. Int. Workshop on Memory Management*, Kinross Scotland (UK), September 1995. http://www-sor.inria.fr/publi/SDGC_iwmm95.html.

[22] S. P. Rana. A distributed solution to the distributed termination problem. *Information Processing Letters*, 17:43–46, July 1983.

[23] Roger Sessions. *COM and DCOM: Microsoft's Vision for Distributed Objects*. Wiley, December 1998. ISBN 0-471-19381-X.

[24] Marc Shapiro, Peter Dickman, and David Plainfossé. SSP chains: Robust, distributed references supporting acyclic garbage collection. Rapport de Recherche 1799, Institut National de la Recherche en Informatique et Automatique, Rocquencourt (France), November 1992. http://www-sor.inria.fr/publi/SSPC_rr1799.html.

[25] Marc Shapiro and Paulo Ferreira. Larchant-RDOSS: a distributed shared persistent memory and its garbage collector. In J.-M. Hélary and M. Raynal, editors, *Workshop on Distributed Algorithms (WDAG)*, number 972 in Springer-Verlag LNCS, pages 198–214, Le Mont Saint-Michel (France), September 1995. http://www-sor.inria.fr/publi/LRDSPMGC_wdag95.html.

[26] R. van Renesse, A. S. Tanenbaum, and A. Wilschut. The design of a high-performance file server. In *Proceedings of the 9th Int. Conf. on Distributed Computing Systems*, pages 22–27, Newport Beach CA (USA), June 1989. IEEE.

[27] Paul R. Wilson. Uniprocessor garbage collection techniques. In *Proc. Int. Workshop on Memory Management*, number 637 in Lecture Notes in Computer Science, Saint-Malo (France), September 1992. Springer-Verlag. ftp://ftp.cs.utexas.edu/pub/garbage/bigsurv.ps.

[28] Ann Wollrath, Roger Riggs, and Jim Waldo. A distributed object model for the java system. In *Conf. on Object-Oriented Technologies*, Toronto Ontario (Canada), 1996. Usenix.

[29] V. Yong, J. Naughton, and J. Yu. Storage reclamation and reorganization in client-server persistent object stores. In *Proc. Data Engineering Int. Conf.*, pages 120–133, Houston TX (USA), February 1994.

Topology-Aware Algorithms for Large-Scale Communication

Luís Rodrigues and Paulo Veríssimo

Faculdade de Ciências, Universidade de Lisboa, Lisboa, PORTUGAL,
{ler,pjv}@di.fc.ul.pt
http://www.navigators.di.fc.ul.pt/

Abstract. When designing communication protocols there is always a
tradeoff between generality and performance. This chapter reports one
approach to achieve right balance between these two aspects, using a
network model that can be applied to the majority of existing large-scale
networks based on reliable high-speed local-area networks interconnected
by slower long-haul connections. The approach consists in making visible
relevant *topological* aspects of the uderlying network infrastructure to
the protocol designer, and is illustrated by several algorithms that use
topology information to achieve improved performance.

1 Introduction

When designing communication protocols there is always a tradeoff between
generality and performance. Generic approaches make few assumptions about
the underlying network. The resulting protocols are easy to port to different
network structures but often exhibit poor performance. On the other hand, tailored solutions exploit particular features of a given class of networks in order
to achieve better performance. However, tailoring has its disadvantages: if the
features exploited are peculiar only to one or two networks, it may be difficult,
if not impossible, to port the resulting protocols to other networks that do not
own these characteristics. The successful design must capture the right balance
between generality and performance.

This chapter reports one approach to achieve this balance, using a network
model that can be applied to the majority of existing large-scale networks based
on reliable high-speed local-area networks interconnected by slower long-haul
connections. This model, that we simply call "WAN-of-LANs", was central to
the design of the NAVTECH architecture. We are going to present a number of
innovative ways to take advantage of it, by making visible relevant *topological*
aspects to the protocol designer.

The chapter is organized as follows. Section 2 presents the NAVTECH framework and network model on which our protocols are based. The next three sections describe protocols exploiting that communication infrastructure. The first
protocol, presented in Section 3, is a clock synchronization protocol that is based
on an hierarchical composition of a protocol tailored to broadcast LANs with a

S. Krakowiak, S.K. Shrivastava (Eds.): Distributed Systems, LNCS 1752, pp. 127–156, 2000.

protocol that makes use of the GPS architecture. The second protocol, presented in Section 4, is a causal order protocol that makes use of topology information to reduce the size of information that needs to be stored and exchanged to provide causal order delivery. The third protocol, presented in Section 5, is a total order protocol that dynamically adjusts the ordering algorithm as a function of the participant location in the network topology. Related work is discussed in Section 6 and Section 7 concludes the chapter.

2   The NavTech Framework

This section describes the main characteristics of an architectural framework called NavTech. The framework specifies architectural constructs and mechanisms to assist the design and execution of dependable distributed applications in large-scale settings. Some of these constructs were the enabling factors of topological-awareness as we describe it in this chapter. In other words, the topology-aware protocols that we will encounter in the following sections were designed having in mind the availability of an infrastructure with the characteristics described here. That is, NavTech is essentially a macroscopic framework made of components such as the Internet, private local area networks, vanilla operating systems, satellite constellations, kept together by the glue of a run-time environment and a few protocols. The principles of NavTech are applicable to known infra-structural networking and computing technologies, and in that sense it is an open architecture, applicable to systems built from COTS components.

2.1   The Scale Problem

NavTech was designed for large-scale applications. Topology issues become more important in the measure that distributed systems grow in span, complexity and number of sites. In order to take advantage from topology, we must identify the implications of scale on the structure of distributed systems, under their several facets: the computation participants; the communication system; the interaction styles.

Computation Participants Scale affects computations in several ways. The most obvious aspect of scale concerns the number of participants in the computation. The number of entities simultaneously involved in a computation varies, according to the type of interaction concerned, but that number is often significantly smaller than the number of sites in the network. For the sake of simplifying our forthcoming analysis, we propose to consider a coarse-grain scale metric, of three "levels": very-large-scale— order of millions and up; large-scale— order of thousands up to the million; small-scale— order of hundreds down.

The communication system characteristics have a fundamental impact on the scale of computations, since they make it extremely difficult, and sometimes even impossible, to reproduce in large-scale the operating conditions that are otherwise found in small-scale systems. In consequence, there is a need for structuring applications in ways that allow reasonably performant operation. Hierarchical organization and clustering according to the topology of the infrastructure, are paradigms addressing this particular issue in NAVTECH.

Communication System A large-scale network such as the Internet forms what we might call the *global network*, for the purpose of large-scale computing. A number of sites in the order of 10^7, and growing, puts it in the very-large-scale level, with a number of *structural* characteristics dictated by its scale and technology: sparse connectivity; limited diffusion capabilities; weak reliability and timeliness; globe-wide distances; public-domain or standard protocols.

In face of these characteristics, we can extract a set of functional communication properties, the most important of which are listed below, deriving both from sheer scale and from technology shortcomings: large communication delay variance; asynchronism; partitioning (e.g. set M of sites reach each other and set N of sites reach each other, neither reaches the other set); non-transitivity (e.g. A reaches B, B reaches C, but A cannot reach C); non-symmetry (e.g. A reaches B, but B cannot reach A).

On the other hand, inside what we might call *local networks*, the infrastructure takes significantly different characteristics that should not be ignored: availability of LAN or MAN technology (including the foreseen role of ATM); dense connectivity (normally broadcast-level); good reliability and timeliness; private operation, enterprise-oriented. Such significant differences should not be ignored by a large-scale architecture. A moderate number of sites puts local networks in the small- to large-scale level.

This analysis identifies a fundamental topological paradigm: many networks exhibit physical organization as a 2-tier WAN-of-LANs.

2.2 Networking Model

The networking model of NAVTECH is based on a few architectural paradigms, which address the scale issues just discussed and put in place a few hooks for topology-awareness: 2-tier networking; clustering; site-participant multiplexing; groups as a scalable construct.

2-Tier WAN-of-LANs The large-scale computing infrastructures will retain a clear duality, which is materialized by several aspects, from administration to technology, in what appears to be a 2-tier infrastructure. Our model of WAN-of-LANs networks, consists of pools of sites with high connectivity links, such as LANS or MANs, or ATM fabrics, interconnected in the upper tier by a point-to-point global network. More concretely, we mean that: the global network is public and runs standard, de jure or de facto, protocols; each local network is run by a single, private, entity [1], and can thus run specific protocols alongside with or in complement to standard ones.

---

[1] E.g.: set of LANs of a university campus, MAN of a large industrial complex, LAN of a regional company department.

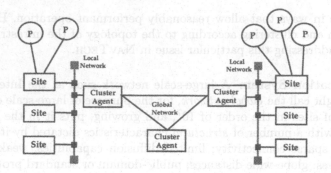

Fig. 1. 2-tier WAN-of-LANs and clustering as followed in NAVTECH

Clustering A fundamental feature of the NAVTECH platform is to take into account the clustering naturally provided by the underlying network. In fact, clustering seems one of the most promising techniques to cope with large-scale, providing the means to implement effective divide-and-conquer strategies. In todays' networks, we identify at least two clustering entities: the *Facility* as a cluster of sites and the *Site* as a cluster of participants.

The first clustering level is obviously compatible with the 2-tier architecture identified in the previous section, and is illustrated in figure 1. Clustering sites that coexist in a same local network can simplify internetwork addressing, communication and administration of these sites. These sites are hidden behind a single entry-point, a *cluster-agent*, a logical gateway that represents the local network members, for the global network. Organization-dependent clustering allows to run specific protocols behind the cluster-agents, without that colliding with the need to use standard protocols in wide-area networking. Global network communication is then performed essentially among cluster-agents.

The second level of clustering consists in taking advantage of a multiplying factor between the number of sites and the (sometimes large) number of participants that are active in communication.

This distinction between *sites* and *participants* is in favor of – and can only be achieved by – a *communication subsystem* approach for structuring the machine's networking. A site-level *protocol server* should take care of all send and receive activities on behalf of the participants residing locally to it.

Sites and Participants The NAVTECH platform supports interactions among entities in different sites (e.g. processes, tasks, etc.). For NAVTECH, these entities, that can be senders or recipients of information, or both, are *participants*. Participants interact via *sites*, which handle all communication aspects on behalf of them, as represented in figure 2. A system built to the site-participant duality provides a framework for defining domains of different synchrony and reliability. For example, intra-site communication is easily made synchronous and reliable, reducing the asynchrony and unreliability problem to inter-site communication.

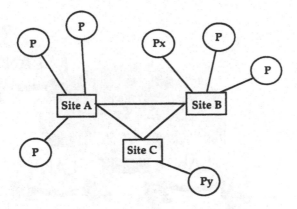

Fig. 2. Site-participant duality

In consequence, while site failure detection is unreliable [4], participant failures can be reliably detected.

Hierarchical Network Model Following the structuring principles outlined above, we can derive a network model that has the following components, as illustrated in Figure 3. Protocol participants are simply designated processes and have disjoint memory spaces. The system is composed of a collection of processes $P = \{p_1, \ldots, p_n\}$. We assume that a unique identifier is associated with each process $p \in P$ (for convenience, we will use the same notation to refer to the process and its identification). We also assume that an order relation $\prec$ can be defined between process identifiers.

Processes are executed in *sites* or *nodes* (we use both terms interchangeably in the discussion). When two processes reside on the same node, messages on to and from these processes to the rest of the network can be filtered by a process on behalf of the operating system (usually, by the kernel itself). The mapping between processes and nodes can be also used for topology-aware failure detection using simple decision rules. For instance, when a node crashes, all processes running on that node are forced to crash.

Nodes are interconnected by two broad classes of *networks*: local networks (for example, using LAN or ATM technologies) and long-haul links. Local-area networks are assumed to have high-bandwidth, low latency and high reliability. Local networks are also less prone to network partitioning than long-haul links. Long-haul links from the the interconnecting mesh that supports communication among local-area clusters. They have lower bandwidth, exhibit higher latency and are prone to partitioning. Some nodes, the cluster-agents, assume the role of gateways, forwarding messages from and to the local networks to the long-haul links. Cluster-agents can be made visible when convenient, as for instance in the causal order protocol.

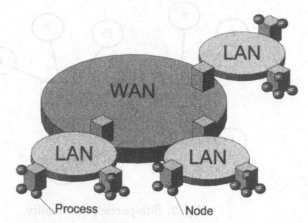

Fig. 3. Communication architecture.

2.3   The Architecture of NavTech

The overall architecture of NavTech is represented in figure 4. The NavTech platform lies on an abstraction of a multipoint network, the *Abstract Network, AN*, created over the physical infrastructure. The *Site Failure Suspector, FS*, is in charge of assessing the connectivity and liveness of sites, and depends on the Abstract Network, by listening to traffic going into each site, and by exchanging information with other FS. The *Site Membership, SM*, depends on information given by the FS module. Based on the latter it creates and modifies the membership of site-groups. The *Communication Support Services, CS*, implement group communication and clock synchronization. All the four modules described are topology sensitive. Protocols may run differently depending on whether: they run in a local network; they run in the global network; this node is a cluster agent. Together, they also form the 'site' part of a node.

The *Participant Membership* module *PM* creates and modifies the membership of participant groups, and validates activity conditions, such as *majority* in a primary partition. The *Participant Failure Detector* module, *FD*, is a module with strictly local operation. Based on probes implemented using available O.S. support, it assesses liveness of participants. The *Activity Support Services* module *AS* implements protocols and algorithms that assist participant activity, such as replication management, mutual exclusion, cooperation awareness, etc. These three modules form the 'participant' part of the node, materializing the site-participant hierarchy. There can be several of these modules mapped onto the site part, as suggested by the grey arrows. NavTech uses groups as its central paradigm. However, participant groups are concerned with distributed applications, and delegate 'communication' on the site group that represents them, which runs the communication protocols. Normally, a site group SG_m is composed of the nodes that host members of participant group G_m. Additionally, there can be several groups of participants mapped onto one site group.

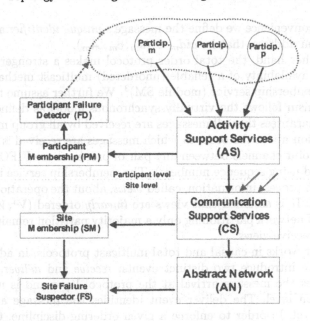

Fig. 4. NAVTECH architecture: 'depends-on' relation

Related Transport Protocols In order to preserve the maximum generality possible, the hierarchical nature of our network model is only made visible when necessary, for example when important performance gains can be achieved. Thus, most of the design follows quite generic assumptions about the companion communication protocols required to support our topology-aware services. Since not all of the protocols we are going to describe rely on the same underlying communication services, we clarify this issue here.

The causal protocol simply assumes that the underlying message passing subsystem is reliable, in the sense that messages sent by a correct process are always received by all correct addressed participants. This assumption is consistent with recent implementations of other causal multicast protocols, which are based on a reliable transport layer (for instance, HORUS [29]). For the causal protocol we do not need to make any assumptions about the order in which messages are received. The identification of the sender $s_m \in \mathcal{P}$ and the set of destination processes $\mathcal{A}_m \subseteq \mathcal{P}$ are always associated with each message m. We also do not impose any restriction on the destination addresses: a message can always be sent to any set of processes in $\mathcal{P}$. Additionally, we assume that each sender assigns a locally generated integer value c_m, to each message, such that if m is sent before n then $c_m < c_n$ (this can be trivially obtained by using a local counter [2] c_p at each process p). Although the pair (s_m, c_m) uniquely identifies a

---

[2] Since this counter is stored in a bit array with limited capacity, we cannot have indefinitely growing counters. However, techniques exist to overcome this problem [15].

message, for convenience we define the message's *unique identifier* also including the destination address, that is, $uid_m \equiv (s_m, c_m, \mathcal{A}_m)$.

On the other hand, the total order protocol makes a stronger assumption, requiring the availability of a reliable (unordered) multicast mechanism and its associated membership service (module SM)[3]. We further assume that the multicast mechanism follows the virtually-synchronous model as defined in [2] and, informally, guarantees that all messages are received by all group members. The only assumption about the order in which messages are received is that all logical point-to-point channels between any pair of processes are FIFO (this can be easily enforced using sequence numbers). The membership service is responsible for giving each process information, called *views*, about the operational processes in the system. It is assumed that views are *linearly* ordered $(V^i, V^{i+1}, ...)$, i.e., that in case of network partitioning only a majority partition remains active and continues to receive views.

As in most works in causal and total multicast protocols, in addition to the *send* event, we introduce two distinct events: *receive* and *deliver*. The receive event identifies the message arrival at the protocol layer and is not visible at the application level. The deliver event identifies the message arrival at the application level. In order to enforce a given ordering discipline, the protocols may have to delay the delivery of received messages.

Simulation Model In order to measure the performance of some protocols we resorted to simulation. For that purpose, MIT LCS Advanced Network Architecture group's network simulator (NETSIM [10]) was used. The network delay $D_{(s,r)}$ between the sender s and the recipient r is represented by a probability distribution function, with a mean value of $\mu_{(s,r)}$, and a variance of $\sigma^2_{(s,r)}$. According to our assumptions about the underlying infrastructure, the distribution function depends on the type of network being used to interconnect each sender-recipient pair. Different network latencies were assigned to local-area network and long-haul links (actual values will be presented when describing the protocols). A node receives its own messages with negligible delay.

3   Topology-Aware Clock-Synchronization

The first example of an algorithm exploiting the WAN-of-LANs network model is a clock synchronization algorithm. Our global time service for large-scale (worldwide) systems based on a topology-aware approach is called CESIUMSPRAY and its principles were already introduced in a previous Chapter. In this section we highlight the topology-aware features of the algorithm.

3.1   Time Service Architecture

The topology-aware clock synchronization exploits the WAN-of-LANs network model in the following way:

---

[3] A number of recent systems [3, 19, 29] also implement total order on top of reliable multicast services.

- At the LAN level, a protocol tailored to local area networks is used. The protocol fully exploits the intrinsic attributes of these networks: error rate is low, transmission delay is bounded but with high variance, median transmission delay is close to the minimum, and message reception is *tight* in absence of errors, meaning that the low-level message reception signal occurs at approximately the same time in all nodes that receive it. This feature can be made fully deterministic when operating from real-time kernels. It is a crucial feature for the mechanism underlying the synchronization algorithm, as will be shown ahead.
- At the WAN level, the GPSs VavStar satellite system is used as the "global network" link between local networks.

The integrated solution combines the LAN-level algorithm with the WAN-level service in a hierarchical manner. CESIUMSPRAY can be implemented on virtually any large-scale distributed computing infrastructure as we see them today— such as the wide-area point-to-point Internet. Given its hierarchical nature based on GPS NavStar, it has virtually unlimited scalability. It is particularly well-suited for large-scale real-time systems.

The architecture of CESIUMSPRAY is shown in Figure 5. The clock synchronization scheme is a hybrid of external and internal synchronization. The top-level of the hierarchy is the source of absolute time, the NavStar GPS, which performs external synchronization by "spraying" its time over the set of GPS-nodes. The second level of the hierarchy is formed by every local network of the system, with the condition that each be provided with at least one GPS-node. The external time resident in the GPS-node is further "sprayed" inside the local network through an internal synchronization algorithm.

3.2 Advantages of Topology-Awareness for Clock Synchronization

Current Internet-based synchronization schemes, such as NTP[17], effective as they may be today, cannot reach the effectiveness of CESIUMSPRAY, because they do not relate the synchronization architecture to the network architecture. For example, the location of external time masters in NTP is not related to the existence of local networks with broadcast properties, such as in CESIUMSPRAY: reading a master clock may mean crossing several Internet gateways; neighbor clocks in the same LAN do not take advantage of that fact.

The topology-aware approach presented here does not suffer these drawbacks. On the other hand, the performance of CESIUMSPRAY synchronization in its current form depends on the assumed real-time capability of the kernels to bound the interrupt delay variance.

4   Topology-Aware Causal Communication

The second example of a topology-aware algorithm, is a causal communication layer that delivers messages in causal order. This layer enforces a *logical precedence* [2]:

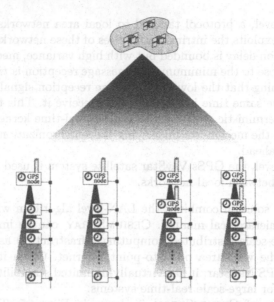

Fig. 5. The architecture of CESIUMSPRAY

Logical precedence: *In a distributed system, in which information is exchanged only by transmitting messages, a message m is said to precede or to be potentially causally related to a message n, represented as m → n, only if: (i) m and n were sent by the same process and n was sent after m or; (ii) m has been delivered to the emitter of n before n was sent or; (iii) there exists x such that m → x and x → n.*

Experience has shown [2, 19, 29] that the design of distributed applications can be simplified if messages are received in order of logical precedence. Since extra complexity would be added to such applications, should the communication subsystem not provide causal delivery, several algorithms have been proposed to implement this ordering discipline [2, 19, 13, 20, 3]. Nevertheless, despite its advantages, the use of causal communication has been somehow limited by the overhead incurred by existing implementations. A major cost of protocols that preserve logical precedence is the size of "history" information that needs to be stored and exchanged to maintain causality, specially in large-scale systems where group addressing is used.

We now show how a topology-aware approach can benefit from the WAN-of-LANs model, allowing to extend previous results on causal history compression using knowledge on the topology of the communication structure. Our compression technique uses the concept of a *causal separator*, a set of nodes of the communication graph that can be used to filter causal information [23]. An implementation of this optimization is presented. Then we show the applicability of this approach to real-life large-scale networks with a hierarchical nature: we present a methodology to model the communication system as a graph, where

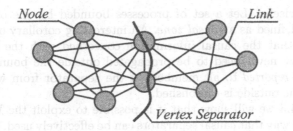

Fig. 6. Vertex separators

causal separators that match the underlying physical and administrative organization are clearly identified.

4.1   Causal Separators

It has been shown that when communication graphs have a process that acts as a gateway, it is possible to decrease the amount of information required to determine temporal relationships [16]. Optimizations based on the communication patterns of processes have also been presented in [28]. Our work extends these results to arbitrary communication structures, making the following contributions:

- we show that, even in graphs that contain cycles, it is possible to reduce the size of the information exchanged by defining *causal separators*, a set of nodes of the communication graph that can be used to filter causal information.
- we present a methodology to model the communication system such that one can make practical use of the previous result.

These two aspects will be dealt with considerable detail in the next two sections. We first provide a global overview of our approach.

We assume that each process is able to communicate directly only with a given subset of system processes $\mathcal{L}_p \subseteq \mathcal{P}$. Two processes not directly linked can communicate indirectly through intermediate hops (usually, automatically selected by a routing algorithm). The complete communication topology can thus be represented by a graph $G(\mathcal{P}, E)$, where processes are the vertices and the communication links between them the edges: there is an edge incident to $\{p, q\}$ if p can send messages to q. We assume that the graph is connected. A set of processes, S, is called a (F_S, B_S) vertex separator, where the sets F_S and B_S are called, respectively, *forward* and *backward* sets, iff $F_S \cap B_S = \emptyset \wedge F_S \cup B_S \cup S = \mathcal{P}$ and $\forall f \in F_S, \forall b \in B_S$ every path connecting f and b passes through at least one vertex of S. In the context of causal communication, we called such vertex separators *causal separators* (see Figure. 6).

In the next sections we will show that a causal separator can work as a barrier that filters all information concerned with messages exclusively addressed to the backward set and "reported" to all members of the separator ("reported" will be defined precisely). Let a set of processes bounded by one or more causal separators be defined as a *causal zone*. An interesting corollary of the previous observation is that the causal information concerned with the elements of a causal zone may never need to be propagated outside the boundaries of that causal zone, if *reported* to all members of the separator from which a causal relation with the outside is established.

In Section 4.3 we will show that it is possible to exploit the WAN-of-LANs model in such a way that causal separators can be effectively used. The technique exploits the physical structure of existing networks, in particular its hierarchical nature, to create a communication graph where causal separators match the underlying physical and administrative organization.

4.2 Causal Order Algorithm

In this section we present an implementation of causal histories that allows to reduce the causal information exchanged using information about causal separators. The interested reader will notice that there are no deep fundamental differences between our representation of causal histories and alternative approaches described in the literature [2, 19]. However, it provides the ground for the implementation of optimizations based on causal separators, the main contribution of our work. Our representation of the causal history, that we called *extended causal history*, stores causal information in three different entities:

- a *causal history*, $\mathcal{H}_p$, a list with the messages that precede the next message to be sent by p;
- the *delivery history*, $\mathcal{D}_p$, a list with the messages that have already been delivered at p and;
- a *carbon-copy* history, $\mathcal{C}_p$, that keeps track of to where causal information has been "reported" (the carbon-copy history is used for compression of causal information, and its use will be detailed later).

The delivery history maintains a record of all messages that were delivered to a given process. The causal history maintains a record of all messages that precede the next message to be sent by a given process. Although the causal history contains the delivery history, different compression rules will be later applied to each, thus we decided to explicitly maintain this information in two different entities (explicit separation between causal and delivery histories is also used in other approaches, for instance [20]). These histories are used in the following way:

Every time a message m is sent by process p, it is timestamped with its sender's causal history, $\mathcal{H}_p$. All messages in $\mathcal{H}_p$ are then said to be "*reported*" to all recipients of m. This information is kept in carbon-copy history, $\mathcal{C}_p$. When a message is received by process q, the recipient compares the message timestamp with its own delivery history and checks whether or not all preceding messages have been already delivered locally. It then delivers or delays the received message accordingly. When a message is delivered, the recipient delivery and causal histories are updated accordingly.

More precisely, causal delivery can be enforced using the delivery and causal histories if the following rules are applied (for clarity, we will defer the use of the carbon-copy history until rule 6 is introduced):

R1 (Initial state): When p starts execution, $\mathcal{H}_p$, $\mathcal{D}_p$, and $\mathcal{C}_p$ are empty. Also, $c_p = 0$. $\square$

R2 (Timestamping): Before being sent by process p, a new *uid* is assigned to message m by incrementing the local counter c_p. Next, m is timestamped with p's causal history, that is, $\mathcal{H}_m = \mathcal{H}_p$. $\square$

R3 (Causal delivery): On receipt of message m sent by process p and times-tamped with a causal history $\mathcal{H}_m$, process $q \in \mathcal{A}_m$ delays the delivery of m until all messages in $\mathcal{H}_m$ that were addressed to q have been delivered at q [4]. More precisely, q delays the delivery of m until the following condition is true: $\forall (i \in \mathcal{H}_m : q \in \mathcal{A}_i)$ i *is-in* $\mathcal{D}_q$; where the *is-in* relation is here defined as: m *is-in* $\mathcal{D} \iff m \in \mathcal{D}$. $\square$

R4 (Record maintenance): When process p sends m it atomically adds m to $\mathcal{H}_p$ and to $\mathcal{D}_q$. When a message, m, is delivered at $q \neq s_m$, m's timestamp, $\mathcal{H}_m$, is added to $\mathcal{H}_q$. Additionally, m is added to $\mathcal{H}_q$ and $\mathcal{D}_q$. $\square$

Rules 1-4 above are enough to enforce causal delivery of messages (see [23] for a proof). However, this solution suffers from a serious drawback as, unless some measures are taken to garbage-collect redundant elements, the causal histories continue to grow indefinitely. In the next paragraphs we present an extra set of rules that allow the garbage-collection of the extended causal history.

We start by compressing the delivery history. The compression rule exploits the fact that messages from the same sender must always be delivered in the order they were sent. From the causal delivery rule, if a message m from process p is delivered to q, then all previous messages from p, addressed to q, were already delivered at q. As a result of this rule, delivery histories do not need to keep more than one message from each sender. More precisely,

R5 (FIFO Delivery): At most one unique message identifier needs to be stored from each sender in the delivery history. When a message m from process p is added to $\mathcal{D}_q$, m replaces the previous message from p delivered at q.

Naturally, since some elements are deleted from the delivery history as new members are added, the definition of "is in $\mathcal{D}$" must be slightly changed. We now say that a message m *is-in* $\mathcal{D}$ if and only if there exists a message in $\mathcal{D}$, from the same sender, with a higher or equal identifier. More precisely, m *is-in* $\mathcal{D} \iff \exists_{n \in \mathcal{D}} : c_m \leq c_n$. $\square$

We now garbage-collect the causal history. The idea is to remove from this history all the elements not strictly required to preserve causal delivery. In doing so, we discard information about the past. The method is an extension of the "last

---

[4] A message can always be delivered without delays to its sender.

send" and "last update" vectors proposed by Singhal and Kshemkalyani [27], also suggested in [28] to optimize the use of vector clocks on overlapping groups. We simply extend this method to arbitrary addressing schemes. The optimization can be informally presented as follows: before being sent, message m is timestamped with its sender's causal history $\mathcal{H}_p$. It will then be delivered to $\mathcal{A}_m$, after all messages in $\mathcal{H}_m$. Any message $n : \mathcal{A}_n \subseteq \mathcal{A}_m$ that carries m in its timestamp, does not need to carry $\mathcal{H}_m$ since it will be delivered after m, thus after all messages in $\mathcal{H}_m$. However, this requires some bookkeeping of whom the messages were reported to. This information can be kept in an additional history, called the *carbon-copy* history, $\mathcal{C}$. The carbon-copy history contains a field for each message in the causal history, storing the list of processes to which the associated message was already "reported" within the timestamp of another message. The carbon-copy history should be updated using the following rule:

R6 (Carbon-copy): Each process, p, keeps a carbon-copy history, $\mathcal{C}_p$, that contains an element $\mathcal{C}_p(m)$ for each message m in $\mathcal{H}_p$. These elements are used according to the following rules:

Extended timestamping (optional): When a message m is timestamped, in addition to $\mathcal{H}_p$, it may also by timestamped with $\mathcal{C}_p$. We refer to the carbon-copy field of m's timestamp as $\mathcal{C}_m$.

Send update: After sending a message m, and before inserting m in $\mathcal{H}_p$, update all fields of $\mathcal{C}_p$ as follows: $\forall (i \in \mathcal{H}_p)$ let $\mathcal{C}_p(i) = \mathcal{C}_p(i) \cup \mathcal{A}_m \cup \{s_m\}$. Then insert m in $\mathcal{H}_p$ and initialize $\mathcal{C}_p(m) = \emptyset$. These updates should be performed in a single atomic operation.

Deliver update: After delivering a message m, processor $q \neq s_m$ updates the carbon-copy fields of previous messages from the same sender as follows:

$$\forall (n \in \mathcal{H}_q : s_n = s_m \wedge c_n < c_m) \text{ let } \mathcal{C}_q(n) = \mathcal{C}_q(n) \cup \mathcal{A}_m$$

Then, it adds all elements n of $\mathcal{H}_m$ to $\mathcal{H}_q$. The carbon-copy fields of these messages are initialized as follows (if extended timestamping is not used, use $\mathcal{C}_m(n) = \emptyset$):

$$\mathcal{C}_q(n) = \mathcal{C}_m(n) \cup \mathcal{A}_m \cup \{s_m\} \cup \bigcup_{i \in \mathcal{H}_q : s_i = s_n \wedge c_i > c_n} \mathcal{A}_i$$

If $n \in \mathcal{H}_m$ is already in $\mathcal{H}_q$ it just updates the existing carbon-copy field, merging $\mathcal{C}_q(n)$ with the result of the previous expression. Finally, q inserts m in $\mathcal{H}_q$ and initialize $\mathcal{C}_q(m) = \{s_m, q\}$. These updates should be performed in a single atomic operation. $\square$

The carbon-copy history is used to compress the causal histories in the following way: (1) messages do not have to be included in a timestamp, if they have already been included in a timestamp of another message sent to the same destination; and (2) when the carbon-copy field of a message completely includes the message's address, that message can be safely removed from the causal history as it has already been reported to all relevant processes. More precisely,

R7 (Timestamp Redundancy): When timestamping a message m, processor p only includes in $\mathcal{H}_m$ the elements of its causal history $i \in \mathcal{H}_p$ not reported to $\mathcal{A}_m$, according to p's knowledge, i.e.: $\mathcal{H}_m = \bigcup i \in \mathcal{H}_p : \mathcal{A}_m \not\subseteq \mathcal{C}_p(i)$.

R8 (History Redundancy): In a causal history, $\mathcal{H}_p$, if there exists a message, m, such that $\mathcal{A}_m \subseteq \mathcal{C}_p(m)$, m can be removed from $\mathcal{H}_p$ and $\mathcal{C}_p$.

4.3 Using the Communication Topology

Causal separators can be exploited to reduce the size of message timestamps as follows. When a member of the causal separator timestamps a message addressed to processes exclusively located in the forward set, it can omit in the timestamp all elements of its causal history that were addressed exclusively to members of the backward set and that were already reported to the other members of the causal separator. More precisely,

R9 (Topological timestamp): Processor p is sending a message m. All messages $n \in \mathcal{H}_p$ for which exists a (F_S, B_S) causal separator[5], S, such that: $p \in S \wedge \mathcal{A}_m \subseteq F_S \wedge \mathcal{A}_n \subseteq B_S \wedge S \subseteq \mathcal{C}_p(n)$, do not need to be inserted in $\mathcal{H}_m$

The compression achieved with the topological timestamping rule can be further improved at the cost of reporting causal information to all the members of the causal separator. In fact, remember that the carbon-copy fields can always be forced to a given desired value just by sending a message to the relevant processes. For proofs of correctness of our rules see [23].

There are a number of challenges associated with the use of our topological timestamping scheme. Firstly, any change to the topology can alter the membership of the causal separators: solutions for this problem are discussed in [23]. Secondly, arbitrary network can have a large number of causal separators: topological timestamping can be applied to all separators or just to a subset of them. Thirdly, causal separators need to be computed before the topological timestamping rule can be applied. Several algorithms to identify vertex separators in a graph are available (for instance, see [8]), but these can be too expensive to be executed frequently during normal system operation.

Thus, our method is better suited for applications where the topology is relatively static or can be computed at compile or configuration time. In this case causal separators may be computed in advance, and the corresponding forward and backward sets prepared and loaded in all causal separator members to allow a fast execution of the topological timestamping rule. A particular case of a relatively static topology, is the one defined by the network infrastructure that connects individual nodes of a distributed system. In particular, the WAN-of-LANs model offers an excellent ground to define causal separators in a meaningful way. We propose a solution for the provision of causal communication in large-scale systems based on the following methodology, that consists in mapping protocol entities onto architectural components:

---

[5] Where F_S and B_S are respectively the forward and backward sets of the separator(see chapter 4.1)

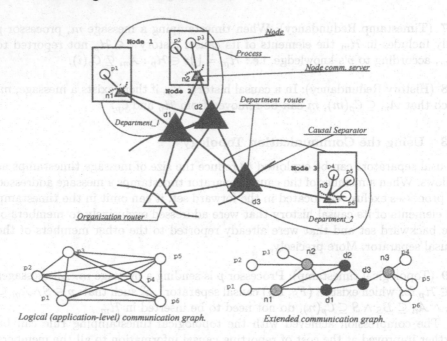

Fig. 7. The communication structure and the communication graph

- the communication entity that connects a node to the network assumes the role of a router process in the communication structure (the site representative in NAVTECH). This process is a causal separator that connects the machine to the network.
- routing of messages between nodes is also implemented by special processes, usually placed in dedicated router nodes (the NAVTECH cluster agent), able to execute topological timestamping as they forward the messages.

Using this methodology, one can build an *extended communication graph* that takes into consideration the organization of the underlying infrastructure. In this graph, new nodes are added, corresponding to communication server and router processes (see an example in Figure 7). Promoting the communication entities to nodes of the (extended) communication graph has several advantages:

- It provides a useful way of mapping the abstract communication graph onto the existing physical and administrative communication structure. This gives the means for the practical and useful identification of causal separators (for instance, node's communication server, department router, etc.).
- The physical communication structure (i.e., the servers and routers, not the application processes) is usually relatively static. This feature provides the basis for an efficient exploitation of topological timestamping and makes the costs associated with dynamic changes of the structure almost negligible.

– It provides a practical way of exploiting communication locality. Using topological timestamping on the structure obtained by adding communication and router processes, it is possible to prevent local information from being propagated on the network. Messages exchanged between processes of the same node are filtered out by the node router, messages exchanged between processes in the same department by the department router, and so on.

In conclusion, we believe that the physical and administrative organization of the physical communication structure can be exploited to support the efficient implementation of topological timestamping. In order to achieve this goal, some communication elements must be promoted to nodes of the communication graph.

4.4 Performance of Causal Separators

In order to evaluate the performance of our approach we resorted to simulation. We measured the average size of timestamps obtained using our extended causal histories and compared these values with the size required by a non-optimized clock-matrix approach [20].

From the several simulation results presented in [23], we have selected a configuration of three LANs connected in such a way that circles exist both at the logical and physical level, as illustrated in Figure 8. If the communication infrastructure is constructed in such a way that, in each broadcast network, both gateways receive all out-going traffic (since these are connected to a broadcast network this can be achieved with negligible cost), the gateways can act as causal separators and filter causal associated with local communication.

The impact of applying topological timestamping is this case is illustrated in figure 8. The figure shows the distribution of message timestamp size in group $G1$ with and without separators. The figure shows also the distribution of the host history size on process $p1$ with and without separators. It can be seen that, without topological timestamp, the causal history of process $p1$ is much larger.

4.5 Advantages of Topology-Awareness for Causal Ordering

Early implementations of logical precedence (also described as the "happened before" relation) were based on logical clocks [14], a technique that introduces a systematic delay in message delivery and that orders more messages than those potentially causally related [26]. To avoid the disadvantages of logical clocks, a new set of algorithms has been proposed, where the information required to precisely define causal relations is piggybacked on the messages exchanged. These approaches are based on causal histories or vector clocks [2, 19, 24, 13, 3]. Recent system have extended these approaches to systems that allow messages to be addressed exclusively to a subset of the existing processes [2, 13, 24, 20]. These early approaches do not take the topology into account and the amount of information that needs to be maintained and exchanged grows quadratically with the number of processes [6].

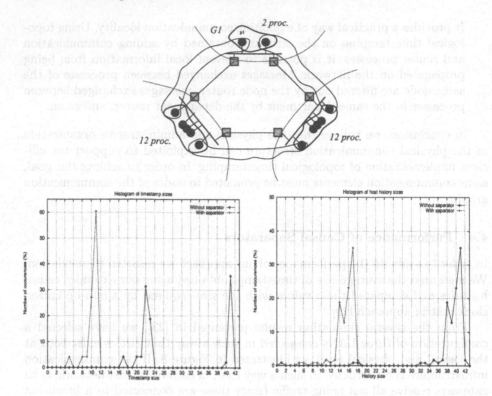

Fig. 8. Three interconnected broadcast networks and impact on group $G1$.

Our technique combines optimizations previously proposed by others [27, 28] with the innovative causal separator concept that allows to fully exploit the WAN-of-LANs model. We exploit the physical structure of existing networks, in particular its hierarchical nature, to create a communication graph where causal separators match the underlying physical and administrative organization. This approach can be applied to existing large-scale systems, fitting the WAN-of-LANs model, providing the means for using topological timestamping with little practical overhead.

5 Topology-Aware Total Order

The third example of a topology-aware protocol is a total order protocol. Totally ordered multicast protocols have proved to be extremely useful in supporting many fault-tolerant distributed applications. For instance, total delivery order is a requirement for the implementation of replicated state-machines [25], which is a general paradigm for implementing fault-tolerant distributed applications.

Although several protocols have been described in the literature [1, 2, 3, 5, 7, 12, 13, 18], few were specifically targeted to operate in (geographically) large-scale systems. In a large scale network processes' traffic patterns are usually heterogeneous. The same applies to the network links: some processes will be located within the same local area network whereas others will be connected through slow links, and thus subject to long delays. In such an environment, none of the previous approaches can provide optimal performance.

The topology-aware total order protocol recognizes that some ordering mechanisms are more appropriate for local-area networks and other more suitable for the wide area network. Since we are targeting a WAN-of-LANs network model, we have designed an hybrid scheme, where each process is able to operate with the ordering mechanism that is most suitable given its position with regard to its peers in the network topology. If all processes are in the same cluster (single or set of interconnected LANs), one mechanism is used. If all processes are in different clusters, another mechanism is used. In intermediate scenarios, different mechanisms are integrated in a hybrid protocol [21].

5.1 Ordering Mechanisms

Among the several algorithms for implementing total ordering, the *token-site* [5, 12] and *symmetric* [19, 7] are the most used approaches. Both methods have advantages and disadvantages.

In the token-site approach one (or more) sites is responsible for ordering messages on behalf of the other processes in the system. This process works as a sequencer of all messages and is often called the *token* site. Token protocols are appealing because they are relatively simple and provide good performance when message transit delays are small (they are particularly well suited for local area networks). However, in a token protocol, a message sent by a process that does not hold the token experiences a delivery latency close to $2D$, where D is the message transit delay between two system processes (i.e., the time to disseminate the message plus the time to obtain either the token or an order number from the token holder). Thus, token-site approaches are inefficient in face of large network delays.

In the symmetric approach, ordering is established by all processes in a decentralized way, using information about message stability. This approach usually relies on *logical clocks* [14] or *vector clocks* [2, 19, 13]: messages are delivered according to their partial order and concurrent messages are totally ordered using some deterministic algorithm. Symmetric protocols have the potential for providing low latency in message delivery when all processes are producing messages. In fact, using a technique called rate-synchronization [21], symmetric protocols can exhibit a latency close to $D+t$, where t is the largest inter-message transmission time. Unfortunately, this also means that all (or at least a majority [7, 18]) of processes must send messages at a high rate to achieve low protocol latency.

In order to illustrate the behavior of both protocols in isolation we have selected the rate-synchronized symmetric protocol of [21] and the non fault-tolerant version of [12] (where a single site issues tickets on behalf of all other processes in the group). The measured latency of these protocols for different network delays is depicted in Figure 9, corresponding to a scenario where 30 processes send messages at a rate of 10 msg/s. It can be seen that, as noted before, the latency

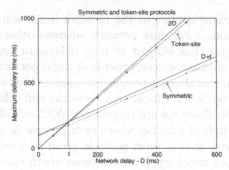

Fig. 9. Latency of symmetric and token-site protocols in isolation.

of the token-site protocol follows the $2D$ line and the latency of the symmetric protocol follows the $D + t$ line. The figure clearly shows that token-site protocols are more favorable when $2D < D + t \equiv D < t$, and that symmetric protocols are more favorable otherwise.

5.2 Static Hybrid Protocol

We now present a hybrid protocol for static topologies, i.e., topologies where traffic patterns, rates and communication delays are known *a priori* and do not change over time. The protocol is extended later to dynamic topologies. The hybrid protocol allows some processes to operate in symmetric mode (these processes are said to be *active*), or also called *sequencers*), and other processes to operate in token-site mode (these processes are said to be *passive*). At a given instant, each passive process is associated with a single active process which issues tickets on its behalf.

The protocol works as follows. Each process has a unique identifier p_i and keeps an increasing sent message counter c_i. Thus, each message is uniquely identified by the pair (p_i, c_i). Messages are multicast, using a virtually-synchronous primitive, directly to all processes of the group. Active processes keep an extra counter: the *ticket number* t_i. Ticket numbers are updated as according to the rate-synchronized symmetric protocol. A ticket is a triplet $(p_i, t_i, (p_j, c_j))$. An active process issues tickets for its own messages and for messages from its associated passive processes. At a given time, each passive process is associated with a single active process, called the passive process *sequencer* (an active process can be a sequencer of more than one passive process). Passive processes multicast their messages to all group processes which then wait for a ticket stating the total order of each message. The ticket is sent by each passive process's *sequencer*. In order to be disseminated to all processes, tickets are piggy-backed in messages sent by active processes. Tickets are ordered as in a symmetric protocol i.e., by increasing order of their ticket numbers, and tickets with the same ticket number are ordered according to the total order of ticket issuers. Finally, messages are delivered by the order of their associated tickets.

```
forall process n set n mode to passive
let a be the process with highest rate; set a mode to active; set changed to true
while (changed is true) do // iteration
    set changed to false
    forall j such that j mode is passive do
        let a be the active process closest to j
        if (D_{(j,a)} + t_j < 2D_{(j,a)}) then
            set j mode to active; set changed to true
        else
            set sequencer of j to a
```

Fig. 10. Mode Assignment Heuristic

The critical part of the hybrid approach is to assign roles to each process. The decision must take into account the rate at which each process is producing messages and network delays between processes. In order to configure the system, a heuristic that analyzes each pair of processes in isolation is used. Consider a process n, subject to a load characterized by a mean inter-message transmission time t_n. Consider that the delay to the nearest (in terms of network delay) active process a is $D_{(n,a)}$. The condition that must be satisfied for process n to assume a passive role is $D_{(n,a)} + t_n > 2D_{(n,a)}$. In this case, inter-message transmission time is longer than the active process' round-trip delay and p can request and obtain a ticket from a before there is a new message to be sent. On the other hand, if $D_{(n,a)} + t_n \leq 2D_{(n,a)}$ since it is sending messages faster than the time required to obtain a ticket from the token-site, n should assume an active role (this not only offers lower latency but provides better load distribution).

The complete algorithm to assign roles can be obtained by applying the previous rule recursively, as described in Figure 10. Initially, all processes are made passive. Since at least one active process must exist in the system, the process (or one of the processes, if more than one exist) with smaller inter-message transmission time is selected as the initial active process. Then, the rule is applied to all other processes of the system to check if some of the processes should be promoted to active. This procedure is executed recursively until no change is made to the network.

5.3   Mode Switching Protocol

In order to apply the hybrid protocol to dynamic topologies, a protocol that allows a process to dynamically switch between active and passive mode is needed. This section describes such a protocol.

There are three types of transitions that can occur in a dynamic hybrid protocol, namely: (i) a passive process can change sequencer; (ii) a passive process can switch to active; (iii) and, an active process can switch to passive. Transitions can occur due to two main reasons: changes in the operational envelope and failures. Transitions due to failures happen when active processes, which are acting as sequencers of other processes, crash. In this case, passive processes associated with the failed sequencer must either select a new sequencer or become active. Transitions due to changes in the operational envelope happen when a process decides to adapt to new load or network delay conditions.

To guarantee correct operation, all active processes in the system must see the same sequence of configurations. Thus, the order in which transitions are executed, with regard to message flow and membership indications, must be agreed before transitions actually take place. In order to reach agreement about the $(i + 1)$th configuration, the properties of the underlying view-synchronous layer (vs-layer) and the total order of messages, established by the ith configuration, are used. The vs-layer advantage is the guarantee that, in case of failures, all surviving processes receive the same set of messages before a new view is installed. This means that each view change is a synchronization point where all processes are guaranteed to have received the same messages. These properties greatly simplify switching protocols. However, no assumptions are made about the consistency of rates and network delay evaluations (i.e., no process can assume that some other process will change state just because such a transition is plausible according to its own local information): all transitions which are not directly triggered by failures must be initiated and disseminated by the switching process.

In order to describe the switching protocol some definitions are needed. Each process j is described by a triplet, called the *process descriptor*, denoted $D_j = (p_j, r_j, rn_j)$, where p_j is the process identifier, r_j is a role (one of *active* or *passive*), and rn_j is a *role-number* (role-numbers start with zero and are incremented every time a process changes roles). A *system configuration*, $C = \{V^i, \bigcup_{j \in V^i} D_j\}$, is defined as a system view plus the process descriptors of all processes in the view. It is also assumed that each process j keeps a record of the last of its own messages that has been delivered, l_j. Finally, it is assumed that a passive process p keeps the process descriptor of its sequencer in a variable called $S(p)$. The following text presents an informal description of the protocol.

Initial Configuration When the hybrid protocol starts, all processes must agree on some initial configuration. The exact configuration is not important since the system is able to reconfigure itself (as long as there is at least one active process in the initial configuration). An initial configuration was used where all processes are active and remain in that state until they have received enough messages to evaluate traffic load and network delays.

Operation in Steady-State In the dynamic hybrid protocol, a process operating in passive mode is not statically assigned to a given sequencer process. Instead, a passive process can instruct any active process to order messages on its behalf, on a message-by-message basis (usually, a passive process only changes sequencer as a result of a configuration change). This confers flexibility to the system and provides fast adaptability to changes in the operational envelope. To allow dynamic binding, data messages are encapsulated in a protocol message with the following format: $\langle type, p_i, c_i, S_i, user\text{-}data \rangle$, where p_i is the source, c_i is the message's sequence number and D_s is the process descriptor of the assigned sequencer for that message (the assigned sequencer will only issue a ticket if it still has the role-number specified in S_i when it receives the message).

Since messages can be transmitted concurrently with events that generate configuration changes, it is possible for the assigned sequencer to fail or increment its role-number before it has the opportunity to issue tickets for a group of messages. In order to cope with these cases, the protocol uses another special message, called a *reassign* message, with the following format: $\langle reassign, p_i,]l_i, c_i], S_{new}\rangle$, where p_i is the source, $]l_i, c_i]$ is a range of message sequence numbers (the specification of this range will be described later on in this section) and S_{new} is the new sequencer for those messages. Reassign messages are only sent when the selected sequencer fails or becomes passive.

If a passive process fails, all of its messages, delivered by the vs-layer before the view change but not yet ordered by its sequencer, are silently discarded by all processes. This procedure is safe, because the properties of the vs-layer guarantee that tickets are totally ordered with respect to the view change.

Both active and passive processes store all received messages in a *pending* queue. Active processes issue tickets for their own messages and for all messages assigned to them in the pending queue (i.e., if the process descriptor in the message matches the process descriptor of that active process). Tickets are ordered as they are received (piggy-backed in the messages of the active processes). Finally, messages are removed from the pending queue and delivered by the order of their tickets. Although only active processes issue tickets, all processes (including passive processes) keep their ticket numbers synchronized according the protocol in [21]: a passive process may need to become active and the protocol exhibits better performance if these numbers are up to date.

Some messages are reserved for protocol usage and are not delivered to the user. The use of such messages will be clarified below. Also, the *reassign* message is never delivered: it is only used to update the sequencer field of all specified messages in the pending queue.

System Reconfiguration Process mode transitions and process crashes induce a sequence of system configurations. In order to voluntarily change their modes, processes broadcast special messages, namely $\langle$ goToActive, $p_i, c_i, S_i\rangle$ and $\langle$ goToPassive, $p_i, c_i, S_i\rangle$ messages. Such messages are sent in total order and their delivery triggers installation of a new system configuration. Processes may also be forced to change their mode due to failure of other processes thus, view changes also trigger installation of a new system configuration. Finally, passive processes may react to configuration changes by selecting a new sequencer. These situations will be addressed in the following paragraphs.

View changes Assume that the system is in configuration C^n is delivered by the vs-layer. A new configuration C^{n+1} is created. If there is no active process in such configuration (i.e, all active processes have failed) process m having the highest process unique identifier in V^{i+1}, is automatically switched to active mode (by setting $r_m = active$ and incrementing rn_m); then, C^{n+1} is installed. If there is a passive process such that $S(p) \notin C^{n+1}$, this process selects a new sequencer m and sets $S(p) = (p_m, r_m, rn_m)$. Additionally, it sends message $\langle reassign, p_p,]l_p, c_p], S(p)\rangle$.

Transition from active to passive In the dynamic hybrid protocol there are two reasons for a process to change from active to passive: (a) its traffic load has decreased to a rate where it is more advantageous to request a ticket from another process; (b) or a nearby process has become active and transmitting at a much faster rate, so that there is no need to continue being an active process. In order to switch to passive mode, process p_i sends a special message $\langle goToPassive, p_i, c_i, S_i\rangle$, stops transmitting and stops issuing tickets, even for messages assigned to itself (these messages will eventually be assigned to another sequencer). It then waits for its own message to be delivered.

When the $\langle goToPassive\rangle$ message is delivered, before creating a new configuration, it should be checked if the sender is the last active process in the group. Note that since several processes can decide to become passive concurrently, all active processes might try to become passive but, since at least one active process must exist, the last one will fail. In the case the message is associated with the last active process, the transition is aborted (and the sender restarts sending messages and issuing tickets). Otherwise, a new configuration C^{n+1} is created by setting $r_i = passive$, and incrementing rn_i. Then, C^{n+1} is installed.

Transition from passive to active A transition from passive to active mode can happen either because a process becomes subject to higher traffic load, making the active mode a better choice, or because all active processes have failed and it is the process with highest identifier.

In the first case, passive process i broadcasts a special $\langle goToActive, p_i, c_i, S_i\rangle$ and stops sending messages. Then it waits until the special message is ordered by its sequencer and delivered. When the message is delivered, a new configuration C^{n+1} is created (by setting $r_i = active$ and incrementing rn_i). Then, C^{n+1} is installed. All messages sent by i after this new configuration are ordered by process i itself.

In case of failure of the only active process, the passive process with highest identifier becomes active as soon as it receives failure indication from the vs-layer. Upon this transition, new active process i issues tickets for all messages it has sent but that were not ordered in previous configurations, i.e., for all messages with sequence numbers in the interval $]l_i, c_i]$.

Change of sequencer A passive process can change its sequencer if some other process becomes active and the round-trip delay to that process is lower than to the previous sequencer. Since data messages specify the desired sequencer, sequencer switching is very simple. To avoid disturbances in FIFO ordering, passive process p stops transmitting temporarily and waits until all its previous messages have been delivered (i.e., it waits until $l_p = c_p$). It then sets its sequencer $S(p)$ to the new desired process descriptor and resumes message transmission.

A passive process p can also switch sequencer if its previous sequencer changes to passive mode. As before, the passive process sets its sequencer $S(p)$ to the new desired process descriptor. Additionally, knowing which message l_i was last ordered by the previous sequencer, it sends a reassign $\langle reassign, p_p,]l_p, c_p], S(p)\rangle$ message instructing the new sequencer to order unordered messages.

5.4 Dynamic Hybrid Protocol

Traffic patterns are likely to change over time in most interactive applications. Components usually react to incoming events by switching between idle periods and high activity periods. Networks delays are also subject to variations, due to load changes (office and night hours, for instance) or link failures (faster routes can become temporarily unavailable). Using the algorithms presented in the previous section, the dynamic hybrid protocol automatically adapts the operational mode of each process to changes both in traffic patterns and in communication links.

Evaluation of System Parameters To allow on-line reconfiguration, processes must be able to evaluate system parameters as traffic load and network delays. The following approach is used: each process timestamps every message with its own local clock at the time of transmission; based on the message's timestamp, all processes can determine the average transmission rate of the sender process. To determine delays in inter-process links, a simple round-trip delay method is used. At every pre-determined fixed interval of time[6], all receiving processes of a given data message respond immediately with a point-to-point null message to the originator process of the first message. This process can then calculate the delay between itself and all recipients. Note that the evaluation of link delays is also required by other components (for instance, for fault-detection), and can be implemented using low-level acknowledgments or synchronized clocks, for instance, using CESIUMSPRAY.

In order to evaluate system parameters based on sample measurements, a simple *mean-shift* detector was used: an initial mean value of rate and delay is calculated using the first k samples from each process[7]; whenever a run of k or more samples fall either all above the mean value or all below it, that mean value is recalculated and used in the next iteration. As the symmetric protocol relies on the fact that all processes must be constantly sending messages, system parameters can be evaluated after a short period of operation. This and other *mean-shift* detectors are described in detail in [11] and, as a future work, we plan to experiment with other detectors to evaluate their performance.

Switching Heuristic Section 5.2 showed how an external observer assign roles to each process in an hybrid configuration. Since an external observer can only be approximated, and to avoid centralized solutions, a heuristic that allows each

---

[6] In our simulations, an interval of a few seconds was used.

[7] In our simulations, we have $k = 7$.

process to make a local switching decision based on its own evaluation of the system state is now presented.

The heuristic is as follows: each process keeps track of its own message rate and of the network delay between itself and all other active processes. If its inter-message transmission rate is smaller than the delay to the closest active, it should switch to active mode, as shown previously. If, on the other hand, its inter-message transmission rate is higher than the delay to the closest active, it should switch to passive mode using the closest active process as its sequencer. To avoid frequent mode changes when the value of inter-message transmission rate is very close to the delay value, the decision to change mode is only made when the difference between these values becomes greater than a given threshold (a threshold of 20% of the delay value was used).

Performance of Total Order In order to test the effectiveness of our approach, the performance of the hybrid protocol is compared with that of the protocols selected in Section 5.1. The results were obtained with a system of five processes, connected by a network as shown in Figure 11 (grey nodes are network relays): processes A, B and C (and processes D and E) are within $D1$ of each other; however, the distance between a process in the first group and a process in the second group is $2D1 + D2$. Each process can be subjected to two different traffic loads, designated respectively by *high*(H) and *low*(L). Nine different scenarios were simulated, differing in relative traffic load of each process. The load of each process in each scenario is shown in the table (for instance, in scenario 1, process A has high load, process D has low load, and so on). In this simulation, the following parameters were used: $D1 = 20ms$, $D2 = 500ms$, a high rate of $100msg/s$ and a low rate of $1msg/s$ (both using a Quasi-Periodic source).

The performance results obtained using the heuristic above are also presented in Figure 11, alongside with results from symmetric and token-site protocols. The system ran continuously while the process load changed with time, making the system evolve through all nine scenarios in sequence. Results are presented for both a Quasi-Periodic and a Poisson message source. In the hybrid approach, every time the load changes in at least one process, roles are reassigned and the affected processes execute the transition algorithm on-line. It can be observed that the hybrid protocol using both types of message sources, out-performs the two other protocols, independently of individual process rates. With the Quasi-Periodic source it shows an almost constant message delivery time, with a temporary increase in message delivery latency upon each change in the operational envelope (this is due to the time required to make local decisions and the disturbance introduced by the switching protocol). With the Poisson source, although more irregular and with a slightly higher delivery time, the results are still better than either the symmetric (which performs poorly with Poisson sources[8]) or

---

[8] Only certain values of the symmetric protocol appear in the figure so as to avoid losing detail in the token-site and hybrid plots.

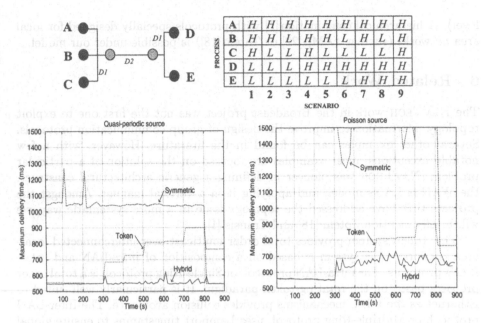

Fig. 11. Dynamic hybrid protocol

token-site protocol. In an extended report [21] simulations results obtained with more elaborate scenarios are presented.

5.5 Advantages of Topology-Awareness for Total Ordering

Among the several algorithms for implementing total ordering, the *token-site* [5, 12] and *symmetric* [19, 7] are the most widely used approaches. Several token-site protocols have been optimized for local area networks [5, 22, 12, 1], so it is fair to say that LAN topology-awareness has been used with success. Previous optimizations for symmetric approaches are not based on topology [7, 18]. A hybrid approach is used by the Newtop protocol [9] where some groups can operate using a symmetric protocol and others using a token-site protocol. We have extended the latter approach by allowing both protocol types within the same group.

Our protocol is able to dynamically adapt to changes in throughput and in network delays while reducing latency through a rate-synchronization policy. The hybrid protocol was simulated for several scenarios, using different network topologies and traffic patterns. Results show that the hybrid protocol can offer significant improvements in message latency. Using simple heuristics, it is possible to make all switching decisions local to each process. Alternative heuristics, for the mode-assignment algorithm and for the switching policies, are currently being studied, to see if they can provide better performance. The protocol can be applied directly to a WAN-of-LANs network (for instance, at the site level of the NAVTECH model) or be used exclusively in the WAN part (at the cluster agent level). A hierarchical combination [1] with protocols specially designed for local area networks (such as xAMp [22] or Totem [18]) is possible under our model.

6 Related Work

The NAVTECH work in the Broadcast project was not the first one to exploit topology information to improve the design of group communication protocols. Several other examples can be found in the literature. However, with a few notable exceptions, most examples are focused on the solution of a particular problem. NAVTECH was pioneer in defining a generic architectural construct, the WAN-of-LANs model, and applying it in a vertical manner. Amongst the projects that have addressed the topology issue in a more systematic way, we will briefly mention Totem [18] and Transis [1].

The Totem system provides total order multicast over interconnected local-area networks. The system is based on a composition of *intra*-LAN and *inter*-LANs protocols. The intra-LAN protocol, or Single-Ring protocol, is a total order protocol based on the rotating-token paradigm. It is particularly well suited to Ethernet as the token mechanisms provides collision avoidance. The Inter-LAN protocol, or Multiple-Ring protocol, uses Lamport timestamps to ensure global total order. The Transis system follows a network model that has similarities with ours. The wide area network is modeled as a hierarchy of multicast clusters, and clusters are arranged in a hierarchical group structure. The work on Transis is complementary to ours: in Transis emphasis was given to efficient local-area communication and hierarchical composition while in NAVTECH emphasis was given on dynamic configuration and filtering of local control data.

7 Conclusions

Making few or no assumptions about the network infrastructure ensures high portability but often yields disappointing performances. The successful design should capture the right balance between generality and performance. In the NAVTECH project, we experimented with a global network model that we have called WAN-of-LANs. The model is simple and general, and can be applied to most existing global infrastructures. Yet, it is powerful enough to allow the protocol designer to exploit its hierarchical nature to improve the performance or reliable communication protocols.

We have designed several proof-of-concepts algorithms that are based on the WAN-of-LANs network model. We have addressed a number of different problems to assess the coverage of the model (namely, clock synchronization, causal order, total order). The applicability of the the WAN-of-LANs network model to the consensus problem is currently under study. Each of our algorithms uses the WAN-of-LANs concept in a different way, but all the solutions follow the general framework provided by the NAVTECH architecture. The experience with these protocols reinforced our belief that the model is appropriate to design efficient group-oriented systems for large-scale networks.

As future work, we intend to benefit from this experience to refine our LAN-of-WANs model, clearly identifying the relevant properties that must be made visible for the benefit of the protocol designer, and which properties must be kept hidden to preserve acceptable portability.

Acknowledgments

The work on clock synchronization was done in collaboration with A. Casimiro. The work on total order protocols was done in collaboration with H. Fonseca, who also provided the simulations for the causal order protocol.

References

[1] Y. Amir, D. Dolev, S. Kramer, and D. Malki. Transis: A communication subsystem for high-availability. In *Digest of Papers, The 22nd Int. Symp. on Fault-Tolerant Computing Systems*, pages 76–84. IEEE, 1993.

[2] K. Birman and T. Joseph. Reliable communication in the presence of failures. *ACM, Transactions on Computer Systems*, 5(1), February 1987.

[3] K. Birman, A. Schiper, and P. Stephenson. Lightweight causal and atomic group multicast. *ACM, Transactions on Computer Systems*, 9(3), August 1991.

[4] T. Chandra and S. Toueg. Unreliable failure detectors for reliable distributed systems. *Journal of the ACM*, 34(1):225–267, 1996.

[5] J. Chang and N. Maxemchuck. Reliable broadcast protocols. *ACM, Transactions on Computer Systems*, 2(3), August 1984.

[6] B. Charron-Bost. Concerning the size of logical clocks in distributed systems. *Information Processing Letters*, 39(1):11–16, July 1991.

[7] D. Dolev, S. Kramer, and D. Malki. Early delivery totally ordered multicast in asynchronous environments. In *Digest of Papers, The 23th Int. Symp. on Fault-Tolerant Computing*, pages 544–553. IEEE, 1993.

[8] Simon Even. *Graph Algorithms*. Computer Science Press, 1979.

[9] P. Ezhilchelvan, R. Macedo, and S. Shrivastava. Newtop: A fault-tolerant group communication protocol. In *Proceedings of the 15th Int. Conf. on Distributed Computing Systems*, pages 296–306. IEEE, 1995.

[10] A. Heybey. The network simulator version 2.1. Technical report, M.I.T., September 1990.

[11] P. John. *Statistical Methods in Engineering and Quality Assurance*. John Wiley & Sons Inc, 1990.

[12] M. Kaashoek and A. Tanenbaum. Group communication in the Amoeba distributed operating system. In *Proceedings of the 11th Int. Conf. on Distributed Computing Systems*, pages 222–230. IEEE, 1991.

[13] R. Ladin, B. Liskov, L. Shrira, and S. Ghemawat. Lazy replication: Exploiting the semantics of distributed services. In *Proceedings of the Ninth Annual ACM Symp. of Principles of Distributed Computing*, pages 43–57, 1990.

[14] L. Lamport. Time, clocks and the ordering of events in a distributed system. *Communications of the ACM*, 21(7):558–565, July 1978.

[15] W. Lloyd and P. Kearns. Bounding sequence numbers in distributed systems: a general approach. In *Proceedings of the 10th Int. Conf. on Distributed Computing Systems*, pages 312–319, Paris, France, May 1990. IEEE.

[16] S. Meldal, S. Sankar, and J. Vera. Exploiting locality in maitaining potential causality. In *Procedings of the 10th ACM SIGACT-SIGOPS Symp. on Principles of Distributed Computing*, pages 231–239, 1991.

[17] David Mills. Network time protocol (version 2): Specification and implementation. Technical Report RFC 1119, DARPA Network Working Group, September 1989.

[18] L. Moser, P. Melliar-Smith, A. Agarwal, R. Budhia, C. Lingley-Ppadopoulos, and T. Archambault. The Totem system. In *Digest of Papers of the 25th Int. Symp. on Fault-Tolerant Computing Systems*, pages 61–66. IEEE, June 1995.

[19] L. Peterson, N. Buchholz, and R. Schlichting. Preserving and using context information in interprocess communication. *ACM Transactions on Computer Systems*, 7(3):217–146, August 1989.

[20] M. Raynal, A. Schiper, and S. Toueg. The causal ordering abstraction and a simple way to implement it. *Information processing letters*, 39(6):343–350, September 1991.

[21] L. Rodrigues, H. Fonseca, and P. Veríssimo. Totally ordered multicast in large-scale systems. In *Proceedings of the 16th IEEE Int. Conf. on Distributed Computing Systems*, pages 503–510, Hong Kong, May 1996. (extended report available).

[22] L. Rodrigues and P. Veríssimo. xAMp: a multi-primitive group communications service. In *Proceedings of the 11th Symp. on Reliable Distributed Systems*, pages 112–121. IEEE, 1992.

[23] L. Rodrigues and P. Veríssimo. Causal separators for large-scale multicast communication. In *Proceedings of the 15th IEEE Int. Conf. on Distributed Computing Systems*, pages 83–91, Vancouver, British Columbia, Canada, May 1995. (extended report available).

[24] A. Schiper, J. Eggli, and A. Sandoz. A New Algorithm to Implement Causal Ordering. In *Proceedings of the 3rd Int Workshop on Distributed Algorithms*, volume LNCS 392, pages 219–232, Nice - France, September 1989. Springer Verlag.

[25] F. Schneider. Implementing fault-tolerant services using the state machine approach: a tutorial. *ACM Computing Surveys*, 22(4):290–319, December 1990.

[26] A. Schwarz and F. Mattern. Detecting Causal Relationships in Distributed Computations: In search of the Holy Grail. Technical report, Departement of Computer Science, University of Kaiserlautern, 1991.

[27] M. Singhal and Kshemkalyani A. An Efficient Implementation of vector clocks. Technical report, Ohio State University, October 1990.

[28] P. Stephenson. *Fast Causal Multicast*. PhD thesis, Cornell Univ., February 1991.

[29] R. van Renesse, Ken Birman, and S. Maffeis. Horus: A flexible group communications system. *Communications of the ACM*, 39(4):76–83, April 1996.

Responsive Protocols for Distributed Multimedia Applications*

Fabio Panzieri and Marco Roccetti

Dipartimento di Scienze dell'Informazione,
Università di Bologna, via Mura A. Zamboni 7, 40127 Bologna, Italy
{panzieri,roccetti}@cs.unibo.it

Abstract. A relevant class of Distributed MultiMedia Applications (DMMAs) can be implemented to support critical activities from which either financial investments, or human lives, or both, may depend. These DMMAs can be distributed across wide geographical distances; owing to their critical nature, the principal requirements they exhibit include the need for scalable services that be both timely and highly available (i.e. responsive). In order to provide support to these DMMAs, we have designed and developed a communication software architecture that meets effectively these requirements. In this paper, we introduce that architecture, and discuss its performance as resulting from a prototype implementation we have developed.

1 Introduction

The implementation of DMMAs is based on the processing and exchange of both *continuous* (or time-dependent) information, such as audio and video data streams, and *discrete* (or time-independent) information, such as streams of text data and still images. In order to support the implementation of these applications, it is required that the application designer be provided with appropriate software that maintain the timing relationships between those data streams, so that their rendering can be synchronized. This requirement introduces complexity in the design of DMMAs distributed across wide area networks, as the communications over these networks are usually asynchronous, i.e. characterized by arbitrary delays.

This requirement can be further aggravated if the DMMAs to be supported are critical applications, such as a video and audio monitoring of crucial sites of a power plant, or a geographically distributed electronic auction bidding system, or a teleconferencing application for supporting cooperative medicine, i.e. applications whose unreliable behaviour may endanger either human lifes, or large financial investments, or both.

Owing to their critical nature, one of the principal concerns in the design of these DMMAs is the provision of responsive services, i.e. services that maintain their availability in the presence of communication or host failures, and

---

* Partial support for this work was provided by the Commission of European Communities under ESPRIT Programme Basic Research Project 6360 (BROADCAST),

provide their users with timely responses. Moreover, these DMMAs require that the data streams (both continuous and discrete) they manipulate be rendered isochronously at a collection (i.e. a *group*) of geographically distant end users. Hence, in addition to the synchronization mechanisms mentioned above, these applications require support for coordinating the isochronous rendering of those streams at their end users. Finally, no assumptions can be made as to the scale of these DMMAs (i.e. the number of users concurrently using them, the number of resources implementing them, the geographical separation among those users or among those resources). Hence, the protocols that support these DMMAs are to be designed so as to provide quality of service guarantees (e.g. reliability, performance) regardless of the DMMA scale.

Needless to say, the variety of requirements that characterizes the DMMAs in general, and the critical DMMAs in particular, is much wider than that mentioned above; for example, these applications may well exhibit requirements for security, efficient information storage, sharing and retrieval (see, for example, [3]). However, in this paper, we shall confine our discussion to the design, implementation, and performance evaluation of a communication protocol architecture, that we have developed, that i) meets the DMMAs' scalability requirement, ii) supports the reliable synchronization and isochronous rendering of multimedia data streams, and iii) provides real-time group communication and membership services for DMMAs. That architecture is fully described and motivated in [17].

This paper is structured as follows. In the next Section we discuss the principal issues we have addressed in the design of our architecture, and motivate our design decisions. Section 3 introduces a prototype implementation of our architecture (based on the IP Multicast protocol). Section 4 discusses the performance results we have obtained from that implementation. Section 5 compares and contrasts our work with related work; finally, Section 6 provides some concluding remarks.

2   Design Issues

The DMMAs mentioned earlier can be based on an asynchronous wide area communication network that interconnects a great variety of nodes, characterized by diverse capabilities. For example, a node may well consist of either a continuous input device (e.g. a camera) directly connected to the communication network, or a multimedia storage server, or a powerful workstation equipped with both continuous and discrete (e.g. a keyboard) I/O devices. These I/O devices can generate/render data streams that may consist either of individual data object sequences (e.g. sequences of audio samples, or video frames, or characters) or of composite multimedia data streams, that represent, for example, a motion video and its sound track, as transmitted by, or stored in, a video server.

Within this scenario, the action of maintaining accurate time relationships among data objects within a single individual stream is generally referred to as *intrastream* synchronization; instead, the action of maintaining accurate time relationships among data objects of different streams (either individual or composite) is referred to as *interstream* synchronization [17]. A variety of algorithms has been proposed for achieving both *intra* and *interstream* synchronization, e.g. [8,20]. These algorithms can be implemented according to one of the following three synchronization policies, termed *synchronization at the source, synchronization at the destination*, and *synchronization at the network*.

Both an analysis of these algorithms and a description of these three policies fall outside the scope of our discussion (the interested reader can refer to the already cited references). Rather, our principal concern is the design of a particular synchronization policy that can support effectively the implementation of *intra* and *interstream* synchronization algorithms. Thus, in the following, we shall use the phrase Composite Multimedia Data Stream (CMDS) to indicate the data object that represents the result of the timely integration of different data streams, regardless of the particular algorithm used to construct it.

In the DMMAs mentioned earlier, the sources and/or destinations (i.e. the I/O devices) of the data streams, that have to be synchronized, may be geographically dispersed. In this context, independent streams of data, originated from these I/O devices, are to be integrated so as to form a CMDS to be rendered isochronously at a collection of output devices.

In order to meet this isochronous rendering (IR) requirement, a real-time multicast service [5,1] can be used for exchanging multimedia data streams within a DMMA. One such service, combined with a real-time group-membership abstraction, provides a useful paradigm for implementing distributed applications. Thus, the architecture we have developed incorporates both a real-time multicast service, that implements the multicasting of CMDSs, and a group membership service, that maintains the group abstraction among DMMA components. These mechanisms can offer a further benefit, as they can be used for constructing adequate fault tolerance support [12] that cope effectively with the critical nature of these applications.

It has been observed that scale is a primary factor that can influence the design and implementation of a distributed system [19]. In particular, mechanisms that work adequately in small distributed systems may fail to do so when deployed within the context of larger systems. Hence, for the purposes of our discussion, we term scalable a system that can provide its services, according to the performance and reliability specifications of those services, regardless of both the number of resources it accommodates, and the geographical separation among these resources.

In order to meet the DMMA scalability requirement, our architecture allows the application designer to structure his/her applications so as to accommodate dynamically an arbitrary number of resources, with no concern for issues of geographical separation among those resources.

In summary, the DMMA requirements introduced above have led us to address the following three principal design issues in the development of our architecture: i) the provision of what we have termed "scalability support", ii) the choice of a particular data stream synchronization policy that meet the IR requirement, and iii) the choice of a particular fault model and group management policy. Below, we discuss each of these issues in turn.

2.1 Scalability Support

In order to deal with scalable DMMAs, we have decided to design algorithms that allow one to structure hierarchically those DMMAs. The rationale behind this decision is that firstly, as shown in [20], hierarchical architectures can scale beyond an order of magnitude than purely centralized or distributed architectures, while continuing to meet the application requirements. Secondly, the hierarchical communication architecture we have developed shields the DMMAs components from the details of the physical communication network by providing them with the abstraction of a tree-structured interconnection infrastructure, that we term k-Augmented M-ary Tree (k-AMT) architecture.

This architecture is structured as a complete M-ary tree (MT) with N leaves, augmented with k additional links (see below). The leaf nodes of the tree represent the multimedia data sources and destinations of a given instance of a DMMA. Nonleaf nodes represent *synchronizers* of multimedia data streams, that implement the synchronization policy mentioned previously. A link between two nodes represents a virtual communication channel between those nodes. Nodes connected by a virtual channel can communicate by exchanging messages.

The abstraction of a MT structured interconnection architecture, can be constructed out of a physical multimedia distributed system, as summarized in the following example.

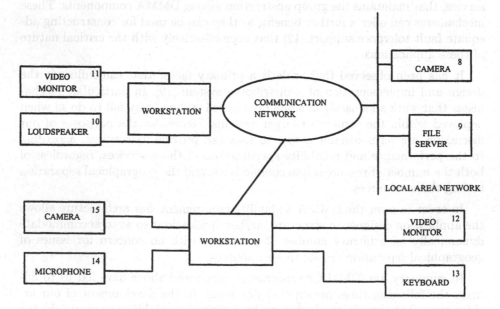

Fig. 1. Multimedia Distributed System

Consider the multimedia distributed system depicted in Figure 1. That system consists of a broadband communication network that interconnects: (i) a workstation equipped with three input devices, namely a camera, a microphone, and a keyboard, and a video monitor output device, (ii) a workstation equipped with two output devices only, i.e. a video monitor and a loudspeaker, and (iii) a multimedia file server and a camera connected to the communication network via a local area network.

For the purposes of this example, we assume that the input and output devices are labeled as illustrated in Figure 1. In addition, we assume $M = 2$, and construct the binary tree illustrated in Figure 2.

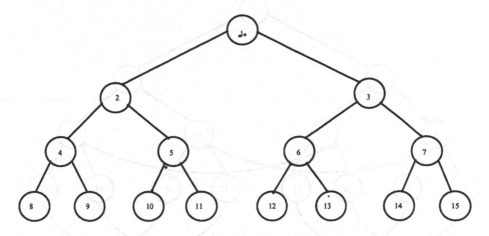

Fig. 2. M-ary Tree

In Figure 2, the root node of that tree is created in one of the workstations (and implemented by a specific synchronizer process); in addition, each I/O device in Figure 1 is represented as a leaf node of that tree. Those devices are clustered in the following four clusters, according to a physical neighborhood criterion, for example. A first cluster consists of the camera and the file server, labeled 8 and 9, respectively, in Figure 1. A second cluster includes the loudspeaker 10, and the video monitor 11; a third cluster includes the video monitor 12 and the keyboard 13. Finally, a fourth cluster consists of the microphone 14, and the camera 15.

The activity of each of these clusters of devices is to be managed by a separate synchronizer process. Hence, in our example, four synchronizer processes are required. A synchronizer process is represented as a node linked to the leaf nodes of the cluster that synchronizer is managing. Thus, the four nodes 4, 5, 6, and 7 in Figure 2 are created.

Owing to our initial assumption that $M = 2$, the activity of each pair of synchronizers is to be coordinated by a further synchronizer process. Thus, two such processes are required in our example; each of these processes can be represented as a node in the tree we are constructing (namely, nodes 2 and 3 in Figure 2), linked to a pair of synchronizers, and to the root node (i.e. node 1 in Figure 2).

The k-AMT abstraction we propose can be derived from the MT abstraction described above by adding at most k spare links to each node in the tree. These k additional links provide the DMMA with sufficient redundancy for tolerating a number of communication faults, which is dependent on k, at the cost of communication bandwidth usage and message overhead. The k-AMT construction algorithm embodied in our architecture is fully described in [17].

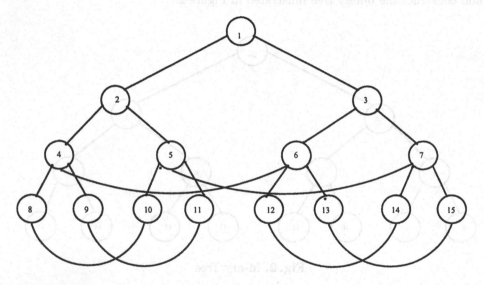

Fig. 3. k-AMT

For example, the k-AMT of Figure 3 can be obtained from the MT of Figure 2 by introducing a $k = 1$ redundancy of the MT links; in particular, the redundant links are those connecting the pairs of nodes (4,6) and (5,7) at level 2, and (8,10), (9,11), (12,14), and (13,15) at level 3. As depicted in Figure 3, the nodes at the end points of these links share a common ancestor other than the parent node. The k-AMT abstraction is constructed by the k-AMTC algorithm described in [17]. Note that the actual configuration of a distributed multimedia system may not fit to form a complete M-ary tree. Hence, the k-AMTC algorithm, when applied to that system, introduces a number of additional leaf nodes, termed virtual leaves, so as to construct the required complete M-ary tree.

2.2 Synchronization Policy

Our approach to multimedia stream synchronization meets the IR requirement introduced earlier, and is based on the use of a scalable, fault tolerant, decentralized synchronization policy, obtained as an extension of the algorithm described in [20]. This algorithm operates on a hierarchical virtual interconnection architecture, structured as an arbitrary rooted tree, and manages synchronized integration of multimedia data streams. In [20], it is assumed that each source generates media packets at a constant rate, and that the communication delays are bounded in a time interval. Under these assumptions, the proposed algorithm minimizes the difference between the generation time of the data packets that are being synchronized, in the absence of globally synchronized clocks. By reducing the packet generation time differences, this algorithm minimizes the buffering time and space requirements of the data packets.

We have extended this algorithm to operate over a k-AMT, and to exploit the k additional links at each node of the k-AMT for transmitting replicas of the individual data streams, in order to overcome problems that may arise from faults of both communication links and nodes. Our synchronization strategy is implemented by a so-called k-AMT Synchronization (k-AMTS) algorithm that operates in two distinct phases, namely a *Collect Phase* and a *Disseminate Phase*. In the Collect Phase, a CMDS is constructed and forwarded by each synchronizer node to both its immediate ancestor and to those nodes directly connected to it via the k additional links. Eventually, the root node of the k-AMT receives a collection of CMDSs, integrates them so as to construct the Final Synchronized Multimedia Data Stream (FSMDS), and multicasts it to its son nodes, thus entering the Disseminate Phase of the k-AMTS algorithm. In the Disseminate phase, each node forwards the FSMDS it receives to both its son nodes and those nodes to which it is directly connected, until the FSMDS reaches the leaf destination nodes. Each leaf node that receives a FSMDS within a known predefined time instant F, will render that FSMDS at time F, otherwise it discards it.

The principal difference between the synchronization strategy we have implemented and that described in [20] is in the redundancy entailed by the transmission of the stream replicas (either CMDSs and FSMDSs) over the k-AMT. In addition, our approach is based on the following four assumptions.

- *A1.* No conditions are placed on the data packet generation rate.
- *A2.* A bounded delay (denoted $D1$) is assumed to be guaranteed by the communication subsystem in the communications between two directly connected sites in the k-AMT architecture.
- *A3.* A bounded processing time (denoted as $D2$) is assumed to be guaranteed for each multimedia data stream which is processed at a given node of the k-AMT architecture. $D2$ may include processing delays such as i) the *collection delay*, i.e. the time elapsed from the acquisition of the data at a k-AMT source node to the delivery of those data to the network transport system of that node (thus, $D2$ includes such delays as those caused by the data digitization and the encoding); ii) the *equalization delay*, which is the time consumed by the synchronization algorithm to produce a CMDS at a given k-AMT site, iii) the *delivery delay*, i.e. the time elapsed between the delivery of a CMDS by the network transport system of a k-AMT node and the rendering of that CMDS at that node. (In section 4, we shall indicate with

$d = D1 + D2$ the overall processing and communication delay which occurs in the communication between two directly connected nodes in the k-AMT architecture.)

– *A4.* The clocks of the processors survive failures, measure the passage of time accurately, and are synchronized, so that the measurable difference between the readings of all non faulty clocks at any instant is bounded by a known constant (denoted ϵ). (Note that this assumption is made realistic by such technological support as that provided by the satellite based GPS [9].) In the following, we shall assume $\epsilon = 0$, without loss of generality.

In summary, the communication subsystem can provide delay guarantees, sufficient buffer space, and a quite accurate clock synchronization by implementing, for example, the delay jitter control scheme described in [7,8]. Moreover, we assume that the basic communication interface supporting the k-AMT architecture provides a multicast real time transport service, such as that introduced in [8], and then developed in [1]. This transport service provides timely multicasting of real time data streams from a sending node to a collection of receiving nodes, directly connected to that sending node in the k-AMT architecture.

To conclude this subsection, we wish to point out that the k-AMTS algorithm meets the IR requirement as it possesses the following three properties, derived from [4].

– *Atomicity* property: every data stream generated by a non faulty source is either played out by all the non faulty destinations or by none of them.
– *Isochronous termination* property: all the data streams generated by non faulty sources at a given time T are played out isochronously, after the same time interval I since T, by all the non faulty destinations.
– *Order* property: all the rendered data streams are rendered by all the non faulty destinations in the same order as they are transmitted.

The motivations for these three properties can be summarized as follows. As the k-AMTS algorithm deals with a data object, i.e. the FSMDS, that is effectively shared among a collection of k-AMT output nodes for rendering purposes, the *Atomicity* property ensures that the consistency of that FSMDS is maintained among those nodes. Instead, the *Isochronous termination* property guarantees that the rendering of the FSMDS can be carried out at the same time by those nodes. Finally, the *Order* property guarantees that the FSMDS is played out maintaining accurately the time relationships among the individual data streams out of which it is constructed. In essence, lack of one of these properties in the k-AMTS algorithm may give rise to inconsistencies in the FSMDS that is rendered by the k-AMT destination nodes; as we consider critical DMMAs that support cooperation among groups of end users, some such inconsistencies may result in disastrous consequences.

2.3 Fault Tolerance and Group Management Policy

Faults have been classified as benign and byzantine faults [14]. Benign faults include *omission* and *timing* faults; byzantine faults are those that exhibit an arbitrary or even malicious behavior.

The fault model we consider for the k-AMT consists of benign faults only, that may occur at the k-AMT links, and at the non root nodes. Typically, these faults may cause message loss, and delays. In particular, an *omission* fault occurring at a k-AMT component (i.e. either a node or a link) causes that a message is never delivered to its destination; instead, a *timing* fault causes that a message is not delivered to its destination within D time units since the time instant at which that message has been sent.

This model captures such faults as audio/video frame loss that may be caused by network congestion [11], for example. The strategy we propose to deal with those faults, described later, is based on the use of the redundant links between k-AMT nodes (this strategy is compared with the Forward Error Correction strategy proposed in [11] in Section 5 of this paper).

In the fault model we propose, faults causing network partitioning will result in omission or timing failures, and will be dealt with accordingly. Transient network partitions will have the same effect; however, when network connectivity is re-established, the components of a DMMA affected by the network partitioning will have to request to join that DMMA in order to resume their activity.

The occurrence of a fault at a k-AMT node may cause timing and omission faults at one or more links that directly connect that node to the k-AMT; thus, in the following, we shall be concerned only with those node faults that have that effect. In addition, we shall assume that those faults are "permanent", i.e. it is either impossible or too expensive (e.g. in terms of additional communication delays) to recover from them within a particular instance of a given DMMA. Finally, faults at the root node can be dealt with either by using conventional replication techniques, or by extending the algorithm proposed in the next Section to incorporate dynamic reconfiguration strategies that, for example, elect an operational node to replace the faulty root node.

In our approach, reliable group communications over the k-AMT are based on the implementation of both the k-AMTS algorithm (introduced above), and a group membership algorithm that maintains the group abstraction among DMMA components. The k-AMTS algorithm transmits CMDSs to their destinations via different routes, transparently to its users, and ensures that the transmitted messages reach their destinations within bounded time intervals, provided that the above mentioned fault hypotheses hold. The group membership algorithm, instead, provides all the non faulty source and destination components of a DMMA (i.e. the leaf nodes of the correspondent k-AMT) with a consistent *view* of their relative group membership, and guarantees time bounded delay of site failure detection and join (see [17] for a formal definition of the proposed group membership view notion).

In essence, in order to provide the group abstraction, our group membership algorithm periodically monitors, at known predefined time instants (termed *membership check times*), the occurrence of possible failures or deliberate disconnections of DMMA components, and requests to join that originate from new components. If the occurrence of any of these events is detected within a monitoring period, a new k-AMT abstraction is constructed at the end of that period. That new k-AMT abstraction will not contain the failed or disconnected components, and include those components whose requests to join have been detected. Finally, our algorithm updates the view of all the DMMA components in the new k-AMT abstraction, prior to the beginning of a new monitoring period.

The implementation of our group management policy over a k-AMT is based on the use of so-called Confirmation Messages (CMs). These messages are periodically transmitted (i.e. at the *membership check times*) from each site in a group to the root node of their k-AMT. Those CMs allow the k-AMT root node to maintain the group membership view of the sites in its own k-AMT, and possibly to reconfigure that k-AMT topology. The CMs' transmission activity over the k-AMT is implemented by the Periodic Confirmation (PC) algorithm. This is a distributed algorithm that operates in two distinct phases, termed *Ascending Phase* and *Descending Phase*. In the *Ascending Phase*, CMs are transmitted from the surviving sites in a given group g to the root of g's k-AMT, i.e. from the leaf nodes of the k-AMT to its root node, via the k-AMT links. In the *Descending Phase*, the updated information about the current group membership view, termed the Final Confirmation Message (FCM), is calculated by the root and then multicast from the root itself to all the surviving members of g, i.e. to the leaf nodes of g's k-AMT, through the k-AMT links.

Our group-membership service satisfies the following five properties.

- *P1: Stability.* After a non faulty site s joins a group g, it remains joined to g until a failure or a leaving of s is detected.
- *P2: Mutual Agreement.* If two surviving sites s and r are joined to the same group g, then these two sites have the same view of the membership of that group.
- *P3: Reflexivity.* A site s, joined to a group g, is required to be a member of that group, that is s is included in the view that s itself has of g.
- *P4: Time Boundness on Join Delay.* There exists a time constant J such that, if a site s issues a request to join a group g at time T, and is surviving until time $T + J$, then s joins g by time $T + J$. Moreover, the group g is also joined by each other site r that requests to join g by time T, and is surviving until time $T + J$.
- *P5: Time Boundness on Failure Detection Delay.* There exists a time constant H such that if a site s, joined to a group g, fails (or leaves) at time T, then each other member r of g, surviving in the time interval $[T, T + H]$, is informed that s is no longer in g by the time $T + H$.

Satisfying the five properties above entails that the following "Correctness" property $C1$ holds:

C1: Correctness. If a site s joins a group g, to which another member r is also joined, then, if both s and r are surviving until time T, both s and r will observe the same view changes (both in the same order, and by the same time).

3 A Prototype Implementation

We have implemented a prototype k-AMT communication architecture using the
C programming language, and the development environment provided by the
SunOS 4.3 (BSD Unix) operating system. Our prototype implementation can be
thought of as structured in the following four principal levels of abstraction.

Level 0, the lower level, consists of the Internet IP Multicast datagram protocol [5]. This protocol implements the transmission of IP datagrams from a
source host to a destination *Host Group*, i.e. a set of hosts identified by a single
IP destination address. An IP Multicast datagram is delivered to the members
of its destination Host Group on a "best effort delivery" basis, as a conventional
unicast IP datagram. Thus, an IP Multicast datagram is not guaranteed to be
delivered to all the members of its destination Host Group; moreover, consecutive IP Multicast datagrams are not guaranteed to be delivered in the same order
as they were sent. The IP Multicast protocol interface, as available through the
SunOS 4.3 socket interface, has been used as the low level transport service in
the implementation of our architecture.

Level 1 incorporates the so-called *Host Synchronization Protocol* (HSP), and
Multicast Virtual Circuit Protocol (MVCP). HSP uses the IP multicast interface to implement a simple clock synchronization algorithm, described in [16], so
as to maintain clock synchronization among all the k-AMT nodes. MVCP uses
the IP Multicast interface to implement timely multicasting of real time data
streams over a *Multicast Virtual Circuit* (MVC). A MVC extends the conventional virtual circuit abstraction by allowing a message source node to establish,
maintain, and release a connection, consisting of multiple virtual channels, with
a group of destination nodes. Messages transmitted over an established MVC
will be delivered to the destination end-points of that MVC in the same order
as they were sent. The MVC abstraction has been implemented based on the IP
Multicast Host Group abstraction.

Level 2 uses the MVCP services to implement the *Augmented Tree Protocol* (ATP), that constructs the k-AMT, and the *Assemblage-Diffusion Protocol*
(ADP), that provides communications over the k-AMT.

Finally, *Level 3* uses the services provided by the ATP and the ADP to implement the Group-Membership Management Protocol (GMMP). This protocol
allows a site to initiate, join and leave a group, and to take part in the coordinated activity of that group. The implementation of the Level 1, 2, and 3
protocols of our architecture is int roduced below, in isolation.

Multicast Virtual Circuit Protocol MVCP implements an interface consisting of the following six primitive operations: *setMVC*, *releaseMVC*, *sendto*,
receivefrom, *addmemb* and *dropmemb*. These primitives allow one to establish,
maintain, release MVCs, and to connect to, and and disconnect from, already established MVCs. In particular, the *setMVC* primitive allows its invoker (namely,
a k-AMT node) to establish a MVC with a set of h distinct k-AMT destination
nodes. The implementation of this primitive transmits a MVC establishment request to those h destination nodes. This request includes information concerning
the maximum communication and processing delay bound d which can be tol-

erated in the communications with the *setMVC* invoker node. Each destination node that wishes to honor that request acknowledges it. Lack of acknowledgement from some destination node, during the MVC establishment phase, causes that *setMVC* raise an exception, termed MVCP *type 1* exception. This exception indicates the number $0 < w < h$ of unacknowledged requests, and identifies those destination nodes lacking the acknowledgement. It is the responsibility of the *setMVC* invoker to handle this exception appropriately, e.g. by either restricting the communications to the $h-w$ available destinations only, or releasing the MVC. A MVC can be released by its initiator by invoking the *releaseMVC* primitive.

When a MVC has been established between a source node and group of destination nodes, the multicasting of data streams from that source to those destinations can take place. The *sendto* primitive implements the multicasting of data streams. Normal termination of this primitive indicates that the data stream has been correctly multicast from the source node to the MVC destination endpoints. Abnormal termination of this primitive can be caused by transmission errors occurring on some, or all, the channels that form a MVC. In this case, an MVCP *type 2* exception is raised that allows the *sendto* invoker node to identify the failed channels within that MVC. The *receivefrom* primitive is invoked by a MVC destination node in order to receive multicast data streams. Normal termination of this primitive indicates that a data stream has been delivered within the predefined delay d. Abnormal termination, instead, indicates that a data stream has been received, and is to be discarded (e.g. that data stream might have been received with a delay greater than d).

Finally, the *addmemb* and *dropmemb* primitives allow their invokers to connect to, and disconnect from, an existing MVC, respectively. These two primitives have been implemented using the *JoinHostGoup* and *LeaveHostGroup* primitives provided by the IP Multicast Protocol interface.

Host Synchronization Protocol (HSP) This protocol maintains clock synchronization among the processors that implement the k-AMT structure. HSP uses the primitives provided by the IP Multicast interface for implementing the distributed clock synchronization algorithm described in [16]. This algorithm guarantees that the measurable difference between the readings of all the clocks of the non faulty processors is bounded by a known constant.

Augmented Tree Protocol The ATP constructs the k-AMT abstraction by implementing the k-AMTC Algorithm introduced earlier. The implementation of the ATP can be summarized as follows. After each node i has identified its M son nodes, and the k peer nodes to which it is to be connected through the spare links, it establishes (using the MVCP interface primitives) a MVC with its parent node, its son nodes, and its k peer nodes.

In addition, each time a new source or destination site requires to join an existing group, firstly the ATP searches for an existing *virtual* leaf node of the corresponding k-AMT. If a *virtual* node exists, the ATP assigns that node to the new site. Otherwise, the k-AMTC algorithm is to be executed to construct a new k-AMT. Instead, if a source or destination site (implemented by a corresponding leaf node in the k-AMT) wishes to leave an existing k-AMT, that node (depending on specific application requirements) can either be considered as a *virtual* node of the k-AMT, or the k-AMTC algorithm can be executed to construct a new k-AMT that does not include that node.

ATP terminates successfully if the construction of the k-AMT has completed successfully. Successful termination of the ATP entails that each node in the k-AMT is ready to execute the message diffusion phases embodied in the k-AMTS and PC algorithms. However, it is worth observing that, during the execution of the ATP, possible MVCP *type 1* exceptions can be raised. ATP intercepts those exceptions, and terminates indicating that the construction of the required k-AMT has failed. In particular, if at least one of these MVCP exceptions is such that $h - w = 0$, then ATP terminates with a failure exception (termed *k-AMT isolated node* exception) indicating that a node is completely isolated. Otherwise, it terminates with a failure exception (termed *k-AMT partial construction* exception) that indicates that the k-AMT construction has failed. (We will not discuss any specific strategy for handling ATP exceptions in this paper.)

Assemblage-Diffusion Protocol (ADP) This protocol supports the communications over a k-AMT by implementing the k-AMTS and the PC algorithms. It implements the two primitive operations *assemble* and *diffuse*. The *assemble* primitive implements the *Collect* phase of the k-AMTS algorithm, and the *Ascending* phase of the PC algorithm. The *diffuse* primitive, instead, implements the *Disseminate* phase of the k-AMTS algorithm, and the *Descending* phase of the PC algorithm.

The *assemble* primitive is invoked by the root node of the k-AMT. The implementation of this primitive causes that each k-AMT node i invoke the MVCP interface primitives in order both to read from its son and peer nodes, and to write to its parent and peer nodes (via the MVC previously established by the execution of the ATP). The termination of the *assemble* primitive is successful if the root node has constructed either the FSMDS, if the k-AMTS algorithm is executed, or the FCM, if the PC algorithm is executed.

The termination of the *assemble* primitive returns a *incomplete assemble* exception if at least one MVCP *type 2* exception has been intercepted by the ADP implementation. (If this occurs, in fact, a node of the communication architecture results to be isolated during the execution of either the *Collect* phase of the k-AMTS algorithm, or the *Ascending* phase of the PC algorithm).

However, whether or not an *incomplete assemble* exception has been raised, the execution of the *assemble* primitive cannot terminate successfully until the root node has constructed either the FSMDS, or the FCM, within the predefined time bound. Thus, a *failed assemble* exception is raised, only if the root of the k-AMT is not able to compose either the FSMDS or the FCM within the predefined time bound. The *failed assemble* exception indicates the identifiers of the failed sites whose data streams (or confirmation messages) have not reached the root.

The termination of the *diffuse* primitive is successful if either the FSMDS or the FCM are delivered to all the destination leaf nodes, within the predefined time bound. The implementation of this primitive can raise an *incomplete diffuse* exception if at least one nonleaf node in the k-AMT is detected to be isolated (i.e. an MVCP *type 2* exception has been raised). Finally, a *failed diffuse* exception can be raised only if at least one destination node has not received either the FSMDS or the FCM, within the predefined time bound (i.e. an MVCP *type 2* exception has been raised at one of the leaf nodes). Note that the exceptions raised by the ADP are propagated back to the root via the k-AMT links.

Group-Membership Management Protocol The GMMP provides the following four primitive operations *join*, *leave*, *initiate*, and *participate*. The *join* primitive can be invoked by a site that wishes to participate to the multimedia data stream exchange activity of an already existing group. The implementation of the *join* primitive causes the requesting site to establish a connection with the root node of the k-AMT that implements that group, and to transmit a join request message to that root node, through that connection. After receiving a join request from a new site, the root of the k-AMT constructs the updated k-AMT abstraction that includes that new site as a leaf node. This operation is carried out within a predefined time interval since the most recent *membership check time*.

The normal termination of the *join* primitive indicates that the invoking site has successfully joined the requested group, and can participate in the coordinated activity of exchanging CMDSs within that group. Abnormal termination of the *join* primitive returns a *join failure* exception, if an MVCP *type 1* exception has been raised in the connection establishment phase.

A site remains joined to a group, until either that site invokes a *leave* primitive, or it is affected by a fault that causes its disconnection from that group. The invocation of the *leave* primitive causes that the invoking site suspend the transmission of the periodic CM, scheduled at the first *membership check time* following that invocation. Thus, the root of the k-AMT will construct, after a fixed known time since the invocation of the *leave* primitive, an updated view that does not include the leaving site.

The *initiate* primitive can be invoked by a site that wishes to start up a new group. The implementation of this primitive causes the invoking site to transmit a "call for participation announcement" to a so-called publicity server [17]. This "announcement" includes a deadline by which the interested sites can confirm their willingness to participate to the new group.

The *participate* primitive allows those interested sites to respond to a "call for participation announcement". The implementation of this primitive causes that the invoking site transmit to the publicity server a "confirmation" message that requests to become a member of the announced group. This primitive terminates successfully if that message is delivered to the publicity server before the relative participation deadline expire. Otherwise the *participate* primitive terminates with a *failed participate* exception. Finally, it is worth noting that even if a site is unsuccessful in participating in the initiation of a new group, it can try to join that group later by invoking the *join* primitive.

After the publicity server has collected the confirmation messages from the interested sites, the root node of the k-AMT that will represent the new group can be elected. Consequently, the ATP interface primitives are invoked by the root node in order to construct the k-AMT communication structure.

4   Experimental Evaluation

The performance of the implementation of the Synchronization and Group communication protocols introduced above has been evaluated using a distributed infrastructure consisting of a 10 Mbs Ethernet interconnecting eight SPARCstation 5 workstations, running the (non real-time) SUN OS 4.3 operating system. The results of this evaluation are discussed below.

As pointed out in [11], the most important metrics that influence the users' perception of multimedia data are: the end-to-end latency of the communications between the participants of a given multimedia application, the number of data discontinuities (i.e. the number of media units belonging to a given multimedia data stream that are never played out), and, finally, the deviations from exact synchronization of audio and video streams. The end-to-end latency is defined as the elapsed time between the acquisition of a data unit at its transmitter, and the rendering of that unit at its receiver. This latency consists of: the *collection delay*, *the network delay*, and *the delivery delay*. The collection delay is the time needed for the transmitter to collect media units and prepare them for transmission (collection may originate, for example, directly from media recorders such as a video camera, or from a multimedia file server). The network delay consists of the amount of elapsed time from the delivery of a media unit to the transport layer interface of the transmitter, to the delivery of that unit to the transport layer interface of the receiver. Finally, the delivery delay is the time the receiver needs to process the media units, synchronize them, and play them out.

The end-to-end latency is to be considered one of the most revealing indicator of the performance of a multimedia system; studies in the field of interactive audio and video demonstrate that it should be kept below 300 milliseconds [8]. Also related to the users' perception of multimedia data streams are the discontinuities in the rendering of the data units that compose those streams. A discontinuity is said to occur when the data unit $n + 1$ is not displayed immediately after the data unit n [11]. This occurs typically when a data unit is lost, or is not delivered at the recei ver in time to be rendered when the playback of the previous unit has completed. Finally, the synchronization among (possibly multiple) audio and video streams is to be considered fundamental in order to ensure that humans perceive the correct temporal ordering of events during a multimedia application. Studies in this field have demonstrated that audio and video should never be more than 100 milliseconds out of synchronization to guarantee the so-called "lip synchronization".

In addition to end-to-end latency, number of data discontinuities, and deviation from exact synchronization, the critical DMMAs we consider require iso chronous rendering of multimedia data streams. Hence, the isochrony in rendering those streams, at a number of possibly geographically separated destination sites, turns out to be an additional parameter of primary importance, in our con text. In view of these observations, the experimental assessment of our protocols we have carried out measures the pe rformance of these protocols with respect to: end-to-end latency, number of discontinuities, deviations from synchronization, and isochronous rendering of data streams at different destinations.

To this end, we have developed three different series of experiments. Each series of experiments consisted of 10 runs of our test programs, executed over two different k-AMT structures (described below), so as to assess the effectiveness of our protocols over different communication topologies.

Essentially, in each run, a very large number of data streams were generated by the k-AMT source nodes, transmitted to the k-AMT root through the k-AMT links, integrated to form CMSDSs (by the synchronizer nodes), and, eventually, FSMDSs, by the root node. The FSMDSs were then transmitted from the root to the destination nodes, and rendered by those nodes. In each experiment, we observed the behavior of our transport and synchronization protocols in a time interval of a fixed length, and measured the total number of FSMDSs that were isochronously rendered at the scheduled play back time by all the destination nodes, out of the total number of data streams that were generated by the source nodes.

In each series of experiments we have assumed a particular value of the *end-to-end maximum latency* D that could be tolerated in the communications between the k-AMT source and destination nodes. Thus, given D, a FSMDS consisting of multimedia data units originated at time O, that could not be delivered to its k-AMT destination nodes by the prescheduled playback time $F = O + D$, was considered affected by an unrecoverable timing fault, and hence discarded.

The first series of experiments was carried out assuming a 500 milliseconds end-to-end maximum latency, and a 75 milliseconds delay d (as defined in Assumption $A3$ in Section 2). The second series of experiments assumed a 300 milliseconds end-to-end maximum latency, and a 50 milliseconds delay d. Finally, the third series of experiments assumed a 150 milliseconds end-to-end maximum latency, and a 30 milliseconds delay d. Moreover, in order to implement the proposed Group Membership Management Protocol, every k-AMT leaf node in each experiment transmitted a Confirmation Message (consisting of eight bytes) at a periodic rate of 33 milliseconds; the relative group membership was calculated by the k-AMT root node, according to the group management policy described in [17], at a rate equal to the maximum end-to-end latency associated to each series of experiments.

As mentioned above, two different k-AMTs were used in each series of experiments. 50% of the experiments were carried out over a k-AMT of depth 3, that included 4 leaf nodes in total, and was characterized by the parameters $M = 2$, and $k = 1$. Thus, the four k-AMT leaf nodes were grouped in two clusters, consisting of two leaf nodes each. Moreover, 1 additional link at each k-AMT leaf node was used for transmitting replicas of the data streams. The scenario within which the multimedia data stream exchange occurred in this first k-AMT structure was as follows. Two leaf nodes of the k-AMT, sharing a parent node, were acting as sources of data streams; instead, the other two leaf nodes were acting as data stream destinations (in essence, the source nodes were simulating a video frame source and an audio frame source, respectively; the destination nodes were simulating the corresponding output devices).

The second k-AMT structure we used was characterized by 8 leaf nodes, depth 4, $M = 2$, and $k = 2$, yielding four clusters of two k-AMT leaves each, and two additional links per k-AMT node. The scenario within which the multimedia data stream exchange occurred was the following. Three leaf nodes of the k-AMT were acting as data stream sources (namely, two video frame sources, and one audio frame source). Two out of these three source nodes shared a grandparent node in the k-AMT; the third source node was situated in a different subtree, instead. Yet again, the remaining five k-AMT leaf nodes acted as data stream destinations.

Table 1. Throughput Statistics - k-AMT with 4 leaves and k=1 ($D = 500$ ms, $d = 75$ ms).

experiments	generated	displayed	lost	lost percentage
experiment 1	10,000	9,908	92	0.92 %
experiment 2	10,000	9,918	82	0.82 %
experiment 3	10,000	9,929	71	0.71 %
experiment 4	16,000	15,842	158	0.99 %
experiment 5	16,000	15,866	134	0.84 %

Each experiment was carried out when the underlying Ethernet was lightly loaded. In addition, each k-AMT node (either source, or destination, or synchronizer) was implemented as a set of communicating processes running in one of the eight Sun SPARC 5 workstations, keeping each different k-AMT leaf node in a separate workstation. Finally, no specific hardware was used for the acquisition and the display of digital video and audio. Instead, we simulated the activities of both digitization and compression at the source nodes, and of decompression and display at the destination nodes. To this end, we assumed the use of color video frames (at a 240 x 256 resolution) compressed in approximately 60 to 64 kilobits, combined with audio frames of 4 kilobits. For the purposes of this simulation, we also assumed that those activities of continuous acquisition and display of the video frames required an average period of 33 milliseconds.

Tables 1, 2, 3, 4, 5, and 6 summarize the results of our experimentation. Each of those Tables is relative to one of the three values of the end-to-end maximum latency introduced above. For each experiment these tables report: i) the total number of data streams that were generated by the source nodes during the time interval in which the experiment was carried out, ii) the total number of FSMDSs that were isochronously played out by all the destination nodes at the same scheduled play out time, iii) the total number of FSMDSs that were either not played out isochronously, or never played out at all by the set of all the destination nodes, and finally, iv) the percentage of "lost" FSMDs. Tables 1, 2, and 3 are relative to the five experiments carried out over our first k-AMT structure, introduced above; instead, Tables 4, 5, and 6 describe the five experiments developed over the second k-AMT structure.

Table 2. Throughput Statistics - k-AMT with 4 leaves and k=1 ($D = 300$ ms, $d = 50$ ms).

experiments	generated	displayed	lost	lost percentage
experiment 6	10,000	9,848	152	1.52 %
experiment 7	10,000	9,872	128	1.28 %
experiment 8	10,000	9,781	219	2.19 %
experiment 9	16,000	15,676	324	2.02 %
experiment 10	16,000	15,548	452	2.82 %

As previously pointed out, the end-to-end latency in interactive audio applications should not exceed 300 milliseconds. In contrast, in non interactive video applications, a maximum delay of 1000 milliseconds can be tolerated [8]. Thus, the results summarized in Tables 1, 2, 4, and 5 show that our reliable transport mechanisms are extremely effective. In fact, Tables 1 and 4 show that, if a 500 milliseconds end-to-end maximum latency is chosen, then only a low average percentage of FSMDSs, (ranging from 0.9% to 2.5%, depending on the specific k-AMT architecture) was either not played out isochronously, or never played out by the destination nodes. Moreover, we observed that approximately the 90% of the total number of "lost" FSMDSs was either effectively lost, or not delivered in time for rendering, *at all* the different destinations. In other words, these experiments confirmed that our communication mechanisms meet satisfactorily the isochronous rendering requirement. Besides, almost no discontinuities were observed, and the audio and video streams were in perfect synchronization.

Table 3. Throughput Statistics - k-AMT with 4 leaves and k=1 ($D = 150$ ms, $d = 30$ ms).

experiments	generated	displayed	lost	lost percentage
experiment 11	interrupted	interrupted	interrupted	interrupted
experiment 12	10,000	8,522	1,478	14.78 %
experiment 13	interrupted	interrupted	interrupted	interrupted
experiment 14	16,000	13,612	2,388	14.93 %
experiment 15	16,000	12,876	3,124	19.52 %

Qualitatively, the results obtained when the end-to-end maximum latency was set to 300 milliseconds were also encouraging. In fact, only an average percentage of FSMDSs ranging from 2% to 4% (yet again, depending on the specific k-AMT architecture) was either not played out isochronously, or never played out at all, and the experienced video and audio discontinuities were sufficiently separate in time not to result noticeable. Moreover, the 88% of the lost FSMDSs were effectively lost *at all* the destination nodes.

Table 4. Throughput Statistics - k-AMT with 8 leaves and k=2 ($D = 500$ ms, $d = 75$ ms).

experiments	generated	displayed	lost	lost percentage
experiment 16	10,000	9,982	198	1.98 %
experiment 17	10,000	9,798	202	2.02 %
experiment 18	10,000	9,818	182	1.82 %
experiment 19	16,000	15,496	504	3.15 %
experiment 20	16,000	15,476	524	3.27 %

In contrast, Tables 3 and 6 show that, in our implementation, the constraint of 150 milliseconds end-to-end maximum latency causes that the synchronization between multiple audio and video data streams become very inaccurate. In fact, with this latency value, a large number of FSMDSs (ranging from 16.5% to 18%) were not delivered in time for isochronous rendering, at the k-AMT destination nodes. Moreover, out of the ten experiments we carried out with this particular latency value, four of them failed, and were interrupted as a very high rate of packet loss was experienced at the system buffers of both the k-AMT synchronizer and destination nodes. That packet loss was likely due to the fact that the reduction of both the end-to-end maximum latency D, and the delay d, caused the SUN OS 4.3 operating system to operate at an unsustainable rate.

Table 5. Throughput Statistics - k-AMT with 8 leaves and k=2 ($D = 300$ ms, $d = 50$ ms).

experiments	generated	displayed	lost	lost percentage
experiment 21	10,000	9,652	348	3.48 %
experiment 22	10,000	9,674	326	3.26 %
experiment 23	10,000	9,701	299	2.99 %
experiment 24	16,000	15,194	806	5.03 %
experiment 25	16,000	15,288	712	4.45 %

To conclude this Section, it is worth pointing out that, owing to the limitations imposed by our hardware and software infrastructure, we were able to carry out our experiments with two k-AMT structures composed of a relatively small number of source and destination nodes. However, the communication mechanisms we designed resulted to be scalable with the number of k-AMT source and destination nodes which were used in our experiments. In fact, a comparison between the results reported in Tables 1 and 2, and those reported in Tables 4 and 5, demonstrate that there are not notable differences between the throughput statistics that were obtained using the two different k-AMT architectures.

Table 6. Throughput Statistics - k-AMT with 8 leaves and k=2 ($D = 150$ ms, $d = 30$ ms).

experiments	generated	displayed	lost	lost percentage
experiment 26	interrupted	interrupted	interrupted	interrupted
experiment 27	10,000	8,104	1,896	18.96 %
experiment 28	10,000	8,354	1,646	16.46 %
experiment 29	interrupted	interrupted	interrupted	interrupted
experiment 30	16,000	13,102	2,898	18.11 %

5 Related Work

Relevant results have been achieved in a number of problem areas concerning the design of distributed multimedia systems; however, there is relatively little work on the problem of supporting critical DMMAs that require an isochronous rendering of real time data, and may need recovery from the loss of video and audio.

For example, the ST family of protocols (namely the ST-II, ST2+ protocols) [6] provide connection oriented, multicast based, real-time mechanisms for receiver-initiated communications; these mechanisms allow receivers to join streams, specify their QOS requirements, and initiate stream establishment and resource reservation. However, both ST-II and ST2+ do not provide explicit support for group communications. Thus, the group abstraction must be supported by higher level protocols; in addition, recovery from the loss of video and audio is outside the scope of these protocols. Finally, no support is provided for guaranteeing the isochronous rendering of multicast multimedia data at geographically separated destinations.

The approach presented by Jeffay et al. in [11] has been proposed and validated principally for point-to-point real time communications. In [11], a Forward Error Correction method is proposed that ameliorates the effects of audio frame losses, and ignores recovery from video frame losses. In particular, audio frames are transmitted multiple times over the same audio channel. Following that policy, the authors report that approximately the 80% of the lost audio frames can be recovered (at the cost of a 10% additional bandwidth) by retransmitting each audio frame twice.

In the Tenet Protocol Suite I [1], fault-handling and recovery mechanisms are proposed for simplex, unicast channels with performance guarantees. Techniques have been devised that reroute connections so as to bypass failed nodes and links, while maintaining the negotiated performance guarantees. Essentially, when a node or a link fail, the system attempts to recover all the different channels that traverse that failed component. However, owing to the unicast nature of the communications in Suite I, no multicast group information is available that can be used to set up the recovery process. This results in parallel and separate attempts to recover the interrupted channels, yielding a very low rate of successfully rerouted connections.

In contrast, in the Tenet Protocol Suite II [1], these failure-recovery techniques are improved by means of a set of new protocols that support multi-party, real time communications. The notion of a real time multicast group (termed *Target Set*) is introduced; this is a real-time analog of the IP Host Group abstraction, (i.e. the list of all the the destinations interested in "listening" to a common session). The Target Set abstraction implements the decoupling between the senders and the receivers of a given DMMA, and provides support for the management of the connections between them. In addition, the Tenet Protocol Suite II provides the so-called *Sharing Group* abstraction, that allows the implementation of some form of resource sharing among those network clients whose resource requests partially overlap. Thus, policies have been proposed for storing appropriate *state* information concerning both the Target Sets and the Sharing Groups in the network components, as well as mechanisms for both reestablishing connectivity of failed channels, and permitting new connections [10].

The above mentioned policies have been designed based on the so-called *fate-sharing* principle [10]. This principle states that it is acceptable to lose the state information associated with an application component, as long as that component is lost as well. This principle has been exploited by the designers of Tenet Protocol Suite II in order to make decisions about the nodes in the network where the appropriate Target Sets and Sharing Groups state information should be placed. For example, critical information associated with the establishment of a given channel is maintained at the channel source node, while the state information concerning a given Target Set is maintained at each destination node. Finally, *Backward Error Recovery* based mechanisms are implemented in the Tenet Protocol Suite II. These mechanisms use the state information distributed across the network in order to overcome the negative effects that may result from failures of network components. In particular, firstly, possible component failures are detected, using *time-out* or *monitoring* based techniques; secondly, based on the available state information, failed multicast trees are repaired or rebuilt, alternative routes computed, failed connections reestablished, and network resources reallocated, in the face of failures that can make part of the network inaccessible. However, backward error recovery based policies, or, in general, *automatic repeat request* (ARQ) schemes which retransmit corrupted packets according to receiver-generated feedback, may result impractical in a time critical multimedia environment, since the overhead caused by the failure detection and repair activities could be unacceptable in most applications. Besides, since ARQ schemes introduce additional delay and jitter to a media stream, additional buffering would be required at the receiver to smooth out its impact.

In alternative to ARQ schemes, it is possible to avoid the use of feedback and retransmissions to control error rates by employing error concealment techniques (e.g. computing a approximate value for missing pieces of the data through interpolation from neighboring values), or using *Forward Error Correction* (FEC) techniques. Planning in advance for error control may typically involve embedding redundant information in the transmitted streams, making packets self-contained, or transmitting critical packets more than once [2,18].

Following these ideas, the Tenet Protocol Suite II designers suggest to employ some *Forward Error Correction* (FEC) technique in conjunction with a multiple-channel reservation scheme for sending multiple redundant copies of the data to the set of destinations. Unfortunately, to the best of our knowledge, not enough details concerning the above mentioned FEC based policy have been made available by the Tenet Suite II designers for assessing its effectiveness. Finally, no support is provided in the Tenet Suite II protocols for the isochronous rendering of real time multimedia data at different destinations.

Another interesting FEC based policy is employed in the INRIA audio tool to recover from loss of audio packets [2]. That tool adjusts the audio packet send rate to the current network conditions, adds redundant information to each packet (under the form of highly compressed versions of a number of previous packets) when the loss rate surpasses a certain threshold, and establishes a feedback channel to control the send rate and the redundant information. The complete process is controlled by an open feedback loop that selects among different available compression schemes, and determines the amount of redundancy needed. Thus, for example, if the network load and the packet loss rate are high, the amount of redundant information carried in each packet is increased by adding to each packet the compressed version of the previous two to four packets. Every 5 seconds, the receiver returns quality of service reports to the sender in order to regulate and adapt the quantity of redundant information being sent.

With our approach to fault tolerance, the experimentation that we have carried out (described in the previous Section 3) has empirically demonstrated that our protocols ensure that: i) no more than a low percentage (from 0.9% to 4%) of audio and video frames are not isochronously displayed at all the destinations of a given DMMA, and ii) the isochronous rendering of audio-video frames can be obtained assuming an acceptable end-to-end latency (i.e. within the range of 300 to 500 milliseconds), even using a poor computing and communication infrastructure.

The provision of support for recovering from the loss of video/audio frames is not the only important requirement to meet in the design of multimedia protocols; thus, we devote the remainder of this Section to discussing further important differences between the general approach we propose to the design of real-time communication support for multimedia applications, and other relevant approaches. To this end, we compare below our approach with those emerging from the *Receiver-initiated Stream Protocol Version II* (Receiver-initiated ST II, for short) proposed in [6], the transport and display mechanism for multimedia conferencing presented by Jeffay *et al.* in [11], and the media mixing strategy proposed by Rangan *et al.* in [20]. In particular, we compare and evaluate these approaches with reference to the following five features:

- communication model;
- end-to-end latency;
- jitter control mechanisms;
- group-membership management mechanisms, and relative additional overheads, and
- satisfiability of the IR requirement.

Communication model. We have proposed a synchronization strategy for DMMAs that support many-to-many real time communications. The proposal by Receiver-initiated ST II, and that by Rangan *et al.* have been explicitly designed and experimented to support the one-to-many and many-to-many real time communication models, respectively. Instead, the approach proposed by Jeffay *et al.* has been mainly tested and validated for a point-to-point real time communications.

End-to-end latency. Studies in the field of interactive audio show that the end-to-end latency should range from 100 to 300 milliseconds. Hierarchical synchronization architectures, such as those proposed by Rangan *et al.*, and us, may introduce additional transport delays, owing to the height of the hierarchy. However, both the the bandwidth required for message reception and transmission at each single node of the communication infrastructure, and the computational cost of the synchronization, are reduced. In addition, experimental measures, such as those presented in [20], and our analysis of Section 3.3.3, show that, in several realistic cases, the end-to-end latency can be kept below 300 milliseconds.

Jitter control mechanism. In our approach, similar to that used in the Receiver-initiated ST II, we assume that is possible to bound the delay jitter below a small upper bound by exploiting, for example, the resource reservation based scheme for delay jitter control proposed by Ferrari [7,8]. In contrast, both the proposals by Jeffay *et al.* and Rangan *et al.* approach the design of real-time communication mechanisms without using resource reservation. In principle, this approach cannot provide guaranteed and predictable QOS. In particular, Jeffay *et al.* propose a "best effort" delivery of digital audio and video protocol that provides mechanisms that dynamically adapt the reception and transmission frame rate to the bandwidth available in the network.

Group management mechanisms. Both Jeffay *et al.* and Rangan *et al.* proposals do not explicitly provide support for group management. Instead, in the Receiver-initiated ST II approach, mechanisms are provided for receiver-initiated communications that allow receivers to join streams, specify their QOS, initiate stream establishment and resource reservation. The authors of the Receiver-initiated ST II have shown that there is a trade off between the scalability of their protocol and the protocol functions. Maximum scalability can be obtained if the origin of the multicast tree (i.e. the source of the DMMA) is unaware of the receivers. In this case, however, some global function cannot be executed by the origin. However, if the origin is aware of all the receivers, it has more control, may execute all the expected global functions but, consequently, the amount of control messages increases. In addition, in the Receiver-initiated ST II protocol, there is not attempt to cope with possible communication faults while executing the group management. In contrast, in our approach, multiple sources and receivers are allowed to initiate the operations for joining and leaving an existing DMMA. The k-AMT root maintains a full control on the group membership management. In addition, confirmation messages flow periodically from the sources and destinations to the k-AMT root, and from the root back to the DMMA sources and destinations, providing robustness of our group membership protocol, in spite of communication faults. Yet again, our analysis in Section 4.4.1 has shown that, fixing the available bandwidth, this periodical flow of control messages causes a "periodical" additional end-to-end latency in the range from 10% to 60%, depending on the particular k-AMT communication architecture.

IR requirement. In the "best effort" approach, proposed by Jeffay *et al.*, the audio and video streams have been evaluated never to be more than 100 milliseconds out of synchronization. The mixing algorithm proposed by Rangan *et al.* provides conditions to be met in order to obtain isochrony. Finally, our approach allows the DMMA designer to meet the IR requirement.

6   Conclusions

In this paper we have introduced both the general design and the prototype implementation of a communication architecture developed to support critical DMMAs. We have shown that this architecture can meet effectively such DM-MAs requirements as those for synchronization and isochronous rendering of multimedia data streams, group management and communications, scalability and dependability. The performance measures of the prototype implementation we have developed show the adequacy of a redundancy based approach to provide critical DMMAs with reliable communications. Future design issues that we will investigate include: the design of k-AMT reconfiguration strategies that deal with failures of the k-AMT root node, the design of QoS negotiation services, and that of appropriate security mechanisms for critical DMMAs.

References

1. A. Banerjea, D. Ferrari, B.A. Mah, M. Moran, D.C. Verma, H. Zhang. *The Tenet Real Time Protocol Suite: Design, Implementation and Experiences*, IEEE/ACM Transactions on Networking, 1996, Vol.4 N. 1, 1-10.

2. J. Bolot, A. Vega Garcia, *"The Case for FEC-based Error Control for Packet Audio in the Internet"*, ACM Multimedia Systems, to appear.
3. G. Coulson, F. Garcia, D. Hutchison, D. Shepherd, *Meeting the Real-Time Synchronization Requirements of Multimedia in Open Distributed Processing*, Distrib. Syst. Eng. Vol. 1, 1994, 135-144.
4. F. Cristian, H. Aghili, R. Strong, D. Dolev, *Atomic Broadcast: from Simple Diffusion to Byzantine Agreement*, Information and Computation Vol. 118, 1995, 158-179
5. S. Deering, *Host Extension for IP Multicasting*, RFC N. 1112 (1992).
6. L. Delgrossi, R.G. Herrtwich, F.O. Hoffmann, S. Schaller, *Receiver-Initiated Communication with ST-II*, ACM Multimedia Systems, Vol. 2, N. 4, 1994, 141-149.
7. D. Ferrari, D. C. Verma, *A Scheme for Real-Time Channel Establishment in Wide Area Networks*, IEEE Journal on Selected Areas in Communications, SAC-8, 1990, 368 - 379.
8. D. Ferrari, *Design and Application of a Delay Jitter Control Scheme for Packet-switching Internetworks*, in Network and Operating System Support for Digital Audio and Video, R.G. Herrtwich (Ed.), LNCS 614, Springer-Verlag, 1992, 72 - 83.
9. I. Getting, *The Global Positioning System*, IEEE Spectrum, December 1993, 36-47.
10. A. Gupta, K. Rothermel (1995) *Fault Handling for Multi-party Real Time Communication*, TR-95-059, International Computer Science Institute, Berkeley (CA), October 1995.
11. K. Jeffay, D. L. Stone, F. Donelson Smith, *Transport and Display Mechanims for Multimedia Conferencing across Packet-Switched Networks*, Computer Networks and ISDN Systems, Vol. 26, N. 10, 1994, 1281 - 1304.
12. T. A. Joseph, K. P. Birman, *Reliable Broadcast Protocols*, in **An Advance Course on Distributed Systems**, S. J. Mullender (Ed.), Addison Wesley Publishing Co., 1989, 313 - 338.
13. H. Kopetz, G. Grunsteidl, J. Reisenger, *Fault-Tolerant Membership Service in a Synchronous Distributed Real-Time System*, Proc. Int. Conf. on Dependable Computing for Critical Applications, Santa Barbara (CA), 1989, 167 - 174.
14. P. M. Melliar-Smith, L. E. Moser, V. Agrawala, *Broadcast Protocols for Distributed Systems*, IEEE Trans. on Parallel and Distributed Systems, Vol. 1, N. 1, 1990, 17 - 25.
15. P.G. Neumann, *On Hierarchical Design of Computer Systems for Critical Applications*, IEEE Trans. on Software Engineering, Vol. SE-12, N. 9, 1986, 905 - 920.
16. F. Panzieri, S.K. Shrivastava, *The Design of a Reliable Remote Procedure Call Mechanism* IEEE Transactions on Computers, Vol. C-31, N. 7, 1992, 692-697.
17. F. Panzieri, M. Roccetti, *Synchronization Support and Group-Membership Services for Reliable Distributed Multimedia Applications*, ACM Multimedia Systems, Vol.5, N. 1, 1997, 1-22.
18. M. Roccetti, et al. *Design and Experimental Evaluation of an Adaptive Playout Delay Control Mechanism for Packetized Audio for use over the Internet*, Multimedia Tools and Applications, Kluwer Academic Publishers, to appear.
19. M. Satyanarayanan, *The Influence of Scale on Distributed File System Design*, IEEE Trans. on Software Engineering, Vol. 18, N. 1, 1992, 1 - 8.
20. P. Venkat Rangan, H. M. Vin, S. Ramanathan, *Communication Architectures and Algorithms for Media Mixing in Multimedia Conferences*, IEEE/ACM Trans. on Networking, Vol. 1, N. 1, 1993, 20 - 30.
21. A. Vogel, B. Kerherve, G. Von Bochmann, *Distributed Multimedia and QOS: A Survey*, IEEE Multimedia, Vol. 2, N. 2, 1995, 10-19.

Programming Partition-Aware Network Applications*

Özalp Babaoğlu[1], Alberto Bartoli[2], and Gianluca Dini[3]

[1] Università di Bologna, Mura Anteo Zamboni 7, I-40127 Bologna (Italy)
Babaoglu@CS.UniBO.IT
[2] Università di Trieste, Via Valerio 10, I-34100 Trieste (Italy)
bartolia@univ.trieste.it
[3] Università di Pisa, Via Diotisalvi 2, I-56125 Pisa (Italy)
dini@iet.unipi.it

Abstract. We consider the problem of developing reliable applications to be deployed in partitionable asynchronous distributed systems. What makes this task difficult is guaranteeing the consistency of shared state despite asynchrony, failures and recoveries, including the formation and merging of partitions. While view synchrony within process groups is a powerful paradigm that can significantly simplify reasoning about asynchrony and failures, it is insufficient for coping with recoveries and merging of partitions after repairs. We first give an abstract characterization for shared state management in partitionable asynchronous distributed systems and then show how views can be enriched to convey structural and historical information relevant to the group's activity. The resulting paradigm, called *enriched view synchrony*, can be implemented efficiently and leads to a simple programming methodology for solving shared state management in the presence of partitions.

1 Introduction

Distributed computing is rapidly becoming the principal paradigm for providing critical services in everyday life and the deployment of future networking technologies will only accelerate this trend. Large geographic extent due to increased globalization and unpredictability of loads imposed by users contribute towards an *asynchronous* characterization for these systems in the sense that communication delays and relative computing speeds cannot be bounded with certainty. Banking, finance, electronic commerce, medical systems, telecommunications, industrial process control and collaborative work are just some of the many sectors that will increasingly rely on large-scale asynchronous distributed systems as their computing infrastructure. Distributed applications to be deployed in such systems are difficult to reason about and to develop. The principal difficulty stems from the fact that in asynchronous distributed systems subject to

---

* Portions reprinted, with permission, from *IEEE Transactions on Computers 46:6*, pp. 642–658, June 1997.

S. Krakowiak, S.K. Shrivastava (Eds.): Distributed Systems, LNCS 1752, pp. 182–212, 2000.
© Springer-Verlag Berlin Heidelberg 2000

failures, inability to communicate cannot be attributed to its real cause — the destination may have crashed, it may be overloaded and thus slow, the communication path may have been disconnected or it may be experiencing long delays [10].

An abstraction that can simplify both reasoning about and implementation of distributed applications is *view synchrony*[1] in the context of process groups [16,6,13] (see also Chapter 3). Two aspects of view synchrony enable it to hide most of the complexities due to failures and asynchrony. On the one hand, it cleanly describes failures and recoveries in the form of changes of the group *view* that are agreed upon by all connected members of the group. On the other hand, view synchrony provides guarantees about the set of messages delivered globally as a function of the view changes that a process observes locally. As such, it permits components of a group to reason globally based solely on local information.

Partitions that may result from communication failures are an insidious characteristic of large-scale distributed systems. Informally, we define a *partitionable system* as one admitting multiple views of the same group to exist concurrently. In such systems, membership of a group may change dynamically not only due to individual process failures and recoveries, but also due to subsets of correct processes becoming disconnected and later re-connecting. This is in contrast to the *primary-partition group membership* model where there can be at most one view of the group active at any time [5,19]. A *partitionable group membership* service allows each collection of mutually-communicating processes to install their own view of the group and lets the application itself decide if it can make progress.

In this chapter we consider programming reliable applications in partitionable asynchronous distributed systems based on process groups and view synchrony. Group members have to maintain state information that is distributed and/or replicated among them. Although view synchrony can be a great aid towards guaranteeing the consistency of this information across failures, recoveries, disconnections and reconnections, many technical problems remain that need to be solved by the application programmer. We first give a novel characterization of these *shared state* problems and we show that view synchrony alone gives little support to cope with them. Thus, most of the burden in solving shared state problems falls on the application programmer and detracts from the simplicity and elegance of view synchrony. We then propose an extension to the basic model by including structural and historical information within views in the form of *subviews* and *subview sets* that are manipulated by processes to reflect the application state and are preserved automatically across view changes by the system. Our extension is called *enriched view synchrony* and offers a simple programming methodology for programming reliable services in parti-

---

[1] The abstraction was first introduced in the Isis system where it is known as *virtual synchrony* [5]. We prefer not to use this term since it is associated with the primary-partition model of group membership that excludes the possibility of progress in multiple concurrent partitions.

tionable asynchronous systems. We illustrate this methodology through detailed examples.

2   System Model and View Synchrony

The system is a collection of processes executing at potentially remote sites that communicate through a network. As a result of failures, processes may crash or the communication network may partition. Crashes cause processes to halt prematurely. Crashed processes may rejoin the computation after recovery and partitions may merge after repairs. We consider an *asynchronous* system in that it is not possible to place bounds on communication delays or relative speeds of processes. We assume that the system being considered is such that it admits a *failure detector* with weak properties that have been shown to be sufficient to solve view synchrony (see Chapter 3).

View synchrony implements the notion of a *process group* and provides *reliable multicast* as the basic communication primitive [16,6,13]. Processes that want to participate in a common computation *join* a named group. They terminate their participation by *leaving* the group. While a member of the group, processes communicate with each other through reliable multicasts. View synchrony includes a membership service that provides consistent information in the form of *views* regarding the components of the group that are currently up and that can mutually communicate. View synchrony abstracts away process and communication failures, both real and due to false suspicions, by delivering to group members *view change* events that are collectively agreed upon.

With the events $mcast(m)$, $dlvr(m)$ and $vchg(v)$ we denote the multicast of message m, delivery of message m and view change to v, respectively. At each process, view synchrony installs new views through $vchg(v)$ events that define a totally-ordered sequence. The last view to be installed in this sequence at a process is called the *current view* of the process. Events are said to *occur in the view* that happens to be current at the time. Views v and w are called *consecutive* if there exists some process common to both views for which w is the next view to be installed after v. View w is called a *successor* of v if there exists a sequence of views leading from v to w such that each adjacent pair of the sequence are consecutive views. It is possible for two views installed at two different processes to be incomparable with respect to the successor relation, in which case they are called *concurrent*. Concurrent views allow us to model diverging views of the group membership due to partitions.

Our discussion is based on the formal specification for view synchrony given by Babaoğlu et al. in Chapter 3 as a set of properties on view installations and message deliveries. The essence of view synchrony can be captured informally by the following property that states how the group membership and reliable multicast services interact:

All processes that survive from view v into the same consecutive view w must have delivered the same set of messages in view v.

With respect to the relative order in which messages are delivered between two consecutive views, we assume that messages multicast by the same process are delivered, if at all, in the order in which they were sent. As it turns out, message ordering guarantees stronger than this FIFO property may only help in *solving* but not *preventing* shared state problems.

The membership service of Chapter 3 guarantees the following *View Coherency* property:

Property (GM3). *(i) If a correct process p installs view v, then either all processes that compose this view also install v, or p eventually installs an immediate successor to v. (ii) If two processes p and q initially install the same view v and p later on installs an immediate successor to v, then eventually either q also installs an immediate successor to v, or q crashes. (iii) When process p installs a view w as the immediate successor to view v, all processes that survive from view v to w along with p have previously installed v.*

We shall replace this property with the following, stronger one:

Property (GM3'). *(i) If a correct process p installs view v containing some process q, then either q installs v or q crashes. (ii) and (iii) are the same as in GM3 above.*

In other words, property GM3' excludes the possibility of views that are not installed by all of their (correct) members, which implies that any pair of concurrent views have empty intersection. The resulting semantics of the membership service is called *strong partial* [16]. We assume this semantics because it simplifies our discussion and examples. However, we shall see that our results, including the enriched view synchrony programming paradigm, remain valid even under the original weaker Property GM3. As an aside, membership services with strong partial semantics are considered undesirable since it is known that they cannot have non-blocking implementations [3].

3   The Shared State Problem

An application is a distributed computation performed by a group of processes that run on top of view synchrony. Without loss of generality, we consider applications that are structured as a single group. The involvement of a process in the application begins when it joins the corresponding group and ends when it leaves the group through the view synchrony primitives *join*() and *leave*(), respectively.Each process has a local state, part of which may be permanent and survive across crashes.

We consider the class of applications that implement *objects*. According to the object-oriented paradigm, an object is an instance of an abstract data type, encapsulating some internal state and exporting to its clients an interface defined through a set of *external operations*. Informally, semantics of an abstract data type may be defined through invariants over the internal state. Thus, the group-based implementation of an object of a certain type can be seen as simulating the logical internal state through a global state distributed over the group members. This in turn requires correct and coordinated interaction among the group members such that invariants remain valid over the global state. How one actually determines the invariants for an abstract data type and implements the related interactions that satisfy them are beyond the scope of this chapter. We assume that these tasks have already been achieved for a group-based implementation of the object with static membership. In other words, if the group does not experience any view changes, then the external operations transform the global state such that the invariants continue to be satisfied.

What complicates the programming task is the possibility of view changes during external operations due to events such as failures, recoveries, joins and leaves. We concentrate on this aspect of the programming job . Clearly, for the object to remain correct despite view changes during its operations, the implementation has to restore the truth of invariants over the global state whenever they are violated. To achieve this, the application relies on a set of *internal operations* that are visible only to the object implementor and are not part of the external interface.

Whether a group member may perform external operations or has to perform internal operations depends, in general, on its local state, its current view composition and the specific application considered. We model these factors by means of *executing modes* of group members. At any time, a group member can be in one of three modes: it is said to be in the NORMAL mode (*N-mode* for brevity) when it can execute all external operations; it is said to be in REDUCED mode (*R-mode*) when it can perform only a (possibly empty) subset of the external operations; finally, the group member is said to be executing in the in the SETTLING mode (*S-mode*) when it has to check the global state, and, if necessary, to reconstruct a new one where the invariants are satisfied by executing the proper internal operations.

We call the reconciliation that is necessary when group members are in *S-mode* the *shared state problem*. We may classify instances of this problem in three categories, that we call *state transfer*, *state creation* and *state merging*. For simplicity, we shall introduce these categories informally, by means of the following examples. A more rigorous treatment of this topic can be found in [4], along with an analysis of the relationship between these issues and existing implementations of view synchrony.

Consider a group of processes that implements files with the two external operations *read* and *write*. For increased availability and reduced latency, the file is partially or fully replicated within the group. Informally, the correctness criteria for this object could be stated as follows: With respect to write operations, the replicated object should behave exactly as if there were only one copy of the file; with respect to read operations, it is acceptable to return any available data, even though it may be stale (missing some of the more recent writes). One possible implementation of this object is to associate with each replica of the file a vote and to define a quorum as a collection of votes that can be obtained in at most one concurrent view.

Suppose that, initially, all group members belong to the same view v_1. In this case, processes are clearly in *N-mode*, because they can perform both read and write operations. Suppose now that v_1 splits in two concurrent views v_2 and v_3 such that only the latter defines a quorum. View v_2 is not conducive to satisfying write operations without the risk of violating some invariant. Therefore, members of v_2 are in *R-mode* as they can perform only a subset of the external operations, that is, the read operation. Suppose, finally, that v_2 and v_3 merge into view v_4 that defines a quorum. This view restores the conditions related to connectivity for performing all of the external operations. However, processes that were in v_2 cannot begin performing external operations soon because their replica could not reflect all updates applied to the file. Processes in v_4 are thus *S-mode* and must execute a proper internal operation. In particular, each process that was in v_2 must compare its local state with the local state of any process that was in v_3 and, possibly, modify it as a consequence of that comparison. We call *state transfer* this particular instance of the shared state problem.

Another significant scenario of the above application is when the quorum view v_3 does not merge with v_2 immediately, but splits instead into concurrent views v_5 and v_6 neither of which defines a quorum. Then, v_5, v_6 and v_2 merge to form quorum view v_7. This situation reflects a different form of the shared state problem because *no* process in v_7 knows whether its local replica is up-to-date or not. For instance, consider a process in v_7 that was in v_2. From its point of view, write operations might have been executed concurrently to the existence of v_2. Processes that were in v_5 and v_6 can reason exactly the same. We call this kind of shared state problem *state creation*, because the global state of the file must be reconstructed from scratch. In this case, each process in v_7 has to compare its state (replica) with that of all the other processes in the view and possibly modify it as a result of this comparison. The situation when all members of a view have just recovered after a crash (total failure) is essentially identical. Identifying which local state is to be used for recreation of the others may require determining the last process to fail [22].

Next consider a different application, that is, a group implementing a database with a single look-up query interface. For performance reasons, the database is fully replicated within the group and the query is performed in parallel by the group members, each being responsible for a portion of the database. The correctness criterion requires that look-ups against the replicated database return exactly the same results as the non-replicated case. In particular, the entire database must be searched before reporting that the value being looked up does not exist. For this example, the only external operation (look-up) can be performed in any view. Thus, *R-mode* does not exist. Any event causing a view change, however, results in a transition to *S-mode* in order to redefine the division of responsibility for portions of the database to be searched by members of the group. An inconsistency in this global state information could result either in reducing efficiency or compromising correctness.

As an example, consider a view v that splits into two successor views v_1 and v_2. This view change requires a redistribution of the responsibility among the members of each resulting view. Otherwise, the portion of database that in v was in charge of processes that now are in v_2 would be never searched in v_1. This, of course, would compromise the correctness of the look-up operations that would be carried out in v_1. A similar reasoning can be made for v_2. Suppose now that v_1 and v_2 merge into view v_4. Also in this case a redistribution of the database among the view members is necessary. Otherwise, pair of processes in v_4, the one coming from v_1 and the other from v_2, could have the responsibility of portions that are completely or partially overlapping. Upon carrying out a query in v_7, these portions would be searched multiple times with the negative effects on the look-up efficiency.

This example shows a global state reconstruction that takes place when processes that continued serving external operations independently in concurrent partitions gather together when the conditions leading to the partition are repaired. An application-specific computation has to be performed in defining a new global state that reconciles the divergence that may have taken place. This reconciliation activity corresponds to the third form of the shared state problem, that we call *state merging*. Depending on the specific application, state merging problem and state transfer problem may present themselves together. The state merging problem cannot arise in applications that are structured around the *primary partition* paradigm, because in such applications there cannot be concurrent views that execute external operations.

In general, whenever a process delivers a view change, the process has to determine whether a shared state problem needs to be solved, and if so, which one. The information provided by view synchrony is typically not sufficient for *classifying* the shared state problem, since views as defined by view synchrony are flat structures and do not contain information regarding past history of processes. For example, suppose that some process p makes the transition from *R-mode* to *S-mode* upon delivery of $vchg(v)$. By reasoning on the composition of view v, the only conclusion p can draw is that the shared state problem must be solved but it is not able to distinguish between a state transfer or a state creation problem since it has no information about whether some processes were in *N-mode*.

Furthermore, view synchrony offers limited support for *solving* the shared state problem, i.e, programming the related internal operation. On the one hand, a process cannot determine the role that other processes in its view will have with respect to the shared state problem. In the above example, if p has to solve a state transfer problem, it does not know which processes in v have an up-to-date state. If p has to solve a state merging problem, it does not know which processes in v have the same state. Processes can obtain this information only through additional protocols that are typically complex and costly [22]. On the other hand, an instance of a shared state problem may interrupt the execution of an external operation or overlap with another instance of the shared state problem (i.e., interrupt an internal operation). Clearly, this asynchrony between the occurrence of the shared state problem and the group activity is a source of significant complexity that may obscure the conceptual simplicity and elegance of view synchrony. Effectively attacking these problems depends mostly on the semantics of the application and programming skills [2].

4   Enriched View Synchrony

In this section we present a novel extension to view synchrony that is aimed at simplifying reasoning about shared state problems. This extension, called *Enriched View Synchrony (EVS)*, requires minor modifications to the view synchrony run-time support and can be implemented efficiently [4]. The cited paper contains also a comparison of EVS and other proposed extensions to the basic view synchrony model as well as a formal specification of EVS. Such a specification is actually given in terms of a membership service in which concurrent views do not overlap, but it can be easily transformed into one for a quasi-strong partial service.

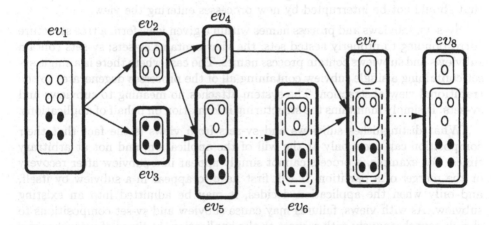

Fig. 1. Basic features of the enriched view synchrony model. Views, subviews and sv-sets are indicated, respectively, through thick, thin and dashed frames. For simplicity, sv-sets that contain a single subview are not traced out as dashed frames. Arrows indicate e-view changes. Solid arrows are used when there is a change in the composition of the e-view (i.e., view change), while dashed arrows are used when there is a change only in the structure of the e-view.

4.1   Basic Properties of Enriched View Synchrony

Our proposed extension to view synchrony is based on the notions of *subviews* and *subview sets* (*sv-sets* for short). Just like views, *subviews* are sets of process names that exist within a given view. Each view is constructed out of at least one subview. Each process belongs to exactly one subview. In other words, subviews do not overlap and they do not span across view boundaries. Subviews in the same view can be grouped together as *sv-sets*. Each subview belongs to exactly one sv-set. Within a given view, subviews and sv-sets never split and they merge only under application control, as described below. Given two consecutive views u and v, processes that are common to u and v and that were in the same subview or sv-set in u remain in the same subview or sv-set also after the installation of v. The example depicted in Fig. 1 illustrates these properties. First, a partition causes e-view ev_1 to split into two concurrent e-views ev_2 and ev_3. When the partition is repaired, (part of) the two concurrent views merge to form e-view ev_5. Note that while the partition divides the processes of ev_1 between ev_2 and ev_3, within each view, black processes remain together in a single subview. The merged e-view ev_5 maintains the structure of the two previous views with respect to subviews and sv-sets. Informally, subviews permit reasoning about which processes belonged to the same view before the installation of a new view. Subview sets, on the other hand, are used by applications to mark those processes involved in some global activity at the time of a view change and that should not be interrupted by new processes entering the view.

Sv-sets, subviews and process names within a given view form a tree structure corresponding to properly nested sets: the view contains sv-sets; sv-sets contain subviews and subviews contain process names. The case where there is a single sv-set containing a single subview containing all of the processes degenerates to the traditional view abstraction. The system attaches no meaning to subviews and sv-sets. It simply maintains the structuring information on behalf of applications.

What distinguishes subviews and sv-sets from views is the fact that their composition can grow only at the will of the application, and not at arbitrary times. For example, a process cannot simply appear in a subview after recovery or the merger of a partition. It will first have to appear in a subview by itself, and only when the application decides, it may be admitted into an existing subview. As with views, failures may cause subview and sv-set compositions to shrink asynchronously with respect to the application, at times of view changes. In Fig. 1, the partition after ev_1 causes the subview to shrink in each of e-views ev_2 and ev_3. After the merge in ev_5, however, processes that were in different subviews or sv-sets in ev_2 and ev_3 continue to belong to different subviews or sv-sets also in ev_5. This is because subviews and sv-sets may merge only in response to application-invoked primitives as described below. It is this aspect of EVS, where subviews and sv-sets expand synchronously with respect to the application, that distinguishes it from traditional view synchrony.

Our extended view synchrony service delivers processes messages and *enriched views* (*e-views* for short) that include the sv-set and subview structure within the view. Traditional view changes correspond to e-view changes where there is a change in the set of processes making up the view. Even when the view membership remains unaltered, e-view change events may be provoked by applications requesting mergers of subviews or sv-sets. When a process first joins a group, it appears within the new view in a new sv-set containing a new subview containing only the process itself. After their initial creation, subviews and sv-sets may be modified by the application through the following calls, which augment the usual view synchrony interface:

SV-SetMerge(*sv-set-list*) Create a new sv-set that is the union of the sv-sets given in *sv-set-list*. Any sv-set in *sv-set-list* that does not belong to the current view is ignored.

SubviewMerge(*sv-list*) Create a new subview that is the union of the subviews given in *sv-list*. The resulting subview belongs to the sv-set of the invoking process. Any subview in *sv-list* that does not belong to the sv-set of the invoking process is ignored.

For example, in Fig. 1, the e-view change from ev_5 to ev_6 is due to a *SV-SetMerge()* call merging two sv-sets, each containing a single subview. The e-view change from ev_7 to ev_8 is due to a *SubviewMerge()* call merging the two subviews of the newly created sv-set. Note that these e-view changes correspond to a scenario where no failures occur thus the composition of the e-view remains unchanged; only the structure of subviews and sv-sets within the view change in response to application invoked calls.

This extended service maintains the semantics of view synchrony regarding view changes and message deliveries, exactly as described in Appendix I. With respect to e-view changes, the following additional properties are guaranteed, which we state informally:

Property (Total Order). E-view change events within a given view (i.e., between two consecutive view change events) are totally ordered by all processes in the view.

Property (Causal Order). E-view change events define consistent cuts of the computation. In other words, causality relations between message multicasts and e-view changes are preserved.

Property (Structure). Subview and sv-set structures are preserved across view changes. In other words, processes that belong to the same subview (sv-set) in a given view remain in the same subview (sv-set) also in the successor view. Moreover, processes that do not belong to the same subview (sv-set) in a given view remain in different subviews (sv-sets) also in the successor view.

4.2 Structuring Applications Based on Enriched View Synchrony

Our proposed extension to view synchrony presents an opportunity for systematic and simplified solutions to shared state problems. It enhances the global reasoning that can be achieved based on local information after view changes and simplifies handling of the asynchrony between view synchrony run-time support and the application.

In terms of the application model used in this chapter, we structure an application according to the following methodology:

1. External operations are performed within a single subview and not across different subviews.
2. Internal operations are performed across subviews belonging to the same sv-set. Upon successful completion of the internal operation, all subviews within this sv-set are merged into a single one.

It follows that the existence of multiple sv-sets within a view signals the necessity for solving a certain instance of the shared state problem. Moreover, the existence of multiple subviews within a given sv-set signals that a shared state problem instance is in progress within this sv-set.

This methodology is illustrated in Fig. 1. Initially, some process in ev_5 creates an sv-set containing the two subviews, signaling that some internal operation is in progress. The resulting e-view change is indicated with the dashed arrow. While this internal operation is in progress, a partition merges and e-view ev_7 is installed. The white process that was in ev_4 can conclude, based solely on local information, that all of the other processes were together in a partition (ev_6) and were engaged in an internal operation before the merge, and thus should not be disturbed.

This methodology simplifies greatly reasoning about shared state problems using only information that is locally available to processes. Note that processes entering an expanding view are not permitted to participate in the computation that might be in progress at the time of the view change because they will appear in a different subview (or sv-set) than the one carrying out external or internal operations. Rather, they have to be "let in" explicitly by the other members in order that the appropriate subviews and sv-sets expand. The Structure Property guarantees that processes remain in the relevant subview (sv-set) across view changes, thus, all surviving processes will continue to participate in the computation and have the same notion of shared state.

As an example, consider the file object introduced in Section 3, and suppose that the implementation of the external operations involves the management of a mutually-exclusive write lock within a quorum view. The shared global state will thus include the identities of the lock manager and the current lock holder (if any). Suppose some process p installs a view v consecutive to u such that v defines a quorum whereas u does not (i.e., p switches from R-mode to S-mode). In traditional view synchrony, upon installing view v, the only conclusion p can draw based only on local information is the fact that v indeed defines a quorum. It cannot distinguish between the following scenarios: (i) a quorum already existed in one of the views prior to v (i.e., a state transfer problem exists); (ii) the shared state was being reconstructed at the time v was installed (i.e., a creation problem exists and an instance of the related internal operation has been interrupted); (iii) a quorum is reborn after it had disappeared temporarily (i.e., a creation problem exists).

With our proposed extensions, process p can draw several relevant conclusions through local reasoning on the view composition and structure. If the new view v contains a subview that defines a quorum, such a subview must contain processes whose notion of shared state is up-to-date. Notice that this is a major advantage since v may contain processes other than p that have just joined v and thus do not know how to obtain an up-to-date shared state. If, on the contrary, v does not contain any subview that by itself defines a quorum, then cases (ii) and (iii) can be distinguished by controlling if v contains an sv-set defining a quorum.

As for the asynchrony between application and run-time support, note that while an operation is being executed, the set of processes participating in it may only shrink — a new view may be delivered by view synchrony at arbitrary times but the composition of subviews and sv-sets may grow only at the will of the application. Therefore, algorithms can be easily designed to run undisturbed across view changes. For instance, in case (ii) above, process p can decide locally to wait for the processes running the creation protocol to complete their task before disturbing them for a copy.

As a further example, suppose that the availability of the replicated object file is further increased by allowing writes in any view. Informally, a write that takes place in a view defining a quorum has a permanent effect. The effects of a write performed in a non-quorum view are tentatively accepted but remain pending. They will become permanent if no write occurred in a concurrent view. Otherwise, they will be discarded. One can read up-to-date and permanent values only in a view defining a quorum.

One possible implementation of this scheme consists of letting a tentative write create a tentative copy, and associating with each tentative copy information reflecting the partial ordering among writes. Version vectors are an example of this information [15] A tentative write becomes permanent by promoting the tentative copies to plain copies and disseminating them to a quorum of processes. A tentative write is rolled back by deleting the tentative copies it produced. When two or more views merge to form a single view, all version vectors in the resulting view are compared in order to detect concurrent writes. Any tentative write that is discovered to have been concurrent with respect to another write is rolled back. Then, the most recent write, if any, is propagated to all members of the view (and the version vectors updated accordingly). If the resulting view defines a quorum, this write is also made permanent.

In this example, the external operations *read* and *write* can be performed in any view, and it follows that processes in a view composed of a single subview are in N-mode while R-mode does not exist. Moreover, any view change that notifies the merging of two or more views produces a transition from N-mode to S-mode. Processes in S-mode compare their version vectors and propagate their copies, if necessary, before returning to N-mode. Since external operations can be performed in any view, processes have to confront only the state merging problem.

Suppose that a process p installs a view v consecutive to two or more views. As stated earlier, with traditional view synchrony, the only conclusion that process p can draw based on local information is whether v defines a quorum or not. With EVS, instead, p may also determine the grouping of v in clusters (e.g subviews) and the clusters that are already involved in a state merging (e.g. sv-sets composed of multiple subviews).

5 Programming Example

In this section we present details of the file object implementation described in Section 3 and in the previous Section. The exercise is useful in that it will illustrate the programming methodology we introduced in previous Section 4.2. We shall use the *state machine* model [21]. This example may thus form the basis of a state machine implementation with several important features that can be informally summarized as follows: (i) ability to reintegrate crashed servers without stopping and re-starting the service; (ii) ability to reconstruct the state of the service after a total failure; (iii) ability to tolerate network partitions; (iv) ability to continue both external operations and internal operations across view changes.

We shall present internal operations in a form independent of the specific example and applicable to a large class of quorum-based applications. Alternative implementations for these operations are outlined and discussed in [4]. Then we shall present external operations that implement the file object according to the state machine model. External operations are also quite general and could be modified easily for other kinds of objects. Finally we shall describe how internal operations should be tailored to this object.

The example of this section is such that external operations cannot be executed in concurrent views, hence the merging problem cannot occur. An example of pseudo-code for handling a merging problem may be found in [4]. That example illustrates how to execute multiple merging operations *in parallel* in the same view, a feature that is very complex to obtain in traditional view synchrony.

5.1 Overview

Let a *quorum sv-set* and a *quorum subview* be, respectively, an sv-set and subview that include enough processes to define a quorum. Based on these definitions and the replicated file specification, the mode of a process can be determined as follows. A process is in

N-mode iff it belongs to a quorum view composed of only one subview;
S-mode iff it belongs to a quorum view composed of multiple subviews;
R-mode iff it does not belong to the quorum view.

Furthermore, the shared state problems that may occur are the creation problem (when a quorum subview disappears for some time) and the state transfer problem (when one or more subviews appear in a view together with a quorum subview).

According to the programming methodology, external operations are executed within subviews. In particular, writes can be executed only in a quorum view composed of only one subview, whereas reads can be executed in any subview, thus returning possibly stale data. Reads are guaranteed to return the current contents of the file only if they are executed in the quorum subview. Internal operations for solving both creation and state transfer problem and reestablishing the consistency of the file contents after the joining of some processes are carried out within a quorum sv-set.

Developing the application based on our methodology requires the implementation of five components:

1. external operations;
2. internal operations;
3. computing the process mode;
4. detecting the shared state problem instances;
5. deciding whether an internal operation has been interrupted.

We achieve this by splitting up each process into two components: the *low-level event manager* (LLEM) and the *high-level event manager* (HLEM). LLEM implements items (3)–(5) by analyzing e-views delivered to the process by the EVS run-time support. LLEM then passes the e-view event, enriched by the outcome of this analysis, to HLEM, that implements (1) and (2).

LLEM collects the results of its analysis into a data structure called Analysis that is a triple *(mode, problem, phase)* of enumerated types. The *mode* variable contains the current mode of the process and it may be any one of *N-mode*, *R-mode* or *S-mode*. The *problem* variable describes which shared state problem needs to be solved and it may be any one of STATETRANSFER, CREATION or NONE. Finally, the *phase* variable describes if the process is involved in an internal operation or if an internal operation is necessary but it has not started yet. The value INPROGRESS specifies the former case, whereas the value RECORDED the latter. If no shared state problem needs to be solved, then both *problem* and *phase* are set to NONE. A crucial point to observe is that LLEM constructs Analysis on the basis of local reasoning only. It is straightforward to deduce from our methodology that the Analysis produced by LLEM when analyzing *ev* is identical at all processes that belong to the same subview in *ev*.

HLEM starts an internal operation when it receives an e-view event from LLEM augmented by a triple whose fields *mode* and *phase* are equal to *S-mode* and RECORDED, respectively (this point will be clarified further below). The value of field *problem* determines which internal operation has to be executed.

Internal operations begin by creating an sv-set that includes the relevant processes. Upon delivery of the corresponding e-view, the *phase* field of Analysis switches to INPROGRESS. Internal operations can proceed across view changes as long as the field *phase* continues to be INPROGRESS, that is, as long as the composition of the sv-set continues to define a quorum. Otherwise the operation aborts.

5.2   Notation

Our algorithms are expressed in a simple pseudo programming language that supports multi-threaded processes. Indentation levels implicitly delimit blocks. The statement **wait-for**(*condition*) synchronizes a thread with the delivery of an event that renders the specified condition true. Upon delivery of an event, the thread executes an uninterruptible code segment called a *handler* that is specified through an **upon**(*event*) statement. Within a handler, we use the notation "Abort **wait-for**" as a shorthand for the forcible termination of the procedure containing the **wait-for**(*condition*) statement that synchronized the executing thread with the current event.

Several ancillary functions are defined. Function SetOfSV-Set() takes an e-view as argument and returns the set of sv-sets contained in that e-view. Function SetOfSV() takes either an e-view or an sv-set and returns the set of subviews contained in its argument. Function *comp*() takes either an e-view, a sv-set, or a subview as argument and returns the set of processes contained in its argument. Function *quorum*() also takes an e-view, a sv-set or a subview as argument and returns the Boolean value TRUE iff the corresponding set of processes defines a quorum. MySV, MySV-Set, and MyPiddenote the current subview, the sv-set and the name of the invoking process. Finally, function *elect*() returns a process chosen deterministically from the set specified as its argument.

Each process is composed of at least two initial threads, corresponding to LLEM and HLEM. HLEM starts an internal operation by spawning a new thread. In general, upon delivery of an event, HLEM forwards this event to the in-progress operations and then, if necessary, starts an internal operation. For the sake of brevity, we omit details concerning inter-thread communication.

In the next section we shall give the details for LLEM and the internal operations carried out by HLEM towards solving the state transfer and state creation problems. In section 5.4 we shall complete the description of HLEM by providing the details for the external operations.

5.3   LLEM and Internal Operations

The pseudo-code for LLEM is given in Fig. 2. Let p denote the executing process. The cases in which p is either R-mode or N-mode are straightforward (lines 4-8). If p is S-mode, its reasoning depends primarily on whether it belongs to a quorum subview (lines 11-16) or not (lines 17-26). In the former case, p reasons on the set of processes that belong to its sv-set but not to its subview (variable *in*, line 12). If this set is not empty, p's sv-set contains multiple subviews. It follows that p is participating in the execution of a state transfer (line 14). Otherwise, the need for a state transfer is recorded (line 16). When p is not in a quorum subview, instead, it first determines whether there is a quorum sv-set (line 18). If there is no quorum sv-set, then a creation algorithm shall be started (line 26). Otherwise, p's reasoning depends on whether it belongs to the quorum sv-set or not. The former implies that p is participating in the execution of an internal operation (lines 19 and 21-24). The latter implies that an internal operation is being executed but p is not participating in it (lines 19-20).

The pseudo-code for the part of HLEM that implements creation is given in Fig. 3. HLEM spawns a thread for executing procedure Creation() upon receiving the triple (*S-mode*, CREATION, RECORDED) from LLEM. In summary, state creation is performed as follows. Processes in the quorum view elect a coordinator that: (i) creates an sv-set encompassing the entire view; (ii) collects

```
1    procedure LLEM()
2
3    upon vchg(ev)
4        if (not quorum(ev)) then
5            Analysis := (R-mode, NONE, NONE);
6        else
7            if (comp(MySV) = comp(ev)) then
8                Analysis := (N-mode, NONE, NONE);
9            else
10               % S-mode
11               if (quorum(MySV)) then
12                   in := {p | p ∈ comp(MySV-Set) ∧ p ≠ comp(MySV)};
13                   if (in ≠ ∅) then
14                       Analysis := (S-mode, STATETRANSFER, INPROGRESS);
15                   else
16                       Analysis := (S-mode, STATETRANSFER, RECORDED);
17               else
18                   if (∃ss ∈ SetOfSV-Set(ev) | quorum(ss)) then
19                       if (MySV-Set ≠ ss) then
20                           Analysis := (S-mode, STATETRANSFER, RECORDED);
21                       else
22                           if (∃sv ∈ SetOfSV(ev) | quorum(sv)) then
23                               Analysis := (S-mode, STATETRANSFER, INPROGRESS);
24                           else Analysis := (S-mode, CREATION, INPROGRESS);
25                   else
26                       Analysis := (S-mode, CREATION, RECORDED);
27       pass vchg(ev) event up to HLEM;
```

Fig. 2. Structure of Low-Level Event Management.

local states from all processes in the sv-set; (iii) decides on a new state and multicasts it within the sv-set; (iv) merges the entire sv-set into a single (quorum) subview. The correspondence between these steps and the pseudo-code in Fig. 3 is straightforward. In particular, note that the primitives for subview and sv-set merging are invoked by the coordinator (lines 4-5 and 11-16). Changes in the view composition during execution of the algorithm are handled simply (lines 22-29). In particular, the algorithm is aborted only if the relevant sv-set does not constitute a quorum any more or if the coordinator leaves the quorum view before creating the sv-set (lines 24-25). In the latter case, another instance of the creation algorithm will be spawned by HLEM. If, instead, the coordinator leaves the quorum view after creating the sv-set, it is taken over by another process (lines 26-29). It can be shown that if the number of view changes is finite and the view continues to define a quorum, then the quorum subview will be eventually created.

```
1    procedure Creation()
2        s := comp(ev);
3        coord := elect(s);
4        if (MyPid = coord) then
5            SV-SetMerge(SetOfSV-Set(ev));
6        wait-for (vchg(ev) | Analysis.phase = INPROGRESS);
7        core-Creation();
8
9    procedure core-Creation()
10       Transfer local state to coord;
11       if (MyPid = coord) then
12           wait-for (receipt of local state from all in s);
13           Select new state among received local states;
14           Transfer new state to all processes in s;
15           wait-for (ack from every process ∈ s, except for myself);
16           SubviewMerge(SetOfSV(MySV-Set));
17       else
18           wait-for (new state from coord);
19           Send ack to coord;
20       wait-for (vchg(ev) | comp(MySV) = comp(MySV-Set));
21
22   upon vchg(ev)
23       if (Analysis.mode ≠ N-mode) then
24           if (Analysis.mode = R-mode or Analysis.phase ≠ INPROGRESS) then
25               Abort thread;
26           s := s ∩ comp(ev);
27           if (coord ∉ s) then
28               coord := elect(s);
29               Abort wait-for and call core-Creation();
```

Fig. 3. State creation algorithm.

We make the following observations. Let ev and ev' be the e-views corre-sponding, respectively, to the formation of the sv-set and its merging into a single subview. The Causal Property of EVS guarantees that a process in the quorum subview will not be delivered a message pertinent to external operations before $vchg(ev')$. Similarly, for instance, the coordinator will not be delivered lo-cal states before the delivery of $vchg(ev)$.

The pseudo-code for the part of HLEM that implements state transfer is given in Fig. 4. This operation is started upon receiving the triple (S-mode, STATE-TRANSFER, RECORDED) from LLEM. In particular, processes in the quorum subview execute procedure State-Transfer-Active() whereas the others execute State-Transfer-Passive(). Processes in the quorum subview elect a coordinator that: (i) creates an sv-set encompassing the entire view; (ii) transfers state to processes that are in the sv-set but not in the quorum subview; (iii) merges the

```
1   procedure State-Transfer-Active()
2       out := {sv| sv ∈ SetOfSV(ev) ∧ sv ∉ SetOfSV(MySV-Set)};
3       coord := elect(comp(MySV));
4       if (MyPid = coord) then
5           SV-SetMerge(MySV, out);
6       wait-for (vchg(ev) | Analysis.phase = INPROGRESS);
7       core-Active();
8
9   procedure core-Active()
10      if (MyPid = coord) then
11          Transfer state to all processes in out;
12          wait-for (ack from every process in out);
13          SubviewMerge(SetOfSV(MySV-Set));
14      wait-for (vchg(ev) | comp(MySV) = comp(MySV-Set));
15
16  upon vchg(ev)
17      if (Analysis.mode ≠ N-mode) then
18          if (Analysis.mode = R-mode or Analysis.phase ≠ INPROGRESS) then
19              abort thread;
20          if (Analysis.problem = STATETRANSFER) then
21              out := out ∩ SetOfSV(MySV-Set);
22              if (coord ∉ comp(MySV)) then
23                  coord := elect(comp(MySV));
24                  abort wait-for and call core-Active()
25          else    abort wait-for and call Creation();
26
27  procedure State-Transfer-Passive()
28      wait-for (vchg(ev) | Analysis.phase = INPROGRESS);
29      Receive state;
30      Send ack;
31      wait-for (vchg(ev) | Analysis.mode = N-mode);
32
33  upon vchg(ev)
34      if (Analysis.mode ≠ N-mode) then
35          if (Analysis.mode = R-mode or Analysis.phase ≠ INPROGRESS) then
36              abort thread;
37          if (Analysis.problem ≠ STATETRANSFER) then
38              abort wait-for and call Creation();
```

Fig. 4. State transfer algorithm. The upper part is executed by processes in the quorum subview, the lower part by processes not in the quorum subview.

sv-set into a single subview. Processes that are not in the quorum subview simply wait for the up-to-date state and for their admission in the quorum subview. Observe that processes joining the quorum view while an internal operation is in progress (either creation or state transfer) will simply wait for the up-to-date state and for their admission in the quorum subview (line 28 of Fig. 4 and lines 18-20 of Fig. 2).

The algorithm exhibits many similarities with the creation algorithm. Primitives for subviews and sv-set merging are invoked by the coordinator (lines 4-5 and 10-13); state transfer is aborted only if the coordinator leaves before enlarging the quorum sv-set or if the quorum sv-set disappears (lines 18-19 and 35-36)[2]; and the coordinator's leaving of the quorum view is managed by electing a new one (lines 22-24). Let p be a process executing the state transfer algorithm from outside the quorum subview. It can be shown that if the number of view changes is finite, then p will eventually belong to the quorum subview or its view will not define a quorum. Moreover, let ev denote the e-view corresponding to the end of state transfer. The delivery of ev lets processes in the quorum view switch to N-mode and thus resume servicing external operations. The Causal Property of EVS guarantees that no messages related to new external operations may be delivered before ev.

5.4   External Operations

In this section we complete the presentation of HLEM by providing details of the external operations that implement the file object. We shall use the *state machine* replication model [21]. As will become clearer later, our state machine implementation is not tailored to the file object and can be easily generalized.

Overview. The implementation of the file object must satisfy the correctness criterion we informally stated in Section 3. That is, with respect to write operations, the file object should behave exactly as if there were only one copy, whereas a read operation returns any available data, even though it may be out-of-date.

To achieve this goal, we impose restrictions on the way read and write operations can be carried out. These restrictions take the form of a replica control policy and a concurrency control policy that we informally state in the following. As for the replica control policy, we allow read operations to be served by any process. On the other hand, if a process serves a given write operation, then every correct process must serve that operation. We say that a given process is correct in a view v, if it belongs to a quorum subview in that view. Notice that, if the process that serves a read operation is correct, the read operation returns up-to-date data.

As for the concurrency control policy, we solve *read-write* conflicts by guaranteeing mutually exclusive-access to to each local replica. On the other hand,

---

[2] Lines 25 and 37-38 handle the case in which the quorum subview disappears but the sv-set in which state transfer was being executed still defines a quorum.

we solve *write-write* conflicts by requiring that if any two processes serve two write operations, they must serve them in the same order.

In the classical state machine model, a client multicasts an operation invocation to all processes. Each process carries out each request autonomously, without interacting with the other processes, and responds. In this example we assume instead that a client willing to access the file sends an operation invocation to any given process, the closer one, for example. The actual invocation will be performed by this process. This structuring allows us to simplify the client code and to keep clients outside of the group. Furthermore, we do not multicast each invocation to all processes but only to processes in the quorum subview. This strategy clearly increases the availability of the file object. Finally, in the case of a read operation, the process selected by the client carries out the operation locally, without multicasting any operation invocation to the remaining processes. This strategy clearly improves the latency of the read operation.

Let p be a process that receives a request from a client. If p is in *N-mode*, then p multicasts the operation request in its subview. If p is either in *S-mode* or in *R-mode*, then p will buffer the request until it goes back into *N-mode*. For brevity, we shall omit the obvious details related to communication between clients and processes, including the possible buffering of client requests.

Given the above structuring, the replica control policy and concurrency control policy can be satisfied by requiring that: (i) operation requests are delivered at correct processes in a total order; (ii) each process serves operation requests in the same order in which they are delivered; and (iii) no response is sent back to a client until the operation has been performed by a quorum of correct processes. In particular, we enforce constraint (i) with a token-based scheme.

Each process maintains a replica of the file object. In addition to the actual file content, each replica is associated with the following information kept in permanent storage: (i) a *tentative content* (*reptc*); (ii) a *quorum subview counter* (*repqs*); (iii) a monotonically increasing *version number* (*repvn*). This information is necessary for coping with failures occurring during the execution of write operations and for reconstructing the state of the file object after total failures. The tentative content *reptc* contains either a null value or a tentative new version of the file. We say that the replica is *stable* in the former case and *tentative* in the latter. Contents of *reptc* are never visible to clients. The quorum subview counter *repqs* identifies the last quorum e-view in which the replica became tentative (see below). At system initialization, all processes are provided with identical replicas, in particular, having $reptc = \perp, repqs = 0, repvn = 0$.

Operation processing is greatly simplified by the fact that all processes in the quorum subview have identical replicas. We shall discuss in a later section the details of Creation and State Transfer that satisfy this assumption. We have structured our example so that, during the execution of a write operation, the quorum subview can only shrink. In other words, no process should join the quorum subview while a write operation is in progress. Satisfying this requirement is not difficult, because it is HLEM itself that decides when to schedule an instance of the StateTransfer-Active() internal operation. As we shall see, however, removing this constraint is not particularly difficult.

Algorithms. Our implementation is based on three software modules: write coordinator (WC), write participant (WP) and token distribution (TD). When the process enters the quorum subview, the main thread of HLEM spawns three threads, one for each module. These threads exist as long as the process continues to belong to the quorum subview. They are aborted when the process leaves the quorum subview, that is, when LLEM produces an Analysis with *mode* field equal to *R-mode*, or an Analysis equal to (*S-mode*, CREATION, RECORDED). For simplicity, we shall omit the code that creates and aborts threads.

For each write operation, the process that multicasts the operation request on behalf of the client is called the *co-ordinator*. Processes that execute that request are called the *participants*. Module WC implements the co-ordinator behavior, whereas module WP implements the participant behavior. Module TD implements a token distribution scheme that totally orders operation requests.

The thread executing the write coordinator module WC is responsible for performing operation invocations on behalf of clients. Each invocation is performed by invoking procedure **Write()** in Figure 5. The co-ordinator acquires the token and multicasts a write request message (WREQ) to all participants, including itself. Then, it sets about waiting for acknowledgement messages (WACK). The receipt of a WACK message from a given participant implies that that participant has updated the file object. Having received a WACK message from a quorum of participants, the co-ordinator multicasts a write commit message (WCOM) and releases the token. At this point, the co-ordinator can return the operation results to the client.

Token requests are directed to a distinguished process in the quorum subview, the *token manager*. The algorithm executed by the token manager is part of module TD and will be discussed below. The **TokenManager** variable of the WP module identifies the token manager and is initialized upon entering the quorum subview, as follows. If the process enters the quorum subview upon completion of the Creation algorithm, then it sets **TokenManager** equal to the result of the deterministic function **select()** applied to the composition of the quorum subview. Otherwise, the process enters the quorum subview upon completion of the State Transfer algorithm, and it acquires the value for **TokenManager** as part of the state received during the state transfer. If the **TokenManager** leaves the quorum subview, all participants determine the identity of the new token manager by re-evaluating **select()**. In this case, each process that has requested but not yet received the token, resends the outstanding request to the new token manager.

The WP module is shown in Figure 6. Variable **qs-cnt** counts the e-view changes delivered since the last creation of the quorum subview. This variable is incremented whenever the process delivers an e-view change and is initialized upon entering the quorum subview, as follows. If the process enters the quorum subview upon completion of the Creation algorithm, then **qs-cnt** is set to zero.

```
1   var      TokenManager: pid;
2            TokenOutstanding: boolean initial(FALSE);
3
4   procedure Write(args)
5      AcquireToken();
6      msg := 〈 WREQ, ClientId, args 〉;
7      v − cast(msg);
8      WriteTerminationCoordinator();
9
10  procedure WriteTerminationCoordinator()
11     wait-for(WACK from a quorum of members of MySV)
12     v-cast(WCOM);
13     send(TokenManager, TREL);
14
15  procedure AcquireToken()
16     TokenOutstanding := TRUE;
17     send(TokenManager, TREQ);
18     wait-for(delivery of TGRANT message);
19     TokenOutstanding := FALSE;
20
21  upon evchg(ev)
22     if(TokenManager ∉ comp(MySV)) then
23        TokenManager := select(comp(MySV))
24        if(TokenOutstanding) then
25           send(TokenManager, TREQ);
```

Fig. 5. State Machine: Processing of operation requests issued by clients (part of Write Coordinator module WC).

Otherwise, the process acquires the initial value for **qs-cnt** as part of the state received during the state transfer. It can be realized easily that **qs-cnt** is kept identical at all processes in the quorum subview.

The replica is accessed through the following auxiliary procedures, not shown for brevity. **MakeTentative(s)** makes the replica of the participant become tentative. That is, it determines from s the tentative new value for the file object, records this value in *reptc* and sets *repqs* equal to the current value of **qs-cnt**. **MakeStable()** makes the replica become stable, that is, the previous value of *reptc* becomes the actual file content, *reptc* is set to ⊥ and *repvn* is incremented.

A participant realises that there is a write operation in progress upon receiving a WREQ message. When its replica has become tentative, the participant responds to the coordinator by means of a WACK message. The participant's replica will become stable upon receiving the WCOM message. Actually, a tentative replica may become stable also upon receiving of "the next" WREQ. As

```
1   var    qs-cnt: integer;
2          Writer: msg initial(⊥);
3          ResponseMsg: msg initial(⊥);
4
5   procedure WriteParticipant()
6      upon delivery(WREQ message msg)
7         if(Writer ≠⊥) then
8             MakeStable();
9         Writer := msg.sender;
10        res := MakeTentative(msg.args);
11        ResponseMsg := 〈 WACK, res 〉;
12        send(Writer, ResponseMsg);
13
14     upon delivery(WCOM message msg)
15        if(msg.vn = vn+1) then
15            MakeStable();
16            Writer := ⊥;
17            ResponseMsg := ⊥;
18
19  upon evchg(ev)
20     qs-cnt := qs-cnt + 1;
21     if(Writer ≠⊥ and Writer ∉ comp(MySV)) then
22        Writer := select(comp(MySV));
23        if(Writer = MyPid) then
24           Spawn a thread that executes WriteTerminationCoordinator()
25                                       and terminates;
26        send(Writer, ResponseMsg);
```

Fig. 6. State Machine: Write Participant module WP.

an example, consider the following sequence of events: (i) process p multicasts a WCOM message mp and releases the token; (ii) message mp experiences high network delays along its way to q; (iii) process r receives mp soon and initiates a new write operation by sending a WREQ message mr; (iv) mr arrives at q earlier than mp. In this case, q handles the WREQ mr as if the WCOM mp was piggybacked into it (and later it will ignore the "real" mp). Similar scenarios are possible because we do not assume any multicast ordering stronger than FIFO [2].

When a participant delivers an e-view change, it must check whether there is a write in progress and the co-ordinator has left the quorum subview. In this case, a new co-ordinator is selected among the components of the quorum subview in order to terminate the write operation. Election is performed by applying the deterministic function **select**() to the composition of the quorum subview. Each participant sends the WACK message to the new co-ordinator, even though it already sent the WACK to the previous coordinator. So doing, the new co-ordinator is instructed about the level of progress of the write operation.

Module TD grants tokens and is shown in Figure 7. The **TokenManager** variable identifies the member of the quorum subview that acts as *token manager*. This variable is kept identical at all processes in the quorum subview and is managed like the analogous variable in the WC module. When the token manager receives a token request message (TREQ), it either grants the token or queues the request in the **RequestQueue**, depending on whether the token is free or not. When the token manager receives a token release message (TREL), it grants one of the outstanding token requests. Pending requests are served FIFO, thus avoiding starvation. Upon an e-view change, requests originated by processes that are not in the current view are removed from the queue. If the current token holder leaves the view, the token is revoked only if no process in the quorum subview created a tentative copy of the file. Otherwise, the token is inherited by the process that will complete the in-progress write operation. The token manager discriminates between these two cases on the basis of the value of the **Writer** variable, that is kept identical to the analogous variable in module WP.

Tailoring Internal Operations. The internal operations for State Transfer and Creation given in Section 5.3 have been purposefully left generic. For instance, they specify neither the state actually exchanged among processes nor the rule for deciding, in the Creation algorithm, which state has to be selected. The tailoring of these operations for the file object just described is accomplished as follows.

The state that the coordinator of the State Transfer algorithm transfers to a process that has to be admitted into the quorum subview consists of the local replica and the values of variables **qs-cnt, TokenManager**. The joining process will use this information for updating its own replica and initializing the necessary variables of modules TD, WC, WP. As an aside, notice that modifying these modules so that processes can enter the quorum subview even while a write operation is in progress is not exceedingly difficult. Essentially, it suffices to include the value of the **Writer** variable among the transferred state.

The state that each process sends to the coordinator of the Creation algorithm consists of the information associated with the local replica, that is, file content, *reptc, repqs, repvn*. The coordinator selects the new state from those associated with the highest *repvn*. If all these states correspond to stable replicas, then any one of them is selected. Otherwise, the tentative replica with highest *repqs* is selected. Intuitively, tentative replicas with identical *repvn* have been created in the order induced by increasing *repqs*. It follows that, when some of the replicas with highest *repvn* are tentative, the one created later is selected.

The fact that the choice operated in the Creation algorithm is indeed safe can be derived from the following, very informal, considerations. Let S denote the set of participants in the creation algorithm and let $OutS$ denote the set composed of

```
1   var   TokenManager: pid;
2         TokenFree: boolean initial(TRUE);
3         TokenHolder, Writer: pid initial(⊥);
4         RequestQueue: queue of pid initial(∅);
5
6   procedure Grant(p: pid)
7         TokenFree := FALSE; TokenHolder := p; Writer := ⊥;
8
9   procedure Release()
10        TokenFree := TRUE; TokenHolder := ⊥; Writer := ⊥;
11
12  procedure GrantSend(p: pid)
13        Grant(p); send(TGRANT, p);
14
15  procedure TokenManager()
16  upon delivery(TREQ message msg)
17        if(TokenFree) then GrantSend(msg.sender);
18        else RequestQueue.put(msg.sender);
19
20  upon delivery(TREL message)
21        p := RequestQueue.get();
22        if(p =⊥) then Release();
23        else GrantSend(p);
24
25  upon delivery(WREQ message msg)
26        Writer := msg.sender;
27
28  upon evchg(ev)
29        if(Writer ≠⊥ and Writer ∉ comp(MySV) ) then
30              Writer := select(comp(MySV));
31        if(TokenManager = MyPid) then
32              Remove from RequestQueue every process p ∉ comp(MySV);
33              if(notTokenFree and TokenHolder ∉ MySV) then
34                    if(Writer =⊥) then
35                          Release();
36                          p := RequestQueue.extract();
37                          if(p ≠ ⊥) then GrantSend(p);
38                    else TokenHolder := Writer;
39        elseif(TokenManager ∉ comp(MySV) ) then
40              TokenManager := select(comp(MySV));
41              if(TokenManager = MyPid and Writer ≠⊥) then
42                    Grant(Writer);
```

Fig. 7. State Machine: Token Distribution module TD.

the remaining group members (recall that S defines a quorum). Let the replica r_a selected by the Creation algorithm be associated with $(reptc_a, repvn_a, repqs_a)$.

Suppose r_a is stable. There can be no process in $OutS$ having a stable replica with $repvn = repvn_a + 1$, because otherwise there would be at least a process in S having such a stable replica or a tentative replica with $repvn = repvn_a$. In either case, r_a would not be selected. Suppose now that r_a is tentative. During the creation algorithm it is not possible to tell whether there is a process in $OutS$ that has made stable r_a. However, making r_a become stable is safe because any other write attempts with $repvn = repvn_a$ and $repqs < repqs_a$ certainly failed: once a write operation has been initiated, either this operation will be completed at a quorum of processes, or the quorum subview will disappear.

Of course, this entire reasoning is based not only on the property that write operations can be completed in at most one view at a time, but also on this stronger property: there cannot be write operations *initiated* in concurrent views. This property is guaranteed by the strong partial semantics assumed for the membership service but it does not hold for the service specified in Chapter 3. Thus, some changes to our algorithms would be needed to make them function under the service specified in Chapter 3. We shall come back to this issue in Section 6.

In case the state selected by the Creation algorithm is associated with a non-null *reptc*, then the "pending write" has to be completed before resuming the service offered to clients. This can be accomplished, for instance, by requiring that the token manager acts as coordinator of this write operation: as soon as a process enters the quorum subview, it sets the **Writer** variable of the WP module equal to the **TokenManager** variable of WC; then the process executes lines 10-12 of Fig. 6); upon receiving the WCOM from the coordinator, client requests can be processed again.

Discussion. Consider a system model in which processes may crash but communication failures cannot occur. In this case, a state machine may complete an operation and respond to the client as soon as the result from *one* server is available [21]. In our scenario this is not possible, because we admit the existence of partitions. Consider a process p that is member of a quorum subview and suppose that p delivers a request message m_{op} related to operation $op(args)$. If p returned the operation results to the client soon, the invariants of the state machine could be violated because, due to a view change, the next quorum subview could exclude p and be composed only by members that have not received m_{op}. In this case, the operation executed by p might not be reflected in the object state.

It is interesting to observe that even if one wanted to implement a *volatile* object, as opposed to a permanent one able to survive across total failures, our structuring would remain almost unaltered. That is, even in that case, the fact that one server has carried out the operation would not suffice to declare that operation as completed: a quorum of responses would still be necessary. The reason is in the fact that the above example depends on the partitionable nature of the system, not on the possibility of all servers simultaneously crashing.

With respect to volatile objects, a solution for partitionable systems in which a single response suffices to declare the operation as completed could be obtained by strengthening the multicast semantics. For instance, by requiring atomicity of message delivery with respect to partitions, such as the *safe* multicast in [1]. By disseminating operation requests via safe multicasts, one is guaranteed that each process in the quorum subview either deliver the request or crashes. Coming back to the above example, when p delivers m_{op}, it could conclude that every other process in the quorum subview either delivers m_{op} or crashes. Therefore, p could execute the operation described by m_{op} and respond to the client immediately. A similar reasoning can be constructed for systems in which there is always at most one view of the group active, i.e., systems that are not partitionable. In this case, one would need a *uniform* multicast [20]. Such solutions, however, have an additional cost hidden into the run-time support. Supporting the stronger semantics required by either a safe or a uniform multicast requires some message-exchange rounds, that we instead perform at the application level.

The state machine approach provides a systematic framework for implementing fault-tolerant services. Our example could be easily generalized to other kinds of objects, not necessarily files. Another fundamental and systematic model is the *primary-backup* approach [14]. In this case, there is a distinguished server, the *primary*, that is responsible for processing *all* requests and for managing the interaction with *all* clients. The processing of each request involves multicasting to all backup's and waiting for their replies, so that the state of all servers is kept in sync. Should the primary crash, or leave the primary view of the group, one of the backups would become the new primary. Modifying our example according to the primary-backup approach is quite simple. Essentially, it suffices to forward all operation requests to an agreed process in the quorum subview that would act as coordinator for all requests. This process could be identified in the same way as the token manager of our example.

6   EVS and Weaker Group Membership Services

So far in this chapter we have considered a view synchrony model based on a strong partial membership service. In this model, any pair of concurrent views has empty intersection. This property clearly eases the programmer task because a process installing a view does not have to consider the possibility that other processes in that view might have installed another different view. Unfortunately, Babaoğlu and *et al.* have shown that non-blocking implementations of strong partial group membership service are impossible to achieve in partitionable asynchronous systems [3]. The EVS abstractions and the related programming methodology are not bound to a membership service with the strong partial property. In fact, they can be well accommodated within a weaker view synchrony model, such as the one described in Chapter 3 that allows the existence of concurrent views with overlapping compositions. EVS retains its power, both as a conceptual framework and as a programming paradigm, also within this model. Of course, two solutions to the same problem that are implemented on different membership services are likely to look differently. Therefore, from a general point of view, algorithms developed for a strong partial membership service cannot be ported unchanged on top of a weaker service. We remark again, however, that the programming methodology of EVS need not be changed.

With respect to our examples, most of them apply unaltered to the membership service of Chapter 3. Essentially, the reason is because our examples make progress when enough messages have been received. For instance, when messages have been received from a set of processes that form a quorum. In other words, the fact that a process p belongs to a given view v is not taken as a proof that p indeed installed v. Such a conclusion is taken only upon receiving in v a message sent by p.

The only necessary changes concern the algorithms based on the assumption that no two concurrent quorum views can exist. Such assumption is present in the solution to the state creation problem. At creation, the **Creation()** procedure must be able to distinguish the most recent one between two or more uncompleted write operations (see Figure 3). An write operation is uncompleted if it has not installed on a quorum of stable replicas. Identifying the most recent uncompleted write operation is necessary because the results of a write operation are sent back to the client as soon as the operation has created a quorum of tentative replicas, no matter whether the operation completes. Our example performs such an identification based on the observation that uncompleted write operations must have initiated in different quorum subviews. Since quorum subviews are totally ordered due to the strong partial property, such an ordering can be used to sort uncompleted write operations. The quorum subview counter is used to reflect the total order existing between quorum subviews on write operations.

In a weaker view synchrony model this is not possible anymore because concurrent quorum views can be scheduled by the group membership service. Two approaches are possible to manage this problem. In both approaches, however, an application writer can exploit the EVS abstractions and programming methodology. In the one approach, the **write()** algorithm is modified so that: (i) participants must acknowledge the reception of WCOMM messages; (ii) the write results can be sent back to the client only when a quorum of processes have acknowledged the reception of the WCOMM message. In this case both LLEM and the creation algorithm would remain unaltered.

An alternative approach leaves the algorithms for the **write()** operation unaltered. With this approach, a quorum of replicas could not suffice to rebuild the shared state of the object upon creation. This takes place when the most recent replicas are tentative replicas generated by two or more uncompleted writes initiated in concurrent quorum subviews. In this situation it is not possible to determine which results, if any, have been sent to the client. The quorum subview will be created in a later instance of the creation algorithm, involving a number of replicas large enough to determine which set of identical tentative replicas, if any, defines a quorum. To cope with this kind of situations, it is necessary to modify both the LLEM (Figure 2) and the Creation() procedure (Figure 3). As to the LLEM, one must observe that now the existence of a quorum sv-set composed of two or more subviews does not necessarily indicate anymore that an activity finalized to rebuilding a shared state in progress. Actually, the Creation() procedure may fail to select the new state (line 13). In that case, the Creation procedure must terminate soon without creating a quorum subview. A new instance of the procedure shall be executed as soon as the quorum view's composition changes. To sum up, in the presence of a quorum view composed of two or more subviews, the LLEM will schedule a state transfer problem if and only if, one of those subviews is a quorum subview. Otherwise, it schedules a creation problem. We do not report the new pseudo-code for brevity.

These approaches embody a different trade-off between efficiency and availability. The first approach allows a quorum of replicas to always make progress. This at the expenses of a more costly write. On the other hand, in the second approach, write operations are implemented efficiently. However, the object may become unavailable after a total failure notwithstanding the existence of a quorum view. It is up to application designers to adopt the first or the second approach depending upon the application requirements, the write operation frequency and the probability that a quorum subviews disappears.

7   Conclusions

Shared state problems such as state transfer, creation and merging, are likely to be an issue in many future applications that have reliability constraints. This is particularly true in partitionable systems such as the Internet, where multiple views of a group may exist concurrently. Even though view synchrony has the potential for being a clean and elegant programming abstraction, this elegance can easily be lost in practice, unless special provisions are made for supporting shared state maintenance.

We have given a characterization for shared state problems in terms of necessary conditions and presented an analysis of related problems that arise in practical applications. We have then presented an extension to view synchrony, called *enriched view synchrony*, explicitly conceived to simplify the task of shared state maintenance in partition-aware applications. Group views delivered to processes are enriched by structural and historical information relevant to the group's activity. Such information is defined by the application and maintained by the run-time support.

In conjunction with a simple programming methodology, local reasoning that is possible upon view changes is greatly improved with enriched view synchrony, even in the case of expanding views. Among others, a process is able to infer whether an algorithm for shared state maintenance shall be run or if it was already in progress before the view change. In the former case, a process can also infer the type of shared state problem and which other processes need to be involved. Moreover, asynchrony between run-time support and application may now be controlled in the sense that shared state problems cannot occur at instants that are inopportune for the application. This in turn simplifies the entire application and not just those parts responsible for handling events that trigger shared state problems. The methodology has been illustrated through a simple example that can be extended to a large class of applications based on the quorum model.

Acknowledgments

This work has been supported in part by the Commission of European Communities under ESPRIT Programme Basic Research Project 6360 (BROADCAST), the Italian National Research Council and the Italian Ministry of University, Research and Technology (MURST) under Project "Design Methodologies and Tools of High Performance Systems for Distributed Applications". We are grateful to Ken Birman for his comments in the early stages of this work and to Rachid Guerraoui for his comments on this chapter.

References

1. Amir, Y., Moser, L.E., Melliar-Smith, P.M., Agarwal, D.A., Ciarfella, P.: The Totem single-ring ordering and membership protocol, ACM Trans. on Comp. Sys., **13** (1995) 311–342.
2. Babaoğlu, Ö., Bartoli, A., Dini, G.: Replicated File management in large-scale distributed systems. In: Tel, G. and Vitányi, P., (eds.): Distributed Algorithms. Lecture Notes in Computer Science, Vol. 857. Springer-Verlag, (1994) 1–16.
3. Babaoğlu, Ö., Davoli, R., Giachini, L.A., Sabatini, P.: The Inherent Cost of Strong-Partial View-Synchronous Communication. In: Hélary, J.M., Raynal, M. (eds.): Distributed Algorithms. Lecture Notes in Computer Science, Vol. 972. Springer-Verlag, (1995) 72–86.
4. Babaoğlu, Ö., Bartoli, A., Dini, G.: Enriched View Synchrony: A Programming Paradigm for Partitionable Asynchronous Distributed Systems. IEEE Trans. on Comp., **46** (1997) 642–658.
5. Birman, K., Cooper, R., Joseph, T., Marzullo, K., Makpangou, M., Kane, K. Schmuck, F., Wood, M.: The ISIS - System Manual, Version 2.1. Department of Computer Science, Cornell University, (1993).
6. Birman, K.: Virtual Synchrony. In: Birman, K., van Renesse, R. (eds.): Reliable Distributed Computing with the Isis toolkit. IEEE Computer Society Press, (1994).
7. Chandra, T.D., Toueg, S.; Unreliable Failure Detectors for Asynchronous Systems. In: Proc. of the 10th ACM Symp. on Princ. of Distr. Comp. (1991) 325–340.
8. El Abbadi, A., Skeen, D., Cristian, F.: An efficient, fault-tolerant protocol for replicated data management. In: Proc. of the 4th ACM Symp. on Princ. of Datab. Syst. (1985) 215–229.
9. El Abbadi A., Toueg, S.: Maintaining Availability in Partitioned Replicated Databases. In: ACM Trans. on Datab. Syst. **14** (1989) 264–290.
10. Fischer, M.J., Lynch, N.A., Paterson, M.S., Impossibility of Distributed Consensus with One Faulty Process. Journal of the ACM **32** (1985) 374–382.

11. Herlihy M., Wing, J.: Linearizability: A Correctness Condition for Concurrent Objects. ACM Trans. on Prog. Lang. and Syst., (1990) 463–492.
12. Keidar, I., Dolev, D.: Increasing the resilience of atomic commit at no additional cost. In: Proc. of the 14th ACM Symp. on Princ. of Datab. Syst. (1995) 245–254.
13. Malki, D., Amir, Y., Dolev, D., Kramer, S.: The Transis approach to high availability cluster communication. Technical Report CS94-14, Institute of Computer Science, The Hebrew University of Jerusalem (1994).
14. Budhiraja, N., Marzullo, K., Schneider, F. Toueg, S.: The Primary-Backup Approach. In: Mullender, S. (ed.) Distributed Systems, 2nd edition, ACM Press, (1993) 199–216.
15. Satyanarayanan, M., Kistler, J.J., Kumar, P., Okasaki, M.E., Siegel, E.H., Steere, D.C.: Coda: A highly available file system for a distributed workstation environment. IEEE Trans. on Comp. **39** (1990) 447–459.
16. Schiper, A., Ricciardi, A.: Virtually-synchronous communication based on a weak failure suspector. In: Proc. of the 23rd Intern. Symp. on Fault-Tolerant Comp. (1993) 534–543.
17. Schiper, A., Ricciardi, A., Birman, K.: Understanding partitions and the "no partition" assumption: In: Proc. of the 4th IEEE Workshop on Future Trends of Distr. Syst. (1993) 354–360.
18. Schiper, A., Sandoz, A.: Uniform reliable multicast in a virtually synchronous environment. In: Proc of the 13th Intern. Conf. on Distr. Comp. Syst. (1993) 561–568.
19. Schiper, A., Sandoz, A.: Primary partition virtually synchronous communication harder than consensus. In: Tel, G. and Vitányi, P., (eds.): Distributed Algorithms. Lecture Notes in Computer Science, Vol. 857. Springer-Verlag, (1994) 39–52.
20. Guerraoui, R., Schiper, A.: Software-Based Replication for Fault Tolerance. IEEE Comp. **30** (1997) 68–74.
21. Schneider, F.B.: Implementing Fault-Tolerant Services using the State-Machine Approach: A Tutorial. ACM Comp. Surveys **22** (1990) 299-319.
22. Skeen, D.: Determining the last process to fail. ACM Trans. on Comp. Syst. **3** (1985) 15–30.

Deploying Distributed Objects on the Internet

Steve J. Caughey[1], Daniel Hagimont[2], and David B. Ingham[1]

[1] Department of Computing Science, University of Newcastle upon Tyne,
Newcastle upon Tyne, NE1 7RU, United Kingdom
{s.j.caughey, dave.ingham}@newcastle.ac.uk

[2] Laboratoire Sirac, INRIA Rhône-Alpes, 655 av. de l'Europe, 38330 Montbonnot, France
Daniel.Hagimont@inrialpes.fr

Abstract. Internet applications are becoming truly distributed as intelligence
moves to the browser and services are being decentralised in order to improve
their performance and availability. As a consequence distributed, object-
oriented technology in the form of language-level support, e.g., Java, or
middleware platforms, e.g., CORBA, is being increasingly deployed.
Underpinning this technology are many years of research, such as that
undertaken by the members of the Broadcast Working Group, into the problems
of distribution in large-scale systems.

In this chapter we outline some of the constraints of large scale systems in
general and the Internet in particular. We then present two case studies that
illustrate the application of distributed, object-oriented technology developed
within the project. The first of these is the W3Objects project in which the
technology is applied to the Web, and the second in which it is applied to
Computer Supported Collaborative Work Internet applications.

1. The Constraints upon Internet Applications

The spectacular growth of the Internet during the early nineties was driven by the rush
to publish services and information on the World Wide Web. Internet applications
were largely market-driven, making use of the established client-server technology to
allow initially dumb clients (Web browsers) to talk to centralised Internet services.
Now however, applications are becoming truly distributed as intelligence moves to
the browser and services become decentralised in order to improve their performance
and fault-tolerance. As a consequence distributed, object-oriented technology in the
form of language-level support, e.g., Java; middleware platforms, e.g., CORBA; and
standards-based components, e.g., ActiveX Controls; is being increasingly deployed.
Underpinning this technology are many years of research, such as that undertaken by
members of the Broadcast Working Group, into the problems associated with Large
Scale Distributed Computing Systems (LSDCS). In this chapter we will explore the
application of some of this research work to Internet applications.

S. Krakowiak, S.K. Shrivastava (Eds.): Distributed Systems, LNCS 1752, pp. 213-237, 2000.

1.1. Characteristics of Internets

We begin by recalling some terminology. *Distributed applications* are composed of two or more computational entities (which we will term *components*), located on two or more computing nodes and capable of co-operating together for some common purpose. This is a very broad definition which encompasses not only tightly-coupled applications composed of distributed processes communicating to perform some well-defined algorithm, but also loosely coupled applications, e.g., Web browsers communicating with servers. We even include in this definition users exchanging documents which they expect to access using some common viewer.

In distributed systems, both computing nodes and network infrastructure may belong to more than one administrative domain. These domains are autonomous to varying degrees depending upon their freedom to make changes, without regard to other domains. This freedom might include the ability to define and modify their own software and hardware components and structure (including that part of the communication network for which they are responsible), and to provide, restrict or deny access to their domain. Where domains have a large degree of autonomy the communication network may be termed an *internet*; and where there is a small degree of autonomy (or a single domain) an *intranet*.

For an intranet a single organisation is effectively in control of the entire system and may therefore ensure (through the enforcement of standards for common languages, services and protocols) successful interworking between its application components. In an internet no single organisation has the authority to enforce standards and instead domains must co-operatively agree interworking standards. This is clearly problematic where many independent domains are present. However, successful examples include the widespread acceptance within many organisations of HTTP and HTML in the Web, and of CORBA and JavaRMI [24] within 'the Internet', the largest internet in existence.

In an intranet, the organisation can ensure that any required end-to-end guarantees between communicating components (such as availability and latency) are satisfied through network support for Quality of Service (QoS) and the provision of sufficient network resource. The lack of provision for end-to-end guarantees within internets means that those systems display the following characteristics:

Variable and unpredictable latency

Autonomous domains are free to place (or accept) whatever load they choose within their domain. (Note that communication between components within some application might pass through a number of intermediate domains). This can cause unpredictable congestion which effects communication latency between components when some part of their communication path is within the affected domain.

Variable and unpredictable availability

Components may be seen to be unavailable due to extended periods of the congestion described above, or due to network failures within any of the domains on the communication path between components. Autonomous domains are also free to restructure their internal organisation as they see fit. This means that they may relocate, rename or even remove components unpredictably as a result of which components could become unavailable.

A heterogeneous environment

In an intranet the organisation can decide to standardise upon particular hardware, operating systems, common services and applications. In an internet, individual organisations make whatever choice is to their particular benefit. This greatly complicates the task of deploying an application across an internet.

A considerable amount of effort has, and is, being expended in developing common standards and protocols intended to overcome some of these end-to-end problems within the Internet. Although work is under way to introduce protocols, e.g., RSVP [20], capable of negotiating and supporting end-to-end QoS, widespread acceptance and deployment of these standards, if it ever happens, is some considerable way off. For the foreseeable future Internet applications will continue to remain highly vulnerable to the characteristics described above, and as a consequence may be unable to provide satisfactory end-to-end guarantees between their constituent components.

In this chapter we will be concerned with techniques which may be used by applications to mask the variable and unpredictable nature of the Internet, and to cope with the inherent heterogeneity. We begin by sketching some general solutions.

The availability of a component within the Internet may be increased through the provision of multiply redundant communication paths via which the component may be accessed. Although the Internet may internally provide many alternative routes between two components, all routes will share some common path, i.e., at a minimum the start and end points of the communication. Replicating a component at a number of locations is a means by which an application can minimise the amount of the path shared between routes from one component to another.

The benefits of this approach are illustrated in Figure 1. In this (and subsequent figures) interacting components are shown as clients (who request some service) and services (which supply some service). This is purely for the purposes of illustration and it should be noted that components may also interact as peers. Figure 1 shows how a client component within an Internet application may continue to obtain service by accessing an alternative replica when the original path to the service is blocked.

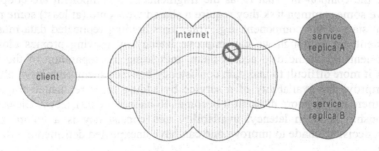

Fig. 1. Increasing service availability by replication

Latency between two communicating components may be improved (and its variance decreased) by simply shortening the Internet communication path between them. One means by which the path could be shortened would be to place interacting components 'close' together for the period of their interaction. (In the face of congestion or planned maintenance, moving a component can also be a means to improve availability). Unfortunately this solution does not make sense for components where i) there is a location dependency, e.g., a user GUI component needs to be co-located with the user's PC, a database server with the database; or ii) the costs of moving the component are prohibitive.

The alternative to improved placement of entire components is improved placement of some part of the component. Where practical a component can be *partitioned* so that a location-independent part (commonly known as a *proxy*) can be used to represent the *real* component in some portion of its interaction with other components. Where a proxy is placed close to components with which the real component needs to interact, then the total communication across the Internet may be greatly reduced. An applet dynamically delivered to supervise form-filling by a particular user, and a 'front-office', statically located close to some set of users in order to pre-process orders before passing them on to the 'back-office', are two examples. Note that proxies themselves are frequently replicated, i.e., there may be many proxies in different locations representing the same component. Proxies which display significant intelligence and independence are often termed *agents*, and these may operate autonomously for large periods of time without communicating with the component they represent.

Figure 2 illustrates the use of partitioning. *Client a* is shown communicating with *service a* via a service proxy; *client b* with *service b* via a client proxy (possibly an agent). The width of the paths shown indicates where the majority of the communication is to occur if the overall communication across the Internet is to be reduced.

In fact there is no clear distinction between the partitioning and replication of a component, i.e., partitions might be partial replicas and vice versa. Indeed a proxy that contains all of the functionality of the component is a complete replica, and a replica that is placed close to other components with which it communicates may be said to be acting as a proxy. We term partitions and replicas collectively as *fragments*.

Unfortunately, although fragmenting a component may be used to improve its availability and latency, doing so introduces the problem of maintaining consistency within the component. That is, as the fragments of a component are cooperating to achieve some common task they require a shared view onto (at least) some part of the current state of the component, e.g., fragments holding replicated data must be kept consistent. So, although we can improve latency by moving proxies closer to the components which need to access them, increasing the separation of the fragments makes it more difficult to maintain consistency between them. Similarly, although we can improve the availability of a service by adding more replicated fragments, the more there are the more difficult it becomes to maintain consistency. Clearly then the relationship between latency, availability and consistency is a complex one and design decisions made to improve one can have unexpected detrimental effects on the others.

Heterogeneity in an internet may be masked by the widespread adoption of a suitably high-level platform which provides a standard interface across a variety of platforms. Two example of this, as we shall discuss later, are the use of Web browsers and of Java.

In the remainder of this section we will focus upon how the characteristics of the Internet described above impact upon CSCW (Computer Supported Collaborative Work) Internet applications and upon the Web. In section 2 we present two case studies which demonstrate the application of object oriented technology to these application domains.

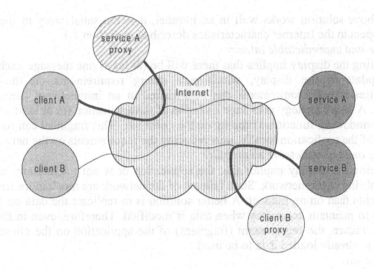

Fig. 2. Service partitioning using proxies

1.2 Internet Application Examples

CSCW

We now consider a subclass of applications that may be distributed on the Internet. These applications are those which provide remote access to a workspace and may potentially be cooperative, i.e., enable the cooperation of a group of users around a common task. Examples of such applications are a cooperative editor which allows multiple users to concurrently share and edit a common document (e.g., a CAD document), or a mail browser application which allows a user to read mail messages (including message archives), and to create and send messages to other users.

The characteristics of these applications are:

- they manage complex data structures that are persistent and may be shared concurrently between several clients. The data can be composed of complex graphs stored, for instance, in a large database.
- the data may be very large, depending on the application. For instance, a document generated by a CAD tool may represent several megabytes.
- the data needs to be loaded on the client site in order to be displayed and sometimes modified.

In an intranet, it is always possible to provide access to such an application using the traditional client-server paradigm. Here, a simple solution is to use remote displaying to enable a client to edit the document from his workstation. Each client can launch the application on the server and redirects the display to its local machine so that the client machine is used just like an X terminal. Sharing and cooperation is only implemented on the server machine. This is the mechanism used in most current CSCW environments.

If the above solution works well in an intranet, it is not satisfactory in the Internet with respect to the Internet characteristics described in section 1.1.

Variable and unpredictable latency

Redirecting the display implies that there will be (at least) one message exchange for each update to the display, which puts strong requirements on the network capabilities. These requirements can be satisfied in an intranet, but cannot in the Internet. A better strategy is to have a version of the application (or at least a fragment for the windowing functions) running on the client site. This fragment can manage the display of the application locally, thus reducing the requirements on the network.

Variable and unpredictable availability

Redirecting the display implies that the application does not tolerate any temporary unavailability of the network. Such failures of the network are much more frequent on the Internet than on an intranet. A better solution is to replicate the data on the client site and to maintain coherency when data is modified. Therefore, even in the case of network failure, the representant (fragment) of the application on the client site can still allow already loaded data to be used.

Heterogeneity

In order to implement the proposed solution, we need to have the application (or some fragments) installed on the client sites. In an intranet, this may be made possible by simply sharing a file system which stores the application. Moreover, in an intranet, the number of machine types is often limited, so that it is possible to install all the required versions of the application for these few types. In the Internet, the fact that the application may be used from any machine in any domain makes it much more difficult to make the application universally available. Furthermore, since Internet domains are administered independently, client machines may use different versions of the same application. Consequently, a solution based on a dynamic deployment of the application (like an applet) seems preferable.

In summary, we observe that the autonomy of the domains involved in the execution of such a cooperative application prevents us from implementing it as we would in an intranet. An internet-based CSCW application must take into account the unpredictability of latency and availability, and the heterogeneity of the environment.

The World-Wide Web

The Web is a distributed hypertext-based information system that is hosted by a large number of distributed, autonomously-managed servers. The Web is responsible for the majority of the network traffic on today's Internet thereby making it the largest example of a LSDCS application. The rapid takeoff of the Web can be partially attributed to the simplicity of the design. The key components of which include the HyperText Transfer Protocol (HTTP), a text-based client-server transport protocol; a location-based resource naming scheme, Uniform Resource Locators (URLs); and a simple text-based mark-up language, the HyperText Markup Language (HTML). In this section, we consider how these features have contributed to the strengths and weaknesses of the Web with respect to the characteristics of the Internet described in section 1.1.

Heterogeneity

Support for heterogeneity is one of the Web's great strengths. Web browsers and servers are available for most common operating systems and machine architectures.

One of the reasons for this is the simplicity of the transport protocol. HTTP is a text-based TCP/IP application protocol and in its early versions consisted of a small number of commands that were easy to implement. In fact, it was feasible for a competent programmer to implement a basic server in a couple of days. A downside of this is the performance penalty incurred in the string manipulation required when serving requests as compared to a binary protocol. Subsequent versions of HTTP have been designed to allow server implementers to maintain backward compatibility with previous versions of the protocol. With the massive number of users it is essential that protocols can be evolved without breaking existing software. More recent developments have incorporated a feature-negotiation mechanism into HTTP, known as the Protocol Extension Protocol (PEP) [17] to allow for evolutionary addition of new features.

The native resource format of the Web, HTML, also facilitates the Web's support for heterogeneity. Authoring Web documents using HTML, at least in the early versions, was possible without the use of specialist editors therefore Web content was created quickly. Similarly, the simple syntax of HTML made it straightforward to parse by Web browsers.

Variable and unpredictable availability

The use of the URL location-based naming scheme for Web resources is the main factor that influences the availability characteristics of the Web. The URL of a Web resource contains the protocol used to access a resource (typically HTTP), the Internet name of the server machine where the resource resides, and the location of the particular resource within the server.

Locational naming schemes are easy to implement as they require little in terms of support infrastructure. Accessing a Web resource requires only the use of the Domain Name Service (DNS) to resolve the hostname to a IP address. This means that the availability of a Web resource is affected only by the availability of the server machine and the network connectivity between the browser and the server. The failure of one Web server does not affect the availability of resources hosted by others. The downside of the use of a locational naming scheme is the lack of tolerance for resource migration. When a resource moves from one server to another or changes location within a server then effectively its name (its URL) changes. Since hypertext links are defined in terms of URLs then resource migration breaks all existing links to the old location.

URLs also imply an inherent one-to-one mapping between name and a single physical copy of a resource. Having a single copy reduces the reliability of the Web since a host failure, a network partition or severe network congestion can render a resource unavailable to all or a proportion of the client base. Since clients access resources by directly specifying the IP address of the server then any failure masking has to be performed at the network-level. Many sites use high availability solutions, such as HP's MC/ServiceGuard [21], which allow services to be failed-over on to a secondary host in the event of failure of the primary. Such solutions only work in closely coupled environments and therefore are unable to mask failures of Internet network links.

Load balancing is also an issue for popular sites where the volume of client requests cannot be satisfied by a single machine. Distributing requests across multiple server machines again requires network-level tricks, such as round-robin DNS [1] or network address translation based approaches [7, 8, 10] to create the illusion of a single URL space on top of a set of distributed servers.

The alternative to location-based naming is an abstract naming scheme in which there is a level of indirection between the name and the physical location of the resource. Supporting this level of indirection requires the use of nameservers that can perform the mapping from abstract name to physical location. Whilst in a small-scale organisation it would be feasible to use a single centralised nameserver to provide name to location mapping for all of the organisation's resources, this is impractical for a system the size of the Web for several reasons: it would be impossible to provide sufficient bandwidth to this centralised nameserver; a single machine could not support the load of all of the name resolution requests; but, most importantly, downtime of the nameserver, network congestion or partitioning would render the entire Web unusable for some or all clients. Therefore implementing abstract naming in the Web requires a distributed highly available name resolution infrastructure. There have been a number of proposals to implement such a scheme using Uniform Resource Names (URNs) that are resolved to URLs but up to present an acceptable approach has not been found.

Variable and unpredictable latency

Caching in the Web, achieved using caching proxy servers, reduces access latency, decreases bandwidth requirements and distributes load. To utilise caching servers, a Web client is configured to indirect all requests via the cache. Similarly, a cache server may be configured to further indirect requests via another cache server, thereby providing multi-level caching. Caching is virtually invisible to clients.

The granularity of the cache path selection is one problem with the current scheme since the same path is used for all resources requested by a client. However, the optimum cache path is likely to be different for different resources since it is dependent on the network topology between client and target resource. Allowing cache paths to be defined on a per resource basis (or per group of resources) would be more flexible in that it would allow network topologies to be taken into consideration. Furthermore, such an approach would allow specialist, e.g., subject specific, cache servers to be deployed that would likely provide higher hit rates. The downside of more flexibility and visibility of caching is the increased burden placed on users to configure cache paths appropriately. One idea for alleviating this problem would be to integrate caching with a high-level naming and metadata scheme whereby metadata could be used to indicate appropriate cache servers, either directly or by inference from the subject area of the resource.

A second problem with the current caching scheme is the inflexibility of the cache consistency protocols. Cache validation in HTTP is polling-based with the ability for some tuning by clients (by specifying acceptable ages) and content providers (by specifying expiry dates). Such a scheme has the advantage that it is easy to implement in a federated system since no collaboration is required between cache servers. However, it is not suitable for all resources, for example, for a resource that is updated infrequently but in an unpredictable manner, polling is inappropriate as it is wasteful of available bandwidth. A better approach would be to support server-driven invalidation using call-back. A more fundamental issue is that current caching, consistent with the Web in general, is only designed to support read-only access. As the Web continues to evolve it is likely that caching for write operations will also be required.

In summary, the incredible success of the Web can be attributed to its very uncomplicated pragmatic design that addressed many of the requirements of LSDCS in a pragmatic, best-effort way. There are a number of ongoing developments to address current limitations, such as HTTP-NG to improve the transport performance, URNs to provide support for resource migration and replication, and XML to add semantic information to Web resources to improve searching and indexing. These new features are being added in an evolutionary way so as to maintain the strengths of the current system.

1.3. Using Distributed Objects for Internet Applications

The use of distributed objects to build large scale distributed applications has been investigated for many years, both at the language and system support levels. Three aspects of the object paradigm make it particularly attractive. Firstly, the model of objects as entities whose only means of communication is through the exchange of messages fits very neatly into a distributed environment. Second, the use of well-defined interfaces is of great assistance when constructing proxies that represent some aspect of real components. Finally, the use of encapsulation provides a structuring mechanism for defining clear recovery boundaries within applications. For these reasons, and others, we will assume throughout the remainder of this chapter, that components (and fragments) of an application are realised as software objects.

A distributed internet application is therefore composed of objects and a network connecting those objects, both of which are under the control of independent domains. In order to deploy distributed objects in a large scale network, several problems have to be solved.

Naming and Binding

Objects and their locations must often identified/discovered at run-time, and objects may move during the lifetime of the application, in order to respond to the variable latency of the network. The main requirement is therefore to allow the access paths between objects to be built dynamically, without compromising the efficiency of remote invocation. The dynamicity of the binding raises in turn the need for distributed garbage collection.

Management of Groups of Objects

Object replication and object group protocols are the main tools used to build highly available applications. Replication is also used to reduce latency, by creating a cached copy of an object close to its callers' location. This in turn raises the need for consistency protocols between replicated objects and for fault tolerant protocols within object groups.

Security
Security constraints must be enforced in the object invocation protocols. Object mobility adds specific difficulties, as objects may move between different protection domains.
Solutions to some of these problems are presented in other chapters of this book [11, 22]. In the next section, we illustrate the use of distributed objects in Internet applications through two systems developed by us, namely, W3Objects and Javanaise.

2. Case Studies

In this section, we present two instances of solutions to some of the problems expressed in 1.3, each of which use variants of Distributed Objects and rely on a widely used infrastructure. The first one, W3Objects, was developed at The University of Newcastle upon Tyne, and is based on the Web infrastructure. The second one, Javanaise, was developed in the Sirac project (INRIA Rhône-Alpes and the Universities of Grenoble), and is based on the Java Virtual Machine.

2.1. W3Objects

Problems similar to those currently being faced by the Web, as described in Section 1.2, have been the focus of extensive research by the distributed computing community over recent years. The W3Objects project, carried out at Newcastle University, was one of the first research initiatives that has attempted to apply these distributed object-oriented computing solutions to the Web. Our work has concentrated on the issues of availability, scalability, latency and manageability of World-Wide Web services [5, 13, 14, 15, 16]. The W3Objects system has been implemented in C++ using *Shadows*, a lightweight ORB-like distributed object platform from Newcastle University [4]. In addition to basic distributed object support, Shadows provides a number of useful facilities including support for migration, referential integrity and garbage collection of objects [4, 5]. Although originally designed for fine-grain, programming-language level objects, in this section we will show how many of Shadows' features have been successfully applied to the larger-grained Web-level entities within the W3Objects system. In this overview, we concentrate primarily on the features that improve availability and reduce latency for Web services.

System Overview
In our model, Web resources are represented as objects (*W3Objects*), which are encapsulated resources possessing internal state and a well-defined behaviour, rather than the traditional file-based entities [13]. Each W3Object may support a number of distinct interfaces, obtained via interface inheritance. Common interfaces may be shared thereby enabling polymorphic access, for example, all W3Objects conform to an HTTP interface, providing methods including httpGet() and httpPost(). The specific implementation of the methods may differ between the different classes of object. For example, a simple W3Object for holding HTML state may simply return

this state in response to a httpGet() request, whereas another may return dynamically generated output based on some computation. Common functional properties such as distribution, persistence caching, and concurrency control are made available to application developers through base classes from which user classes can inherit.

W3Objects are organised and named within *contexts*, which may be nested. W3Object server processes (*W3OServers*) are simply active contexts. Objects are accessed using RPC and addressed using *W3References*, which are themselves objects. Internally, the minimum information held by a W3Reference includes the communication end-point of the W3OServer and the name of the object within that server. All inter-object references, such as those representing hypertext links are internally managed as W3References. The protocol that operates between a reference and an object is customisable. In this section, we will present three reference types: our basic reference which provides support for referential integrity; a fault-tolerant reference to improve availability; and a caching reference that can be used to reduce access latency.

Web Access to W3Objects

Web access to W3Objects is provided though a gateway, implemented as a plug-in module for an extensible Web server, such as Apache [2]. The gateway is fully compatible with the CGI interface allowing standard HTML forms to be used to create user interfaces to services. The Web server is configured to pass requests for part of the URL space (for example, URLs beginning /w3o/) to the gateway module. The remainder of the URL identifies the name of the required service and any parameters to be passed to it. The module then binds to the requested named object within a nameserver (a standard context) and invokes the appropriate method on it, e.g., httpGet() or httpPost(). Additional data associated with the request, including URL-encoded data from the client and environment data generated by the Web server is grouped together as a request object that is passed as a parameter to the HTTP interface operations. The nameserver forwards the request to the destination object, which performs the necessary computation and returns the results to the client, via the server. Figure 3 below illustrates the architecture through an example W3Objects site.

Improving Availability through Advanced Referencing

Earlier in this chapter, it was shown how the use of URL-based naming increases the likelihood of broken hypertext links due to resource migration or deletion. Our design addresses these issues through the W3Reference naming scheme which provides referential integrity and garbage collection for W3Objects [5].

The desired behaviour is for holders of references to be guaranteed referential integrity and for unreferenced objects to be garbage collected. W3Objects achieves this by maintaining binding information between objects. Reference counting is used to detect unreferenced objects. W3References, when created, perform an explicit *bind* operation on the object they refer to (thereby incrementing that object's reference count) and perform an *unbind* operation whenever the reference is deleted (thereby decrementing the count).

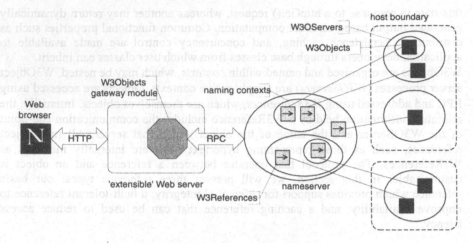

Fig. 3. Architecture of a W3Objects site

W3Objects are referenced from some root (typically a *root nameserver*) either directly, via W3References, or by being contained within another W3Object. This reference containment is used to support hypertext links between objects. Figure 4 below shows two servers, W3OServer 1 contains a root nameserver which contains references to objects held in context 2. One of these objects contains references to 2 further objects: reference 3 to a local object; and reference 4 to a remote object held within W3OServer 2. All of these objects are therefore reachable from some root.

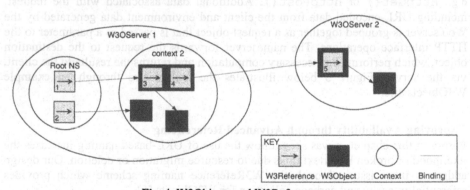

Fig. 4. W3Objects and W3References

Support for resource migration

One of the issues highlighted in Section 1.2 was the autonomous nature of the Web, in that resources are managed within independent domains. Each service provider is free to migrate and move resources within its domain. Our reference counting approach can be used to ensure that a resource owner is aware when resources are externally referenced and therefore can make intelligent decisions when considering deleting resources; if an externally-referenced object has to be deleted, it can be replaced with a *gravestone*, providing alternative information rather than simply becoming a broken link as is the case with the current URL-based referencing. Many broken links occur through resource migration rather than deletion. Our referencing scheme supports this transparently; an object may be moved from one location to another (potentially to some remote site). Our service guarantees that object moves are transparent to all other objects, i.e., references to the moved object continue to be valid.

Whenever an object is moved, a W3Reference is left behind at the old location and this automatically forwards invocations (without involving the invoker) to the new location. Further moves of the object may cause a chain of such references to be created (in a similar manner to that used by SSP chains [22]), leading ultimately to the real object. An example is shown in the figure below, which shows the steps that occur when an object is moved. In step 1, the object is migrated from context 2 to context 3 and an indirection reference (reference 2) is automatically introduced into the referencing graph. This indirection reference automatically forwards requests to the new location of the object. Whenever an invocation follows such a chain these indirections are short-cut as shown in step 2. Following a short-cut, intermediate references which are no longer referenced are automatically garbage collected.

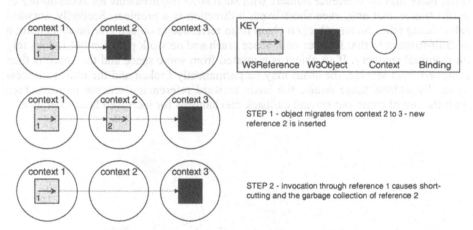

Fig. 5. Object migration and reference short-cutting

Reference chains can be extended in the backward direction through message exchange as shown in the figure below. Whenever a reference is to be passed to some party, e.g., from context 2 to context 1, the holder of the reference concerned first creates a new reference locally which is bound to the existing reference (step 1). As binding occurs within the local address space no external messages are required. The new reference is then passed in a message to a party in context 1 and the chain extended in the backward direction (step 2). However, in order to avoid invocations through the new reference having to follow the indirection, a hint is included within the reference, which allows the old reference to be bypassed. Note that it is the chain through the original reference which guarantees referential integrity whilst the hint is a simple optimisation for improved performance. The path from the hint may itself contain indirections (if the target object has migrated) and so *all* invocations, whether along the chain or via the hint, cause short-cutting.

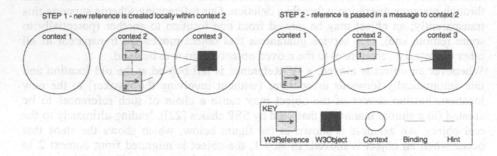

Fig. 6. Creating references – extending the chain backwards

Although our short-cutting mechanism efficiently removes indirections at invocation time, there may be reference holders with such strict requirements for accessibility or performance, that any, even short-lived, indirection is a problem. Secondly, forward referencing relies on an unbroken chain from reference to object. Our implementation is fault-tolerant in that it copes with space crash and network partition but it does rely on eventual recovery. If an object is migrated from some space and the space is then removed from service, the chain may be permanently broken and the object inaccessible. To address these issues, the basic forward referencing scheme is augmented with the use of name servers and callback mechanisms for increased fault-tolerance.

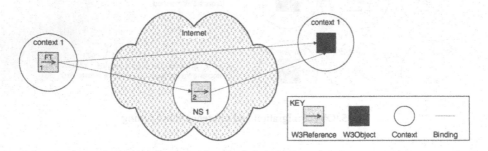

Fig. 7. Fault-tolerant references and nameservers for increased availability

Improving fault-tolerance

Name servers have two functions. Firstly, they may be used to maintain the binding between some name and an object, i.e., by tracking object location; this is how name servers are used within the Web server gateway module shown earlier. The second use of name servers is to provide alternative paths to an object so as to improve availability.

Reference 1 in the diagram above is a fault-tolerant variant of the basic W3Reference that supports multiple paths to the target object. An invocation performed on this reference will first be attempted directly but if the target is unreachable, the alternate path via reference 2 in nameserver NS 1 will be attempted. This mechanism improves availability and increases fault-tolerance. However, if the object is migrated, then a common path will be introduced. This situation is illustrated in Figure 8 below.

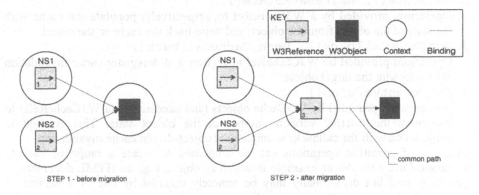

Fig. 8. Migrating nameserver-referenced objects

Although each name server will be updated on the first access of the object via their reference, until this happens they continue to share the common path (and, if some of the name servers are being used *only* to provide alternative paths, the update may not occur *until* the primary path fails - precisely the occasion at which a common path is most undesirable). To combat this problem, it is possible to allow the object to automatically inform all references (including nameserver references) when a migration occurs. Clearly there is a trade-off here: if the object performs the necessary updates during the migration then a burden is imposed on the migrator (in terms of delay) and by all of its reference holders (in that they cannot access the object whilst it is migrating). However, if the updates are delayed until some time after the migrate then a common path will exist until the updates occur.

Improving Latency through Caching
The deficiencies with the native caching mechanisms of the Web were highlighted in Section 1.2. To address these issues, the W3Objects system provides support for a highly-customisable *open caching* scheme that can be used to implement a wide-variety of caching protocols. Like the majority of W3Objects' features, our caching mechanisms overlay on to the existing Web infrastructure without interruption. The caching mechanism is implemented as a variation on our basic referencing scheme, that is, the basic referential integrity protocol between a reference and an object is augmented with support for caching features. The W3Objects library provides a W3Cache base class from which user classes can derive. This class provides a set of primitive caching operations that can be used, in conjunction with appropriate concurrency control, to create application specific caching protocols. W3References for W3Cache objects (known as *W3CacheRefs*) are provided (by virtue of the target

object being a W3Cache) with operations to drive the client end of the caching protocol. The set of caching related operations are listed below:

1. `CreateW3CacheRef()`
   An operation provided by the W3OServer to allow W3CacheRefs to be created, a parameter specifies the target object, i.e., W3OServer end-point and object name.
2. `GetState()`, `WriteBackState()`
   Operations provided by a W3CacheRef to, respectively, populate the cache with the state of the object from the object, and write-back the cache to the object.
3. `RegCacheCallback()`, `DeregCacheCallback()`
   Operations provided by W3CacheRef to register and deregister cache invalidation callbacks with the target object.
4. `IncrementVersion()`
   An operation provided by W3Cache objects (and accessible via W3CacheRefs) to increment the internal version number of the object state. This is used in conjunction with the callbacks to implement object-driven cache invalidation.

This set of primitive operations can be combined to create a range of caching schemes. First, consider an example in which an object, e.g., an HTML document, is generally read but occasionally may be remotely updated by one of a number of clients. During an update period a client may perform many state changes to the object. Without the use of caching, each state change would require remote communication to the target object. Using our scheme, the client application would create a new W3CacheRef bound to the target object, attempt to acquire a write-lock on the object, and if successful, retrieve the state of the object to populate the W3CacheRef. Subsequent invocations would be performed locally, i.e., on the W3CacheRef. When the client terminates the update session, the state of the cache is written back to the object, the lock released and the W3CacheRef can be discarded.

Secondly, consider an application for which it is appropriate to allow clients to continue to read cached stale copies of a resource whilst it is in the process of being updated, but refreshes those caches after the updates are complete. To create a read-only cache that is kept consistent in this manner the client requests, as before, that a local server create a proxy bound to the remote object. The client then requests that the proxy register a callback with the object and then obtain a copy of the object's state (correct as of the time of the last synchronisation event, i.e., write lock set or release). Our client may then invoke read-only operations upon the proxy, all of which occur locally. Whenever some other client updates the object (which automatically increments the version number) the object invokes a callback to invalidate each of its caches. The next operation invoked upon the proxy refreshes the now invalid cache by automatically obtaining the new state of the object. Whenever the client has finished with his cache he requests that the proxy deregister the callback. Finally, the client requests that the local server discard the proxy.

In the examples above the implementation requires the client to explicitly drive every step of the protocol. However, the application programmer can hide the protocol details from the client. For example, the object could offer simpler caching operations than the ones described here which hide complexity, e.g., in the first example the two operations `CreateWriteCache()` and `RemoveCache()` might be sufficient.

As well as allowing clients to drive cache refreshes by explicitly requesting the proxy obtain a new copy of the state, another operation allows clients to specify an acceptable age for the cache. When a cache handles an invocation a refresh of the cache occurs automatically if the cache is 'older' than the acceptable age. (This is similar to the use of the max_age field in HTTP).

As we have already described, clients may create or access W3OServers within the network. Clients may also create or access proxies within those servers that are bound to an object. Servers may be created to act as cache servers and used by co-operating clients as a shared cache store. As caches may be bound to caches, many levels of cache may be constructed into complex hierarchical trees.

Summary

W3Objects addresses the issues of availability, scalability and latency of Web services. We use the forward referencing mechanism described above to ensure referential integrity within the W3Object domain. Holding a reference guarantees that the target object will persist, despite space and communication failures and will remain accessible (at least, eventually) via the reference. As we show in [5], our mechanism is totally distributed and completely scaleable. The basic mechanism caters for object movement, requiring no additional messages at migration time, and the minimum message overhead on invocation. The use of nameservers and callbacks allows additional guarantees concerning the availability and performance of specific objects to be obtained. The flexible open caching mechanisms allow clients to make caching decisions for individual resources and explicitly drive the consistency protocol for their cache in order to obtain optimal performance. Cache hierarchies may be created and used by groups of clients to obtain higher performance and other benefits of sharing. These mechanisms offer a very high degree of flexibility over caching at the expense of additional complexity as perceived by a Web client and/or application programmer. However, users are free to make decisions about whether to accept this trade-off on a per resource basis, and choosing to do so has a minimal performance effect on access to all other resources. Further information about the W3Object caching facilities can be found in [6].

2.2 Javanaise

In this section, we present Javanaise, a system developed within the Sirac project at INRIA [12]. Javanaise aims at providing adequate support for distributed shared objects on the Internet; it therefore addresses the issues previously described.

In order to present this experiment, we will first overview the motivation for Javanaise and then describe the design and implementation.

Motivations

The main objective of Javanaise is to implement system support for object sharing on the Internet. Today, sharing objects on the Internet is closely linked with the Web (essentially URLs) and Java. This is mainly because they provide, respectively, a global naming scheme and machine independent code, thus helping overcome the problems of heterogeneity. Therefore, a first step to providing distributed shared objects on the Internet was Java-RMI [24] which allows remote method invocation between Java objects. Remote object references may be exchanged and a mechanism called *object serialisation* [18] allows distributed programs to exchange copies of objects (as in Sun RPC [19]). However, distributed applications that use RMI are based on the client-server architecture, which does not allow objects to be cached and therefore accessed locally. It is possible to manage object replicas using the object serialisation facility, but the coherence between the replicas has to be explicitly managed by the application programmer. As mentioned in 1.2, object caching is one of the key features required by distributed applications, especially over the Internet, where latency and bandwidth are highly variable.

In order to assist the programmer, Javanaise provides a system-level service which implements the abstraction of a distributed shared Java object space. This service provides the same abstraction and interface as the RMI service of Java, but extends its functionality by allowing shared objects to be cached on the accessing node. Objects are copied on demand to the requesting nodes and are cached there, until invalidated by the consistency protocol. With this system support, the programmer can develop his application as if it were to be executed in a centralised configuration. Then, the application can be configured for a distributed setting without any (or with minor) modification to the application source code. This configuration is performed by annotating the interfaces of the objects that are distributed, specifying the synchronisation and consistency protocols to be applied to these objects. The system is implemented on top of Java and consists of a proxy generator which is used to generate indirection objects (proxies) for the support of dynamic binding, and a few system classes that implement consistency protocols and synchronisation functions.

The main benefits of Javanaise are:

1. Dynamic deployment. Since Javanaise is based on Java, applications can be dynamically deployed to the client nodes from the node that hosts the application, provided a Java virtual machine is available; thus applications do not have to be installed on a machine prior to execution.
2. Caching. The system support of Javanaise allows shared Java objects to be cached on co-operating nodes, thus enabling local invocation on distributed objects and reducing latency.
3. Transparency. A distributed application can be developed as if it were to be run centralised. Distribution and synchronisation are expressed separately from the application code. This also enables adaptation of existing centralised applications in order to run distributed.

Design of Javanaise

The design of Javanaise is based on an abstraction called a cluster, which is used as a unit for application structuring, and which allows the costs of system-level operations to be amortised.

Managing clusters.

The goal is to efficiently manage distributed replicas of Java objects while keeping distribution transparent to the application programmer. The following problems must be solved.

1. Managing object replicas requires mechanisms for object faulting, invalidating and updating in order to ensure consistency. These mechanisms should be hidden to the application programmer, who should only manipulate Java references as if every object were local.
2. Previous experiments with the management of distributed fine grained objects have shown that efficiency is closely linked with object clustering. A *cluster* of objects

is a group of objects which is managed as a whole at the system level; thus the cost of the system mechanisms is factored for all the objects within a cluster. However, clustering works well only if objects co-located within the same cluster are effectively closely related.

The mechanisms to be factored are related to naming, binding and consistency. In order to be able to dynamically bind a reference to a remote object, a unique name must be associated with each object, thus allowing the object to be located and copied to the requesting node. In order to implement object binding[1], indirection objects are created, thus allowing object faults to be triggered if the reference is not yet bound. Consistency-related messages have to be exchanged between co-operating nodes in order to invalidate and update copies according to a consistency model.

Managing clusters of objects is a means for amortising these costs (indirection objects, messages) over a group of inter-dependent objects. Inter-dependence means here that if one object of the group is accessed, most of the objects included in the group are likely to be used in the near future.

Application dependent clustering

The simplest way to address the object clustering issue is to provide system support that allows any object to be stored in any cluster. The system exports to applications a cluster management interface allowing objects to be stored in, or migrated to, any cluster. From the programmer's point of view, managing clustering is complex and most of the time leads to a default policy which is inefficient and does not actually use the flexibility of the clustering interface.

In Javanaise, the approach is to allow application specific clustering policies while keeping it transparent to the application programmer. The approach, called *application dependent clustering*, is based on the observation that object-based applications tend to manage logical graphs of objects in their data structures. For example, a structured editor [9] manages chapters that are composed of sections, themselves composed of subsections and paragraphs. Some of these graphs should be managed as clusters by the system since they correspond to closely related objects according to the application semantics.

In Javanaise, a cluster is an application-defined graph of Java objects. A cluster is identified by a Java reference to an initial object (called a *cluster object*) and the graph that defines the cluster is composed of all the Java objects that are accessible from the cluster object (the transitive closure). The boundaries of this graph are defined by the leaves of the graph and by the references to other cluster objects. A reference to another cluster object is called an *inter-cluster reference* (Figure 9). The Java objects within a cluster are called *local objects*.

A cluster object is an instance of a class (defined by the programmer) which has been defined (when the application is configured to be run distributed) as being a cluster class. Only interfaces of cluster objects are exported to other cluster objects, which means that the interface of a cluster object may only include methods whose reference parameters are references to cluster objects. Therefore, local objects in one cluster are only accessible from objects within the cluster.

---

[1] without modification to the Java virtual machine

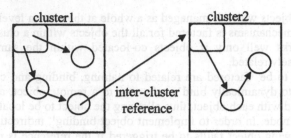

Fig. 9. Management of clusters in Javanaise

With RMI, as for Javanaise, configuring the application for distribution involves specifying which classes are Remote (resp. Cluster). Then, only Remote objects are globally visible and the applications only pay the cost of objects declared Remote.

The basic difference between Javanaise and RMI is that Javanaise provides cluster caching. This means that a cluster is loaded on the client node the first time it is used, and is accessed locally thereafter. Furthermore, Javanaise enforces object consistency whenever objects are cached on different machines, as is shown in a further section.

Application programming

The programmer develops applications using the Java language without any language extension nor explicit use of system support classes (libraries). An application can be debugged and tested locally (on one machine).

Configuring the application for distribution first consists of specifying which classes are cluster classes (just like an RMI user specifies which classes are Remote). The configurator should take into account the data structures managed in the application, i.e., the links between the classes that compose the application. However, this separation between the configuration and the application code makes it possible to experiment with different configurations for the same application without any modification to the application.

Since an application is developed as if it were centralised, synchronisation and consistency aspects are not considered. A second step in the configuration process is to associate a synchronisation and a consistency protocol with each cluster. This is done at the level of the interfaces of the cluster classes. The interfaces of the cluster classes are annotated with keywords that define the consistency and synchronisation protocols associated with the clusters.

Several protocols have been implemented. In the single writer / multiple readers protocol, it is possible to associate a mode (reader or writer) with each method in the interface of a cluster. When the method is invoked on a cluster instance, a lock in that mode is taken and a consistent copy of the cluster is brought to the local host. Two different versions of this protocol allow the cluster to be made consistent either with invalidation on write or with update broadcasting. Another protocol implements an exclusive access protocol (a unique copy in the whole system). Experiments with different consistency/synchronisation protocols are contemplated.

Implementation of Javanaise

Since a cluster is a graph of Java objects, the implementation of Javanaise uses the Java serialisation mechanism to dynamically copy clusters to a requesting node. This is detailed in the rest of this section.

Managing cluster binding

Since clusters are fetched dynamically from remote nodes, the problem is to ensure dynamic binding of inter-cluster references.

The implementation relies on *proxy* objects [23] which are transparently inserted between the referenced cluster and the cluster which contains the reference. In Javanaise, a proxy contains a Java reference that points to the referenced cluster object if it is already there, and is null if not. It also contains a unique name associated with the cluster, allowing the cluster to be located and a copy to be brought on the local host.

The class of the proxy object is generated from the interface of the cluster class to which it points. This proxy implements the same interface as the cluster object. Each method invocation is forwarded to the actual cluster object if the reference is already bound, i.e., if the Java reference in the proxy is not null. If this Java reference is null, then a function of the runtime system is invoked in order to check whether the cluster is already cached (subsequent to the binding of another inter-cluster reference). A copy of the cluster is fetched if required and the Java reference in the proxy object is updated.

This proxy is called a *proxy-out object*. Proxy-out objects are stored in the cluster which contains the reference to the cluster.

Managing cluster consistency and synchronisation

The problem is to manage invalidates and updates of clusters according to a consistency protocol.

A cluster can be invalidated on one node (Java virtual machine) simply by assigning to null the Java references in the proxy-out objects that reference the cluster. All the Java objects included in the invalidated cluster would then be automatically garbage collected by the Java runtime system. However, this would require searching for all the proxy-out objects that point to the invalidated cluster, a complex and inefficient process. Instead, Javanaise manages another type of proxy called a proxy-in object, which is inserted between the proxy-out object and the cluster it points to. A proxy-in object is stored in the cluster which is referenced. Similarly to proxy-out objects, a proxy-in object forwards method invocations to the referenced cluster if its internal Java reference is not null. If this Java reference is null, then a function of the runtime system is invoked in order to fetch a consistent copy of the cluster and the Java reference in the proxy-in object is updated. Figure 10 illustrates this architecture with proxy-in and proxy-out objects.

Then, a cluster invalidation on one node simply consists in assigning to null the Java reference in its associated proxy-in object.

Therefore, Javanaise has to deal with two kinds of cluster faults:

1. proxy-out faults. When the Java reference in a proxy-out object is null, a copy of the referenced cluster is fetched. This copy of the cluster includes a proxy-in object pointing to the cluster object.

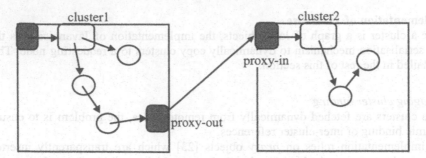

Fig. 10. Consistency of cluster objects in Javanaise

2. proxy-in faults. When the Java reference in a proxy-in object is null, a copy of the referenced cluster is fetched. This copy of the cluster does not include a copy of the proxy-in object which is already there.

In both cases, the consistency protocol may require the cluster to be invalidated (or updated) on some other nodes, using its proxy-in object on that node.

In most cases, a synchronisation scheme is associated with the consistency protocol. For instance, the *entry consistency* protocol [3] requires applications to lock objects, and guarantees objects coherence only when a lock is taken. Such a synchronisation scheme is implemented in the proxy-in object. Javanaise provides a set of consistency/synchronisation protocols and allows the association of one of them with each cluster. For instance, with the single writer / multiple readers protocol, an access mode (read or write) can be associated with each method in a cluster interface, which means that a lock on the cluster must be taken before entering the method. This locking strategy in managed in the proxy-in object which knows which lock is being held on the current node. An invalidation on one node is a lock request to the proxy-in object, that may block until all locks are released on that object.

Managing reference parameter passing

In the interface of a cluster object, methods may only have reference parameters that are references to cluster objects. When such a reference is passed at execution time, the system ensures that a reference which enters a cluster will point to a proxy-out object. This is ensured by the proxy-out objects for onward parameters and the proxy-in objects for backward parameters (Figure 11).

In Figure 11, a local object in *cluster1* (1) performs an invocation (*c3 = c2.meth()*) on *cluster2*. The invoked method returns a Java reference stored in *cluster2* (2), which is a reference to *cluster3*. In order to be able to store a reference to *cluster3* in *cluster1*, the system must create a proxy-out which points to *cluster3* (3). This proxy-out object is created by the proxy-out in *cluster1* which is associated with the reference to *cluster2* (4). An onward reference parameter would be managed similarly by the proxy-in object in *cluster2*.

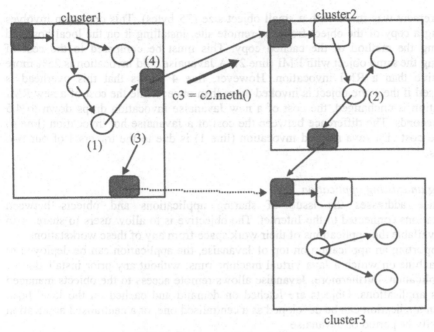

cluster1

(4)

c3 = c2.meth()

(1)   (3)

cluster2

(2)

cluster3

Fig. 11. Parameter passing in Javanaise

When managing proxy-out objects for entering parameters in a cluster, the system must guarantee that all the references to a cluster C within the cluster point to the same proxy-out object. This is especially important when comparing two variables that contain cluster references (within one cluster). To do this, Javanaise manages in each cluster a table which registers the proxy-out objects which already exist in the cluster. When a reference enters the cluster and if an associated proxy-out object already exists in the cluster, then this proxy-out object is used and no additional proxy-out object is created. Therefore, it avoids having two proxy-out objects associated with the same external reference in one cluster.

Evaluation and Experience

Basics costs
Table 1 gives the costs of the basic operations that are relevant to Javanaise.

(1)	Java method invocation	1.45 µs
(2)	RMI invocation	4000 µs
(3)	Javanaise invocation (cold)	5000 µs
(4)	Javanaise invocation (hot)	4.5 µs

Table 1. Basic costs of operations in Javanaise

Line 3 gives the cost of a method invocation in Javanaise in the case the object (a cluster) which is remote, i.e., not yet cached locally (cold invocation). This measurement was made with a small object size (75 bytes). This operation involves fetching a copy of the object from the remote site, installing it on the local host and invoking the method of the cached copy. This must be compared to the cost of invoking the same object with RMI (line 2). A Javanaise cold invocation is 25% more expensive than a RMI invocation. However, line 4 shows that this overhead is amortised if the same object is invoked more than once; while the cost of a new RMI invocation is unchanged, the cost of a new Javanaise invocation drops down to 4.5 microseconds. The difference between the cost of a Javanaise hot invocation (line 4) and the cost of a Java method invocation (line 1) is due to the traversal of our two proxies.

Porting an existing application

Javanaise addresses the issue of sharing applications and objects between workstations connected to the Internet. The objective is to allow users to share or to keep available the applications of their work space from any of these workstations.

By supporting an application on top of Javanaise, the application can be deployed to any machine on which a Java virtual machine runs, without any prior installation of the application. Furthermore, Javanaise allows remote access to the objects managed by this applications. Objects are fetched on demand and cached on the local host. Such an application can be developed as a centralised one, or a centralised application can easily be ported on Javanaise.

To experiment with Javanaise, an existing graphical mail browser application has been ported on Javanaise. This application consists of 10700 lines of Java code. It uses a POP server to get the electronic mail and provides traditional facilities such as folders for messages. When a user reads and sends messages, he may archive the messages in different folders and browse old messages in his folders. In the original centralised application, all the messages and the folders are stored in files on the site where the application is installed. This application is supposed to be launched only on that site. On top of Javanaise, the application can be launched from any machine and the folder objects are fetched on demand and transparently managed by the runtime of Javanaise.

This experiment showed that it was very easy to port an application on top of Javanaise. It took actually two days to complete the port of the mail browser application.

References

1. P. Albitz and C. Liu, "DNS and BIND in a Nutshell," O'Reilly and Associates, 1992.
2. "The Apache Project web site." <URL:http://www.apache.org/>
3. B. N. Bershad et al., "The Midway Distributed Shared Memory System," Proceedings of the 38th IEEE Computer Society International Conference (COMPCON'93), pp. 528-537.
4. S. J. Caughey, G. D. Parrington and S. K. Shrivastava, "Shadows: A Flexible Support System for Objects in a Distributed System," Proceedings of 3rd IEEE International Workshop in Object-Orientation in Operating Systems (IWOOOS'93), Ashville, North Carolina, U.S.A., pp.73-81, Dec. 1993. <URL:http://arjuna.ncl.ac.uk/group/papers/p028.ps>
5. S. J. Caughey and S. K. Shrivastava, "Architectural Support for Mobile Objects in Large Scale Distributed Systems," Proceedings of the 4th IEEE International Workshop on Object

Orientation in Operating Systems (IWOOOS'95), pp. 38-47, Lund, Sweden, 1995. <URL: http://arjuna.ncl.ac.uk/group/papers/p044.ps>

6. S. J. Caughey, D. B. Ingham, and M. C. Little, "Flexible Open Caching for the Web," Computer Networks and ISDN Systems, vol. 29, no. 8-13, pp. 1007-1017, 1997. <URL: http://arjuna.ncl.ac.uk/group/papers/p055.pdf>

7. "Cisco LocalDirector," Cisco Systems, Inc. White paper, 1996.

8. O. M. Damani et al., "ONE-IP: Techniques for Hosting a Service on a Cluster of Machines," Proceedings of the 6th International World Wide Web Conference, Santa Clara, California, USA, April 1997.

9. D. Decouchant et al., "Griffon: A Cooperative, Structured, Distributed Document Editor," Technical Report 93-20, Bull-IMAG, 1993.
    <URL:http://sirac.imag.fr/~hagimont/papers/93-20-griffon-RT.ps.gz >

10. K. Egevang and P. Francis, "The IP Network Address Translator (NAT)," RFC 1631, Network Information Center, SRI International, May 1994. <URL:ftp://ds.internic.net/rfc/ rfc1631.txt>

11. P. Felber, R. Guerraoui and A. Schiper, "Replication of CORBA objects", Chapter 11, this book.

12. D. Hagimont and D. Louvegnies, "Javanaise: distributed shared objects for Internet cooperative applications," Proceedings of Middleware'98, pp. 339-354, 1998.

13. D. B. Ingham, M. C. Little, S. J. Caughey, and S. Shrivastava, K., "Bringing Object Oriented Technology to the Web," World Wide Web Journal, vol. 1, no. 1, pp. 89-105, 1995. <URL: http://arjuna.ncl.ac.uk/group/papers/p049.html>

14. D. B. Ingham, S. J. Caughey, and M. C. Little, "Fixing the "Broken-Link" Problem: The W3Objects Approach," Computer Networks and ISDN Systems, vol. 28, no. 7-11, pp. 1255-1268, 1996. <URL: http://arjuna.ncl.ac.uk/group/papers/p050.html>

15. D. B. Ingham, S. J. Caughey, and M. C. Little, "Supporting Highly Manageable Web Services," Computer Networks and ISDN Systems, vol. 29, no. 8-13, pp. 1405-1416, 1997. <URL: http://arjuna.ncl.ac.uk/group/papers/p056.html>

16. M. C. Little, S. Shrivastava, K., S. J. Caughey, and D. B. Ingham, "Constructing Reliable Web Applications using Atomic Actions," Computer Networks and ISDN Systems, vol. 29, no. 8-13, 1997. <URL: http://arjuna.ncl.ac.uk/group/papers/p054.html>

17. W3C, "PEP - An Extension Mechanism for HTTP," <URL: http://www.w3.org/ Protocols/PEP/>

18. R. Riggs et al., "Pickling State In The Java System," Computing Systems, vol. 9, no. 4, pp. 313-329.

19. rpcgen - An RPC Protocol Compiler, Sun Microsystems, Inc., 1988.

20. IETF Network Working Group, Resource ReSerVation Protocol (RSVP), Version 1 Functional Specifications, <URL:ftp://ftp.isi.edu/in-notes/rfc2205.txt>

21. B. Sauers, "Understanding High Availability," Hewlett-Packard Company, 1996.

22. M. Shapiro, F. Le Fessant and P. Ferreria, "Recent advances in distributed garbage collection", Chapter 5, this book.

23. M. Shapiro, Structure and encapsulation in distributed systems: the proxy principle, 6th International Conference on Distributed Computing Systems, pp 198-204, Boston, May 1986.

24. A. Wollrath, R. Riggs, and J. Waldo. A Distributed Object Model for the Java System, Computing Systems, vol. 9, 4, 1996, pp. 265-290.

Integrating Group Communication with Transactions for Implementing Persistent Replicated Objects

Mark C. Little and Santosh K. Shrivastava

Department of Computing Science
University of Newcastle, Newcastle upon Tyne, NE1 7RU, England

Abstract. A widely used computational model for constructing fault-tolerant distributed applications employs atomic transactions for controlling operations on persistent objects. There has been considerable work on data replication techniques for increasing the availability of persistent data that is manipulated under the control of transactions. Process groups with ordered group communications (process groups for short) has also emerged as a model for building available distributed applications. High service availability can be achieved by replicating the service state on multiple processes managed by a group communication infrastructure. These two models are often seen as rivals. This paper examines whether a distributed transaction system can profit from process groups for supporting replication of objects. A general model of distributed objects is used to investigate how objects can be replicated for availability using a system that supports transactions (but no process groups) and a system that supports process groups (but no transactions). A comparative evaluation reveals how a distributed transaction system can exploit group communications for obtaining a flexible approach to supporting replication of objects.

Keywords: distributed systems, fault-tolerance, persistent objects, group communication, atomic transactions, replication

1. Introduction

A widely used computational model for constructing fault-tolerant distributed applications employs atomic transactions (atomic actions) for controlling operations on persistent (long-lived) objects. There has been considerable amount of work done on data replication techniques for increasing the availability of persistent data that is manipulated under the control of transactions [1]. The process group with ordered group communications (process groups for short) has also emerged as a model for building available distributed applications [e.g., 2-8]. High service availability can be achieved by replicating the service state on multiple server processes that are managed by an underlying group communication infrastructure.

These two models are often seen as rivals; for example a recent paper suggested that transactional systems are a better alternative to process groups [9], a claim hotly denied by the supporters of the process group approach [10]. There have been

S. Krakowiak, S.K. Shrivastava (Eds.): Distributed Systems, LNCS 1752, pp. 238-253, 2000.

attempts to 'unify' the two models, the main thrust of the work being to enrich group communication with some transactional flavour [11]. This paper also explores the role of the two models in building fault-tolerant distributed applications. We do it in very focussed manner, dealing with just the replication of persistent objects, exploring the overall system design issues that have not been addressed by previous studies.

Our approach to exploring ways of using transactions and group communications together is quite pragmatic: we actually investigate how transaction systems can make use of process groups, rather than the other way round as hinted in [11]. We envisage that future distributed applications will increasingly rely on the so called 'middleware services' for support for naming, concurrency control, event management, persistence etc. Further, CORBA, the industry backed distributed object architecture has adopted transactions as the application structuring paradigm for manipulating long-lived objects, and transaction services are already available on CORBA platforms alongside other services mentioned before. In addition, given the availability of CORBA group communication services (such as [12, 13]), we have the possibility of supporting object replication in more than one way. For applications that are programmed using transactions, it is then worth investigating if any benefits can be gained by exploiting group communication for replicating transactional objects. We show that this is indeed the case. Our ideas on how transaction systems can make use of group communication for supporting high availability distributed applications are therefore directly applicable to CORBA and similar architectures. An earlier version of this paper has appeared in [14].

We begin by presenting a model of distributed object system without replication. We do not claim that our model is 'universal', but that it is representative of a sufficiently wide class of real systems. We then investigate how objects can be replicated for availability in two types of systems: (i) a system that supports transactions but no process groups; object replication approaches used here will be termed transaction based (or *TR-based* for short); and (ii) a system that supports process groups but no transactions; object replication approaches used here will be termed group communication based (or *GC-based* for short). We then evaluate the two approaches. This evaluation enables us to understand how a distributed transaction system can exploit group communications for obtaining a flexible approach to supporting replication of objects. We do not assume any special hardware support for replication (e.g., mirrored disks, tightly coupled primary-backup processor clusters etc.), but consider just a distributed collection of processors with secondary storage.

2. Models

2.1. Assumptions

It will be assumed that the hardware components of the system are computers (nodes), connected by a communication subsystem. A node is assumed to work either as specified or simply to stop working (crash). After a crash, a node is repaired within a finite amount of time and made active again. A node may have both stable (crash-proof) and non-stable (volatile) storage or just non-stable storage. All of the data stored on volatile storage is assumed to be lost when a crash occurs; any data stored on stable storage remains unaffected by a crash.

We model the communication environment as either *asynchronous* or *synchronous*. In an asynchronous environment connected and correctly functioning processes are capable of communicating in *bounded but unknown* time (i.e., the time interval between the sending of a message and its reception by the receiver cannot be estimated accurately) whereas in a synchronous environment connected and correctly functioning processes are capable of communicating with each other in *bounded and known time*. A network will be said to be *partitionable*, if correctly functioning processes are not able to communicate (e.g., due to physical breakdown such as a crash of a gateway node and/or network congestion). In an asynchronous environment, even without partitions, timeouts and network level 'ping' mechanisms cannot act as an accurate indication of process failures (they can only be used for *suspecting* failures); whereas in a synchronous environment, assuming no partitions, judiciously chosen timeouts together with network level 'ping' mechanisms can act as an accurate indication of process failures. In this paper we will make the assumption of asynchronous, partitionable communication environment; however, we assume that a partition in a network is eventually repaired.

We will consider the case of *strong consistency* which requires that the states of all replicas that are regarded as *available* be mutually consistent (so the persistent states of all available replicas are required to be identical). Object replicas must therefore be managed through appropriate replica-consistency protocols to ensure strong consistency.

2.2 Distributed Non-replicated Objects

An object is an instance of some class. The class defines the set of *instance variables* each object will contain and the *operations* or *methods* that determine the externally visible behaviour of the object. The operations of an object have access to the instance variables and can thus modify the internal state of that object. An operation invocation upon a remote object is performed via a remote procedure call (RPC).

We assume that objects are *persistent*, by which we simply mean that they are long-lived entities. Objects are assigned unique identifiers (UIDs) for naming them. We further assume that some application specific naming service can map an application level object name (a string) to the corresponding UID. We do not discuss such a naming scheme further here, and assume that an application can always obtain the UIDs of objects it is manipulating.

A persistent object not in use is assumed to be held in a *passive* state with its state residing in an object store (a stable object repository) and *activated* on demand (i.e., when an invocation is made) by loading its state from the object store to the volatile store, and associating an *object server* process for receiving RPC invocations. To be able to access a persistent object, an application program must be able to obtain information about the object's location. We assume that the application program can request this information from a *binding service* by presenting it with the UID of the object. Once the application program (client) has obtained the location of the object it can direct its invocations to that node. It will be the responsibility of that node to activate the object (if the object was in a passive state). Thus, a number of system services are required to support distributed computations structured out of objects. We enumerate them below:

- *RPC service*: provide an object invocation facility;
- *Object Storage service*: provide a stable storage repository for object states; a state can be retrieved by presenting the service with the UID of the object.
- *Binding service*: provides a mapping from a given UID to the necessary information required for binding to the object (this information is: host name of the object server, host name of the object store, see below). The binding service is assumed to run at a well known address.

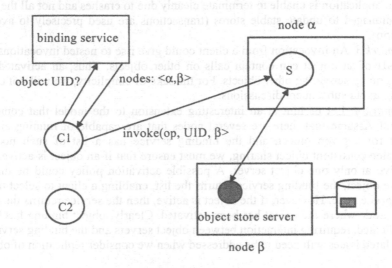

Figure 1: Object binding.

We assume that for each persistent object there is a node (say α) which, if functioning, is capable of running a server for that object (in effect, this would require that the node has access to the executable code for the object's methods). If α receives an invocation from the client, and the object is passive at α, then the object needs to be activated before the invocation can be performed; this requires allocating a server and if necessary loading the executable code for the object and then fetching the object state from some object store. We will assume that there is a node (say β) whose object store contains the state of the object; we do not require that α be the same as β. Thus, we assume that the binding service maps a given UID to location related information, namely the pair <α, β>. Fig. 1 illustrates the steps involved for the case of an object that is passive: client C1 presents the UID of an object to the binding service; sends the invocation (to perform operation 'op') to node α. This node allocates a server S and gets the state from the object store at β, before S can perform the operation. During the termination of an application, the new states of objects are migrated to their object stores.

We assume that objects can be shared between clients, and an object server is responsible for enforcing concurrency control on its objects (e.g., shared read but exclusive write). In the above example, if some client C2 invokes the same object, then that invocation will be sent to α who will direct the invocation to the activated copy being managed by S.

Remark 1: In the object model presented above, for a given set of objects, the binding service requirement is simple as it needs to provide read only access to location information. We assume that a copy of the information is also held on stable store (see below).

Remark 2: The model goes a long way towards supporting the ability to recover from *total crashes*: even if all of the nodes crash, the system can eventually bootstrap itself with information held on stable stores remaining consistent, provided partitions eventually heal and crashed nodes eventually recover. Some inconsistency can creep in if an application is unable to terminate cleanly due to crashes and not all the servers have managed to update stable stores (transactions are used precisely to avoid this situation).

Remark 3: An invocation from a client could give rise to nested invocations, as the methods of an object can contain calls on other objects. Thus, an activated object could end up activating other objects. For the sake of simplicity, we will not consider nesting in our subsequent discussions.

Remark 4: Let us hint at an interesting extension to the model that complicates matters! Assume that there are several nodes that are capable of running an object server for a given object, and the binding service has a list of such nodes. To guarantee consistent object sharing, we must ensure that if an object is active, then it is active at only one object server. A possible activation policy could be that for a passive object, the binding service returns the list, enabling a client to select the most appropriate node. However, if the object is active, then the service returns the identity of the node where the object has been activated. Clearly, object binding has become complicated, requiring interaction between object servers and the binding service; this and related issues will need to be addressed when we consider replication of objects.

2.3. Object Replication

In the scheme shown in fig. 1, an object can potentially become unavailable to the client if any of the communication paths get disrupted due to partitions or any of the nodes hosting α, β, or the binding service crash. We will assume that we do not have direct control over communication resources, so we will investigate exploitation of redundancy in the form of multiple machines capable of running servers for an object and multiple machines capable of storing the state of an object.

The binding service needs to maintain sufficient information about replicas to enable clients to be bound to available replicas. We assume that for every persistent object, the binding service maintains two sets of node related data: (i) Sv_A: for an object A, this set contains the names of nodes each capable of running a server for A; and, (ii) St_A: this set contains the names of nodes whose object stores contain states of A. The way this information is maintained by the binding service will depend on which replication approach is in use (TR-based or GC-based). We now consider two ways of activating an object (assume that A is currently passive, i.e., not in use).

(i) *Single copy activated*: This represents the case where only the state of an object is replicated (see fig. 2). Activating A will consist of creating a server at the node which is a member of Sv_A (say α) and loading the state from any of the nodes in St_A. If the server crashes, then a new one is created at some other node in Sv_A.

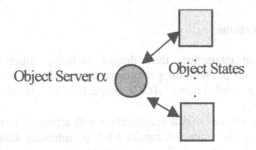

Figure 2: Object state replication.

(ii) *Multiple copies activated*: Activating A consist of creating servers at one or more nodes listed in Sv_A (let $Sv_{A'}$, where $Sv_{A'} \subseteq Sv_A$, be the set of such nodes), and loading the state of the object from the node in St_A.

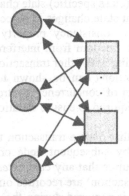

Figure 3: Server and state replication.

A process group, such as the group of servers, $Sv_{A'}$ must be managed as a single entity. There are two well-known group management policies: (i) *Active replication:* In active replication, all the functioning members of the group perform processing [15]. Of course, it is necessary that all the functioning members receive client invocations in the same order and that the computation performed by each replica be deterministic. (ii) *Primary-backup replication:* Here, only one replica, the *primary* (coordinator), carries out processing. The primary regularly checkpoints its state to the remaining replicas (cohorts). If the failure of the primary is detected, then the cohorts elect one of them as the new primary to continue processing. In both the cases, the initial membership of the group, (e.g., $|Sv_{A'}|$) is $2K+1$, $K \cdot 1$. If partitions cause the group to be broken into sub-groups, then only the *majority* sub-group with at least $K+1$ members (if any) remains functioning while other sub-groups delete themselves. Clients with access to the majority group can continue to make forward progress.

The binding service must be replicated 2K+1 times, and only the clients with access to the majority of name service replicas (K+1) can make forward progress.

2.4. Atomic Transactions

An atomic transaction guarantees that, despite failures, either all of the work conducted within its scope will be performed or it will all be undone. Atomic transactions have the well known *ACID* properties of *Atomicity, Consistency, Isolation and Durability*.

Atomicity property ensures that a computation will either be terminated normally (*committed*), producing the intended results (that is, intended state changes to the objects involved) or *aborted* producing no results (no state changes to the objects). This atomicity property may be obtained by the appropriate use of backward error recovery, which can be invoked whenever a failure occurs that cannot be masked. Typical failures causing a computation to be aborted include node crashes and communication failures such as the continued loss of messages.

It is assumed that, in the absence of failures and concurrency, the invocation of an operation produces consistent (class specific) state changes to the object. Transactions then ensure that only consistent state changes to objects take place despite concurrent access and any failures. This consistency property goes hand in hand with the isolation property that ensures freedom from interference: each transaction accesses shared objects without interfering with other transactions. In other words, the effect of concurrently executing transactions can be shown to be equivalent to some serial order of execution. Some form of concurrency control policy, such as that enforced by two-phase locking [1], is required to ensure isolation and consistency properties of transactions.

It is reasonable to assume that once a transaction terminates normally, the results produced are not destroyed by subsequent node crashes. This is ensured by the durability property, which requires that any *committed* state changes (i.e., new states of objects modified in the transaction) are recorded on stable (crash-proof) storage. A (two phase) commit protocol is required during the termination of a transaction to ensure that either all the objects updated within the transaction have their new states recorded on stable storage, or, if the transaction aborts, no updates get recorded. Atomic transactions can also be nested; the effects of a nested transaction are provisional upon the commit/abort of the outermost (*top-level*) atomic transaction.

2.5. Process Groups

A *group* is defined as a collection of distributed entities (objects, processes) in which a member entity can communicate with other members by multicasting to the full membership of the group. A desirable property is that a given multicast be *atomic*: either all or none of the functioning members are delivered the message. An additional property of interest is guaranteeing *total order*: all the functioning members are delivered messages in identical order. As an example, these properties are ideal for replicated data management: each member manages a copy of data, and given atomic delivery and total order, it can be ensured that copies of data do not diverge. However, as we discuss below, achieving these properties in the presence of failures is not simple.

Suppose a multicast is interrupted due to the crash of the member making the multicast; this can result in some members not receiving the message. Member crashes should ideally be handled by a fault tolerant protocol in the following manner: when a member does crash, all functioning members must promptly observe that crash event and agree on the order of that event relative to other events in the system. In an asynchronous environment this is impossible to achieve: when members are prone to failures, it is impossible to guarantee that all functioning members will reach agreement in finite time [16]. This impossibility stems from the inability of a process to distinguish slow members from crashed ones. Asynchronous protocols can circumvent this impossibility result by permitting processes to *suspect* process crashes and to reach agreement only among those processes which they do not suspect to have crashed [17].

A group therefore needs the services of a *membership service* that executes an agreement protocol to ensure that functioning members within any given group will have identical views about the group membership. The membership service also ensures that the sequence of views installed by any two functioning member processes of a group that do not suspect each other are identical. Network partitions can lead to the group of processes to partition themselves into several subgroups of mutually unsuspecting processes. In a *primary partition membership service*, members of one subgroup (primary subgroup) continue to function while members of the other subgroups are deemed faulty. A normal way of deciding on a primary is to select the subgroup with the majority of the members of the original group. A *partitionable membership service* on the other hand permits the subgroups of processes to coexist and later merge (see [18] for discussion on partitionable membership service). We will assume a primary partition membership service.

The failure model of process groups differs from that used in transaction model in one important way: when a member of a group fails by crashing, it looses all its state (i.e., members have no stable states).

3.   TR-Based and GC-Based Replication

For comparative evaluation, we will now investigate how replication schemes of broadly similar functionality can be implemented in TR (a system that supports transactions but no process groups) and GC (a system that supports process groups but no transactions) and then compare the two. We will use single copy activation scheme with state replication for the TR-based approach (fig. 2). Since only a single server is activated (a backup is created only if the failure of the original server is suspected), there is no need to rely on group communication for managing the server. We will use primary-backup replication scheme (both server and state replication, fig. 3) for the GC-based approach. Here the primary server does the processing and a backup takes over if the primary fails, so the scheme resembles the single copy activation scheme to be used in TR.

3.1. TR-Based Replication

As stated before, the replication scheme to be considered here requires only a single copy of the object to be activated. As regards to state replication, replicated data management techniques that go hand in hand with transaction commit processing [1] provide an integrated solution to object state management. The binding service plays a central role here, by maintaining up-to-date Sv and St related 'group view' information. We assume that it is possible to update Sv and St related information for objects maintained by the naming and binding service. For example, it should be possible to exclude the name of a node currently in St_A if the node is found not to contain the latest (committed) state of the object (say the node has crashed). We assume that the binding service itself is built out of one or more persistent objects, so the above state changes are (naturally) performed under the control of transactions. For now we will assume that the service is available, and discuss later the issues concerning its replication.

Here is an overview, for the simple case of a client accessing some object A: assume object A is passive and this is recorded in the binding service. The client's binding request to A then returns the sets Sv_A and St_A enabling a client to select the most appropriate server node. The client directs its invocation to some such node in Sv_A (say α); α allocates a server and loads the state from any node in St_A. (This has been discussed already for the case of non-replicated objects, see fig. 1). The identity of the activated server (α) must be registered with the binding service, so that subsequent binding requests to A return α in place of Sv_A. At commit time, an attempt is made to copy the updated state of the object at α to the object stores of all the nodes in St_A. To ensure that St_A contains the names of only those nodes with mutually consistent states of A, the names of all those nodes for which the copy operation failed must be removed from St_A. A transaction using A will abort if α crashes (or is suspected to have crashed) during execution. Restarting the transaction could cause A to be activated at some node α' in Sv_A. These aspects are discussed further below with the help of fig.4.

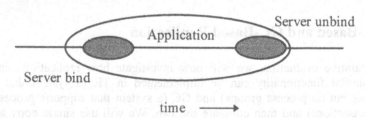

Figure 4: Binding and unbinding performed using nested transactions.

Binding: Prior to contacting the binding service the client (say C_1)begins an application level transaction. To guarantee consistency in the presence of concurrent bind requests for the same object, binding has to be an atomic operation. This is achieved by C_1 performing the binding related operations mentioned earlier from within a transaction (this is the nested transaction 'server bind' in fig. 4). So, if the object is passive, and C_1 manages to get a server at α, then the binding service update to record that the object is active at α is performed as apart of this nested transaction; at the same time, a 'use count' for this object maintained by the service is set to one (indicating one user). A subsequent bind request (say from C_2) to this activated object will return the address of node α. C_2, as a part of its bind transaction, will try to connect to the server at α, and if this succeeds, the 'use count' is incremented and the bind transaction is terminated. If C_2 is unable to connect, then it suspects a crash of the server and is free to select some other node from Sv_A to activate the object, and the entry for α is replaced by the identity of the new node (with a 'use count' of one). Note that if C_2's suspicion is incorrect and the server at α is functioning (say there is a temporary partition) then there is an inconsistency (the object has been activated at more than one place) that must be resolved. This is done at commit time as we will describe shortly. If the application level transaction aborts after binding, any binding related updates to the binding service are undone.

Unbind: Unbinding is also performed as a transaction (see fig. 4) executed during commit processing of the application level transaction. The client contacts the binding service to check for any binding inconsistency: if this is detected, then the client aborts. Otherwise, the client decreases the 'use count'. If the use count reaches zero, then the server can be told to passivate the object and the binding service can treat the object as passive again. Commit processing also involves updating all the states held at nodes $\in St_A$. The names of any nodes where these updates fail are removed from the set St_A kept at the binding service. This ensures that the set always maintains the names of node with the latest state of the object.

The binding service itself must be available at all times. This requirement can be met by replicating the service on $2K+1$ distinct nodes. To eliminate the requirement of the service itself requiring a binding system for replicated objects, three simplifying restrictions can be made: (i) the nodes storing Sv and St related data objects also run servers for them; (ii) every client is expected to 'know' the locations of these nodes (that is the binding service addresses are well known); and (iii) client updates to binding data are allowed only if a majority of the replicas can be updated (else the client action aborts). This also means that a client has to contact a majority of the binding servers to be sure to obtain the most recent binding information. This is the well known quorum consensus replication approach [1, 19]. Forward progress is not possible if the majority assumption cannot be met, and application level processing must block till enough nodes recover and/or partitions heal.

In summary: the binding service is used transactionally to activate, bind, unbind and passivate objects in a consistent manner; the set of nodes in Sv for an object provide redundancy for server creation and the set of nodes in St provide redundancy in storage. So long as a client has access to the binding service, an object A remains available provided the client has access to at least one node in Sv_A and that node has access to at least one node in St_A.

A final observation: the scheme illustrated by fig. 4 has a shortcoming in that the binding information concerning an object remains locked for the entire duration of the application level transaction (because the service access is performed as nested transactions). If this is considered a concurrency control bottleneck, then an alternative concurrency control scheme is possible whereby the bind and unbind transactions are run as 'nested top level' transactions; these details are discussed elsewhere [20, 21].

3.2.   GC-Based Replication

We will first describe the basics of the primary-backup passive replication scheme using a process group and then discuss how such groups can be used in our object model. Since process groups explicitly deal with message passing, we will describe and illustrate the scheme in terms of messages; the treatment given here is based on [22].

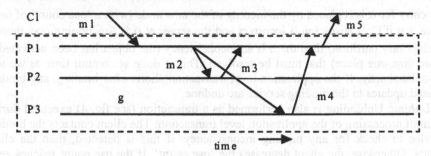

Figure 5: Primary-backup passive replication.

We assume that clients know the name of the primary within the replica group (P_1 in the replica group g with three members, P_2 and P_3 are backups, fig. 5). The client sends its request message (m_1) to the primary. The primary carries out the work, updates its state and then multicasts a message (m_2) containing state changes performed. P_2 and P_3 update their states and send acknowledgements to the primary (messages m_3, m_4). The primary then sends the response message (m_5).

If the primary is suspected to have failed, then the membership service of the group will reformulate the group with the primary removed. Any deterministic algorithm can be used by the members for deciding the next primary. The atomic delivery property of multicasts ensures that backups remain in 'step'. For example, assume the primary crashes during the multicast of m_2; if P_2 is delivered the message, then P_3 will also be delivered m_2. Continuing with this scenario, the client waiting for the response will eventually timeout. Assume it somehow finds out the name of the next primary and resends its request. If the primary has received m_2, then it sends the response message (without redoing the work).

Returning to our object model: referring to fig. 3, we can see that two groups to manage a replicated object are suggested: a server group and a state group (let us denote them as Gs and Gt respectively). However, since it is the server group that performs the computation, a simplification is possible and the need for Gt can be dispensed. Since a process group manages its membership view information, the binding service is no longer required to maintain current membership information for activated groups. The binding service must however maintain the information about whether a group has been activated or not, and for an activated group, who the primary is. Further, the binding service maintains the list St that must only contain the names of nodes with the latest states of persistent objects. Here are the possible steps involved in activating and using an object (A).

The client contacts the binding service, and receives the sets Sv_A, and St_A. The client constructs a list of 2K+1 nodes in Sv_A, with one listed as primary and requests one of them (say α) to create a group; α creates the group (Gs), and registers the name of the primary with the binding service. The primary of Gs acts as a client to obtain the persistent state of the object from any node $\in St_A$. It then multicasts the state to other members of Gs. The client sends requests to the primary of Gs (these are normal object invocations, and handled as discussed earlier with respect to fig. 5). If the group elects a new primary, then the newly elected primary registers its identity with the binding service, deleting the name of the old one.

When a client finishes using A, it explicitly sends a 'disconnect' invocation to the primary of Gs. The group must now make the object state persistent by updating the object stores named by St_A (this corresponds to the commit operation of the transaction system). There are two steps involved here: (i) the primary updates the object stores named by St_A, and then makes a list of nodes where the updates have not succeeded; and (ii) the primary removes the names of these nodes from the St_A set maintained by the binding service.

When a group determines that it has no more users (this is possible to calculate provided connected clients survive and are able to communicate with the group), the primary of the group can unregister its name from the binding service, and the group can be destroyed.

In this scheme, forward progress is possible despite partitions and node failures provided a primary subgroup of Gs survives and remains connected with the client; further, this group must be able to access the binding service and at least one object store in St_A. If this is not possible then consistency cannot be guaranteed. For example, suppose that during step (ii) above all the group members crash (call it a *group failure*), as a result, the St_A list of the binding service is not updated as required. In that case the list cannot be guaranteed to contain the names of nodes with the latest states of persistent objects. This problem can be handled by maintaining, in a careful manner, group configuration information on stable store, such that the primary group configuration can be reconstructed after a group failure; this way the group can resume the interrupted operation (papers [23, 24] discuss how to enhance process groups with the capability of recovering from group failures). One problem still remains: as there is no support for backward recovery, if a client crashes, then there is no automatic way of restoring any states of objects.

The binding service itself can be made available quite simply: we assume that a process group with 2K+1 members with well known addresses is created at start up time and remains in operation.

4.   Integrated Replication Schemes

4.1.   Comparative Evaluation

We evaluate the two schemes discussed in the previous section by considering their effectiveness in meeting requirements of the ability to recover from total crashes (even if all the nodes crash, the system can eventually bootstrap itself with information held on stable stores remaining consistent, provided partitions eventually heal and crashed nodes eventually recover) and availability (objects remain accessible even if partitions have not yet healed and nodes have not yet recovered).

Replication using transactions: Transactions are ideally suited to meeting the requirement of ability to recover from total crashes (not surprising as they have been designed specifically for the very same purpose). Transactions ensure that shared information held on stable store is manipulated consistently despite failures. This is a powerful facility that can be utilised for building those facilities that are not directly supported by transactions. Transactions do not provide direct support for maintaining replica group related information, so we have to build a subsystem (transactional binding service in our case) that does exactly that. The mechanism for making the binding service available is rather heavyweight, requiring clients to read from a majority to be sure of obtaining the latest copy of the information.

Transactions can be used in a limited (but quite effective) manner for supporting availability. Their way of dealing with server failures (suspected or real) is to push the problem to application level transactions bound to the server; an affected transaction can abort and rebind to a new server, so that forward progress can be made. Transactions do not provide any direct support of agreeing over failure suspicions, so any consistency problem caused has to be pushed again to applications. In the scheme discussed here, inconsistent server bindings are checked at commit time and offending transactions aborted.

Replication using group communications: In contrast to transactions, process groups provide a very elegant way of managing replicas in the most general case of partitionable environments where functioning processes can be wrongly suspected to have failed. So long as the formation of a primary server subgroup is possible, server failures can be masked from clients.

Coordinated backward recovery is not an integral feature of process groups, so there is no direct way of dealing with client failures (real or suspected). Process groups cannot directly support the ability to recover from total crashes. As indicated earlier, to do this would require enhancing process groups with support for maintaining views on stable store, such that groups can be reconstructed even after group failures.

In summary, transactions are good at dealing with total crashes, but extra effort is required for maintaining replica group related information and ensuring that inconsistent bindings do not occur due to servers wrongly suspected to have crashed. Process groups are good at managing replica server groups, but need additional support for dealing with total crashes and client failures.

4.2.   Using Transaction Systems with Process Groups

In the light of the analysis presented in the previous subsection, we discuss how the two system models can be used together. For the reasons given in the introduction, we will investigate how transaction systems can make use of process groups, and what practical benefits can be gained. We assume that transactions are used directly by application programmers and process groups are essentially hidden from application programmers.

Transactions provide a very effective solution to dealing with all the exceptions that cannot be masked: abort and retry. We have used this approach here for dealing with server failures and recovering from inconsistent bindings to servers. Since applications use transactions any way, why not exploit transactions for handling problems of replication? This is the application of the well known 'end to end argument in system design' [25]: see if application level mechanisms can be used for handling lower level problems. However, the 'end to end argument' does not preclude the use of specific lower level mechanisms for masking exceptions, if these mechanisms enhance efficiency. A transaction system can profitably make use of process groups for supporting replication in at least three ways:

(i) *Supporting binding service replication*: A process group with 2K+1 members can be used to maintain the binding service. Clients now only need to contact the primary, and the need for reading from K+1 replicas and voting is eliminated.

(ii) *Fast switch over from a failed server*: A process group can provide a faster way of switching to a backup in the event of the failure of the primary. As described previously, in a transaction system, this would entail the transaction aborting and then rebinding. Commercial transaction systems in fact do make use of primary-backup process groups in a very specialised manner: a primary-secondary pair is used in a non-partitionable communication environment (so carefully chosen timeouts can be relied upon for failure detection). Process groups can provide this functionality in the general setting of 2K+1 replicas in a partitionable communication environment.

(iii) *Supporting Active Replication*: Active replication is often the preferred choice for supporting high availability of services where masking of replica failures with minimum time penalty is considered highly desirable. Active replication requires that all the functioning members of a server group receive client invocations in the same order. A process group can provide this facility.

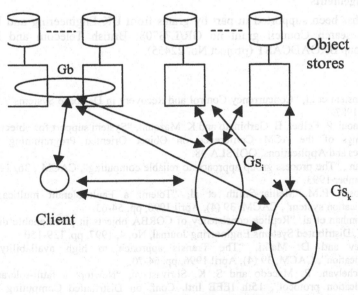

Figure 6: Use of process groups.

A general scheme for the exploitation of process groups is depicted in fig. 6; here Gb is the group for managing the transactional binding service and Gs (i..k) are the server groups that are created on demand as discussed earlier. We have designed a toolkit for CORBA with the above architecture in mind [26]. The default implementation supports pure transaction approach discussed in section 3. Our toolkit has all the necessary hooks for exploiting the services of a process group, such as a CORBA group service [12, 13], enabling a client (more precisely, a client proxy) to invoke a group using group specific multicasts if required.

5.   Concluding Remarks

We have carried out this investigation to understand how transactions and group communications (process groups) can be exploited to construct high availability distributed applications. In particular, we have investigated how a transaction system can benefit from an underlying group communication system. As we show, although transactions can be used for supporting replication of persistent objects without the need of process groups, if the underlying infrastructure does support process groups, then these can be exploited effectively for binding service replication, providing faster switch over to backups and for supporting active replication. A recent paper has investigated the use of group communication in a fully replicated database system [27]. Although the distributed system model used in that paper is different to what is assumed here (the unit of replication is the entire database, so no binding service is required), the study reinforces the observation made here that transaction systems can benefit from group communication services.

Acknowledgements

This work has been supported in part by grants from UK Engineering and Physical Sciences Research Council grant no GR/L73708, British Telecom and ESPRIT working group BROADCAST (project No. 22455).

References

1. P.A. Bernstein et al, "Concurrency Control and Recovery in Database Systems", Addison-Wesley, 1987.
2. R. Guerraoui, P. Felber, B. Garbinato and K. Mazouni, "System support for object groups", Proceedings of the ACM Conference on Object Oriented Programming Systems, Languages and Applications, OOPSLA 98.
3. K. Birman , "The process group approach to reliable computing", CACM , 36, 12, pp. 37-53, December 1993.
4. L.E. Moser, P.M. Melliar-Smith et al, "Totem: a Fault-tolerant multicast group communication system", CACM, 39 (4), April 1996, pp. 54-63.
5. P. Narasimhan et al, "Replica consistency of CORBA objects in partitionable distributed systems", Distributed Systems Engineering Journal, No. 4, 1997, pp. 139-150.
6. D. Dolev and D. Malki, "The Transis approach to high availability cluster communication", CACM, 39 (4), April 1996, pp. 64-70.
7. P. Ezhilchelvan, R. Macedo and S. K. Shrivastava, "Newtop: a fault-tolerant group communication protocol", 15th IEEE Intl. Conf. on Distributed Computing Systems, Vancouver, May 1995, pp. 296-306.

8. F. Cristian, "Synchronous and asynchronous group communication", CACM, 39 (4), April 1996, pp. 88-97.
9. D. R. Cheriton and D. Skeen, "Understanding the limitations of causally and totally ordered communication", Proc. of 14th ACM Symp. on Operating Systems Principles, Operating Systems Review, 27 (5), pp. 44-57, December 1993.
10. Rebuttals from Cornell, Operating Systems Review, 28 (1), January 1994.
11. A. Schiper and M. Raynal, "From group communication to transactions in distributed systems", CACM, 39(4), April 1996.
12. P. Felber, R. Guerraoui, and A. Schiper, "The implementation of a CORBA object group service", Theory and Practice of Object Systems, 4(2), 1998, pp. 93-105.
13. G. Morgan, S. K. Shrivastava, P. D. Ezhilchelvan and M.C. Little, "Design and Implementation of a CORBA Fault-tolerant Object Group Service", Proceedings of 2nd IFIP International Working Conference on Distributed Applications and Interoperable Systems, DAIS'99, Helsinki, June 1999.
14. M.C. Little and S K Shrivastava, "Understanding the Role of Atomic Transactions and Group Communications in Implementing Persistent Replicated Objects", Advances in persistent Object Systems, ed. R. Morrison, M. Jordan and M. Atkinson, Morgan Kaufman, ISBN: 1 55860 585 1, 1999, pp. 17-28.
15. F.B. Schneider, "Implementing Fault-Tolerant Services Using the State Machine Approach: A Tutorial", ACM Computing Surveys, 22(4), December 1990, pp. 299-319.
16. M. Fischer, N. Lynch, and M. Paterson, "Impossibility of Distributed Consensus with One Faulty Process", J. ACM, 32, April 1985, pp 374-382.
17. T.D. Chandra and S. Toueg, "Unreliable failure detectors for reliable distributed systems", J. ACM, 43(2), 1996, pp. 225-267.
18. O. Babaoglu, R. Davoli and A. Montresor, "Group communication in partitionable systems: specification and algorithms", Chapter 3 of this book.
19. D. K. Gifford, "Weighted Voting for Replicated Data", 7th Symposium on Operating System Principles, December 1979.
20. M.C. Little, D. McCue and S.K. Shrivastava, "Maintaining information about persistent replicated objects in a distributed system", ICDCS-13, Pittsburgh, pp. 491-498, May 1993.
21. M. C. Little and S. K. Shrivastava, "Object replication in Arjuna", Broadcast Project deliverable report, Vol.2, October 1994, Dept. of Computing Science, University of Newcastle upon Tyne, UK (http://www.newcastle.research.ec.org/broadcast/trs/year2-deliv.html#a2.1)
22. R. Guerraoui and A. Schiper, "Software-based replication for fault tolerance", IEEE Computer, April 1997, pp. 68-74.
23. I. Keider and D. Dolev, "Efficient message ordering in dynamic networks", ACM Symp. on Principles of Distributed Computing, PODC, May 1996.
24. P Ezhilchelvan and S K Shrivastava "Enhancing Replica Management Services to Tolerate Group Failures", The 2nd IEEE International Symposium on Object-oriented Real-time distributed Computing, ISORC'99, Saint-Malo, May 99, pp. 263-268. (also, Chapter 4 of this book).
25. J.H. Saltzer, D.P. Reed and D.D. Clark, "End to end argument in system design", ACM Trans. on Comp. Syst., 2(4), Nov. 1984, pp. 277-288.
26. M.C. Little and S K Shrivastava, "Implementing high availability CORBA applications with Java", IEEE Workshop on Internet Applications, WIAPP'99, San Jose, July 1999.
27. B. Kemme and G. Alonso, "A suite of replication protocols based on group communication primitives", Proc. 18th IEEE Intl. Conf. on Distributed Computing Systems, ICDCS'98, Amsterdam, May 1998, pp. 156-163.

Replication of CORBA Objects*

Pascal Felber**, Rachid Guerraoui, and André Schiper

Département d'Informatique
Ecole Polytechnique Fédérale de Lausanne
1015 Lausanne EPFL, Switzerland

Abstract. Distributed computing is one of the major trends in the computer industry. As systems become more distributed, they also become more complex and have to deal with new kinds of problems, such as partial crashes and link failures. While many middleware architectures have emerged to answer the growing demand in distributed technologies, most of them do not provide any kind of fault tolerance mechanisms. In this paper, we discuss the addition of object group support to CORBA. We describe three approaches: integration, interception, and service, and we argue is favor of the latter. We present the architecture of an Object Group Service (OGS) that provides for fault tolerance and high availability through object replication. This service enables the application developer to deal with invocations to replicated objects in a completely transparent way. We describe the major components of OGS: messaging, monitoring, consensus, group membership, and group multicast. We finally discuss the implementation of the service and its performance.

1 Introduction

1.1 Context

The last few years have seen the emergence of several programming environments that greatly reduce the complexity of developing distributed software. These environments, regrouped under the term *middleware* as they appear between application programs and operating system services, provide high-level facilities for developing distributed applications without having to deal with low-level details, such as remote communication and object location. They use object-oriented concepts to abstract the complexity of the system and promote modularity and reusability. These environments offer frameworks for integration of heterogeneous distributed components. Examples of these middleware architectures are OMG's CORBA [OMG98a] and Microsoft's DCOM [Ses97].

---

* Research supported by OFES under contracts number 96.0454 and 95.0830, as part of the ESPRIT project OpenDREAMS II (project 25262), respt. ESPRIT BROADCAST-WG (number 22455).

** Current affiliation is Oracle Corp., 1000 SW Broadway, Suite 1200, Portland, OR 97205.

S. Krakowiak, S.K. Shrivastava (Eds.): Distributed Systems, LNCS 1752, pp. 254–276, 2000.
© Springer-Verlag Berlin Heidelberg 2000

1.2   Motivations

Existing object-oriented middleware environments essentially deal with point-to-point invocations. While this interaction style complies with the invocation model of object-based systems, some types of applications need to invoke *several objects* at once. In particular, communication facilities have shown to be necessary for *object replication*.

One-to-many interactions can be provided by group communication. Group communication manages groups of objects and provides primitives for sending messages to all members of a group, with various reliability and ordering guarantees. A group constitutes a logical addressing facility: messages can be issued to a group without having to know the number, identity, or location of individual members. Groups can be used for *replication*: a set of replicas constitutes a group, but are viewed by clients as a single entity in the system.

CORBA does not currently provide any support for replicated objects. Systems that require replication support must do all the necessary design and implementation in the application, with no guarantee of either interoperability or portability. Providing group support in CORBA reduces the burden on designers and implementers of fault tolerant applications. Applications benefit from the power of groups (high availability, fault tolerance, etc.) while preserving the key features of object-oriented middleware environments (simple development process, distribution transparency, component integration, etc.). This work pioneers the ongoing efforts of the OMG to support fault tolerance in CORBA using entity redundancy [OMG98b].

1.3   The Object Group Service

In this paper, we present different approaches followed by existing systems to support replication in the CORBA middleware environment. All these systems use *group communication* mechanisms to provide replication. We classify these approaches according to three categories: the *integration* approach, the *interception* approach, and the *service* approach, and we argue that only the latter complies with the modular, component-based architecture promoted by CORBA.

Then we present the design of a CORBA *Object Group Service* (OGS), that provides replication support through group communication for standard off-the-shelf CORBA environments. The OGS environment specifies an architecture and a set of interfaces for object groups. The OGS architecture does not define a single monolithic component; it is decomposed into several CORBA services that provide various facilities for reliable distributed computing, and that are used for the actual implementation of group communication. In particular, the *Object Monitoring Service* provides distributed failure detection mechanisms, and the *Object Consensus Service* allows several CORBA objects to solve distributed agreement problems [GS96]. This decomposition into several independent components promotes modularity and reusability, and extends the use of OGS to areas other than group communication. OGS is currently available for Orbix [ION97] and VisiBroker [Vis98].

1.4   Roadmap

This paper is organized as follows: Section 2 presents background concepts about CORBA, object replication, and group communication. Section 3 discusses related work about object groups and replication support in CORBA. Section 4 describes our *Object Group Service* (OGS), and its different components. Section 5 gives an overview of the different configuration options of OGS. Section 6 presents the performance of the current OGS implementation. Finally, the concluding section summarizes the main characteristics of OGS and relates it to the ongoing standardization efforts for object group support in CORBA.

2   Background

2.1   The Object Management Architecture

The *Object Management Architecture* (OMA) [OMG98a], specified by the *Object Management Group* (OMG), is a conceptual infrastructure for building portable and interoperable software components, based on open standard object-oriented interfaces. Figure 1 shows the five major parts of the OMA reference model.

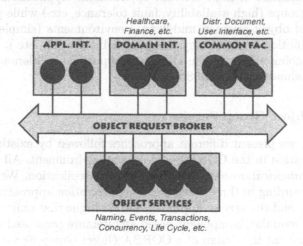

Fig. 1. The OMA architecture

Commercially known as CORBA, the *Object Request Broker* (ORB) is the communication heart of the OMA. It enables heterogeneous objects to transparently invoke remote operations and receive replies in a distributed environment. The ORB also provides the environment for managing objects, advertising their presence, and describing their metadata. Each object interface is specified in the OMG *Interface Definition Language* (IDL), which is implementation independent. Clients use *object references* to identify remote objects and invoke operations on them.

The *Object Services* are a collection of interfaces and objects supporting basic functionalities useful for most CORBA applications. A CORBA service is basically a set of CORBA objects with their corresponding IDL interfaces, and these objects can be invoked through the ORB by any CORBA client. Services are not related to any specific application but are basic building blocks, usually provided by CORBA environments. Several services have been designed and adopted as standards by the OMG.

The *Common Facilities* are a collection of interfaces and objects providing end-user-oriented capabilities useful across many application domains. The *Domain Interfaces* are meant to be used in vertical application domains. Finally, the *Application Interfaces* are interfaces specific to end-user applications.

2.2 Replication

The idea of using redundancy as a mean of masking the failures of individual components dates back to von Neumann [vN56]. With redundant copies, a replicated entity can continue providing services in spite of the failure of some of the copies, without affecting its clients. Redundancy may appear at different points in the architecture, such as redundancy of computational and storage resources, redundancy of communication links between these resources and their clients, redundancy of transient application components.

In distributed systems, the two best known replication policies are *active* and *primary-backup* replication [GS97]. A replicated object is represented by a set of copies. This set may be static or dynamic. Static replication means that the number and the identity of the copies do not change during the lifetime of the replicated object. Dynamic replication is more powerful since copies may be added or removed at runtime.

2.3 Group Communication

Groups were first introduced in the V-Kernel [CZ85], as a convenient addressing mechanism. They were later extended to handle replication in the Isis system [Bir93]. The key idea of *group communication* is to gather a set of processes or objects into a logical group, and to provide primitives for sending messages to all group members with various ordering guarantees. A group constitutes a logical addressing facility since messages can be issued to groups without having to know the number, identity, or location of individual members. Groups have proven to be very useful for providing *high availability* through *replication*: a set of replicas constitutes a group, viewed by clients as a single entity in the system. Through the group abstraction, the failure of a replica is made transparent to the client; in addition, read-only accesses to a replicated object can transparently be performed through the closest replica.

The key mechanisms underlying the group paradigm are *group multicasts* and *dynamic group membership*. A well-known example of a group multicast primitive is the *total order multicast*, which ensures that the requests issued to a group are received by all the members of the group in the same order.

Dynamic group membership allows the modification of the group composition at run-time (e.g., when objects crash or recover). Group members are notified whenever a member joins or leaves the group so that each member knows the current composition of the group. This mechanism is called a *view change*. Since the members of a group usually share a common state, a new member has to receive the current state from the group when joining it. This is performed by a *state transfer* mechanism that transmits the state from a current member of the group to the new one. Hence, group members must provide operations for "getting" and "setting" their state.

3 Object Groups in CORBA

Although no *standard* support for object groups is available, several systems provide replication of CORBA objects based on group communication. This section introduces the different design alternatives for managing object groups in CORBA, evaluates them, and describes how they have been used by existing systems.

3.1 A Coarse Classification

The CORBA object model defines an object as an entity with a well-defined interface that may be remotely invoked using an *object reference*. An object reference is an *"object name that reliably denotes a particular object. An object reference identifies the same object each time the reference is used in a request, and an object may be denoted by multiple, distinct references"* [OMG98a]. This means that the CORBA specification does not permit an object reference to designate a set of objects, and it does not provide ways for clients to invoke several objects at once using an object reference. CORBA only deals with point-to-point remote invocations.

The absence of mechanism that permits to multicast requests to groups of CORBA objects complicates the design and implementation of many applications that have requirements for reliability and high-availability. Only the CORBA *Object Transaction Service* (OTS) provides fault tolerance to a limited extent through transactional mechanisms, but unlike group-based systems, it does not achieve high availability.

During the last couple of years, several systems have been developed to augment CORBA with groups. We can classify these systems according to three main categories, each of which represents a different approach to group communication in CORBA [FGG97]:

1. The *integration approach* integrates an existing group communication system within an ORB.
2. The *interception approach* intercepts messages issued by an ORB and maps them to a group communication toolkit.
3. The *service approach* provides group communication as a CORBA service beside the ORB.

We now describe these three approaches and existing systems that implement them. A more exhaustive discussion of these approaches can be found in [Fel98].

3.2 Integration Approach

With the integration approach (Fig. 2), the ORB functionality is enhanced by a group communication toolkit. The ORB directly deals with object groups and references to object groups. CORBA requests are passed to the group communication toolkit that multicasts them from clients to replicated servers, using proprietary mechanisms. The group toolkit is "integrated" into the ORB.

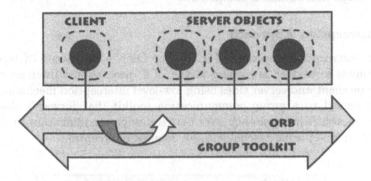

Fig. 2. Integration approach

Two systems are based on the integration approach: Orbix+Isis, [II94] which is a commercial system from Iona Technologies and Isis Distributed Systems[1], and Electra [Maf95], a free CORBA programming environment written in C++. In these systems, only one of the replies is returned by default to the client in order to keep the group invocation transparent.[2] However, a client aware of the group is also able to access all the replies, if necessary. The basic idea is to extend the IDL language mapping and to generate two types of functions from IDL definitions: (1) standard functions that conform to the language mapping and (2) special functions with sequences of values for *out* and *inout* parameters. The client uses the function with the signature that corresponds to its needs. If the client is not aware of groups, it uses only standard functions.

Although appealing for its ease of development (there is no need to build a new group system from scratch) and its transparency (an object group is not distinguishable by a client from a singleton object that implements the same interface), this approach is not fully CORBA compliant, and results in proprietary systems. In addition, the integration approach adopted by Electra and

---

[1] Orbix+Isis has been recently discontinued.

[2] This makes sense if groups are used for replication.

Orbix+Isis uses non-standard language-specific constructs,[3] causing application code to be also not portable. Furthermore, most existing group toolkits are not adapted to a CORBA environment: they are designed for process groups instead of object groups, and they do not provide adequate primitives for group-to-group communication, making it difficult to support client replication [GFGM98].

An interesting variant of the integration approach, which has not been explored by existing systems, would consist in providing a second object adapter in addition to the *Basic Object Adapter*. We would then have the basic adapter for standard objects and a dedicated adapter — a *Group Object Adapter* — for group member objects. This approach would be more compliant with the CORBA specification, since it would isolate all group management functionalities in a single non-standard component.

3.3   Interception Approach

With the interception approach (Fig. 3), the ORB is not aware of replication. ORB requests formatted according to the IIOP protocol are intercepted transparently on client and server sides using low-level interception mechanisms; they are then passed to a group communication toolkit that forwards them using group multicasts. This approach does not require any modification to the ORB, but relies on OS-specific mechanisms for request interception.

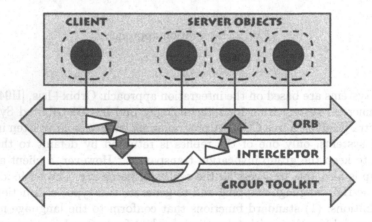

Fig. 3. Interception approach

Eternal [MMSN98] is a system based on the interception approach. It operates on top of the Unix operating system, and works with standard CORBA implementations. Eternal exploits the Unix /proc interface to monitor the operating system calls made by an object to establish an IIOP connection over

---

[3] These constructs are quite different in Electra and Orbix+Isis; application code written for one is not portable to the other.

TCP/IP, and to communicate IIOP messages over that connection. Eternal intercepts the IIOP messages before they reach TCP/IP, and passes them to the Totem group communication system [MMSA+96], which multicasts the messages to the object groups containing the replicas. Any group communication system that provides guarantees similar to those of Totem can be used instead.

The drawback of this approach lies mainly in its low-level interception mechanisms: while these mechanisms can be implemented on most Unix systems, they are not portable to any other operating systems.

3.4   Service Approach

The service approach, which has been adopted and developed in the context of OGS, provides explicit group support through a CORBA service [FGG96] (Fig. 4). Unlike the integration approach, a CORBA service is mostly specified in terms of IDL interfaces, and does not depend on implementation language constructs. The ORB is not aware of groups, and the service can be used with any compliant CORBA implementation. The service approach complies with the CORBA philosophy, by promoting modularity and reusability. Note that a service does not have to be centralized: it can be made of several objects, located at different hosts on the network, that work together at providing the complete service. This is important when dealing with fault tolerance, since a centralized service would be a single point of failure.

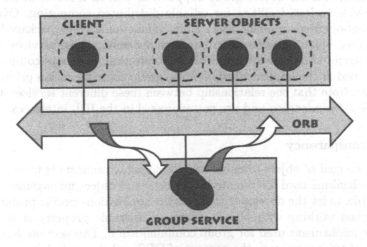

Fig. 4. Service approach

CORBA's open architecture allows us to easily define and implement new services. The process of specifying a new service consists in isolating the requirements, choosing the right abstractions, and specifying the interfaces for these abstractions. The OMG has published guidelines for designing object services and their interfaces [OMG97].

The service approach has also been adopted in the *Distributed Object-Oriented Reliable Service* (DOORS) [CHY+98], currently in development at Bell Labs. Our work on CORBA fault-tolerant services has significantly influenced many of the proposals that have recently been made to the OMG in the context of its undergoing standardization effort towards fault-tolerant CORBA [OMG98b].

4   The Object Group Service

4.1   Overview

The *Object Group Service* (OGS) is a CORBA service that provides group management and communication facilities in a CORBA environment. It is composed of a set of generic IDL-specified interfaces. With OGS, clients can send invocations to object groups without knowing the number and identities of group members. In addition, OGS provides support for *transparent group invocations*, allowing clients to invoke operations on object groups as if they were invoking singleton objects. OGS is based only on standard CORBA mechanisms and is thus portable to any compliant ORB implementation. OGS may be used from any programming language that is supported by CORBA, or from any system that supports the CORBA *Internet Inter-Orb Protocol* (IIOP).

More precisely, the OGS environment specifies an architecture and a set of IDL interfaces for object group support, as well as a set of object services that provide various facilities for reliable distributed computing. OGS uses a component-oriented approach. Basic units of functionality are packaged as CORBA services, which represent distributed components. These services, which include distributed agreement protocols and detection of remote component failure, are used in the implementation of the group communication primitives (see Sect. 4.3). Note that the relationship between these different services are *implementation dependencies*, and are not expressed in the IDL interfaces.

4.2   Transparency

A common goal of object-oriented middleware environments is to hide the low-level mechanisms used for remote invocations and object management as much as possible, to let the developer focus on the application-specific problems. Similarly, when working with object groups, a desirable property is to hide the complex mechanisms used for group communication. This section describes the concept of transparency in the context of OGS and the underlying mechanisms used to provide it.

Transparency in OGS. *Transparency* is the property of a system to be invisible, i.e., the degree to which application programs are unaware of the system. Transparency appears at different levels in the OGS architecture [GFGM98] and may be classified as follows:

- *Plurality transparency:* the application objects have the illusion that they deal with singleton objects, although they interact with object groups.
- *Behavior transparency:* the application objects are not aware of the replication policy and the protocols run by OGS in order to make the system behave consistently.
- *Type transparency:* requests are performed via direct method invocations on the server's interface, rather than by explicit calls to a group communication API (e.g., via a multicast() operation), and explicit packing and unpacking of operation parameters into and from messages. Type transparency means that the application does not need to perform type conversions.

Full transparency is achieved if the application program is completely unaware of the group service. OGS provides full client-side transparency, without even requiring the client code to be recompiled [Fel98].

The Benefits of Transparency. Transparency provides a number of properties that are useful, if not necessary, to develop distributed applications with object groups. Some of the benefits of transparency are outlined below.

- *Ease of use.* Applications do not need to be written with replication in mind.
- *Less error prone.* Application programmers do not need to write error prone code for inserting and extracting data into and from requests.
- *Reuse of existing code.* Existing client code can be reused without modification. Server code requires only minor modifications. Objects from existing frameworks can be made groupable by using multiple inheritance of interfaces and implementations.
- *Encapsulate behavior in the group.* OGS knows about the operations invoked on object groups, and can associate different semantics to distinct requests on behalf of the object group. The protocols may vary depending on the invoked operation without the client's knowledge.

The Limitations of Transparency. Client transparency is generally considered as a "good thing" for object replication. However, server transparency has several drawbacks for complex systems. When dealing with replica configuration, failure detection mechanisms, or advanced synchronization between replicas, explicit group management support is required. In some cases, transparent replication can make systems suffer reduced performance due to the lack of control over how replication is performed.

4.3   OGS Components

OGS implements group communication using a set of CORBA services. These services are not organized in a layered architecture, but as a set of orthogonal components with *usage relationships* between each other (*component-oriented* approach). Figure 5 presents an abstract view of the major components defined in the OGS architecture. Although this is not clearly visible on the figure, each component is specified independently and they all interact with each other through the ORB. The application may use any of these components directly. These components are:

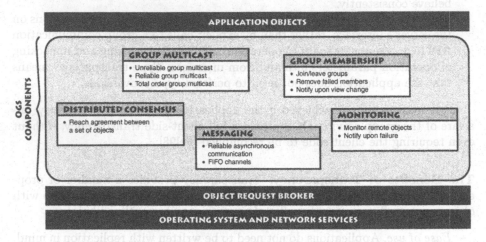

Fig. 5. Overview of the OGS architecture

1. A *Messaging Service* that provides non-blocking reliable point-to-point and multicast communication.
2. A *Monitoring Service* that monitors objects and provides failure detection mechanisms in CORBA.
3. A *Consensus Service* [GS96] that allows a set of application objects to solve the so-called distributed consensus problem [CT96]. This service is used to implement group multicast and membership protocols.
4. A *Group Service* that provides both *group multicast* and *group membership*.

The dependencies between these components are *implementation-specific*, and do not appear in the IDL interfaces of the services. All these components are described in details in [Fel98]. In the following, we focus on the group service only.

4.4 The Group Service

The *group service* is the core of the OGS environment. It is the service that actually provides object group support, and which the application programmer has to deal with. It implements two functionalities:

– *Group membership* manages the life cycle of object groups. It maintains the updated list of all correct group members. It provides support for joining and

leaving groups, view change notification, and state transfer. A group membership service is generally associated with a failure detection mechanism for detecting group member failures.
- *Group multicast* provides support for sending multicast invocations to all the members of a group, with various reliability and ordering guarantees.

The group multicast and group membership services interact closely. In particular, multicast operations are defined on object groups rather than on sets of unrelated objects, thus involving group membership. Therefore, both services are contained in the set of interfaces forming the group service.

Group Membership. The role of a group membership service is to manage memberships in a distributed system on behalf of the processes that compose it. OGS supports dynamic groups, i.e., the composition of the groups can change over time. New members can join an existing group, explicitly leave it, or may be implicitly removed from the group because of a failure. Objects that wish to join a group do so by contacting the membership service, which updates the list of group members. Once admitted to the group, an object may interact with other group members. Finally, if the object fails or leaves the group, the membership service will again update the list of group members. Dynamic group membership involves two kinds of protocols:

- A *view change protocol*, which is run each time the composition of a group changes. It ensures that every correct member of the group receives a *view change notification*, indicating the new composition of the group as a list of group members with mutually consistent rankings. View changes are totally ordered with each other.
- A *state transfer protocol*, which is an atomic operation occurring during view change, when a new member joins an existing group. It consists in obtaining the state from a current group member, and giving it to the new member. This protocol ensures that the state of all group members is kept consistent upon membership changes. The view change protocol can terminate only after a state transfer is completed.

The group membership interfaces define how OGS and group members interact. They are essentially composed of two types of objects (Fig. 6): (1) service-specific[4] *group administrator* objects that enable group members to change their status in the group (e.g., join and leave the group); and (2) application-specific *groupable* objects that enable OGS to call back to the application for view change and state transfer protocols. The GroupAdministrator interface is implemented by the service, and is used as a black box by the application. A group administrator is assigned to a single group at creation time, but there may be several

---

[4] We distinguish *service-specific* objects, defined and implemented by the service and accessed by the application through their IDL interface, from *application-specific* objects, implemented by the application and supporting some interface defined by the service.

group administrators on the same host or in the same process. The Groupable interface must be implemented by application objects that want to be members of a group.

Group Multicast. Group multicast provides primitives for sending invocations to groups instead of singleton objects. OGS provides a rich set of group multicast primitives, adapted to various types of applications. OGS implements groups as open structures, and allows non-member objects to issue multicast invocations to groups. Multicast primitives can be classified according to their degree of *reliability* and their *ordering* guarantees. In addition, OGS provides two communication models: *untyped* and *typed* invocations.

Multicast Reliability. Reliable multicast is a key mechanism for developing replicated applications. In the context of group communication, it means that all correct group members deliver the same set of messages *(agreement)*, that this set includes all messages multicast to the group by correct objects *(validity)*, and that no spurious messages are ever delivered *(integrity)* [HT93].

OGS provides both unreliable and reliable multicast primitives. The unreliable primitives may be useful for read-only operations. Reliable multicast, in itself, does not ensure that group consistency is preserved; it is generally combined with an ordering guarantee.

Multicast Ordering. In addition to reliability, message ordering is an important concern when dealing with one-to-many communication. The state of an object generally depends on the order in which it receives requests, and some special multicast primitive must be used to maintain a consistent ordering of requests received by all group members. The current version of OGS provides unordered, FIFO, and totally ordered multicast primitives.

Multicast Replies. Just as an invocation to a singleton object may return a value, a multicast invocation may return a set of values (one from each target object). The client may want to wait only for the first reply, for several replies, or even for no replies. OGS provides the following options for the number of replies expected by the client:

- *All-replies multicast invocations* wait for replies from all group members.
- *Majority-of-replies multicast invocations* wait for a majority of replies from the group members.
- *One-reply multicast invocations* wait for the first reply from any group member.
- *Zero-reply (synchronous) multicast invocations* wait for the operation to complete on one group member, but does not return any reply to the client.
- *One-way multicast invocations* do not wait for any reply from the group members, and do not block the client's execution thread.

With either majority-of-replies or all-replies multicast invocations, OGS might need to modify the expected number of replies if a server crashes while the invocation is processed. The zero-reply synchronous invocation style is useful for flow control to avoid that the object group becomes congested; it blocks the sender until the message is processed, allowing the receivers to decongest.

Untyped Interfaces and Explicit Invocations. The untyped invocation interface of OGS allows clients to send untyped messages to group members. An object that wishes to send a multicast to an object group must explicitly pack the data of the message into a value of type any, and pass it to OGS, which will perform the multicast. On the server side, OGS delivers this message by passing the any value to group members through their deliver() operation.

This invocation interface is flexible since the client can place any kind of data in the message, and can easily specify the semantics associated with the multicast invocation and the expected number of replies. The drawback of this model is that the application programmer must *explicitly* pack all parameters associated with the server's invocation in a message (marshaling), and extract these parameters on the server side (unmarshaling), which is a painful and error-prone task. In addition, this untyped invocation interface exposes group communication to the client application, while a common goal to most group-based systems is to hide groups from clients.

Typed Interfaces and Transparent Invocations. The typed invocation interface of OGS provides group transparency to clients, which can issue invocations to object groups as if they were invoking singleton objects. The client directly invokes operations of the server's interface using static stubs, and OGS delivers multicasts by directly invoking the relevant operation of the server, using static skeletons. OGS transparently filters messages and returns a single reply to the client. Of course, typed communication does require that all servers implement the same IDL interface.

Although less flexible than the untyped invocation interface, this model is much easier to use. The application developer does not need to perform the marshaling and unmarshaling of the request (these operations are performed transparently by OGS), and can benefit from the type safety of CORBA's static invocation interface. The client cannot specify the semantics to associate with a multicast invocation but, as we will see in the next paragraph, this may be favourably replaced by server-specified invocation semantics.

Server-Specified Invocation Semantics. As mentioned in Sect. 4.2, OGS provides server-specified invocation semantics: the server may associate specific semantics to each individual operation of its interface when using the typed version of OGS.[5] For instance, if an operation does not change the state of the server (read-only operation), the server may decide to deliver the invocation without

---

[5] By default, OGS uses a total order multicast for invocations with unspecified semantics.

ensuring total order. Since the server implements the operations, it knows their properties and the client does not need to be aware of them. Furthermore, the server can optimize client requests based on their semantics; for instance, two update operations do not have to be totally ordered with each other if they are commutative (e.g., they modify disjoint parts of the server's state). This approach is an improvement over the traditional model where a client asks for the strongest ordering guarantees for a message when it is unsure of the exact semantics of the associated operation.

4.5   OGS Components and Interactions

OGS combines support for group membership and group multicast in a single set of interfaces. Figure 6 presents a simplified high-level view of OGS components. OGS interfaces are classified according to three categories, associated with the different views of the service:

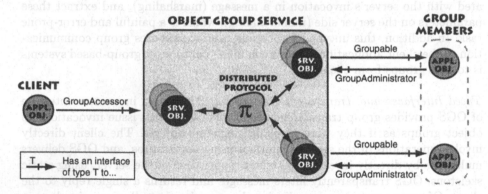

Fig. 6. OGS components overview

1. *Client interfaces* (`GroupAccessor`) allow clients to interact with object groups.
2. *Member interfaces* (`GroupAdministrator`) are a superset of client interfaces, and allow servers to manage the group's life cycle (e.g., join and leave groups).
3. *Service interfaces* (`Groupable`) define interfaces that the member objects must implement for OGS to issue callbacks to them.

Group accessors and administrators are service objects. Performing a multicast to the group initiates a distributed protocol between group accessors and administrators, which ensures that messages are delivered to the members according to some condition (e.g., total order). The `Groupable` interface must be implemented by application objects.

The IDL interfaces of the group services are described in [Fel98]. OGS interfaces are defined in two modules: the first one, mGroupAccess, is used by group clients and defines operations to communicate with object groups; the second module, mGroupAdmin, is used by group members and defines operations for administrating object groups. Interfaces from the mGroupAdmin module inherit from interfaces defined in mGroupAccess. Inheritance is used because the client depends on less functionality than the full interface offers.

Figure 7 illustrates the interfaces and operations of the complete OGS specification in a class diagram. Inheritance relationships clearly show that server-side interfaces inherit from client-side interfaces.

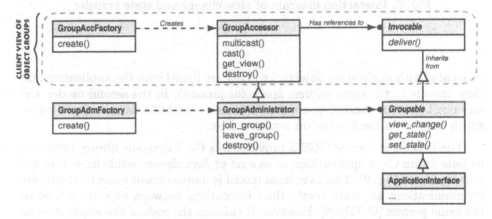

Fig. 7. Class diagram of OGS interfaces

The interaction diagram of Fig. 8 illustrates the view change and state transfer mechanisms on two members. Initially, the group is empty. A first member object joins the group (1), and receives the new view (2). A second member object joins the group (3), which is not empty anymore, leading to both a state transfer protocol (4, 5), and a view change notification (6).

5   OGS Configuration

Invocations to object groups are performed by OGS. Client messages are sent via group accessor objects, and server messages are delivered via group administrator objects. Group accessors and administrators are *service objects* that form the visible part of the OGS runtime system, which is presented in this section. The application developer can configure this runtime system in a number of ways, leading to different degrees of flexibility, efficiency, transparency, or reliability. Examples of OGS programs using various configurations can be found in [Fel98].

To conceal efficiency and flexibility, OGS provides two execution models: a *linkable* model and a *daemon* model. In the first model, the service objects are

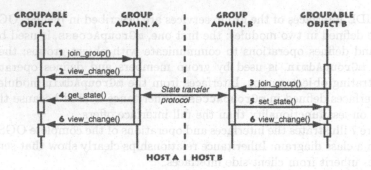

Fig. 8. Interaction diagram of view change and state transfer

co-located with application objects, i.e., they are linked with the application and they execute in the same address space (or process). In the second model, the service objects are located in another process — the OGSd daemon program — which may be on the local or on a remote host.

The linkable version of OGS is provided as a C++ dynamic library (OGSl) to be linked with C++ applications, or as a set of Java classes usable from Java applications (see Fig. 9). This execution model is more efficient since inter-process communications are more costly than invocations between objects located in the same process [GFGM98]. However, it enforces the code of the application to be written with the same programming language as the library and to support multi-threading.

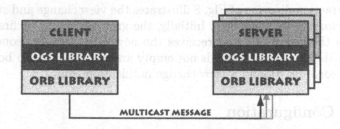

Fig. 9. The co-located execution model

The *daemon* execution model, with two separate processes, has the advantage of decoupling the service from the application, enabling several applications running on the same host to use the same resources. It also allows user applications written in another programming language, such as Smalltalk, to use the

C++ or Java service. Figure 10 illustrates the use of the OGS daemon on the client side, while the service is linked with the application on the server side.[6]

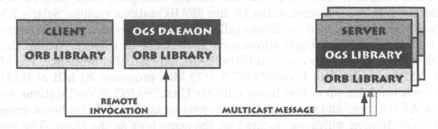

Fig. 10. The remote execution model

The co-located execution model mainly benefits from its efficiency, while the remote execution model provides language heterogeneity. But the choice of the execution model also affects reliability. As matter of fact, with the co-located execution model, the application does not need to care about potential link failures or crashes of service objects, since OGS cannot fail independently from the application.

If the application and the service objects are located on different machines, the application must handle network, machine, and OGS daemon process failures. Therefore, using a remote daemon requires the communication link between the application and the daemon to be reliable (this hypothesis is realistic in a local area network).

6 OGS Performances

This section presents the performance of the OGS implementation on VisiBroker [Vis98] (some performance measurements of OGS on Orbix [ION97] may be found in [FGS98]).[7] We focus on client multicast invocations, i.e., the cost of invocations through OGS, from a client to a group of objects. We compute the overhead of using OGS over using plain CORBA invocations, and we investigate the source of this overhead.

These measurements focus on OGS performance. They do not analyze the intrinsic cost of invocations going through the ORB in detail. Exhaustive performance measurements and analysis of CORBA latency with different ORBs may be found in [GS98].

---

[6] Note that the servers could also use an OGS daemon.

[7] Due to some limitations in the current version of Orbix, we could not perform all the tests presented in this section with the Orbix version of OGS.

6.1   System Configuration

Our performance measurements have been performed with the C++ version of OGS, compiled with VisiBroker 3.2. Testing took place on a local 10 Mbit Ethernet network, interconnecting 13 Sun SPARCstations running Solaris 2.5.1 or 2.6, under normal load conditions (all workstations were running X Windows, as well as several user applications such as netscape or emacs). Among these workstations, there were four Sun UltraSPARC 30 (250 Mhz processor, 128 MB of RAM), and nine Sun UltraSPARC 1 (170 Mhz processor, 64 MB of RAM). For tests involving up to four hosts, only the UltraSPARC 30 workstations were used. All the client and server applications were located on different hosts, except the OGS daemon which was located on the same host as the client. The tests have been run with the *TCP-no-delay* option that sets all sockets to immediately send requests, instead of buffering them and sending them in batches.

6.2   Test Scenarios

Our performance tests evaluate the latency of multicast invocations issued by a client to an object group when no failure occurs. These invocations use the various semantics provided by OGS: total order (using two different algorithms [Fel98]), reliable, and unreliable; and three different modes of invocations: untyped invocations with the OGS library, untyped invocations with the OGS daemon, and typed invocations with the OGS daemon. The group size varies from one to ten members. The client waits for a single reply from the servers, except with the optimistic active replication algorithm, with which the client waits for a majority of replies.

The test program operates as follows: a single client executes several rounds, in each of which it issues a fixed number of synchronous invocations (typically 100). The client waits for a reply from each request before issuing the next invocation. The total time of each round is divided by the number of invocations issued during the round to obtain the latency of a single invocation. We kept the value of the best round. Since there is only one client, invocations are not performed concurrently and OGS cannot benefit from its consensus-based total order algorithm that can order several requests at once. Therefore, this test is not a good measure of the total throughput of OGS with this algorithm.

6.3   Performances Measurements

In Sect. 4.2, we have classified transparency according to three categories: behavior transparency, plurality transparency, and type transparency. We analyze the costs of the OGS architecture according to this classification: we first evaluate the cost of the various multicast primitives of OGS (behavior); plurality transparency is analyzed in details in [Fel98]; we finally evaluate the performance overhead induced by the use of dynamic typing facilities in OGS (type).

The Cost of Behavior. The semantics of multicast invocations depend on the behavior of an object group. Figure 11 illustrates the cost of the different OGS untyped invocation primitives, with the library execution style and different group sizes.

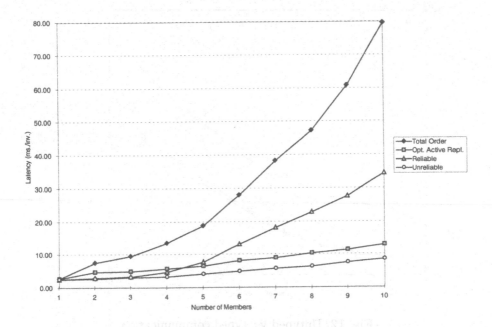

Fig. 11. Comparing OGS multicast primitives

This figure shows that the latency of total order and reliable multicast grows faster than the latency of the other primitives. This is due to the fact that the former primitives are based on a simple reliable multicast algorithm; the complexity of the number of messages for this algorithm is $O(n^2)$ for n participants.[8] In contrast, the optimistic active replication algorithm [Fel98] has been optimized so that is does not use the same reliable multicast primitive when there is no failure. Its cost grows thus linearly, similarly to the unreliable multicast primitive.

Note that the cost of an invocation to a single object issued directly through VisiBroker is about three times lower than the same invocation going through OGS to a group with a single member.

The Cost of Typing. Type transparency is an important feature of OGS because it hides groups from the application developer, and makes it possible to reuse existing applications without having to modify the client. In the current

---

[8] Note that this cost could be reduced by using a "smarter" algorithm.

version of OGS, typed communication is available only for the daemon execution style. Figure 12 compares the latency of untyped totally ordered requests (library and daemon execution styles) with that of typed requests.

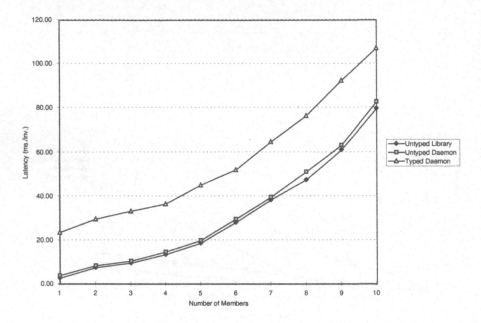

Fig. 12. Untyped vs. typed communication

This figure illustrates that there is a fixed overhead of about 1 millisecond for using the daemon (Untyped Library vs. Untytped Daemon). This corresponds to the latency of a (single) two-way invocation through the ORB. The typed version of OGS adds an overhead of about 20 milliseconds. This overhead results from the use of the DSI and the DII[9] for type transparency, and is *independent* of the group size. This is due to the fact that the DSI and the DII are used only once on the client and the server side.

Another source of overhead comes from request management. When profiling OGS, we noticed that a non-negligible part of the time required for remote invocations is spent in constructing requests. We also observed that working with untyped any values has a significant impact on performance. Unlike other IDL types, any values are augmented by a typecode information that contains details about the actual type of the value. This information increases the size of the messages sent on the network. Moreover, validity checks upon data extraction slow down the remote invocation process.

---

[9] DSI = Dynamic Skeleton Interface; DII = Dynamic Invocation Interface.

7   Conclusion

Distributed computing is one of the major trends in the computer industry. As systems become more distributed, they also become more complex and have to deal with new kinds of problems, such as partial crashes and link failures. Many of these problems can be solved by replicating critical components.

To answer the growing demand in distributed technologies, several middleware environments have emerged during the last few years. These environments however lack support for one-to-many communication primitives, which are necessary to implement object replication. Augmenting a middleware architecture by adding support for object groups provides straightforward support for replicating distributed objects.

We have presented here an open architecture for object group support in CORBA, based on a component-oriented approach. This architecture is generic and can be applied to other middleware environments than CORBA. The *Object Group Service* (OGS) defines an object group model and specifies a set of interfaces adapted to group communication in middleware environments. OGS is decomposed into several components that together provide higher-level services. This decomposition promotes modularity and reusability, and complies with the CORBA architectural model.

OGS provides support for dynamic group membership and for group multicast with various reliability and ordering guarantees. In addition, OGS proposes several execution styles and various levels of transparency. CORBA objects can easily be made groupable using interface inheritance. Client applications can communicate with object groups in the same way as they do with singleton objects. A prototype implementation of OGS is freely available at `http://lsewww.epfl.ch/OGS/`.

References

[Bir93]   K.P. Birman. The process group approach to reliable distributed computing. *Communications of the ACM*, 36(12):36–53, December 1993.

[CHY⁺98]   P.E. Chung, Y. Huang, S. Yajnik, D. Liang, and J. Shih. Doors: Providing fault tolerance for corba applications. In *IFIP International Conference on Distributed Systems Platforms and Open Distributed Processing (Middleware'98)*, September 1998.

[CT96]   T.D. Chandra and S. Toueg. Unreliable failure detectors for reliable distributed systems. *Journal of the ACM*, 43(2):225–267, 1996.

[CZ85]   D.R. Cheriton and W. Zwaenepoel. Distributed process groups in the V kernel. *ACM Transactions on Computer Systems*, 3(2):77–107, May 1985.

[Fel98]   P. Felber. *The CORBA Object Group Service: A Service Approach to Object Groups in CORBA*. PhD thesis, École Polytechnique Fédérale de Lausanne, Switzerland, 1998. Number 1867.

[FGG96]   P. Felber, B. Garbinato, and R. Guerraoui. The design of a CORBA group communication service. In *Proceedings of the 15th IEEE Symposium on Reliable Distributed Systems*, pages 150–159, October 1996.

[FGG97]   P. Felber, B. Garbinato, and R. Guerraoui. *Special Issues in Object-Oriented Programming*, chapter Towards Reliable CORBA: Integration vs. Service Approach, pages 199–205. dpunkt-Verlag, 1997.

[FGS98]   P. Felber, R. Guerraoui, and A. Schiper. The implementation of a CORBA object group service. *Theory and Practice of Object Systems*, 4(2):93–105, 1998.

[GFGM98]   R. Guerraoui, P. Felber, B. Garbinato, and K. Mazouni. System support for object groups. In *Proceedings of the ACM Conference on Object Oriented Programming Systems, Languages and Applications (OOPSLA'98)*, 1998.

[GS96]   R. Guerraoui and A. Schiper. Consensus service: a modular approach for building agreement protocols in distributed systems. In *Proceedings of the 26th International Symposium on Fault-Tolerant Computing (FTCS-26)*, pages 168–177, June 1996.

[GS97]   R. Guerraoui and A. Schiper. Software-based replication for fault tolerance. *IEEE Computer*, 30(4):68–74, April 1997.

[GS98]   A. Gokhale and D. Schmidt. Measuring and optimizing CORBA latency and scalability over high-speed networks. *IEEE Transactions on Computers*, 47(4):391–413, April 1998.

[HT93]   V. Hadzilacos and S. Toueg. *Distributed Systems*, chapter 5: Fault-Tolerant Broadcasts and Related Problems, pages 97–145. Addison-Wesley, 2nd edition, 1993.

[II94]   IONA and Isis. *An Introduction to Orbix+Isis*. IONA Technologies Ltd. and Isis Distributed Systems, Inc., 1994.

[ION97]   IONA. *Orbix 2.2 Programming Guide*. IONA Technologies Ltd., Mar 1997.

[Maf95]   S. Maffeis. *Run-Time Support for Object-Oriented Distributed Programming*. PhD thesis, University of Zurich, February 1995.

[MMSA+96]   L.E. Moser, P.M. Melliar-Smith, D.A. Agarwal, R.K. Budhia, and C.A. Lingley-Papadopoulos. Totem: A fault-tolerant multicast group communication system. *Communications of the ACM*, 39(4):54–63, April 1996.

[MMSN98]   L.E. Moser, P.M. Melliar-Smith, and P. Narasimhan. Consistent object replication in the Eternal system. *Theory and Practice of Object Systems*, 4(2):81–92, 1998.

[OMG97]   OMG. *CORBAservices: Common Object Services Specification*. OMG, 1997.

[OMG98a]   OMG. *The Common Object Request Broker: Architecture and Specification*. OMG, February 1998.

[OMG98b]   OMG. *Fault tolerant CORBA Using Entity Redundancy, Request For Proposal*. OMG, Apr 1998. http://www.omg.org/techprocess/meetings/schedule/Fault_Tolerance_RFP.html.

[Ses97]   R. Sessions. *COM and DCOM: Microsoft's Vision for Distributed Objects*. John Wiley & Sons, 1997.

[Vis98]   Visigenic. *VisiBroker for C++ 3.2 Programmer's Guide*. Visigenic Software, Inc., Mar 1998.

[vN56]   J. von Neumann. Probabilistic logics and the synthesis of reliable organisms from unreliable components. In C. E. Shannon and J. McMarthy, editors, *Automata Studies*, pages 43–98. Princeton University Press, 1956.

Constructing Dependable Web Services

David B. Ingham[1], Fabio Panzieri[2] and Santosh K. Shrivastava[1]

[1]Department of Computing Science, University of Newcastle upon Tyne,
Newcastle upon Tyne, NE1 7RU, United Kingdom
{dave.ingham, Santosh.Shrivastava}@ncl.ac.uk
[2] Dipartimento di Scienze dell'Informazione, Universita' di Bologna,
Mura Anteo Zamboni 7, 40127 Bologna, Italy
panzieri@cs.unibo.it

Abstract. This paper discusses the issues involved in supporting high-volume, highly-reliable, Web services. Such services pose a number of diverse technical challenges. The paper discusses how recent research ideas from distributed computing can be deployed at the various levels of the architecture to yield an overall solution.

Keywords. objects, fault-tolerance, reliability, transactions, process groups.

1. Introduction

The majority of today's Web sites offer read-only access to relatively small amounts of infrequently-changing information. Also, since the load experienced by these sites is usually small, services can generally be hosted as a background task on a general purpose workstation. Such services are generally not overly concerned about the levels of quality of service presented to their users. Conversely, there exists a much smaller number of extremely popular sites that experience very high loads and, in order to maintain their popularity and reputation, tend to be concerned about the quality of service experienced by their users.

The quality of service (QoS) as perceived by the users of a Web service is dependent on a number of factors. Perhaps the most important of these relate to performance and reliability. Users expect services that are continuously available and appear responsive to their requests. A service that is frequently unavailable may have the effect of tarnishing the reputation of the service provider or result in loss of opportunity. Furthermore, from the user's perspective, a service that exhibits poor responsiveness is virtually equivalent to an unavailable service. QoS also encompasses the quality of the information provided, a specific instance being the integrity of hypertext linking between resources.

The users of sites that offer more advanced services, such as electronic shops, personalised newspapers, customer-support systems etc., have additional QoS requirements. The content provided by such services tends to be dynamically generated in response to some read/write interaction between the user and the service. From the user's perspective, it is desirable that the generated content is consistent. Examples of undesirable behaviour include forgetting that the user does not like frames or losing items from a user's shopping basket. The issue here is data integrity;

S. Krakowiak, S.K. Shrivastava (Eds.): Distributed Systems, LNCS 1752, pp. 277-294, 2000.

a service must ensure consistency in the face of concurrent access and occasional system failure. More severe problems can be envisaged for services that involve complex back-office processing. It would not be acceptable, for example, for a component failure within a merchant's service to cause a customer to be billed for a product that was not delivered.

This paper discusses the issues involved in supporting high-volume, highly-reliable, Web services. Such services pose a number of diverse technical challenges. The paper discusses how recent research ideas from distributed computing can be deployed at the various levels of the architecture to yield an overall solution. A short version of this paper has appeared in [1].

2. Problem Understanding

Service providers are looking to computer vendors to provide low-cost, scalable fault-tolerant solutions. The prime requirement is to minimise reliance on specialist equipment and techniques for delivering core services. Indeed, an ideal solution would make use of 'standard' middleware services (e.g., CORBA services for persistence, transactions etc.). Research results on distributed objects and software implemented fault-tolerance techniques hold the promise of providing such solutions. However, the task of constructing such solutions using general-purpose, low cost components, such as commodity UNIX servers, middleware services etc. is extremely challenging.

The central problem is that any software implemented distributed fault-tolerance technique consumes resources (a combination of network bandwidth, processing power and disk storage) that otherwise would be available for normal use. For example, object replication introduces extra messages between replicas (required for replica synchronisation) and message logging introduces either extra messages or disk writes (or both). This frequently makes a fault-tolerant solution unacceptably sluggish (unresponsive) compared to its non-fault-tolerant version. This is particularly so for the case of Web sites: popular Web sites are heavily loaded with client requests, and the last thing that one wants to do is to increase the message traffic. Thus software implemented distributed fault-tolerance techniques must be applied with care. It is therefore important to understand the constraints under which solutions to dependable Web services need to be developed.

Fig. 1 shows a typical non-redundant system, where clients have low bandwidth paths to the Web server. The service will be unavailable to a given client if the server is down, or there is an internet routing problem that prevents the client from contacting the server. The service will not be responsive to a given client if the route is congested or the server is overloaded.

How can the service be made responsive and available? We will assume that message routing and bandwidth allocation within the Internet itself is not entirely under our control, so a practical way of handling unavailability and the unresponsive problems would be to introduce redundancy, namely by replicating the server at distinct sites and ensuring that a client (somehow) gets bound to the 'nearest' lightly loaded server (see fig. 2).

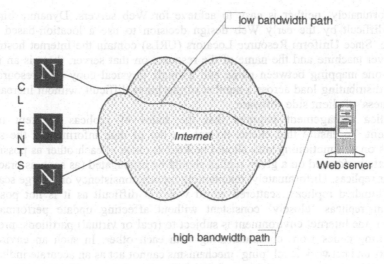

Fig. 1. A non-redundant system

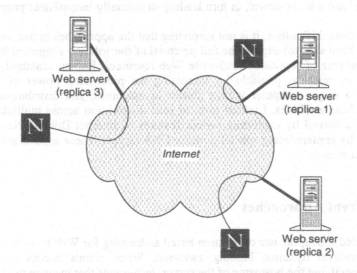

Fig. 2. Redundant system

The success of the above solution will depend on how well we succeed in achieving the following two goals:

(i) Load sharing/distribution: Dynamically binding the client to the 'right' Web site replica. Where 'right' web site choice would be based on: the need to distribute the overall load amongst the available replicas; and, the need to provide a low latency, least congested path between the client and the replica.

(ii) Consistency Management: Replica management technique that somehow manages to keep (important information within) replicas mutually consistent.

Unfortunately, neither is easy to achieve for Web servers. Dynamic binding is made difficult by the early Web design decision to use a location-based naming scheme. Since Uniform Resource Locators (URLs) contain the Internet hostname of the server machine and the name of the resource on that server, there is an inherent one-to-one mapping between name and a single physical copy of a resource. This makes distributing load across a number of machines difficult, without increasing the 'smartness' of client side software.

Replica management requires that the states of replicas be kept mutually consistent. To ensure that clients do not get out of date information, the states of replicas on all functioning sites should be kept as close to each other as possible. So, an update performed on a given replica should be propagated (as soon as practicable) to other replicas. Unfortunately, maintaining replica consistency on a large scale (e.g., a few hundred replicas, scattered world wide) is difficult as it is not possible to maintain replicas 'closely' consistent without affecting update performance. In addition, the Internet environment is subject to (real or virtual) partitions, preventing functioning nodes from communicating with each other. In such an environment, timeouts and network level 'ping' mechanisms cannot act as an accurate indication of node failures (they can only be used for *suspecting* failures). This could lead to the members of a group of sites hosting replicas to form mutually inconsistent views of who is 'up' and who is 'down', in turn leading to mutually inconsistent propagation of updates.

Given these difficulties, it is not surprising that the approaches in use today do not (have not been able to) exploit the full potential of the solution suggested by fig.2 for the general case of replicated read-write Web resources. Rather, scalability has been achieved as much as possible by increasing the processing power of a site, by replacing a single computer with a cluster of machines, and distributing the load amongst these machines. Limited form of load distribution across multiple sites has also been achieved by exploiting certain features of Internet Domain Name Service (DNS) or by implementing special-purpose DNS servers. These aspects are discussed in the next section.

3. Current Approaches

As indicated above, the use of location based addressing for Web resources has made application-level dynamic binding awkward. Since clients access resources by directly specifying the hostname of the server, techniques that manage to bind a client to one of a set of servers dynamically (without any significant increase in Internet message traffic) need to manipulate host name to IP address binding and/or message routing within the Internet. A number of network-level solutions have therefore been developed to enable a number of machines to share IP addresses. Their use in scalable Web servers is discussed below.

3.1 Clusters

A locally distributed cluster of machines (a set of machines) with the illusion of a single IP address and capable of working together to host a Web service provides a practical way of scaling up processing power at a given site. Fig. 3 illustrates a typical solution that relies on the router to distribute the load using a technique known as Network Address Translation (NAT).

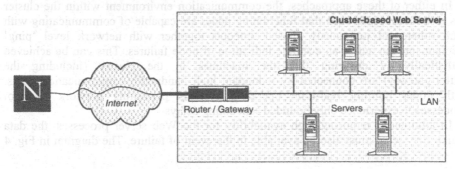

Fig. 3. Workstation Cluster

NAT is a technique for dynamically altering the destination address of a particular IP packet at a network border (at the router/gateway). The mechanism operates by editing the IP headers of packets so as to change the destination address before the IP to host address translation is performed. Similarly, return packets are edited to change their source IP address. Such translations can be performed on a per session basis so that all IP packets corresponding to a particular session are consistently redirected.

This technology can be applied to Web service load distribution over a host cluster. All clients communicate with the service by specifying a single IP address (the address of the router/gateway). At the gateway to the Web cluster network, the gateway can redirect incoming requests to one of a number of slave hosts. An example of a commercial product supporting this technology is the *LocalDirector* from Cisco. LocalDirector performs redirection in an intelligent manner by monitoring the response times of the server hosts and directing requests so as to maximise the QoS as perceived by the client. In the event of a host failure, its response time becomes infinite and receives no subsequent requests until it returns to service.

3.2 Fault-Tolerance

The above technique has a single point of failure (the router/gateway), and little can be done about it other than using hardware level solutions to make the router/gateway fault-tolerant.

In addition, techniques must be devised for enabling working machines to take on the load of machines that fail. As indicated earlier, a convenient way of achieving this form of load distribution is to enrich the router with failure detection capability. The router is required to maintain knowledge of functioning machines and use it for distributing the load.

An alternative, decentralised approach that does not rely on the router for load distribution is also possible. This approach exploits that fact that the networking software of a machine (say A) can be configured to respond, in addition to its own, to the IP address of some other machine in the cluster (say B). Machine A monitors B and if B fails, starts responding to requests directed to B. In a two machine cluster A and B can be made to watch each other to tolerate a single machine failure.

In either of these approaches, the communication environment within the cluster has to be engineered such that functioning nodes are capable of communicating with each other, and judiciously chosen timeouts together with network level 'ping' mechanisms can act as an accurate indication of node failures. This can be achieved realistically by ensuring that the machines in the cluster (including the router/gateway) are connected by redundant high bandwidth communication paths, with nodes running real-time operating systems permitting network protocol processes to experience only bounded scheduling delays.

In addition to requiring high availability for the Web server processes, the data which they serve must also be available in the event of failure. The diagram in Fig. 4 illustrates two possible data distribution configurations.

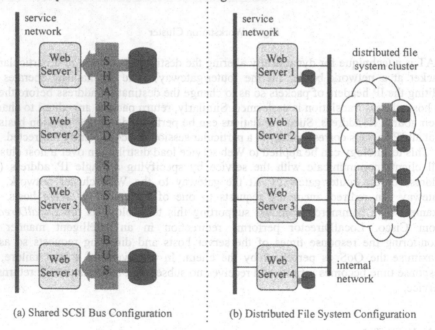

(a) Shared SCSI Bus Configuration   (b) Distributed File System Configuration

Fig. 4. Data distribution configurations

The shared SCSI bus configuration, shown in Fig. 4(a), is a suitable configuration for a server cluster where it is possible to partition the data among the server machines. Under normal operating conditions each Web server obtains an exclusive reservation on its primary disc, i.e., server 1 serves data from disc 1, etc. In the event of a host failure, say, server 1, then in addition to taking over the IP address of the failed host, as previously described, the designated replacement machine, say, server 2, reserves the disc of the failed host in addition to its own. Server 2 is then capable of serving any requests for server 1's data in addition to its own.

The alternative to partitioning the data set is to configure all machines to serve the same data. There are two ways of supporting this configuration, either through the use of multi-port discs (only suitable for small configurations) or by using distributed file systems, configured to share a master copy of the data among the servers. In the latter approach, a two tiered configuration is required as shown in Fig. 4(b). The data set is stored within a distributed file system, with the data being distributed across a number of servers as load demands. Each of the Web server hosts mount and serve the same data set from the distributed file system. AFS appears to be best suited to this task by virtue of its client side caching features that allows copies of frequently accessed data to be cached on the local discs of the Web servers. This dramatically improves performance since read-only operations can be performed locally. Write operations are *written-through* to the master copy and cache-consistency mechanisms ensure that *dirty-data* is not accessed. In this configuration the distributed file system is required to be highly available. This can be achieved using the shared SCSI bus techniques described previously.

3.3 Load Distribution across Multiple Sites

Directing clients to the most appropriate server is achieved in several ways. In many current sites, users are asked to indicate their geographical location or a preference for a particular server and then select an appropriate URL from a list presented on a Web page. More automated solutions, although not entirely satifactory, are possible and discussed below.

A very simple approach to load distribution is to make use of the redirect command in the HTTP protocol to re-direct incoming users to one of a number of available servers. The client makes an initial connection to the main server, i.e., the publicised URL. The server responds with a redirect instruction to one of the available hosts and then the client makes all subsequent requests to that host. This mechanism has the disadvantage of making visible the URLs of all of the server machines, which could be stored in hotlists, indexed by search engines etc., therefore defeating subsequent load balancing.

Another common form of load distribution currently in use for Web service provision is based upon exploitation of a feature of the Domain Name Service (DNS) that is responsible for mapping domain names (host names) to IP addresses. DNS allows a host name to be mapped on to one of serveral IP addresses, out of which a given IP address is chosen in a round-robin manner (therefore two consecutive requests will receive different answers). This provides a simple way of load distribution.

There are, however, two main problems associated with this technique. Firstly, the DNS service is organised as a hierarchy; a client passes all resolution requests to a local DNS server, if this server cannot resolve a name it passes the request to another server using well-defined rules. This process continues until the request arrives at the server responsible for resolving the name in question (the *primary*). It is this server that performs the DNS round-robinning. The response is then passed back down the chain to the client's DNS server. To improve efficiency, DNS utilises caching techniques so that each server in the path between client and server will cache responses from servers further down the chain. The worst case scenario from the perspective of the load sharing is that a DNS server close to the primary caches one of the responses and continues to serve a single IP address thereby resulting in one host receiving a disproportionate percentage of the load. To alleviate this problem, the time-to-live value associated with a DNS entry can be tuned; by shortening the time-to-live the impact of caching can be reduced. However, there is a trade-off associated with this technique, since the lower the time-to-live value, the greater the load on the DNS server.

The other main problem is concerned with maintaining service availability in the event of host failures. The DNS service was designed to support data that infrequently changes; it is not well equipped to propagate changes quickly throughout the system of co-operating servers. Therefore, in the event of a server crash, it is not possible to update the whole DNS system, in a timely fashion, to remove the name of that server from the server set, therefore, many clients will continue to direct their requests for the service to the deceased machine and after appropriate network-level time-outs will receive a 'service not available' message.

A new commercial product from Cisco, the DistributedDirector, aims to perform automatic selection of the optimum server for a particular client by utilising routing information inherent in the network. DistributedDirector can operate in two modes, as a DNS server, suitable for redirecting multiple application protocols, and as a HTTP redirector. In DNS mode, it acts as the primary nameserver and replies with a single address of the appropriate server. In HTTP mode, it acts as a Web server, accepting incoming HTTP requests and returning HTTP code 302 (temporarily moved) to redirect clients to the appropriate server.

In order to determine the optimum server for a particular client several different metrics are used, the most interesting use a proprietary protocol to query software agents running on the gateway devices closest to each of the distributed servers. The query contains the client address and the agents use the routing table information to determine the number of hops between the client and the particular server. The DistributedDirector collates the responses and chooses the host that is *closest* to the client. In order for this technique to work it requires that the appropriate agent software is running at each of the distributed sites, this naturally requires Cisco gateway systems.

3.4 Summary

The fault-tolerance techniques that have been discussed in here are mainly concerned with masking process and host failures from clients. For a Web server that is solely providing read-only access to data, these mechanisms are sufficient. However, the provision of read/write services requires additional mechanisms to guarantee integrity of data in the presence of failures during write operations. Similarly, with multiple servers potentially accessing data concurrently, techniques are required to provide serialised access to data to prevent corruption. The techniques used for enabling working machines to take on the load of machines that fail are difficult to scale beyond a small configuration (a few machines on a LAN) as the communication environment within the cluster has to be engineered carefully to ensure accurate failure detection. DNS servers do not maintain server availability or load information, so in DNS round-robin technique it is possible that client requests can continue to be directed to overloaded or failed servers.

4. Software Implemented Fault Tolerance and Distributed Objects

As we remarked earlier, service providers are looking to computer vendors to provide low-cost, scalable fault-tolerant solutions that would make use of 'standard' middleware services. Object Management Groups's (OMG's) Common Object Request Broker Architecture (CORBA) specification provides one such industry standard for building applications from distributed objects [2,3]; two of its main features are:

(i) *Object Request Broker (ORB)*, which enables objects to invoke operations on objects in a distributed, heterogeneous environment. This component is the core of the OMG reference model. Internet Inter-ORB-Protocol (IIOP) has been specified to enable ORBs from different vendors to communicate with each other over the Internet.

(ii) *Common Object Services*, a collection of 'middleware' services that support functions for using and implementing objects. Such services are considered to be necessary for the construction of any distributed application. These include transactions, concurrency control, persistence, and many more.

In this section we review two complementary approaches to structuring software implemented fault-tolerant distributed systems and what run time support can be made available via CORBA middleware services. The term software implemented fault-tolerance will be used here to refer to the software techniques for tolerating (hardware, software) component faults; for general principles, reference may be made to [4]. A component will be assumed to either work correctly or fail by stopping. The two approaches are transactions on distributed objects and process groups. Transactions provide a means of atomically updating distributed data items in the presence of failures [5]. Process groups provide consistent view management and atomic multicast facilities that can be used for managing a group of machines [6].

4.1 Transactions on Distributed Objects

A widely used computational model for constructing fault-tolerant distributed applications employs atomic transactions (atomic actions) for controlling operations on persistent (long-lived) objects. Each object is an instance of some class. The class defines the set of *instance variables* each object will contain and the *operations* or *methods* that determine the externally visible behaviour of the object. The operations of an object have access to the instance variables and can thus modify the internal state of that object. Distributed execution is achieved by invoking operations on objects which may be remote from the invoker by using remote procedure calls (RPCs). An atomic transaction guarantees that, despite failures, either all of the work conducted within its scope will be performed or it will all be undone. Atomic transactions have the well known *ACID* properties of *Atomicity, Consistency, Isolation and Durability*.

Atomicity property ensures that a computation will either be terminated normally (*committed*), producing the intended results (that is, intended state changes to the objects involved) or *aborted* producing no results (no state changes to the objects). This atomicity property may be obtained by the appropriate use of backward error recovery, which can be invoked whenever a failure occurs that cannot be masked.

Typical failures causing a computation to be aborted include node crashes and communication failures such as the continued loss of messages.

It is assumed that, in the absence of failures and concurrency, the invocation of an operation produces consistent (class specific) state changes to the object. Transactions then ensure that only consistent state changes to objects take place despite concurrent access and any failures. This consistency property goes hand in hand with the isolation property that ensures freedom from interference: each transaction accesses shared objects without interfering with other transactions. In other words, the effect of concurrently executing transactions can be shown to be equivalent to some serial order of execution. Some form of concurrency control policy, such as that enforced by two-phase locking [4], is required to ensure isolation and consistency properties of transactions.

It is reasonable to assume that once a transaction terminates normally, the results produced are not destroyed by subsequent node crashes. This is ensured by the durability property, which requires that any *committed* state changes (i.e., new states of objects modified in the transaction) are recorded on stable (crash-proof) storage. A (two phase) commit protocol is required during the termination of a transaction to ensure that either all the objects updated within the transaction have their new states recorded on stable storage, or, if the transaction aborts, no updates get recorded. Atomic transactions can also be nested; the effects of a nested transaction are provisional upon the commit/abort of the outermost (*top-level*) atomic transaction.

The above object and transaction model provides a natural framework for designing fault-tolerant systems with persistent objects [2,7]. In this model, a persistent object not in use is normally held in a *passive* state with its state residing in some object store (which could be a file system or a database) and *activated* on demand (i.e., when an invocation is made) by loading its state and methods from the object store to the volatile store, and associating an *object server* process for receiving RPC invocations. An ORB together with relevant CORBA services support such a model. The Object Transaction Service (OTS) standard is of particular relevance here. The OTS provides interfaces that allow multiple distributed objects to cooperate in a transaction such that all objects commit or abort their changes together.

In the object model discussed above, a persistent object can become temporarily unavailable due to failures such as a crash of the object store, or network partition preventing communications between clients and the object server. The availability of an object can be increased by storing its state in more than one object store. A number of replica consistency techniques have been developed [5]. For the case of strong consistency where the states of all replicas that are regarded as available need to be kept mutually consistent, to tolerate K replica failures, in a non-partitionable network, it is necessary to maintain at least K+1 replicas, whereas in a partitionable network, a minimum of 2K+1 replicas are necessary to maintain availability in the partition where clients have access to the majority of the replicas (the service/object becomes unavailable in all of the other partitions).

4.2 Process Groups

Process groups with ordered group communications also provide a set of facilities for building available distributed applications. The building of such applications is considerably simplified if the members of a group have a mutually consistent view of the order in which events (such as message delivery, process failures) have taken place. Below we present some relevant concepts pertaining to process groups.

A *group* is defined as a collection of distributed entities (objects, processes) in which a member entity can communicate with other members by multicasting to the full membership of the group. A desirable property is that a given multicast be *atomic*: either all or none of the functioning members are delivered the message. An additional property of interest is guaranteeing *total order*: all the functioning members are delivered messages in identical order. As an example, these properties are ideal for replicated data management: each member manages a copy of data, and given atomic delivery and total order, it can be ensured that copies of data do not diverge. However, as we discuss below, achieving these properties in the presence of failures is not simple.

Suppose a multicast is interrupted due to the crash of the member making the multicast; this can result in some members not receiving the message. Member crashes should ideally be handled by a fault tolerant protocol in the following manner: when a member does crash, all functioning members must promptly observe that crash event and agree on the order of that event relative to other events in the system. In an asynchronous environment this is impossible to achieve: when members are prone to failures, it is impossible to guarantee that all functioning members will reach agreement in finite time [8]. This impossibility stems from the inability of a process to distinguish slow members from crashed ones. Asynchronous protocols can circumvent this impossibility result by permitting processes to *suspect* process crashes and to reach agreement only among those processes which they do not suspect to have crashed [9].

A group therefore needs the services of a *membership service* that executes an agreement protocol to ensure that functioning members within any given group will have identical views about the group membership. The membership service also ensures that the sequence of views installed by any two functioning member processes of a group that do not suspect each other are identical. A few words on the treatment of partitions. Despite efforts to minimise incorrect suspicions by processes, it is possible for a subgroup of mutually unsuspecting processes to wrongly agree (though rare it may be in practice) on a functioning and connected process as a crashed one, leading to a 'virtual' partition. There is thus always a possibility for a group of processes to partition themselves (either due to virtual or real network partitioning) into several subgroups of mutually unsuspecting processes. In a *primary partition membership service*, members of one subgroup (primary subgroup) continue to function while members of the other subgroups are deemed faulty. A normal way of deciding on a primary is to select the subgroup with the majority of the members of the original group.

Design and development of process groups with the accompanying membership service has been an active area of research [e.g., 10,11,12]. In the world of distributed objects, process group ideas can be mapped easily to *object groups*, and there have been many recent research efforts to enrich CORBA with object groups [e.g., 13, 14,15]. In particular, it has been shown that support for object groups can be provided by a middleware CORBA service [13, 15]. Unlike transactions however, currently there is no OMG standard for an object group service. OMG is currently considering proposals for fault tolerance in CORBA [16] that would require facilities for managing groups of objects [17].

5. Applications of Transactions and Process Groups

We discuss below how middleware services of transactions and process (object) groups can be used for providing low-cost, scalable fault-tolerant solutions. We use an example from e-commerce (online auctions) to illustrate the ideas.

5.1 Fault-Tolerant Clusters

Process groups provide a generic solution to decentralised configuration management of arbitrarily large processor clusters. Membership service, at the granularity of processors, can be used for enabling each functioning processor to maintain mutually consistent membership and processor load information. Any deterministic algorithm can be used by each of the processors to determine how the incoming requests can be shared. In a simple scheme, the router/gateway (that uses NAT technique) translates the incoming packet addresses to a broadcast address and broadcasts them on the cluster LAN, and can leave it to the machines to decide who should serve the request. An alternative scheme would require the router/gateway also to be a member of the processor group, and thus maintain membership and load information; based on this information, the router can forward the incoming request to a member processor.

5.2 Wide Area Load Distribution

The techniques discussed above can also be used for creating general purpose, open solutions for wide area load distribution in place of rather specialised, proprietary solutions exemplified by the DistributedDirector product discussed earlier. The DNS server and Web servers can be made members of a group to enable the DNS server to maintain membership and load information. This way the probability of the server directing requests to failed or overloaded Web servers is minimised. A generalisation is possible where by a number of DNS servers can be incorporated in the group for maintaining mutually consistent membership and load information, thereby obtaining tolerance against DNS server failures and partitions.

5.3 Replica Management

Object replicas must be managed through appropriate replica-consistency protocols to ensure that object copies remain mutually consistent. Consistency could be either *strict* (an update at any replica is propagated to other copies 'straight away'), or *lazy* (updates are propagated in background). A major advantage of strict consistency is that clients always get consistent, fresh information. Unfortunately, strict consistency reduces update performance, so does not scale well. Lazy consistency on the other hand can scale well, but freshness of information at any given replica cannot be guaranteed.

Any practical system is likely to contain a mixture of the two [18]. For example, one could imagine maintaining strict consistency within a 'primary' cluster, with remaining clusters being updated lazily. However, certain data items across all the replicas may well need to be kept strictly consistent. Lazy updates could be carried out as a series of transactions initiated by the primary. Both transactions and process groups provide complementary mechanisms for implementing replica consistency [19,20,21]. Additional work is required for developing scalable mixed consistency solutions.

5.4 Reliable Internet Applications

So far in our discussions, we have concentrated on issues concerning reliability of Web servers. However, this is only a part of the story. Typically, a distributed application will also involve processing at a client's side, so issues of client side reliability need to be taken in to account. For example, if a user purchases a cookie (a token) granting access to a newspaper Web site, it is important that the cookie is delivered and stored if the user's account is debited; a failure could prevent either from occurring, and leave the system in an indeterminate state. Providing *end-to-end transactional integrity* between the client (browser) and the Web server is important: in the previous example, the cookie *must* be delivered once the user's account has been debited. Providing such a guarantee was difficult with the original "thin" client model of the Web, where browsers were functionally barren. With the advent of Java it is now possible to empower browsers so that they can fully participate within transactional applications [22].

We conclude this sub-section by briefly describing how CORBA services can be used to provide generic facilities for the construction of fault-tolerant distributed applications in the Internet environment. Given the increasing use of the Internet and the Web for electronic commerce, of particular interest are workflow systems that are widely used by organizations that need to automate their business processes. However, currently available workflow systems are not scalable, as their structure tends to be monolithic. Further, they offer little support for building fault-tolerant applications, nor can they inter-operate, as they make use of proprietary platforms and protocols. Recent work on *transactional workflow systems* has shown that they can be designed and implemented as a set of CORBA services to run on top of a given ORB [23,24]. Wide-spread acceptance of CORBA and Java middleware technologies make such systems ideally suited to building dependable Internet applications.

5.5 Example Application: Internet Auctions

Buying and selling of goods through auctions is an age old custom, and it should not come as a surprise to learn that Web sites offering auctioning services are fast emerging all over. Auctions involve competitive bidding among buyers and sellers of goods. As described in [25], the most common trading models used in real-life auctions are the so-called "open-cry", the "sealed-bid", and the "Dutch" models. Variations of these models include the "Vickrey" auctions, the "Discriminative" (or "Yankee") auctions, and the "Non-discriminative" auctions. The implementation of these trading models in a geographically distributed context, gives rise to a number of design and implementation problems at the system architecture level. Specifically, the system scalability, its responsiveness, and the consistency of the data the system manipulates (e.g. the objects on sale, the submitted bids) must be guaranteed.

Concerning responsiveness, a distributed auction application may require support for real-time communications among multiple buyers and a single seller, as well as communications among multiple buyers and multiple sellers, depending on the particular model of trading. There could also be requirement for *fairness* dictating that all buyers must be granted an equal opportunity to buy the goods offered by a seller [26].

In this sub-section, we discuss how the replicated Web server architecture of fig. 2 can be used to meet data integrity, responsiveness, and scalability requirements of auction services. Allowing users to bid at any of the servers is the principal way of achieving scalability and responsiveness, as the total load is shared amongst many servers. We will consider implementation of open-cry auctions only; implementation of other types of auctions is discussed in [27].

A real-life open-cry auction can be described as follows. The auctioneer and the participants gather in the same location (typically, remote participants can be represented by local agents who act on their behalf).

The auctioneer starts the auction by setting an asking price for an item on sale, and requests bids from the floor. Periodically, the auctioneer increments that asking price to the value of the highest bid received from the floor, and starts a new auction round. The auctioning of an item terminates when no more bids are submitted for that item, within a time interval from the last received bid. Thus, the auctioning of each item may take multiple rounds.

In this type of auction, the auctioneer and all the participants can hear and see each other, and bids are made, and selected (usually through verbal communication and gestures). Thus, each bidder is aware of the bids submitted by the other bidders and can decide his/her bidding strategy, based on the bids of the other auction participants.

All the participants have the same view of the items being sold by auction, and of the proposed bids; in addition, they experience the same communication delays among them, and between them and the auctioneer, and share the same notion of "time"; thus, bidders can adhere to the time constraints imposed by the auctioneer (i.e. the limited time interval to make a bid).

5.5.1 Replicated Auction Services

For our electronic auction system, we require that participants (users) from all over the world should be able to take part in an auction. We adopt an "asynchronous" model of auction service that does not require that all the users be available for auction at the "same time" as in conventional open-cry or Dutch auctions. We replicate the auction service across a number of 'auction servers'. Data integrity is achieved by ensuring atomic interactions between a bidder and a server and by keeping replicated data mutually consistent. In this model, each site (representing a branch of the auctioneer) provides a number of services for taking part in an auction through an *auction server*, as depicted in fig. 5.

Essential state information concerning an auction in progress is replicated at the branches. The auction servers are required to co-operate with each other in order to maintain the consistency of the replicated data. The state information maintained by a server for a given auction in progress will have two components: site specific local state (e.g., bids submitted at that site), and a copy of the shared state which must remain consistent with respect to the copies at other servers.

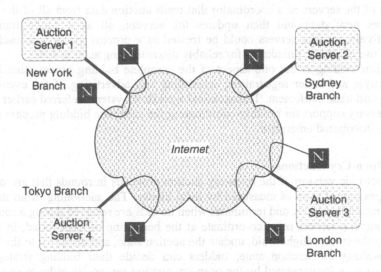

Fig. 5. Replicated auction server architecture

Thus, in this model, the responsibility of the auctioneer is confined to the provision of highly available services that maintain a consistent view of what we can term the "auction state", i.e. the object on sale, the current object price, etc.

In essence, for each object on sale, the auction servers will display that object, its current price and a deadline by which the participants have to place their bids. We assume that servers maintain the same view of the external time with some known accuracy. When the set deadline expires, the servers will exchange collected bids with each other in order to determine the winning bid, update the auction state, and start the new cycle for accepting new bids, if necessary.

An auction participant can connect to any branch, get information on items currently on sale by auction, and submit a bid. It is the responsibility of the auction participants to examine the auction state, and to place their bids before the deadlines expire.

Two principal protocols are required in order to implement this model; namely a Browser-to-Server Protocol (BSP), and a Server-to-Server Protocol (SSP).

The BSP allows a bidder to submit a bid for a particular item on sale. In order to guarantee consistency of the auction state, the bid submission operation is to be executed atomically, i.e. either the bid is correctly delivered to the auction server, or the operation has no effect (in either cases, the invoker of the operation is notified of the termination of the operation). BSP can use an atomic transaction to ensure that the bid submission operation performed from the browser of the bidder is executed atomically. [22] describes how end-to-end transactional integrity between a browser and a server can be achieved.

The SSP manages the information exchange among the auction servers. This protocol is responsible for maintaining the consistency of the shared state among those servers; in particular, it allows those servers to reach consensus on the values contained in the shared state, and provides atomic update of the shared state at all servers. There are several ways of implementing SSP. A transactional approach could use one of the servers as a coordinator that reads auction data from all of the servers, composes new state and then updates the servers, all as a single transaction. Alternatively, auction servers could be treated as a process group with each server making use of atomic broadcasts for reliably disseminating auction state.

Auction bidding is but one aspect of the complete bidding process that includes initial buyer and seller registration, scheduling and advertising of the event, actual bidding and trade settlement. Transactional workflow systems referred earlier provide the necessary support for reliably coordinating the complete bidding process across a globally distributed enterprise.

5.5.2 Open-Cry Auctions

Our electronic version of the open-cry auction proceeds in rounds that are triggered by the passage of time as measured by local clocks. The auctioning of an item may require multiple rounds, and terminates when no bids are received during a round.

The auction servers must co-ordinate at the beginning of each round, in order to agree on the current highest bid, update the auction state, and display it to the bidders. By consulting the auction state, bidders can decide their bidding strategy. The (skeleton) code implemented by the open-cry auction servers, in order to sell an item by auction, is illustrated in Fig. 6. The shared auction state consists of the auctioned object, its associated deadline, and the set of submitted bids that meet the winning bid criterion (termed "valid" bids, below).

```
/* OPEN-CRY AUCTION INITIALIZATION */
current_price := initial_price; /* set initial value */
cycle
    set_deadline;
    no_bids := TRUE; /* initialize Boolean variable */
    display_object_on_sale;
    accept_bids;
    when deadline-expires do
    {
        COLLECT_BIDS;
            /* only accept valid bids;
               exchange bids with other servers;
               if at least one bid has been received at a
               server, set no_bids to FALSE */
        if no_bids then TERMINATE
            /* if no new bids then select winning bid
               based on previous bids */
        else
            current_price := RESOLVE(collected_bids)
    }
end cycle
/* CLOSE OPEN-CRY AUCTION */
```

Fig. 6. Open-cry Auction server skeleton code

The action COLLECT_BIDS involves the co-operation among the servers in order to exchange the received bids. In particular, as part of the execution of the action

COLLECT_BIDS, the shared auction state must be updated atomically at all the sites. Thus, COLLECT_BIDS will be implemented using the server-to-server protocol (SSP). It is worth observing that, in open cry auctions, a bid can be accepted (i.e. it is deemed valid) only when its value is greater than the current_price of the item being sold by auction.

Once the auction set has been made mutually consistent, any deterministic algorithm can be used locally by each server to resolve the bids and to reach an identical decision. this permits each server to locally perform the RESOLVE and TERMINATE actions.

6. Concluding Remarks

We have reviewed current approaches to building high-volume, highly-reliable, Web services. These approaches either use proprietary solutions and/or *ad hoc* techniques that do not scale well. Service providers are looking to computer vendors to provide low-cost, scalable fault-tolerant solutions. The prime requirement is to minimise reliance on specialist equipment and techniques for delivering core services. We have discussed how software implemented fault-tolerance techniques (transactions and process groups) can be applied for creating scalable solutions.

Acknowledgements

This work has been supported in part by Hewlett-Packard Laboratories, Bristol, Nortel Networks, Harlow, the Italian Consiglio Nazionale delle Ricerche (CNR), the Italian Gruppo Nazionale Informatica e Matematica (GNIM), ESPRIT working group BROADCAST (project No. 22455), ESPRIT projects C3DS (project no. 24962) and MultiPLECX (Project No. 26810).

References

1. D. Ingham, F. Panzieri and S.K. Shrivastava, "Constructing dependable Web services", IEEE Internet Computing (to appear).
2. R. Orfali, D. Harkey and J. Edwards, "The essential distributed objects", John Wiley and Sons Ltd., 1996.
3. "CORBAservices: Common Object Services Specification", OMG Document Number 95-3-31, March 1995.
4. F. Cristian, "Understanding fault tolerant distributed systems", CACM, February 1991.
5. P.A. Bernstein et al, "Concurrency Control and Recovery in Database Systems", Addison-Wesley, 1987.
6. K. Birman , "The process group approach to reliable computing", CACM , 36, 12, pp. 37-53, December 1993.
7. G.D. Parrington, S.K. Shrivastava, S.M. Wheater and M.C. Little, "The design and implementation of Arjuna", USENIX Computing Systems Journal, vol. 8 (3), pp. 255-308, Summer 1995.

8. Fischer, M., Lynch N., and Paterson, M., "Impossibility of Distributed Consensus with One Faulty Process", J. ACM, 32, April 1985, pp 374-382.

9. T.D. Chandra and S. Toueg, "Unreliable failure detectors for reliable distributed systems", J. ACM, 43(2), 1996, pp. 225-267.

10. L.E. Moser, P.M. Melliar-Smith et al, "Totem: a Fault-tolerant multicast group communication system", CACM, 39 (4), pp. 54-63, April 1996.

11. P. Ezhilchelvan, R. Macedo and S. K. Shrivastava, "Newtop: a fault-tolerant group communication protocol", 15th IEEE Intl. Conf. on Distributed Computing Systems, Vancouver, pp. 296-306, May 1995.

12. D. Dolev and D. Malki, "The Transis approach to high availability cluster communication", CACM, 39 (4), April 1996, pp. 64-70.

13. P. Felber, R. Guerraoui and A. Schiper, "The implementation of a CORBA object group service", Theory and Practice of Object Systems, 4(2), 1998, pp. 93-105.

14. P. Narasimhan, L, E. Moser and P. M. Melliar-Smith, "Replica consistency of CORBA objects in partitionable distributed systems", Distributed Systems Eng., 4, 1997, pp. 139-150.

15. G. Morgan, S.K. Shrivastava, P.D. Ezhilchelvan and M.C. Little, "Design and Implementation of a CORBA Fault-tolerant Object Group Service", Proc. of Second IFIP International Working Conference on Distributed Applications and Interoperable Systems, DAIS'99, Helsinki, June 1999.

16. http://www.omg.org/techprocess/meetings/schedule/Fault_Tolerance_RFP.htm

17. L.E. Moser, P.M. Melliar-Smith and P. Narasimhan, "A Fault tolerance framework for COBRA", Proc. of 29th Symp. On Fault Tolerant Computing, FTCS-29, Madison, June 1999.

18. J. Gray, P. Helland, P. O'Neil and D. Shasha, "The dangers of replication and a solution", ACM SIGMOD Record, 25 (2), pp. 173-182, June 1996.

19. P. Felber, R. Guerraoui and A. Schiper, "Replication of CORBA objects", Chapter 11 of this book.

20. M.C. Little and S. K Shrivastava, "Understanding the Role of Atomic Transactions and Group Communications in Implementing Persistent Replicated Objects", Advances in persistent Object Systems, ed. R. Morrison, M. Jordan and M. Atkinson, Morgan Kaufman, ISBN: 1 55860 585 1, 1999, pp. 17-28. See also, Chapter 10 of this book.

21. B. Kemme and G. Alonso, "A suite of replication protocols based on group communication primitives", Proc. 18th IEEE Intl. Conf. on Distributed Computing Systems, ICDCS'98, Amsterdam, May 1998, pp. 156-163.

22. M.C. Little and S. K. Shrivastava, "Java Transactions for the Internet", 4th USENIX Conf. on Object Oriented Technologies and Systems, COOTS, Santa Fe, April 1998.

23. D. Georgakopoulos, M. Hornick and A. Sheth, "An overview of workflow management: from process modelling to workflow automation infrastructure", Intl. Journal on distributed and parallel databases, 3(2), pp. 119-153, April 1995.

24. S. M Wheater, S. K Shrivastava and F. Ranno "A CORBA Compliant Transactional Workflow System for Internet Applications ", Proc. Of IFIP Intl. Conference on Distributed Systems Platforms and Open Distributed Processing, Middleware 98, (N. Davies, K. Raymond, J. Seitz, eds.), Springer-Verlag, London, 1998, ISBN 1-85233-088-0, pp. 3-18.

25. M. Kumar, S.J. Feldman, "Internet Auctions", Proc. 3rd USENIX Workshop on Electronic Commerce, Boston (MA), Aug. 31 - Sept. 3, 1998, pp. 49-59.

26. J.P. Banatre M. Banatre, G. Lapalme, F. Ployette, "The design and building of Enchere, a distributed electronic marketing system", CACM, Vol. 29, NO. 1, pp. 19-29, Jan. 1986.

27. F Panzieri and S K Shrivastava, "On the provision of replicated Internet auction services", IEEE Intl. Workshop on Electronic Commerce, WELCOM'99, Lausanne, 19 October, 1999.

Support for Distributed CSCW Applications

François J. N. Cosquer[1†], Paulo Veríssimo[2], Sacha Krakowiak[3], and Loïc Decloedt[4††]

[1]Axlan
[2]Universidade de Lisboa
[3]Labo. Sirac (Institut National Polytechnique de Grenoble, INRIA, Université Joseph Fourier)
[4]Dolphin Integration
[†]the work reported here was done while the author was at INESC
[††]the work reported here was done while the author was at INRIA Rhône-Alpes

Abstract. This chapter reports on advances made in the field of distributed systems technology for the computational support of CSCW applications, with emphasis on distributed synchronised applications (i.e. same time, different place). The main concepts are first recalled, and illustrated by the description of two CSCW platforms developed in Broadcast: NAVCOOP, based on a group-oriented communication layer, and CoopScan, based on software agents. Finally, the techniques for enhancing a legacy interactive application with facilities for distributed cooperation are discussed and illustrated by two examples.

1 Introduction

The exponential growth of interconnected networks such as the Internet has led to the emergence of a computing infrastructure with enormous potential for hosting a wide range of distributed applications. Computer Supported Cooperative Work, CSCW for short, is a multi-disciplinary area which includes disciplines such as sociology, psychology, linguistics and computer science, and aims to understand and improve the task productivity of a group of individuals. CSCW applications, or collaborative applications for short, are software systems that allow multiple users to work together. Because of its multi-user/multi-site nature, CSCW applications rely on distributed software architectures and implementations.

There have been many attempts over the years to assist the collaborative applications developer. These range from models trying to define all aspects of multi-user activity over a common task to low level system support for data transmission [10]. This effort is aimed at grouping what is identified as key functionality or common services into support platform so-called groupware toolkits, platforms or environments in order to reduce the implementation effort.

This chapter reports on the advances made in the field of distributed systems technology for the computational support of CSCW applications. We provide insight into CSCW application development and runtime support with emphasis on distributed synchronised applications (i.e. same time, different place). We discuss our experience through the presentation of concrete examples.

We begin this chapter by presenting a survey of CSCW applications and tools, followed by a presentation of the overall software system architecture of a CSCW support system. Two experimental CSCW platforms are then described including both

S. Krakowiak, S.K. Shrivastava (Eds.): Distributed Systems, LNCS 1752, pp. 295–326, 2000.

architecture and implementation considerations. A section on real-life CSCW applications scenarios based on dedicated support platforms concludes the presentation.

2   Survey

After a quick definition of terminology, this section gives an overview of the main collaborative tools and applications, from which we derive the main requirements.

2.1   Basic Terminology for Cooperative Work

Organising a computer-based collaborative activity, often referred to as a *session*, first of all implies the existence of mechanisms for scheduling events. This functionality is referred to as *session management*. Usually, the *initiator* starts a session by registering it with the system, as opposed to the *attendees*, who simply connect to a session. Any user taking part in a session is known as a *participant*. groups The mechanisms required to support a session while it is running, i.e. the management of the shared workspace, are called *active session support*.

The shared workspace is defined as the environment (text, graphical objects, tools) in which the collaboration takes place. Multimedia channels that enable the exchange of sound and video data are also becoming more common.

One frequently supported mechanism for access control is the *floor*. The floor identifies the active user in a conversation, while *floor control* refers to the mechanisms and policy under which the floor changes. In addition to the floor, a complete range of facilities is necessary to enable and mediate the collaboration over the shared workspace. For example, *social roles* are application-specific mechanisms used to enforce access rules over the shared workspace. They correspond to application level entities used for concurrency control. Roles can be used for moderating the manipulation of the *telepointer*, which is a cursor that appears on more than one display.

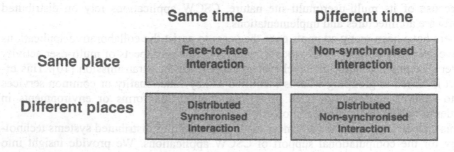

Fig.1. The time/space matrix

A classification, known as the time/space matrix (Fig. 1), organises CSCW systems in four categories according to the location of the interacting persons (same place or different places) and the interaction characteristics (people active at the same time or at different times). Face-to-face interaction (same time and same place) corresponds to meeting-room technology. A physical bulletin board is an illustration of *non-synchronised* interaction (same place, different time), while the electronic mail system is an example of distributed *non-synchronised* interaction (different place, different time).

Distributed *synchronised* interaction (same time, different place) covers applications such as teleconferencing. Examples are given below.

2.2 Collaborative Tools and Applications

Multi-user talks are visual communication programs. They are one of the simplest types of tool for collaboration. As opposed to electronic mail, the electronic version of the paper-based mail system, multi-user talk tools represent a perfect example of highly synchronised cooperation. A basic type of synchronised communication for two users is available through the Unix talk program.

Shared drawing tools extend a basic drawing tool to support multiple users who are visually sharing the editing window. This idea corresponds to a computerised distributed version of the traditional white-board which can be found in most meeting rooms. The relative difficulty of implementing such a tool is related to the amount of access control rules to be built in. Many systems of this kind are available today; a comparative study is presented in [12]. The criteria compared include the kind of interaction (synchronised/non-synchronised), the type of input allowed (video, pixel, structured graphics), and the storage facilities.

Cooperative editing gives users the ability to share, i.e. edit, a data file (text or code) by modifying, possibly simultaneously, selected parts. The aim is to guarantee that the contributions from multiple users will reach a (final) coherent state, i.e. a meaningful article or a working computer programme. Besides the ability to share data files, the tools must provide users with features allowing cooperation. For example, most editing tasks require the ability to work alternately in isolation and in a group. This means that tools may have to support both synchronised and non-synchronised mode. We will concentrate here on the synchronised interaction aspects.

There are at least two reasons why synchronised operations are needed in the context of shared editing. First, the inputs of each user on a document may have a direct influence on the work of co-editors; and second, as pointed out in [14], users demonstrate a natural tendency to check what other users are doing.

Group Decision Support Systems more often referred to as GDSS, help a community of users to make decisions or to elaborate ideas about unstructured problems (often called brainstorming sessions). The characteristic features of these systems are voting and issue analysis tools. Typically, the tools provide a way to define an idea, propose it to the group and evaluate it. The sequence of these operations need not be pre-determined since an idea can be refined or evolve through discussion and comments. However, GDSS tools must guarantee progress and the quality of the final decision.

Therefore, one important and challenging design issue is to select the appropriate representation of knowledge and the kind of relationship between knowledge entities. Furthermore, a number of phases have to be defined and the tools must use a number of rules to ensure the session is making progress. The way the data is presented to the users depends directly on the choices associated with these design issues.

Concurrent Engineering (CE) designates the activities of a (possibly geographically distributed) team of people aiming to accomplish the concurrent design of several phases of a common product. More than just supporting one specific task such as drawing or text editing, CE tools involve the notion of a more elaborate task and are usually composed of a set of tools.

By allowing and structuring concurrent activities and organising synchronisation phases and negotiations, it is hoped that better products in terms of quality, costs and time-to-market will emerge. Software tools have been developed to allow the collaboration of these virtual teams, prompting the advent of an area known as Computer Support for Concurrent Engineering. Many examples of such systems can be found in the literature [13]. The systems most familiar to computer scientists are undoubtedly the Computer-Supported Concurrent Software Engineering tools [9]. These allow team-level development, testing and debugging all through the software life cycle. For flexibility reasons, they are integrated in the personal working environment of each individual and provide some collaborative features such as common viewing of source for editing or debugging, and shared outputs for synchronised work. Multimedia support can be added to enhance the collaboration.

Teleconferencing tools have text and graphic interaction channels and real-time voice and/or video stream. Depending on their interfaces and their complexity, these tools range from the electronic classroom to desktop conferencing. The latter usually requires video channels and sophisticated control and interaction modes in order to reach the full power of standard teleconferencing facilities with desktop computers. However, for many reasons, such as cost-effectiveness, ease of set-up and the potential to reach a large number of people located all over the world, these systems have attracted more attention over the past few years. This is reflected in the business world by the penetration of Integrated Office Collaboration tools such as Lotus Notes and on the Internet by the proliferation of software based products such as Microsoft NetMeeting.

Multimedia channels are useful for verbal and some aspects of visual cooperation. Use of multimedia can partially serve some aspects of collaboration awareness but is not absolutely necessary. However, issues concerned with continuous data (audio/video) storage, synchronisation and transmission lie outside the scope of this chapter. We concentrate on the cooperation aspects using standard computer systems equipped with graphical screen, mouse and keyboard.

2.3   Requirements for CSCW Application Support

We can identify the following high level requirements for CSCW applications support:

- Need for shared data management with flexible access control: most distributed platforms (databases, file systems, replicated data management, etc.) are built for masking distribution. This systems-oriented transparency is opposed to the collaboration awareness nature of CSCW applications. Access control has to take into account the multi-user aspects from a cooperation perspective (user-centered) as opposed to the traditional system-oriented perspective. Examples of mechanisms

which have proved useful in order to minimise conflicts for cooperative applications are listed below:
- roles for structuring hierarchy;
- reservation mechanisms;
- showing intentions;
- user level policies (social protocols).
- Need for efficient multi-party communication: most distributed platforms are oriented more towards inter-process point-to-point communication. Efficient multi-party communication is needed for:
  - improving overall tool responsiveness due to the distribution of data;
  - providing user-level informal communication channel;
  - interjections-like accesses in a shared window (example of how collaboration awareness can help to mediate access control over the shared space).
- Need for audience management: little effort has been devoted to registration and dynamic user membership representation in traditional distributed platforms. Audience management includes issues related to :
  - registration and scheduling: who can join, what, how, etc.
  - keeping track at runtime of who is in, who leaves, etc.

CSCW applications are distributed in nature and have needs common to many distributed applications: message passing, identification and naming, addressing, mobility, etc. Furthermore, synchronised collaboration over large-scale distributed systems requires support environment which encompass asynchronism, delays and partition or failure in general. It is therefore important to relate the CSCW support to existing distributed systems technology.

3   Architecture

After the presentation of CSCW applications, we now discuss the design approach and an overall software system architecture. The goal is to present the software layers involved in the support for CSCW applications and discuss architectural choices. The implementation of specific support platforms is discussed in more detail in Sect. 4.

3.1   The Design Approach

Generic middleware has become a key component to building distributed applications. However, the characteristics of CSCW applications require specific functionality that can be embedded in support platforms. This functionality is provided through a set of abstractions representing the cooperation model and accessed through generic mechanisms that hide the intrinsic complexity of such multi-user/multi-site applications. The objective is to reduce the prototyping effort, thus leading to better implementations and faster evaluations of CSCW applications. The use of support platforms should improve product quality and thus contribute to end-user acceptance

The way to provide platform functionality differs according to what are considered to be the most privileged application domain and research issues. In this chapter, we focus on support platforms developed with distributed systems technology.

3.2   The Overall Layering

A view that has emerged over the years is that distributed applications rely on a variety of distributed computing services and application development environments referred to as middleware. Middleware is the software layer that provides the "glue" between the distributed applications components across different networks and operating systems. We have refined this global architecture for CSCW applications. The software layering is used from the point of view of the application support. It makes it easier to present and understand interaction. (see Fig. 2 below).

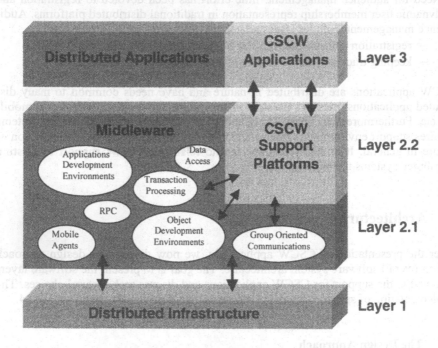

Fig. 2. The layered architecture

Applications are at the top of the stack (layer 3). At the bottom, we find the distributed infrastructure (layer 1) composed of OS and network software, which provides unreliable data transfer between processes. The middle part (layer 2) is split in two:

> *Layer 2.1* (generic middleware services), which provides reliable data transfer, transactions (ACID properties), code mobility, etc., and helps the developers to deal with low level issues such as failure and concurrency.
> *Layer 2.2* (dedicated or application-class specific middleware), which implements active session support and session management. Examples of implementation of layer 2.2 are given in Sect. 5.

The advantage of this layered architecture is to separate basic mechanisms (usually embedded in the generic middleware) from application domain specific policies. The specific CSCW policies are embedded in the CSCW support platforms and rely on the generic middleware layer.

3.3 Architectural Choices

As mentioned earlier, the functionality of CSCW support platforms can be subdivided in Session Management and Active Session Support
Session management deals with issues linked with registration and scheduling of the collaboration phases both before and with audience management at runtime. The architectural issues are very similar to directory services such as X500 and LDAP .
Regarding the active session support, the main choice lies in whether a centralised versus a replicated software architecture should be used. The pros and cons of centralised vs. replicated software architecture have long been discussed. Concerning more specifically the support for CSCW applications, the important decision factors for optimal performance are:

- expected number of participants using the application simultaneously
- the size and speed of the network
- the fault-tolerance requirements

The centralised architecture has a simple design, but it is does not scale well and is not resilient to failures. Therefore a replicated software architecture is preferred in most cases.
Another important point is whether the CSCW support will allow running existing applications without modifications. This option is useful when developers do not have access to the source code of the application Such constraint implies that the support of the cooperation is achieved by a wrapper that intercepts calls to the graphical/windowing environment. An illustration of such design choices is further discussed in Sect. 5.2. The next section presents two concrete examples of CSCW support platforms.

4 Implementing Support Platforms

In this section we present two different approaches of CSCW support platforms, illustrated by examples. The NAVCOOP platform relies on a group oriented communication layer, while the coordination layer of CoopScan is based on software agents.

4.1 NAVCOOP: Large Scale Interaction Support

The main thrust of NAVCOOP is synchronised large-scale interaction support. Our main design options were based on the following:

- Separation of user interface and control, based on dialog independence.
- Provision of support through mechanisms and feedback, which could be easily integrated in current applications.

Furthermore, the emphasis on large-scale setting means that in order to maintain co-operation one must encompass asynchronism, delays and partitions. This means providing mechanisms and services such as the ones listed below:

- Connectivity feedback to users
- Partition detector, with particular attention to *minimising* partition detection errors
- Possibility for multiple partitions to operate simultaneously
- Support for controlling progress in each partition
- Level of Service for specification of degradation

Due to a beneficial relationship between what is provided by a group communication system and the cooperative applications requirements [6], we selected NavTech as the generic middleware to base our design and implementation.

The emphasis of NAVCOOP is large-scale distribution support which naturally led us to a replicated architecture (process and data). Each node runs its own copy of NAVCOOP and an instance of each cooperative application it is participating in.

The overall NAVCOOP architecture is depicted in Fig. 3. Two NavTech components, namely the *membership services* and the *node failure suspector*, are shown because of the key services they provide to NAVCOOP.

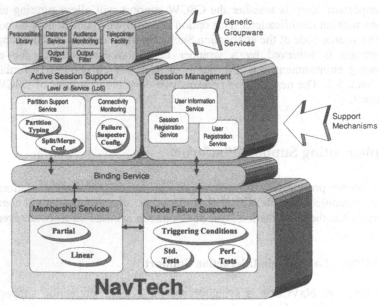

Fig. 3. The NavCoop architecture

The NavCoop platform is composed of the following blocks:
- *The support mechanisms*, which represent the base components of NavCoop. These are composed of the failure suspector configuration, the partition support, the Level of Service and the binding service.
- *The generic services*, which are built using the NavCoop support mechanisms. The distance and audience monitoring services provide group awareness modules dedicated to large-scale interaction. The personality library is a high-level interface for simplifying the configuration of connectivity requirements. Finally, a partition-resilient telepointer service is provided, illustrating the benefits of NavCoop for implementing enhanced versions of already existing cooperation artefacts .

The session management, which is necessary for ensuring the registration of sessions and the connection of users.

Support Mechanisms
To tackle problems relating to connectivity and partitions, we have developed support mechanisms using the flexibility offered by the NavTech platform.

Connectivity Monitoring deals with the configuration of the NavTech failure suspector and the associated connectivity specification. The failure suspector is designed to evaluate a number of operational parameters. Each parameter characterised by a set of variables such as sample rate, threshold (maximum acceptable value), etc. Each node runs the performability tests to every other node involved in the computation. The number of samples for which the threshold is execeeded (TE) is recorded for each parameter.

The overall connectivity to a remote node is measured by a Disturbance Index (DI). The DI is the weighted sum of the TEs (threshold exceeded), the weight indicating the importance of the parameter. The set of DI values are computed periodically and used to build a Local Connectivity Vector (LCV). In order to reduce the probability of incorrect failure detection further, failure suspectors exchange periodically their Local Connectivity Vectors to build a Global Connectivity Matrix, or GCM. The GCM indicates how every node perceives the connectivity to every other node. Activation of the membership module depends on a condition referred to as *triggering condition*, which is a function of GCM values. More information on the configuration of failure suspectors can be found in [7].

PSS: Partition Support Service deals with partition processing specifications and the runtime support using the membership service. Once the system has partitioned, resulting in isolated subgroups, the applications should still have mechanisms that preserve the notions of control, coordination and cooperation. The mechanisms provided by PSS rely on strong-partial membership service at the communication level, which allows virtual synchrony as the baseline consistency paradigm. NavCoop implements partition *levels* [1,2,...n] which reflect the relative importance of the partitions. Partition *typing* applies the idea of a social role (or *role*), a concept found in cooperative applications to model the relative importance of each user. The role is materialised by two variables: the *identity* of a participant, and its *weight*. A partition is specified using a combination of both weight and identify of its set of participants.

The importance of partitions, expressed by the levels and specified by types, is translated into (application-specific) progress specifications. These mechanisms are complemented by a configuration interface called the *split/merge rules table*, which allows the programmer to specify how the application should respond to a partition event at runtime. More information on PSS can be found in [8].

Level of Service (LoS) defines the operational envelopes. The LoS combines the failure suspector configuration with the partial membership services and the associated PSS. The configurations of both mechanisms are suitable for specifying and supporting coherent degradation at runtime. Matching membership views with actions being performed at runtime can be seen as an extra degree of freedom for the programmer. The triggering of the membership is based on the GCM, the Global Connectivity Matrix. This allows the programmer to specify the notion of what the group should be as a whole. Suspicion weights indicate the relative importance of users, thereby closely matching the real-life situation of face-to-face meetings. When network events occur, the PSS level and rules preserve the notion of animation and control necessary to the progress of the applications. In a way, this suggests the use of the PSS and the configuration of FS not simply as passive modules reacting to low-level events but as runtime instrumentation for tuning the application resource requirements.

Binding Service is the thin layer necessary to support the mechanisms and resulting generic services. It keeps three mapping: users (i.e. names) to processes (i.e. NAVTECH representation); roles (i.e., tag representation) to users; roles to weights.

Generic Services

Generic Services are application-independent. *Personality Library* provides a way of modelling different user connectivity requirements. This simplifies the interface to the parameterisation of the FS and encourages the reuse of the FS parameters by a whole range of applications.

Typical default threshold values, weights and sample rates are defined using known specifications of responsiveness and estimated bandwidth for the target applications [Rodden 92]. We modelled cooperative personalities based on *responsiveness* (roundtrip delay) and *talkativeness* (throughput). Depending on the expected type of activity during a cooperation session, a user can be modelled as any combination of these attributes. The classification is given in the Table 1 below.

Table 1. The cooperative personalities library

Characteristics	Responsiveness (roundtrip)	Talkativeness (throughput)
Extravert	High	High
Demanding	High	Low
Verbose	Low	High
Laconic	Low	Low

Choosing a personality connectivity requirement is done by means of a selectable programming parameter which greatly simplifies the task of the programmer. The actual values were preset using estimations. *Distance Service* allows a local measure of link connectivity to be visually monitored. It is an application-independent service that enhances collaboration awareness. It is implemented by intercepting the FS output and using new feedback techniques. Early experiments led to a GUI analogy for the distance service, inspired by a hill, on which people walk up and down. Participants are aligned in ascending order from left to right as they get more distant from the viewer (Fig. 4). The "distance" can be defined by any (combination) of the operational parameters of the Failure Suspector. *Audience Monitoring Service* complements the distance service by keeping track of which participants are in the current working group. In order to avoid paying the cost of the underlying membership service, the audience monitoring service relies on the information provided by the GMC (Global Connectivity Matrix).

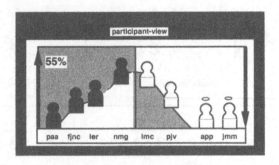

Fig. 4. Distance service GUI

The value of membership of a node is generated using the suspicion information, which is an average of all LCVs (Local Connectivity Vector) for that node. The value corresponding to each user can then be displayed as shown in Fig. 5. The icons use the following convention: full icon for no suspicion (high global connectivity) which gets emptier as the suspicion (of connectivity problem) increases. This representation metaphor gives users an overview of the situation at a glance.

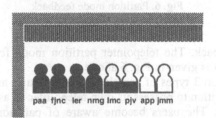

Fig. 5. Audience monitoring service GUI

Telepointer facility is the result of experiments with ways of incorporating feedback. In order to improve the level of support further at runtime, we explored how connectivity and partition level information could be integrated in existing artefacts such as a telepointer. We combined the partition typing information   provided by   the PSS with standard cooperative modules using new feedback techniques for improving

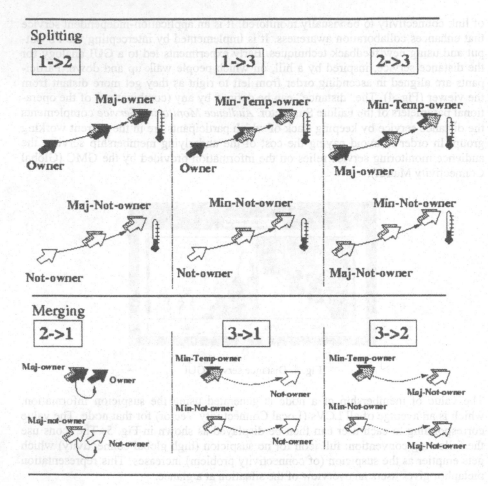

Fig. 6. Partition mode feedback

group awareness feedback. The telepointer partition mode feedback for telepointer owners and non owners is given in Fig. 6 above.

The example is based on 3 types of partitions (initial, major and minor). The default policy allows each partition to possess its own telepointer so as to preserve animation during partition mode. The users become aware of partitioning when they see a change in the telepointer shade. The combination of shadowing with black, grey, and white informs the user about its current capabilities in the presence of partitioning, as depicted in the Figure. These depend on the split and merge rules table, which defines the different transitions allowed.

This functionality allows users to proceed smoothly in the presence of temporary network disruptions and guarantees a WYGIWIG-like paradigm on a per group basis.

Session Management
Session management includes all activities dealing with the session before its activation. These range from registration, advertisement and connection protocol to the user information service. NAVCOOP session management is organised in three services.

- *Session Registration Service* is responsible for providing mechanisms to the initiator for registering sessions.
- *User Information Service* allows users with granted permission to access the session table where all the sessions are listed. They can consult all or some of the advertisement parameters of the different sessions (type of session, content, start-up requirements, etc.). This service is very similar to the news systems. The difference lies in the fact that moderation is made at the level of the session registration service which is in charge of registering the information. This provides flexible access control which is not present in the current news system.
- *User Registration Service* deals with the functions associated with user connection to a session. This includes the interface to the various types of connection procedure (the UCP parameters), as well as the issues related to de-registration.

Summary
NAVCOOP is a groupware platform that provides support for building robust CSCW applications. NAVCOOP relies on the services offered by the underlying group-oriented system. The group-oriented communication layer and its configurable components have allowed us to build a support platform which can assist the programmer when dealing with complex problems related to network disruptions. The main features of this replicated architecture are:

- A partition detector with special care to minimising partition detection errors.
- Support for controlling progress in multiple partitions.
- Level of Service (LoS) for specification of degradation.
- Connectivity feedback to users.

The benefits and applicability were tested by porting an existing Group Decision Support System application to the NAVCOOP platform. This experience is presented in Sect. 5.1.

4.2   CoopScan: A Generic Platform for Synchronous Groupware

CoopScan [4, 5] is a generic platform designed for the development of cooperative applications, with the following objectives.

- The platform should allow existing interactive applications to be readily integrated, with a low development cost and a low production delay.
- The platform should be flexible, i.e. it should allow easy modification and customisation of the cooperation protocols (data access, floor control, join and leave, etc.).
- The platform should allow the participants to use several applications at the same time.

The class of target applications may be characterised as follows.

- Cooperation between participants is essentially based on shared information and direct communication.

- Interaction is synchronous, i.e. all participants have an identical view of shared data and modifications to these data are immediately reflected in all views.

Examples include cooperative document editing and cooperative CAD.

The main design decisions were dictated by the above requirements. The response time constraints inherent to synchronous interaction led to choose a replicated architecture over a centralised one. The requirement of fast integration motivated the choice of a high-level application integration scheme based on application related events, instead of a low-level scheme based on display related events. The next two sections respectively present the architecture of the platform and the mechanisms for application integration and protocol customisation.

Architecture

CoopScan is organised in three levels: the GUI layer at the top, the application layer at the bottom, and the coordination in the middle. As explained in the introduction, the architecture is totally replicated; this means t hat each layer contains a module on each participant node, as represented on Fig. 7.

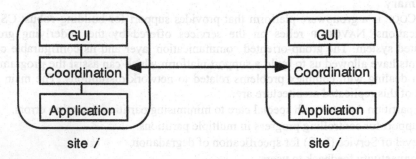

site *i*   site *j*

Fig. 7. General organisation of CoopScan

The coordination layer is itself organised as a set of agents (in this context, an agent is simply an autonomous active entity that interacts with other agents and with its environment). The interactions are specified by an event-reaction model: for each agent, we specify a set of events to which the agent may react; this reaction is described by a predefined script, the execution of which may cause other events to be generated. This organisation is modular, portable, and easily adaptable to changing requirements.

Cooperative work using the CoopScan platform is organised in sessions: a session is a period of time during which the users may interact and share resources. In order to add flexibility, we represent a user by an actor playing a role; the actor is the abstraction of a user independently of any specific function, and a role defines the function of an actor with respect to other actors (e.g. manager, editor, etc.). An actor may successively play several roles. This aspect is detailed in the next section.

We first describe how actors access shared resources (e.g. documents) during a session. We then explain how sessions are started and closed.

Actions on shared resources are actually executed through applications that use these resources. An actor may simultaneously use several applications (e.g. a text editor and a voice communication system, etc.). An actor is connected to a site and is associated with a local agent on that site; the local agent performs the actions requested by the actor on the local resources. Each local agent is associated with a remote agent on each site that participates to the session: remote agents are in charge of duplicating on remote sites the modifications made by local agents.

An actor starts a session by specifying the sites that participate to the session. A session agent is created on each of these sites. Session agents perform administration tasks: they create the local and remote agents, they maintain information related to the state of a session, and they are in charge of dynamic aspects such as floor management and actor joining and leaving.

The organisation of the coordination layer of CoopScan is described on Fig. 8. In this figure, the box labeled "Actor" also include the user interface (GUI).

The tasks of the agents may be detailed as follows: a local agent filters all operations performed by an actor. If the operation only affects private (non-shared) data, it is simply propagated to the application. If it affects shared data, the local agent first checks the current access rights (depending on the actor's role, on the status of the data, etc.). If access is allowed, the local agent performs the operation, and propagates it to the remote agents. The local agent attached to an actor interacts with other actors' local agents in order to perform cooperation related tasks (e.g. token transmission, change of access rights, etc.).

A remote agent waits for orders from the local agent from which it depends. When it receives the description of an operation on shared data, it performs the operation through the relevant application.

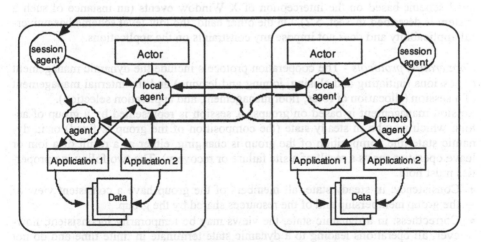

Fig. 8. The agent organisation of CoopScan

The session agent, on a site, is in charge of administration, group management, and floor allocation. It provides an interface for administration requests, such as requesting a new connection, requesting the floor, or starting a new application. In its initial state, a session agent waits for a connection request. When the request arrives, the agent starts a new session or joins an existing session (depending on the origin and parameters of the request), and switches to an active state, in which it executes the coordination protocols. The agents that are part of a session on different sites communicate through messages in order to build a global view of the session and to implement the coordination protocols.

Application Integration and Cooperation Protocols

Application integration. As mentioned earlier, CoopScan uses a high-level integration scheme. This means that it may only accept "open" applications, i.e. applications that export a high-level interface, both in terms of input (operations to be performed on the data) and of output (events or upcalls resulting from an internal change of state). The upcall interface allows internal changes to be detected and propagated to remote instances of the application, through the agent mechanism described in the previous section.

The high-level integration scheme has the following benefits.

- Flexibility and adaptability. The modular organisation allows easy modification of the system. For example, a fine degree control may be exerted on the cooperation policies and protocols. Specific protocols based on a semantic knowledge of the applications may be easily introduced.
- Platform independence. The system does not depend on the characteristics of the underlying platform as regards user interface (e.g. window system) and resource management.
- Low network traffic. Only application-related events need to be exchanged between the nodes.

These advantages are apparent if one compares the CoopScan architecture with a low-level scheme based on the interception of X Window events (an instance of such a system is described in Sect. 5.2). On the other hand, the low-level scheme has universal applicability and does not impose any constraints on the applications.

Cooperation protocols - The cooperation protocols include the dynamic management of sessions (initiating and closing, joining and leaving) and the internal management of a session (allocation of roles, floor management, and application selection).

Session management is based on groups. A session is represented by a group of actors, which may be in steady state (the composition of the group is fixed) or in dynamic state (the composition of the group is changing, either as a result of a join or leave operation, or as a result of a site failure or recovery). The two following properties must hold.

- Consistency: in steady state, all members of the group have a consistent view of the group membership and of the resources shared by the group.
- Correctness: in a dynamic state, the views may be temporarily inconsistent; however, all operations leading to a dynamic state terminate in finite time and do not create deadlocks.

We have formally verified [11] that the protocols of CoopScan ensure consistency and correctness, under the assumption that communication failures do not create network partitions.

Within a session, three main roles are defined: chair, participant, and floor holder. The chair is the initiator and manager of a session; the chair role may be reallocated through election, e.g. following a site failure. Floor allocation is managed through a specific protocol. In CoopScan, several such protocols are used, and the session chair may dynamically select a new protocol. Two standard protocols are initially provided; they are based on a unique token. In the explicit selection protocol, the token is allocated by the session chair. In the implicit selection protocol, the token is allocated by the current token holder, using a FIFO scheme based on request arrival time.

The actors that are part of a session form a group called the root group of the session. Within that group, it is possible to define subgroups, based on the usage of a specific common application and the sharing of the corresponding resources. While an actor may only be part of a single session at a time, it may be member of several subgroups within a session, in order to use different applications.

Summary

CoopScan is a generic platform for synchronous groupware using a high-level integration scheme, based on application-related events, and using a fully replicated architecture. While the use of CoopScan is restricted to "open" applications, our experience shows that the main advantages are the ease of integration of new applications and the flexibility provided by the modular organisation in agents, which allows a wide range of cooperation policies to be implemented and tested.

The CoopScan architecture is generic in the sense that most functions provided by the platform can be reused for various applications. The session agent and most of the local agent (about 75% of the functions) are independent from the application. The dependency from the application interface is concentrated in a small part of the local agent and in the remote agent; for the latter, the adaptation to new interface is straightforward, and defined by a standard procedure.

Our main experience has been with applications using both document sharing (through the structured document editor Thot, or through a Web browser) and audio communication. A full-scale system based on the CoopScan prototype has also been developed by France Télécom.

4.3   Conclusion

We conclude this section by a brief comparison of the NAVCOOP and Coopscan platforms, based on our experience. Both platforms use a replicated architecture, and provide generic services to the applications. However, the design goals were different. NAVCOOP aims at providing a set of services for preserving the quality of communication in large-scale applications, in the face of variable network conditions, including partitions. These services rely on elaborate system support modules, based on membership services and failure suspectors. On the other hand, the emphasis in CoopScan was on flexibility, not on large scale support. The main goal was to allow rapid development and tuning of cooperative applications by integration of legacy software. The organisation into specialised agents makes it very easy to identify the local changes to be done, both for integrating new applications and for customising a cooperation policy. It is assumed, however, that the applications have an open structure with explicit interfaces (if not, techniques described in Sect. 5.2 are applicable).

The techniques used in the two platforms appear to be complementary. Thus it could be possible to combine group awareness and fault tolerance with flexibility, by developing an agent layer on a platform providing group services. However, the scalability problems (in terme of number of participants, not of geographical deployment) remain to be solved.

5   Building CSCW Applications Efficiently

Many cooperative applications are not developed from scratch, but by enhancing an existing (interactive) application with cooperative capabilities. There are two main benefits to this approach: making a smooth transition for the users by preserving a familiar environment; reusing existing code, thus reducing development costs. On the other hand, integrating cooperative facilities into an application designed for a stand-alone usage may be problematic, since cooperation introduces synchronisation and data sharing constraints that potentially interfere with the deep structure of the application.

To address these problems, two main approaches have been proposed:

- The first approach attempts to modify the internal operations of the application to adapt it to a cooperative mode. This approach has the potential of a better adaptation to the cooperative mode, both in terms of performance and functionality. However, it requires a good understanding of the structure of the initial application, and the ability to modify its internals; in addition, it may also require that the internal functions provide specific information (e.g. callbacks when an information is modified). These constraints may preclude the use of this method.
- The second approach takes a more external view, and aims at developing a framework for enhancing an application with cooperative capabilities, with minimal interference to its original program. This approach is much less constraining; however, it is subject to two risks: the performance cost may be prohibitive, and it may not be possible to integrate all the needed additional capabilities if access to the internal structure of the application is restricted.

In order to illustrate the pros and cons of the two different approaches we present below an example of each category. Firstly, the NGTool experiment is presented in which collaboration was enhanced by substituting application communication layer by the support platform thus modifying some of the application internals. Secondly, the XCoop experiment is given in which the collaborative functionality was developed intercepting X-windows events without modifying the source code.

5.1   Synchronised Techniques for GDSS: The NGTool Experiment

NGTool [2, 3] is a GDSS (Group Decision Support System) which helps a group to structure ideas about a problem. The NGTool provides synchronised operations over a display space shared by users, one of which known as the *moderator*. A NGTool functionality closely models the Nominal Group Technique, a structured behavioural science technique for group consensus forming. The NGTool session is composed of 4 phases: generation of ideas, discussion, voting, and final decision. The NGTool runs on Unix workstations over the Internet and uses X Windows and the OSF Motif toolkit.

We selected the NGTool for our experiment because it is a collaborative application that exhibits highly synchronised cooperation phases, requires (large-scale) distribution support, and is easy to modify since the source code was available

NGTool first prototype was implemented using a centralised server-based message bus for communication. This choice affected the performance during synchronised phase and put a single point of failure on the whole system. Furthermore, NGTool provided no functionality to cope with unpredictable and high-variance transmission delays observed in today's large scale networks. This lack of concern for the underlying operational conditions could often lead to unfair access to the information of the shared workspace or even to the complete breakdown of a session.

The NGTool application requirements had to be adapted to the communication conditions associated with large-scale interaction. Users need to be more aware of the communication constraints inherited by the large-scale operation. If users can ascertain or predict from observations what the current message delays during the session are, they can modify their behaviour and expectances accordingly.

The NGTool experiment described here illustrates the benefits of using NAVCOOP, a dedicated support platform described in Sect. 4.1, by showing how the NGTool session proceeds "normally" through the following steps: 1) adapting to network delays; 2) adapting to partition; and 3) merging and repair (graceful and late merge).

Porting NGTool to NAVCOOP
As mentioned above, the original implementation of the NGTool relied on a message bus based on a centralised communication server and did not provide any functionality for dealing with large scale interaction. The porting of a collaborative application such as the NGTool to NAVCOOP is illustrated in Fig. 9.

The NGTool application configuration is comprised of the substitution of the communication layer and the implementation of the partition specific feedback (optional). The NAVCOOP platform configuration is comprised of the parameterisation of NAVCOOP base support mechanisms and the tuning of NAVCOOP Generic Services.

Substitution of the communication layer
The first integration task involved the substitution of the communication layer used by NGTool. The existing prototype implementation of NGTool used *Message Bus* for inter-process communication.

Message Bus uses a centralised server with which every cooperative process has to register. The server keeps a list of all registered links to processes. The server constantly listens to each link in round-robin turns.

When it receives a message on one link it forwards the message to every other link using point-to-point TCP connections. There is no ordering enforced between messages processed by the centralised server.

Our first concern was to preserve the simplicity of the interface. In order to hide the possible complexity of the NavTech primitives, it was decided to implement a simple send/receive interface at NAVCOOP level. Causal ordering was selected for the multicast primitive. It has the basic property for implementing the consistency of the workspace. The communication interface part of NGTool was modified according to the new underlying support. The start-up phase of the NGTool code was modified and no longer involved a centralised *Message Bus* server but the NAVCOOP/NavTech services.

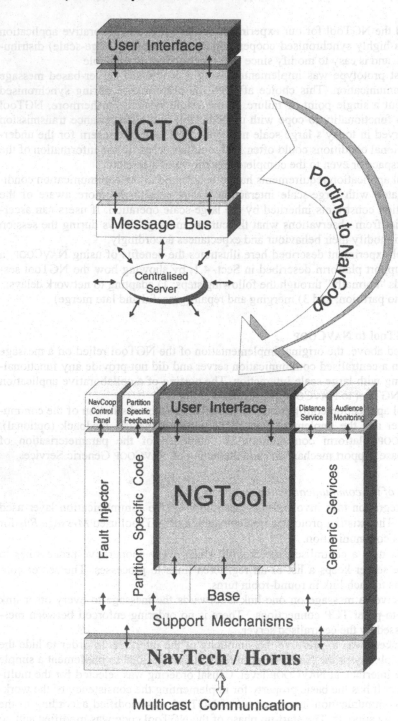

Fig. 9. Porting NGTool to NavCoop

The start-up was initiated at the NAVCOOP level, which handled the registration of the group with the Horus name server (*dirserver*). Finally, NGTool was modified to accept the local delivery of sent messages which was not the case with *Message Bus*.

Implementation of the partition-specific feedback (optional)
After the communication layer was substituted with the NAVCOOP/NavTech platform, the application had to be modified to implement the application upcalls specific to partition split and merge events as explained in Sect. 4.1. Since NGTool was not originally designed for surviving partition events, a minimal interface change was made. An extra *partition call* was implemented, which corresponds to the NAVCOOP upcall COOP_level(). On each COOP_level() call, the corresponding split/merge function is also passed as an argument. The application then invokes the code that matches the transition.

Furthermore, when implementing and experimenting with the partition processing, we decided to inform the users visually of the occurrence of partition in the application itself. The idea was to enhance NAVCOOP generic services by introducing feedback that would attract the users' attention. The first experiments used a notice pop-up window which users had to acknowledge. This was found to be too intrusive to the progress of the NGTool session. A little icon gave instant feedback on partition mode without disrupting the current flow of the collaboration.

Parameterisation of NAVCOOP base support mechanisms
The parameterisation consists of 1) setting the failure detector parameters (performability tests, the sample rate, etc.) and the triggering agreement conditions (suspicion weights, global suspicion quorum); 2) defining the partition levels and corresponding split/merge functions. For the NGTool experiment we defined two types of partition, *moderated* and *non-moderated*. Thus, at run time, the application only differentiates two kinds of progress depending on the presence of the moderator. The NGTool designer made this decision since the application is strongly coordinated by the moderator. This results in the fact that moderated partitions always have higher privileges than non-moderated partitions.

Tuning of NAVCOOP Generic Services
The Distance Service tuning involved choosing the distance unit, i.e. the operational parameter that represents the distance and associated parameters (mountain foot, mountain foot and screen update frequency). The *roundtrip delay* was chosen to define the distance service. This choice was made after careful observations of typical NGTool sessions. It was found that very little bandwidth is used by the exchange of information involved in shared space management updates. The response time is the key element for maintaining the notion of control and coordination during the synchronised phased. The roundtrip represents a good approximation for modelling the distance and thus provides realistic feedback on the connectivity status. Finally, the roundtrip delay is an intuitive model for representing distance and as such was appealing for the first experiments. The screen update frequency has to take into account the disruptive effect of fast-moving objects on the screen. This consideration led us to implement a low-pass filter, thus isolating the end user from abrupt changes that

could affect the interpretation of the distance service. The rule adopted was that there should be at least three updates for abrupt connectivity changes.

The Audience Monitoring delivers a global view of the connectivity situation. It was decided to display three levels on the User Interface: full icon for no (failure) suspicion, half-full icon for suspicion above 50% and empty icon when the user has been removed from the current view and is no longer part of the working group. A filter was configured to map the current global suspicion to a three-level value. The screen update frequency was chosen to be consistent with the distance service. However, any lower frequency would also be acceptable.

Integration and Testing

Experimental set-up

One of our main concerns was to validate the NAVCOOP approach using a representative scenario of a real-life situation. This meant running a realistic session situation which involved users performing actions according to the NGTool policy. Taking into account the scenario presented above, it was decided that the experimental set-up should include three users with one workstation each. The session was composed of a moderator and two participants. Each user would run his/her own NGTool/NAVCOOP processes. Our experience has shown that any test including at least three users is a fair representation of a typical NGTool session when in final use.

NAVCOOP control panel

The control panel was designed for manipulating a number of parameter values at runtime. Each node involved in the computation runs a control panel. The parameters include the distance update frequency, the audience monitoring update frequency and the fault-injector parameters. Runtime parameter modification allowed us to explore a wider range of values and obtain immediate feedback on their impact.

The fault injector

Implementation of the fault-injector was designed to enable emulation of large-scale environment events. Events such as message delay and message loss could be emulated in our LAN environment. Internally, the fault injector models the connections between nodes as a graph of point-to-point links. This reflects more closely the long-haul interconnection topology used today. The fault injector allows delays over the various (logical) links connecting the cooperative users to be created and partitions to be emulated. The combined functionality of the control panel and the fault injector allowed us to conduct experiments and test our approach, while obtaining immediate usage feedback at runtime.

Evaluation

Programmer perspective

Two main programming aspects should be considered: first, the configuration task; second, the interface-related issues. On the basis of our experience, the configuration process still remains complex, especially for a novice user. It requires a clear under-standing of the problems and of the functionality provided by NAVCOOP.

Failure Suspector configuration: The choice of the operational parameters as well as the associated variables was difficult. The NGTool experiment resulted in a clearer definition of the relations between the various parameter values. The configuration provides a powerful tool for closely modelling the connectivity requirements.

Partition Support Service: Although partition levels and split/merge rules were defined according to the particular semantics of the application (graceful and late merges), the NAVCOOP PSS allows the problems associated with partitions to be tackled in a structured and manageable way.

Distance and audience monitoring services: as intended originally, these generic services could be integrated in a "plug-and-play"' fashion. They were easy to adapt, and the main lesson of the NGTool experiment was to include the control panel as a module of the NAVCOOP platform.

As regards the interface, our main goal was to provide simplicity, allowing the pro-grammer to concentrate on cooperation issues. Our experience has shown that appli-cation programmers want easy-to-use interfaces. The simplicity of the NAVCOOP interface made the porting of the NGTool application relatively straightforward.

User perspective

As we only have a limited experience, we will restrict our comments to general ob-servations based on our experience with NGTool, which also includes in-house and public demonstrations.

Distance and audience monitoring services: The feedback provided by these services was particularly well accepted. This reflects the fact that the chosen distance unit is an intuitive parameter that facilitates interpretation. We also learned two addi-tional lessons from the usage: first, it is very important to isolate the users from in-consistencies that may occur at lower layers; second, with respect to the UI represen-tation chosen, we now intend to provide other UI analogies, which users will be able to select at runtime. This suggestion came from (a minority of) users who found it difficult to relate to the current presentation of connectivity data.

Mechanisms The failure suspector functionality is not directly perceived by the users. When a membership view changes, which results in NAVCOOP partition events, it is propagated to the application by a possible change of working levels. As for the application programmers, we first of all need the users to accept the (conse-quences of) problems related to the underlying infrastructure. The benefits obtained from the enhanced functionality at runtime largely compensate for the burden other-wise caused by the possible breaking down of the session.

In general, we found that user reactions depended mainly on their background, i.e. distributed systems or CSCW. Distributed systems people expect to manipulate low-level information to provide strong properties to programmers. People from coopera-tive work focus more on the flexibility aspect of the control and coordination strate-gies. The main lessons learnt for end users is that cooperative applications should consider the existence of working envelopes. NAVCOOP support enforces this behav-iour, which appears to be a suitable solution for running distributed synchronised cooperative applications over current technology.

Summary
The NGTool experiment related in this section illustrated how a collaborative application can be enhanced by using a dedicated underlying support platform such as NAVCOOP. The positive findings of the NGTool experiment are highlighted below.

Focusing on the needs of application builders showed that groupware application designers are more concerned with the collaboration and data presentation aspects. Hence, providing a simple interface to the system support layer is a key requirement. In this respect, the port of NGTool to NAVCOOP was straightforward.

The need for a uniform configuration approach became apparent with the interdependence of NAVCOOP modules. We found that all configurations are inter-related and should be defined with exactitude, a task that is far from easy in practice.

The need for runtime tuning appeared as an important feature. Although not included at first in the NAVCOOP architecture, the experience of the NGTool experiment prompted us to include the runtime customisation of services.

In conclusion, it is important to show a strong concern for end users in order to gain wide acceptance for the support platforms from collaborative applications developers.

5.2   Cooperative CAD Application: The XCoop Experiment

The application discussed in this section is a CAD tool designed to visualise layouts of integrated circuits masks developed under X-Window. The code of the application was not available in source form, and therefore the use of the "external" approach was mandatory. We have actually developed a generic framework to convert an interactive stand-alone application working under X Window into a cooperative one. Since many interactive applications use X-Windows, the results have a wide applicability.

Principles and Design Decisions
The application is a tool for the visualisation of layouts of integrated circuit masks, The original version operated in a single-user mode. The requirements of the client were to enable a group of users to share the views of the circuits and to exchange comments and documents. The constraints were that, for commercial reasons, it was not possible to modify the code of the application, and that the number of its instances in simultaneous operation was limited. This led to a solution based on a single copy of the application and on an interposition layer in which the cooperation is managed.

Design Principles
The X-Window system defines a communication interface between a client application and a graphical server that manages a display and user input (Fig. 10 a). The application and the server interact through a network. The principle of XCoop is to interpose a software layer between the application and the multiple X-Window servers, which preserves the application-server interface (Fig. 10 b).

The interposition layer acts as a virtual server. It maintains the illusion of a single server for the application, and replicates the graphical output of the applications on the participant servers. This is achieved by maintaining a unique "abstract state" shared by the application and by all servers. The function of XCoop is to ensure that this abstract state is correctly perceived by all servers and consistently modified. The interposition layer intercepts the messages generated both by the application and the server. The requests issued by the application are selectively broadcast to the servers.

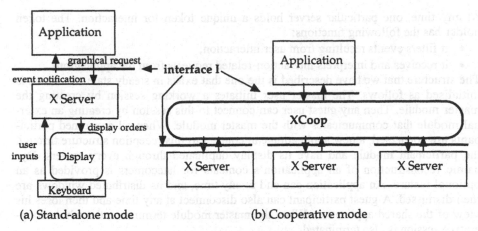

(a) Stand-alone mode   (b) Cooperative mode

Fig. 10. Overall structure of XCoop

The events issued by the servers are aggregated into a single channel and delivered to the application. The details are explained in the next section.

Architecture of XCoop

XCoop provides a unified interface between the application and the connected servers. It operates as a virtual server that simulates a unique display for the application but is internally distributed between several terminals. In addition, XCoop is able to support the concurrent execution of several different applications. To this effect, XCoop acts as an application multiplexer: a specific connection is maintained with every server for each connected application; this connection is used to transmit application-specific requests and to retrieve application-dependent events.

A cooperative work session is described by a modular structure, with one module per user (usually one module per participant site). The module associated with a user manages the user's server (communication with the application, graphical resource management, inter-user communication). In order to simplify communication management and inter-module cooperation, one specific module (located on the site on which the application runs) acts as a master. This structure is described on Fig. 11. The role of the master module is

- to manage multiple applications and to maintain an abstract state for each application; this state is the unique reference for the application, and its modifications are propagated to the servers;
- to dispatch the graphical requests from the application to the servers;
- to propagate the events from the servers to the applications; these events may possibly modify the abstract state.

The role of an external module is

- to translate the requests of an application into commands for the server, doing format conversion as required (details in Sect. 3);
- to filter events generated by the server (some events are handled locally, others are transmitted to the application);
- to maintain a consistent state on the local server.

At any time, one particular server holds a unique token for interaction. The token holder has the following functions:

- it filters events resulting from user interaction;
- it receives and interprets interaction-related requests from the applications.

The structure that we have described is the one that exists in steady state. A session is initialised as follows. The master user initiates a working session by creating the master module. Then any guest user can connect to this session by creating an external module that communicates with the master module. When all concerned participants are connected, a new application can connect to this reception structure through the participant module and have its display duplicated through every servers. Dynamic reconstruction of an application's contents for latecomers is provided as an optional feature. An application can end at any time, and its distributed windows are then dismissed. A guest participant can also disconnect at any time and then loses his view of the shared application. When the master module terminates, the whole cooperative session is also terminated.

In addition to these distribution features, direct communication facilities (cooperative whiteboard and dynamic edition wrappers) have been included. The cooperative whiteboard is a shared graphical space where any participant can import screen copies and draw elementary graphics. Dynamic edition wrappers are transparent windows that can be dynamically integrated into the top-level windows created by a shared application. These wrappers enable a participant to cooperatively draw onto the graphics contents of the application or to index some specific parts.

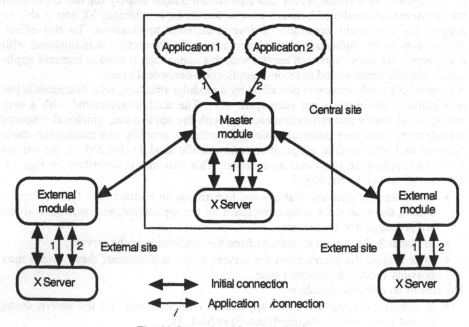

Fig. 11. Internal architecture of XCoop

Finally, XCoop is highly configurable to take in account heterogeneous work conditions from one session to another. For example, different servers can have different colour management policies. Communication bandwidth and latency are also an important factor for performance and the ability to adapt the platform to a range of performance levels can be decisive.

Implementation
Communication in XCoop is based on sockets; a different socket pair is allocated for each application to facilitate communication multiplexing betwen applications. In order to implement the architecture described above, two main aspects must be considered: transferring information between the different modules, and performing the mapping between abstract and concrete states, with possibly heterogeneous resources. These aspects are examined in the rest of this section.

Request Handling
An application may send three types of requests:
a) global update requests for graphical display, which should be sent to all servers;
b) investigation or update requests on the reference state of the graphical resources; these requests are handled on the master server and are not propagated;
c) requests related to the interaction (e.g. modification of the position of the cursor); these requests are only propagated to the token holder.
These requests are directed to the master server, which dispatches them according to their type. This is done with the help of a dispatch table.
Requests from a server to an application have the function of event propagation. There are three types of events.
1. events related to interaction, e.g. pointer and keyboard events (generated by the server that holds the token);
2. events related to the management of the application's resources, e.g. notification of keyboard configuration changes, creation and destruction of windows, etc.;
3. events requesting a reaction from the application, e.g. display refresh.
These events are locally filtered by the external module associated with the server, which may or not propagate them to the application. For instance, events of type b) are handled locally, except for those occurring on the master server, which are propagated to the application.

Resource Management
In order to achieve the two-way mapping between the common abstract state of an application (managed by the master module) and the concrete state (managed by the local X server), two problem must be solved:
1. ensure that resources are correctly referenced in the requests exchanged between servers and applications.
2. interpret the events that trigger a change of state, and propagate this change.
Resource designation
The master handles abstract resources, while the external modules manipulate concrete ones. Since the requests exchanged between the server and the application contain references to resources, these references need to be converted to the adequate format. This is done through translation tables that associate abstract to concrete resources. Depending on resource types, these tables are static (set up at the beginning of a session, and valid through the session) or dynamic (updated continuously).

Examples of statically managed resources are windows, colour maps, pixmaps. These resources are designated, in the X Window environment, by a local identifier Xid, composed of a base value and a resource-specific offset. The base value is different for each server but the offset of the resource is the same. Therefore, the mapping for statically managed resources is straightforward.

Examples of dynamically managed resources are colour cells. Since they are allocated independently on each server, there is no uniform naming policy to assist the mapping between different servers. The solution for such resources is to maintain dynamic translation tables on each server.

Requests and events may include, as parameters, both simple values and references to graphical resources. Only the latter need to be translated. Therefore, a template describing he parameter types and formats is associated with each type of request or event.

Consistent state management

In order to maintain a consistent state on the master server (abstract state) and on the other servers (concrete state), the events that modify the state need to be interpreted. The problem is that the events associated with the operation of X servers have a very low semantic level. Dependencies between graphical resources are not directly expressed in the X messages, but have to be reconstructed. For example, a window can be associated with a colour map that maps pixels to colour definitions. But this map is not specified in the graphic requests that act on the window: it is managed by the X server and modified by a specific X request. Therefore, we need to create, for each window, a descriptor in the form of a complex data structure that summarises the state of the window (size, position, colour map, other internal information) and to update this structure after each operation. For example, if the token holder modifies the size of a window, this change of state is registered and propagated to the other servers.

The heterogeneity of platforms and X servers has to be taken into account. This raises problems that have been solved for common cases, such as the management of pop-up menus or the equivalence of colours. In each case, a specific consistency protocol has been developed.

Direct Communication

Additional tools are provided to improve communication between users. These tools include a shared graphical space and some edition wrappers. The shared space consists in a cooperative graphic whiteboard in which any participant can import a portion of its screen; a set of tools (pointer, hand-drawing, text-writing) is also available. The changes made by a user are propagated to every whiteboard. Edition wrappers are transparent windows that can dynamically be integrated onto the top-level windows of a shared application. These windows offer the same graphic features as the cooperative editor but their integration into the window structure of an application significantly improves the ergonomy for the users.

Session and Floor Management

Several applications may be active at the same time. Each of them is part of a different session. For each session, XCoop maintains a data structure, distributed over the servers involved in the application, that contains the connection descriptors (Unix sockets) and resource management data (base values for resource identifiers, identifiers of default resources, default colour map, etc.). This structure is created at session start (a session may be started by any user, by a request to the master server). When a user connects, he is shown the list of current sessions, and he may join one of them.

Floor management is implemented by a token passing mechanism. A different token holder is defined for each session. In a session, each participant site contains a pointer to the current token holder and the list of participants who requested it. Several protocols are provided for the allocation of the token (centralised on the master site, explicit by release, implicit after a period of inactivity of the current holder).

Experience and Lessons Learnt

Status and Performance

The XCoop prototype is presently 35000 lines long and was developed in 1.5 man • years. It draws on the experience of XTV, a former research prototype [1]. XCoop is written in C, using the X-Window and Motif libraries, and have been deployed successfully over several Sun platforms and workstations.

A performance evaluation of the prototype has been done with GDSDisplay, a visualisation tool for layout design, using Sun architectures with different types of X servers (Sun station consoles, NCD terminals and X emulators on PC under Windows 3.1), across high-bandwidth and low-bandwidth networks.

A first observation is that server heterogeneity does not a significantly affect the cooperation. Minor problems concerning colour displaying have been observed with emulators under Windows but the main functionalities were preserved. Major compatibility problems comes from applications that allocate all available colour cells, like Netscape. Indeed, the allocation capacity of external servers is often exceeded. But in general, applications allocate a reasonable number of colours.

Measurements on a local area network show that response time is increased by a factor of 2 to 3 for two users, with respect to single user interaction. In practice, the maximum number of users on a local network is limited to five. The degradation factor rises to about 5 on a low-bandwidth network (64 Kbit/s), but the application remains usable in a context of a limited use. Relaxing the constraints on window consistency greatly improves performance, almost to the level of single-user interaction.

User Feedback

The XCoop prototype seems to answer an unsatisfied demand. Users are happy to preserve their familiar working environment, with the addition of cooperative functions and communication tools. In summary, the new functionality provided by XCoop compensates the lost of efficiency it entails.

The limitations of its approach make the current prototype more adapted to short-time sessions rather than to a long-range design process. On the one hand, users are not yet used to work in integrated cooperative environment; in their current practice, their activity of common work is very limited in time. On the other hand, the performance degradation caused by the use of XCoop is acceptable for limited sessions but would make users uncomfortable for continued work. Another characteristic is that the cooperative sessions generally involve more discussion and information exchange than actual design, as the main design decisions are made "off-line".

Users like to keep control of their own data. Indeed, as they generally share private documents, they prefer keeping a close control on the modifications made during the common session. So, the centralised architecture in which one user controls the external applications and shared data fulfils the needs for controlled rights. This approach enables to export views on large amounts of data without duplicating them.

Finally, this approach has many other applications than remote conferences. It can also be useful for teaching needs, remote demonstration, and user support. The main constraint is that the complexity of interactions should remain moderate.

Summary

The XCoop system illustrates an approach for the conversion of a single user interactive application to a multi-user cooperative mode. This approach may be characterised as follows.

- The code of the original application is not modified, and minimal assumptions are needed on the semantics of the application.
- The participants do not share actual data, but only views on the data through a graphical interface; the management of data remains centralised.
- Additional communication services may be integrated into the application in order to improve interaction between users.

The drawback of this approach is that its generality affects efficiency, especially if the application creates a large amount of graphical data. In addition, the very low abstraction level and information contents of the X Window messages make it difficult to interpret them in terms of the application's semantics. It is hard to separate the events related to the application from those generated by the management of the display. One possible improvement of the approach would be applicable in the case where the code of the application is accessible and may be modified. It would then be possible to identify application-related requests and to separate them from those linked to display management. A modular organisation of the system could be then proposed, along the following lines.

- Application dialog component: interprets application's requests, translates them into graphical requests, intercepts events to be transmitted to the application.
- Graphical management component: shares the graphical contents of an application between participants; managed distributed graphical resources; enforces consistency according to a specified (modifiable) policy.
- Additional communication services: provide facilities such as shared whiteboard, edition wrappers, etc.; do not interfere with the application, only with the graphical component.
- Communication layer: provides communication services to the other components.

These components would provide a framework within which an application may be integrated. The main advantage of this organisation is that it separates application-specific communication from that related to display management. It also improves the configurability of the system.

In conclusion, the advantages of the proposed approach in terms of genericity and encapsulation have been recognised for several CAD related applications, and an industrial product derived from XCoop is currently being developed

6   Conclusions

This chapter has reported on advances in the research of supporting technologies for CSCW applications, made in the Broadcast project. After a number of years of very active research on applications in this area in the past decade, the time was ripe for the definition of platforms. Accumulated experience provided insight on the common denominators that could support a desirably wide spectrum of CSCW applications. Two such platforms were presented here, and the experimental tests that were run with applications were also reported. The results are encouraging and allow us to consider *CSCW support* as a fundamental piece of today's middleware for open large-scale application design.

Acknowledgments
The CoopScan system has been developed in the Bull-IMAG laboratory. This project was partially supported by France Télécom. The main contributors to the development of the Coop-Scan prototype were Slim Ben Atallah and Rushed Kanawati.
The XCoop system has been developed within the Storia programme, a joint effort of INRIA Rhône-Alpes and ST Microelectronics, partially supported by the French Ministry of Industry.

References

1. H. Abdel-Wahab and M. Feit, "XTV: A Framework for Sharing X Window Clients in Remote Synchronous Collaboration", *Proc. IEEE TriComm*, Chapel Hill, NC, 1991, pp. 159-167
2. P. Antunes, N. Guimarães, "NGTool – Exploring Mechanisms of Support to Interaction", *First Cyted-Ritos Int. Workshop on Groupware CRIWG*, Lisbon, Portugal, 1995.
3. P. Antunes, N. Guimarães, "Structuring Elements for Group Interaction", *2nd Conference on Concurrent Engineering, Research and Applications (CE95)*, Washington, 1995.
4. R. Balter, S. Ben Atallah, R. Kanawati, "System Architecture for SynchronousGroupware Development'", Symbiosis of Human and Artifact - *Proc. of the 6th International Conference on Human-Computer Interaction (HCI'95)*, Vol. 20A, Y. Anzai, K. Ogawa et H. Mori, ed., pp. 371-379, Elsevier, Tokyo, July 1995.
5. S. Ben Atallah, R. Kanawati, R. Balter, M. Riveill, "CoopScan : une plate-forme générique pour le développement de collecticiels'", *Septièmes Journées de l'Ingénierie de l'Interaction Homme-Machine (IHM'95)*, pp. 21-26, Cépaduès-Éditions, Toulouse, October 1995.
6. F.J.N. Cosquer, P. Veríssimo, "The Impact of Group Communication Paradigms in Groupware Support", *Proc. of the 5th Workshop on Future Trends of Distributed Systems*, IEEE CS, Cheju Island, Korea, 1995.
7. F.J.N. Cosquer, L. Rodrigues, P. Veríssimo, "Using Tailored Failure Suspectors to Support Distributed Cooperative Applications, *Proc. of the 7th International Conference on Parallel and Distributed Computing and Systems*, Washington, pp. 352-356, 1995.
8. F.J.N. Cosquer, P. Antunes, P. Veríssimo, "Enhancing Dependability of Cooperative Applications in Partitionable Environments", *Proc. of the 2nd European Dependable Computing Conference (EDCC-2)*, Italy, 1996.
9. P. Dewan, J. Riedl, "Towards Computer-Supported Concurrent Software Engineering", *IEEE Computer*, pp 17-27, 26(1), 1993.
10. C.A. Ellis, S.J. Gibbs, G.L. Rein, "Groupware, Somme Issues and Experiences", *Communications of the ACM*, 34(1), pp 38-58, 1991.

11. A. Kerbrat, S. Ben Atallah, "Formal Specification for a Framework for Groupware Development", *8th International Conference on Formal Description Techniques for Distributed Systems and Communication Protocols (FORTE'95)*, pp. 303-310, Montréal, Canada, October 1995.

12. C. Peng, "Survey of Collaborative Drawing Support Tools", *Computer Supported Cooperative Work*, pp. 197-228, 1(3), 1993.

13. Y.V. Ramana Reddy, K. Srinavas, V. Jagannathan, R. Karinthi, "Computer Support for Concurrent Engineeering", *IEEE Computer*, pp 12-16, 26(1), 1993.

14. M. Stefik, G. Foster, D. Bobrow, K. Kahn, S. Lanning, L. Suchmann, "Beyond the Chalkboard: Computer support for collaboration and problem solving in meetings", *Communications of the ACM*, pp. 32-47, 30(1), 1987.

Component-Based Programming of Distributed Applications

Valérie Issarny[1], Luc Bellissard[2], Michel Riveill[2], and Apostolos Zarras[1]

[1] INRIA, IRISA, Campus de Beaulieu, 35042 Rennes Cédex, France
[2] IMAG-INRIA, INRIA, 655 Avenue de l'Europe, 38330 Montbonnot, France

Abstract. The software architecture research domain arose in the early 90s and seeks solutions for easing the development of large, complex, software systems based on the abstract description of their software architectures. This research field is quite recent and there still does not exist a consensus on what should be the description of a software architecture. However, guidelines are already provided. In particular, it is now accepted that an architecture definition decomposes into three types of elements: component, connector, and configuration, which respectively correspond to a computation unit, an interaction unit and an architecture. It is also admitted that the description of an architecture should rely on a well-defined set of notations, generically referred to as architecture description languages. This document gives an overview of the capabilities offered by development environments based on the architecture paradigm. In a first step, we examine basic features of architecture description languages, which may be seen as their common denominator although existing languages already differ from that standpoint. We then concentrate on two specific environments, developed by members of the BROADCAST working group, which aim at easing the implementation of distributed applications out of existing components. The Aster environment from the Solidor group at INRIA-IRISA provides means for the systematic synthesis of middleware from non-functional requirements of applications. The Olan environment from the Sirac group at INRIA-Grenoble offers support for the deployment of distributed applications composed of heterogeneous software elements.

1 Introduction

The ever increasing complexity of distributed applications calls for methods and tools for easing their development. In that framework, industrial consortia have emerged so as to provide application developers with standard distributed software architectures. In general, such a standard specifies a base distributed system for communication management, a set of services for distribution management (e.g., naming service), and a set of tools for application development (e.g., Interface definition language). The definition of a standard architecture then serves as a guideline for the implementation of a programming system. A well known example of standard distributed architecture is the OMA (*Object Management*

S. Krakowiak, S.K. Shrivastava (Eds.): Distributed Systems, LNCS 1752, pp. 327–353, 2000.
© Springer-Verlag Berlin Heidelberg 2000

Architecture) [33] from the OMG (*Object Management Group*) for the development of distributed applications relying on client-server type interactions.

A more ambitious approach to the development of complex distributed applications is the one undertaken in the software architecture research field of software engineering. Instead of concentrating on the definition of a specific architecture, the ongoing research work aims at providing a sound basis for the specification of various styles of software architectures (e.g., see [35,40]). An architectural style identifies the set of patterns that should be followed by the system organization, that is, the kinds of components to be used and the way they interact. Although the software architecture field is continuously evolving, it is now accepted that the description of an application architecture decomposes into at least three abstractions (e.g., see [39]):

(*i*) *Components* that abstractly define computational units written in any programming language,

(*ii*) *Connectors* that abstractly define types of interactions (e.g., pipe, client-server) between components,

(*iii*) *Configuration* that defines an application structure (i.e., a software architecture or configuration-based software) in terms of the interconnection of components through connectors.

Development environments that are based on the software architecture paradigm then integrate an *Architecture Description Language* (ADL) that allows application specification in terms of the three above abstractions, together with runtime libraries that implement base system services (including primitive connectors). Such an application description fosters software reuse, evolution, analysis and management.

In the light of research results in the software architecture field, configuration-based description of distributed applications constitutes a promising approach for facilitating the development of correct, complex distributed applications. The next section provides a general definition of ADLs together with an overview of research work in the area. Sections 3 and 4 then concentrate on two specific development environments based on the architecture description of distributed applications. Section 3 presents the Aster environment, which is being developed within the Solidor research group at INRIA-IRISA. The Aster environment offers a set of tools for the systematic synthesis of middleware from the formal specification of non-functional properties (e.g., security, availability, timeliness) as respectively required by distributed applications and provided by available middleware services. Section 4 discusses the Olan environment from the Sirac research group at INRIA-Grenoble. The Olan environment provides means to deploy a distributed application over a given infrastructure with respect to the application's configuration. Finally, Section 5 offers some conclusions.

2   Description of Software Architectures

Research effort in the software architecture domain aims at reducing costs of developing large, complex software systems. Towards that goal, formal notations are being provided to describe software architectures, replacing the usual informal description of software architectures in terms of box-and-line diagrams. These notations are generically referred to as *Architecture Description Languages* (ADLs). Basically, an ADL allows the developer to describe the gross organization of his system in terms of coarse-grained architectural elements, abstracting away the elements' implementation details. Except this general definition and despite the increasing interest in the software architecture domain since its appearance in the early 90s, it still does not exist a consensus on what is an ADL. As previously mentioned, prominent elements of a software architecture subdivide into the three following categories: component, connector and configuration. However, some ADLs do not model connectors as first-class objects in which case connectors are implicitly defined within configurations through the connections (or bindings) among components. In general, existing ADLs differ depending on the aspects that are targeted for the construction of software architectures. We identify at least two research directions, which are sometimes both covered by the same ADL:

(*i*) Architecture analysis that relates to the formal specification of architecture behavior. Work in this category further subdivides into the analysis of the properties provided by either components, connectors, or configurations.

(*ii*) Architecture implementation that relates to the implementation of an application from the description of its architecture.

The interested reader is referred to Chapter 2 of [1] and [30] for a survey of existing ADLs and associated CASE tools. An overview of work on the formal specification of the behavior of architecture elements may further be found in [19].

In general, most existing ADLs should rather be seen as complementary rather than as competitive. As a consequence, this has led to the definition of an architecture description interchange language so as to allow the developer to combine the various facilities provided by different ADLs, for the construction of his applications [17]. The following provides a general definition of ADLs, based on existing work in the area, together with a brief overview of work relating to the implementation of applications from their architectural description. However, we do not intend to be exhaustive from the standpoint of ADLs taken as references since the number of proposed ADLs is quite large and the number of related projects keeps growing (see [15] for an overview of latest results). Examples specifically considered in the following are Aesop [16], Aster [20], Darwin [27], Olan [6], Rapide [26], Sadl [32], UniCon [39], and Wright [2].

The following paragraphs give a general definition of component, connector and configuration as offered by existing ADLs knowing that the corresponding language constructs vary according to ADLs. For illustration purpose, we take the example of a Distributed Information System (DIS). However, simplified declarations will be provided, which are sufficient to exemplify ADL features. Basically, a DIS is composed of a set of clients interacting with a possibly distributed server for information access; we further assume that the interaction protocol among components is RPC-like. Thus, the DIS may be seen as a special instance of a client-server architecture and corresponds to various specific architectures depending on the instantiation of the DIS architectural elements. For instance, examples of DIS incarnations include the Web, distributed file systems, and online services providing access to discrete data.

2.1   Component

A component may be either primitive or complex: a complex component is equivalent to a configuration; and a primitive component corresponds to either a computation unit or a data store, whose implementation details (e.g. programming language, supporting platform, ...) are abstracted away. The description of a primitive component gives the component interface. In general, the interface specifies the interaction points (e.g. port in UniCon) of the component with respect to the communication protocol that is used (i.e. it prescribes the expected type of connector).

The other feature of a component that is of equal interest is its functional behavior. Here, the component's interface states the list of operations (or services) provided for other components and the list of operations required from other components. Let us remark that the latter definition of component interface may be seen as an extension of an IDL (Interface Definition Language) interface. Even closer to this ADL definition of component falls *Module Interconnection Languages* (MILs) that were introduced in the 70s for the implementation of large-scale software [14]. Simply stated, a MIL allows the developer to abstractly describe the configuration of his application through bindings among the functions offered and provided by the components. Hence, when the ADL definition is oriented towards application implementation such as UniCon (as opposed to ADLs aimed at architecture analysis), it appears to closely resemble a MIL except it integrates the notion of connector. Let us further remark that this distinction falls short when a development environment that is based on a MIL enables to build applications that may run above various (possibly distributed) platforms. For instance, the Polylith environment [36] belongs to this category of environments. The distinction that can then be made between a MIL-based and an ADL-based environment for application deployment above a given platform is that the know-how about the platform usage is within the corresponding connector for the former, while the latter requires wrapping the platform so as to make it accessible through the API specified by the environment for use by components. Hence, the connector notion enables the development of adequate CASE tools for the generation of interfacing code among components and the underlying platforms as abstracted by connectors. Such a facility is for instance supported by the Aster and Olan environments, as further addressed in the two next sections. On the other hand, to our knowledge, the wrapping of platforms within MIL-based environments is realized in an ad'hoc manner, on a case-by-case basis. In the following, despite the aforementioned distinction between MIL and ADL-based development, when concerned with implementation-oriented ADLs, we include

MILs in this category. To be more precise, implementation-oriented ADLs and MILs may be referred to under the generic term of *configuration languages* [10].

The definition of component interfaces –be they interaction-, functional-related, or both– may simply take the form of operation signatures or be more precise by formally specifying the behavior of operations [34,13]. Other attributes may further be stated in the declaration of components. For instance, when concerned with architecture implementation, the ADL provides way to specify the implementation file that corresponds to the component.

For illustration, Figure 1 gives a description of the client component of the DIS example. For the sake of generality, we do not take the syntax of a specific ADL but instead use a self-explanatory syntax, and merge the component's interaction- and functional-related specification. The *client* component declaration specifies a component interface, which may be instantiated through different implementations.

```
component interface client =
  port
      Declares the port used for interaction, e.g., client-type port
  functional
      Declares the operations offered/required by the client component,
      e.g.: operations for opening, closing a connection,
      for reading, writing information
  interaction
      Declares the port used for accessing the declared operations,
      which prescribes whether they are offered or provided by the
      component. In the example operations given above, they are all
      required and use a client-type port.
```

Fig. 1. An example of component description

In general, software reuse being one of the primary objectives of ADL-based development environments [18], ADLs can support reuse by modeling abstract components as types and instantiating them multiple times in an architecture description [30]. Enhanced support for software reuse may further be offered through subtyping and parameterized types. All the ADLs taken into consideration for this chapter distinguish component types from instances. On the other hand, not all offer subtyping and parameterization: the former is supported by Acme, Aesop, Aster, and Rapide, and the latter is supported by Acme, Darwin, and Rapide.

2.2   Connector

Similarly to a component, a connector may be either primitive or complex. A primitive connector corresponds to a communication protocol of the target execution platform. For instance, over a Unix platform, there will be a connector describing a pipe. The description of a primitive connector includes the connector interface, which may further formally specify the connector's behavior [2]. In addition, if the architecture description is to be used for the architecture's implementation, the implementation corresponding to the connector is given.

A complex connector is a connector that is built from a set of connectors and components. A typical example of complex connector is a middleware that comprises a set of services for enhanced management of component interoperation [7]. As a more precise example, we may consider a CORBA Distributed Processing Environment (DPE) composed of some Common Object Services (COSs) interconnected by the CORBA Object Request Broker (ORB). Thus, the properties provided by a connector relate to: (*i*) properties of the base underlying communication protocol (e.g. asynchronous message passing, RPC, pipe, ...), and (*ii*) to additional non-functional properties (e.g. dependability, security, timeliness, ...) characterizing the embedded services [21].

For illustration, Figure 2 gives the definition of the connector describing an RPC-based transactional middleware providing atomicity, and isolation properties, as for instance offered by the CORBA ORB combined with the Object Transaction Service (OTS) and Concurrency Control Service (CCS).

```
connector interface TransactionalServiceMdw =
    role
        Declares the roles offered for achieving interaction among
        components, e.g., client-type and server-type roles as
        offered by RPC-based middleware
    non-functional
        Specifies the additional operations provided by the middleware
        for the enforcement of some non-functional (or quality)
        properties over the interactions, e.g., operations for creating,
        committing, and aborting a transaction in the case of the
        considered middleware
```

Fig. 2. An example of connector description

As for the definition of components, enhanced reuse is provided by the ADL if connectors are modeled as types. However, let us recall here that not all the ADLs define connectors as first-class entities, in which case connectors are defined in-line within the configuration, hence prohibiting connector naming, subtyping or reuse in general. Among the ADLs taken as examples, Acme, Olan, Sadl, UniCon, Wright and the latest Aster version model connectors explicitly, which is realized according to one of the following two forms: (*i*) definition of an extensible type system in terms of communication protocols and independent of implementation (e.g. Acme, Aesop, Wright); (*ii*) definition of a set of types based on their implementation mechanisms (e.g. Aster, Olan, Sadl, UniCon).

2.3   Configuration

The description of a configuration consists in interconnecting a set of components so as to bind the operations that are required by some configuration components to the corresponding operations that are provided by other components of the configuration. These interconnections (or bindings) are further realized through connectors, hence specifying the communication protocols that are used for the resulting interactions among components. As for components and connectors, formal specification of configuration behavior has given rise to a number of proposals, providing ways to reason about correctness of architecture refinement [32] and about legal dynamic changes to architectures [25], and to carry out behavioral analysis of architecture properties [26,2,24].

For illustration, Figure 3 gives the definition of a configuration for the DIS example where the definition of the client component that is used is the one given previously.

A configuration ultimately corresponds to the abstract description of an application. However, as exemplified by the DIS configuration, it generally defines a software architecture from which various applications (or more specialized configurations) may be derived by refining the description of embedded components and connectors. Such a feature is crucial from the standpoint of both design and software reuse. A configuration constitutes the blueprint for the implementation of a specific application. The choice for a given blueprint then results from various factors such as the functionalities targeted for the application or the execution platform to be used for execution.

2.4   Implementation of Applications from Architecture Description

Implementation of applications from their architectural description is one area of active research in the software architecture domain. Basically, the implementation of an application from its architectural description consists of generating appropriate stub code for the realization of component interactions *via* connectors (*e.g.* see [12] for an overview although this reference addresses application implementation from its description using a MIL). One of the most difficult parts in the implementation of an application from the description of its software architecture lies in the integration of possibly heterogeneous architectural elements, which may be partly simplified through the use of component-based middleware architectures such as CORBA or EJB. This issue is being examined by various research groups of the field. It is currently simplified in most prototypes

```
connector interface service =
  role
      Declare client- and server-type roles
component interface server =
    port
        Declares a server-type port
    functional
        Declares operations for opening, closing sessions, and
        for information access
    interaction
        Declares that all the operations use the server-type port

configuration DIS(typeInt N) =
  component
      The DIS configuration is made of a number of
      client components and a server component
  connector
      Declares a service connector per client component
  binding
      Each client component port binds to the client
      role of the connector it is associated to.
      The server role of all the connectors are bound
      to the role of the server component
  functional binding
      Binds the operations of each client component with
      the corresponding operations of the server component
```

Fig. 3. An example of configuration description

of ADL-based development environments by integrating architectural elements
aimed at the same platform although different platforms may be targeted by
a prototype. The Darwin environment currently supports the construction of
distributed systems above the Regis [28] (A specific platform developed at Im-
perial College) and CORBA platforms. The Aster [20] and Olan [6] prototypes
also support the implementation of applications above CORBA platforms. The
Olan environment further provides base solutions for the integration of heterogeneous architectural elements through dedicated declarations within connectors,
which is further detailed in Section 4. The UniCon environment.[39] deals with
lower level platforms by addressing specifics of the underlying operating system.
In particular, it enables the implementation of applications requiring real-time
scheduling capabilities (Real-Time Mach operating system in the case of the
UniCon prototype) [40]. The implementation of an application from its architec-

tural description does not prescribe any specific execution platform. Platforms that are supported by an environment result in general from design and implementation decisions for the given prototype based on different factors such as the types of applications that are targeted or the implementation effort required for the integration of architectural elements.

3   Synthesizing Middleware from Non-functional Requirements

Middleware services provided by infrastructures such as CORBA, DCOM or EJB can all be characterized by the functionality they provide when combined into a middleware. The principal idea of the systematic middleware synthesis that is being investigated within the Aster research activity[1] is to match this functionality against the demands of the application. Based on the match, an appropriate set of middleware services is selected and combined to form the middleware with desired properties. Thus, the entire synthesis process is driven by demands of the application that is to use the middleware.

In the current practice, specification of properties provided by a middleware is semi-formal, consisting of a description of the middleware interface and a description of the middleware behavior. The interface description is formal, given in an interface definition language specific to the infrastructure. The behavior description is informal, given in a natural language. Such an informal description is not useful for the systematic customization of middleware, as it lacks precision and makes automated reasoning about required and provided properties virtually impossible. So as to remedy this problem, we employ the basic concepts introduced in the software architecture paradigm. The input of the systematic customization is an architecture description of the application that, apart from the definitions given previously, includes a specification of the requirements on the properties of the middleware connectors that mediate the interaction among the components (i.e. non-functional properties required by the application). We also rely on the recursive nature of the architecture description to specify how the middleware connectors are built from the middleware services.

Figure 4 depicts an architecture description using the Aster ADL[2] of the example application we use throughout this section to demonstrate the systematic synthesis of middleware. The example application is a specialization of the DIS example used in the previous section and describes a (simplified version) of a distributed file system. The specification describes two component types, *FileClient* and *FileServer*, and a connector *ReliableConnector*. The *FileServer* component type provides an interface that exports a set of basic operations for accessing files, the *FileClient* component type requires the same interface so as to issue requests for accessing files. The *ReliableConnector* definition requires

---

[1] Information about the Aster activity may be found at the URL: http://www.irisa.fr/solidor/work/aster.

[2] The syntax taken for the Aster ADL is based on the one of the TINA-ODL object definition language, which is itself an extension of the OMG's IDL.

```
interface FileSystem {
    void fopen (in string name, out handle file);
    void fread (in handle file, in long size, out sequence<octet> data);
    void fwrite (in handle file, in sequence<octet> data);
    void fclose (in handle file);
};

object FileClient { requires FileSystem FS;};
object FileServer { provides FileSystem FS;};
connector ReliableConnector { property CModel, TModel; };

configuration Application
{
    instances
        Server FileServer;
        Client FileClient;
        Connector ReliableConnector;
    bindings
        Client.FS to Server.FS through Connector;
};

property CModel { ReliableComm; };
property TModel { Atomicity, Isolation; };
```

Fig. 4. An example architecture description

the connector to provide properties *ReliableComm* for reliable communication, and *Atomicity* and *Isolation* for the atomicity and isolation properties known from the flat ACID transaction model. The configuration part of the description defines two components, *Client* and *Server*, of the *FileClient* and *FileServer* component types. The interfaces of those components are bound together through a connector of the *ReliableConnector* type.

3.1 Property Specification

Until now, our definition of properties provided by or required from a middleware connector has been rather intuitive. To precise the term, we first define *observable behavior* of a middleware as a sequence of events that influence the application components. Ideally, the middleware would be completely encapsulated and the observable behavior would be defined as the interaction that takes place through the middleware interfaces. Typically, however, the middleware can also influence the application components through the operating system, libraries or other shared resources. This makes our definition of the observable behavior include not only the interaction through the interfaces, but also the indirect influence on the state of the components, the activities executing within the components, etc. Based on the definition of observable behavior, a property of a middleware is then simply a constraint on this behavior. Expressed in a natural language, examples of such constraints can be:

- Whenever a request is issued by a source component for delivery, it is eventually delivered to the destination component once. No request is delivered unless issued. This constraint intuitively defines a property of reliable communication.
- When a set of requests is processed by a set of components and processing of any request of the set ends with failure, the state of the components at the end of processing the requests will be the same as at the beginning of processing the requests. This constraint reflects the atomicity property from the ACID transaction model.
- While a set of requests is processed, no request not belonging to this set will be processed by the components processing this set. This constraint reflects the isolation property from the ACID transaction model.

Formalized Specification The formalized specification of a middleware property in temporal logic follows the approach of defining constraints on the observable behavior. The events that make up the observable behavior are described by temporal logic predicates that hold whenever the particular event happens, the constraints on the observable behavior are expressed by temporal logic formulas. In this paper, we employ the temporal logic notation found in [29]. Here is a brief list of operators used:

- Boolean operators $\wedge$ (and), $\vee$ (or), $\neg$ (not), $\Rightarrow$ (implies), with their usual meaning.
- Quantifiers $\forall$ (for all), $\exists$ (exists), with their usual meaning.
- Operators $\oplus P$ (next), $\ominus P$ (previous), stating that P holds at the very next time in the future, resp. that P held at the just passed time in the past.
- Operators $\Diamond P$ (eventually), $\Diamondblack P$ (once), stating that P holds at some time in the future, resp. that P held at some time in the past.

Here is further a brief list of symbols and predicates used:

- A set of components of the application, $\mathcal{C}$.
- A set of possible states of a component $C \in \mathcal{C}$, Σ_C.
- A set of requests exchanged by components, $\mathcal{R}$.
- Predicates characterizing components, namely:
  - $[\sigma_C]$, holding when $C \in \mathcal{C}$ is in state $sigma_C \in \Sigma_C$.
  - $export(src, dst, req)$, holding when $src \in \mathcal{C}$ exports request $req \in \mathcal{R}$ to $dst \in \mathcal{C}$.
  - $import(src, dst, req)$, holding when $dst \in \mathcal{C}$ imports request $req \in \mathcal{M}$ from $src \in \mathcal{C}$.
- Predicates characterizing requests, namely:
  - $failure(req)$, holding if $req \in \mathcal{R}$ reports a failure.

The above notations make it possible to formally specify a middleware property as a temporal logic formula that describes constraints on the observable behavior. Following our example, the specification of the reliable communication property in temporal logic is[3]:

$$ReliableComm \equiv \forall src, dst \in \mathcal{C}, req \in \mathcal{R} :$$
$$(export(src, dst, req) \Rightarrow$$
$$\Diamond(import(src, dst, req) \wedge \neg \ominus \Leftrightarrow import(src, dst, req) \wedge$$
$$\neg \oplus \Diamond import(src, dst, req))) \wedge$$
$$(import(src, dst, req) \Rightarrow \Leftrightarrow export(src, dst, req))$$

The two remaining properties from our example, atomicity and isolation, are specified in a similar way. We use three additional predicates in the specification to denote involvement of a component in processing a set of requests, and beginning and end of processing the requests[4]:

- $involved(C, S)$ holds if $C \in \mathcal{C}$ is involved in processing $S \subset \mathcal{R}$, formally $\exists src \in \mathcal{C}, req \in S : \Diamond \Leftrightarrow import(src, C, req)$.
- $begin(C, S)$, $end(C, S)$ holds when $C \in \mathcal{C}$ begins, resp. ends, processing requests from $S \subset \mathcal{R}$.

$$Atomicity \equiv \forall S \subset \mathcal{R}, C \in \mathcal{C} \mid involved(C, S) :$$
$$\exists req \in S \mid failure(req) \Rightarrow$$
$$\exists \sigma_C \in \Sigma_C \mid (\Diamond \Leftrightarrow ([\sigma_C] \wedge begin(C, S))) \wedge (\Diamond \Leftrightarrow ([\sigma_C] \wedge end(C, S)))$$

$$Isolation \equiv \forall S \subset \mathcal{R}, req \in \mathcal{R} - S, src \in \mathcal{C}, dst \in \mathcal{C} \mid involved(dst, S) :$$
$$(import(src, dst, req) \wedge \oplus \Diamond begin(dst, S)) \vee$$
$$(end(dst, S) \wedge \oplus \Diamond import(src, dst, req))$$

Property Matching The primary use for the formalized property specification is an automated matching of properties provided by the middleware against properties required by the application. A middleware providing property P can be used in an application requiring property R if any observable behavior that satisfies the constraints characterizing P also satisfies the constraints characterizing R. In this case, we say that P *refines* R. Formally, the refinement is expressed as an implication between the constraints. Let P denote the constraints characterizing property P and R the constraints characterizing property R. Then, P matches R if $P \Rightarrow R$. Although formally precise, this definition of property matching does not reflect the differences between the specification of provided and required properties.

A specification of a required property is something perceived by the application designer. Typically, such a specification is short and abstract, not going

---

[3] For sake of brevity, we presume that each request is unique, i.e. the same request cannot be issued more than once.

[4] In a full property definition, these predicates would be related to e.g. *begin*, *commit* and *abort* operations provided by the middleware connector.

into detail unless it is necessary for application functionality. On the other hand, a specification of a provided property is associated with a specific middleware, and is therefore very detailed so as to describe the middleware precisely. The difference in the level of detail can often lead to a situation where none of the provided middleware properties quite satisfies the specification of the required property simply because this specification does not allow for minor differences that are not, in fact, vital for the application. This is the case in our example, where the specification of the *ReliableComm* property requires absolutely reliable delivery that cannot be provided in a realistic environment. Instead, the available middleware will guarantee slightly weaker property of at-most-once or at-least-once delivery, which is probably what the application designer had in mind when specifying the requirement anyway. Similarly, the available middleware might provide atomicity as long as the number of components involved is less than 32767 or other handy limit. Again, such a service would not meet the requirements for atomicity as specified by *Atomicity*, even though the limit is probably something the application designer would not mind. To overcome this drawback, we introduce a concept of an *ideal behavior* as a behavior that the middleware would exhibit if there were no failures in neither the hardware nor the software the middleware relies on, and if there were no resource shortages. We do not further detail specification of middleware behavior, the interested reader is referred to [43].

When built solely on the predicates introduced at the beginning of this section, the temporal logic specifications tend to grow quickly in size even for relatively simple middleware properties. The specifications are then not only difficult to write and read, but the proofs of relationships between them become computationally expensive. In a sense, this is similar to building a program out of too primitive statements, and can be solved by introducing predicates that describe complex events and conditions, as was done in the case of the *involved*, *begin* and *end* predicates in the example above. What predicates are used then depends on the domain of the property the temporal logic formula describes. For instance, formulas describing communication properties can take advantage of a predicate stating what transport protocol the middleware uses, rather than specifying the format of the messages on the wire.

3.2   Middleware Architecture

With the formalism for specifying middleware properties in place, we now focus on the description of the middleware architectures that provide specific properties. The goal is to provide a middleware architecture description associated with, and later on selected by, the properties that it provides. Once selected, the architecture description is used to assemble the middleware as per the application requirements. In principle, there is no significant difference between architecture description of middleware and architecture description of any other software system. Employing this fact, we use the same architecture description language to describe the middleware structure as the one we use to describe the structure of the entire application in Figure 4. In our example, a middle-ware architecture that provides reliable communication, atomicity and isolation is required. Focusing on the CORBA infrastructure, as mentioned in the previous section, such a middleware can be built from an ORB and the OTS and CCS services.

Reusing Middleware Architectures A middleware architecture often reuses properties that are provided by other middleware architectures. In our example, we can consider the ORB component alone as a middleware architecture that provides reliable communication. The rest of the example then builds on top of the reliable communication to provide the atomicity and isolation properties. Any middleware architecture that provides reliable communication compliant with the CORBA standard can be used in place of the ORB component. To re-flect this, we allow a component definition within the middleware architecture to refer not only directly to a specific middleware service, but also indirectly to any other middleware architecture that provides specific properties required from the component. This, in fact, is a recursive application of the principle where a connector definition lists required properties rather than specifying a particular connector to be used. A fragment of a middleware architecture description illus-trating our example is presented on Figure 5. The description does not detail the interconnection of the OTS and CCS services as, although the two services are specified independently by OMG, they cannot in fact be implemented sepa-rately. The *Binding* interface denotes the interface the middleware architecture is to bind within the application, its definition is therefore taken from the appli-cation architecture description. The *TSIdentification* interface is a standardized interface used to connect an ORB with an OTS service, its functionality is de-scribed by the *TSPortability* property.

From Architecture to Implementation To assemble a middleware on the implementation level, we require the implementations of the middleware services to export operations defined in the middleware architecture description[5]. The implementations are then linked together with a binding code generated from the architecture description. This process is complicated by the fact that some of the interface definitions within the middleware architecture are derived from the interface definitions of the application components connected by the middle-ware. In our example on Figure 5, these are the interfaces of type *Binding*. Some of the middleware services come with a specialized tool for generating imple-mentation based on the interface description, such as an IDL compiler available with an ORB. Such tools, however, may not be available for every middleware service used within the architecture, or may not accept input in the form used within the architecture description. To overcome this problem in the systematic synthesis framework, we introduce a macro language that makes it possible to

---

[5] We also require the implementations to provide certain housekeeping operations such as operations for service initialization and shutdown.

```
    interface Transaction {
      void begin ();
      void commit ();
      void abort ();
    };

    object OTSCCSBlock {
      provides Binding ServerIn, Transaction Control;
      requires Binding ServerOut, TSIdentification Ident;
    };
    object ORBBlock {
      provides Binding ClientIn, TSIdentification Ident;
      requires Binding ServerOut;
      property ReliableComm, TSPortability;
    };

    configuration Middleware
    {
      provides Binding ClientIn, Transaction Control;
      requires Binding ServerOut;
      instances
          OTSCCS OTSCCSBlock;
          ORB ORBBlock;
      bindings
          ClientIn to ORB.ClientIn;
          Control to OTSCCS.Control;
          ORB.ServerOut to OTSCCS.ServerIn;
          OTSCCS.ServerOut to ServerOut;
          OTSCCS.Ident to ORB.Ident;
    };
```

Fig. 5. An example middleware architecture

parameterize those parts of the middleware implementation that depend on the specific application interfaces [42]. The macro language can be used to provide expected input for the available implementation generation tools, or to generate the middleware implementation directly, as the situation requires. Taking our example into the ORBIX environment, the implementation of the ORB component is partially generated from the application interface description by the ORBIX IDL compiler. The output of the IDL compiler needs to be further supplemented with the binding code that sets up connection between the application components. Figure 6 provides fragments of both the IDL compiler input and the C++ binding code defined using the macro language. The *$(Macro)* macros expand according to the specific application architecture, in our example scenario this means the *$(Interface.Name)* macro expands to *FileSystem* etc.

```
interface $(Interface.Name) {
  $(Iterate $(Interface.Operations Op
    $(Op.Type) $(Op.Name) ($(Op.Args));
  )
};

$(Proxy.Name)::$(Proxy.Name) () {
  pReference =
    $(Proxy.Type)::_bind (":$(Target.Component)","$(Target.Host)"); };
```

Fig. 6. Usage of macros for ORBIX ORB

3.3 Middleware Repository

Selecting from the available middleware architectures based on the properties they provide leads to a need of a repository that contains the available middleware architectures together with descriptions of the properties they provide, and that can be searched with the required properties as a search key.

The middleware repository needs to be organized in a way that allows for efficient searching. This issue is even more emphasized by the fact that the middleware properties are matched using a theorem prover, which is computationally expensive. In traditional databases, efficient search is achieved by exploiting an ordering on the search keys. In the middleware repository, the search keys are middleware properties that can be partially ordered using the refinement relation from Section 3.1. The refinement allows to structure the repository as a lattice, allowing to employ search methods that are more efficient than a linear search [31]. Apart from properties provided by existing middleware architectures, the lattice structure of the repository also contains abstract properties that are not associated with any particular architecture. The abstract properties are used to group the detailed middleware properties into domains. The reason for introducing abstract properties is twofold. Since the properties typically provided by middleware architectures are qualified as not related by the refinement relation, the lattice structure built only from these properties would be rather shallow and thus of little help when trying to make the search efficient. The abstract properties make the lattice structure deep enough to warrant more efficient searching [20]. The abstract properties also make it easier to browse the middleware repository. The domains defined by the abstract properties provide an ample navigation aid to the application designer, who will typically want to browse the available properties before specifying the application requirements rather than providing the definitions of the required properties straight away. Within the repository, a middleware architecture is linked to those nodes of the refinement lattice that define the properties provided by the architecture. As detailed in Section 3.2, the middleware architecture is represented by a formalized architecture description whose every component is associated either with a specific middleware service or with a list of properties the component is to provide.

3.4 Middleware Integration

Based on the repository, the systematic middleware synthesis takes part in three steps:

- First, the repository is searched based on the properties required by the application, and a middleware architecture that provides these properties is retrieved.
- Second, the retrieval is repeated recursively to replace every middleware component in the architecture that is specified by its properties with an architecture that those properties specify. The recursion stops when all components of the middleware architecture are associated with specific middleware services.
- Third, the middleware services are combined together according to the retrieved middleware architecture to form the synthesized middleware.

Note that at each step of the process, multiple valid results can be obtained if the repository provides multiple middleware architectures that satisfy the same requirements. In this case, the developer is asked for selecting the most suitable architecture among the eligible ones.

3.5 Discussion

This section has provided an overview of the features offered by the ADL-based Aster development environment so as to support the systematic customization of middleware given the non-functional requirements imposed by the application under construction. The Aster prototype described in [20] is currently being enhanced regarding the middleware selection process, including the use of the STeP theorem prover [11] and the efficient implementation of the middleware repository. The reader further interested by detailed specification of non-functional properties may refer to [8,9] and [38] for security and fault-tolerance related properties, respectively.

Except the benefits of characterizing non-functional properties within architecture description from the standpoint of middleware synthesis, this is also beneficial from the standpoint of the software design process. As illustrated in [38], the specification of non-functional properties may serve as a basis for characterizing generic architectures aimed at the enforcement of non-functional properties, which may be conveniently combined with an application architecture so as to produce the overall architecture of a given software system. Open issues regarding the proposed approach include the combination of possibly interfering non-functional properties within an architecture [22]. Another issue relates to the practical use of the Aster environment where software developers are in general reluctant to the use of formal specifications. The aforementioned issues are currently being examined within the Aster research activity.

4   Deploying Distributed Applications

In the previous section, we have presented an approach to the systematic synthesis of middleware with respect to the applications requirements. Given the middleware to be used by an application, it is further required to conveniently deploy the application's components. In addition, enhanced software reuse is supported if the environment enables to encapsulate legacy software within components. This section gives an overview of the Olan environment[6], which offers the ADL-based Olan Configuration Language (OCL) [4,41] and a number of tools for the deployment of configurations, possibly made up of legacy software [3].

4.1   Olan Configurations

From an OCL description, the OCL compiler generates the stub classes for the components and the connectors (if these do not already exist) needed by the application. These are stored in a distributed repository. The compiler also generates a script (called the deployment script) that contains orders and guidelines for the deployment of the application in a distributed environment. The remainder of this section details the execution structures which are generated for components and connectors, as well as the interpretable deployment scripts.

Execution Structures Basically, two kinds of structures can be distinguished at runtime: the execution structures for components encapsulating legacy software and their binding to the underlying communication systems, and the execution structures for connectors in charge of integrating a particular communication schema between components. In the current prototype, execution structures are implemented as objects programmed in the Python interpreted language [37]. Object orientation is a convenient way to manage customizable classes of components and connectors. Let us now detail the components and connectors execution structures.

A component is represented by an object that is responsible for managing the interface with the encapsulated code as well as the communications with other components via connectors. The main characteristic of such an object is to be configurable and its purpose is to allow dynamic positioning of the interconnections with other components as well as dynamic loading of integrated software. In between the component object and the various integrated software (called modules), is the stub, that homogenizes parameters format, and the wrapper that knows how to access the encapsulated modules according to the kind of integrated software. Stubs and wrappers are automatically generated by the compiler. According to the kind of modules (or classes), the work to be performed by the programmer to have his code integrated, ranges from almost nothing to the explicit redirection of the outgoing calls to the wrapper.

---

[6] Information about the Olan activity can be found at the URL: http://sirac.inrialpes.fr.

The main role of connectors is to bind a set of potential senders to a set of potential receivers for communication schemes based on service request or event notification broadcast. A connector is represented by two main kinds of Python objects: the service adapters (resp. notification) and the sender/receivers objects The *adapters* represent both the entry and exit points for the connector structure. On a sender side, they provide a function that allows a given component to initiate a communication as described in OCL. On a receiver side, they have the ability to call a given function (representing either a provided service or a notification handler), provided by the component. The adapters are also in charge of executing the user-level code which may have been added to the connector description (e.g. code for data flow adaptation). The sender/receiver objects are in charge of:

- Encapsulating the use of the communication system,
- Handling the possible control flow translations (e.g. when a sender asks for an asynchronous service request while the receivers provide the service in a synchronous way), and
- Handling remote communication according to the placement of the interconnected components.

Deployment Scripts The deployment script (also called configuration machine script) contains a list of commands that can be executed by the Olan Configuration Machine (OCM). Those commands correspond to the requests for the creation of components and connectors execution structures and the interconnection between the components, according to the architectural requirement expressed in OCL. The command for the creation of components requires several information from the script: the name of the component in order to be able to find the associated execution structure and the administration parameters that characterize the node and context of creation. The interconnection parameters contain the name of the connector to be instantiated and the list of components (and the services name) that must be bound together. Several other kind of commands can be found in the deployment script corresponding to every abstractions of OCL (e.g. attribute assignment, creation of composite structures, ...).

For illustration, Figure 7 gives a script, which comes from an application described with OCL named *Appli*, where two primitive components *Component1* and *Component2* are defined (the first one with a required service named *Notify1* and an attribute named *Attr1* of type string, and the second with a provided service named *React1*). There is one instance of each component and they are interconnected together with the *asyncCall* connector. The value 'foo' is assigned to the first component attribute. The administration parameters indicate that the first component instance must be created on a node whose Internet name is '*db?.inrialpes.fr*', and whose processor usage is less than 10% with less than 10 users connected to the machine. In addition, the user for which the component should be created must have '*admin*' as login name.

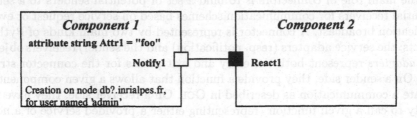

```
## Primitive Component creation and administration parameters
nInfo = ( 'name':  "(node.name [1:] == "db") and  ## constraints on Node
          (node.name[3:-1] == ".inrialpes.fr")",
   'IPAdr': "true",
   'platform': "true",
   'osType': "true",
   'osVersion': "true",
   'CPULoad': "node.CPULoad <= 10",
   'UserLoad': "node.UserLoad <= 10"
   )
uInfo = ('name': 'user.name == "admin"','uid': "true",
   ## constraints on User
   'grpId": "true")
CreatePrimitiveComponent('Appli_Component1Impl:Appli_Component1Impl:_1',
         uInfo, nInfo)
## Interconnections
## component1.Notify1() -> component1.React1() using asyncCall
Bind('Appli:AppliImpl_asyncCall_1:AppliImpl_1_52',
   [('Appli_Component1Impl:Appli_Component1Impl:_1', 'Notify1', 'itf')]
   [('Appli_Component2Impl:Appli_Component2Impl:24', 'React1', 'itf')])
## Attribute assignment \\
SetAttribute('Appli\_Component1Impl:Appli\_Component1Impl:\_1', \\
   '\_a\_Attr1',
   "('string*', 'foo')")
```

Fig. 7. Example of a deployment script

4.2   The Olan Configuration Machine

The OCM machine is in charge of creating and configuring components and connectors instances, according to the configuration constraints expressed in the deployment script produced by the OCL compiler. More precisely, the OCM performs the following tasks:

- Deploying components: for each component, the OCM tries to find a relevant node able to host it, according to its placement constraints.
- Installing components: the installation step consists of the creation of the components execution structures and the assignment of their initial parameters. Components can be created at various time: initially, at the beginning of the execution, or during execution if the OCL description contains dynamic component instantiation.
- Setting interconnections: once components are created on the various nodes, the setting of interconnections consist in creating a connector execution structure according to the user-specified communication mechanism and the optional insertion of the code in charge of data flow transformation. Let us mention that connector structure can be spanned on multiple nodes, depending on the component location.
- Support for the application execution: this final step allows users to launch an application execution and handles the authorized connections or withdrawals of users in a running session.

The general architecture of the OCM relies on several abstract machines: the *component machine* in charge of managing the components execution structures, the *connector machine* in charge of handling the configuration of interconnections and a *repository* allowing a distributed access to the components core implementation and the OCL compiler generated structures. Each node able to host an application execution contains an instance of the OCM. It relies on an Object Request Broker when remote communication between computer nodes are required. The ORB is used whenever remote configuration machines need to communicate with each other, for example at the deployment step when querying nodes or at the installation step when creating components remotely. However, the ORB is not used for the communication between components during the application execution (unless the application designer has specified its use in an interconnection).

Functions of the OCM Machine Three management functions are carried out by the OCM:

- The management of the distributed environment, called a *cell*,
- The control of the deployment and execution of a single distributed application, called a *session*,
- The management of the part of a distributed application that executes on a given node for a given user, called a *context*.

A distributed environment is managed by a set of *Cell Servers*, one per node for each cell. One particular Cell Server (called the Master Cell Server), is responsible for managing the join and the withdrawal of nodes inside the cell. A Cell Server provides features for the following tasks:

- Instrumenting the local node with predefined sensors that return information corresponding to the management attributes. Information returned by sensors can be either static (e.g. the name, the IP address) or dynamic (e.g. the average load, the number of logged users).

- Specifying policies for the evaluation of administration parameters contained in the OCL description. The criteria for eligible nodes may differ according to the cell administrators.
- Managing the deployment of an application within the cell according to the scripts for the application. This task is performed through calls to the Session management level.

A given distributed application that is currently being executed is called a *session*. A session is represented and managed by one *session server*. The session server provides services for the support of the installation and configuration of components and connectors of the application. Some of these services, like the creation of a component require the use of the context management level. Each time a user launches an application, he specifies the name of the session in which he wants the application to be executed. This may thus correspond to either the launching of a new session, or to the incoming of a new user into an existing session. More precisely, the launch of an application execution is managed through an additional script produced by the OCL compiler, which is given in Figure 8.

```
Start(applicationName, serviceName, args):
  If the given session already exists
      Get the reference of the local Session Server
      Ask for the execution of the given service
  Else
      Create a new Session Server
      perform the application deployment
      Ask for the execution of the given service
```

Fig. 8. Script for launching an application

A *context* represents the part of an application that executes for a given user on a given node. In other words, a context is an execution space for components, which ensures that components belonging to distinct users will not execute in the same address space, for protection reason. A context is managed by a *context server*, which is in charge of the actual creation and initialization of components within the context. A context server is also responsible for the creation and initialization of the parts of the connectors that involve the components it manages.

4.3   Discussion

A prototype implementation of the OCL compiler and Configuration Machine has been achieved using the Python language [37]. Using Python is of a particular interest for rapid prototyping due to facilities such as dynamic typing, reflexivity features, easy manipulation of complex structures such as lists, dictionaries, etc. Another major interest is the portability of Python code across various platforms (flavors of Unix, NT, W95,...). However, the price to pay is the poor performance at runtime due to the interpretive approach. The configuration machine uses ILU [23], a CORBA compliant ORB, for its own communication purposes. However, ILU is not used for the actual execution of the application, except if the architecture contains explicit use of a connector based on ILU mechanisms. The component and connector structures are also implemented in Python. Stubs and wrappers may be implemented both in Python and in the native language of the integrated software modules. Finally, the implementation of the communication protocol within connectors depends on the kind of connector which is used. For instance, there are multiple implementations of a remote synchronous call: one using sockets, another one using sun RPC, and a third one using ILU.

It should be noted that good performances at runtime were not expected from this experiment. The choice of the various implementation languages and tools were mainly motivated by the objective of rapid prototyping. The lessons drawn from our experiments mainly concern: the feasibility of the approach; the ease of application configuration; the flexibility of the deployment procedure; the transparent use of a distributed environment.

The prototype has been used for the construction of two applications: a cooperative document editor [5] and an electronic mail facility. The choice of these applications was motivated by the wish to address real-life scenarios which actually require heterogeneous components to be integrated within a distributed environment. The first scenario consists in transforming an existing single-user interactive application (e.g. a document editor or a CAD tool) to be used within a distributed groupware environment. No change can be applied to the code of the application itself (as usually only binary code is available). A way to achieve this goal consists in replicating the application on each user node, and building a coordination function defined as a set of cooperating components also replicated on each node. These components communicate together to achieve the control of the coordination between them, but they are the only one allowed to interact with the instance of the application of their node. The second scenario consists in extending an existing application (in this case an electronic mail browser) with additional facilities, acting autonomously on behalf of the end-user (e.g. for filtering and/or forwarding messages according to parameters customized by the user). Here again, the application itself cannot be changed and new functions are implemented as a set of cooperating components (also called agents here because of their specific role) which interact with existing software modules (i.e. the sendmail program, and the Netscape mail browser in this scenario). In both cases, the Olan environment has proved to be helpful for the following reasons:

- The OCL compiler greatly aids in providing wrappers to encapsulate existing binary code thus integrating legacy applications in a distributed environment (e.g. the Netscape browser and the editor in the previous scenarios)
- The Olan Configuration Machine also revealed to be very helpful in the implementation of the deployment process of the distributed application configurations. In the previous scenarios, nothing related to the distribution has to be implemented by the component programmer. Everything concerning distribution is externalized and the remote communications are handled by connectors.

In addition, it should be noted that an OCL description facilitates the reusability at the architecture level. This is a major advantage as it allows easy customization of an application for a specific use. Customization can be achieved in two ways: at the component level, to provide new facility, functionally equivalent to the former one, but implementing new policies; at the connector level, to change the communication schema between a set of interrelated components. For example, in the cooperative editor application, the component in charge of implementing the floor-passing policy can be changed on demand. Moreover, the same architecture may be reused to extend an existing CAD application towards a groupware environment. This does not require to redevelop the whole application from scratch.

5   Conclusion

This chapter has given an overview of work in the software architecture field. Using Architecture Description Languages, an application is abstractly described as a configuration that consists of a set of components characterizing computation units, which are interconnected through connectors that define communication protocols. Associated to ADLs are methods and tools for architecture analysis. Analyses that can be performed include:

- Correctness of bindings among components, ensuring that the behavior of an operation provided by a component matches the one expected by the component that uses it.
- Correctness of component interconnection through connectors, ensuring that the behavior provided by a connector matches the one expected by the components that use it with regard to both interaction and non-functional properties.
- Compatibility among configurations, ensuring that a configuration is a specific instance of another.
- Behavioral analyses of architectures so as to prove properties relating to liveness, and safety.

Another area of active research in the field of ADLs, which has been the main focus of this chapter, is the provision of tools for the implementation of distributed applications from their architectural description. In particular, we have presented features of the Aster and Olan ADL-based development environments, developed by BROADCAST members. The Aster environment provides support for the systematic synthesis of middleware from the (non-functional) requirements stated within the architectural description of an application. Such requirements serve for the selection of necessary middleware services, which are then composed with the application components. The Olan environment provides tools for the deployment of applications, including those made out of legacy software, over a distributed architecture.

The software architecture research field is quite recent and there is still much work to be done for it to address the overall requirements of distributed application construction. However, existing results already demonstrate that it is a promising approach. In particular, this research field is shown to offer a convenient testbed for the development of a number of CASE tools, which not solely ease the design and implementation of distributed software systems but are also applicable to real such systems.

References

1. R. Allen. *A Formal Approach to Software Architecture*. PhD thesis, Department of Computer Science, Carnegie-Mellon University, Pittsburgh, PA, USA, 1997.
2. R. Allen and D. Garlan. A formal basis for architectural connection. *ACM Transactions on Software Engineering and Methodology*, 6(3):213–249, 1997.
3. R. Balter, L. Bellissard, F. Boyer, M. Riveill, and J.Y. Vion-Dury. Architecturing and configuring distributed applications with olan. In *Proc. IFIP Int. Conf. on Distributed Systems Platforms and Open Distributed Processing (Middleware'98)*, 1998.
4. L. Bellissard, S. Ben Atallah, F. Boyer, and M. Riveill. Distributed application configuration. In *Proc. 16th International Conference on Distributed Computing Systems*, 1996.
5. L. Bellissard, S. Ben Atallah, A. Kerbrat, and M. Riveill. Component-based programming and application management with Olan. In *Proceedings of the Object Based Distributed and Parallel Computation Franco-Japan Workshop (OBDPC'95)*, 1995.
6. L. Bellissard, F. Boyer, M. Riveill, and J. Vion-Dury. System services for distributed application configuration. In *Proceedings of the Fourth International Conference on Configurable Distributed Systems*, 1998.
7. P. A. Bernstein. Middleware: A model for distributed system services. *Communications of the ACM*, 39(2):86–98, 1996.
8. C. Bidan and V. Issarny. Security benefits from software architecture. In *Proceedings of* COORDINATION *'97: Coordination Languages and Models*, pages 64–80, 1997.
9. C. Bidan and V. Issarny. Dealing with multi-policy security in large open distributed systems. In *Proceedings of the Fifth European Symposium on Research in Computer Security*, pages 51–66, 1998.
10. J. Bishop and R. Faria. Connectors in configuration programming languages: Are they necessary. In *Proceedings of the Third International Conference on Configurable Distributed Systems*, pages 11–18, 1996.

11. N. Bjorner, A. Browne, M. Colon, B. Finkbeiner, Z. Manna, M. Pichora, H. M. Sipma, and T. E. Uribe. STeP: The Stanford Temporal Prover Educational Release. Technical report, Stanford University, 1998. 1.4-a edition.
12. J. R. Callahan and J. M. Purtilo. A packaging system for heterogenous execution environments. *IEEE Transactions on Software Engineering*, 17(6):626–635, 1991.
13. Y. Chen and B. H. C. Cheng. Facilitating an automated approach to architecture-based software reuse. In *Proceedings of the IEEE International Conference on Automated Software Engineering*, pages 238–245, 1997.
14. F. DeRemer and H. Kron. Programming-in-the-large versus programming-in-the-small. *IEEE Transactions on Software Engineering*, 2(2):80–86, 1976.
15. P. Donohe, editor. *Software Architecture*. Kluwer Academic Publishers, 1999.
16. D. Garlan, R. Allen, and J. Ockerbloom. Exploiting style in architectural design environments. In *Proceedings of the ACM SIGSOFT'94 Symposium on Foundations of Software Engineering*, pages 175–188, 1994.
17. D. Garlan, R. Monroe, and D. Wile. ACME: An architecture interchange language. Technical report, Department of Computer Science, Carnegie-Mellon University, Pittsburgh, PA, USA, 1997. http://www.cs.cmu.edu/afs/cs/project/able/www/papers.html.
18. D. Garlan and D. E. Perry. Introduction to the special issue on software architecture. *IEEE Transactions on Software Engineering*, 21(4):269–274, 1995.
19. V. Issarny. Configuration-based programming systems. In *Proceedings of SOFSEM'97: Theory and Practice of Informatics*, pages 183–200, 1997.
20. V. Issarny, C. Bidan, and T. Saridakis. Achieving middleware customization in a configuration-based development environment: Experience with the Aster prototype. In *Proceedings of the Fourth International Conference on Configurable Distributed Systems*, pages 275–283, 1998.
21. V. Issarny, C. Bidan, and T. Saridakis. Characterizing coordination architectures according to their non-functional execution properties. In *Proceedings of the Thirty First Hawaii International Conference on System Sciences*, pages 275–285, 1998.
22. V. Issarny, T. Saridakis, and A. Zarras. Multi-view description of software architectures. In *Proceedings of the Third ACM SIGSOFT Software Architecture Workshop*, 1998.
23. B. Janssen and M. Spreitzer. ILU 2.0alpha10 Reference Manual. Technical report, Xerox Corporation, Palo Alto, CA, 1996.
24. J. Kramer and J. Magee. Exposing the skeleton in the coordination closet. In *Proceedings of* COORDINATION *'97: Coordination Languages and Models*, pages 18–31, 1997. LNCS 1282.
25. D. Le Métayer. Software architecture styles as graph grammars. In *Proceedings of the ACM SIGSOFT'96 Symposium on Foundations of Software Enineering*, pages 15–23, 1996.
26. D. C. Luckham, J. J. Kenney, L. M. Augustin, J. Vera, D. Bryan, and W. Mann. Specification and analysis of system architecture using Rapide. *IEEE Transactions on Software Engineering*, 21(4):336–355, 1995.
27. J. Magee and J. Kramer. Dynamic structure in software architecture. In *Proceedings of the ACM SIGSOFT'96 Symposium on Foundations of Software Engineering*, pages 3–14, 1996.
28. J. Magee, J. Kramer, and M. Sloman. REGIS: A constructive development environment for distributed programs. *Distributed Systems Engineering*, 1(5):663–675, 1994.
29. Z. Manna and A. Pnueli. *The Temporal Logic of Reactive and Concurrent Systems*. Springer-Verlag, 1992.

30. N. Medvidovic and R. Taylor. A framework for classifying and comparing architecture description languages. In *Proceedings of the Joint European Software Engineering Conference - ACM SIGSOFT Symposium on Foundations of Software Engineering*, pages 60–76, 1997.

31. A. Mili, R. Mili, and R. Mittermeir. Storing and retrieving software components: A refinement based system. In *Proceedings of the Sixteenth International Conference on Software Engineering*, pages 91–100, 1994.

32. M. Moriconi, X. Qian, and R. A. Riemenschneider. Correct architecture refinement. *IEEE Transactions on Software Engineering*, 21(4):356–372, 1995.

33. OMG. Object management architecture guide (OMA guide). Technical Report 92.11.1, OMG, 1992. http://http.omg.org.

34. D. E. Perry. The Inscape environment. In *Proceedings of the Eleventh International Conference on Software Engineering*, pages 2–12, 1989.

35. D. E. Perry and A. L. Wolf. Foundations for the study of software architecture. *ACM SIGSOFT Software Engineering Notes*, 17(4):40–52, 1992.

36. J. M. Purtilo. The Polylith software bus. *ACM Transactions on Programming Languages and Systems*, 16(1):151–174, 1994.

37. Rossum Van R. Python Reference Manual. Technical report, Dept. AA., CWI, 1995.

38. T. Saridakis and V. Issarny. Developing dependable systems using software architecture. In *Software Architecture*, 1999.

39. M. Shaw, R. DeLine, D. Klein, T. Ross, D. Young, and G. Zelesnik. Abstractions for software architecture and tools to support them. *IEEE Transactions on Software Engineering*, 21(4):314–335, 1995.

40. M. Shaw and D. Garlan. *Software Architecture: Perspectives on an Emerging Disciplines*. Prentice Hall, 1996.

41. J.-Y. Vion-Dury, L. Bellisssard, and V. Marangozov. A component calculus for modelling the olan configuration language. In *Proc. Second Int. Conf. on Coordination Models and Languages, (COORDINATION'97)*, 1997.

42. A. Zarras and V. Issarny. A framework for systematic synthesis of transactional middleware. In *Proceedings of Middleware98 - IFIP International Conference on Distributed Systems Platforms and Open Distributed Processing*, pages 257–274, 1998.

43. A. Zarras, P. Tuma, and V. Issarny. Using software architecture for the systematic synthesis of middleware. Submitted for publication, 1999.

OPENflow: A CORBA Based Transactional Workflow System

Stuart M. Wheater, Santosh K. Shrivastava, and Frederic Ranno

Department of Computing Science, University of Newcastle upon Tyne,
Newcastle upon Tyne, NE1 7RU, England.
{Stuart.Wheater, Santosh.Shrivastava, Frederic.Ranno}@newcastle.ac.uk

Abstract. The paper describes an application composition and execution environment implemented as a transactional workflow system that enables sets of inter-related tasks to be carried out and supervised in a dependable manner. The paper describes how the system meets the requirements of interoperability, scalability, flexible task composition, dependability and dynamic reconfiguration. The system is general purpose and open: it has been designed and implemented as a set of CORBA services. The system serves as an example of the use of middleware technologies to provide a fault-tolerant execution environment for long running distributed applications.

1 Introduction

There is growing interest in providing computer support for an organisation's business processes such as customer order processing, product support, stock taking and so forth. Workflow systems are normally used for this purpose to co-ordinate and monitor execution of multiple tasks arranged to form business processes. We will discuss issues in the design of a fault-tolerant application composition and execution environment for business processes whose executions could span arbitrarily large durations. We are particularly interested in the domain of electronic commerce applications in the Internet/Web environment. The Internet frequently suffers from failures which can affect both the performance and consistency of business processes (or applications) run over it. A number of factors need to be taken into account in order to make these applications fault-tolerant. First, most such applications are rarely built from scratch; rather they are constructed by composing them out of existing applications and protocols. It should therefore be possible to compose an application out of component applications in a uniform manner, irrespective of the languages in which the component applications have been written and the operating systems of the host platforms. Application composition however must take into account individual site autonomy and privacy requirements. Second, the resulting applications can be very complex in structure, containing many temporal and data-flow dependencies between their constituent applications. However, constituent applications must be scheduled to run respecting these dependencies, despite the possibility of intervening

S. Krakowiak, S.K. Shrivastava (Eds.): Distributed Systems, LNCS 1752, pp. 354-374, 2000.

processor and network failures. Third, the execution of such an application may take a long time to complete, and may contain long periods of inactivity (minutes, hours, days, weeks etc.), often due to the constituent applications requiring user interactions. It should be possible therefore to reconfigure an application dynamically because, for example, machines may fail, services may be moved or withdrawn and user requirements may change. Fourth, facilities are required for examining the application's execution history (e.g., to be able to settle disputes). So, a durable 'audit trail' recording the interactions between component applications needs to be maintained. Taken together, these are challenging requirements to meet!

Bearing the above observations in mind, we present the architecture of *OPENflow* workflow system designed and implemented by us. Our system meets the requirements of *interoperability, scalability, flexible task composition, dependability* and *dynamic reconfiguration* implied by the above discussion. Currently available workflow systems are not scaleable, as their structure tends to be monolithic. Further, they offer little support for building fault-tolerant applications, nor can they inter-operate, as they make use of proprietary platforms and protocols. Our system represents a significant departure from these; our system architecture is decentralized and open: it has been designed and implemented as a set of CORBA services [1,2,3].

2 Workflow Management Systems

Workflows are rule based management software that direct, coordinate and monitor execution of tasks representing business processes. Tasks (activities) are application specific units of work. A Workflow schema (workflow script) is used explicitly to represent the structure of an application in terms of tasks and temporal dependencies between tasks. An application is executed by instantiating the corresponding workflow schema.

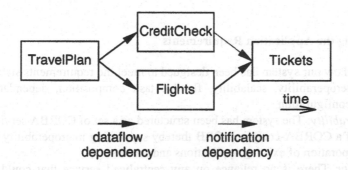

Fig. 1. Inter-task dependencies

Imagine an electronic travel booking workflow application. Fig. 1 shows its 'activity diagram' depicting the *temporal dependencies* between its four constituent applications (or tasks), *TravelPlan*, *CreditCheck*, *Flights* and *Tickets*. Tasks *CreditCheck* and *Flights* execute concurrently, but can only be started after the *TravelPlan* task has terminated and supplied the necessary data, so these two tasks have *dataflow dependencies* on the *TravelPlan* task. Task *Tickets* can only be started after *Flights* task has terminated and supplied the necessary data and task *CreditCheck* has terminated in an 'ok' state. In this case, task *Tickets* has a dataflow dependency on *Flights*, and a restricted form of dataflow dependency (called *notification dependency*) on *CreditCheck*.

There are several organizations involved in the above application (customer organization, travel agency, credit card agency, etc.). Each organization may well possess its own workflow system for carrying out its activities. A specific way of executing this application could be: the travel agency has the application description (workflow script) and is responsible for coordinating the overall execution and it itself executes tasks *TravelPlan* and *Tickets*; its workflow system will invoke *CreditCheck* task and *Flights* task at other organizations.

Clearly, there is a need for a standard way of representing application structure and sending and receiving 'work items', if organizations are to cooperate. Standardization efforts are therefore underway. The Workflow Management Coalition (WfMC), an industry-wide consortium of workflow system venders, has proposed a reference model that defines interfaces with the aim of enabling different workflow systems to inter-operate (Lawrence 1997). Unfortunately, it is a rather centralized model, not suitable for wide-area distribution [4]. The Object Management Group (OMG), the consortium of IT vendors and users, has adopted a standard that rectifies this deficiency [5]. Our system serves as an example of the use of middleware services to construct a workflow system that provides a fault-tolerant application composition and execution environment.

3 System Overview

3.1 Meeting the Application Requirements

We discuss how our system has been designed to meet the requirements stated earlier, namely: interoperability, scalability, flexible task composition, dependability and dynamic reconfiguration.

- *Interoperability*: The system has been structured as a set of CORBA services to run on top of a CORBA-compliant ORB thereby supporting interoperability including the incorporation of existing applications and services.
- *Scalability*: There is no reliance on any centralized service that could limit the scalability of workflow applications.
- *Flexible Task Composition*: The system provides a uniform way of composing a complex task out of transactional and non-transactional tasks. This is possible because the system supports a simple yet powerful *task model* permitting a task to perform application specific input selection (e.g., obtain a given input from one of

several sources) and terminate in one of several outcomes, producing distinct outputs.

- *Dependability*: The system has been structured to provide dependability at *application level* and *system level*. Support for application level dependability has been provided through flexible task composition mentioned above that enables an application builder to incorporate alternative tasks, compensating tasks, replacement tasks etc., within an application to deal with a variety of exceptional situations. The system provides support for system level dependability by recording inter-task dependencies in transactional shared objects and by using transactions to implement the delivery of task outputs such that destination tasks receive their inputs despite finite number of intervening machine crashes and temporary network related failures.

- *Dynamic Reconfiguration*: The task model referred to earlier is expressive enough to represent temporal (dataflow and notification) dependencies between constituent tasks. Our application execution environment is *reflective*, as it maintains this structure and makes it available through transactional operations for performing changes to it (such as addition and removal of tasks as well as addition and removal of dependencies between tasks). Thus the system directly provides support for dynamic modification of workflows (*ad hoc workflows*). The use of transactions ensures that changes to schemas and instances are carried out atomically with respect to normal processing.

3.2   System Architecture

The workflow management system structure is shown in fig. 2. Here the big box represents the structure of the entire distributed workflow system (and not the software layers of a single node); the small box represents any node with a Java capable browser. The most important components of the system are the two transactional services, the workflow repository service and the workflow execution service.

Workflow Repository Service: The repository service stores workflow schemas and provides operations for initializing, modifying and inspecting schemas. A schema is represented according to the model described in the next section, in terms of tasks and dependencies. We have designed a scripting language that provides high-level notations (textual as well as graphical) for the specification of schemas. The scripting language has been specifically designed to express task composition and inter-task dependencies of fault-tolerant distributed applications whose executions could span arbitrarily large durations [6].

Workflow Execution Service: The workflow execution service coordinates the execution of a workflow instance: it records inter-task dependencies of a schema in persistent atomic objects and uses atomic transactions for propagating coordination information to ensure that tasks are scheduled to run respecting their dependencies. Its design is discussed in section 6.

These two facilities make use of CORBA Object Transaction Service (OTS). The implementations for OTS used for the workflow management facility are OTSArjuna (for C++) or JTSArjuna (for Java), which are OTS compliant version of Arjuna distributed transaction system built by us [7]. In our system, application control and management tools required for functions such as instantiating workflow applications, monitoring and dynamic reconfiguration etc., (collectively referred to as administrative applications) themselves can be implemented as workflow applications. Thus the administrative applications can be made fault-tolerant without any extra effort. A graphical user interface to these administrative applications has been provided by making use of Java application or applets which can be loaded and run by any Java capable Web browser.

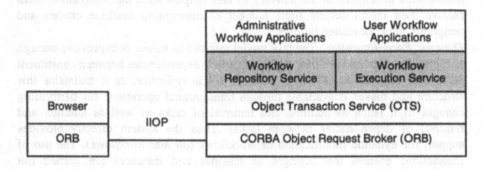

Fig. 2. Workflow management system structure.

4 Repository Service

A workflow schema must be expressive enough to be able to represent temporal dependencies of applications. The schema represents a workflow application as a collection of tasks and their dependencies. A task is an application specific unit of activity that requires specified input objects and produces specified output objects. As indicated earlier, dependency could be just a *notification* dependency (indicating that the 'down-stream' task can start only after the 'up-stream' task has terminated) or a *dataflow* dependency (indicating that the 'down-stream' task requires in addition to notification, input data from the 'up stream' task). We next present the *task model*, highlighting first some of its features that enable flexible ways of composing an application:

- *Alternative inputs*: A task can start in one of several initial states, representing distinct ways in which the task can be started, each associated with a distinct set of input objects. This is useful to introduce time related processing (e.g., a set of 'normal' inputs and a set for an exceptional input such as a timer enabling a task to wait for normal inputs with a timeout).
- *Alternative input sources*: A task can acquire a given input from more than one source. This is the principal way of introducing redundant data sources for a task and for a task to control input selection.

- *Alternative outputs*: A task can terminate in one of several output states, producing distinct outcomes. Assume that a task is an atomic transaction that transfers a sum of money from customer account A to customer account B by debiting A and crediting B. Then one outcome could be the result of the task committing and the other outcome could be an indication that the task has aborted.
- *Compound tasks*: A task can be composed from other tasks. This is the principal way of composing an application out of other applications. Individual tasks that make up an application can be *atomic* ('all or nothing' ACID transactions, possibly containing nested transactions within, with properties of: Atomicity, Consistency, Isolation and Durability) or *non-atomic*.
- *Genesis tasks*: A genesis task is a specialised form of compound task that acts as a place holder for a task structure, represented as a workflow schema. Its main purpose is to enable dynamic (on demand) instantiation of that schema. Structuring an application in terms of genesis tasks then provides an efficient way of managing a very large workflow, as only those parts that are strictly needed are instantiated. Genesis tasks can also be utilised to specify workflow applications that contain recursive executions, that is a task structure whose execution will potentially cause the execution of its own structure as one of its sub-tasks.

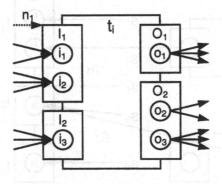

Fig. 3. A task.

A task is modeled as having a set of *input sets* and a set of *output sets*. In fig. 3, task t_i is represented as having two input sets I_1 and I_2, and two output sets O_1 and O_2. A task instance begins its life in a *wait* state, awaiting the availability of one of its input sets. The execution of a task is triggered (the state changes to *active*) by the availability of an input set, only the first available input set will trigger the task, the subsequent availability of other input sets will not trigger the task (if multiple input sets became available simultaneously, then the input set with the highest priority is chosen for processing). For an input set to be available it must have received all of its constituent input objects (i.e., indicating that all dataflow and notification dependencies have been satisfied). For example, in fig. 3, input set I_1 requires three dependencies to be satisfied: objects i_1 and i_2 must become available (dataflow dependencies) and one notification must be signaled (notifications are modeled as data-less input objects). A given input can be obtained from more than one source (e.g., three for i_3 in set I_2). If multiple sources of an input become available simultaneously, then the source with the highest priority is selected.

A task terminates (the state changes to *complete*) producing output objects belonging to exactly one of a set of output sets (O_1 or O_2 for task t_i). An output set consists of a (possibly empty) set of output objects (o_2 and o_3 for output set O_2).

Task instances, which represent applications, manipulate references to input and output objects. Such tasks are associated with one or more implementations (application code); at run time, a task instance is bound to a specific implementation.

A schema indicates how the constituent tasks are 'connected'. We term a source of an input an *input alternative*. In fig. 4 all the input alternatives of a task t_3 are labeled s_1, s_2, ..., s_8. An example of an input having multiple input alternatives is i_1, this has two input alternatives s_1 and s_2. Note that an input alternative could be from an output set (e.g., s_4) or from an input set (e.g., s_7); the latter represents the case when an input is consumed by more than one task.

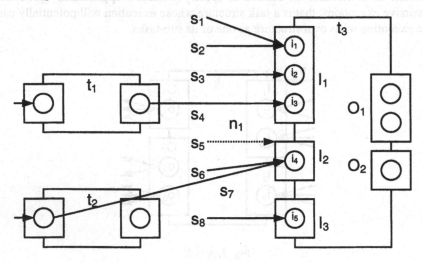

Fig. 4. A Workflow schema indicating inter-task dependencies.

The notification dependencies are represented by dotted lines, for example, s_5 is a notification alternative for notification dependency n_1.

To allow applications to be recursively structured, the task model allows a task to be realized as a collection of tasks, this task is called a *compound task*. A task can also be a *simple task* (primitive task), a genesis task or a compound task composed from simple, genesis and compound tasks. A compound task undergoes the same state transitions as a simple task. Fig. 5 illustrates a compound task, t_1, composed of tasks t_2 and t_3. A given output of a compound task can come from one or more internal sources (*output alternatives*). If multiple output sets become available simultaneously, then the source with the highest priority is selected.

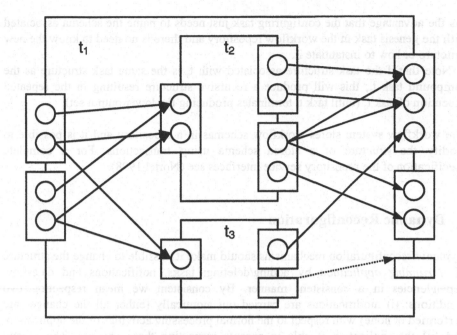

Fig. 5. A compound task.

As stated earlier a genesis task can act as a place holder for a task structure (a workflow schema), so enabling dynamic (on demand) instantiation of that task structure, at the point when the genesis task starts. Fig. 6 shows a genesis task, t_3 which is contained within a compound task t_1. If task t_2 terminates producing the upper output set, this will cause task t_3 to be started; t_3 being a genesis task, this will cause the instantiation of the schema associated with t_3. The task structure associated with a genesis task can be determined at run time. This would allow, for example, task t_2 to change the task structure which is associated with task t_3, so causing major reconfiguration of the application's task structure. The use of genesis task in this way

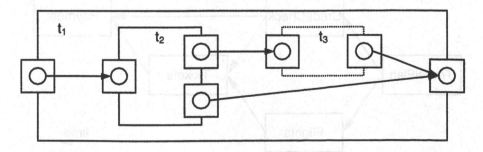

Fig. 6. A genesis task.

has the advantage that the configuring task just needs to name the schema associated with the genesis task in the workflow repository and there is no need to know the new structure or how to instantiate it.

Note that if the task structure associated with t_3 is the same task structure as the compound task t_1, this will produce a recursive structure resulting in the repeated execution of task t_2 (until task t_2 terminates producing the lower output set).

The workflow system stores workflow schemas in a repository and it is possible to modify the structure of a stored schema using transactions. For a complete specification of the repository service interfaces see (Nortel 1998).

5 Dynamic Reconfiguration

Dynamic reconfiguration mechanisms should make it possible to change the structure of a *running application* by adding/deleting: tasks, notifications and data-flow dependencies in a consistent manner. By consistent we mean respecting two conditions: (i) modifications are carried out atomically (either all the changes are performed or none) with respect to the normal processing activities of the application; and (ii) the application is able to execute respecting these changes. The second condition is slightly subtle, and is discussed further. Referring to fig. 1, assume that the task *Flights* needs to be replaced by a task *TrainJourney*, with the same input-output dependencies; such a change can be performed provided the *Flights* task has not yet started. Take another example: assume that electronic payment facilities are available and it is desirable to extend the application with a new task (*Payment*) with the dependencies as shown in fig. 7. Once these changes have been performed, the run time system should ensure that *Payment* task does receive its inputs. So for example, if the changes are performed after *CreditCheck* has terminated, its outputs should still be made available for consumption by *Payment*.

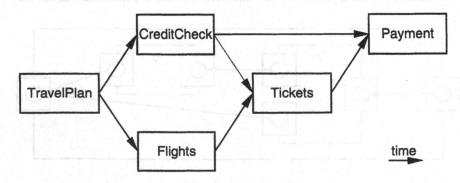

Fig. 7. Dynamic reconfiguration.

Below is the list of possible changes that can be performed on a workflow instance:

(a) The implementation bound to a simple task can be changed.
(b) Tasks can be added or removed from workflow instances.
(c) The constituent tasks of a compound task can be changed.
(d) Input alternatives can be added and removed from a task.
(e) The priority associated with input alternatives of a task can be changed.
(f) Output alternatives can be added and removed from a compound task.
(g) The priority associated with output alternatives of a compound task can be changed.
(h) The task structure associated with a genesis task can be changed.

These changes must be performed consistently, by which we mean respecting two conditions: (i) modifications to a workflow schema instance are carried out atomically (either all changes are performed or none) with respect to the normal processing activities; and (ii) the application is able to execute respecting these changes.

We use transactions to respect condition one. In addition, the following restrictions need to be observed to respect condition two.

- *R1*:   The implementation bound to a simple task can be changed, provided the task is in the wait state.
- *R2*:   The task structure bound to a genesis task can be changed, provided the task is in the waite state.
- *R3*:   Input alternatives cannot be added, removed or in anyway modified for tasks that are in state *active* or *complete*.
- *R4*:   Output alternatives cannot be added, removed or in anyway modified for a compound task that is in *complete* state.

6 Execution Service

The workflow execution service coordinates the execution of a workflow instance: it records inter-task dependencies of a schema in persistent atomic objects and uses atomic transactions for propagating coordination information to ensure that tasks are scheduled to run respecting their dependencies. The dependency information is maintained and managed by *task controllers*. Each task within a workflow application has a single dedicated task controller. The purpose of a task controller is to receive notifications of outputs (and inputs) from other task controllers and use this information to determine when its associated task can be started. The task controller is also responsible for propagating notifications of outputs of its task to other interested task controllers. Each task controller maintains a persistent, atomic object, *TaskControl* that is used for recording task dependencies. A task controller is an active entity, a process, that contains an instance of a *TaskControl* object (however, to simplify subsequent descriptions, no distinction between the two will be made). The structure is shown in fig. 8. For example, task controller tc_3 will co-ordinate with tc_1 and tc_2 to determine when t_3 can be started and propagate to tc_4 and tc_5 the results of t_3.

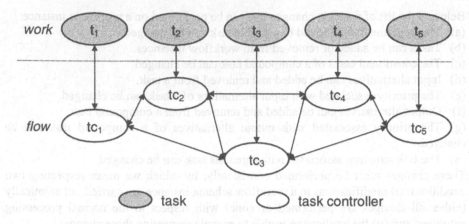

Fig. 8. Tasks and task controllers.

In addition to *TaskControl*, the workflow execution service maintains two other key objects: instances of *Resource*, and instances of transactional objects *Task*. Objects whose references are to be passed between workflow tasks are derived from *Resource*. *Task* objects represent the workflow tasks which make up a workflow application (*Task*s are 'wrapper' objects to real application tasks). The most important operation contained within the *Task* interface is *start*, which takes as parameters: a reference to a *TaskControl* and a sequence of *Resource* references. The *TaskControl* reference is that of the controller of the task, and the sequence of *Resource* objects are the input parameters to the workflow task.

The state transition diagram for a task controller is shown in fig. 9. The *TaskControl* object provides a *get_status* operation that returns its current state. During the initial setup phase, operations can be performed on the task controller to set inter-task dependency information. If task controller (tc_i) depends on an input from the input or output set of some task controller (tc_j) it must 'register' with tc_j by invoking *request_notification* operation of tc_j (a complementary, 'unregister' operation is available for deregistering). When the relevant input/output object of tc_j becomes available, tc_j invokes the *notification* operation of tc_i to inform input availability.

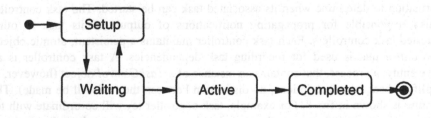

Fig. 9. Task controller state diagram.

Once a task controller has been setup, it enters the waiting state. The waiting, active and complete states correspond respectively to the waiting, active and complete states of a task. The task controller uses the *start* operation to start its task. Upon termination, a task invokes the *notification* operation of its controller to pass the results. Fig. 10 shows the interaction for some of task controllers and tasks of fig. 9.

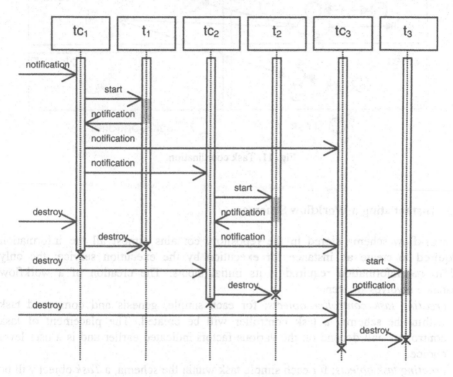

Fig. 10. Interactions between task controllers and tasks.

A novel feature of our system is that task controllers of an application can be grouped in an arbitrary manner. Fig. 11 show a possible configurations.

Nodes *B*, *C* and *D* are depicted, in fig. 11, as using a distributed coordination scheme, where a controller is co-located with the corresponding *Task* object, whereas a centralized scheme is being used by node *A*, where all the controllers have been grouped together at a given machine. A suitable configuration can be selected using the workflow administration application that is responsible for instantiating a schema (see below). The choice of a given schema could depend on various factors (e.g., dependability, performance, monitoring, administrative convenience etc.), and is left to the users and administrators. If dependability is crucial to the workflow application, then the task controllers can be placed on multiple machines so that the failure of a single machine will have a minimal effect on the progress on the workflow application. If the monitoring of the progress of the workflow application is more important than its dependability, then the task controllers can be grouped on the

monitoring machine so reducing communications overhead. In most cases the
placement policy for the task controllers within the workflow application will be a
compromise between these two extremes.

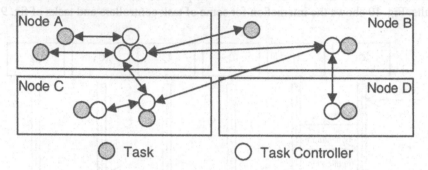

Fig. 11. Task coordination.

6.1 Instantiating a Workflow Schema

A workflow schema stored in the repository contains almost all the information
required to create an instance for execution by the execution service; the only
additional information required is its initial inputs. The creation of a workflow
instance involves six steps:

- *creating task controller objects*: for each simple, genesis and compound task
  within the schema, a task controller will be created. The placement of task
  controllers will depend on the various factors indicated earlier and is a user level
  choice.
- *creating task objects*: for each simple task within the schema, a *Task* object will be
  created and bound to appropriate implementation (application code of the task).
- *assigning tasks to their task controllers*: tasks need to be assigned to task
  controllers so that the initiation and termination of the tasks can be controlled. A
  task is assigned to a task controller by invoking the *set_task* operation of the task
  controller with an object reference to the task as a parameter.
- *assigning task controllers of genesis tasks with task definitions*: task controllers of
  genesis tasks need to be assigned a task definition, this task definition being
  instantiated by the task controller, when the task is started. A task controller is
  assigned a task definition by invoking the *set_task_definitions* operation of the task
  controller with an object reference to the task definition as a parameter.
- *linking task controllers to form the structure of the workflow schema*: Task
  controllers must be initialized with inter-task dependency information contained in
  the schema. Task controllers possess operations such as *set_input_alternative* and
  set_output_alternative (*set_output_alternative* only appropriate to task controllers
  of compound tasks); these are performed on a 'down-stream' task controller to
  initialize it with the information about the "source" of a dependency ('up-stream'

task controller). Once this information has been provided, a 'down-stream' task controller will invoke the *request_notification* operations on all the source 'up-stream' task controllers to register itself as a sink of dependencies.

* *providing the initial input*: the execution of a workflow instance will not start until the input conditions of the "root" task controller have been satisfied. This will be an application specific activity.

6.2 Workflow Execution

The execution of a workflow application is controlled by the exchange of notifications between task controllers and tasks. Notifications are generated when a controller of a task, either simple, genesis or compound, selects an input set or produces an output set. As stated earlier, these notifications are sent from an 'up-stream' task controller to a 'down-stream' task controller by the former invoking the *notification* operation on the latter. The parameters of the *notification* invocation contains information indicating: the source of the notification, the identity of the input/output set which caused the notification, and the objects which constitutes the input/output set contents. Referring to fig. 4, assume that the input set maintained by the task controller for task t_2 becomes ready; in this case, the task controller will invoke the *notification* operation on the controller of t_3.

A novel dependability feature of our system is that for an atomic task (i.e., the task is performed as transaction), its task controller can provide the guarantee that the task as well as some or all of its notifications are performed atomically. Fig. 12(a) shows a schema. Assume that task *t1* is not transactional; then dependencies *A* and *B* will generate two notification transactions (*A* and *B*, fig. 12(b)) as we have discussed already. If however, task *t1* is transactional, then if desired, the execution of this transaction as well as the two notification transactions can be enclosed within an outermost transaction *T* (fig. 12(c)). Thus it can be arranged that the effects of the task's execution will only be committed if all of the notifications are completed successfully. This allows the successful completion of an atomic task to be predicated on the completion of a set of "required notifications". Such a facility may well be attractive in electronic commerce applications.

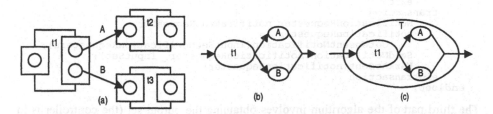

Fig. 12. Atomic notifications.

The actual algorithm used by a task controller to control its task (either simple, genesis or compound) is very simple; an important feature of this algorithm is that it can be restarted after failure. The following pseudo code describes the algorithm.

The following variables represent the state required to control a task, all variable being persistent and manipulated by transactions:

```
Boolean                               isSimpleTask;
sequence Alternative<>                inputAlternatives;
Boolean                               inputSetSelected;
ObjectSet                             inputSet;
sequence NotificationRequester<>      inputSetNotificationRequesters;
TaskDefinition                        taskDefinition;
Boolean                               instantiateDefinition;
sequence Alternative<>                outputAlternatives;
Boolean                               outputSetProduced;
ObjectSet                             outputSet;
sequence NotificationRequester<>      outputSetNotificationRequesters;
```

The first part of the algorithm involves collecting notifications to form an input set. This corresponds to the activity of a task controller in its 'waiting' state; the controller is repeatedly checking if any of its input sets is complete. Note that error handling in not included in the pseudo code.

```
// Collect notifications to form input set
if not inputSetSelected then
    loop
        transaction
            inputSetSelected := CheckForInputSet(inputAlternatives);
            if inputSetSelected then
                inputSet := BuildInputSet(inputAlternatives)
            endif
        endtransaction
    when inputSetSelected exit
        ProcessNotification(inputAlternatives)
    endloop
endif;
```

The second part of the algorithm involves sending notifications to all task controllers which are interested in the contents of the input set (this would be the case for shared inputs, e.g., input set of task *t2*, fig. 4 or if the input set belongs to a compound task, fig. 5).

```
// Send notifications to requesters of input set
loop
    when not ExistUnsentNotification(inputSetNotificationRequesters)
        exit
    transaction
        NotificationRequester notificationRequester;
        notificationRequester :=
            GetUnsentNotification(inputSetNotificationRequesters);
        SendNotification(notificationRequester, inputSet);
        MarkAsSent(notificationRequester)
    endtransaction
endloop;
```

The third part of the algorithm involves obtaining the output set (the controller is in state 'active'). This is done in one of three ways depending on whether the task is a simple task, a genesis task or a compound task. For a simple task this involves: beginning a transaction, starting the task with the input set, collecting the results some time later, then committing the transaction (assuming all has gone correctly). For a genesis task, this involves instantiating the task structure in its associated task definition, starting their executions and obtaining the results. For a compound task, this simply involves collecting notifications to form an output set.

```
// Obtain output set
if not outputSetProduced then
    if isSimpleTask then
        // Invoke task and obtain output
        transaction
            StartTask(inputSet);
            CollectResults(outputSet);
            outputSetProduced := true
        endtransaction
    else if isGenesisTask then
        // Instantiate task defintions and obtain output
        if not instantiateDefinition then
            transaction
                InstantiateDefinition(taskDefinition);
                instantiateDefinition := TRUE
            endtransaction
        endif;
        transaction
            StartSubTaskController(inputSet);
            CollectResults(outputSet);
            outputSetProduced := true
        endtransaction
    else // isCompoundTask
        // Collect notifications to form output set
        loop
            transaction
                outputSetProduced:=
                    CheckForOutputSet(outputAlternatives);
                if outputSetProduced then
                    outputSet := BuildOutputSet(outputAlternatives)
                endif
            endtransaction
        when outputSetProduced exit
            ProcessNotification(outputAlternatives)
        endloop
    endif
endif;
```

The fourth and final part of the algorithm involves sending notifications to all task controllers which are interested in the contents of the output set (the task controller switches to state 'complete').

```
// Send notifications to requesters of output set
loop
    when not ExistUnsentNotification(outputSetNotificationRequesters)
        exit
    transaction
        NotificationRequester notificationRequester;
        notificationRequester:=
            GetUnsentNotification(outputSetNotificationRequesters);
        SendNotification(notificationRequester, outputSet);
        MarkAsSent(notificationRequester)
    endtransaction
endloop;
```

In summary, our system provides a very flexible and dependable task coordination facility that need not have any centralized control. Because the system is built using the underlying transactional layer, no additional recovery facilities are required for reliable task scheduling: provided failed nodes eventually recover and network partitions eventually heal, task notifications will be eventually completed. For a complete specification of the execution service interfaces, see [8].

7 Administration Applications

As stated earlier, in our system, application control and management tools required for functions such as instantiating workflow applications, monitoring and dynamic reconfiguration etc., (collectively referred to as administrative applications) themselves can be implemented as workflow applications. This is made possible because the repository and execution services provide operations to examine and modify the structure of schemas and instances respectively. A graphical user interface (GUI) has been provided for these applications.

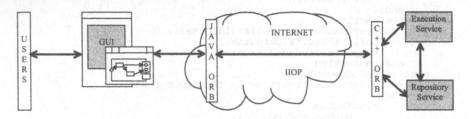

Fig. 13. Graphical User Interface.

The GUI has been implemented as a Java applet and as a result it is platform independent, and can be loaded and run by any Java capable Web browser (see fig. 13). This component of the toolkit is important as it makes it easier to use the workflow system, enabling a user to specify, execute and control workflow applications with minimal effort [9].

One of the purposes of the GUI is to help the designer compose the specification of a workflow application. The specification of a workflow application can be performed either from scratch by specifying all of the application components (in our script notation [6], these are object classes, task classes, tasks and compound tasks) and the relationships between them or by composing the application out of existing components which have been already specified. Existing component specifications can be obtained from the workflow repository.

The GUI can be used to view graphical representations of tasks and their instances, which can then be modified, using a forms style interface to input the required modifications. Fig. 14 shows a screen dump from the Java application showing the graphical representation of a task. Here compound tasks are represented by double line rectangles.

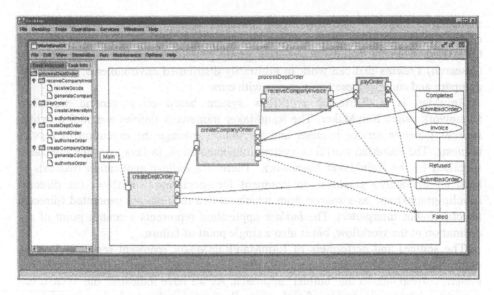

Fig. 14. Graphical representation of a task.

A navigation system is also available that lets users zoom in and out of a specification. Zooming in on a compound task lets users see its component tasks, while zooming in on a simple task displays its task class as well as all the dependencies it is involved in. The zoom-out is the reverse action: zooming out lets users see the embedding workflow.

Consistency checking and simulation tools are also available. The script semantics is expressed using LTSA (Labelled Transition Systems Analysis) tool [10], which enables system designers to carry out behavioural analysis. This tool kit can be used for checking for safeness, reachability, deadlocks and liveness. The simulator allows animating of the script in a variety of ways.

The GUI can be used for observing the execution of an application. This is possible because the GUI can access the *TaskControl* objects of the workflow execution service and hence can display the starting and completion states of tasks (recall that *TaskControl* objects store information on dependencies and task states). In addition to this simple monitoring, the GUI can also be used for driving the workflow administrative applications for dynamically modifying the execution of an application by forcing certain tasks to abort (when possible) or even by adding/removing tasks and dependencies as discussed earlier.

8 Related Work

The workflow approach to coordinating task executions provides a natural way of exploiting distributed object and middleware technologies [11,12]. However, currently available workflow systems are not scaleable, as their structure tends to be monolithic. There is therefore much research activity on the construction of decentralized workflow architectures. Systems such as ours, RainMan [4] and ORBWork from the METEOR research group [13] represent a new generation of (research) systems that can work in arbitrarily distributed environments. We briefly compare and contrast these two systems with ours.

RainMan is a distributed workflow system based on a generic workflow framework called RainMaker. The RainMaker framework defines a model in which *sources* generate service requests and *performers* manage the execution of service requests. The RainMan workflow system implementation, in Java, uses the interfaces specified by the RainMaker framework. There is a *builder* application that acts as both an interactive graphical environment for specifying workflows (as directed acyclic graphs) and as a *source* from which service requests are generated (directed acyclic graphs interpreter). The *builder* application represents a central point of co-ordination of the workflow, but is also a single point of failure.

The sources and performers of RainMan/RainMaker represent respectively, task controllers and tasks of our system. The centralized coordination configuration of our system corresponds to the 'builder' approach. As we have indicated, our system can support arbitrary placement of task controllers, so can be made immune from a central point of failure. There is no support for fault tolerance in RainMan.

ORBWork is a CORBA based workflow enactment system for the $METEOR_2$ workflow model. In the $METEOR_2$ model the workflow system's runtime is divided into two types of components: *task managers* and *tasks*. The purpose of a *task manager* is to control/schedule the execution of a *task* within a workflow application. The specification of the control/schedule is stored in Workflow Intermediate Language (WIL). The WIL is used to automatically generate code fragments (C++) which are combined with ORBWork task manager code to create programs which can be used to control the workflow application. $METEOR_2$ model distinguishes different types of *tasks* components depending on their behaviour, for example, transactional, non transactions or user tasks. For each behavioural set an appropriate *task manager* is specified, with an appropriate IDL interface.

The task managers and tasks of ORBWork correspond to task controllers and tasks respectively of our system. However, unlike our system, ORBWork does not implement a transactional task coordination facility: task managers and tasks are not transactional CORBA objects. Therefore, as we have stated earlier, our system does not need special recovery facilities to deal with failures. Naturally, recovery facilities need to be implemented in ORBWork; the cited paper describes its design.

There are two features of our system that distinguishes it from the rest: i) The use of a transactional task coordination facility means that the system naturally provides a fault-tolerant 'job scheduling' environment. ii) Our system is reflective: computation structure is maintained by the system at run time and exposed in a careful manner for dynamic control. The execution service directly maintains the structure of an application within task controllers making it available through transactional operations. This makes the provision of system monitoring and dynamic workflows relatively easy.

9 Concluding Remarks

We have described the design and implementation of an application composition and execution environment that enables sets of inter-related tasks to be carried out and supervised in a dependable manner. The system meets the requirements of interoperability, scalability, flexible task composition, dependability and dynamic reconfiguration. The system has been structured to provide dependability at *application level* and *system level*. Support for application level dependability has been provided through flexible task composition discussed earlier that enables an application builder to incorporate alternative tasks, compensating tasks, replacement tasks etc., within an application to deal with a variety of exceptional situations. Support for system level dependability has been provided by recording inter-task dependencies in transactional shared objects and by using transactions to implement the delivery of task outputs such that destination tasks receive their inputs despite finite number of intervening machine crashes and temporary network related failures; this also provides a durable audit trail of task interactions. Thus our system naturally provides a fault-tolerant 'job scheduling' environment that maintains a durable history of application interactions. Our system architecture is decentralized and open: it has been designed and implemented as a set of CORBA services. Wide-spread acceptance of CORBA and Java middleware technologies make our system ideally suited to building Internet applications.

Acknowledgements

This work has been supported in part by grants from Nortel Technology, Engineering and Physical Sciences Research Council, ESPRIT CaberNet, ESPRIT working group BROADCAST (project No. 22455), ESPRIT Project MultiPLECX (Project No. 26810) and ESPRIT LTR Project C3DS (project no. 24962). Mark Little has played a key role in making the OTS compliant versions of Arjuna. Support from colleagues Samantha Merrion, Dave Stringer, Harold Toze and John Warne at Nortel Technology, Harlow is gratefully acknowledged.

References

1. F. Ranno, S .K. Shrivastava and S.M. Wheater, "A system for specifying and coordinating the execution of reliable distributed applications", Distributed Applications and Interoperable Systems, eds: H. Konig, K. G. Geihs and T. Preuss, Chapman and Hall, ISBN 0 412 82340 3, 1997, pp. 281-294.
2. S.M. Wheater, S.K. Shrivastava and F. Ranno "A CORBA Compliant Transactional Workflow System for Internet Applications ", Proc. Of IFIP Intl. Conference on Distributed Systems Platforms and Open Distributed Processing, Middleware 98, (N. Davies, K. Raymond, J. Seitz, eds.), Springer-Verlag, London, 1998, ISBN 1-85233-088-0, pp. 3-18.

3. S.K. Shrivastava and S.M. Wheater, "Architectural Support for Dynamic Reconfiguration of distributed workflow Applications", IEE Proceedings – Software, Vol. 145, No. 5, October 1998, pp. 155-162.
4. S. Paul, E. Park and J. Chaar, "RainMan: a Workflow System for the Internet", Proc. of USENIX Symp. on Internet Technologies and Systems, Dec. 1997.
5. IEEE concurrency paper: IBM
6. F. Ranno, S.K. Shrivastava, and S.M. Wheater, "A Language for Specifying the Composition of Reliable Distributed Applications", 18th IEEE Intl. Conf. on Distributed Computing Systems, ICDCS'98, Amsterdam, May 1998, pp. 534-543.
7. G.D. Parrington, S.K. Shrivastava, S.M. Wheater and M.C. Little, "The design and implementation of Arjuna", USENIX Computing Systems Journal, vol. 8 (3), pp. 255-308, Summer 1995.
8. Nortel and University of Newcastle upon Tyne, "Workflow Management Facility Specification", OMG document number bom/98-03-01, March 1998.
9. F. Ranno, "A language and toolkit for the specification, execution and monitoring of dependable distributed applications", Phd thesis, Department of Computing Science, University of Newcastle upon Tyne, June 1999.
10. J. Magee and J. Kramer, "Concurrency: state models and Java programs", John Wiley and Sons, 1999.
11. D. Georgakopoulos, M. Hornick and A. Sheth, "An overview of workflow management: from process modelling to workflow automation infrastructure", Intl. Journal on distributed and parallel databases, 3(2), pp. 119-153, April 1995.
12. J.P. Warne, "Flexible transaction framework for dependable workflows", ANSA Report No. 1217, 1995.
13. S. Das, K. Kochut, J. Miller, A. Seth A and D. Worah, "ORBWork: A reliable distributed CORBA-based workflow enactment system for METEOR2", Tech. Report No. UGA-CS-TR 97-001, Dept. of Computer Science, University of Georgia 1997.

Improving the Effectiveness of Web Caching

Jean-Marc Menaud, Valérie Issarny, and Michel Banâtre

INRIA

IRISA, Campus de Beaulieu, 35042 Rennes Cedex, France
{jmenaud,issarny,banatre}@irisa.fr

Abstract. The bandwidth demands on the (WORLD-WIDE) WEB continue to grow at an exponential rate. It is thus becoming crucial to provide solutions improving the WEB latency. In that framework, the most promising low cost solution lies in the use of caches at the level of the clients, network and servers. Caching effectiveness then relies upon adequate cache management so as to keep in the cache the WEB objects that are the most likely to be re-accessed. However, the effectiveness of a single cache remains poor as it is in general no higher than 40%. One way to further improve caching effectiveness is thus to make caches cooperate so as to increase the probability of retrieving an object at the caching level. The cache cooperation protocol must then be such that it induces a negligible load for the network and cooperating caches.

This paper presents our solutions to improving the effectiveness of WEB caching concerning both cache management and cache cooperation. Regarding cache management, we propose two novel algorithms that exploit the latest results about WEB usage, enabling us to undertake replacement decisions that are more accurate than the one taken by existing algorithms. From the standpoint of cooperating caches, we propose a cooperation protocol, which minimizes the associated network bandwidth, processing load, and storage consumption among caches.

1 Introduction

The ever-increasing popularity of the INTERNET is raising an urgent need for solutions aimed at masking the resulting traffic congestion and hence allowing improved response time. Two types of solutions have been explored: (*i*) increasing the bandwidth of the network links, which is of limited help due to the associated financial cost and technical problems; (*ii*) using caches over the INTERNET for replication of the most frequently accessed data. Although more affordable than the first solution, the actual benefit of caches for improving response time over the INTERNET still remains negligible [27]. Various approaches have been examined in order to increase the effectiveness of caches. These include the use of large caches and of more efficient cache management techniques. However, such approaches may only have a limited impact since most of the documents are accessed only once [2]. Furthermore, the use of large caches raises financial and technical problems. Other efforts have been focusing on the prefetching of data within caches but the resulting traffic overhead is too costly (*e.g.* [18]).

S. Krakowiak, S.K. Shrivastava (Eds.): Distributed Systems, LNCS 1752, pp. 375–401, 2000.
© Springer-Verlag Berlin Heidelberg 2000

Another way to increase cache effectiveness is not to propose solutions at the level of a single cache but rather to make a set of caches cooperate. Because they take advantage of the network topology, the most popular types of cooperative cache systems are the hierarchical and the transversal ones, which are both implemented by the Squid software [25] from the Harvest project [7]. This paper introduces solutions to increasing the effectiveness of WEB caching, addressing support both at the level of a single cache and at the one of cooperating caches. Our solutions result from the study of Web traces and of their analyses that were published before 1999. It should be clear that proposing the most effective solution to Web caching is still an open issue and will certainly remain so for quite a while. Given that the number of both Web sites and Web users keeps growing at an exponential rate, it is almost impossible to determine an accurate pattern of Web accesses (*e.g.*, degree of sharing, most frequently accessed documents). Henceforth, we are far from being able to define an analytical model of Web accesses, which could serve as a basis for designing Web caching policies. However, available Web traces enable to accurately compare various Web caching techniques as done in the following.

From the standpoint of cache management, we propose novel replacement algorithms that take advantage of a survey on WEB usage (Section 3). In particular, it has been noticed that the wide majority of requests handled by a WEB server relates to few documents. Thus, this raises the existence of hot WEB objects, which may be exploited to favor the replacement of cold objects. In addition, regarding documents stored within WEB caches, it appears that 40% of the objects are images. Given that an image may be degraded at low cost using JPEG-like algorithms, without affecting considerably the resulting document readability, image degradation is an appealing alternative to object removal within a cache.

From the standpoint of cooperating caches, the major drawback of used techniques is that they introduce a significant bandwidth and workload overhead as they rely on the exchange of messages among all the cooperating caches to locate an object. Recent proposals address this performance penalty through a centralized knowledge of the cache system state, which induces a significant network and storage load for state management. On the other hand, a distributed solution to cooperative caching may be devised, yet introducing a bearable bandwidth and storage overhead. We propose such a solution, which is based on the adequate distribution of the state of the overall cooperating caches (Section 4).

Prior to present our solutions to improving effectiveness of WEB caching together with performance evaluation using simulation, the next section gives a more thorough introduction to caching in the WEB. Finally, we conclude in Section 5, summarizing our contribution and addressing our current and future work.

2   Caching in the Web

Basically, a cache is a software that is in charge of storing on disks, data elements that are accessed by a number of clients. The *cache management* policy drives data replacement within the disk so as to preferably keep in the cache, the data elements that are the most likely to be re-accessed. Within the WEB, there are three types of caches in use, which are located at the three points of the client-server interaction (*i.e.*, at the level of the client, network, and server). These caches are further detailed in the following subsection. Given that most of the WEB documents are accessed only once [2], techniques complementary to cache management have been proposed. In particular, due to the network topology, the idea of making network caches cooperate has emerged. Subsection 2.2 sketches base cooperative cache systems that have been proposed for network caches. Finally, Subsection 2.3 gives criteria that are used to measure the effectiveness of caching techniques, which will be used throughout this paper to compare various caching techniques.

2.1   Web Caches

WEB caches subdivide into client, network, and server caches. A client cache executes on the client machine and is in general integrated in a browser. It aims at improving the response time for the client's WEB requests. Client caches enable to efficiently handle document re-accesses (*e.g.* backward and forward re-accesses). On the other hand, since client caches are non-shared, they have no impact on the response time for newly accessed documents. One way to improve the WEB latency when accessing a document for the first time, is to use predictive prefetching techniques. Predictive prefetching consists of anticipating the client requests so as to prefetch a document on the WEB server before the client actually requests it. Predictive prefetching subdivides into: *user-directed prefetching* where prefetching decisions are based on user-provided hints [23]; and *automatic prefetching* where prefetching decisions are based on information gathered at the level of the WEB server (*i.e.* documents that are frequently accessed together) [19,4]. Prefetching has been shown to drastically reduce the time taken to get a requested WEB document. For instance, the technique proposed in [19] improves the WEB mean latency of up to 60%. However, it has also been shown that predictive prefetching causes a non-negligible increase in the network traffic due to erroneous prefetching decisions. Moreover, prefetching techniques are hardly compatible with network caches, which are considered as a key element to reducing the WEB latency.

In general, a client never interacts directly with the server holding the document it requests for. Instead, the request is issued to a network cache, which is shared by a number of clients. Thus, the client may benefit from earlier access to the same document by clients sharing the cache. If the cache owns a requested object, then it transfers the object to the client. Otherwise, the cache sends the request to the server, and gets the object. Then, in parallel, the cache stores the object on its disk and forwards it to the client.

The purpose of server caches differs from the one of client and network caches. It aims at reducing the processing capacity required for the server node, through (partial) replication of the server over a number of nodes that are physically distinct in terms of both network and machine. Thus, the primary goal of a server cache is not to improve the WEB latency but to reduce the server node's workload. To our knowledge, the distribution of user requests among server caches is not achieved according to load criteria but is instead based on a simple distribution scheme [13]. The DNS server owns a list of cache servers, and, upon a connection, the least recently used cache is selected to actually handle the request. This basic strategy enables to significantly decrease the server nodes' load while being easy to install and administrate; it is thus commonly used as it is for instance the case in the NCSA server [14].

The effectiveness of a WEB cache in particular depends on the cache replacement algorithm that is used. Ideally, the algorithm must keep in the cache the objects that will be re-accessed by the cache's clients. In the light of latest results about WEB usage, we have proposed novel cache management strategies which are more accurate than existing solutions regarding the undertaken replacement decisions (see Section 3). It is important to note that the various WEB caches are complementary rather than competing. In particular, it has been shown in [1] that the best way to achieve scalability over the INTERNET is to couple client, network, and server caches, data compression techniques, and possibly increase the bandwidth of the network links. The next subsection outlines yet another complementary method, which lies in the introduction of cooperative network cache systems.

2.2 Base Cooperative Cache Systems

The hierarchical approach to network cache cooperation is among the pioneering one and has been proposed by P. Danzig [8] in the light of a study on the INTERNET traffic in the USA. Results of this study showed that the INTERNET traffic can a priori be reduced by 30% through the introduction of a cache on every network node. The hierarchical structure of the cache system then came from the hierarchical organization of national networks. In a hierarchical cache system, a cache gets a missing requested object by issuing a request to the cache at the upper level in the hierarchy. The process is iterated until either the object is found or the root cache is reached, which may ultimately contact the object's server. The object is then copied in all the caches that got contacted when returned to the client. A transversal system enriches the hierarchical one by integrating a set of sibling caches, which are close in terms of latency time, at each level of the hierarchy (see Figure 1). Then on a cache miss, a cache not only contacts its ancestor cache but also its siblings.

Hierarchical and transversal cache systems are being evaluated on various national networks such as RENATER in France and JANET in the UK. Early results show that hierarchical systems bring actual benefit but there is no significant result for transversal systems. The effectiveness of a transversal system mainly depends on the number of siblings and hence on the number of caches

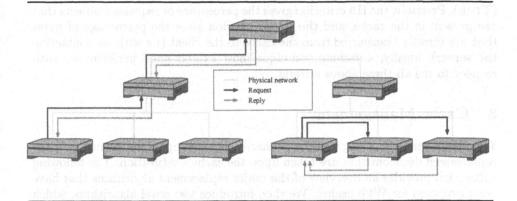

Fig. 1. Cooperative caching

composing the system. But, network administrators voluntarily set this number to 3 or 4 in order to limit the bandwidth overhead caused by the cooperation protocol of the transversal system. This overhead is a direct consequence of how a cache miss is handled in the implementation artifact: a request message is sent to all the siblings, and each of them replies by a hit or miss message, depending on the presence or absence of the requested object. Thus, the number of messages that are exchanged to get a global information about an object within a transversal system is equal to $2 \times (N-1)$ with N being the number of siblings. This network overhead is far too costly and cannot be reduced since multicast is prohibited due to technical and security problems [25]. Another critical factor of a transversal system is the resulting workload for cache machines: a cache has to handle messages received from its siblings in addition to messages received from its clients. Actually, the workload of a cache in a transversal system is increased by a factor of N in terms of handled requests. Based on the aforementioned evaluation of transversal systems, we have designed a new protocol for transversal cooperation so as to gain the foreseen benefit of such cache systems while having negligible network and machine overhead, and providing a scalable solution (see Section 4).

Although transversal cooperative caching was initially proposed for network caches, it is important to note that it applies as well for server caches. In the same way, transversal cooperation among client caches may also be exploited at the level of an organization.

2.3   Measuring Caching Effectiveness

So as to propose an evaluation of various Web caching techniques from the standpoint of their effectiveness, we use the following usual criteria: the *Hit Rate* (HR), the *Weighted Hit Rate* (WHR) and the mean response time to user requests

(TIME). Precisely, the HR criterion gives the percentage of requested objects that are present in the cache, and the WHR criterion gives the percentage of bytes that are directly transferred from the cache to the client (*i.e* without contacting the server). Ideally, a caching technique must exhibit good performance with respect to the all three above criteria.

3   Cache Management

The effectiveness of a single cache primarily depends upon the accuracy of the replacement decisions that are taken upon the cache's saturation. The following subsection provides an overview of the major replacement algorithms that have been proposed for WEB caches. We then introduce two novel algorithms, which respectively take advantage of the existence of hot WEB pages, and of the fact that 40% of the documents stored within a WEB cache are degradable images.

For evaluation of the replacement algorithms discussed in this section, we have run simulations using the UC Berkeley traces [12]. These traces were collected over a 18-days period, starting November 1st, 1996. During this period, about 10,000 different persons have been accessing the WEB over the INTERNET, issuing about 2,500,000 requests for a total data volume of about 1 TeraByte. For confidentiality purpose, traces have been modified using cryptography techniques. Precisely, the HTTP requests have been replaced by their MD5 code [17] and the IP addresses of clients and servers have been replaced by anonymous addresses. We selected these traces because they enable to have a highly accurate evaluation of the replacement algorithms effectiveness from the standpoint of TIME. Actually, unlike most of the other available WEB traces, the UCB traces gives the time at which requests are issued and at which responses are received. Thus, it allows us to precisely infer the mean response time for client requests. Finally, the simulations were run on a 100 MHz PC PENTIUM running the NT 4.0 operating system.

3.1   Replacement Algorithms

Existing replacement algorithms for WEB caches subdivide into two categories depending on whether the replacement decision is based on a single criterion or on a set of criteria.

Single-Criterion Algorithms: Single-criterion replacement algorithms rely on the selection of a criterion according to statistical analysis of users behaviors. The main algorithms in use are the LRU, LFU, SIZE, and LAT algorithms whose performances in terms of HR, WHR and TIME are given in Table 1. Table 1 further gives the performances of the PERFECT algorithm, which corresponds to an ideal cache with an infinite storage capacity, and hence serves to set the optimal caching effectiveness.

The LRU (*Least Recently Used*) algorithm remains the most used one. For storing an object within a full cache, the LRU algorithm iteratively removes the

Algorithms	Hᴿ	Wʜʀ	Tɪᴍᴇ
Pᴇʀꜰᴇᴄᴛ	30.2	28.7	8.97
Lʀᴜ	24.6	21.4	10.54
Lꜰᴜ	25.3	21.8	10.62
Sɪᴢᴇ	26.0	18.4	9.43
Lᴀᴛ	24.7	20.4	9.51

Table 1. Effectiveness of the single-criterion replacement algorithms

least recently used object until there is enough place available. In some situations, this replacement strategy leads to remove a large number of small-size objects so as to store a large object. In order to avoid such a drift, Lʀᴜ algorithms that further take into account the objects sizes have been proposed. These include the Lʀᴜ-Mɪɴ algorithm that is presented in the next subsection.

Instead of considering the time a cached object was last accessed for replacement decision, the Lꜰᴜ (*Least Frequently Used*) algorithm considers the number of times a cached object was accessed. Then, for storing an object, the algorithm iteratively removes the least frequently accessed object until there is enough place available in the cache. This algorithm has the same drawback as the Lʀᴜ algorithm; it does not take into account the objects sizes. In addition, let us remark that since most of the cached objects are accessed only once, the behavior of the Lꜰᴜ algorithm becomes close to the one of a simplistic random algorithm.

Unlike the two previous algorithms, the Sɪᴢᴇ algorithm takes replacement decisions based on the size of the Wᴇʙ objects. Upon the cache saturation, the largest object is removed from the cache, and the removal process is iterated until there is enough place available to store the new object. Despite its simplicity, this algorithm is among the most efficient of the single-criterion replacement algorithms as shown in Table 1.

The Lᴀᴛ (*Latency Access Time*) algorithm was the first replacement algorithm taking into account the time taken to get an object. Upon the cache saturation, the objects that are first removed from the cache are the ones whose access time is the lowest. The object's access time is based on the previous access times observed for the object. The major drawback of this algorithm is that it induces a significant management overhead. In addition to the storage of the objects' access times, the selection of the object to be removed causes a large processing overhead. This algorithm thus decreases the cache's efficiency and scalability. Moreover, since most of the objects are accessed only once, the access time that is estimated for an object is in general wrong. This has led the *Network research group* at Virginia Technology Blackburg to propose an estimation of objects access times with respect to servers and not the objects

Algorithms	HR	WHR	TIME
PERFECT	30.2	28.7	8.97
LRU-MIN	25.9	20.2	10.20
HYB	25.4	22.0	9.31

Table 2. Effectiveness of the multi-criteria replacement algorithms

themselves [28]. Such a solution decreases the algorithm's memory consumption and further allows to estimate the access time for a newly requested object.

Considering performance evaluation of the above algorithms, given in Table 1, we see that the SIZE algorithm gives a good HR because it removes the largest objects and hence enables to store more objects within the cache. The LRU and LFU algorithms further give a good WHR because, in general, large objects that get re-accessed, are in a small time interval. Finally, the LAT algorithm is effective with respect to TIME because any object that has a high access time is kept in the cache.

Multi-criteria Algorithms: In general, single-criterion replacement algorithms are efficient with respect to a single caching effectiveness criterion. Thus, one way to have a cache replacement algorithm that is efficient from the standpoint of HR, WHR, and TIME, is to make replacement decisions according to the conjunction of some criteria. Among existing multi-criteria algorithms, we present the two most efficient ones, *i.e.*, LRU-MIN and HYB, whose performances are given in Table 2.

The LRU-MIN algorithm minimizes the number of objects to be removed upon the cache saturation. Let V be the size of the object O to be placed in the cache, and L be the –possibly empty– list of the cached objects whose size is greater than V. If the list is non empty then an object is removed according to the LRU strategy. Otherwise, the value V is divided by two and the object list L is updated accordingly. Then objects of L are removed according to the LRU strategy until either O can be stored within the cache or L is empty. In the latter case, the algorithm iterates.

The HYB (*HYBrid*) algorithm takes into account a number of factors for object removal: object access time, object access frequency, and object size [6]. The objects that get removed from the cache are those which are optimal with respect to the three above factors. The algorithm is further generic in that it allows to weigh the importance of each of the factors in the removal process. The main drawback of this algorithm is that it induces a large processing overhead as for the LAT single-criterion algorithm. In particular, this has led to apply the optimization proposed for the LAT algorithm to the HYB algorithm [28]: access times are considered with respect to the servers and not to the objects.

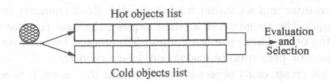

Hot objects list

Evaluation
and
Selection

Cold objects list

Fig. 2. The LRU-HOT algorithm

As shown by the performance measures given in Table 2, none of the two above algorithms exhibit good performance with respect to all three effectiveness criteria, *i.e.*, HR, WHR, and TIME. The two next subsections introduce two novel replacement algorithms, which enable to significantly increase the overall caching effectiveness, *i.e.*, regarding all the effectiveness criteria.

3.2 LRU-Hot

The survey about WEB usage presented in [3] shows that the requests issued to a WEB server relates to a small number of documents, highlighting the existence of *hot objects*. We thus have designed a replacement algorithm based on this criterion. The major difficulty then resides in identifying hot objects within a cache. We were not able to devise a reliable method to automatically differentiate hot and cold objects at the cache level. On the other hand, a WEB server can easily and efficiently detects its hot objects, by simply associating an access frequency to each of its objects. This has thus led us to use a solution based on server cooperation. An object is considered as being hot if its access frequency exceeds a given threshold (*e.g.*, 0.10 was chosen for our performance evaluation[1]), and as being cold otherwise. Then, when a server transfers an object, it includes a binary flag within the MIME header of the HTTP response message, notifying whether the object is hot or cold.

The resulting replacement algorithm, called LRU-HOT, relies on the management of two object lists that respectively give hot and cold objects (see Figure 2). In each list, the objects are ordered according to their *re-accessibility*, which depends upon the time the object was last used, in a way similar to the LRU strategy. Thus, the re-accessibility of a stored object periodically decreases. The idea is then to make the re-accessibility of cold objects decrease faster than the one of hot objects. However, updating the re-accessibility values of objects must

---

[1] This frequency value is set according to access frequency values observed for objects in WEB servers; it appears that most frequently accessed objects are those with an access frequency of at least 0.10 while the access frequency of remaining objects drops to 0.02.

induce a bearable processing overhead. We thus chose to use two reference counters: a base counter and a counter for hot objects. Both counters are initialized to 0. Then, upon the reception of a client request, the base counter is increased by one. On the other hand, the hot counter is increased by one every α (e.g., 2 was chosen for our performance evaluation) client requests.

When a hot (resp. cold) object is stored within the cache, it is added to the hot (resp. cold) object list and is assigned an *access value* that is equal to the base counter value. The objects of the hot and cold lists being ordered according to the decreasing order of their access value, the newly received object becomes the head of the list to which it is added. In the same way, when a stored object gets re-accessed, the object is moved up to the head of its embedding list, and its access value is updated with the current base counter value.

Upon the cache's saturation, the LRU-HOT algorithm computes the re-accessibility values for the two objects that are the tail of the hot and cold lists. Let *tail_hot* and *tail_cold* denote the access values associated to the tail object of the hot and cold lists, respectively. We get the following re-accessibility values for these two objects:

$$hot\_value = tail\_hot - hot\ reference\ counter$$
$$cold\_value = tail\_cold - base\ reference\ counter$$

Then, the object that is removed from the cache is the one that has the smallest re-accessibility value. If the cache can still not host the newly received object, the algorithm iterates until there is enough place available.

Performance evaluation of the LRU-HOT algorithm using simulation requires to know the access frequency of each object. For every object of the UCB traces, this frequency has been set to the number of times the object was accessed divided by the number of times the server owning the object was accessed. The objects' access frequencies are thus biased since they are computed with respect to the specific set of clients that were traced and not with respect to the overall requests handled by servers contacted by traced clients. It follows that evaluating the LRU-HOT algorithm using the overall traces would not be fair for the other algorithms. Hence, we have run simulations for a subset of the clients that were traced. Precisely, we chose 1,000 clients at random among all the clients, and the requests issued by these clients were used for the evaluation of all the replacement algorithms.

As shown in Table 3, the LRU-HOT algorithm performs better than existing replacement algorithms from the standpoint of HR, WHR, and TIME when taken as a whole. It is further important to note the simplicity of the algorithm. Additional improvements could be envisioned for the algorithm. For instance, the selection of removed objects could be based on the objects' actual access frequencies instead of the basic binary hot status. However, this would lead to a major storage and processing overhead. Another point relates to the evaluation of the α parameter used for keeping hot objects longer than cold objects within the cache. So far, this value has been set arbitrarily two 2 based on the authors' intuition. It would be interesting to examine a fine tuning of this value.

Algorithms	HR	WHR	TIME
PERFECT	30.2	28.7	8.97
LRU-HOT	27.1	23.5	9.41

Table 3. Effectiveness of the LRU-HOT algorithm

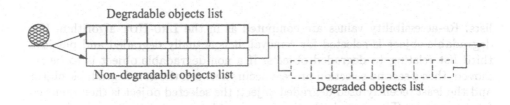

Fig. 3. The LRU-QOS algorithm

3.3 LRU-QoS

The LRU-HOT algorithm has been proposed in the light of the observation of the documents that are requested from WEB servers. The statistical analysis of WEB caches further shows that 40% of the documents that are stored are images, which may be degraded at low cost using a JPEG-like algorithm. We thus have devised a replacement algorithm, called LRU-QOS, based on object degradation so as to save the disk space used by degradable objects. Various kinds of objects are degradable besides images (*e.g.*, video). In a first step, we have only implemented degradation of image objects. However, let us remark that it is trivial to modify the implementation of the proposed replacement algorithm so as to integrate degradation of various object types.

The principle of the LRU-QOS algorithm is similar to the one of LRU-HOT (see Figure 3). In the same way, the algorithm manages two lists: one relating to degradable objects (*i.e.* images) and the other to remaining objects. The base idea then consists of keeping as long as possible non-degradable objects at the expense of the degradable object quality. For image degradation, we choose to degrade an image by a factor of 50% although a higher factor could be taken while ensuring image readability. Here again, we use two reference counters: a base counter and a counter for non-degradable objects, the latter being increased two times less frequently than the former. Upon the cache's saturation, either a degradable or a non-degradable object is chosen according to the respective re-accessibility values of the tail objects in the degradable and non-degradable

Algorithms	HR	WHR	TIME
PERFECT	30.2	28.7	8.97
LRU-QOS	25.6	23.1	10.01
LRU-HOT+QOS	27.3	24.1	9.39

Table 4. Effectiveness of the LRU-QOS and LRU-HOT+QOS algorithms

lists. Re-accessibility values are computed as in the LRU-HOT algorithm. If a degradable object is selected for removal, it is actually degraded and put in a third list relating to degraded objects. If a non-degradable object is to be removed, then a second selection process occurs between the non-degradable object and the least recently used degraded object; the selected object is then removed from the cache. The second selection criterion that we use here is subjective and consists of setting that the cache stores no more degraded objects than degradable ones. Finally, the removal/degradation process iterates until there is enough place available in the cache.

Performance evaluation given in Table 4 shows that the LRU-QOS algorithm enables to improve caching effectiveness although the benefit is not as drastic as with the LRU-HOT algorithm. Different variants of the LRU-QOS algorithm can be considered. For instance, one could consider to degrade a bunch of images at once rather than a single image. Parameters of the algorithm could further be tuned in a finer way, including the degradation factor, the frequency with which the non-degradable reference counter is updated, and the size of the degraded object list.

Finally, let us consider the combination of the two algorithms we have introduced, leading to the LRU-HOT+QOS algorithm whose performances are given in Table 4. Precisely, this algorithm subdivides each of the degradable, non-degradable, and degraded object lists into two sub-lists corresponding respectively to hot and cold objects (see Figure 4). The selection process for object removal/degradation then consists of applying the LRU-HOT strategy on sublists, and the LRU-QOS strategy among the lists.

As was already stated, our algorithms performs better than existing algorithms from the standpoint of HR, WHR, and TIME when taken as a whole. However, the LRU-HOT algorithm has the drawback of requiring cooperation from the server; in the absence of server cooperation, its performance will be close to the one of the LRU algorithm since objects received by non-cooperating servers will be considered as cold. Practically, it is thus better to implement a LRU-HOT+QOS algorithm within caches.

Regarding the performance measures given for the PERFECT algorithm, one can notice that the effectiveness of a single cache is bounded. Precisely, the HR of a single cache with respect to the cache size is a logarithmic function [20]. Hence,

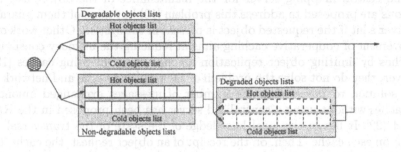

Fig. 4. The LRU-HOT+QOS algorithm

although *a priori* beneficial, increasing the size of a cache has a bounded impact on the effectiveness of a single cache. Another more promising way to make caching more effective is to have a system of cooperating caches as discussed in Subsection 2.2. In this way, the number of clients of a cache increases, leading to a higher hit rate for the cache system. Existing work in this area together with our proposal to make more effective cooperative caching is discussed in the next section.

4   Cooperative Caching

We have seen that cooperative cache systems subdivide into complementary hierarchical and transversal systems. Although appealing, transversal cooperative caching suffers from the introduction of significant cache and network load since each cooperating cache has to handle the requests issued by its siblings in addition to the ones received from its clients. Solutions to this performance penalty have recently been proposed; they are outlined hereafter. Due to our focus on transversal caching, the term *cache system* will be used to mean *transversal cache system* in the remainder.

4.1   Improving the Performance of Transversal Cache Systems

To our knowledge, the CRISP proposal [11] was the first to address a solution to the ICP bandwidth overhead problem of (transversal) cache systems. This solution lies in the use of a centralized mapping server, which maintains the list of all the objects present in each of the cooperating caches. Thus, for a local cache miss, only 2 requests (central mapping server interrogation and response) are needed to localize an object. However, this solution has several drawbacks: it requires a specialized machine, the central mapping server, which can easily becomes a bottleneck; moreover, it needs strong synchronization among caches and the central mapping server for the maintenance of the object list. Many solutions are proposed to address this problem [10] but none of them guarantees to deliver a hit if the requested object is present in the system. Other work on the improvement of cooperative caching aims at reducing the memory consumption of caches by limiting object replication among the cooperating caches [15,21]. However, they do not solve the problem of the resulting cache and network load.

A solution to minimizing the number of messages exchanged among sibling caches without using a centralized server has been proposed in the RELAIS project [22]. It lies in the local knowledge of the state of the transversal cache system on each cache. Then, on the receipt of an object request, the cache is able to locally identify whether the object is in the transversal cache system, based on its knowledge of the system's state. Should the object be within one of the cache's siblings, a request is issued to it in order to get a copy of the object. Local knowledge of the system's state has the advantage of introducing negligible workload for siblings when a cache handles an object request. However, such a local knowledge induces high memory consumption for storing the system state. It further causes a non negligible network load since messages need to be issued to siblings each time a cache is updated.

A protocol similar to the one of RELAIS but that induces less memory consumption has been proposed in [9]. The idea of this protocol is to encode the objects' URLs using Bloom filters [5] to reduce the size of the cache system state. Thus, the system state is encoded as a list of 4 bits signatures instead of a list of URLs. However, this space saving is at the expense of an approximation of the system state: several URLs may have the same encoding. Furthermore, this protocol still suffers from the same drawback as the RELAIS protocol; it causes a non negligible network load for update of the system state stored by the caches. In order to minimize the resulting overhead, only the code of the removed and added objects are transferred, and update messages are not sent on every cache update but at regular time intervals (*i.e.*, about every five minutes). Notice that differing the update of the system state within caches decreases the efficiency of cooperative caching; it may lead to consider as absent an object whilst the object being actually stored within one of the caches.

In the following, we describe our solution to transversal cooperation based on the idea of having a local knowledge of the system state, while minimizing the resulting memory consumption and network load.

4.2   Design Principles

One way to alleviate the penalty of using local knowledge of the whole system state from the standpoint of memory consumption, is to fairly distribute this knowledge among the caches composing the transversal system. Let us denote by $\mathcal{A}(C_i)$, the set of sibling caches for which cache C_i knows locally the content, $\mathcal{A}(C_i)$ including C_i. In other words, for each cache C_j of $\mathcal{A}(C_i)$, C_i maintains a list, which gives the objects identities that are present on C_j. Let us further denote by $\mathcal{S}$, the set of caches composing the transversal system. Then, to get knowledge of the whole system state and hence to locate an object that is not within a cache of $\mathcal{A}(C_i)$, C_i must contact a set of caches, noted $\mathcal{D}(C_i)$, as exemplified in Figure 5. The value of $\mathcal{D}(C_i)$ should then be such that:

$$\mathcal{A}(C_i) \bigcup \cup_{(\forall C_j \in \mathcal{D}(C_i), j \neq i)} \mathcal{A}(C_j) = \mathcal{S} \tag{1}$$

Thus, a cache C_i in the system can know the state of another cache C_x if C_i maintains locally a list for C_x or if one of the caches contacted by C_i, noted C_j (*i.e.* $C_j \in \mathcal{D}(C_i)$), maintains a list for C_x (*i.e.* $C_x \in \mathcal{A}(C_j)$). Note that when $\forall C_i \in \mathcal{S} : \mathcal{A}(C_i) = \{C_i\}$, we are in the presence of a traditional transversal system while when $\forall C_i \in \mathcal{S} : \mathcal{A}(C_i) = \mathcal{S}$, we are in the presence of a transversal system with local knowledge of the whole system state on each cache (*e.g.* systems proposed in [22,9]). Our objective is to find a *scalable* solution that is a tradeoff between these two alternatives in terms of object retrieval latency, memory consumption, and message exchanges.

Let us first examine the issue of object retrieval latency in the worst case, where we omit communication between the client and its cache since the associated latency is the same for any cache system. In a traditional transversal system, the object retrieval latency is equal to 4 message exchanges (considering that the time taken to retrieve an object within a cache is negligible compared to the cost of message exchanges): (*i*) For retrieving an object, a cache C_i sends, in parallel, the object request to its siblings, (*ii*) each sibling replies by a hit or a miss message depending on whether it holds the object or not, (*iii*) C_i sends a message to get the object, to one of the caches that replied by a hit, (*iv*) the object is finally sent to C_i. We observe the same latency using distributed knowledge of the system state. The only difference lies in the achievement of the first two steps: C_i sends messages to every cache C_j of $\mathcal{D}(C_i)$ instead of all the system caches, each C_j then returns the list of caches that own the object with respect to the object lists held for the caches of $\mathcal{A}(C_j)$.

Let us now consider the issue of memory consumption. For every cache C_i of $\mathcal{S}$, we want the cardinal of $\mathcal{A}(C_i)$, noted $|\mathcal{A}(C_i)|$, to be much smaller than $|\mathcal{S}|$. Furthermore, the scalability criterion requires load balancing, which leads to set an identical value for the cardinal of every $\mathcal{A}(C_i)$.

In the worst case, the number of messages that are sent by a cache upon the treatment of an object request, to locate the object, is equal to $|\mathcal{D}(C_i)|$ and hence we want the cardinal of $\mathcal{D}(C_i)$ to be much smaller than the one of $\mathcal{S}$. Furthermore, as for the cardinals of the $\mathcal{A}(C_i)$s, the cardinals of all the $\mathcal{D}(C_i)$s should be identical so as to meet our scalability criterion.

Figure 5 gives an example of a transversal system with distributed knowledge of the system state, for a system composed of 4 caches. Setting such a system depends upon the evaluation of $\mathcal{D}(C_i)$ and $\mathcal{A}(C_i)$ for every cache C_i of $\mathcal{S}$. Furthermore, the value of these sets must satisfy the aforementioned condition of load balancing, and should be such that the number of messages sent for updating the system state on a cache update is minimal.

It can be shown [16] that we have an optimal system meeting our scalability requirement if $|\mathcal{A}(C_i)| = \sqrt{|\mathcal{S}|}$ and $|\mathcal{D}(C_i)| = \sqrt{|\mathcal{S}|} - 1$, the number of exchanged messages on a cache update being then of $\sqrt{|\mathcal{S}|} - 1$. With such values, the network

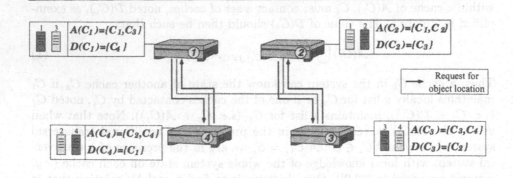

Fig. 5. Exploiting distributed knowledge of the system state

load to get an object within a cache is equal to $3 \times (\sqrt{|S|} - 1)$ messages, while
it is equal to $2 \times (|S| - 1)$ messages in a traditional transversal system.

4.3   Dealing with Cache Updates

Up to this point, we have not addressed the protocol used for updating the
distributed system state in the presence of cache update. In the following, we
introduce an update protocol whose bandwidth cost is negligible.

Let us first consider the addition of an object $\mathcal{O}$ within a cache C_i, C_i must
a priori send an update message to every cache C_j whose set $\mathcal{A}(C_j)$ includes
C_i. Beforehand, for getting $\mathcal{O}$, C_i already sent messages to caches belonging to
$\mathcal{D}(C_i)^2$. Caches belonging to $\mathcal{D}(C_i)$ can anticipate that $\mathcal{O}$ will be within C_i since
C_i requested for it. The two cases where the anticipation is wrong is when either
(*i*) $\mathcal{O}$ no longer exists or (*ii*) C_i did not get $\mathcal{O}$ due to some failure (*e.g.*, temporary
communication failure). The latter case is too rare to have a real incidence on
the correctness of anticipation and is thus not considered. The former case can
be seen as a special value for the object and is hence cached in place of an actual
object value. Thus, whenever a cache C_i is requested an objet $\mathcal{O}$ by a sibling
cache C_j, it can anticipate that C_j will hold C_i. Setting further the following *Rule
1*, this allows us to withdraw the network load that was expected for handling
the addition of an object within a cache.

Rule 1: *For every C_i in S, if C_i is in $\mathcal{D}(C_j)$ then C_j is in $\mathcal{A}(C_i)$.*

In other words, a cache C_i that is directly contacted by another cache C_j, *i.e.*
$C_i \in \mathcal{D}(C_j)$, to get an object, maintains the state of this cache, *i.e.* $C_j \in \mathcal{A}(C_i)$.

---

[2] As will be shown in Subsection 4.5, this is because a cache C_i that searches remotely
for an object seeks the object, in parallel, within the caches of both $\mathcal{A}(C_i)$ and $\mathcal{D}(C_i)$.

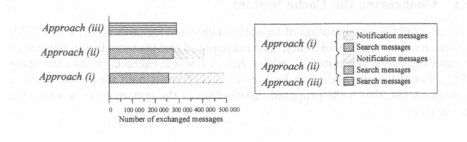

Fig. 6. Number of exchanged messages with different notification policies for object removal

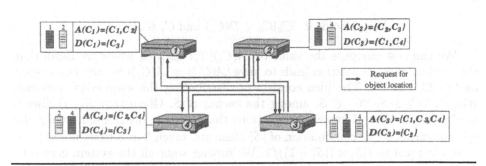

Fig. 7. Distributed knowledge of system state

Let us now examine removal of an object within a cache C_i of the system. Using simulation, achieved in the framework detailed in Subsection 4.6, we have compared three approaches: (i) notification to caches of $\mathcal{D}(C_i)$ upon the object's removal, (ii) notification of the object removal to a cache of $\mathcal{D}(C_i)$ when such a cache requests for the object while the object is not present, (iii) absence of notification to caches of $\mathcal{D}(C_i)$ with periodical emission of C_i's state to caches of $\mathcal{D}(C_i)$. Figure 6 gives performance results obtained through simulation for the three solutions; it shows that the third solution gives better performance in terms of the overall bandwidth use, and was thus preferred for our protocol.

Figure 7 gives an example of a system composed of 4 caches, with distribution of the system's state according to Rule 1. As previously, setting such a system depends on the evaluation of $\mathcal{A}(C_i)$ and $\mathcal{D}(C_i)$ for every cache C_i of $\mathcal{S}$, where we recall that Rule 1 leads to have: $C_j \in \mathcal{D}(C_i) \Leftrightarrow C_i \in \mathcal{A}(C_j)$ for every C_i of $\mathcal{S}$.

4.4 Configuring the Cache System

Let us detail the computation of an optimal cardinal for both $\mathcal{A}(C_i)$ and $\mathcal{D}(C_i)$, under the criterion of scalability. The principle of our protocol lies in the use of a knowledge relation, noted K, where $K(i,j)$ holds if cache C_i knows the state of C_j. For the cache system to be correct, $K(i,j)$ must hold for all the pairs of system caches. Given the proposed distribution of the system state, we are able to set that:

For two caches C_i and C_j of $\mathcal{S}$, $K(i,j)$ holds if either:
$C_j \in \mathcal{A}(C_i)$, or
$\exists C_k | C_k \in \mathcal{D}(C_i)$ and $C_j \in \mathcal{A}(C_k)$.

Since $C_i \in \mathcal{A}(C_i)$ always holds for any cache C_i of $\mathcal{S}$, we may simplify the above and get:

$K(i,j)$ holds if $\exists C_k | C_k \in \mathcal{D}(C_i)$ and $C_j \in \mathcal{A}(C_k)$.

We can now compute the value of $|\mathcal{A}(C_i)|$ for each C_i where we recall that the load balancing condition leads to have $|\mathcal{A}(C_i)| = |\mathcal{A}(C_j)|$ for any two system caches C_i and C_j. The idea consists of distributing the knowledge relations, $K(i,j)$, $\forall C_i \in \mathcal{S}$, $\forall C_j \in \mathcal{S}$, among the caches of $\mathcal{S}$. Given that $K(i,i)$ always holds, the number of knowledge relations that must be distributed among the system caches is the combination of $|\mathcal{S}|$ elements, taken 2 at a time, noted $\binom{|\mathcal{S}|}{2}$, which is equal to $(|\mathcal{S}| \times (|\mathcal{S}| - 1))/2$. We further want all the system caches to manage the same number of relations, leading to have $(|\mathcal{S}| - 1)/2$ knowledge relations per cache. We are now able to infer the value of $|\mathcal{A}(C_i)|$ for every C_i of $\mathcal{S}$. By construction of $\mathcal{A}(C_i)$ and $\mathcal{D}(C_i)$, there are $\binom{|\mathcal{A}(C_i)|}{2}$ knowledge relations per cache, which should be equal to $(|\mathcal{S}| - 1)/2$. Hence, we obtain:

$$|\mathcal{A}(C_i)| = \sqrt{|\mathcal{S}| - 3/4} + 1/2, \forall C_i \in \mathcal{S} \tag{2}$$

From the above, we are able to infer $|\mathcal{D}(C_i)|$. By construction, each cache C_j of $\mathcal{D}(C_i)$ knows the state of C_i, i.e., $C_i \in \mathcal{A}(C_j)$, and of some other caches. Thus, when C_i issues a request to a cache $C_j \in \mathcal{D}(C_i)$, only $(|\mathcal{A}(C_j)| - 1)$ cache states known by this cache are significant for C_i to get knowledge of the whole system state. It follows that we should have:

$$|\mathcal{A}(C_i)| + (|\mathcal{D}(C_i)| \times (|\mathcal{A}(C_j)| - 1)) = |\mathcal{S}| \tag{3}$$

Hence, we get:

$$|\mathcal{D}(C_i)| = |\mathcal{A}(C_i)| - 1, \forall C_i \in \mathcal{S} \tag{4}$$

Given the values of $|\mathcal{D}(C_i)|$ and $|\mathcal{A}(C_i)|$ for all the system caches, it is straightforward to map the communication graph used by our protocol over the cache system, leading to set up the cooperation architecture. It amounts to compute

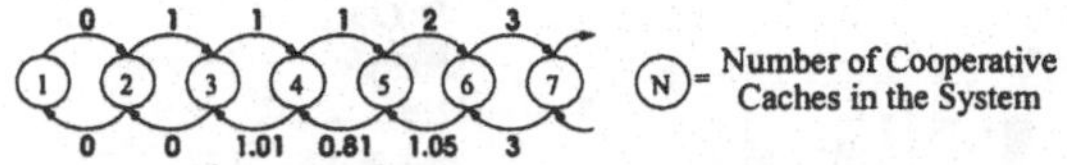

Fig. 8. Reconfiguration cost

an adjacency matrix such that the resulting boolean matrix has $|\mathcal{A}(C_i)|$ rows evaluating to true, $|\mathcal{D}(C_i)|$ lines evaluating to true, and $K(j, k)$ holds for any two caches C_j and C_k of $\mathcal{S}$. In other words, the matrix must contain $\binom{|\mathcal{S}|}{2} + |\mathcal{S}|$ elements evaluating to true with appropriate values for $|\mathcal{A}(C_i)|$ and $|\mathcal{D}(C_i)|$, $\forall C_i \in \mathcal{S}$. The matrix computation is based on a game algorithm using the branch and bound method: the algorithm searches an adjacency matrix with successive tests, and terminates when a valid matrix for our construction criteria is found.

Unlike traditional cache systems, our approach to transversal cooperation introduces an interdependency among caches. In particular, removal of a cache due to failure must be addressed. In general, addition or removal of a cache requires to update the cooperation architecture, which implies the exchange of cache states (i.e. lists corresponding to cache states) between some caches. To cope with this issue, we have designed a dynamic reconfiguration method minimizing the resulting network load. The reconfiguration method is computed by one of the cooperative caches, selected among alive caches. The proposed reconfiguration method subdivides into two algorithms that respectively deal with the addition and removal of a cache. The original cooperation architecture is given by the adjacency matrix of size $|\mathcal{S}|$. In the presence of a cache addition, the reconfiguration computes a valid adjacency matrix of size $(|\mathcal{S}| + 1)$ such that the number of cache states to be exchanged is minimal. The removal of a cache is handled according to the same principle. A valid adjacency matrix of size $(|\mathcal{S}| - 1)$ must be computed while minimizing the resulting network load. Figure 8 gives the average number of states (in the link's label) that are exchanged between caches to cope with the addition and removal of a cache, for a system composed of up to 7 caches. For instance, adding a cache to a system made of 4 caches requires to exchange a single cache state. The proposed evaluation shows that the bandwidth used for reconfiguration is negligible (if reconfigurations are rare), compared to the one used by the transversal system.

4.5 The Complete Protocol

The cooperation protocol resulting from the use of a fair distributed knowledge of the system state is depicted in Figure 9. When a cache C_i receives an object request, it checks whether the object is locally present (1). If so, the object is sent to the client. Otherwise, the object is sought within the lists corresponding to the

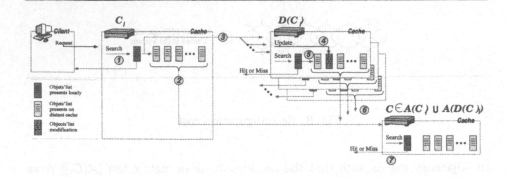

Fig. 9. The cooperation protocol

states of the caches belonging to $\mathcal{A}(C_i)$ (2). In parallel, a request for the object is sent to each cache of $\mathcal{D}(C_i)$ (3). A cache C_j receiving such a request updates the list corresponding to the state of C_i (4), i.e., C_j anticipates the presence of the object within C_i. C_j then searches for the object locally and within the state held for the caches belonging to $\mathcal{A}(C_j)$ (5). If the object is within C_j, C_j sends a hit to C_i while it sends a *miss* to C_i otherwise. Furthermore, for each cache C_k of $\mathcal{A}(C_l)$, $l \in \{i,j\}$, that has (supposedly) the object, C_l sends a request message to C_k (6). Then C_k either replies by a hit or a miss to C_i depending on whether the object is present or absent within the cache (7).

Note that the object retrieval latency in the worst case is now equal to the time taken by 5 message exchanges instead of 4 as discussed in Subsection 4.2. This results from our handling of cache update. The knowledge of the state of the caches in $\mathcal{A}(C_i)$ for any cache C_i is now an approximation of the cache's state. Thus, when a cache C_j of $\mathcal{D}(C_i)$ gets an object request from C_i, it cannot send a hit or a miss on behalf of the caches in $\mathcal{A}(C_j)$, to C_i. Instead, C_j sends a request message to these caches, which reply directly to C_i. The penalty of one message is negligible from the standpoint of latency since the time taken for message exchanges between sibling caches is in general far less than the one between a cache and the server.

For illustration of the proposed cooperation protocol, let us consider a system composed of 7 caches (see Figure 10). Each cache of the system must maintain the states of 3 caches (i.e. $|\mathcal{A}(C_i)| = 3$) and send requests to 2 caches (i.e. $|\mathcal{D}(C_i)| = 2$) to get knowledge of the whole system state. Let us now consider that there is a miss on cache C_1. Then, C_1 seeks the object within the lists it has for the states of C_5 and C_7 (i.e. $\mathcal{A}(C_1) = \{C_1, C_5, C_7\}$), and, in parallel, sends request messages to C_4 and C_2 (i.e. $\mathcal{D}(C_1) = \{C_4, C_2\}$). If C_1 believes the object is present within either C_5 or C_7, or both, C_1 sends a request message to C_5 and/or C_7. Upon the receipt of the request from C_1, C_i, $i \in \{2,4\}$, updates the

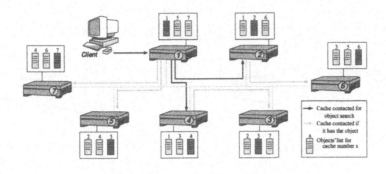

Fig. 10. An example with 7 caches

state of C_1 and seeks locally the object. Depending on the presence or absence of the object, C_i either sends a hit or a miss to C_1. In parallel with the local search, C_i seeks the object within the state held for caches of $\mathcal{A}(C_i)$ (*i.e.* cache C_6 for C_2, and cache C_3 for C_4). If the object is supposed to be within such a cache, a request message is sent to it and the cache will send a hit or a miss to C_1 depending on its actual local state.

4.6 Evaluation

This section proposes an evaluation of a transversal system integrating our cooperation protocol. We base our evaluation on a comparison with the ICP transversal cooperation protocol [26]. For both protocols, the replacement algorithm run by caches is the LRU algorithm. Our comparison falls in two steps: (*i*) comparison from the standpoint of algorithmic complexity, and (*ii*) comparison through simulation so as to show the benefit of our solution in terms of caching effectiveness.

Algorithmic Complexity: The ICP transversal cooperation protocol requires that a cache issues a request to all its siblings to get knowledge of the whole system state. Thus, the network load is $O(N)$ with N being the number of caches composing the system, *i.e.*, $N = |S|$. In the same way, the workload for each cache is $O(N)$ since each cache has to handle requests from its siblings, in addition to the requests received from its clients.

Let us consider a centralized system where one of the caches (say C_1) has a local knowledge of the whole system state for cooperation , *i.e.* $|\mathcal{A}(C_1)| = N = |S|$. With such a system, the workload for C_1 is $O(N\ Log(N) + N)$ and the network load is $O(1)$ (ignoring state update).

Finally, using our cooperation protocol, the network load is $O(\sqrt{N})$ since the number of requests that are issued to get a global knowledge is equal to

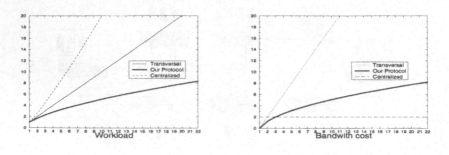

Fig. 11. System comparison in terms of complexity

$\sqrt{N - \frac{3}{4}} - \frac{1}{2}$ given the value set for $\mathcal{D}(C_i)$. Furthermore, the complexity for the workload is $O(\sqrt{N} \ Log(\sqrt{N}))$ since, upon an object request, $\sqrt{N}$ caches get contacted and each of them performs a search within $\sqrt{N}$ lists for a cost equal to $O(Log(\sqrt{N}))$.

In addition to the algorithmic complexity, we can evaluate the needs in memory size of the systems, for an optimal search time. The search time is optimal if all the lists maintained by a cache are in main memory (hence, avoiding disk accesses). Let us assume that each cache stores 400,000 objects, and that the length of an object identifier (URL) is 50 bytes, the memory consumption per list is equal to 20 MBytes. Thus, 40 MBytes per cache is required with 7 cooperative caches, 60 MBytes with 13 caches, and 200 MBytes with 111 caches. As a comparison, a centralized server, like CRISP [11], requires for the mapping server 140 MBytes with 7 cooperative caches, 260 MBytes with 13 caches and 2,220 MBytes with 111 caches.

For illustration purpose, Figure 11 gives the bandwidth (resp. workload) cost for each cooperation protocol, for systems whose number of caches ranges from 1 to 21. It can be noticed that for a system composed of 21 caches, 40 messages are exchanged to get knowledge of the whole system state when using the ICP cooperation protocol while only 8 messages are required with our protocol. In general, the efficiency of our solution is proportional to the square root of the number of caches composing the transversal system. Thus, our protocol significantly decreases the bandwidth and workload induced by transversal cooperation. In order to further validate our solution, we have run simulations so as to study the behavior of our system in a real environment.

Simulation: The proposed simulations were achieved using traces collected on a cache located at the Technical State University of Virginia [24]. These traces are representative of the WEB accesses performed by the 3 following groups of

University members: (*i*) students, (*ii*) professors, and (*iii*) students using a WEB browser during sessions of a class on multimedia. For our evaluation, we have used the traces corresponding to the accesses performed by the members of the first group. The number of computers used by this group were equal to 31, and traces were collected between April and October 1995, which gives traces over a 185-days period. During this period, 188,674 requests were sent by users and the total size of the objects that were transferred was equal to 2.26 GBytes. In order to evaluate the efficiency of our proposal, we have subdivided the traces of the single cache that were available into 6 sets of traces. This subdivision was done according to the IP number of client machines, and each set of traces was assigned to a virtual cache. Each virtual cache was further assigned a disk capacity equal to 10% of the capacity required to avoid cache replacement, giving a cache size of 30 MBytes. Let us remark that the number of cooperating caches is set to 6 caches due to the traces that we have been using. We are about to run experiment with the UCB traces that we used for evaluation of the replacement algorithms (see Section 3) so as to run simulations for 32 cooperating caches. Furthermore, this experiment will use our prototype that is under testing. Still concerning the evaluation of our protocol, the period for the emission of cache content for cache update (see Subsection 4.3), was set to a week (precisely, each Sunday at midnight). Finally, the simulations were run on a 100 MHz PC PENTIUM running the NT 4.0 operating system.

Two kinds of simulations were run: (*i*) one aims at comparing two transversal systems using respectively the protocol of ICP and ours, for a system composed of 6 caches, (*ii*) the other aims at comparing the two aforementioned cache systems from the standpoint of caching effectiveness, *i.e.* evaluating the hit rate of the two systems for the same bandwidth cost.

Evaluation for a fixed number of cooperating caches: Considering a fixed number of cooperating caches, the two transversal systems should *a priori* exhibit the same performances in terms of HR and WHR since both systems have the same storage capacity and their composing caches run the same replacement algorithm. However, one might envision that the management data required by our cooperation protocol alter the storage capacity of the overall system. Simulation results showed that our protocol does not incur such a penalty and hence both systems have similar performances, *i.e*, the HR and WHR were respectively equal to 30.93%, 18.92% for both systems under our simulations.

As shown in Table 5, the main difference between the two cache systems lies in the bandwidth consumption and workload overhead. For identical results in terms of HR, the base transversal system consumes a bandwidth that is 138 % higher than the bandwidth consumed by a system integrating our cooperation protocol[3]. Thus, it increases by 82 % the number of requests treated by each of the cooperative caches.

---

[3] This follows from the fact that a cache miss leads to send 5 request messages in the base system while only 2 are sent with our system.

System	Workload (mean per cache)	Bandwidth consumption (in number of messages)
Icp	22,700	211,330
Our protocol	12,474	88,424
Gain	-45.05%	-58.15%

Table 5. Caching effectiveness for a fixed number of cooperating caches

Evaluation for a fixed bandwidth cost: Let us now evaluate our system from the standpoint of caching effectiveness for a fixed bandwidth cost. This cost is given in terms of request messages exchanged among caches, which determines the maximal number of cooperating caches. If we set this cost to 4 messages, our protocol enables to have a single transversal system composed of 6 caches while the Icp protocol leads to have 2 transversal systems made of 3 caches. Let us further extend to a cache system, the criteria used for the evaluation of the effectiveness of a single cache (*i.e.*, HR and WHR). We get the following additional criteria for evaluation:

- The *Sibling Hit Rate* (SHR) that gives the percentage of objects sought by a cache that are present in the cache system.
- The *Sibling Weighted Hit Rate* (SWHR) that gives the percentage of bytes obtained by a cache from the cache system over the total number of bytes obtained from the network (*i.e.* the remote server and the set of siblings).
- The *Group Hit Rate* (GHR) that gives the percentage of requested objects that are present in the cache system,
- The *Group Weighted Hit Rate* (GWHR) that gives the percentage of bytes that are directly transferred from the cache system to the client (*i.e.* without contacting the server).

Simulation results showed that the efficiency of the cache system in terms of HR equals 30.93% in the absence of cooperation, 35.77% with transversal cooperation based on the Icp protocol, and 40.90% with transversal cooperation based on our protocol.

Table 6 further shows the complete results of the mean caching effectiveness for the two systems. In general, our simulation results about the efficiency of the cache systems showed that the system based on our protocol is in the average 2.12 times more efficient than the other system in terms of HR, and is 2.49 times more efficient in terms of WHR. Depending on the number of caches composing the system and the associated system configuration, the improvement gained by our cache system ranges from 82% to 132%. Let us notice that to get the proposed results, our system actually increases the bandwidth cost of at most 4%, which is due to the absence of update of the distributed system state on object removal.

	Workload	HR	WHR	SHR	SWHR	GHR	GWHR
Mean	ICP	12150	30.93%	18.92%	6.98%	4.97%	**35.77%**	**22.82%**
per	Our protocol	12474	30.93%	18.92%	14.56%	10.61%	**40.90%**	**27.37%**
cache	*Gain*	**2.66%**	0%	0%	112.44%	149.73%	**14.22%**	**21.41%**
Bandwidth consumption (in number of messages)							
ICP				84532			
Our protocol				88424			
Gain				**4.60%**			

Table 6. Caching effectiveness for a fixed bandwidth cost

The efficiency of our system is a direct consequence of the number of caches composing the transversal system. Even better results could be exhibited with a system composed of more caches. Unfortunately, the traces we have been using to run our experiment were not suited to run the evaluation of such transversal systems. Further experiment will thus be run with our prototype, which is currently under testing, based on the UCB traces. In particular, we will then be able to evaluate and compare the fetching delay associated to our protocol and to the one of ICP.

We are currently working on the enhancement of the cooperation protocol so as to cope with heterogeneous architectures of cooperating caches, including caches having different capacities. Another concern is to dynamically compute the cooperation graph underlying the proposed protocol. In particular, this would allow to couple caches that frequently share common objects.

5   Conclusion

WEB caching is an appealing low cost technique for improving the WEB latency. Caching effectiveness then depends upon the replacement algorithm that is used for cache management, which has to keep in the cache the objects that will be re-accessed. However, the effectiveness of a single cache is bounded by the percentage of objects that are actually re-accessed. One way to increase this percentage is either to have a larger storage capacity for caches or to have a set of cooperating caches. The latter solution is the most cost-effective, which has given rise to cooperation protocols for the WEB.

This paper has presented novel solutions for increasing caching effectiveness at the level of both a single cache and cooperating caches. We have introduced two novel replacement algorithms that performs better than existing ones from the standpoint of the resulting hit rate (HR), weighed hit rate (WHR), and response time for client requests (TIME) when considered as a whole. We further have proposed a new protocol for transversal cooperation among caches, which induces low network load, and low storage and processing overhead for caches, compared to alternative proposals. We have presented a performance evaluation of our solutions using simulation. We are currently testing a prototype, which integrates our replacement algorithms and cooperation protocol within the Squid software. We will then run experiment using this prototype so as to further assess the benefits of our solutions.

Our future work relates to devising a generic cache management strategy for WEB caches so as to adapt the strategy to the cache behavior. In particular, we believe that the effectiveness criterion that matters for a cache depends upon the type of the cache. If we consider a client cache, the most important criterion is TIME since the client is primarily interested in having a requested document in a short time interval. Let us now examine a network cache. From the standpoint of the provider, what matters is to save network bandwidth and to make documents available to clients in a timely manner. Thus, WHR and TIME should be optimized. Finally, regarding a server cache, it must minimize the accesses to the database server while responding in a timely manner. Hence, a server cache must optimize HR and TIME. Another factor of adaptation for cache management relates to caches that serve as both a server and a network cache. For such a cache, the management strategy must thus adapt to requests depending on whether they relate to network or server caching. We are currently designing a generic algorithm for WEB cache management, enabling adaptation of the strategy according to the aforementioned criteria.

References

1. G. Abdulla, M. Abrams, and E. A. Fox. Scaling the World Wide Web. IEEE. 1996.
2. M. Abrams, C. R. Standridge, G. Abdulla, S. Williams, and E. A. Fox. Caching Proxies: Limitations and Potentials. *Proceedings of the 4th International World-Wide Web Conference.* 1995.
3. M. Arlitt and C. Williamson. Web Server Workload Characterization : The Search for Invariants. *ACM SIGMETRICS Conference.* 1996.
4. A. Bestavros. Speculative Data Dissemination and Service to Reduce Server Load, Network Traffic, and Service Time for Distributed Information Systems. *Proceedings of the 1996 International Conference on Data Dissemination.* 1996.
5. B. Bloom. Space/time trade-offs in hash coding with allowable errors. *Communications of the ACM*, 13(7). July 1970.
6. J.-C. Bolot, S.M. Lamblot, and A. Simoniai. Design of efficient schemes for the World Wide Web. *Proceedings of ITC 15.* 1997.
7. A. Chantkuthod, P. B. Danzig, C.Neerdaels, M. F. Schwartz and K. J. Worrell. *A Hierarchical Internet Object Cache.* Technical Report 95-611-University of Southern California, Boulder, California, USA. 1996.
8. P. Danzig, R. S. Hall and M. F. Schwartz. A Case for Caching File Object Inside Internetworks. *Proceedings of ACM Sigcomm'93.* 1993.
9. L. Fan, P. Cao , J. Almeida, and A. Broder. Summary Cache : A Scalable Wide-Area Web Cache Sharing Protocol. *Computer Communication Review, a publication of ACM SIGCOMM*, 28(4). October 1998.

10. S. Gadde, J. Chase and M. Rabinovich. *Directory Structures for Scalable Internet Caches.* Technical Report CS-1997-18-Duke University, Durham, North Carolina, USA. November 1997.
11. S.Gadde, M.Rabinovich, and J. Chase. Reduce, Reuse, Recycle: An Approach to Building Large Internet Caches. *Proceedings of the Sixth Workshop on Hot Topics in Operating Systems (HotOS-VI).* 1997.
12. S. Gribble and E. Brewer. *UCB home IP HTTP traces.* Available at http://www.-cs.berkeley/gribble/traces/index.html. June 1997.
13. E. D. Katz, M. Butler et R. McGrath - A Stable HTTP Server : The NCSA prototype. *Computer Networks and ISDN Systems,* 27. 1994.
14. T. Kwan, R. McGrath and D. Reed. NCSA's World Wide Web Server : Design and Performance. *IEEE Computer.* 1995.
15. R. Malpani, J. Lorch, and D. Berger. Making World Wide Web Caching Servers Co-operate. *Proceedings of the 4th International World-Wide Web Conference.* 1995.
16. J-M. Menaud, V. Issarny, and M. Banatre. A New Protocol for Efficient Transversal Web Caching. *Proceedings of DISC'98 (Formerly WDAG) - 12th International Symposium on Distributed Computing.* 1998.
17. A. Menezes, P. Van Oorschot, and S. Vanstone. Handbook of Applied Cryptography. *CRC Press.* 1997.
18. J. C. Mogul. Hinted Caching in the Web. *Proceedings of the 7th ACM SIGOPS European Workshop.* 1996.
19. V. N. Padmanabhan and J. C. Mogul. Using Predictive Prefetching to Improve World Wide Web Latency. *SIGCOMM Newsletter.* 1996.
20. G. Pierre and M. Makpangou. Saperlipopette!: A Distributed Web Caching Systems Evaluation Tool. *Proceedings of Middleware'98.* 1998.
21. D. Povey and J. Harrison. A Distributed Internet Cache. *Proceedings of the 20th Australian Computer Science Conference.* 1997.
22. The Relais Group. *Relais: Cooperative Caches for the World Wide Web.* Available at http ://www-sor.inria.fr/projects/relais. 1998.
23. D. Steere and M. Satyanarayanan. Using Dynamic Sets to Overcome High I/O Latencies during Search. *Proceedings of the 5th Workshop on Hot Operating System Topics.* 1995.
24. *Trace Files of WWW Traffic.* Available at http://www.cs.vt.edu/~chitra/www.html.
25. D. Wessels. Configuring Hierarchical Squid Caches. Available at http://squid.nlanr.net/ Squid/Hierarchy-Tutorial. 1997.
26. D. Wessels and K. Claffy. *Internet Cache Protocol (ICP), version 2.* National Laboratory for Applied Network Research/UCSD. September 1997.
27. S. Williams, M. Abrams, C. R. Standridge, G. Abdulla, and E. A. Fox. Removal policies in network caches for World Wide Web documents. *Proceedings of ACM Sigcomm'96.* 1996.
28. R. Wooster and Abrams M. *Caching that Estimates Page Load Delay.* Network Research Group, Virginia Tech Blackburg, Available at http ://www.cs.vt.edu/ chitra/docs/www6r. 1996.

Mobility and Coordination for Distributed Java Applications

Paolo Ciancarini, Andrea Giovannini, and Davide Rossi

Dept. of Computer Science, University of Bologna,
Mura Anteo Zamboni, 7 - 40127 Bologna, Italy
{cianca,rossi}@CS.UniBO.IT

Abstract. A mobile agent is a piece of code which can move among the nodes of a network of computers, looking for data and services. There are currently several programming languages and systems to develop applications including mobile agents. They are widely different, and it is not easy to understand *how* they differ. We propose a taxonomy classifying different kinds of mobile entities according to how they can move and how they can interact with their environment.

We then introduce Macondo, a platform for mobile agents including interaction primitives based on coordination technology. In fact, Macondo is based on MJada: a coordination tool for Java extended to deal with agent mobility. We use our taxonomy of mobility to compare Macondo with other well known systems to program mobile agents.

1 Introduction

When a new technology is introduced, the invention of a clear taxonomy to understand and distinguish the available paradigms and technologies is fundamental for its wide acceptance. This is the case of the new technology of languages for programming *mobile agents* [1,2]. There are currently several languages and systems allowing to develop mobile agents. They are widely different, however it is not easy to understand *how* they differ. A paper that contains a taxonomy for systems based on mobile code is [3]. Such a taxonomy includes three categories only: remote evaluation, code on demand, and agent mobility. In *remote evaluation* a requester sends some code to a service provider, which executes the code and returns the result to the requester. In *code on demand*, a requester asks for some code to a code provider, which returns the code to the requester. In *agent mobility*, a computing entity including both code and some computational state moves from a computational environment to another one, where it activates again.

Here we propose a new programming language for agent mobility. In order to show its originality with respect to some existing platforms for programming mobile agents, we define a novel taxonomy, finer-grained than the one described above, and that is able to classify different kinds of mobile entities and the related programming language support. In fact, different programming languages for mobile agents offer mobility primitives acting on different kind of entities [1].

S. Krakowiak, S.K. Shrivastava (Eds.): Distributed Systems, LNCS 1752, pp. 402–425, 2000.
© Springer-Verlag Berlin Heidelberg 2000

For instance, standard Java applet code mobility is different from agent mobility as defined in Aglets [4].

We propose the following taxonomy for mobile entities.

- **mobile data**: data is usually mobile in client-server architectures; for instance, when a WWW browser downloads an HTML page from a server, this is mobility of data, since HTML is not Turing-equivalent; interestingly, data mobility is analogous to passage by value in conventional programming languages.
- **mobile reference**: using a WWW browser the user can "move" to a different WWW page or to a different directory. In this case what moves is just a reference to a WWW resource, like an HTML document or a directory. Another example is the name of a communication channel passed from a process to another process. In fact, a reference can also be seen as the endpoint of a communication channel: this kind of mobility is expressed by the π-calculus [5]. This kind of mobility is analogous to passage by reference in conventional programming languages.
- **mobile code**: when a WWW browser downloads a Java object from a server, this is mobility of code. Java applets are the most known example of mobile code applications. Their main advantage is the possibility to build a dynamic environment where code is downloaded on demand, without having to preinstall it.
- **mobile code and store**: in this case the mobile entity consists of both code and store; we include in the store the value of variables and, possibly, also a code entry point (what is usually called the *state* of an object). This is the form of mobility offered by most Java mobile agent systems.
- **mobile closure**: a *closure* is the complete run time description of a computation, made of code representation and a mapping between language identifiers and resource values. If an identifier refers to a network resource and the corresponding closure is moved, then the connection is maintained during migration. Obliq [6] is a language that supports closure migration.
- **mobile code, store, and execution state**: this happens when it is possible to move both the store and the complete scheduling state of the entity, including all threads. This will be an important feature in distributed systems where migration has to be transparent to the execution of an entity, for instance in load balancing systems. This form of mobility is called *strong*; this technology is used in Telescript [7].
- **mobile ambient**: in [8] Cardelli and Gordon propose a new process algebra, namely the *ambient calculus*, in order to describe in a uniform way mobile agents, their interaction environments, and their mobility. For instance, it is possible to model the transfer of a set of running programs, called an *ambient*, from a personal computer to a laptop, that is, from a container ambient to another one [9]. In the same way we can express the mobility of the laptop ambient. A similar kind of mobility is available in the language Bauhaus [10].

Mobile agents systems can also offer different kinds of linguistic support for controlling mobility, namely to define the itinerary that an agent has to travel. An *itinerary* consists of a sequence of *locations* which an agent travel through. For instance, traveller agents are useful to design workflow applications because they can represent "active documents" following some given workflow [3].

We have devised the following classification to distinguish among three levels of mobility control:

- **planned mobility**: the agent itinerary is statically predefined. The agent can have a single entry point or multiple entry points bound to each location to visit. A planned itinerary can be fixed or dynamically mutable. When it is fixed the itinerary to trave is represented by a list of locations; when it is mutable it is a tree of locations. In both forms, using itineraries can decouple application specific code from mobility code;

- **spontaneous mobility**: the agent itinerary is not statically predefined, but computed at run-time. The most known example of spontaneous mobility is the go() instruction in Telescript. Using iteratively spontaneous mobility primitives is different from following a planned itinerary, because it is impossible to pre-determine the sequence of locations where the agent will move, since it can decide to migrate to a new location at runtime. Spontaneous mobility is useful when an agent must cope with unavailability of resources. For instance, if the current location of an agent is heavily loaded then it can autonomously decide to migrate to a new location with a lighter workload to get better services;

- **controllable mobility**: The agent migration is forced by an authority in some location, using some I/O mechanisms to communicate with a remote agent. By authority we mean either the "owner" (or creator) of a mobile agent, which for instance could be interested in some partial result, or a "host", which could be interested in hosting a mobile agent. This means that there are two types of controllable mobility: sender-controlled and receiver-controlled mobility. In the first case the agent is sent to a location different from the authority's location, as in the case of a shopping agent sent by a user in locations containing items to buy. In case of receiver-controlled mobility the agent is "called" in the authority's location, as in the case of an applet requested by a browser.

In this paper we introduce a platform for programming mobility of code and store in Java. Such a platform, that we call Macondo, is based on a coordination language extended to deal with agent migration. We use the above taxonomy of mobility to compare Macondo with other well known systems to program mobile agents.

This paper is organized as follows: Section 3 presents Macondo; Section 4 outlines a simple application; Section 2 gives an overview of the most important Java-based mobile agent systems, presenting also a comparison with Macondo; finally, Section 5 concludes the paper outlining our future work.

2   Mobile Agents Platforms

There are several platforms to program mobile agents in Java. In this section we give an overview of the main Java-based platforms available, namely Concordia, Aglets, Voyager, Odyssey, and Mole. We compare these tools with Macondo, focusing on their primitives for mobility and interaction among agents.

2.1   Overview of Existing Systems

Concordia Concordia is a framework for mobile Java agents developed by Mitsubishi [11].

A Concordia agent can move itself only by an itinerary, which is a sequence of pairs (location, method), where at each location is executed the corresponding method. This way application code is completely decoupled from mobility issues, but we think that in some situations the availability of a Telescript-like go() method could be very useful.

Interaction between Concordia agents is supported by asynchronous distributed events and collaboration. While events provide a mean for agents to communicate in a flexible manner, the collaboration framework enables collaborative activities between agents. For a collaboration to take place it is needed a collaboration point, that is a distributed Java object, which provide a method called by other agents. Then the object collects partial results submitted by agents and compute the collective result. Finally, this result is communicated to all the other agents via another method call. We think that this framework is not sufficiently adequate in order to deal with complex coordination patterns.

Run time support for Concordia agents relies on Conduit Servers. Each server is then built upon several component, called *manager*, that handle agent mobility, security, communication and persistence.

Now an example of a Concordia agent follows. It can be seen that mobility is expressed using an itinerary. The itinerary is kept separated from the agent, leading to a clean separation between agent application code and mobility primitives.

```
public class myAgent extends Agent {
    // some data

    public myAgent() {
        // initialize data
    }

    public void method1() {
        ...
    }
```

```
    public void method2() {
        ...
    }

    public void method3() {
        ...
    }
}
```

Agent initialization is managed in the following code, together with agent itinerary and information about auxiliary classes.

```
public class TestLaunch {
    public static void main(String args[]) {
        myAgent agent = new myAgent();
        Itinerary itinerary = new Itinerary();
        itinerary.addDestination(new Destination("host1",
            "method1"));
        itinerary.addDestination(new Destination("host2",
            "method2"));
        itinerary.addDestination(new Destination("host3",
            "method3"));
        String agentsCodebase = ...;
        String relatedClasses[ ] = {...};
        BootStrap.launchAgent(agent, itinerary,
            agentsCodebase, relatedClasses);
    }
}
```

More information on Concordia is available at:
http://www.meitca.com/HSL/Projects/Concordia.

Aglets IBM's Aglets Workbench is one of the first and most known projects on mobile Java agents [4]. The main design goal was to develop a programming model for mobile agents mirrored from Java applets.

The Aglets API is mainly based upon the concepts of aglet, proxy, context, and message. An *aglet* is an autonomous mobile Java object which can move between different hosts. A *proxy* is used to refer to an aglet, in order to protect the aglet itself from indiscriminate accesses and to provide location independence. A *context* is the execution environment of aglets and can protect hosts from malicious aglets. A *message* is an object used for communications between aglets. It can be used for synchronous and asynchronous communication. Multicast is also supported via message subscribing.

The life cycle of an aglet is defined by a sequence of well defined events, that are creation, cloning, dispatching, retraction, activation, deactivation, disposal, and messaging. An aglet can react to these events via methods that can be overridden by the programmer, leading to a great flexibility. However, the programmer has to deal with all complexities introduced by events.

The Aglet communication mechanism is simple and flexible, but for some applications which require complex coordination among agents it is quite limited.

The following example shows the source code of an aglet which moves between several hosts using an itinerary. It can be seen that an aglet supports only a single entry point. This is a limitation, not present for instance in Concordia, that forces the usage of a multiple-choice statement in order to determine the method to execute in each location.

```
public class myAgent extends Aglet {
    // some data

    public myAgent() {
    }

    public void method1() {
        ...
    }

    public void method2() {
        ...
    }

    public void method3() {
        ...
    }

    SeqPlanItinerary itinerary;

    public void onCreation(Object init) {
        itinerary = new SeqPlanItinerary(this);
        itinerary.addPlan("atp://host1", "method1");
        itinerary.addPlan("atp://host2", "method2");
        itinerary.addPlan("atp://host3", "method3");
        itinerary.startTrip();
    }

    public boolean handleMessage(Message msg) {
        if (itinerary.handleMessage(msg)) {
            // itinerary has handled the message
            return true;
        } else if (msg.sameKind("method1")) {
            method1();
            return true;
        } else if (msg.sameKind("method2")) {
```

```
            method2();
            return true;
        } else if (msg.sameKind("method3")) {
            method3();
            dispose();
        } else return false;
        return true;
    }
}
```

More information on Aglets is available at:
http://www.ibm.co.jp/trl/aglets.

Voyager Voyager is an Object Request Broker which supports mobile agents. The recently added CORBA support and the planned DCOM interoperability make Voyager a powerful platform for distributed computing.

The Voyager distributed object oriented model is based on interfaces, as in Java RMI. Remote methods of an object are thus grouped in one or more Java interfaces. Automatic generation of interfaces is supported using an utility.

One of the main features of Voyager agents is that the target of a migration can be a program but also a Java object. The migrating object can thus move to the destination, obtaining a reference to the target object and then starting local direct communication with the object.

Voyager allows also to invoke a method on a moving object. In order to achieve it, an agent leaves a *forwarder* in each location touched. An invocation directed to an obsolete location will be transparently forwarded to the new location of the agent. Subsequent invocation will refer to the new location.

Another interesting feature of Voyager is that the moveTo() method, used for migration, can specify a method to be invoked on the agent at destination. This way an agent can have multiple entry point. Itineraries are not supported in Voyager.

Voyager communication is based on different flavors of remote method invocations, namely synchronous, oneway, future (asynchronous), oneway multicast and publish/subscribe invocations.

While communication support in Voyager is very powerful and flexible, we think that this approach is limited in open distributed systems. In such systems it is impossible to know in advance the interface of an agent, while this is required in order to support direct communication.

```
public class myAgent extends Agent implements ImyAgent{

    // list of destinations to visit
    Vector itinerary = new Vector();

    // index of current destination
    int     index = 0;
```

```
public void addToItinerary(String address) {
    itinerary.addElement( address );
}

public void launch() {
    next();
}

private void next() {
    if( index < itinerary.size() ) {
        Address destination =
            (Address)itinerary.elementAt(index++);

        try {
            if (index == 0) {
                moveTo(destination, "method1");
            } else if (index == 1) {
                moveTo(destination, "method2");
            } else if (index == 2) {
                moveTo(destination, "method3");
            }
        } catch(VoyagerException exception) {
            ...
        }
    }
}

public void method1() {
    ...
}

public void method2() {
    ...
}

public void method3() {
    ...
}
}
```

The ImyAgent interface source code is omitted, since it simply contains agent public methods signature.

```
public class TestLaunch {
    public static void main(String[] args) {
        try {
```

```
        ImyAgent agent = (ImyAgent)Voyager.construct(
            "myAgent","localhost/Fred");
        agent.addToItinerary("host1");
        agent.addToItinerary("host2");
        agent.addToItinerary("host3");
        agent.launch(); // send the agent on its way

        Voyager.shutdown();
    } catch( VoyagerException exception ) {
        System.err.println( exception );
    }
  }
}
```

More information on Voyager are available at:
http://www.objectspace.com/voyager.

Odyssey General Magic was the first company working on mobile agents with the Telescript language. Because of the fact that Telescript was a proprietary language and the success of Java, General Magic decided to develop Odyssey, a mobile Java agents system based on the concepts of Telescript.

An Odyssey system is based on agents and places. Agents can move between places using a go() method or itineraries. Differently from other systems places have also to be implemented, leading to very flexible systems.

Agents communicate with other agents and places using local method invocation. It is also possible to exchange object references inside a place, but the mechanism does not provide any synchronization between participants.

An interesting feature of the Odyssey run time system is the support for multiple transport mechanism. The standard one provided is Java RMI but are also supported Microsoft DCOM and CORBA IIOP.

Odyssey is a very well designed tool but suffers the lack of more sophisticated communication and coordination mechanism.

For instance, the example of an Odyssey agent follows. The Odyssey Worker class represents an agent which uses an itinerary in order to move.

```
public class myAgent extends Worker {

    public myAgent(Task[] itinerary)
            throws OccupancyDeniedException {
        super(itinerary);
        ...
    }

    public void method1() {
        ...
    }
```

```
    public void method2() {
        ...
    }

    public void method3() {
        ...
    }

}
```

Agent launch and itinerary initialization are managed by the following program.

```
public class TestLaunch {
    public static void main(String[] args) {
        Task itinerary = new Task[3];

        itinerary[0] = new Task("host1", "method1");
        itinerary[1] = new Task("host2", "method2");
        itinerary[2] = new Task("host3", "method3");

        try {
            new myAgent(itinerary).start();
        } catch (OccupancyDeniedException.exc) {
            // agent is refused
            . . .
        }
    }
}
```

As in Concordia it is possible to specify a direct mapping between destinations and agent entry points.

More information on Odyssey are available at:
http://www.genmagic.com/html/agent_overview.html.

Mole Mole is a mobile agents system developed at University of Stuttgart [12]. Mole supports two kind of agents: mobile agents and system agents. While mobile agents migrate between different hosts, system agents are stationary and represent the interface with the services provided by hosts.

Mobile Mole agents do not support itineraries and can have only a single entry point, like Aglets.

Communication between agents takes place exchanging message objects. Two kind of messages are provided, Message and RPCMessage, where the latter is used to simulate remote method invocation. Services offered by system agents can be registered on a shared dictionary, then looked up by other agents.

Other interesting features of Mole are orphan detection, that is a mechanism used to detect and remove agents from the systems, and an original code migration architecture. Mole authors are also currently working on agent groups, security and transaction semantics for mobile agents.

Like the other systems presented, Mole does not currently provide any advanced support for agent coordination.

The following example shows a Mole agent.

```
public class myAgent extends UserAgent {

    LocationName[] itinerary = {
        new LocationName("host1"),
        new LocationName("host2"),
        new LocationName("host3")};

    int index = 0;    // index of current destination

    public myAgent() {
        ...
    }

    public void start() {
        ...

        if (index == 0) {
            migrateTo(itinerary[index++]);
        } else if (index == 1) {
            method1();
            migrateTo(itinerary[index++]);
        } else if (index == 2) {
            method2();
            migrateTo(itinerary[index++]);
        } else if (index == 3) {
            method3();
        }
    }

    public void method1() {
        ...
    }

    public void method2() {
        ...
    }
```

```
public void method3() {
    ...
}
```
}

Since Mole agents don't support neither itineraries nor multiple entry points, the previous code is more complicated than, for example, Odyssey agents' source code.

More information about Mole are available at: http://www.informatik.uni-stuttgart.de/ipvr/vs/projekte/mole.html.

3   Introducing Macondo

Macondo is a framework for distributed computing in Java, based on mobile agents and coordination technology. Several existing tools for mobile agents in Java provide *ad hoc* communication and collaboration mechanisms for the agents. The main feature of Macondo is that the mobile agents support is completely decoupled from the coordination support. The latter is provided by MJada, a powerful Linda-like coordination language. MJada can be used in coordinating multiple concurrent threads in the same program or different distributed Java programs, like applets and Macondo agents.

3.1   Mobile Agents in Macondo

The main design goals for mobile agents support in Macondo are simplicity and flexibility. The agent model we adopted is based on two concepts, namely *agents* and *places*.

Agents are autonomous programs that move themselves to different places in order to perform their proper tasks. Agents are created by extending Macondo `Agent` and `Traveller` classes. A `Traveller` agent extends `Agent` to define an *itinerary*, that is a sequence of mappings between locations and tasks.

Execution environments for agents are represented by `Place` objects. A `Place` can be used as a stand alone server or can be extended by the programmer in order to provide more advanced services.

Now we present a simple example of a mobile agent in Macondo.

```
import macondo.mak.*;

public class MyAgent extends Agent {

    public MyAgent() {
        // . . .
    }

    // this is executed at destination:8000
```

```
public void work() {
    // do some work . . .
}

public void init() {
    // do some initialization
    // . . .

    // then go working at destination:8000
    try {
        go("destination", 8000, "work");
        // this is never reached
    } catch (Exception e) {
        e.printStackTrace();
    }
}
}
```

A key method of the Agent class is go(), which when invoked moves the agent in a different place, specified by *host name* and *port number*. The last argument is the name of the method invoked when the agent arrives at the destination place. In this way we can provide multiple entry points into an agent, differently from other systems, like Aglets and Mole, which support only a single entry point into an agent.

The go() method is a spontaneous mobility primitive. The init() method is called when the Macondo run time system executes the agent.

The following source code example shows a Traveller agent and the use of itineraries for planned mobility in Macondo.

```
public class myTraveller extends Traveller {
    ...

    // this code is executed at host1:8000
    public void a() {
        ...
    }

    // this code is executed at host2:9000
    public void b() {
        ...
    }

    // this code is executed at host3:8000
    public void c() {
        ...
    }
```

```
public void init() {
    Itinerary i = new Itinerary();
    i.add(host1,8000,"a");
    i.add(host2,9000,"b");
    i.add(host3,8000,"c");
    setItinerary(i);

    // start moving
    doTrip();
}
}
```

The main advantage of itineraries is the decoupling between application code and mobility primitives, which leads to a cleaner coding style.

We remark the simplicity of agent programming in Macondo and the flexibility offered by the go() method and itineraries, provided by the Traveller class.

3.2   Coordination in Macondo

Coordination technology is an effective solution for developing applications in open distributed systems. In this section we present MJada, a language based on Java which includes mechanisms for mobility and for coordination.

MJada is itself an extension of Jada, a coordination language [13] that has been used as a coordination kernel in the context of the UE Open LTR PageSpace project [14]. Jada introduces Linda-like coordination in Java. Jada is realized as a set of Java classes and is not based on the use of a preprocessor, like other Linda-based implementations. This has the advantage of allowing programmers using Jada to continue to refer to the standard Java object-oriented programming model. As in Linda, interactions among agents are based upon the exchange of tuples in a tuple space.

MJada adds to Jada the support for coordination among mobile agents. The MJada coordination medium is the tuple space, like in Linda. However, Linda uses only one tuple space, although physically distributed. Instead, MJada supports *multiple nested tuple spaces*, which form a hierarchical coordination structure based on the TupleSpace object. Hence a TupleSpace offers some "navigation" methods that allow a thread or an agent to navigate the coordination structure, expressing itineraries as sequences of names similar to UNIX file system names. Names are expressed by paths, so both "/space" and "/chapter/section" are valid names. A TupleSpace object can be created with

```
TupleSpace tuple_space = new TupleSpace();
```

An agent can connect a tuple space with the join() method. For instance, after the following statement

```
tuple_space.join("space1");
```

all operations on tuple_space will be relative to the tuple space called *space1*.

Tuple space names can be specified as relative paths but also as absolute paths. For instance, if the current tuple space is "/working_space" and join is called with argument "/games_space", then following operations are performed on space "/games_space". It is also possible moving to the encompassing space specifying ".." as the join() argument. Finally, a name can have multiple items like "space2/space3". For flexibility additional methods are provided to move to the encompassing tuple space, leave(), or to the root tuple space, leaveAll().

A tuple is represented by the Tuple class and contains a set of Java objects. We can create a tuple as follows:

```
Tuple tuple = new Tuple("Hello!", new Integer(1));
```

Tuples can be inserted in a tuple space with the out() method.

```
tuple_space.out(tuple);
```

Tuples are retrieved from a tuple space using an associative mechanism: when an agent calls the in method it has to pass it a tuple that is used as a matching pattern. The in method returns a tuple (if any) that matches the given pattern (the same applies to the read method; the difference between read and in is that in removes the returned tuple from the tuple space).

In order to have flexible matching operations we introduce the concepts of *formal* and *actual* tuple items: a *formal item* is an instance of the Class class (the meta-class used in Java). Any other object is an *actual item*.

Two tuples match if they include the same number of items and each item of the first tuple matches the corresponding item of the second tuple.

For instance, the following is a template tuple with an actual field of class String and a formal field of class Class

```
Tuple template = new Tuple("Hello!", new Integer(0).getClass());
```

This tuple matches both:

```
Tuple alpha = new Tuple("Hello!", new Integer(3));
Tuple beta = new Tuple("Hello!", new Integer(7));
```

Tuples can be read or withdrawn from a space using the following methods

- Result read(Tuple formal)
- Result in(Tuple formal)

Differently from Linda, disruptive MJada operations do not return a result tuple, but a placeholder for that tuple represented by the Result class. The placeholder can then be used to test result availability, to fetch a result or to kill the request. Trying to fetch a tuple that is not available will block the calling thread, resulting in the same coordination mechanism used in Linda.

Tuple spaces in MJada can either be "local", namely shared among concurrent threads running in the same Java Virtual Machine, or "remote", namely running on a (possibly) remote host and accessed via an ad-hoc proxy class in a way that is similar to the one used by RMI.

The main feature of MJava to support mobile agents coordination is the ability of transparently abort and resend a request for a pending **in** or **read** operation among migrations. Thus, if an agent performs:

```
Result result=remote_tuple_space.In(my_tuple);
```

and the requested tuple is not available at call time, it can migrate to another place and the **result** object will still refer to a valid **in** operation performed on the remote tuple space.

MJada provides also multiple-result operations that allow one to read or withdrawn all tuples that match a given template.

- **Enumeration readAll(Tuple formal)**
- **Enumeration inAll(Tuple formal)**

Result tuples can then be fetched using Java enumerations. Linda does not have any similar operation.

In addition to the previous basic tuple operations Jada introduces a new coordinative computing framework based on tuple *collections*. A tuple collection, represented by the **TupleCollection** class, defines a sequence of tuples having the same signature. In order to build a tuple collection we write

```
TupleSpace space = new TupleSpace();
Tuple pattern = new Tuple(new String().getClass(),
    new Integer.getClass());
TupleCollection tc = new TupleCollection(space, pattern);
```

where **space** is the tuple space where collected tuples reside and **pattern** is a tuple which define the tuples' signature. Tuples can be inserted in a collection using the **add()** method

```
tc.add(new Tuple("Hello!", new Integer(1)));
```

If the specified tuple has a signature different from the collected one, an exception is thrown. The main feature of collections is that tuples can be read or withdrawn in the same order they were inserted with *iterator* objects. Two predefined iterators are provided, **ReadIterator** and **InIterator**, but more advanced iterators can be added to the framework, provided that they implements the **nextTuple()** method. For instance, the following code reads all tuples from the previous collection

```
TupleIterator iterator = tc.readIterator();
Tuple result;
```

```
while( ... ) {
    // get next tuple in this collection
    result = iterator.nextTuple();

    // use tuple items
    ...
}
```

Tuple collections and iterators capture a recurrent pattern of coordinative programming, that is consuming a sequence of tuples, and simplify noticeably the source code.

Iterators are not built using a constructor, but with a *factory* method of the TupleCollection class. The main advantage is the possibility to develop extended collection classes which use the same factory method to create iterators.

Iterators are also a well known *design pattern* [15] used to encapsulate access and traversal logic of an object container. Thus different iterators implements different access policies, leading to an improved design of the system.

The main feature of ReadIterator and InIterator is that the nextTuple() method is blocking. This way we can define an iterator that reads all tuples already inserted in the collection, but also all tuples that will be inserted in the future. The same result is obtained in other coordination languages like for instance Linda using an index as a tuple field; iterators offer a more elegant solution.

3.3 Relating Mobility and Coordination

An agent can use a remote MJada tuple space with a client/server architecture. The SpaceServer class represents a remote TupleSpace, whereas the SpaceClient class allows one to interact with such servers.

In figure 1 we show an abstraction of the Macondo runtime.

The runtime software architecture includes two kinds of servers:

- an *agent server* (rounded box) is a host for agents (circles); an agent can move from an agent server to another agent server.
- a *tuple space server* (ellipse) is a container of nested tuple spaces; agents can manipulate tuple spaces to communicate using Macondo.

In the picture we see three agent servers with some agents and two tuple space servers with some tuple spaces.

The servers are completely uncoupled: the same hosting JVM can run any number of agent servers and/or tuple space servers.

The picture shows the uncoupling of the mobility infrastructure from the coordination infrastructure. An agent can travel through agent servers, keeping a connection to a tuple space server. Its itinerary can be "planned", meaning that it visits a predefined list of servers. Its itinerary can be "spontaneous" (namely implementing *subjective mobility*, a term suggested by Cardelli), meaning that

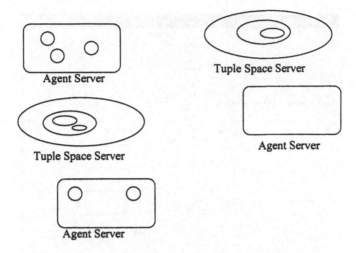

Fig. 1. Software Architecture of Macondo

it computes at runtime the next server to visit. Its itinerary can be "controllable" (implementing *objective mobility*), meaning that an authority controls its itinerary at runtime using a tuple space to communicate with the agent.

Using our taxonomy, we see that the current version of Macondo combines code+store mobility plus closure mobility, because an agent can keep a reference to a tuple space even after moving. Interestingly, such a picture suggests what we need to implement more complex mobility styles in Macondo. If we could move an agent server from a JVM to another JVM, this would be a case of code+store+execution state mobility. Finally, if we could move a tuple space from a server to another one transparently with respect to all connected agents this would be a case of ambient mobility.

4   A Case Study for Macondo

An application field where mobile agents and coordination technology are especially effective is groupware. In order to show a meaningful programming example in this section we will describe a Meeting Scheduler system, a simple groupware application that assists several users in scheduling a meeting.

A meeting initiator proposes a range of dates for holding the meeting to potential participants. The "advertising" for the meeting is done using traditional systems, like e-mail or WWW. The initiator also specifies a host where a service called *Meeting Scheduler Place* is running. Such a service will hosts agents involved in the meeting scheduling process. The figure 2 shows the interface used by the meeting initiator to set up the service Meeting Scheduler Place: she has to insert the number of expected participants and a range of dates for meeting definition.

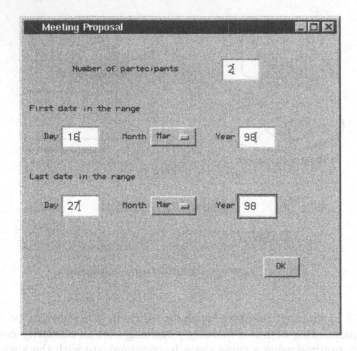

Fig. 2. The GUI used to set up the Meeting Scheduler system

The system provides two kinds of agents, namely the *scheduler* agent and the *participant* agent. Participant agents are set up by users invited to a meeting with their preferences; then they migrate to the host specified by the meeting initiator.

Preferences are typed in using the interface shown in figure 3. Each user can specify

1. a set of preferred date for the meeting to take place, marked with white circles in the interface;
2. a set of dates on which the meeting could not be attended, marked with red circlesl;
3. a set of dates on which the meeting could be attended if necessary, marked with pink circles;

The first set of dates constitutes the *preference set*, while the others form the *exclusion set*.

In order to enhance the flexibility of the system a user can also specify that, if a conflict occurs, its agent can reduce automatically the exclusion set removing dates in (3) or it can extend the preference set with all dates not belonging to the exclusion set.

The scheduler agent resides in the Meeting Scheduler Place and performs the real scheduling task, asking other agents for preferred and excluded dates and managing conflicts when they arise. In figure 4 the architecture of the system is shown.

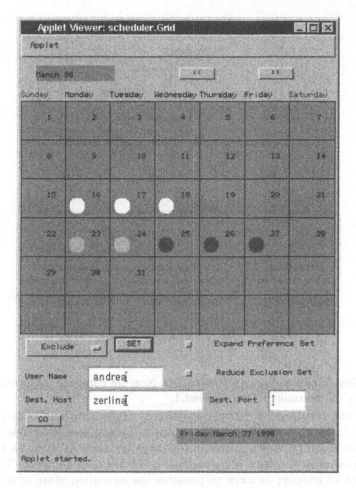

Fig. 3. The GUI used by participants to initialize agents with their preferences

Agent mobility and coordination are heavily exploited in the Meeting Scheduler system. Mobility lets participant agents migrate to a common place in order to engage high bandwidth communication. Using agents it also possible to solve issues of wide distribution of users. Complex interactions for scheduling take place using the coordination facilities of MJada.

A main advantage of Macondo is its flexibility for rapid application development. For instance, the Meeting Scheduler system has been easily extended from a single-meeting prototype to a version supporting multiple meetings, where a participant agent migrates to different places in order to schedule different meetings. The system can also support new kind of agents, as long as they follow the defined coordination protocol for the scheduling activity. This is an intrinsic feature of the generative communication used in MJada.

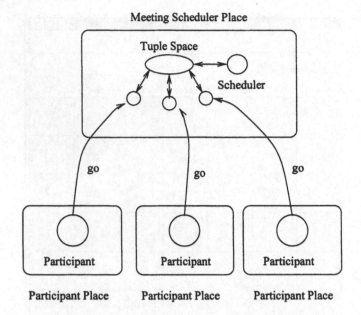

Fig. 4. The Meeting Scheduler system

Comparing Mobile Agents Platforms Now we compare the presented systems using the taxonomy given in Sect.1.

Regarding the kind of entity transmitted, single data and code migration are trivial in Java. Navigation inside multiple tuple spaces in MJada is a form of reference mobility, which misses in the other systems. All systems allows the migration of code, the *behaviour*, and store, the *state*, of an agent. This is due to the lack of support in Java to preserve the execution state of a program. Closure migration is also unavailable in Java systems since the language doesn't allow to define code block closures. None of the presented systems support the migration of interaction and execution ambients of agents. Its implementation in MJada would require the migration of Place objects, properly restarting the agents contained, and MJada tuple spaces.

In the following table we compare existing Java mobile agents systems with Macondo from the point of view of mobility linguistic support.

Type of mobility	Concordia	Aglets	Voyager	Odyssey	Mole	Macondo
Planned	Yes	Yes	No	Yes	No	Yes
Spontaneous	No	Yes	Yes	Yes	Yes	Yes
Controllable	No	Yes	Yes	No	No	Yes

With the exception of Concordia, all systems provide Telescript-like spontaneous mobility.

The remote method invocation capabilities of Voyager support controllable mobility in a natural way. Aglets also support controllable mobility by the use of a proxy: invoking a dispatching method on the proxy causes the migration of the corresponding aglet to the specified destination. All the other systems do not support such a kind of mobility.

The following table compares interaction support for agents for the Java mobile agents systems we presented, included Macondo, focussing on interaction features of such systems.

Interaction Features	Concordia	Aglets	Voyager	Odyssey	Mole	Macondo
Remote method invocation	No	Simulable	Yes	No	Simulated	Simulable
Messaging to mobile agents	No	No	Yes	No	No	No
Distributed Events	Yes	No	Yes	No	No	Simulable
Publish/Subscribe	No	Yes	Yes	No	No	Simulable
Meeting	No	Yes	Yes	Yes	Yes	Simulable
Coordination/Collaboration	Yes, limited	No	Yes, open	Only local	No	Yes, open

The previous points will be now described.

- **Remote Method Invocation**: this is a feature directly supported only by Voyager in a very flexible manner. Mole allows agents to exchange special RPCMessages, thus simulating RMI. In the same way message passing in Aglets can be used to implement method invocation. Odyssey does not provide any remote communication mechanism, while Concordia communication is based on events. Using MJada we can simulate remote method invocation in a simple and elegant way;
- **Java messaging to mobile agents**: this is a unique feature of Voyager, described above. Since communication in MJada is generative, mobility and locality issues are not difficult to handle;
- **Distributed events**: only Concordia and Voyager support distributed events. In particular, Voyager uses the event delegation model developed for JavaBeans. This paradigm can be expressed with MJada primitives in a very simple manner;
- **Publish/Subscribe**: Voyager and Aglets allows to subscribe a particular subject for a method invocation or for a message. This kind of message selection is very similar to tuple exchange;
- **Meeting**: this is a concept originally introduced in Telescript and consists of a direct method invocation between agents in the same execution environment. Aglets, Voyager, Odyssey and Mole support itineraries while Concordia do not. Meeting can be simply expressed in MJada using tuple exchange;
- **Coordination/Collaboration**: Voyager and Macondo provide very open coordination and collaboration frameworks. While Voyager uses distributed

events and remote method invocation, MJada is based on Linda, the coordination language *par excellence*. Exchanging an object reference in Odyssey is similar to Linda primitives, but Odyssey does not provide blocking operations. Concordia offers some explicit support for agent collaboration, but it is quite limited.

5   Conclusions

The rapid growth of cellular telephony and the wide diffusion of PDA devices opens new and challenging opportunities: just think how easy would be to put a picoJava processor and a pen driven graphical user interface into such a toy. But having the hardware is useless without having an operating environment that can support users' applications. And applications tailored for these easy-to-connect but mostly off-line devices have to deal with some kind of code mobility (we usually refer to the use of these devices as *nomadic computing* [16]).

Is still unclear if we really need to migrate Turing-equivalent entities in order to support this new generation of applications, but we try to archive this extreme goal to examine strong points and weaknesses of the mobile agents paradigm.

In this context we have shown how we deal with mobility in Java using a mobile agent platform: Macondo, and a coordination language: MJada. We plan to use these tools to develop more interesting applications in the context of nomadic computing and collaborative work.

References

1. T. Thorn Programming Languages for Mobile Code *ACM Computing Surveys*, 29(3):213–239, 1997
2. G. DiMarzoSerugendo and M. Muhugusa and C. Tschudin A Survey of Theories for Mobile Agents *World Wide Web Journal*, 1(3):139–153, 1998
3. A. Fuggetta and G. Picco and G. Vigna Understanding Code Mobility *IEEE Transactions on Software Engineering* 24(5):342–361, 1996
4. D. Lange and M. Oshima Mobile Agents with Java: the Aglets API *World Wide Web Journal* 1(3):111–121, 1998
5. C. Fournet and G. Gonthier and JJ. Levy and L. Maranget and D. Remy A Calculus of Mobile Agents *Proc. 7th Int. Conf. on Concurrency Theory (CONCUR)* 406–421, 1996
6. L. Cardelli A language with distributed scope *Proc. 22nd ACM Symposium on Principles of Programming Languages (POPL)* 286–298, 1995
7. P. Lloyd and R. Whitehead Transforming Organizations Through Groupware Springer-Verlag, Berlin, 1996
8. L. Cardelli and A. Gordon Mobile Ambients Proc. of Foundations of Software Science and Computation Structures (FoSSaCS), European Joint Conferences on Theory and Practice of Software (ETAPS'98), 140–155, 1998
9. S. Hild and P. Robinson Mobilizing Applications *IEEE Personal Communications* 4(5):26–34, 1997
10. N. Carriero and D. Gelernter and S. Hupfer Collaborative Applications Experience with the Bauhaus Coordination Language *Proc. HICSS30, Sw Track* 310–319, 1997

11. D. Wong and others Concordia: An Infrastructure for Collaborating Mobile Agents *Proc. First Int. Workshop on Mobile Agents (MA 97)* 86–97, 1997
12. J. Baumann and others Communication Concepts for Mobile Agents Systems *Proc. First Int. Workshop on Mobile Agents (MA97)* 123–135, 1997
13. P. Ciancarini and D. Rossi Coordinating Java Agents Over the WWW *World Wide Web Journal* 1(2):87–99, 1998
14. P. Ciancarini and R. Tolksdorf and F. Vitali and D. Rossi and A. Knoche Coordinating Multiagent Applications on the WWW: a Reference Architecture *IEEE Transactions on Software Engineering* 24(5):362–375, 1998
15. E. Gamma and R. Helm and R. Johnson and J. Vlissides Design Patterns Addison-Wesley, 1995
16. R. Bagrodia and W. Chu and L. Kleinrock and G. Popek Vision, Issues, and Architecture for Nomadic Computing *IEEE Personal Communications* 2(6):14–27, 1995

PerDiS: Design, Implementation, and Use of a PERsistent DIstributed Store*

Paulo Ferreira[1], Marc Shapiro[2], Xavier Blondel[2]**, Olivier Fambon[3],
João Garcia[1]***, Sytse Kloosterman[2], Nicolas Richer[2]†, Marcus Robert[4],
Fadi Sandakly[5], George Coulouris[4], Jean Dollimore[4], Paulo Guedes[1],
Daniel Hagimont[3], and Sacha Krakowiak[3]

[1] INESC
Rua Alves Redol 9, 1000 Lisboa, Portugal
{paulo.ferreira,joao.c.garcia,paulo.guedes}@inesc.pt
[2] INRIA Rocquencourt
Domaine de Voluceau, Rocquencourt BP 105, Le Chesnay Cedex 78153, France
{marc.shapiro,xavier.blondel,sytse.kloosterman,nicolas.richer}@inria.fr
[3] INRIA Rhône-Alpes
ZIRST - 655, Avenue de l'Europe, 38330 Montbonnot Saint-Martin, France
{olivier.fambon,daniel.hagimont,sacha.krakowiak}@inrialpes.fr
[4] QMW
Queen Mary and Westefield College, Mile End Road, London, E1 4NS, UK
{marcusr,george,jean}@dcs.qmw.ac.uk
[5] CSTB
BP 209, 290 Route de Lucioles, F-06904 Sophia Antipolis Cedex, France
sandakly@cstb.fr

Abstract The PerDiS (Persistent Distributed Store) project addresses
the issue of providing support for distributed collaborative engineering
applications. We describe the design and implementation of the PerDiS
platform, and its support for such applications.

Collaborative engineering raises system issues related to the sharing of
large volumes of fine-grain, complex objects across wide-area networks
and administrative boundaries. PerDiS manages all these aspects in a
well defined, integrated, and automatic way. Distributed application programming is simplified because it uses the same memory abstraction as
in the centralized case. Porting an existing centralized program written
in C or C++ is usually a matter of a few, well-isolated changes.

We present some performance results from a proof-of-concept platform
that runs a number of small, but real, distributed applications on Unix

---

* This work was supported by Esprit under the PerDiS project (n° 22533),
http://www.perdis.esprit.ec.org/. The partners in the PerDiS consortium are: CSTB,
INRIA Rhône-Alpes, INESC, QMW College, INRIA Rocquencourt, IEZ. Two are
from the building industry: CSTB is a research institute, and IEZ is a CAD tool com-
pany. The others are research institutes or university departments in Informatics and
Telecommunications. The Principal Investigator is Marc Shapiro.
** Student at CNAM Cédric.
*** Student at IST, Technical University of Lisbon.
† Student at Université Paris-6, LIP6.

and Windows NT. These confirm that the PerDiS abstraction is well adapted to the targeted application area and that the overall performance is promising compared to alternative approaches.

1   Introduction

The PerDiS project seeks to support distributed, cooperative engineering applications in the large scale. It aims to demonstrate cooperative computer-aided design (CAD) of buildings within a virtual enterprise.[1]

Single-user CAD applications are in widespread use today in architecture and building firms. The design for a building contains numerous fine-grain objects (100 bytes–10 Kb each), typically running into megabytes even for a relatively simple building. Objects are densely interconnected by pointers; for instance a wall object contains a pointer to its adjacent walls, ceiling, and floor, as well as to its windows, doors, pipes and other fittings.

In current practice, sharing of information in a VE is mostly limited to faxes or sending diskettes by post.[2] On a smaller scale, an enterprise might share files through a distributed file system over a local network, but is hindered in this case by the lack of consistency and concurrency control.

The industrial demand for distributed, collaborative CAD tools is high. Many developments, including one by PerDiS partner CSTB [1], are based on remote object invocation, using Corba [16], DCOM [29] or Java RMI [34]. A client application running on a workstation invokes objects, stored in a server, through remote references. Applied to the CAD domain this results in abysmal performance, and server scalability problems. Remote objects are especially inappropriate in the virtual enterprise, where the object server may be located across a slow WAN connection. Applications must be completely re-engineered (in devious ways) in order to get decent performance. Furthermore, none of the remote-object systems adequately address persistence or concurrency control.

Collaborative engineering in a VE raises a number of exciting system issues. The goal of this research is to address them in a fully integrated, automated, efficient and easy-to-use platform. Application programmers should be able to concentrate on application semantics, without worrying about system issues. Existing centralized CAD applications must port easily without complete re-engineering. The platform should provide fast, consistent access to data, despite concurrent access. Persistence must be guaranteed for as long as objects are needed. The platform should automate distribution, storage, and input-output. The system should work well in the large scale, tolerating faults such as net-

---

[1]   A virtual enterprise (VE) is a consortium of small enterprises, or of small departments of larger enterprises, working together for the duration of a construction project. The members are often geographically dispersed, even located in different countries.

[2]   Users are limited not only by the absence of interchange standards or of high-speed networks, but also by a prudent distrust between members of the VE.

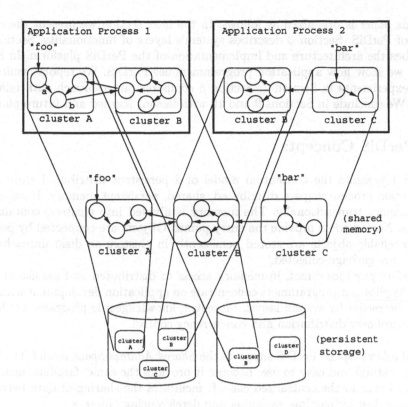

Fig.1. PerDiS abstractions

work slowdowns and disconnections, crashes, and providing an adequate level of security.

In a VE, collaboration follows a stylized, sequential pattern. Typically, a small group of architects located at a single site do the initial design, performing many updates during a limited period of time. Then, the design is passed along to structural engineers, another small group, possibly in a different site. They then pass their results on to another group, and so on. There is a high degree of temporal and spatial locality. There is also some real concurrency, including write conflicts, which cannot be ignored; for instance working on alternative designs in parallel is common practice.

To better understand the PerDiS approach, consider a typical application scenario from the building industry area. Architects and engineers from different companies collaborate on a design, working at different locations, either concurrently or at different times. Tentative or alternative designs are created, tried out, abandoned. The constructors on site consult the plans, making on-the-spot modifications, which should be reflected back to the engineering offices.

In response to these requirements, the PerDiS project proposes a new abstraction, the *Persistent Distributed Store*.

This paper is organized as follows. In the next section we present the concepts of PerDiS. Section 3 describes system's layers of functionality. Section 4 describes the architecture and implementation of the PerDiS platform. In Section 5 we show how application programmers use PerDiS. We report results of some experiments in Section 7. Section 8 compares our approach with related work. We conclude in Sections 9 and 10 with lessons learned and future plans.

2   PerDiS Concepts

Figure 1 presents the conceptual model of a persistent distributed store. An application process maps a distributed, shared, persistent memory. It accesses this memory transactionally. The memory is divided into clusters, containing objects. Named roots provide the entry points. Objects are connected by pointers. Reachable objects are stored persistently in clusters on disk; unreachable objects are garbage-collected.

PerDiS provides direct, in-memory access to distributed and persistent objects. Application programmers concentrate on application development without being distracted by system issues. Moreover, knowledgeable programmers have full control over distribution and concurrency control.

Shared address space PerDiS supports the *Shared Address Space* model [11]. It is simple, natural and easy to use, because it provides the same, familiar, memory abstraction as in the centralized case. It facilitates the sharing of data between programs, just by naming, assigning and dereferencing pointers.

PerDiS provides the illusion of a shared memory across the network and across time, by transparently and coherently caching data in memory and reading and writing to disk.

Clusters An application allocates an object within a cluster of the shared memory. A cluster groups together objects that belong together for locality, concurrency control, garbage collection and protection.

The intent is that a cluster will be used just like a document or a file in current operating systems, providing the user with mnemonic access to important data. Applications divide their data among clusters in whatever way is most natural and provides best locality. For example, in our cooperative engineering applications, objects for each major section of a building will be stored in a separate cluster.

Persistence by reachability The PerDiS memory is persistent. Even programs running at different times share data simply by mapping memory and working with pointers. The application programmer does not need to worry about flattening object graphs into files, nor about parsing ASCII representations into memory.

An object may point to any other object. The system ensures that pointers retain the same meaning for all application processes. To combine persistence with real pointers while retaining flexibility, many systems do *swizzling*, i.e., automatically translate global addresses into pointers [27,33]. PerDiS is designed to provide swizzling but the current implementation simply relies on fixed address allocation [11].

Starting from some *persistent root* pointer identified by a string name, a process navigates from object to object by following pointers. For instance, an application might navigate the graph illustrated in Figure 1. Starting from the root foo in cluster A, one can navigate through the objects, e.g. invoke foo->a->b->print(). This would access cluster B.

Any object reachable through some path from a persistent root must persist on permanent storage. This is called *Persistence By Reachability* (PBR) [3]. Unreachable objects are garbage-collected (see Section 4.4).

Transactions and concurrency control To relieve application programmers from dealing with the hard issues of concurrent updates, an application runs as a sequence of one or more transactions. It can read and write memory without interference from concurrently-running processes. Transactions ensure that if a single transaction updates multiple clusters, either the transaction commits and all the updates are applied, or it aborts and it is as if none has occurred.

For completeness, PerDiS supports transactions with the usual ACID transactional semantics. However, the ACID model is not well suited to our application area, so we plan to support more sophisticated transactions that allow more concurrency while reducing the probability of aborts.

Security A VE is a co-operation between different companies, for the limited purpose of designing and constructing some building. These same companies might be simultaneously competing for some other building. Data and communication must be protected.

PerDiS poses new security problems because applications access local copies of objects (via a DSM mechanism) instead of accessing them as remote objects protected by servers (more details in Section 4.5).

Ease of programming It is a requirement to minimize programming restrictions, and to support standard, non-modified programming languages and compilers. Pointers in C and C++ (or even assembly language) are supported; there is no requirement to use special pointer types (e.g., C++ smart pointers [17]), and dereferencing a pointer costs the same (once data has been loaded) as in the machine's native virtual memory. Pointer arithmetic is legal. However, pointer-hiding (e.g., XORing pointers, casting a non-pointer into a pointer, or a union of a pointer and a non-pointer) would defeat garbage collection and is illegal.

Our performance goals are modest: within the limits of our locality model (see Section 1), PerDiS should support applications much better than a remote-object client-server system. The main focus is on simplicity, ease of use, and adaptation to the needs of the application area.

App. 1   App. 2   App. 3   ...

4	C env.	C++ env.	Java env.	...
3	Access Methods		
2	Object Support		
1	Distributed File System		

(Unix)   (NT)

Fig. 2. Layers of the PerDiS design

3   Design

PerDiS provides the logical layers of functionality shown in Figure 2. PerDiS is hosted on traditional operating systems (OS), currently Unix and NT. Of the host OS, PerDiS uses only the local file service for storing its data, and TCP/IP sockets for communication with remote nodes (a node is a machine participating in a PerDiS platform.) The distributed sharing of data is managed by PerDiS, independent of the host OS.

3.1   Secure Transactional File System

Layer 1 of the PerDiS design provides a secure, distributed file system with transactional semantics [2]. Each cluster is stored in its own file with access restricted to the PerDiS Daemon by OS protection.

Each cluster has a PerDiS specific access control list (ACL), and an application process will gain access to a cluster only if the user presents credentials matching the ACL. Furthermore, a node will classify other nodes as trusted or untrusted. Communication with a trusted node uses a lightweight protocol. When communicating between untrusted nodes, each one double-checks that the other one is doing the right thing; for instance one node will not accept updates from a node that cannot prove ownership of a write lock. More details about the security architecture are in Section 4.5.

The PerDiS platform provides cooperative caching. A cluster can be stored anywhere, and even saved on local disk for fault tolerance and availability. However, it is a requirement, for security and legal reasons, that every cluster has a designated *home site*. The home site is guaranteed to store the most recent, authoritative version of the cluster.

3.2   Object Support

Layer 2 provides support for objects, i.e., collections of contiguous bytes. It is independent of any particular programming language, but it attaches meta-data to an object, for use by the language-specific support of Layer 4 (language-specific runtime service).

Layer 2 knows about the pointers contained in an object; the data is otherwise uninterpreted by this layer. It supports pointer persistence (swizzling), persistence by reachability, and garbage collection.

It is transparent whether a pointer points within the same cluster or into another cluster; however cross-cluster pointers are known to be more costly than intra-cluster ones. Application programmers can control the cost of following pointers by increasing locality within the same cluster.

3.3   Access Methods

Layer 3, also language-independent, provides naming of roots and access to objects in memory. The latter is very similar to what is found in a traditional DSM.

Its link_root primitive names a pointer with a URL [4], thus making it a root. Later, an application can enter the system via any root by providing its URL to the open_root primitive.

Two alternative memory access methods are provided. The first is based on an explicit API, whereby an application process calls the hold primitive to declare intent to operate on some data. As the application navigates through the object graph (starting from a root), it calls hold for each object. The arguments to hold include the extent of the object and the access mode (e.g., read or write). If the object indicated by hold is in a cluster that has not yet been accessed, this layer calls Layer 1 to open the new cluster (thereby checking access rights), thus providing seamless access across cluster boundaries. It calls Layer 1 to perform transactional concurrency control accessing the byte range in the specified mode, to record the access with the transaction manager, and to load the data into memory. It calls Layer 2 (Object Support) to do pointer swizzling, which in turn up-calls the language-specific runtime of Layer 4 to do type-checking.

The second access method, called the "compatibility interface" makes it easy to make existing centralized C or C++ programs distributed and persistent. A program can choose not to explicitly call hold. On initial entry via open_root, the corresponding cluster is opened and its pages protected against all access. As the application follows a pointer, the operating system might signal a page fault to this layer, which is handled as an implicit hold covering the whole faulting page.

3.4   Language-Specific Run-Time Services

Layer 4 provides language-specific run-time services, such as allocation of typed objects and type-checking procedures. It takes advantage of the hooks provided by Layer 2 (object support) to store the type information for each object. The swizzler, in Layer 2, up-calls this layer at swizzling time to ensure that pointers are correctly typed.

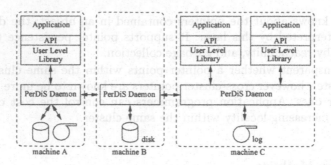

Fig.3. PerDiS platform design

4   Architecture and Implementation of the PerDiS Platform

PerDiS is a large, long-term project with ambitious goals. The major portion of the design is available in the prototype platform, although some parts are not implemented yet (see Section 6), most notably swizzling and fault-tolerant caches.

4.1   Structure

The PerDiS architecture is multi-process and peer-to-peer. Figure 3 illustrates the breakdown into processes, which isolates crucial platform functions from applications, and applications from one another, while providing reasonable performance. This breakdown is very much orthogonal to the layered design of Section 3; indeed, a bit of each layer can be found in each process.

A node runs a single *PerDiS Dæmon* (PD), and any number of application processes. Applications interact with PerDiS through an API layer, which interfaces to the *User Level Library* (ULL). A ULL communicates only with its local PD.

The ULL provides memory mapping, transactions, private data and lock caching, swizzling and unswizzling, and the "creative" part of garbage collection (see Section 4.4). When the application needs locks or reads or writes stored data, its ULL makes requests to the local PD.

A PD provides a data and lock cache shared by all applications at this node, maintained coherent with other PDs. It logs the results of transactions. It also contains security modules, and the "destructive" part of garbage collection. A PD communicates with other PDs over the network. They exchange notification messages for locks, updates and garbage collection. They cooperate to locate the home site of a cluster.

To illustrate the responsibilities of ULL and PD, consider a typical application scenario. An application starts a new transaction. This creates an instance of a transaction manager in the ULL, and causes the PD to start a log. Then

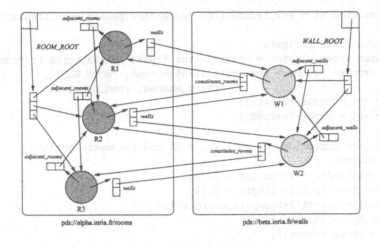

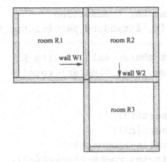

Fig.4. Distributed data example: rooms and walls

the application opens a cluster. When the application performs **hold** (either explicitly or through a page fault), and the data is not already cached in the ULL, the ULL requests the corresponding data from the PD. The ULL also requests locks to maintain consistency of its cache with the PD. If the PD does not have some data or lock in its cache, it fetches it from another cache or from the cluster's home site. When the application commits, it sends garbage collection information, updates and locks to the PD.

4.2 API

We will illustrate the PerDiS API through a simple example. Figure 4 displays the data structures, and Figure 5 contains the source code. Suppose that we represent a building by **room** and **wall** objects. Each **room** points to adjacent rooms and to its own walls, and each **wall** points to adjacent walls and to the rooms it encloses. We arbitrarily decide to store all **room** objects in cluster **pds: //alpha.inria.fr/rooms** and all **wall** objects in cluster **pds://beta.inria. fr/walls**. The URLs identify the cluster's home site and file name. We give each

```
transaction *t = new_transaction (&standard_pessimistic_transaction);

// open root, navigate
cluster *room_cluster = open_cluster ("pds://alpha.inria.fr/rooms");
list<*room> *rooms = open_root (list<*room>, "ROOM_ROOT",
                                intent_shared, room_cluster);
room *r1 = rooms->first();
room *r2 = rooms->second();

// Change dimensions of wall W1 of R1 and recompute surface
and volumes
r1->walls->first()->height = 2.72;
r1->walls->first()->length = 3.14;
r1->walls->first()->compute_surface();
r1->compute_volume();
r2->compute_volume();

// commit, and start another transaction
t = renew_transaction (t, &standard_pessimistic_transaction);

// Add new room R3 that shares wall W2 with R2
room *r3 = pds_new (room, room_cluster) room;

rooms->insert(r3);
r3->adjacent_rooms->insert(r2);
r2->adjacent_rooms->insert(r3);
r3->walls->insert(r2->walls->second());
walls->second()->constitutes_rooms->insert(r3);

end_transaction(t, COMMIT);
```

Fig.5. Source code for example

cluster a persistent root (respectively, ROOM_ROOT and WALL_ROOT) that points to all its objects.

The call to **new_transaction** starts a transaction; the argument requests a pessimistic transaction using the compatibility interface (see Section 3.3). The sequence open_cluster;open_root opens the root of the room cluster. The application navigates from the root and changes a wall's dimensions; note that the wall cluster does not need to be opened explicitly. The application recomputes affected surfaces and volumes. The primitive **renew_transaction** commits the current transaction and atomically starts a new one, retaining all its locks, data, and mappings. Then we create a new **room** in **room_cluster**; the macro **pds_new** calls the PerDiS primitive **allocate_in** to reserve space in the cluster, then calls the C++ initialization directive **new**. The new room is inserted into the corresponding data structures. Finally, the program commits. For simplicity, we (incorrectly) neglected to check for errors; for instance renew_transaction might fail because the first transaction cannot commit.

This example shows that the PerDiS approach is powerful and elegant. Thanks to caching, all data manipulation is local and distribution is transparent. Local and cross-cluster references are normal pointers. Instead of bothering with distribution, persistence, memory-management, etc., programmers focus on problem solving and application semantics.

Although the argument to hold is typically an object or a page, it can in fact be an arbitrary contiguous address range, from a single byte to a whole cluster. Thus, the application can choose to operate at a very fine grain to avoid contention (at the expense of overhead for numerous hold calls), or at a very large grain to improve response time (increasing however the probability of false sharing and deadlock, and increasing the amount of data to be logged at commit time). Programmers have full control, if desired, over distribution through the hold primitive and through the cluster abstraction.

4.3   Transactions and Caching

An application can request either pessimistic or optimistic concurrency control [21]. It can also request different kinds of locking behaviour, including non-serializable data access, but we will ignore this issue here for the sake of brevity.

A PD caches data and locks accessed by transactions executing at its site. In the current implementation, PDs maintain a sequentially-consistent coherent cache, along the lines of entry consistency [5]. The granularity of coherence is the page.

Transactions run on top of this coherent cache. An application process running a transaction gets a private, in-memory scratch copy of the pages it accesses. An application may update its scratch copy (assuming its write intents were granted). The transaction manager (in the ULL) sends changed data regions to the log (in the PD). When the transaction commits, it flushes any remaining updates, then writes a commit record on the log. The updates are applied to the cache and to disk.

A scratch copy is guaranteed to be coherent when initially copied in from the cache, and again at commit: taking a transactional lock on some datum translates into taking an entry-consistency lock on the corresponding page(s) in the cache. The timing of the entry-consistency locking is different for optimistic and pessimistic transactions. A pessimistic transaction takes a read or write lock as soon as the application issues hold, and releases the locks at commit or abort. This blocks any conflicting concurrent transaction. In an optimistic transaction, hold reads each page and its *version number* atomically. The transaction takes entry-consistency locks only at commit time; at that time it checks that no version numbers have changed (otherwise the transaction must abort); it performs its updates and releases the locks. Every commit, whether optimistic or pessimistic, increments the version numbers of all pages it modifies. The above guarantees serializable behaviour for both kinds of transactions.

Once the commit record is recorded in the log, the commit is successful. Logged modifications are then applied to the cache, and finally to the files at the clusters' homesites. Our current implementation guarantees the ACID properties on both the optimistic and pessimistic transaction models. If a PD or a node crashes, a recovery procedure reads the log; transactions whose commit record is on the log are re-done, and those that are still pending are undone. However, caches are not yet fault-tolerant, and a data request sent to a node that has crashed will abort the requesting transaction.

4.4 Garbage Collection

Manual space management, implying potential storage leaks and dangling pointers, is unacceptable in a persistent store. Any leakage would persist and accumulate, overwhelming the store. Dangling pointers (caused by an application program erroneously deleting a reachable object) would make the store unsafe, causing programs to fail unexpectedly, possibly years after the error. In PerDiS instead, storage is managed automatically, using the Larchant distributed garbage collection algorithm [19,20]. Larchant is based on meta-information that supplements pointers, called stubs and scions. A stub describes a pointer that points out of a cluster, and a scion a pointer into a cluster. Stubs and scions are also used by the swizzler.

The algorithm is divided into a "constructive" and a "destructive" part. The constructive part, known as *stub-scion creation* [8], detects a new inter-cluster pointer assigned by the application, creates the corresponding stub, and sends a message to the downstream cluster requesting creation of a scion. Before a transaction's updates are commited, they are analyzed by the stub-scion creation module.

The destructive part, called *garbage reclamation*, runs in the PD. It traces the set of clusters currently cached, using their scions and their persistent roots as starting points for tracing the graph. Objects not visited are unreachable and are deleted. Any given execution of the reclaimer only detects a subset of the actual garbage, but as the contents of caches vary over time, most garbage is deleted with high probability.

The garbage collector must be aware of caching and concurrency, because an object might not be reachable at a particular site but still be reachable globally. It must also carefully order its actions because of possible global race conditions. This is explained in more detail in the Larchant articles [19,20].

4.5 Security

The PerDiS platform protects whole clusters according to user-specified access rights and provides secure communication between PDs. Communication is secured against eavesdropping, impersonation, tampering and replay by attackers from within or outside the VE. The VE is composed of several trust domains.

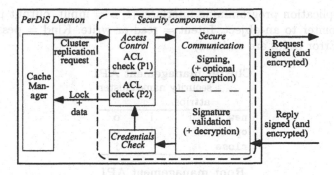

Fig.6. Security operations when requesting a cluster copy

This domain-based trust model enables the encryption and authentication mechanisms to be optimized for the different levels of trust existing within and between organizations.

Access Control We adopt a role-based model for access control, described in detail in [12]. To summarise: all the cooperative activities carried out by users are assigned to *tasks* and access rights are specified for the roles that users may play within a particular task. A person called a task manager digitally signs *role-in-task* certificates stating which users may play each role. Delegation of roles is supported by the use of task-related delegation certificates. The certificates for each user-level task are stored in a designated cluster and are therefore accessible to the PerDiS security system at participating sites.

Access rights for each cluster are specified in an ACL and access control is applied before a copy is supplied. The access rules are:

- For a PD to obtain a copy of a cluster from another PD the principal behind the requestor must have *read* access rights. This check is applied whenever a PD attempts to acquire a read lock for a cluster and hence get a copy of the data.
- For a PD to obtain a write lock, the principal behind it must have *write* access rights.
  In both cases the access control check is applied at the PD initiating the cluster request in order to give immediate feedback to the application, but because of the lower level of trust between PDs in different domains the check is also applied at the remote PD before granting a lock. This second check can be omitted for PDs in the same domain.
- In addition, a check is needed to ensure that the data accompanying a lock is a genuine version of the relevant cluster. This will be true if the PD granting a lock is backed by a principal that has *write* access rights. (The PD wouldn't have been able to get the lock without those rights). This check is applied by a PD whenever it receives a lock.

Table1. Application programming interface. (I, o = input, output parameter. Object = pointer to an object. Intent = read or write. Kind = pessimistic or optimistic. Error codes are omitted)

Cluster management API

	security	name	cluster attribs.
new	i	i	o
open		i	o
close			i

Root management API

	name	cluster	type	object	intent
link	i	i		i	
open	i	i	i	o	i
unlink	i	i			

Data allocation and access API

	cluster	type	object	intent
allocate	i	i	o	
hold		i	i, o	i

Transaction API

	kind	t'action	status
new	i		o
renew	i		i, o
end		i	i

Figure 6 shows the security management components within a PD and illustrates their operation to secure a cluster request from the local Cache Manager providing data for an application running on behalf of a principal P1.

After P1's rights have been checked locally, the request is signed, (optionally) encrypted and it is dispatched to the PD currently holding a lock on the required data. The security components at the PD receiving the request validate the request, check P1's credentials and if they allow the access, the second PD returns a signed (and optionally encrypted) reply. Finally, the credentials of the principal behind the second PD are checked at the first PD before the lock and data are passed to the Cache Manager.

Trust management Ultimately, the trust between the participants in a collaborative activity rests on the public keys of the individual users. But to avoid the need for costly bootstrapping of shared keys we establish local trust domains within which a session key is shared between the PDs involved in any PerDiS activity. A trust domain might for example comprise a small organisation or a department of a larger one. The users cooperating on a particular joint task will not generally all be in the same trust domain.

Within a trust domain the assumption of correct PDs on all local computers enables a shared session key to be used and removes the need for the duplication of access control checks described above. But between trust domains the authentication of replication requests requires the use of public key encryption, at least to establish secure channels.

Replication requests may be queued and the request queue may migrate with the lock on a cluster. Hence a PD that sends a replication request cannot be sure that the reply will come from a PD inside the trust domain. We have devised a secure protocol that deals with this issue and is optimised for the local case. Briefly, the sending PD signs (and optionally encrypts) all request messages using the shared session key for the local trust domain. A responding PD in the same trust domain can authenticate the request immediately. If the responding PD turns out to be in another trust domain, it must initiate an additional authentication exchange using the public keys of the two principals involved. The protocol is described in detail in Coulouris et al. [13].

5   Programming with PerDiS

The PerDiS platform supplies application programmers with a whole range of functionalities: object persistence, distribution, caching, transactions, and security. These features are exposed to an application programmer via an explicit API (see Table 1). The interface is *unobtrusive*: very few lines of code are needed to exploit the PerDiS functionality. The PerDiS API consists of four major parts: cluster and persistent root management, data allocation and access, and transactions. More details can be found in the Programmer's Manual and in the PerDiS design documents [18,23].

5.1   API

For cluster manipulation, API functions exist to create a new cluster, to open an existing cluster, and to close an open cluster. Cluster creation requires parameters to specify the security attributes for the cluster, together with its URL.

Since PerDiS' persistence model is based on persistence by reachability, we offer API functions to manage persistence roots. Linking a root associates a name with a pointer. Unlink removes the name; in this case, data reachable only from that root is eventually garbage collected. Opening a root requires, in addition to a name and a cluster, the root object's type. This allows verification of the expected root object type against the actual stored type.

The way data allocation is implemented depends on the programming language. For C and C++ applications we provide alternatives to `malloc` and `new`, respectively. To allocate data in a cluster, one passes a cluster and the type of the object to be allocated. Note that an API for explicit de-allocation of data is deliberately missing, since this is done by the garbage collector only.

All access to the PerDiS store must occur within the context of a transaction. Transactions can be started, terminated and *re-newed*. Renew atomically commits and starts a new transaction, retaining the locks, data and mappings of the committed transaction. PerDiS supports different kinds of transactions; starting a transaction requires parameters setting its behaviour. The main parameters specify when and how data locks are taken (as explained in Section 4.3).

5.2   Porting Applications

In general, porting an existing centralized C or C++ application to the PerDiS platform requires data and code conversions, which are both straightforward.

Data conversion requires only small modifications to the application's original I/O modules: (i) create a cluster in place of a file, (ii) perform memory allocation within an appropriate cluster, (iii) create at least one persistent root. These changes can usually be done with very little effort.

Code conversion can be done in several ways, playing on the trade-off between conversion effort and concurrency. We outline the simplest conversion, which takes very little effort (but reduces the level of concurrency): (i) embed the application in a pessimistic transaction that uses the "compatibility interface" (see Section 3.3), (ii) open persistent roots, (iii) replace writes into a file with renew_transaction or commit. Again, this involves very few modifications at clearly identifiable places. Thanks to the compatibility mode, data access is trapped using page faults and locks are taken automatically.

These limited modifications bring many gains. In particular, there is no more need for flattening data structures, explicit disk I/O, or explicit memory management. In addition, data distribution, transactions and persistence come for free.

This approach was used to port the applications presented in Section 7.

6   Status

The PerDiS project started in December 1996 and is scheduled as a three-year project. It occupies the equivalent of 8 full-time persons in 6 different institutions across Europe. Time and resources have been obviously insufficient to fully implement the ambitious goals listed above, which however constitute the criteria by which we measure design and implementation decisions.

The source code of the current release is freely available from http://www. perdis.esprit.ec.org/download/. It contains some 20,000 lines of C++ and runs on Solaris, Linux, HP/UX and Windows-NT. It is acceptably stable and supports a number of applications, as reported in Section 7.

The platform is intended as a proof-of-concept implementation, and it is not surprising that its performance is not satisfactory yet. Some issues that will be improved are fault tolerant caching, swizzling, type management, performance and elegance.

Table2. VRML application. For each test set, we provide: (a) Size of SPF file (Kb); number of SPF objects and of polyloop objects. (b) Execution times in seconds: stand-alone centralized version; PerDiS and Corba port, 1 and 2 nodes. (c) Memory occupation in Kbytes (PerDiS 1st column: in memory, 2nd column: in persistent cluster). (d) Number of allocation requests, in thousands (PerDiS 1st column: in memory, 2nd column in persistent cluster)

Test	size	SPF objects	PolyLoops
cstb_1	293	5 200	530
cstb0rdc	633	12 080	1 024
cstb0fon	725	12 930	1 212
demo225	2 031	40 780	4 091

(a) Test applications

Test	Std-Alone	PerDiS 1	Corba 1	PerDiS 2	Corba 2
cstb_1	0.03	1.62	54.52	2.08	59.00
cstb0rdc	0.06	4.04	115.60	4.27	123.82
cstb0fon	0.07	4.04	146.95	5.73	181.96
demo225	0.16	13.90	843.94	271.50	1452.11

(b) Test application execution times (s)

Test	Std-Alone	PerDiS in mem.	pers.	Corba
cstb_1	2 269	2 073	710	26 671
cstb0rdc	2 874	2 401	1 469	51 054
cstb0fon	3 087	2 504	1 759	59 185
demo225				

(c) Test application memory occupation (Kb)

Test	Std-Alone	PerDiS in mem.	pers.	Corba
cstb_1	62	49	14	1 100
cstb0rdc	128	101	29	2 180
cstb0fon	153	121	35	2 543
demo225				

(d) Test application allocations (thousands)

7   Applications

In this section we present some experiments with applications. These experiments allow us to evaluate the difficulty of building distributed and persistent applications with PerDiS, to compare with other methods and to measure the platform's performance.

7.1   AP225 to VRML Mapping Application

SPF-AP225 is a standard ASCII file format for representing building elements and their geometry; it is supported by a number of CAD tools. The application presented here reads this format and translates it into VRML (Virtual Reality Modeling Language), to allow a virtual visit to a building project through a VRML navigator.

We chose this application because it is relatively simple, yet representative of the main kernel of a CAD tool. We compare the original, stand-alone centralized version, with a Corba and a PerDiS version.

The stand-alone centralized version has two modules. The *read module* parses the SPF file, and instantiates the corresponding objects in memory. The *mapping module* traverses the object graph to generate a VRML view, according to object geometry (polygons) and semantics. The object graph contains a hierarchy of high-level objects representing projects, buildings, storeys and staircases. A storey contains rooms, walls, openings and floors; these are represented by low-level geometric objects such as polyloops, polygons and points.

In the Corba port, the read module is located in a server which then retains the graph in memory. The mapping module is a client that accesses objects remotely at the server. To reduce the porting effort, only five classes were enabled for remote access: four geometric classes (Point, ListOfPoints, PolyLoop, and ListOfPolyLoops), and one (Ap225SpfFile) allowing the client to load the SPF file and to get the list of polyloops to map. The port took two days. The code to access objects in the mapping module had to be completely rewritten.

In the PerDiS port, the read module runs as a transaction in one process and stores the graph in a cluster. The mapping module runs in another process and opens that cluster. The port took only one day; we used the method outlined in Section 5.2, with no modification of the application architecture. The PerDiS version has the advantage that the object graph is persistent, and it is not necessary to re-parse SPF files each time. The VRML views generated are identical to the original ones.

The stand-alone centralized version is approximately 4,000 lines of C++, in about 100 classes and 20 files. In the Corba version, only 5 of the classes were made remotely accessible, but 500 lines needed to be changed. In the PerDiS version, only 100 lines were changed.

Table 2 compares the three versions for various test sets and in various configurations. Compared to the stand-alone centralized version, performance is low, but this is not surprising for a proof-of-concept platform. Compared to a remote-object system, even a mature industrial product such as Orbix, the PerDiS approach yields much better performance.[3] Memory consumption in the PerDiS version is almost identical to the stand-alone one, whereas the Corba version consumes an order of magnitude more memory.

---

[3] Note that in Table 2 the PerDiS numbers do not include commit times so that we can compare them fairly with the numbers obtained with CORBA, which were obtained without transactions.

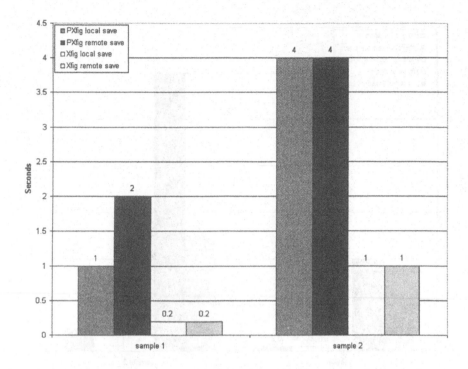

Fig.7. PXfig vs. Xfig save time. The figure compares the time to save drawings using PXfig and Xfig (PXfig local/remote = local/remote home site; Xfig local/remote = local file/NFS file)

In Table 2, Std-Alone represents the original, stand-alone application; PerDiS-1 and 2 are the port to PerDiS; both processes run on the same machine, but the cluster's home is either on the same node or on a different one. Corba-1 and 2 are the port to Corba, with the server running on the same machine as the client or on another machine. Size represents the size of the SPF file in kilobytes. Objects is the number of objects in the SPF file, of which Loops represents the number of elementary polyloops. Execution times are in seconds. Allocation sizes are in Kbytes, and allocation requests in thousands. The memory allocation numbers for PerDiS and Corba add up the consumption of both processes.

The one-machine configuration is a Pentium Pro at 200 MHz running Windows-NT 4.0. It has 128 Mbyes of RAM and 100 Mbytes of swap space. In the two-machine configuration for Corba, the server runs on the same machine as above. The client runs on a portable with a Pentium 230 MHz processor, 64 Mbytes RAM and 75 Mbytes swap space, running Windows-NT 4.0. In the two-machine configuration for PerDiS, both processes run on the first machine, whereas its home site is on the second one.

This experience confirms our intuition: the persistent distributed store paradigm performs better (in both time and space) than an industry-standard

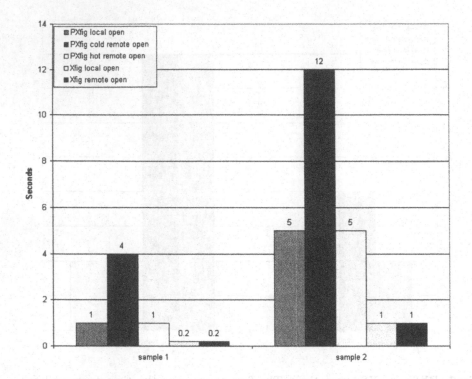

Fig.8. PXfig vs. Xfig open time. The figure compares the time to open drawings locally and remotely (PXfig hot/cold = hot/cold PD cache)

remote-invocation system, for data sets and algorithms that are typical of distributed VE applications. It also confirms that porting existing code to PerDiS is straightforward and provides the benefits of sharing, distribution and persistence with very little effort.

7.2 Persistent Xfig

Xfig is a simple drawing tool written in C, freely available on the Internet in source code format. The version ported to PerDiS is Xfig 3.2. We call our port to PerDiS *persistent Xfig (PXfig)*.

We choose Xfig because it is relatively simple and well-written. We expect it to be representative of the behaviour of the class of drawing tools. PXfig allows users to work together on a shared drawing. The port followed the guidelines presented in Section 5.2.

To convert allocation in a transient heap to allocation in a persistent one, 191 lines of code were modified (0.31% of total). 1809 lines were added to provide a graphical interface, e.g. to open a cluster containing a drawing and to commit or abort. We modified 24 source files, out of a total of 141, and we created 8 new

Table3. PXfig vs. Xfig storage requirements. The fields are: number of objects; size of Xfig text file (KB) and size of PerDiS cluster (KB)

	Objects	Xfig file	PXfig cluster
sample 1	4511	83.6	181.9
sample 2	21326	274.4	653.4

source files. PXfig preserves the capability to work with classical Xfig drawings. Consequently, code to parse and flatten Xfig file format remains in PXfig sources; if we removed this backward compatibility, at least 4000 lines of code (6.3% of total) could be deleted.

We present in Figures 7 and 8 a performance comparison between Xfig and PXfig. All the measurements were done on two Sun UltraSparcs at 140 Mhz with 128Mb of memory, running Solaris 2.5 and connected by a 100MB Ethernet. Two complex Xfig drawings, named sample1 and sample2 were used to measure basic operation speed. Table 3 shows the size and number of graphics objects for each sample.

For each test, the measurements were repeated with both the explicit and compatible API but we found no significant performance differences (in all cases we have used only pessimistic transactions). Note also that the results for remote open and remote save for classical Xfig are based on NFS.

The conclusion of this experience is that Xfig was quite easy to port, allowing distributed cooperative edition of Xfig drawings. Note the size increase between Xfig and PXfig files in Table 3, which represents a negative (if not unexpected) consequence of using a binary format. Performance of PXfig is acceptable for an interactive drawing tool. We expect future optimizations of the platform to improve performance significantly.

7.3 Genome Application

LASSAP[4] is an application that searches through a database of genome sequences for a match with a particular pattern. In the original implementation, sequences are stored in a text file, which LASSAP parses at each execution.

We ported LASSAP to PerDiS to see how our system will behave outside the targeted application area. LASSAP should benefit from PerDiS by running multiple searchs in parallel without re-parsing the database every time.

The original version of LASSAP parses the data for a single sequence and stores it into a statically-allocated object. This object is large enough for the biggest possible sequence. After comparing one sequence, the next one overwrites the previous one in the same location.

Porting LASSAP was far harder and less beneficial than expected. For the PerDiS port, we kept the same object type, but we dynamically allocate a new object for each sequence. This in itself required major changes in the code. Since

---

[4] LArge Scale Sequence compArison Package, http://www.gene-it.com

we did not change the object type, and the original is generously sized, a lot of memory is wasted, causing poor performance because of the cost of allocation and of the loss of locality. We don't present any figures here because they do not provide much insight.

This experience teaches us that applications that use overlayed static data structures are not easy to port to PerDiS.

8   Related Work

Given that the distributed sharing of objects is an active research area, PerDiS can be compared to many different kinds of systems.

8.1   Distributed File Systems and DSMs

The differences between PerDiS and a distributed file system (DFS) should now be clear: Layer 1 of PerDiS provides a DFS; its other layers add support for objects, for DSM functionality, and for language-specific functionality.[5]

Differences with a DSM are also clear. DSMs have been most successful in supporting multi-threaded parallel programs, whereas PerDiS facilitates sharing between different programs.

Many of the ideas in PerDiS are direct descendents of the so-called Single-Address Space Operating Systems (SASOS) such as Opal [11], Grasshopper [14], or EOS [22]. The main difference with PerDiS lies in the integration of persistent object systems and object-oriented database concepts, e.g., transactions, persistence by reachability and garbage collection. This is why our system uses transactions and incorporates a security architecture. We also provide persistence by reachability, essential for the long-term safety of the store.

8.2   Object-Oriented Databases, Persistent Object Systems, and Object-Based Systems

Object-oriented databases (OODBs) [35] such as O_2 [15], Thor [25], GemStone [9], or ObjectStore [24] share many of the same goals as PerDiS. OODBs support complex data types, persistently preserving the structure and type of data. However, they are very heavyweight, and often come with their own specialized programming language.

Moreover, an OODB typically manages a database as a tightly encapsulated data unit, residing on a specific server entrusted with crucial functions such as security, recovery and schema enforcement. Transactions can access multiple databases, but this is an infrequent and heavyweight action. In contrast,

---

[5]   Let us emphasize that, in contrast to well-known DFSs such as NFS, AFS, or Sprite, our Layer 1 is a *transactional* and *secure* DFS. Our experience shows that transactions cannot be efficiently layered on top of a standard DFS, and that security permeates the whole system and cannot be added as an afterthought.

the PerDiS shared object world is diffuse, being composed of clusters which are dynamically opened according to application navigation. PerDiS accommodates this world of data *without frontiers* by distributing server functions across cooperative caches, performing schema validation incrementally, and permitting applications to customize their transaction semantics.

As an example, compare PerDiS and ObjectStore. Both provide coherent distributed access to shared objects, exploit client caching, and rely on page fault interception to swizzle pointers. However, ObjectStore is a full-featured system for database management, whereas PerDiS is intended to support object sharing for a diverse range of applications, of which CAD is the primary motivating example.

Persistent object systems such as Mneme [26], Shore [10], Texas [31] and PJama [28] have a similar lightweight approach to PerDiS. However, most of these such systems do not address the issues of distribution and security, they are mostly client-server based, and are limited to traditional transaction models which are too restrictive to the applications we are considering.

Object-based systems such as Comandos [32], SOS [30], or Emerald [7], for example, have tried to simplify the construction of applications that handle persistent and distributed data. However, they do not support replicated data, they are mostly client-server based, objects are acessed by remote invocation, and security has not been fully considered from the beginning.

8.3 Remote Object Systems

Remote object systems such as Corba [16], DCOM [29] or Java RMI [34] let a client invoke objects located on a remote server by Remote Procedure Call (RPC) [6]. RPC solves the problems of identification and remote access. However, every remote data access is burdened with communication to the server, which becomes a performance and availability bottleneck. This makes the client-server architecture inadequate for interactive CAD and cooperative applications, especially upon the WAN connections typical of a VE. In addition, RPC does not support coherence of data viewed by multiple clients. Finally, it imposes an interface definition language to program remote data access, separate from the programming language. Some of the above systems provide transactional and/or persistence services, but they are poorly integrated into the system, being very heavy-weight and awkward to use.

9 Future Work

Concurrent engineering transactions are of long duration; they sometimes need to read data that is being actively modified by another transaction. They are interactive, implying that aborts are perceived as intolerable by users.

In future work, we plan to allow a transaction that would abort under the standard ACID policy, to be committed tentatively until its results are either reconciled with the store or definitely abandoned. Thus, the work done within a transaction might not be completely lost.

We also have a list of functionalities which are planned for future research. These include support for versioning and reconciliation of write conflicts, sharing data between heterogeneous machine types, schema evolution, and automatic reclustering. We plan to provide each cluster with its own choice of policies, for replication and coherence control, concurrency control, swizzling and garbage collection.

Some open questions remain. For instance, persistence by reachability is the cleanest persistence model, but it is not clear how programmers can make the most effective use of it.

10 Conclusion

We presented PerDiS, a new persistent distributed store providing support for cooperative applications in the framework of a virtual enterprise.

PerDiS automatically manages distribution, persistence, memory management, caching and security in a well defined, integrated, and automatic way. Distributed programming is very simple because PerDiS provides the same memory abstraction as in the centralized case. Although on the one hand the platform provides transparency to programmers who prefer to let the system take care of the difficult issues, it also provides powerful primitives that provide full control to the knowledgeable application programmer.

PerDiS integrates in a novel fashion different techniques, such as distributed shared memory, transactions, security, and distributed garbage collection. This unique combination makes porting of existing centralizaed applications very easy. In addition, these applications have an increased functionality because they can make full use of PerDiS. We also achieve good overall performance because we cache data, taking advantage of the locality characteristics of the application area.

References

1. Virginie Amar. *Intégration des standards STEP et CORBA pour le processus d'ingénierie dans l'entreprise virtuelle.* PhD thesis, Université de Nice Sophia-Antipolis, September 1998.
2. João Garcia, Paulo Ferreira, and Paulo Guedes. The PerDiS FS: A transactional file system for a distributed persistent store. In *Proc. of the 8th ACM SIGOPS European Workshop*, Sintra, (Portugal), September 1998.
3. M. P. Atkinson, P. J. Bailey, K. J. Chisholm, P. W. Cockshott, and R. Morrison. An approach to persistent programming. *The Computer Journal*, 26(4):360–365, 1983.
4. T. Berners-Lee, L. Masinter, and M. McCahill. Uniform resource locators (URLs). Request for Comments 1738, December 1994.
5. B. Bershad, M. J. Zekauskas, and W. A. Sawdon. The Midway distributed shared memory system. In *Proc. of the 1993 CompCon Conf.*, 1993.

6. A. D. Birrell and B. J. Nelson. Implementing Remote Procedure Calls. *ACM Transactions on Programming Languages and Systems*, 2(1), February 1984.
7. A. Black, N. Hutchinson, E. Jul, and H. Levy. Object structure in the Emerald system. In *ACM Conference on Object-Oriented Programming Systems, Languages and Applications*, Portland, Oregon, October 1986.
8. Xavier Blondel, Paulo Ferreira, and Marc Shapiro. Implementing garbage collection in the PerDiS system. In *Int. W. on Persistent Object Systems: Design, Implementation and Use*, Tiburon CA (USA), August 1998.
9. P. Butterwoth, A. Otis, and J. Stein. The GemStone object database management system. *Com. of the ACM*, 34(10):64–77, October 1991.
10. Michael J. Carey, David J. DeWitt, Michael J. Franklin, Nancy E. Hall, Mark L. McAuliffe, Jeffrey F. Naughton, Daniel T. Schuh, Marvin H. Solomon, C. K. Tan, Odysseas G. Tsatalos, Seth J. White, and Michael J. Zwilling. Shoring up persistent applications. In *Proc. Int. Conf. on Management of Data (SIGMOD)*, pages 383–394, Minneapolis MN (USA), May 1994. ACM SIGMOD.
11. J. S. Chase, H. E. Levy, M. J. Feely, and E. D. Lazowska. Sharing and adressing in a single address space system. *ACM Transactions on Computer Systems*, 12(3), November 1994.
12. George Coulouris, Jean Dollimore, and Marcus Roberts. Role and task-based access control in the PerDiS project. In *W. on Role-Based Access Control*, George Mason University, VA (USA), October 1998. ACM.
13. George Coulouris, Jean Dollimore, and Marcus Roberts. Secure communication in non-uniform trust environments. In *ECOOP W. on Dist. Object Security*, Brussels (Belgium), July 1998.
14. Alan Dearle, Rex di Bona, James Farrow, Frans Henskens, Anders Lindström, John Rosenberg, and Francis Vaughan. Grasshopper: An orthogonally persistent operating system. *Computing Systems*, 7(3):289–312, 1994.
15. O. Deux et al. The O₂ system. *Communications of the ACM*, 34(10):34–48, October 1991.
16. Digital Equipment Corporation, Hewlett-Packard Company, HyperDesk Corporation, NCR Coporation, Object Design, Inc., and SunSoft, Inc. The Common Object Request Broker: Architecture and specification. Technical Report 91-12-1, Object Management Group, Framingham MA (USA), December 1991.
17. Daniel R. Edelson. Smart pointers: They're smart, but they're not pointers. In *C++ Conference*, pages 1–19, Portland, OR (USA), August 1992. Usenix.
18. Marc Shapiro et al. The PerDiS API. `http://www.perdis.esprit.ec.org/deliverables/sources/interfaces/pds_api.h`, May 1997.
19. Paulo Ferreira and Marc Shapiro. Garbage collection and DSM consistency. In *Proc. of the First Symposium on Operating Systems Design and Implementation (OSDI)*, pages 229–241, Monterey CA (USA), November 1994. ACM.
20. Paulo Ferreira and Marc Shapiro. Modelling a distributed cached store for garbage collection. In *Proc. of the 12th European Conf. on Object-Oriented Programming (ECOOP)*, Brussels (Belgium), July 1998.
21. Michael Franklin, Michael Carey, and Miron Livny. Transactional client-server cache consistency: Alternatives and performance. *ACM Transactions on Database Systems*, 22(3):315–363, September 1997.
22. Olivier Gruber and Laurent Amsaleg. Object grouping in EOS. In *Proc. Int. Workshop on Distributed Object Management*, pages 184–201, Edmonton (Canada), August 1992.

23. Sytse Kloosterman and Xavier Blondel. *The PerDiS Reference Manual, version 2.1.* INRIA, B.P. 105, 78150 Le Chenay Cedex, France, 2.1 edition, May 1998. ftp://ftp.inria.fr/INRIA/Projects/SOR/PERDIS/PLATFORM/PPF-2.1/ppf-2-1-manual.ps.gz.

24. Charles Lamb, Gordon Landis, Jack Orenstein, and Dan Weinreb. The ObjectStore database system. *Communications of the ACM*, 34(10):50–63, October 1991.

25. Barbara Liskov, Mark Day, and Liuba Shrira. Distributed object management in Thor. In *Proc. Int. Workshop on Distributed Object Management*, pages 1–15, Edmonton (Canada), August 1992.

26. J. Eliot. B. Moss. A performance study of the Mneme persistent object store. *ACM Transactions on Information Systems*, 8(2):103–139, April 1990.

27. J. Eliot B. Moss. Working with persistent objects: To swizzle or not to swizzle. *IEEE Transactions on Software Engineering*, 18(8):657–673, August 1992.

28. Tony Printezis, Malcom Atkinson, Laurent Daynes, Susan Spence, and Pete Bailey. The design of a new persistent object store fir pjama. In *International Workshop on Persistence for Java*, San Francisco Bay Area, California (USA), August 1997.

29. Roger Sessions. *COM and DCOM: Microsoft's Vision for Distributed Objects.* Wiley, December 1998. ISBN 0-471-19381-X.

30. Marc Shapiro, Yvon Gourhant, Sabine Habert, Laurence Mosseri, Michel Ruffin, and Céline Valot. SOS: An object-oriented operating system — assessment and perspectives. *Computing Systems*, 2(4):287–338, December 1989.

31. K. Singhal, S. Kakkad, and P. Wilson. Texas: An efficient, portable persistent store. In *Proc. of the Fifth International Workshop on Persistent Object Systems Design, Implementation and Use*, pages 13–28, San Miniato Pisa (Italy), September 1992.

32. Pedro Sousa, Manuel Sequeira, André Zúquete, Paulo Ferreira, Cristina Lopes, José Pereira, Paulo Guedes, and José Alves Marques. Distribution and persistence in the IK platform: Overview and evaluation. *Computing Systems (Fall 1993)*, 6(4), 1993.

33. Paul R. Wilson and Sheetal V. Kakkad. Pointer swizzling at page fault time: Efficiently and compatibly supporting huge address spaces on standard hardware. In *1992 Int. Workshop on Object Orientation and Operating Systems*, pages 364–377, Dourdan (France), October 1992. IEEE Comp. Society, IEEE Comp. Society Press.

34. Ann Wollrath, Roger Riggs, and Jim Waldo. A distributed object model for the java system. In *Conference on Object-Oriented Technologies*, Toronto Ontario (Canada), 1996. Usenix.

35. S. Zdonik and D. Maier. *Readings in Object-Oriented Database Systems.* Morgan-Kaufman, San Mateo, California (USA), 1990.

The University Student Registration System: A Case Study in Building a High-Availability Distributed Application Using General Purpose Components

Mark C. Little, Stuart M. Wheater, David B. Ingham, C. Richard Snow,
Harry Whitfield, and Santosh K. Shrivastava

Department of Computing Science, Newcastle University,
Newcastle upon Tyne, NE1 7RU, England.

Abstract. Prior to 1994, student registration at Newcastle University involved students being registered in a single place, where they would present a form which had previously been filled in by the student and their department. After registration this information was then transferred to a computerised format. The University decided that the entire registration process was to be computerised for the Autumn of 1994, with the admission and registration being carried out at the departments of the students. Such a system has a very high availability requirement: admissions tutors and secretaries *must* be able to access and create student records (particularly at the start of a new academic year when new students arrive). The Arjuna distributed system has been under development in the Department of Computing Science for many years. Arjuna's design aims are to provide tools to assist in the construction of fault-tolerant, highly available distributed applications using atomic actions (atomic transactions) and replication. Arjuna offers the right set of facilities for this application, and its deployment would enable the University to exploit the existing campus network and workstation clusters, thereby obviating the need for any specialised fault tolerant hardware.

Key words: available systems, distributed system, fault-tolerance, atomic transactions, replication.

1. Introduction

In most British Universities, the process of registering all students as members of the institution is largely concentrated into a very short period of time. At the University of Newcastle, the registration period occupies a little over a week in September, at the start of the academic year. The purpose of the registration process is to determine which students will be taking courses within the University, and for the administration to keep its records up-to-date. From the students point of view, registration enables them to acquire the necessary authorised membership of the University, and where relevant, obtain their grant cheques. It is usually the case that students will register for particular courses, or modules, at the same time, and the

S. Krakowiak, S.K. Shrivastava (Eds.): Distributed Systems, LNCS 1752, pp. 453–471, 2000.

information collected is used by members of the teaching staff to construct class lists, etc.

Prior to 1994, registration involved students being registered in a single place within the University, where they would present a form which had previously been filled in elsewhere by the student and their department. After registration this information was then transferred to a computer system. In 1993, the University decided that the entire student registration process was to be computerised (electronic registration) for the Autumn of 1994. The decision was also made to decentralise the registration process so that the end users of the course data, the various University departments, would have more control over the accuracy of the data entered. It was also expected that the delay before the final data could be delivered back to the departments would be considerably reduced. Although the same registration forms were issued to students, available data concerning each student had already been entered in the system database. At the registration, using unique student number as a key, student data was retrieved from the database and updated as necessary.

Needless to say that the registration process is extremely important to the University and the students: the University cannot receive payments for teaching the students, and students cannot receive their grants or be taught until they have been registered. Thus the electronic registration system has a very high availability and consistency requirement; admissions tutors and secretaries *must* be able to access and create student records (particularly at the start of a new academic year when new students arrive). The high availability requirement implies that the computerised registration system must be able to tolerate a 'reasonable' number of machine and network related failures, and the consistency requirement implies that the integrity of stored data (student records) must be maintained in the presence of concurrent access from users and the types of failures just mentioned. It was expected that most human errors, such as incorrectly inputting data, would be detected by the system as they occurred, but some "off-line" data manipulation would be necessary for errors which had not been foreseen. Tolerance against catastrophic failures (such as complete electrical power failure, or a fire destroying much of the University infrastructure) although desirable, was not considered within the remit of the registration system.

A solution that would require the University buying and installing specialist fault-tolerant computing systems, such as Tandem [1] or Stratus [2] was not considered economically feasible. The only option worth exploring was exploiting the University's existing computing resources. Like most other universities, Newcastle has hundreds of networked computers (Unix workstations, PCs, Macs) scattered throughout the campus. A solution that could make use of these resources and achieve availability by deploying software-implemented fault-tolerance techniques certainly looked attractive.

The Arjuna distributed system [3,4,5] has been under development in the Computing Science Department at the University since 1986. The first public release of the system was made available in 1991, and since then the system has been used by a number of academic and commercial organisations as a vehicle for understanding and experimenting with software implemented fault-tolerance techniques. Arjuna provides a set of tools for the construction of fault-tolerant, distributed applications using *atomic actions* (*atomic transactions*) [6] for maintaining consistency of objects and replication of objects maintaining availability. Arjuna runs on Unix workstations, so it offered the promise of delivering the availability and consistency required by the student registration system without requiring any specialist computing equipment. In the summer of 1994 we (recklessly?) convinced the University to go electronic and committed ourselves to delivering a system that would run on a cluster of Unix workstations and provide transactional access to student records from PC and Macintosh front end machines located in various departments.

This paper describes the design and implementation of the student registration system built as an Arjuna application. The registration system been in use since October 1994, and during each five day registration period approximately 14,000 students are registered. The system illustrates that software implemented fault tolerance techniques can be deployed to build high availability distributed applications using general-purpose ('off-the-shelf') components such as Unix workstations connected by LANs. Although distributed objects, transactions and replication techniques that have been used here are well-known in the research literature, we are not aware of any other mission-critical application that routinely makes use of them over commonly available hardware/software platforms.

2. Failure Assumptions

It is assumed that the hardware components of the system are computers (nodes), connected by a communication subsystem. A node is assumed to work either as specified or simply to stop working (crash). After a crash, a node is repaired within a finite amount of time and made active again. A node may have both stable (crash-proof) and non-stable (volatile) storage or just non-stable storage. All of the data stored on volatile storage is assumed to be lost when a crash occurs; any data stored on stable storage remains unaffected by a crash.

The communication environment can be modeled as either asynchronous or synchronous. In an asynchronous environment message transmission times cannot be estimated accurately, and the underlying network may well get partitioned (e.g., due to a crash of a gateway node and/or network congestion) preventing functioning processes from communicating with each other; in such an environment, timeouts and network level 'ping' mechanisms cannot act as an accurate indication of node failures (they can only be used for *suspecting* failures). We will call such a communication environment *partitionable*. In a synchronous communication environment, functioning nodes are capable of communicating with each other, and judiciously chosen timeouts together with network level 'ping' mechanisms can act as an accurate indication of node failures. We will call such a communication environment *non-partitionable*.

The student registration system can be viewed as composed of two sub-systems: the 'Arjuna sub-system' that runs on a cluster of Unix workstations and is responsible for storing and manipulating student data using transactions, and the 'front-end' sub-system, the collection of PCs and Macs each running a menu driven graphical user interface that users employ to access student data through the Arjuna sub-system (see fig.1).

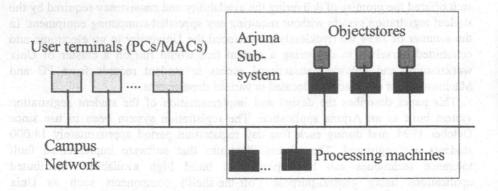

Figure 1: The student registration system.

The Arjuna-subsystem was engineered to run in a non-partitionable environment by ensuring that the entire cluster of machines was on a single, lightly loaded LAN segment; this decision was made to simplify the task of consistency management of replicated data (as can be appreciated, the problem of consistency management is quite hard in a partitionable environment). The current configuration consists of eight Unix workstations, of which three act as a triplicated database (object store). On the other hand, the front-end system was expected to run in a partitionable environment; however, we assume that a partition in a network is eventually repaired. We had no control on the placement of user machines, so we could not assume a non-partitionable environment for user machines. Note that there are no consistency problems if a front-end machine gets disconnected from the Arjuna sub-system, as the latter sub-system can abort any on-going transaction if a failure is suspected.

3.   Arjuna Overview

3.1.   Objects and Actions

Arjuna is an object-oriented programming system, implemented in C++ [3,4,5], that provides a set of tools for the construction of fault-tolerant distributed applications. Objects obtain desired properties such as concurrency control and persistence by inheriting suitable base classes. Arjuna supports the computational model of *nested atomic actions* (nested atomic transactions) controlling operations on persistent (long-lived) objects. Atomic actions guarantee consistency in the presence of failures and concurrent users, and Arjuna objects can be replicated on distinct nodes in order to obtain high availability.

The object and atomic action model provides a natural framework for designing fault-tolerant systems with persistent objects. When not in use a persistent object is assumed to be held in a *passive* state in an object store (a stable object repository) and is *activated* on demand (i.e., when an invocation is made) by loading its state and methods from the persistent object store to the volatile store. Arjuna uniquely identifies each persistent object by an instance of a *unique identifier* (*Uid*).

Each Arjuna object is an instance of some class. The class defines the set of *instance variables* each object will contain and the *methods* that determine the behaviour of the object. The operations of an object have access to the instance variables and can thus modify the internal state of that object. Arjuna objects are responsible for their own state management and concurrency control, which is based upon multiple-readers single-writer locks.

All operation invocations may be controlled by the use of atomic actions that have the well known properties of *serialisability*, *failure atomicity*, and *permanence of effect*. Furthermore, atomic actions can be nested. A commit protocol is used during the termination of an outermost atomic action (*top-level action*) to ensure that either all the objects updated within the action have their new states recorded on stable storage (committed), or, if the atomic action aborts, no updates are recorded. Typical failures causing a computation to be aborted include node crashes and continued loss of messages caused by a network partition. It is assumed that, in the absence of failures and concurrency, the invocation of an operation produces consistent (class specific) state changes to the object. Atomic actions then ensure that only consistent state changes to objects take place despite concurrent access and any failures.

3.2. Distribution

Distributed execution in Arjuna is based upon the *client-server* model: using the remote procedure call mechanism (RPC), a client invokes operations on remote objects which are held within server processes. Distribution transparency is achieved through a stub generation tool that provides client and server stub code that hides the distributed nature of the invocation. The client stub object is the proxy of the remote object in the client's address space; it has the same operations as the remote object, each of which is responsible for invoking the corresponding operation on the server stub object, which then calls the actual object.

Arjuna creates server processes automatically on demand, as invocations to objects are made. When a client first requests an operation on a remote object, it sends a message to a special daemon process called the *manager*, requesting the creation of a new server, which is then responsible for replying to the client. All subsequent invocations from that client are then sent to this server. The created server is capable of loading the state of the object from object store where the object state resides (state loading normally happens as a side effect of the client managing to lock the object). What happens if the client does not get a response? This could be because of one of several reasons, such as: (i) it is a first invocation, and the manager is busy with other requests, so it has not yet got round to creating the server; (ii) the server has not yet finished computing; (iii) the server's machine has crashed (in which case no response will come). If no reply is forthcoming after waiting for a while, the client uses a ping mechanism to determine if the destination machine is working (see below) and retries only if the machine is determined to be working, else a fail exception is returned. Normally, client's response to this exception will be to abort the current transaction. The length of time which the client should wait is therefore crucial to the performance of the system. If the time-out interval is too short, requests will be repeated unnecessarily, but if it is too long, the client might wait a long time before realising that the server machine has crashed.

In order to better distinguish between the case where the machine has crashed and the machine is merely running slowly, Arjuna installs a dedicated daemon process on a machine, the *ping daemon*, whose sole responsibility is to respond to "are you alive" ping messages. Whenever a client has not received a response to an RPC request, it "pings" the destination machine. If ping fails to produce a response -even after several retries - then the machine is assumed to have failed and no RPC retries are made.

3.3. Object Replication

A persistent object can become *unavailable* due to failures such as a crash of the object server, or network partition preventing communications between clients and the server. The *availability* of an object can be increased by replicating it on several nodes. Arjuna implements *strong consistency* which requires that the states of all replicas that are regarded as available be mutually consistent (so the persistent states of all available replicas are required to be identical). Object replicas must therefore be managed through appropriate replica-consistency protocols to ensure strong consistency.   To tolerate K replica failures, in a non-partitionable network, it is necessary to maintain at least K+1 replicas of an object, whereas in a partitionable network, a minimum of 2K+1 replicas are necessary to maintain availability in the partition with access to the majority of the replicas (the object becomes unavailable in all of the other partitions) [6]. As the Arjuna sub-system was assumed to run in a non-partitionable network, K+1 replicas were required (K = 2 was considered sufficient for this particular application).

The default replication protocol in Arjuna is based upon *single-copy passive replication*: although the object's state is replicated on a number of nodes, only a single replica (the primary server) is activated, which regularly checkpoints its state to the object stores where the states are stored. This checkpointing occurs as a part of the commit processing of the application, so if the primary fails, the application must abort the affected atomic action. Restarting the action results in a new primary being activated.

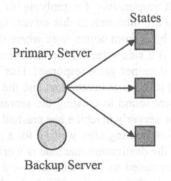

Figure 2: Passive replication.

This is illustrated in Fig. 2, where an object's state is replicated on three object stores. All clients send requests to the primary, which loads the state of the object from any one of the replicated object stores. If the state is modified it is written back to those stores when the top-level action commits. Stores where the states cannot be updated are excluded from subsequent invocations until they have been updated by a recovery mechanism. If the primary server fails then a backup server gets created. As long as a single state and server replica are available, the object can be used. Replication in Arjuna is discussed in more detail in [7,8].

4.   System Architecture

Based upon the experiences of the manual registration process, it was anticipated that 100 front-end machines would be necessary for the purposes of the registration exercise, resulting in a maximum of 100 simultaneous users. These machines (PC-compatible machines and Apple Macintosh systems), would be distributed throughout the University campus. For each of these two types of machine, a user-friendly interface program (*front-end*) was written, which would display the equivalent of the original paper registration form. The student data would be retrieved from an information store, written using Arjuna. In the following sections we shall examine this architecture in more detail.

4.1   The Student Information Store

It is important that the student information is stored and manipulated in a manner which protects it from machine crashes. Furthermore, this information should be made accessible from anywhere in the campus, and kept consistent despite concurrent accesses. Therefore, a distributed information store (the *registration database*) was built using the facilities provided by Arjuna. The database represents each student record as a separate persistent object (approximately 1024 bytes), the *StudentRecord*, which is responsible for its own concurrency control, state management, and replication. This enables update operations on different student records (StudentRecord objects) to occur concurrently, improving the throughput of the system. Each StudentRecord object was manipulated within the scope of an atomic action, which was begun whenever a front-end system requested access to the student data; this registration action may modify the student record, or simply terminate without modifying the data, depending upon the front-end user's requirements.

Each StudentRecord has methods for storing and retrieving the student's information:

- *retrieveRecord*: obtain the student data record from the database, acquiring a *read* lock in the process.
- *retrieveExclusiveRecord*: obtain the student data record, acquiring a *write* (*exclusive*) lock.
- *storeRecord*: store the student data in the database; if a record already exists then this operation fails.
- *replaceRecord*: create/overwrite the student data in the database.

460   Mark C. Little et al.

These methods are accessed through a server process; one server for each object.

To improve the availability of the database, it was decided to replicate each StudentRecord object, as described in Section 2. We decided to replicate the object states on three machines dedicated to this purpose (HP710s), the object stores. The system could therefore tolerate the failure of two object store machines. In addition, each primary server had two backup servers as described below.

As previously described, the registration system was expected to cope with 100 simultaneous users. Each such user has a dedicated Arjuna *client* process running on one of five HP710 Unix workstations of the Arjuna sub-system (the processing machines, see fig. 1) that is responsible for initiating transactions on student data. Because each StudentRecord is accessed through a separate server process this requires the ability to deal with 100 simultaneous processes. The same five workstations were used for this purpose to distribute this load evenly. These machines were also used for backup StudentRecord servers; each StudentRecord object was allocated a primary server machine, with backup server machines in the event of failures. If a server machine failed, load was evenly redistributed across the remaining (backup) machines; each primary has two backups.

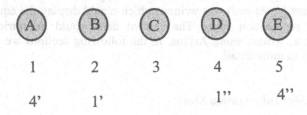

Figure 3: Server replica distribution.

Fig. 3 illustrates the server replication for 5 StudentRecord objects numbered 1 to 5. Machine A is the primary server for student number 1, with the first backup on machine B, and the final backup on D. Similarly, for student number 4, the primary server machine is D, with primary and secondary backups A and E respectively.

Each student is identified within the University, and to the database system, by a unique *student number*. With a suitable hashing function, the student number was found to provide a uniform distribution of primary servers across the available server machines. When a primary machine failure was detected, the client process recomputes the location of the new primary server for the student object based upon the new number of available machines. This mapping of student number to server location was performed dynamically while doing an 'open' on a StudentRecord.

4.2   The Registration Service

At the start of each registration day each front-end system is connected by a TCP connection to one of the five HP710 UNIX systems. One process for each connected front-end is created on the UNIX system; this process is responsible for interpreting the messages from the front-end and translating them into corresponding operations on the registration database. This is the Arjuna *client* process mentioned earlier, and typically existed for the day. In order to balance the load on these systems, each user was asked to connect to a particular client system. If that system was unavailable, then the user was asked to try a particular backup system from among the other machines.

Client processes, having received requests from the front-end systems, are then responsible for communicating with Arjuna server processes which represent the appropriate StudentRecord objects. As described earlier, the location of each server process was determined by the student number. If this is a request to open a student's record, then the client process starts an atomic action within which all other front-end requests on this student will occur. The server process exists for the duration of the registration action. The mapping of processes to machines is illustrated in fig. 4. In summary, the Arjuna sub-system thus consists of eight machines, of which three are used exclusively as object store machines.

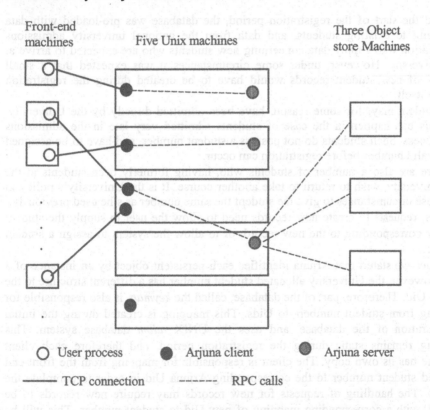

Figure 4: Client, server and user processes.

Included with the front-ends were 2-5 *swipe-stations*[1], which were introduced in the second year of operation. Registration forms were modified to include a bar-code

---

[1] The exact number of stations varied with the number of students.

containing the student's registration number. This was used by the swipe-stations to quickly determine the status of a student. These stations were only used to read the student's data, and therefore no modification of the data occurred.

5.   Registration Operation

Having described the overall system architecture we shall now examine the operation of the registration system, showing how existing students were registered, new students were added to the system, and the data was examined.

5.1   Initial Set-Up

Prior to the start of the registration period, the database was pre-loaded with data pertaining to existing students, and data from the national university admissions organisation who supply data concerning new students who are expected to arrive at the University. However, under some circumstances it was expected that a small number of new student records would have to be created during the registration process itself:

- A student may, for some reason, have been admitted directly by the University. This can happen in the case of students admitted very late in the admissions process. Such students do not possess a student number, and have to be assigned a valid number before registration can occur.
- There are also a number of students who, having formerly been students at the University, wish to return to take another course. It is the University's policy in these circumstances to give the student the same number as s/he used previously.

Thus, requests to create new records need to allow the user to supply the student number corresponding to the new record, or to allow the system to assign a student number.

Earlier we stated that Arjuna identifies each persistent object by an instance of a *Uid*. However, the University allocated student number has a different structure to the Arjuna Uid. Therefore, part of the database, called the *keymap*, is also responsible for mapping from student numbers to Uids. This mapping is created during the initial configuration of the database, and uses the UNIX *ndbm* database system. This mapping remains static during the registration period, and therefore each client machine has its own copy. The client is responsible for mapping from the front-end supplied student number to the corresponding Arjuna Uid in order to complete the request. The handling of requests for new records may require new records to be created, with a corresponding mapping of new Uid to student number. This will be described later.

5.2   Student Record Transactions

The front-end workstations run a program which presents the user with a form to be completed on behalf of a student. The initial data for this form is loaded from the registration database, if such data already exists within the system, or a new blank form is presented in the case of students not previously known to the system. The form consists of a variety of fields, some of which are editable as pure text, some of which are filled from menus, and some of which are provided purely for information and are not alterable by the user.

A registration activity consists of the following operations:
 (i) either opening (asking to retrieve) the record, or creating a new record.
 (ii) displaying the record on the screen of the front-end system.
 (iii) either closing it unmodified, or storing the record in the database.[2]

Any such activity is executed as an atomic action. The actual operations will be described in more detail later but we present an overview here:

- *Open*: retrieves an existing record from the database. This operation is used when the record may be modified by the front-end system, and therefore a write-lock is obtained on the database object.
- *New*: for students not already registered in the database this operation allows a new record to be created and modified before being stored.
- *Close*: terminates the atomic action without modifying the record in the database.
- *Store*: stores the record in the database, and terminates the atomic action.
- *Read*: retrieves an existing record from the database, in read-only mode. This operation is typically used by the swipe-stations, and does not allow modification of the record. Therefore, the Arjuna client immediately invokes a *Close* request upon receiving the student data.

In order to start the processing of a record, the user is required to enter the student number, which is the user's method of keying into the student record database. A registration activity is started upon receipt by an Arjuna client of an *Open* or *New* request from a front-end; the client starts an atomic action and the object corresponding to that record is activated. This involves the creation of a server process, which is then requested to retrieve the object from the object store. The architecture described above clearly implies that there is one instance of a client for each active front end. Thus, there should be at most one such active object extant for each client. Although the workstation programs were intended to avoid the possibility of multiple *Open* calls being made, it was decided to insure against erroneous behaviour on the part of the front-end by implementing the client program as a simple finite state machine. Thus, following an *Open* request, further *Open* requests are regarded as inadmissible until a subsequent *Close* or *Store* operation has been performed. Similarly, *Close* and *Store* operations are regarded as invalid unless there has previously been a successful *Open* request. This is illustrated in Fig. 5.

The StudentRecord object is responsible for ensuring that the record is locked at the start of a transaction, and Arjuna automatically releases the lock when the transaction completes (either successfully, or as a result of some failure condition). As stated previously, *Read* operations obtain *read* locks on the student object, whereas *Open* and *New* operations obtain *write* locks.

---

[2] A *Delete* operation is also provided, but was disabled during the registration period.

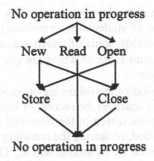

No operation in progress

New   Read   Open

Store   Close

No operation in progress

Figure 5: Possible sequences of registration operations.

6. The Operations

In the following sections we shall examine in detail the front-end operations, and how they interact with the StudentRecord objects in terms of the protocol described previously and the operations it provides.

6.1 Open

The *Open* operation is used to retrieve a record from the database given the student number. This operation assumes that the record exists, and one of the failure messages that may be returned indicates that there is no record corresponding to the given student number. The *Open* operation first has to interrogate the *keymap* to map the student number into a corresponding Arjuna *Uid*. If an Arjuna *Uid* is successfully located, an atomic action is started, and a *retrieveExclusiveRecord* call is made to the appropriate server, chosen according to the supplied student number. The server will try to obtain a lock on the record and get the state of the StudentRecord from the object.

The *retrieveExclusiveRecord* call will either succeed, in which case the record is delivered to the front-end, or it will fail, causing an error message to be returned to the front-end and the atomic action to abort. The reasons why this call may fail are that the record does not exist, or the record is locked in a conflicting mode. If *retrieveExclusiveRecord* indicates that the record is locked, then this information is relayed directly back to the user via an appropriate message; the user then has the option of retrying, or attempting some other activity. The remaining failure is basically a time out, indicating a "no reply". This is interpreted by the client as a failure of the server. If this occurs, then the client attempts to access the record using one of the backup servers, as described previously.

The server process created in response to the *retrieveExclusiveRecord* call remains in existence until the client informs the server that it is no longer required. This will happen either because the *retrieveExclusiveRecord* call itself fails, or because the front-end user finishes the registration activity through the *Store* or *Close* operation.

The life of the server, the object, and the atomic action is precisely the duration of a registration activity.

6.2   Read

The *Read* operation is similar to *Open*, but invokes the *retrieveRecord* operation on the StudentRecord object. Because this obtains the StudentRecord data for read-only operations, such as required by the swipe-stations, the client automatically issues a *Close* request. This helps to reduce the time for which the record is locked, which could prevent other users from manipulating the data. This is the only operation which the front-end can issue which encapsulates an entire atomic action, i.e., when the student data is finally displayed the registration atomic action, student record object, and server have all been terminated.

6.3   Store

The *Store* operation is used to *commit* the atomic action and transfer the data, possibly modified by the user, into the object store database. The *Store* message generates a *replaceRecord* call to the server, which may fail because the server has crashed. This is a potentially more serious situation than if the server crashes before a *retrieveExclusiveRecord* call is made, since this represents a failure while an atomic action is in progress. All modifications made between retrieval and the attempt to save the record will be lost, but the atomic action mechanism will ensure that the original state of the record is preserved. If the *Store* fails, an appropriate message will be displayed at the front-end and the user has the option to restart the registration activity.

6.4   Close

The *Close* operation is used simply to end the registration atomic action. It is used in the situation where a user has retrieved a record, has no further use for it, but does not wish to modify it. The *Open* operation will have started a new atomic action, and have caused a server process to be created. The *Close* terminates the atomic action (causes it to *abort*) and also causes the server process to terminate. The *Close* operation cannot fail even if the server crashes; a failed server will simply impact on performance since aborting the action includes sending a message to the server asking it to terminate.

6.5   New

As mentioned previously, some students may appear at registration having no record in the database. There are two possible reasons for this, and hence two variants of the *New* operation:

  (i) the student is returning unexpectedly for another year, and already has a valid student number given in a previous year.

(ii) the student is new to the University and does not have a student number. Therefore, the system allocates a new student number from a pool of "spare" numbers.

In case (ii), the pool of numbers is known before the registration begins, and blank records are pre-created and registered with the system; the mapping from Uid to student number is also known and written in the *keymap* database. In order to ensure that simultaneous *New* requests obtain different student numbers, the system uses another (replicated) Arjuna object: an *index* object, which indicates the next available student number in the free pool. This is an increment operation that atomically updates the index and returns the new number to the user.

However, in case (i) a new Arjuna object representing the student record has to be created and stored in the database, and the appropriate mapping from student number to Arjuna Uid stored in an accessible place. Because each client has its own copy of the *keymap* database, the creation of new *keymap* entries poses a problem of synchronising the updates to the individual copies of the *keymap* database on the various client machines. It was decided that the problems associated with the *New* operation could be solved by administrative action, and by accepting a single point of failure for this minor part of the operation[3]. An alternative *ndbm* database called *newkeymap* was created in a shared file store, available to each Arjuna client system via NFS. This database contained the mappings between new database object Uids and their corresponding student numbers. It was read/write accessible to users, and was protected from simultaneous conflicting operations via appropriate concurrency control.

Any *Open* request must clearly be able to observe changes made to the database as a whole, and therefore it will have to search both the *newkeymap* and the *keymap* databases. If the shared file service becomes unavailable, no new student records can be created, and neither is it possible to access those new student records which have already been created. It would be possible to minimise this difficulty by merging the *newkeymap* and *keymap* at times when the system is quiescent.

Given the new (or front-end supplied) student number, a corresponding StudentRecord object is created with a blank record. The front-end user can then proceed to input the student's information. In order to ensure that there would never be any conflict over multiple accesses to *newkeymap*, and therefore to the new number pool, it was also decided that the *New* command should be disabled on each front-end system except one, which was under the direct control of the Registrar's staff. This machine had several backups.

7.   Testing and Live Experience

During the development of the front-end programs, tests were done to ensure that the front-end software performed satisfactorily. However, the timetable for the whole operation meant that it was impractical to mount a realistic test using the intended

---

[3] In excess of 12,000 students were registered over the registration periods and approximately 200 of these were added using *New*.

front-end systems themselves, involving as it would a human operator for each such station. However, it proved relatively straightforward to construct a program to run on a number of Unix workstations around the campus, which simulated the basic behaviour of the front-end systems as seen by the registration database. Each simulated front-end system would retrieve a random record, wait a short period of time to simulate the action of entering data, and then return the record to the system, possibly having modified it.

It had been estimated that over the registration period, the system would be available for some 30 hours. In this time, it was expected that of the order of 10,000 students would be registered, and that the database would need to be about 15 Mbytes in size. In some cases, the student record would need to be accessed more than once, so that it was estimated that approximately 15,000 transactions would take place. We therefore anticipated that the expected load would be of the order of 500 transactions per hour, or a little over six per workstation per hour. This however would be the average load, but it was felt that it would be more realistic to attempt to simulate the peak loading, which was estimated as follows: the human operator would be required to enter data for each student in turn; the changes to be made to each record would range from trivial to re-entering the whole record. In fact, in the case of students for whom no record was pre-loaded, it would be necessary for the whole of the students data to be entered from the workstation. It was therefore estimated that the time between retrieval and storing of the record would be between 30 seconds and 5 minutes.

7.1   Simulated Operation

A program was written which began by making a TCP connection to one of the Arjuna client machines. It then selected a student number at random from the *keymap* data base, retrieved the corresponding record, waited a random period of time, and then returned the record with a request either to store or simply to close the record. This final choice was also made at random. After performing the simulated transaction a fixed number of times, the program closed the TCP connection and terminated. The program recorded each transaction as it was made, the (random) time waited, the total time taken and the number of errors observed.

The object of this test was to discover at what point the system would become overloaded, with a view to "fine-tuning" the system. At the level of the Arjuna servers, it was possible to alter a time-out/retry within the RPC mechanism (i.e., between client and server) to achieve the optimal performance, and also to tune the ping daemon described earlier.

The front-end simulation therefore arranged for the record to be retrieved, a random interval of time uniformly distributed in the range 30 to 300 seconds was allowed to elapse, and the record was then returned to the system[4]. The variable parameters of the system were:

---

[4] With the addition of the swipe-stations, we reduced the estimated minimum time to 1 second, and tested the system with 10,000 simulated transactions in 2.5 hours.

- the range of values for the time between retrieving and storing the record.
- the probability that the returned record would have been modified.
- the number of transactions to be performed by each run of the program.

7.1.1   Results

The Arjuna ping daemon was described in Section 3.2. The failure of a machine is suspected whenever a ping daemon fails to respond (after several retries) to an "are you alive" message. In order to reduce the probability of incorrect failure suspicion due to network and machine congestion it was important to tune the timeout and retry values which the ping daemon used. By running the tests at greater than expected maximum load it was possible to tune these values to reduce the possibility of incorrect failure suspicion.

The longest run of the test program carried out a total of 1000 simulated transactions, which took approximately 2 hours to complete. With 10 such processes running, this represented 10000 transactions in about 2 hours, or 5000 transactions per hour. This was far in excess of the expected average load during live operation, and approximately twice the expected maximum transaction rate. From these results, we tuned Arjuna to detect a crashed machine in 10 seconds. Because the simulated load was greater than that expected during registration, we were confident that we could differentiate between overloaded and crashed machines during registration.

7.2   Live Operation

The live experience was acquired by observing, and to some extent participating in, the operation of the system during actual registration. At its peak, the system had over 100 simultaneous users performing work, and on average there were approximately 60. Many of the problems that arose during this period were unrelated to the technical aspects of the system. Such problems were: incorrect operation of the system by its operators, including attempting to repeat operations because the response was not perceived to be satisfactory, failure to install the latest version of the software on the workstations, and similar problems. In fact overall the system performed extremely well, with good performance even in the presence of failures.

There was one major difficulty that arose during the first year of operation which caused the system to be shut down prematurely (about half an hour earlier than scheduled). This occurred at the time when, and because, the system was heavily loaded, which resulted in slower than expected response times. The original figures for the number of registration users and hence the expected rate of transactions were exceeded by over 50%. Because the system had not been tuned for this configuration, server processes began to incorrectly suspect failures of object store machines. Since the suspicion of failure depends upon timeout values and the load on the object store machine, it was possible for different servers to suspect different object store machine failures. This *virtual partitioning* meant that some replica states diverged instead of all having the same states, and therefore it was possible for different users to see inconsistent states. Using timestamps associated with the object states it was possible to reconcile these inconsistencies, and the system was re-tuned to accommodate the extra load.

Although no hardware failures occurred during the first year, in the second year the registration system successfully coped with two machine failures. The machines which we were using for registration were shared resources, available for use by other members of the University. One of the Arjuna client machines had a faulty disk which caused the machine to crash when accessed over NFS. This occurred twice during the registration period when other users of the machine were running non-registration specific applications which accessed the NFS mounted disk.

7.2.1 Performance Graphs

The following graphs are based upon the statistics gathered from the 1995-1996 registration period. Graph 1 shows the total number of transactions (*Open/Save*, *Read/Close*, *New/Save*) performed during each hour of the registration operation. The registration system was active for 10 days, and each working day was of 13 hrs duration; the first 5 days were the main period when students presented themselves for registration, whereas the last 5 days were used more for administration purposes. Each day is represented by two peaks, representing the main morning and afternoon sessions, with the minimum occurring when students went to lunch.

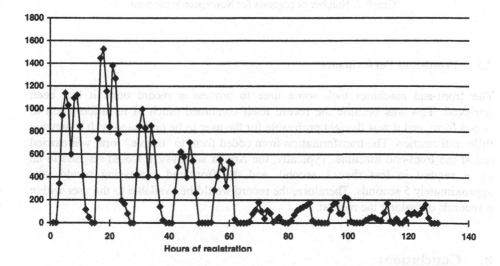

Graph 1: Number of transactions per hour.

As can be seen from the graph, the main period occurred on the second day, when approximately 10,000 transactions occurred, with an average rate of about 750 transactions per hour. The large number of transactions, and the high transaction rate can be attributed to the swipe stations, which only performed *Read/Close* operations.

Graph 1 showed all transactions which occurred during a given registration day. Graph 2 shows the number of *New/Save* operations which occurred. Most new students were registered during the first two days, with approximately 400 being registered in that period.

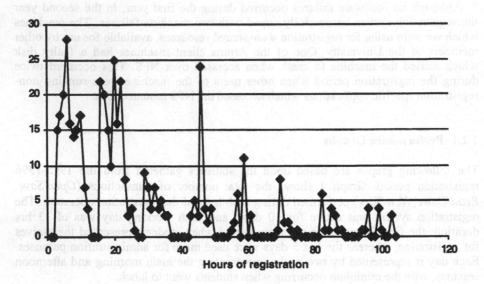

Graph 2: Number of requests for New records per hour.

7.3   Front-End Performance

The front-end machines took some time to process a record once it had been retrieved. This was because the record itself contained much of its information in coded form, and it was thought preferable for the user to be presented with somewhat fuller information. The transformation from coded form to "usable" form was carried out at the front-end machine. Typically, the Arjuna sub-system would respond to an *Open* request in less than 1 second, and the front-end processing would take approximately 5 seconds. Therefore, the record would be available to the user within 6 seconds of making the request.

8.   Conclusions

The system described here has been used every year since 1994. The University has committed to continuing to use the registration system, and some considerable effort has gone into making the system manageable by non-Arjuna experts. The Arjuna system was used in this application to provide high reliability and availability in case of possible failure of certain components. When failures did occur, the use of atomic transactions and replication guaranteed consistency and forward progress. The system has performed well even at maximum load, and the occurrence of failures has caused minor glitches, to the extent that most users did not realise anything had happened. In the context of the ultimate purpose of the exercise, namely the completion of the registration process, the outcome was exactly what we could have wished for. This positive field experience does indicate that it is possible to build high availability distributed applications by making use of commodity components, such as networked Unix workstations and relying entirely on software implemented fault-tolerance techniques for meeting application specific availability and consistency requirements.

Acknowledgements

We thank the staff from the University's Management Information Services for willingly taking part in this 'adventure'. The work on Arjuna system has been supported over the years from research grants from EPSRC and ESPRIT.

References

1. C. J. Dimmer, "The Tandem Non-stop System",   Resilient Computing Systems, (T. Anderson , ed.), pp. 178-196, Collins, 1985
2. D. Wilson, "The STRATUS Computer system",   Resilient Computing Systems, (T. Anderson , ed.), pp. 208-231, Collins, 1985.
3. S. K. Shrivastava, G. N. Dixon, and G. D. Parrington, "An Overview of Arjuna: A Programming System for Reliable Distributed Computing," IEEE Software, Vol. 8, No. 1, pp. 63-73, January 1991.
4. G. D. Parrington et al, "The Design and Implementation of Arjuna", USENIX Computing Systems Journal, Vol. 8., No. 3, pp. 253-306, Summer 1995.
5. S. K. Shrivastava, "Lessons learned from building and using the Arjuna distributed programming system," Int. Workshop on Distributed Computing Systems: Theory meets Practice, Dagsthul, September 1994, LNCS 938, Springer-Verlag, July 1995.
6. P.A. Bernstein et al, "Concurrency Control and Recovery in Database Systems", Addison-Wesley, 1987.
7. M. C. Little, "Object Replication in a Distributed System", PhD Thesis, University of Newcastle upon Tyne, September 1991. (ftp://arjuna.ncl.ac.uk/pub/Arjuna/Docs/Theses/TR-376-9-91_EuropeA4.tar.Z)
8. M. C. Little and S. K. Shrivastava, "Object Replication in Arjuna", BROADCAST Project Technical Report No. 50, October 1994.
   (ftp://arjuna.ncl.ac.uk/pub/Arjuna/Docs/Papers/Object_Replication_in_Arjuna.ps.Z)

Quality of Service and Electronic Newspaper: The Etel Solution

Valérie Issarny, Michel Banâtre, Boris Charpiot, and Jean-Marc Menaud

INRIA

IRISA, Campus de Beaulieu, 35042 Rennes Cedex, France
{issarny,banatre,jmenaud}@irisa.fr

Abstract. Making electronic newspapers available to users is an attractive business for newspaper editors. The production of electronic newspapers may *a priori* be realized at low cost using the editor's news base, while enabling to attain a larger audience. However, the success of an electronic newspaper in a commercial setting depends upon the provided quality of service. The newspaper must guarantee to its users, both content quality in terms of reading comfort, and access quality in terms of response time. This paper presents the Etel electronic newspaper whose main design objective is to guarantee high quality of service to users. Content quality is achieved through the design and production of electronic editions in close collaboration with a newspaper editor. Access quality is realized through the design and implementation of a dedicated client-server distributed system. The proposed distributed system exploits the specifics of electronic newspapers. Precisely, most newspaper readers systematically consult the various editions of their usual newspaper in the same way (*e.g.* a reader may consult his newspaper by first reading local and then sport pages). In the context of an electronic newspaper, this means that we can safely assume the existence of user profiles in terms of access patterns to newspaper editions. This feature allows us to propose profile-based automatic prefetching and load balancing strategies, which together enable to offer a highly responsive and scalable distributed system.

1 Introduction

The ever-increasing use of computing facilities by the general public makes attractive the electronic production of newspaper editions. Among benefits, this allows a newspaper editor to attain a much larger audience, and to offer additional services to its customers by exploiting together its information base and processing capacities. Various electronic newspapers are now available over the INTERNET, either *via* proprietary online services (*e.g.* AMERICA ON LINE) or the World Wide Web (*e.g.* USA TODAY). The success of an electronic newspaper depends upon the *quality of service* it provides to its users. The electronic version of a newspaper must guarantee a quality that makes the electronic version at least as attractive as a paper version. In other words, reading an electronic newspaper should be as convenient as reading a conventional newspaper from

S. Krakowiak, S.K. Shrivastava (Eds.): Distributed Systems, LNCS 1752, pp. 472–496, 2000.

the customers' standpoint. Meeting such a requirement implies to offer an adequate layout for pages of the electronic newspaper as well as to display requested pages in a timely manner. Let us examine available electronic newspapers from that perspective:

- The layout of electronic newspapers varies depending on whether the editor chooses a Web view or a newspaper view. In the fist case, pages are classical HTML pages, possibly including frames. In the second case, the editor decides to have a presentation of the electronic newspaper that is close to the one of a newspaper, with changes made so as to have a layout that fits in a screen.
- The timely delivery of pages is still an open issue. Newspapers available *via* the Web cannot guarantee satisfying response time due to the current limitation of the Web from this standpoint. Newspapers available *via* proprietary online services in general exhibit better response time through adequate server configuration, but still remain dependent upon the INTERNET bandwidth.

While the provision of a newspaper having a satisfactory layout may be considered as being achieved by existing electronic newspapers, the delivery of an electronic newspaper in a timely manner is yet to be solved.

This paper presents the Etel electronic newspaper that has been designed so as to offer a high quality of service to users. The provided quality of service lies in two complementary results: (*i*) pages of the electronic newspapers are automatically produced using the database of a newspaper editor, according to quality criteria set by the editor; (*ii*) pages are delivered to users over a client-server distributed system that has been specifically designed so as to ensure fast response time while optimizing resource usage. The next section gives an overview of the Etel electronic newspaper, precising the targeted quality of service together with resulting design decisions. Section 3 then details the primary constituents of the Etel distributed system, introducing the mechanisms used for ensuring timely delivery of the newspaper pages to a large number of users (*i.e.* in the order of tens thousands) together with their performance evaluation. Finally, we conclude in Section 4, summarizing our contribution and addressing our current and future work.

2   The Etel Electronic Newspaper and Its Quality of Service

The quality of service of an electronic newspaper can be evaluated according to two complementary criteria:

- The *content quality* that relates to the quality of the displayed information according to the user's particular interest as well as the information presentation.
- The *access quality* that refers to the ability to guarantee fast response time to users.

Achieving the former relates to the production of the newspaper's pages. The latter appertains to the distributed system over which the pages are transferred from the server to clients. Ideally, access quality should be guaranteed in the presence of failure so as to propose a highly available service to users. Up to now, adequate support for fault tolerance has not been integrated in the Etel system as we preferred to concentrate on the issue of ensuring fast response times to users. The following subsections detail design decisions that were made for the Etel newspaper service with respect to offering both content and access qualities to users.

2.1 Providing Content Quality

Content quality bears upon the users' interest in the information they are given access to, and the associated reading comfort. Thus, providing content quality to users is a subjective criterion that is user-specific. However, meeting the expectation of a given user population may be achieved through appropriate design decisions.

Although the acceptance of a newspaper with respect to its content is a user-specific matter, we may foresee the adhesion of a population of users by producing the electronic newspaper in collaboration with a newspaper editor. The electronic newspaper is expected to gain acceptance at least with the newspaper's usual readers. The Etel newspaper has been designed in close collaboration with the Ouest-France editor, that is the major French local newspaper editor. Thus, Etel editions are produced using the Ouest-France information base. Furthermore, in order to best match users interests, every customer subscribing to the Etel newspaper service may specify the topics in which he is interested so as to give him access to individualized editions. This user-specific information is known as the *user's profile* [15]. Ensuring content quality further requires to address the reading comfort of the electronic newspaper from the users' standpoint (*e.g.* how convenient is the reading of pages, the retrieval of information). Regarding existing electronic newspapers, reading comfort is achieved by choosing either a Web view or a newspaper view. In our opinion, the former approach has several drawbacks. In particular, it does not exploit the expertise of newspaper editors who have a long experience in offering attractive information presentation. This has led us to undertake the latter approach. From the standpoint of producing pages that fit within a screen, it has been realized by designing pages in close collaboration with Ouest-France, building upon the Ouest-France newspaper's layout[1]. Another factor that has to be taken into account when producing an electronic newspaper ensuring content quality is the resulting cost for the newspaper editor. A requirement of the Ouest-France editor was to have an *automatic production* of the electronic newspaper, by exploiting the information base used for producing paper versions.

---

[1] Let us remark that the Etel approach to the production of electronic editions can be re-used by other editors, it amounts to change the layout of pages accordingly.

Based on the above, the implementation of the Etel electronic newspaper had to achieve the following functions to ensure content quality to its customers, while meeting Ouest-France requirements:

(*i*) Coupled production of paper and electronic editions, *i.e.* production of the two versions from the same data.

(*ii*) Customization of the electronic edition according to the user's profile.

(*iii*) Presentation of the information according to screen display, which combines the advantages of both the paper version (*e.g.* layout) and the electronic support (*e.g.* interactivity).

Regarding the third point, let us mention that the electronic newspaper gives access to a set of interactive services, derived from the general information embedded in usual newspapers (*e.g.* theater and TV programs, weather forecast). The system further offers encyclopedia-like services, which exploit the information base of the newspaper editor. In particular, such services allow users to query for customized thematic newspaper-like documents.

For the automatic production of electronic editions, we exploit the fact that the structure of a newspaper is invariant. Distinct editions of a newspaper offer information relating to a fixed set of topics, which is organized as a hierarchy. This hierarchy serves to place associated articles within a given edition. For instance, the Ouest-France newspaper offers news relating to the following set of general topics: international, national, local, sport, and miscellaneous, which further subdivide into more specialized topics. Hence, the structure of a newspaper may be defined using two complementary data structures:

(*i*) The *logical data structure* that defines the hierarchy of topics covered by the newspaper.

(*ii*) The *physical data structure* that defines the mapping of the newspaper's logical data onto the newspaper's physical support (*e.g.* screen, paper).

In the Etel framework, the logical data structure is unique while there are two physical data structures characterizing respectively the paper and electronic versions of the newspaper. The production of a given edition then relies upon relating the articles of the day to the logical data structure, and producing the edition according to the physical data structure. Focusing on electronic editions, they are produced as PDF files, using the following software tools:

− XPress[2] that is aimed at press editing, with plug-ins for the generation of the editions' pages as PDF files, based on the newspaper's logical and physical data structures and the articles of the day.

− Acrobat[3] for the presentation of the so-built editions on the user's display.

[2] http://www.quark.com
[3] http://www.adobe.com/Acrobat/

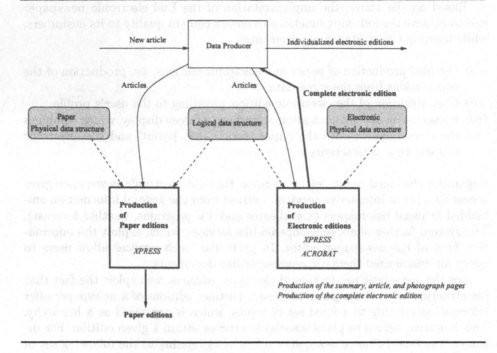

Fig. 1. Production of the newspaper editions

Figure 1 depicts the production of newspaper editions using the database of articles, and the logical and physical data structures. Concerning the electronic editions, the production tool produces the base daily edition. This edition is then individualized for each user by taking the subset of the base edition that relates to the topics in which the user is interested.

An electronic edition is organized as a set of pages (*i.e.* PDF files) where each page corresponds to either a summary, an article, or a photograph (see Figure 2). A summary page roughly corresponds to a page of the paper version. In addition, except for the newspaper's first page, each summary page relates to a specific topic (*e.g.* the summary page of Figure 2.*a* relates to the *Pays d'Alençon* local topic). The content of a summary page differs from the one of its corresponding paper page by summarizing every article into the article's title and photograph (if any), and hyperlinks to the corresponding article and photograph (*e.g.* Figures 2.*b* and 2.*c* give the article and photograph pages for the article entitled *Belote : les qualifiés pour la finale* relating to the local sub-topic *Le Méle-sur-Sarthe* of the summary page). Every page further integrates a frame on the right-hand side of the screen, listing customized hyperlinks to a set of topics according to the user's profile.

a) A summary page

b) An article page

c) A photograph page

Fig. 2. A sample of Etel pages

A page of an electronic edition subdivides into a number of PDF files. Each article leads to produce: (*i*) a file containing the text of the article for both the summary and article pages, and (*ii*) two files per photograph associated to the article, embedding respectively the full-page-size and small-size photographs. A summary page is then made of the sets of PDF files associated to its articles but files embedding full-page size photographs.

2.2 Providing Access Quality

As for the content quality criterion, the access quality of an electronic newspaper is also user-specific: the time taken to read an electronic newspaper edition must be close to the one that would be taken to read its counterpart paper edition. Ideally, this means that a requested page of an electronic edition is made available to a user in a time interval that does not exceed the one taken to consult a given paper page. The only way to meet this ideal timeliness requirement is to have the electronic newspaper locally available on the user's machine before the user accesses the newspaper. However, such a solution is not practical due to the newspaper's storage needs. Precisely, a Ouest-France daily edition actually decomposes into 40 regional editions whose topics may either be shared by a subset of regional editions or be specific to one edition in the case of village-specific

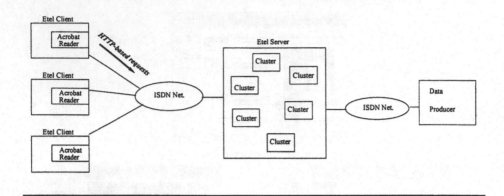

Fig. 3. Architecture of the Etel distributed system

topics. The ensemble of Ouest-France daily editions leads to the production of about 400 pages, each having an average size of 80 Kbytes. The Etel newspaper further enables a user profile to embed an evolving set of topics relating to distinct Ouest-France regional editions. In addition, we want the service to be accessible from a large variety of terminals including those having a low storage capacity (*e.g.*, Web phone, set-top-box). Thus, we had to design and implement a client-server distributed system, dedicated to Etel, so as to guarantee timely delivery of requested pages to clients from the server, in a way that approaches the ideal case without requiring large storage capacity for user machines. Precisely, timeliness requirements in the context of an electronic newspaper subdivide into the following constraints:

- *Timeliness* at the level of each user, *i.e.* providing fast response time to every user.
- *Scalability* of the server, *i.e.* supporting a large number of users at the lowest cost in terms of resource needs, while maintaining timeliness guarantees.

Timeliness and scalability constraints are addressed through the following design decisions for the Etel distributed system whose architecture is depicted in Figure 3:

- Every Etel client runs a *predictive prefetching strategy* for performing server accesses, which is aimed at providing timeliness guarantees.
- The Etel server that handles pages delivery to users upon client requests is structured as a distributed server composed of a set of autonomous clusters. The server further runs a specific *load balancing strategy* aimed at providing scalability guarantees.

- The networking infrastructure is based on private networks. Precisely, the interconnections among the Etel clients and server, and between the Etel server and the database server (*i.e.* the Ouest-France server storing the information base) are achieved through an ISDN network. Furthermore, the machines (*i.e.* PCs) composing a cluster are interconnected through a high-speed ATM network.

The use of an ISDN network for the interconnection of clients to the Etel server may be seen as a restriction compared to an INTERNET-based interconnection. However, meeting timeliness constraints of the Etel electronic newspaper requires to have guarantee about the available network bandwidth, which is not currently achievable over INTERNET. Let us notice that this restriction is temporary, the Etel distributed system will be run over INTERNET as soon as a resource reservation protocol will be available over it. In particular, this perspective, which is targeted by Ouest-France, has led us to base the Etel system on the Web infrastructure: the protocol used for interaction among Etel clients and server is based on HTTP. In addition, we are currently working on the production of the electronic newspaper pages as HTML files instead of PDF files.

The next section details the Etel distributed system for which our main design objective was to meet the aforementioned timeliness and scalability constraints. Our solution bears upon the specifics of an electronic newspaper. Precisely, according to information provided to us by Ouest-France, most newspaper readers systematically consult the various editions of their usual newspaper in the same way (*e.g.* a reader may consult his newspaper by first reading local and then sport pages). In the context of an electronic newspaper, this means that we can safely assume the existence of user profiles in terms of access patterns to newspaper editions. In the remainder, such profiles are qualified as *access profiles*, while the term *profile* is used to refer to the set of topics usually consulted by a user.

3   The Etel Distributed System

For the design of the Etel distributed system, we exploited the existence of both user profiles and user access profiles to conveniently drive data distribution over the system's elements. On the client site, the user's access profile serves to anticipate the user's access and hence realize automatic predictive prefetching [20]. This leads the Etel system to make a page available on the client site before the user actually requests the page. On the server site, the set of user profiles may be processed so as to group together users having close profiles, which further serves to define corresponding data groups that are distributed over the server's clusters [6].

3.1   Enhancing Response Time Through Prefetching

The main component provided within the Etel system so as guarantee timely delivery of pages to users lies in the implementation of an automatic predictive prefetching policy exploiting users' access profiles, within clients. We first give an overview of existing proposals in the area of predictive prefetching, and point out the novelty of our solution compared to them. We then detail the proposed policy and discuss its integration within the Etel system.

Background: The prefetching strategy that we propose is based on previous work on file system prefetching. Proposals in this area are briefly sketched below and are followed by an overview of existing prefetching techniques for the Web.

File prefetching is recognized as an effective technique for improving file access performance. Existing techniques fall into two categories:

(*i*) *Application-directed prefetching* where prefetching decisions are made according to hints provided either by applications [5,25] or by users [28].

(*ii*) *Automatic prefetching* where prefetching decisions are initiated by the operating system [10,17,19].

While application-directed prefetching strategies rely on user-provided hints for anticipating file accesses, automatic prefetching strategies anticipate file system requests based on past file accesses. More precisely, automatic strategies rely on the management of a directed *access graph* that captures the correlation between file accesses: a node in the graph corresponds to a file and an arc between two nodes denotes an *access dependency*. Then, given the access to a file denoted by a node *A* of the graph, all the files denoted by nodes that are pointed by arcs leaving *A* are likely to be accessed and hence are eligible for prefetching. In order to differentiate eligible files, the arcs of the access graph are generally weighed by the number of times (or frequency) the pointed node is accessed after the origin node. Thus, each arc gives the probability of a particular file being opened soon after another file, which serves ordering files that are eligible for prefetching. Existing automatic techniques differ in the way dependencies are identified. First, dependencies can be identified at the granularity of either the file server as in [11,17] or of the client as in [19]. In the latter case, independent accesses (performed by different processes) are distinguished, while they are grouped in the former. Another difference among existing proposals lies in whether a dependency is identified when an access follows immediately another [17,19] or is performed within a given lookahead period of a number of accesses after another [11]. The performance of an automatic prefetching technique is conditioned by the accuracy of prefetching decisions. While a high accuracy can be expected from application-directed prefetching, the accuracy of automatic prefetching depends upon the actual repetition of access patterns within applications. Another point that impacts on the performance gained with prefetching relates to the interaction between prefetching and caching. Prefetching and caching strategies must be integrated so as to avoid prefetch decisions leading to harmful cache replacement [5,25,16].

Prefetching techniques for the Web can be classified in a way similar to techniques proposed for file systems:

(*i*) *User-directed prefetching* consists of making prefetching decisions based on user-provided hints [28].

(*ii*) *Automatic prefetching* consists of making prefetching decisions based on information gathered at the level of Web servers [24,3].

Both user-directed and automatic strategies are close to their file system counterpart: prefetching decisions are either based upon user-provided hints or an access graph that serves making prefetching decisions for Web files. However, there is a noteworthy difference regarding automatic strategies, which results from the abstraction level at which the prefetching strategy takes place. Unlike automatic file system strategies, automatic Web strategies do not require any kernel modifications. To our knowledge, all the existing automatic prefetching strategies that are dedicated to the Web, implement management of the access graph on the server. However, they differ depending on whether there is one graph per active client [24] or a single graph that is global to the server [3]; we refer to the former as an *individual strategy* and to the latter as a *global strategy*. Existing proposals also differ in the way prefetching decisions are made: the server either decides unilaterally to send together with the requested file, the files that are likely to be accessed next [3], or just notifies the client of these files [24]. In the latter case, it is the client that decides to prefetch the files based on local environmental factors such as the content of the local cache or the current system load. Using Web traces, its has been shown that the individual prefetching strategy proposed in [24] improves the Web mean latency of up to 60% but causes an increase in the network traffic. Similar results were observed for global strategies [3]. As for file system prefetching, the actual benefits of a prefetching strategy for the Web lie in the accuracy of prefetching decisions. Ideally, the prefetching decisions should correspond to the actual requests, hence leading to a significant latency improvement without increasing the network traffic and server load. Here again, higher accuracy is expected from a user-directed strategy. However, we believe that an automatic strategy is preferable because it leads to a more comfortable service for users.

The accuracy of automatic prefetching decisions for a distributed information system is highly conditioned by the redundancy of performed accesses, which is itself dependent upon the type of service that is accessed. This calls for service-specific strategies, which provides an appealing tradeoff between a user-directed and an automatic strategy. By focusing on one type of service, *i.e.* an electronic newspaper, we are able to anticipate at a high degree the future user behavior in a systematic way. Precisely, distinct editions of a newspaper have all the same structure, which is based on the ordering of topics within the newspaper; editions differ only by their articles. Furthermore, a newspaper reader usually consults distinct editions according to the same pattern, which reflects his personal interest in each topic. In the context of an electronic newspaper, this means that the same hyperdocument graph is used to represent the various personalized newspaper editions made available to a given user, and that the user usually

accesses the hyperdocument according to the same pattern[4]. In a way similar
to the proposal of [24], we introduce an individual strategy for realizing automatic prefetching in Etel. However, there are two key differences. In the work
of [24], the access graph reflects the user's past accesses during a single session
and is managed on the server. In our strategy, the access graph is a permanent
data structure that registers the user's past accesses over distinct sessions and
is managed on the client. This results in a twofold improvement:

(i) Prefetching decisions are more accurate because they rely on the observation
    of the user access pattern for a longer period. In particular, notice that the
    strategy of [24] is effective only when a user re-accesses files of the Web
    server during the same session. Higher accuracy is further offered through
    the use of a statistical method in addition to the access graph for computing
    predictions.
(ii) Better load balance is achieved between the client and the server because
    the server does not manage user-specific information.

In addition, we have designed a client caching strategy and a client-server protocol that are integrated with our prefetching strategy, which together minimize
the penalty of prefetching that is the resulting traffic increase.

Our prefetching strategy is primarily aimed at an electronic newspaper service and hence will provide optimal performance for this type of service only.
Nonetheless, we argue that for other services, it will perform at least as well
as alternative individual prefetching strategies. In the same way, re-accesses are
reflected by the access graph. Differences will be observed with global strategies.
They may allow more accurate prefetching decisions when access patterns of
different users overlap. Notice that such a feature of access patterns is the main
assumption governing the implementation of Web proxy caches. In general, we
see a global prefetching strategy as complementary to an individual one rather
than as competing. In particular, in the case of an electronic newspaper, the
existence of a global strategy enables to take into account the possible access to
temporary hot news topics, relating to subjects that are usually of no interest
for the user (e.g., increasing enthusiasm of the French for football during the
1998 World cup).

Profile-Based Prefetching: An automatic prefetching strategy lies in the
definition of the following components:

– An *access graph* for keeping track of past accesses.
– A *prediction algorithm* that predicts future accesses given the user's current
  access, the access graph, and complementary statistical data.
– A *prefetching algorithm* that prefetches data according to the result returned
  by the prediction algorithm.

---

[4] Let us remark that the hyperdocument graph derives from the logical data structure
(see § 2.1); it is the subset of the logical data structure that includes only the topics
read by the user.

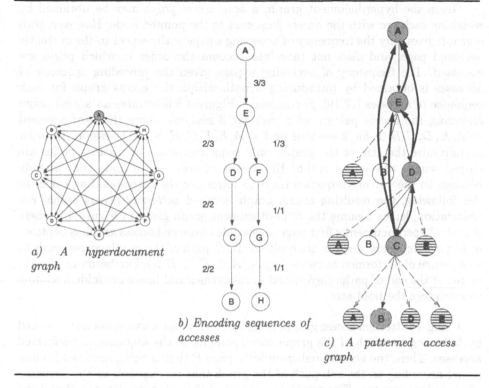

a) A hyperdocument graph

b) Encoding sequences of accesses

c) A patterned access graph

Fig. 4. Graphs relating to a hyperdocument

Prior to detail the above constituents, we outline the design elements for the proposed strategy.

As stated previously, a newspaper edition is characterized by an hyperdocument, which is structured as a set of *pages* and each page contains a set of *hyperlinks* that determine the pages that are accessible from it. Each page further gives information relating to a particular topic (*e.g.* international politics, national economics, sports, ...). Hence, the content of each page is updated daily but the hyperdocument structure is invariant. As shown in Figure 4.*a*, a hyperdocument can be represented as a directed graph where each node corresponds to a page and an arc to a hyperlink. A user then consults the hyperdocument pages according to an order that reflects his personal interest for the corresponding topics. Notice that the hyperdocument graph is fully connected; this is due to the presence of the frame listing customized hyperlinks within each page (see Subsection 2.1). Let us recall that, in the general case, a newspaper page decomposes into a number of text files and of image files. From the standpoint of automatic prefetching, this means that a prefetching decision is made with respect to a page, possibly leading to prefetch an ensemble of files.

Given the hyperdocument graph, a *base access graph* may be obtained by weighing each arc with the *access frequency* to the pointed node. However, such a graph gives only the frequency of accessing a page with respect to the currently accessed page, and does not take into account the order in which pages are accessed. The frequency of accessing a page given the preceding sequence of accesses is obtained by introducing a path within the access graph for each sequence of accesses [17,19]. For instance, Figure 4.*b* illustrates an access graph encoding the access pattern of a user for 3 sessions where the user accessed $< A, E, D, C, B >$ for 2 sessions and $< A, E, F, G, H >$ for 1 session. In order to minimize the size of the graph, only sequences made of distinct nodes are stored within the access graph. Hence, the re-access to a node that already belongs to the current sequence leads to introduce the corresponding cycle. In the following, the resulting access graph is called *patterned access graph*. For illustration, let us assume the hyperdocument graph given in Figure 4.*a* where A is the hyperdocument's first page; a possible patterned access graph is depicted in Figure 4.*c* where weights are omitted. Each path of the graph corresponds to a sequence of performed accesses (*e.g.* $< A, E, D, C, B >$). Furthermore, shaded nodes at the end of paths correspond to re-accesses and hence are folded, leading to introduce the bold arcs.

Using a patterned access graph, *access prediction* for a user session is achieved by following the path of the graph corresponding to the sequence of performed accesses. Then, the access prediction for a page P that is being accessed is computed according to the sub-path of the graph that corresponds to the sequence of preceding accesses. The terminal node N of the sub-path denotes P and the prediction for P is the set of pages pointed by arcs leaving N. For instance, let us consider the graph of Figure 4.*c* and let us assume that the user is consulting page D subsequently to the sequence $< A, E >$. The prediction for D then contains the set of pages A, B, C and E. Pages in the prediction are further ordered according to the decreasing weights (*i.e.* access frequencies) of the arcs from D to these nodes (*i.e.* the greater the access frequency is, the more the pointed node is likely to be accessed). However, the shortcoming of using access frequencies for predicting future accesses is that it may take time to capture changes in the user's access pattern. A change in the access pattern is taken into account in the access prediction only when the order of the access frequencies becomes modified. In order to detect earlier access pattern changes in the prediction process, we use a method based on *statistical quality-control charts* [29], *i.e.*, the generic *Exponentially Weighting Moving Average* (EWMA) approach [7]. Briefly stated, statistical quality-control charts are aimed at both controlling that a fabrication process is stable with respect to the required quality specification, and reducing the number of products that do not conform with the product's specification. In our framework, the quality that is considered is the accuracy of the user's access pattern as reflected by the patterned access graph compared to the user's actual access pattern. By attaching a statistical control chart to each arc of the patterned access graph, we are able to detect that the user access pattern with respect to a given arc deviates from what is reflected by the access frequency weighing the arc. For instance, let us consider a user consulting a hyperdocument whose structure is depicted by the graph of Figure 4.*a*. Let us further assume that this user has been consulting page *B* after accessing the first page *A* for about 100 sessions and that he has then been accessing page *C* after the first page *A* for the 20 last sessions. Computing the access prediction for the first page *A* with respect to access frequencies leads to rank *B* before *C* although the user's access pattern for the last sessions tends to show that the user now accesses *C* after *A* rather than *B*. Such a change in the access pattern is detected using the statistical control charts attached to the arcs leaving the node denoting the first page *A*. Then, the access prediction with respect to a page *P and* the preceding sequence of accesses is a sequence of pages that are ordered according to their decreasing probability of being accessed immediately after *P*. For each page of the sequence, this probability is computed according to the access frequency and associated control chart, weighing the arc leading to that page [20].

Given a computed prediction, *prefetching* is carried out as follows. The prediction is read sequentially from the first element up to at most the size of the client's cache in terms of page entries. On each iteration step, the page that is given by the prediction's element, is searched within the client cache. If the page is absent then a request for the corresponding files is issued to the server, while no action is taken otherwise

Improvement of the service response time using the proposed automatic prefetching strategy depends on two factors: (*i*) the accuracy of predictions and (*ii*) the interference of the prefetching strategy with the other resource management policies affecting the service. From the standpoint of the former factor, high prediction accuracy is expected based on the undertaken statistical approach (see Subsection 3.3 for evaluation of prediction accuracy). The latter factor relates to the management of the client cache and to the client-server protocol. First, the caching and prefetching strategies must be closely coupled so as to avoid the removal from the cache of a file that is about to be accessed. The resulting coupling lies in the implementation of a replacement algorithm undertaking replacement decisions with respect to the prediction computed for the next access. In addition, prefetching requests must not prevail over the user's actual requests, which requires actual requests to be treated with higher priority by the client-server protocol. This has led us to propose a novel client-server communication protocol implementing a priority-based parallel communication scheme [22]. This protocol enables to suspend an ongoing prefetching request when the user's request does not match the prediction. The protocol further shares out the network bandwidth among a set of requests so as to enable parallel prefetching of the pages of a given prediction that have an almost identical probability of being accessed.

Integration within Etel: Regarding integration in the Etel system, the predictive prefetching strategy interacts with the client Acrobat software with a dedicated plug-in, which handles the user's access requests. The following actions are undertaken upon each request:

– *Action 1:* The requested page is made available to Acrobat using the following algorithm. The page is first searched within the client cache. If the page is
absent, it is examined whether it is currently being prefetched (*i.e.* miss-on-
prefetch). If not, the page is requested to the server and the corresponding
request is given the highest priority by the client-server protocol.
– *Action 2:* The patterned access graph is updated so as to integrate this new
access.
– *Action 3:* If the prefetching step for the current page is still executing, it is
terminated[5]. The prefetching process with respect to the requested page is
then initiated.

3.2 Enhancing Scalability Using Load Balancing

In addition to offer timely delivery of the newspaper pages to the user, another
primary concern in the design of the Etel distributed system was to guarantee
scalability of the Etel newspaper service. The scalability of a system determines
the system's ability to offer a collective service without degrading the service's
individual quality. In our context, this means that the Etel newspaper must be
made available to a large number of users without affecting the mean response
time offered to each user. The following subsection outlines base distribution
management policies that we chose for implementation of the Etel server. We
then detail the load balancing strategy that we specifically designed for the Etel
server, together with its integration within Etel.

Background: As already pointed out in Subsection 2.2, the Etel server is structured as a set of autonomous clusters, where each cluster is composed of a number of processing elements interconnected by a high speed network. This design
choice was motivated by various factors:

– Clustering is recognized as a useful technique for improving scalability when
applied to either data or processing elements.
– The configuration of the server may easily be changed so as to face new
environmental factors. In particular, new processing elements may be added
at low cost when the number of system users is increasing significantly.
– The computing infrastructure of the Ouest-France editor is geographically
distributed over a number of sites, each site producing distinct local news.
Hence, each of these sites may be used to host a cluster.

Clustering of processing elements is not sufficient to address the scalability constraints of Etel. We must further deal with the distribution of the newspaper
data and of the client requests over the clusters. Base distributed system techniques are eligible here: data replication and load balancing. Data replication

---

[5] Let us notice that the termination of a prefetching step does not imply termination
of the corresponding prefetching requests; these requests are only suspended and are
later either resumed or terminated, based on the prefetching decisions for the newly
requested page.

consists of having multiple copies of a data over distinct processing elements. Concurrent accesses to a data may then be scheduled over the various processing elements storing the data, with respect to load balancing and access latency considerations. The drawback of data replication is that it requires to manage replica consistency. However, there is no need for consistency management in the Etel system. Clients perform only read accesses. Thus, the consistency issue raises only when a new edition is produced, *i.e.* when the content of the new edition is distributed over the various clusters. Clusters being autonomous, a user interacts only with one cluster, which renders useless inter-cluster consistency. Finally, regarding intra-cluster consistency, a new edition is produced at night, and thus at off-peak hours. It follows that we have decided to not deal with consistency management in the Etel system since it has a negligible impact on the overall quality of service of the Etel newspaper.

Although data replication and load balancing are *a priori* eligible techniques for improving scalability, they must be used in an appropriate way to be actually beneficial. For instance, data replication must not lead to overload the clusters' storing elements. In the same way, the load balancing strategy should not introduce processing overhead when processing elements are handling requests. Our approach to offer scalability guarantees using clustering, replication, and load balancing techniques relies on exploiting the user profiles in terms of accessed topics. Knowing the topics that are the most frequently accessed by each user, we are able to identify groups of clients such that the clients of a group read similar pages[6]. In the same way, we are able to identify groups of pages such that the pages of a group are all accessed by some set of clients. Groups of pages constitute units of load balancing for data distribution over clusters while groups of clients constitute units of load balancing for request distribution over clusters. Achieving a high degree of scalability for the Etel server then lies in the adequate computation of user and page groups. The next subsection introduces our technique for computing these groups, and the associated load balancing strategy.

Profile-Based Load Balancing: Our objective is to compute groups of clients and associated page groups given user profiles. The grouping strategy should be such that it enhances scalability of the cluster-based server. In other words, we must compute groups so as to be able:

---

[6] One could have considered exploiting access profiles as for predictive prefetching, instead of base profiles to compute client and data groups. However, we have not yet foreseen the benefits of such an approach compared to the resulting complexity in terms of both memory consumption and computation. Practically, using access profiles would lead to group clients based on similar access patterns and not just interest in similar topics. Hence, this may allow increased scalability should the server's storage capacity be smaller than the storage capacity required for Etel, which is not the case. Furthermore, scalability would be actually increased if the access profile integrated the time of the day the client accesses Etel, which is not currently taken into account.

- To map page groups onto clusters, according to the clusters' storage capacities, in a balanced way, while ensuring that the resulting distribution of user requests among clusters will also be balanced.
- Upon the initiation of a user session, to assign the corresponding client requests to a cluster, according to the cluster's load and the page group stored by the cluster.
- To guarantee fast response times to user requests, *i.e.* ensuring local availability of the requested page within the cluster.

The aforementioned requirements may be achieved by providing a grouping strategy computing a hierarchy of page groups that is such that:

- Every page group is accessed by a *significant* number of users, *i.e.* a page group belongs to a significant number of user profiles. This enables the system to enforce a balanced processing load among the clusters.
- Within the hierarchy, page groups are related in terms of common pages, which enables to identify a number of page groups equal to the one of clusters without sacrificing the resulting load balance.

Remark that a page may belong to various computed page groups, which determines the replication of pages based on their popularity among users. In addition, a single user profile may include distinct page groups, which provides the adequate framework to deal with processing load balancing among the server's clusters. Other requirements for the grouping strategy is that it should have minimal spatial and temporal complexities, and should be dynamic so as to efficiently handle changes at the level of either the users base or the server configuration.

Existing algorithms for computing client and/or page groups relate to the data analysis [18,9,26,14,12] and data mining [1,27,21,8] domains. An evaluation of the various eligible algorithms with respect to our criteria, is proposed in [6]. Based on the result of this evaluation, our algorithm is based on associative data mining [2,13,4]. Briefly stated, associative data mining computes a set of inference rules among database elements (or *items*), according to the transactions stored in the database where each transaction contains a set of database elements (or *itemset*). In the Etel context, an item corresponds to a newspaper topic and a transaction corresponds to a user profile. An inference rule of the form $I \Rightarrow J$ means that most transactions containing the itemset I also contain the itemset J. In general, an inference rule is associated with its *support*, which gives the number of transactions verifying the rule, and its *confidence*, which gives the probability with which a transaction containing I will also contain J. A classical data mining algorithm decomposes in two phases:

- In the first phase, the algorithm computes the sets of elements that are *frequent* within transactions. Frequency is determined according to a given support threshold. This process is done iteratively by computing at the kth step, the frequent sets containing exactly k elements. The process terminates when a frequent set cannot be identified for the given number of elements.

– The second phase consists of identifying inference rules given the frequent sets computed in the first phase. Basically, an inference rule of the form $I \Rightarrow J$ is identified if the number of frequent sets verifying this rule is greater than a given threshold.

In the Etel context, the above first phase of the algorithm computes data groups of increasing size, and each group identifies a set of topics that are all accessed by a number of users exceeding the given threshold. In other words, it gives us with groups of topics that are significant (or frequent) enough to be used as a basis for the distribution of the corresponding pages and of user requests over the server's clusters. However, existing algorithms return a set of independent groups (e.g. [2]). In order to get a hierarchy of groups, we modify the algorithm's first phase so that it structures computed groups according to a tree structure, in a way similar to the proposal of [4]. The modification consists of establishing a hierarchical relations among (frequent) groups containing k topics and those containing $k + 1$ topics. The unique ancestor of a group containing $k + 1$ topics among eligible groups of k topics is selected according to an ordering among topics: the additional topic of a descendant is greater than all the topics of its ancestor. The ordering among topics is set arbitrarily; for instance, it can be the alphabetical order over topic names. Given the aforementioned modification, we are able to compute a hierarchy of groups for an algorithmic complexity of $O(N)$, N being the number of registered users. However, the data mining algorithm is not suited for the dynamic computation of groups. Any modification within the set of user profiles leads to recompute the whole hierarchy. One way to deal with this issue consists of periodically executing the algorithm. Such a solution is suitable only if the modifications of profiles occurring between two algorithm executions do not affect significantly the current grouping. We cannot make this assumption, which has led us to propose a second adaptation of associative data mining so as to make the algorithm dynamic. Our algorithm dynamically builds the group hierarchy using recursive procedures for the addition, removal, and modification of a user profile. By construction, a tree node is necessarily a frequent group whose level in the tree determines its size. Let us consider the introduction of a user profile that includes the topics of a frequent group whose corresponding node is at level k. Depending on the topics given in the user profile, this may lead to identify a frequent group of $k + 1$ topics, and hence to create a descendant–if it does not exist already. Thus, each node of the tree stores the number of clients whose profile contains the topics of its associated group and an additional topic (which has to be greater than all the topics of the group). However, in order to minimize the memory space used by the algorithm, this information is not kept for all the additional topics. The number of clients gets counted once the corresponding group can potentially become frequent. The frequency potential is evaluated with respect to the data mining principle: a frequent group of size $k + 1$ is necessarily composed of frequent groups of size k. Hence, a group of size $k + 1$ can be considered as being potentially frequent only once all the groups of size k that it contains are themselves frequent.

Given the hierarchy of topic groups computed using our dynamic data mining algorithm, the load balancing strategy decomposes into:

- The distribution of an Etel edition (*i.e.* the electronic version of the 40 Ouest-France daily regional editions) on the server's clusters, upon the edition's publication, which happens at night[7].
- The distribution of the users' requests upon users connections, on the server's clusters.

Let us first detail distribution of the Etel edition. The objective here is to map topic groups (or page groups) onto clusters so as to avoid the overloading of clusters in terms of processing and storage usage. This is achieved by distributing the leaves of the group hierarchy over the clusters. Since the number of leaves in general exceeds the one of clusters, page groups of the leaves are grouped based on ancestor commonality, using the group hierarchy. In addition, so as to optimize the placement of page groups with respect to the resulting processing and storing load, the grouping of inner page groups is done with respect to the distance among profiles of associated users [6]. Notice that the mapping of groups onto clusters needs not be computed each day; a computed mapping is valid as long as the group hierarchy remains unchanged. Given the mapping of page groups onto clusters, the pages of the edition are transferred to clusters accordingly. For the distribution of pages among the machines of a cluster, this is realized by distributing the pages over each machine in turn. This simplistic choice is due to the fact that an efficient cooperation protocol is implemented among the cluster's machines. Efficiency comes from the use of an ATM network but also from the cooperation algorithm, which is based on the one introduced in [23]

Concerning distribution of the users' requests, it consists of choosing a cluster for every user upon the user's connection. The cluster is selected based on the groups it hosts and on its current processing load. Among clusters that host a group which is contained in the user's profile, the one whose associated group is the largest is selected in priority. However, if its current load does not enable it to host the client, remaining clusters are considered, still based on the size of the groups they host. When more than one cluster is eligible, the least loaded cluster is selected. Finally, once a cluster is chosen for a client, the least loaded machine of the cluster is selected for handling the client's requests.

Integration within Etel: Integration of the profile-based load strategy within Etel lies in the following elements:

- A centralized server for user authentication, which further chooses the machine that will handle the user's requests, according to the distribution of requests introduced previously.

---

[7] Distribution of an edition could also have to be initiated when the hierarchy of groups changes or when one of the cluster fails. We do not consider these cases because their frequencies of occurrence are less than the one of edition production.

- A centralized server, which stores the users' profiles and maintains the hierarchy of topic groups. This server is the *Data Producer* of Figure 3, which further distributes edition pages over the clusters according to the approach discussed previously.
- A client-server communication protocol implemented on all the machines of the clusters, according to the priority-based parallel communication scheme discussed in Subsection 4.
- A cooperation protocol among the machines of each cluster, which is an adaptation of the one proposed in [23].

3.3   Evaluation

Regarding evaluation of the Etel service, we are interested in assessing the benefit of the proposed prefetching and load balancing strategies with respect to the service's mean response time and scalability. Ideally, such an assessment should be based on performance measures of the service using actual user traces. However, we do not have such traces for the Etel service as it is currently being tested by a restrictive user panel. Precisely, the panel is composed of a small group of newspaper professionals, hence requiring few support from the underlying distributed system for offering high mean response time and scalability. Another option would be to use traces from other newspaper services but these are confidential for obvious reasons. Hopefully, the Ouest-France editor has provided us with the results of a (confidential) sample survey about readers habits. We thus used these results as a basis for the generation of user profiles, which although not real are close to the reality. In that framework, the electronic newspaper service gives access to a hyperdocument whose structure is the one depicted in Figure 4.*a*, which corresponds to the structure of individualized Ouest-France editions. Each page has further an average size of 80 Kbytes. Finally, following users reading habits as reflected by the Ouest-France survey, a user reads an average number of 7 pages per session, and the size of the corresponding access graph is less than 80 Kbytes.

Let us first consider the evaluation of the profile-based prefetching strategy. The main criterion for assessing its benefit is to measure the accuracy of the predictions that are computed with respect to the users' requests. Towards that goal, we have generated various user access profiles, which differ in terms of the stability of the user's access patterns over distinct sessions. In addition, for comparison purpose, we implemented two prediction algorithms: one using a base access graph (*i.e.* hyperdocument graph with arcs weighed with the corresponding access frequency), and ours using a patterned access graph (*i.e.* base access graph that is enriched so as to differentiate sequences of accesses) with EWMA control charts attached to arcs. Notice that the prediction accuracy obtained with the base access graph correspond roughly to the results that would be obtained with the strategy of [24]; the difference lies in the fact that our access graph is permanent. Figure 5 compares prediction accuracy using the base access graph and the EWMA-based patterned access graph. The figure gives the percentage of computed predictions that rank first the actually requested page

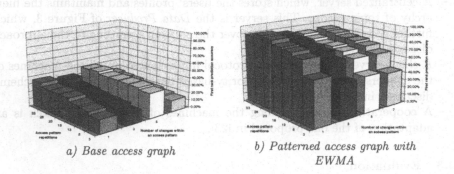

a) Base access graph   b) Patterned access graph with
                                        EWMA

Fig. 5. Prediction accuracy

according to access pattern evolution. An access pattern evolution is characterized both by the number of sessions during which the user performs the same
sequence of page accesses (*i.e.* repeats the same access pattern) and by the number of changes occurring within the sequence of accesses compared to the value
of the sequence at the previous session (*i.e.* changes in the access pattern). For
each evolution, 1000 sessions were run, a user accessing 7 pages per session and
the access graph being null at the first session. Using the EWMA-based patterned access graph, up to 92% of the pages that are actually requested by the
user appear first in the prediction when the user access pattern changes unfrequently (*i.e.* a sequence of accesses is repeated over 28 sessions and there is a
single modification in the sequence when the user's access pattern changes), and
is no lower than 44% when the user access pattern changes frequently (*i.e.* a
sequence of accesses is repeated over 3 sessions and there are 7 modifications
in the sequence when the user's access pattern changes). On the other hand,
using the base access graph, this percentage falls to at least 40%. Still considering the base access graph, it can be noticed that results are non-intuitive with
respect to the number of changes within the sequence of accesses; best results
are observed when there are 5 changes. This is due to the fact that the graph is
fully connected and to the distribution of access frequencies over such a graph.
The results we obtain for prediction accuracy are important from the standpoint
of the server load increase caused by the prefetching strategy. Given that the
user's actual access is predicted at the first rank for a majority of accesses using
the EWMA-based patterned access graph, this allows to offer a highly responsive
service even when only the first element of a prediction is prefetched.

Table 1 gives the service's mean response times in seconds, given a 64 Kbit/sec.
ISDN network, and a non-overloaded server (*i.e.*, the cluster machine selected for
the client is able to handle the client requests in a timely manner). Results are
provided for a user taking 5 seconds for consulting a page and for a client cache
enabling the prefetching of up to 3 pages. We give results for two access pattern

System model	Unstable pattern	Stable pattern
No prefetching	10.00	10.00
Base graph & Sequential communication	6.00	3.20
Base graph & Parallel communication	5.00	2.80
EWMA-based patterned graph & Sequential communication	2.50	0.20
EWMA-based patterned graph & Parallel communication	2.10	0.15

Table 1. Mean response time

evolutions. The *unstable* (resp. *stable*) access pattern corresponds to the access pattern where each sequence of accesses is repeated for 3 (resp. 33) sessions prior to be changed, and a single modification occurs at each change. For each evolution, 1000 sessions were run, the user accessing 7 pages per session and the access graph being null at the first session. Furthermore, results are provided for both access graphs and using both priority-based sequential and priority-based parallel communication schemes. When using the parallel communication scheme, priorities for the 3 parallel prefetching requests are respectively set to 50%, 30% and 20%[8]. Results show that the EWMA-based patterned access graph combined with a parallel communication scheme gives better performance.

Let us finally examine the benefit of our profile-based load balancing strategy with respect to scalability, i.e., the number of clients that can be accommodated by the service without sacrificing mean response times offered to users. From that perspective, Figure 6 gives the server's mean response time (*i.e.*, the mean time taken for sending back the page requested by a client, once the request is received) with respect to the number of clients, for (*i*) a simple load balancing algorithm, called DYN, which dynamically assigns a machine to a given client with respect to the machines' load for the duration of a session and for (*ii*) our algorithm, called PROFILE. For each algorithm, we ran simulations for various server configurations, which differ according to the number of clusters and to the number of machines per cluster. Notice that the configuration with one cluster of one machine corresponds to a centralized server, which is given as a reference point. For remaining configurations, results show that our algorithm performs better than the two others.

---

[8] Notice that priorities are not assigned according to the access frequencies. This is to better compare results using the base access graph with the ones using the EWMA-based patterned access graph.

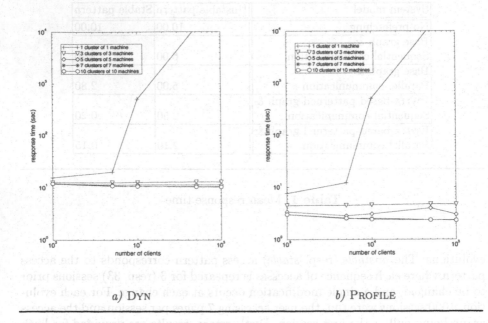

a) DYN   b) PROFILE

Fig. 6. Scalability and timeliness guarantees

4   Conclusion

This paper has presented the Etel electronic newspaper whose main design goal
was to offer high quality of service to Etel users. The Etel quality of service
lies in the provision of both content and access quality. Content quality relates
to the quality of the displayed information regarding both its significance and
its readability from the user's standpoint. The Etel content quality is achieved
through the design and production of individualized electronic editions in close
collaboration with the French Ouest-France newspaper editor. It follows that
both the layout and content of the electronic editions benefit from the expertise
of the newspaper editor. Access quality lies in ensuring timely delivery of the
electronic newspaper pages to users, so as to make the reading of the electronic
newspaper as comfortable as the one of a classical newspaper. The Etel access
quality results from the design of the dedicated Etel client-server system, which
exploits the specifics of electronic newspapers for data distribution among the
system's resources. Specifically, each Etel client runs a profile-based predictive
prefetching policy that exploits the user profile in terms of reading habit for
anticipating the user requests, and hence makes pages available on the client
machine before the pages are actually requested by the user. In addition, the
Etel server is composed of a set of clusters, and runs a profile-based load bal-

ancing strategy. This strategy exploits the knowledge of user profiles in terms of accessed pages to store together jointly accessed pages within clusters and then assigns each client to the cluster that stores most of the pages read by the corresponding user. The combination of the profile-based prefetching and load balancing strategies enable to provide a highly scalable system offering timely delivery of newspaper pages to users.

The Etel electronic newspaper service is being tested by a user panel since early spring 1999. Ultimately, the Etel electronic newspaper should become a commercial product, made available by the TC MultiMédia Company, subsidiary of Ouest-France. Another activity based on the Etel newspaper service that has been carried out is the enhancement of the service so as to make it available to mobile users. Towards that goal, we have exploited the infrastructure for mobile users developed in the framework of the FollowMe Esprit RITD project[9].

Acknowledgments

The authors would like to thank Frédéric Leleu who is the designer of the profile-based predictive prefetching strategy. They also acknowledge the participation of Jean-Paul Routeau and Michel Le Nouy who were in charge of the development of the Etel prototype.

References

1. R. Agrawal, T. Imielinski, and A. Swami. Mining association rules between sets of items in large databases. *ACM SIGMOD*, 1993.
2. R. Agrawal and R. Srikant. Fast algorithms for mining association rules. In *Proc. of the 20th International Conference on Very Large DataBases*, 1994.
3. A. Bestavros. Speculative data dissemination and service to reduce server load, network traffic and service time for distributed information systems. In *Proc. of the 1996 International Conference on Data Engineering*, 1996.
4. S. Brin, R. Motwani, J. D. Ullman, and S. Tsur. Dynamic itemset counting and implication rules for market basket data. *ACM SIGMOD*, 1997.
5. P. Cao, E. W. Felten, A. Karlin, and K. Li. A study of integrated prefetching and caching strategies. In *Proc. of the 1995 ACM SIGMETRICS Conference*, 1995.
6. B. Charpiot. *Rpartition thmatique des accs un systme d'informations distribues.* PhD thesis, Universit de Rennes I, 1998.
7. S. Crowder. A simple method for studying run-length distributions exponentially weighted moving average charts. *Journal of Quality Technology*, 1987.
8. C. Faloutsos, M. Ranganathan, and Y. Manolopoulos. Fast subsequence matching in time-series databases. In *ACM SIGMOD*, 1994.
9. E.W. Forgy. Cluster analysis of multivariate data: Efficiency versus interpretability of classifications. *Biometric Society Meetings Riverside*, 1965.
10. J. Griffioen and R. Appleton. Reducing file system latency using a predictive approach. In *Proc. of the 1994 Summer USENIX Technical Conference*, 1994.

---

[9] http://hyperwav.fast.de/followme

11. J. Griffioen and R. Appleton. The Design, Implementation and Evaluation of a Predictive Caching File System. Technical report, Department of Computer Science, University of Kentucky, Lexington, KY, 1996.

12. A. Guttman. R-trees: a dynamic index structure for spatial searching. In *ACM SIGMOD*, 1984.

13. M. Holsheimer, M. Kersten, H. Mannila, and H. Toivonen. A perspective on databases and data mining. In *Proc. of the 1st International Conference on Knowledge Discovery and Data Mining*, 1995.

14. L. Hubert. Monotone invariant clustering. *Psychometrika*, 38(1), 1973.

15. T. Kamba, K. Bharat, and M. C. Albers. The krakatoa chronicle: An interactive, personalized, newspaper on the web. In *Proc. of the 4th International World Wide Web Conference*, 1995.

16. T. Kimbrel, A. Tomkins, R. H. Patterson, B. Bershad, P. Cao, E. W. Felten, G. A. Gibson, A. R. Karlin, and K. Li. A trace-driven comparison of algorithms for parallel prefetching and caching. In *Proc. of the 2nd Conference on Operating System Design and Implementation (OSDI)*, 1996.

17. T. M. Kroeger and D. E. Long. Predicting file system actions from prior events. In *Proc. of the 1996 Winter* USENIX *Technical Conference*, 1996.

18. L. Lebart, A. Morineau, and K. M. Warwick. Multivariate descriptive statistical analysis. *Willey Series in probability and mathematical statistics*, 1984.

19. H. Lei and D. Duchamp. An analytical approach to file prefetching. In *Proceedings of the 1997 Winter* USENIX *Technical Conference*, 1997.

20. F. Leleu. *Techniques d'anticipation des accs un service d'informations distribues. Application un service de presse crite lectronique.* PhD thesis, Universit de Rennes I, 1997.

21. M. Mehta, R. Agrawal, and J. Rissanen. Sliq: A fast scalable classifier for data mining. In *5th International Conference on Extending Database Technology*, 1996.

22. J-M. Menaud. ParaComm : une bibliothèque de communication d'anticipation des accès. In *Actes de la 1ère Conférence française sur les systèmes d'exploitationn (CFSE'1)*, 1999.

23. J-M. Menaud, V. Issarny, and M. Banâtre. A new protocol for efficient transversal web caching. In *Proc. of DISC'98 (Formerly WDAG -) 12th International Symposium on Distributed Computing*, 1998.

24. V. N. Padmanabhan and J. C. Mogul. Using predictive prefetching to improve World-Wide Web latency. *SIGCOMM Newsletter*, 1996.

25. R. H. Patterson, G. H. Gibson, E. Ginting, D. Stodolsky, and J. Zelenka. Informed prefetching and caching. In *Proc. of the 15th ACM Symposium on Operating System Principles (SOSP)*, 1995.

26. J. Mac Queen. Some methods for classification and analysis of multivariate observations. In *5th Berkeley Symposium on Mathematical Statistics and Probability*, 1967.

27. R. Srikant and R. Agrawal. Mining quantitative association rules in large relational tables. In *ACM SIGMOD*, 1996.

28. D. Steere and M. Satyanarayanan. Using dynamic sets to overcome high I/O latencies during search. In *Proc. of the 5th Workshop on Hot Operating System Topics*, 1995.

29. E. Yashchin. Some aspects of the theory of statistical control schemes. *IBM Journal of Research and Development*, 31, 1987.

FlexiNet:
A Flexible, Component-Oriented Middleware System

Richard Hayton, Andrew Herbert

Citrix Systems (Cambridge) Ltd
Poseidon House
Castle Park
Cambridge
CB3 0RD, United Kingdom

Richard.Hayton, Andrew.Herbert@citrix.com

Abstract. The FlexiNet Platform is a Java middleware platform that features a component based internal structure with strong emphasis placed on reflection and introspection at all levels. This allows programmers to tailor the platform for a particular application domain or deployment scenario by assembling strongly typed components. In this paper we give an overview of the FlexiNet architecture, highlighting how its approach differs from other middleware architectures, and illustrate the benefits that result from the new approach.

Introduction

The authors are members of the ANSA Project, supported by the ANSA Consortium. The ANSA Project started in 1985 with the ambition of developing standards and prototypes for what is now called middleware. The project took a prominent role in the definition of the ISO Reference Model for Open Distributed Processing [5] and the early stages of definition of CORBA within the Object Management Group (OMG) [1]. We have therefore seen distributed processing grow from its seed in the research community to a maturing industrial technology. Pleased as we are to see our results contribute to the mainstream, we have reservations about the monolithic structure and inflexibility of current products compared to our original concepts. The FlexiNet platform grew out of an effort to go back and re-apply the ANSA architectural approach to the contemporary view of middleware. Our aim was to see if we could produce a platform that competes favourably in terms of function and offers significantly better capabilities in terms of tailoring, extension and optimisation..

We believe we have succeeded in our aim and in the following sections give an outline of the key features of the FlexiNet architecture. To put the work in context, we begin by reviewing our perceptions of the limitations of existing middleware.

Generally, research middleware platforms provide application programmers with facilities for just one model for distributed programming, for example remote procedure call, or message passing or process groups. In consequence, compact, efficient and scalable implementations are often achieved. By contrast, industrial

S. Krakowiak, S.K. Shrivastava (Eds.): Distributed Systems, LNCS 1752, pp. 497-508, 2000.

middleware platforms address the need for a ubiquitous infrastructure and provide an integrated set of capabilities including, for example, transactions, replication, authentication, privacy, auditing and others.   The result is typically monolithic, inefficient and complex.

Since different applications require different combinations of middleware features, a compositional approach in which only the middleware services needed by an application need be made available is appropriate. In CORBA, for example, a set of nested choices is offered in CORBA Object Services. Each Object Service extends the core Object Request Broker with additional capabilities such as persistence and transactions. The benefit of the CORBA framework of Object Services is that it is comprehensive. The disadvantage is that it is unnecessarily rigid because the order in which capabilities have to be assembled is fixed and this rules out some implementation choices. Moreover, the core Object Request Broker is required to contain support for the data structures and protocols required by each Object Service whether it is used or not. Thus, in addition to causing bloat and inefficiency in the implementation, developers are forced to manage more capabilities than they necessarily need in any particular situation.

A further aspect of inflexibility comes from the use of stubs in Object Request Brokers to provide access transparent invocation. A stub converts an invocation into an untyped byte array representation to be passed on to a communications layer in the case of a remote service. Discarding language level typing and introspection facilities in this way makes it hard to provide developer-written protocols and mechanisms that can coexist with standard stubs. Specifically, it can be difficult to tie together application level events, middleware events and communications events. For example Iona's Orbix Object Request Broker's filters and transformers [2] provide a means to modify how communication events are handled in Orbix. However, no conventions or data structures are defined for relating filter events   (i.e., pre-stub events) to transformer events (i.e., post-stub events). Behaviour at the filter level is modelled by CORBA type codes and dynamic type checking of these has to be managed by the developer rather than delegated to the programming language.

Inherent in the design of distributed systems is the need to make appropriate trade-offs between the competing goals of abstraction and application control. Abstraction in middleware is generally associated with distribution transparency. Abstraction/transparency makes life easier for developers by hiding the engineering details of interaction models behind a generic invocation interface (e.g., method invocation). In essence, the infrastructure manages distribution. Application control, by contrast, allows developers to optimise the infrastructure when it is beneficial to do so, for example by providing heuristics for error cases. Control requires that implementation aspects of a distribution transparency should be exposed. Unfortunately current systems either impose a 'one size for all' transparency or expose the low level 'systems' mechanisms in all their complexity.

The FlexiNet Platform is a Java middleware system built to address some of the above issues of configurable middleware and application deployment. Its key feature is a component based 'white-box' approach with strong emphasis placed on reflection and introspection at all levels. This allows programmers to tailor the platform for a particular application domain or deployment scenario by assembling strongly typed components. The FlexiNet component developer operates within the language type system and is saved from having to conduct the book-keeping that would otherwise been needed to remember relationships between components.

Related Work

The core of FlexiNet is the binding mechanism by which components are linked together and our approach to encapsulating distributed objects. There are many other research systems offering flexible binding, particular with respect to performance and resource tradeoffs. Traditionally this work has been driven either from a quality of service perspective [3] or from an aim to simplify protocol implementation by building complex protocols out of simpler micro-protocol engines. In these contexts binding can be at the generic buffer and communication channel level. FlexiNet differs in that it provides flexibility at a higher level. In addition to controlling protocol level choices management of higher level distribution transparency mechanisms based on transactions, replication, security, persistence, mobility and so forth can be managed. In providing these capabilities as components we have to intercept and transform application level invocations and tie together different protocols, transparency mechanisms and system services in a consistent and structured manner.

The key advantage that FlexiNet has over other schemes is the Java Virtual Machine itself. This provides a great deal of the support we need, in particular for introspection (runtime examination and control of types) and reflection (generic invocation of methods). It allows FlexiNet to provide a middleware framework that extends the core language features, and is internally strongly typed – rather than having to separately manage the infrastructure type system as with CORBA (i.e., via typecodes). The disadvantage of course is that effectively FlexiNet is a Java language specific platform. (While there are mappings of other languages to the Java Virtual Machine, none of then can be regarded as main stream implementations). However, by way of mitigation, in distributed Internet applications, Java is a common choice because of its suitability for network programming and platform independence. Since this is the focus of our work, we are prepared to trade the benefits gained against the restriction to a single language.

Computational Model

We use different computational model for Java than Javasoft's Remote Method Invocation (RMI) [6]. We adopt the ODP notion of interfaces as the access points for objects, and provide transparent interface proxies. When parameters are passed to a method, we pass references to interfaces by reference, and pass object values by copying. This enables FlexiNet to follow Java language model as closely as possible, without introducing 'special' tag classes to indicate remote interfaces, or value objects, as is done in RMI. The benefit of determining the parameter semantics by choosing between an object or an interface (for copy or reference semantics respectively) within the context of a particular call can be seen when mobile objects are considered. Using the tagged object approach, each object would be statically classified as either a server or a data object. It is therefore not possible to have the concept of a mobile server object – since it would be tagged as a 'server' and could never be transmitted as data when moving from one location to another.

Selective Transparency

Since FlexiNet remote method invocation offers similar semantics to local method invocation, we have access transparency at the lowest level. This uniformity helps keep application code separated from 'systems' code, making it easier to move applications from one environment to another. To take control, the application programmer can inject particular mechanisms, both at runtime using an explicit binding facility and at design time by controlling the mixture of protocols and transparency components used. Resources can be managed by restricting the allocation policies for, and sizes of, resource pools assigned to selected components. We describe this capability as 'selective transparency', since the developer can choose how strongly system components are tied to (and visible to) application components. Binding decisions can be taken directly by system components or handed off to third parties where this is appropriate. The former is appropriate for autonomous systems, the latter for managed infrastructures (e.g., a trusted computing base).

Bindings

An interface on a remote object is represented in FlexiNet by a local proxy object. Typically, this is a simple stub object that turns a typed invocation into a generic (but fully typed) form and then passes the request to the top layer of a protocol stack. Our stubs are very lightweight compared to other systems, and in particular the stub is not responsible for the 'on-the-wire' representation of the invocation, and embodies no implicit or explicit policy about how the call will be handled. Since stubs are so simple, we generate stub classes on demand within client processes, by introspection on the interface definition dynamical linking. A stub class can be shared by all protocols that treat service objects in a similar way.

FlexiNet protocol stacks are correspondingly more complex than those of a traditional 'heavyweight stub' system, since we make them responsible for all aspects of call processing. This includes high level features, such as management of replication, in addition to basic actions such as the serialisation of invocation parameters and execution of a remote procedure call protocol.

The layers of a FlexiNet communication stack can be viewed as a set of reflective meta-objects. Each meta-object in turn manipulates the invocation as a data structure before it is ultimately invoked on the destination object using Java Core Reflection [8] (thereby removing the need for a server-side stub or skeleton). Using reflection has a number of advantages. Middleware (or application) components may examine or modify the parameters to the invocation using and protected by the Java language typing system. Debugging is made straightforward as information is kept 'in clear'. Splitting omnibus middleware protocols into components is simplified, as the language typing support provides the necessary machinery to ensure consistency of use and to reduce cross dependencies in the code.

Figure 1 illustrates how a communication stack can be assembled as a number of meta-objects that perform reflective transformations on an invocation. Meta-objects can be fully general Java objects and are fully type-safe. For example a replication meta-object might extract replica names from an interface and then perform invocations on each replica in turn. As this processing is performed in terms of generic invocations, there is no need for each of these calls to pass through stubs and so the code can be both straightforward and efficient.

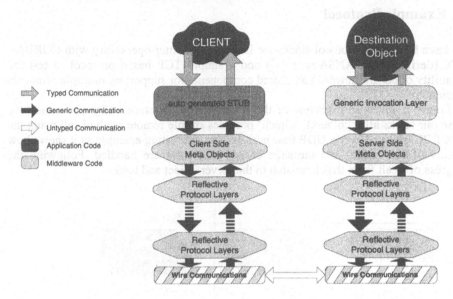

Fig. 1. A Reflective Protocol Stack

At the top of the client side stack, an invocation consists of the abstract name of the destination interface, the method to be invoked, and the parameters to the method as an array of objects. Interface names are arbitrarily complex objects that can be resolved by a protocol stack to provide a route from the client to the destination interface (or interfaces for replicated objects).

As the call proceeds down the stack, each layer can manipulate the invocation. By the bottom of the stack, the original abstract name will have been resolved to an appropriate endpoint or connection identifier, and sufficient information will have been serialised into a buffer to allow reconstruction of the invocation on the server.

On the server, the reverse process takes place, so that ultimately the destination object, method and parameters are available.

Many RPC protocols maintain state across a number of calls, for example a UDP based protocol may keep a record of unacknowledged replies, and a TCP based protocol might maintain a connection. FlexiNet provides *sessions* as an abstraction for managing this information, so that a stack can retain client-related information over the duration of a number of calls. Sessions also provide an in-call mutex for use by the layers to ensure that per-client resources are cleanly allocated and freed across a number of essentially independent components. Use of this mutex enables conflicts between communication events on the way up the stack and application events on the way down the stack to be avoided. In other work, our colleagues have had experience adding security features to a number of RPC protocols. They have found that a suitable session structure greatly eases this kind of post-hoc protocol modification and its omission from CORBA and RMI is a considerable oversight.

An Example Protocol

We have developed protocol stacks for IIOP [1] (for inter-operability with CORBA), REX (derived from ANSAware [7]) and a simple TCP based protocol to test the suitability of our framework and shared components for supporting multiple protocols efficiently.

Figure 2, gives an overview of the 'Green' protocol stack. (By convention we name our stacks after colours). 'Green' provides simple remote method call using the REX RPC protocol over a UDP transport. It is an interesting example as it shows how aspects of call based, and message based, exchanges are handled. Following the progress of a call from the client stub to the server object and back:

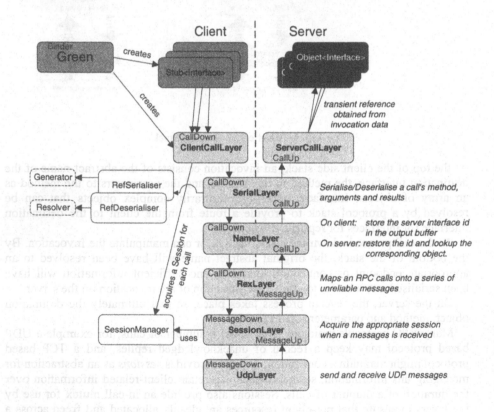

Fig. 2. The Green binder and protocol stack

1. Initially a call is made on a client stub. The nature of this call will depend on the semantics of the interface, and the stub is responsible for converting this into a

generic representation that may later be executed using Java Core Reflection. This de-couples the type of the object being invoked from the implementation of the protocol stack, and enables reuse of standard reflective components.

2. The stub will then call the top of the protocol stack. At this stage the arguments to the call, and the method class are available, and reflective classes may be called. For example, the arguments may be validated, or modified. There may be a number of reflective layers, for example to multiplex the call over a number of replicas, or perform other client-side processing. In the Green protocol, however, there is no reflective tinkering, and the call passes directly to the Client Call Layer.

3. The Client Call Layer acquires an appropriate session on which to perform the call. Sessions group a number of invocations that share the same service endpoint, to allow various optimisations. Other layers may utilise the session structure to cache information relating to a particular endpoint (for example encryption keys).

4. There may be additional reflective layers to further manipulate the call (e.g., per replica in the case of a multicast protocol). After this manipulation, the call passes to the Serial Layer, which serialises (marshals) the method and parameters into an output buffer.

5. The Name Layer comes next and extracts de-multiplexing information from the name of the interface being referenced (e.g., an interface id), and stores this in the output buffer. The subpart of the name used to locate the peer layer in the server is then passed, together with the other call parameters, to the next layer down. This separates the different levels of multiplexing, keeping the system modular.

6. The REX layer acts as a gateway between reliable call and return method invocation, and unreliable one way messaging. The REX layer contains sufficient state to manage lost or duplicate messages, and utilises the session structure to map a series of message onto a number of invocations.

7. There may again be a number of additional (per message) layers (for example to encrypt or compress the outgoing message, before it reaches the session layer). The session layer stores information to allow the session to be re-established on the server. Using the mutex, the Green protocol stack ensures that only one call or message per session will be in progress above the session layer. This simplifies the coding of session related functions, and reduces the number of race conditions (such as duplicate messages or simultaneous messages and timeouts) that the programmer must deal with.

8. Finally, the UDP Layer sends the message as a single UDP packet to the server.

9. On the server, the message is received in the UDP Layer. A new thread is started to listen for further messages, and the thread that received the message is sent up the stack to process the request. When it arrives in the REX layer, it is identified as a new request, and a timeout is set for acknowledgement (REX piggy-backs acknowledgements on replies). The message is converted to a call, and is passed up to the Name layer, which reads the interface id, and identifies the object being called. The call arguments and method are de-serialized in the next layer, and then the Call Layer invokes the method on the service object. The result of the invocation (normal or exception) unwinds the call stack: in the serialisation layer, the result is serialised, and in the REX layer, a message containing the result is constructed. The message is passed down to the Session Layer and treated in an identical way to any other outgoing message (whether it represents a request, reply or protocol message).

10.On the client, the REX layer eventually receives a reply message that it can pair with the original request. The original thread is then woken and unwinds up the stack. Eventually, the result is returned to the client using standard Java means.

Binders

In the discussion so far, we have describe how a binding to a remote interface is represented, and how an invocation may be processed. In an invocation, it may be necessary to serialise references to local and remote interfaces. During deserialisation, proxies must be constructed to represent these exported references. This is the mechanism by which all bindings (other than an initial built-in reference to a trader) are constructed.

The object responsible for generating names for interfaces is called a 'Generator'. The object responsible for resolving names is called a 'Resolver'. The more familiar term, Binder, is used to refer to objects that are capable of both generation and resolution of names. A typical binder will both generate names and convert names generated by other (compatible) binders into the (stub, stack) pair previously described. A FlexiNet binder is therefore a factory for bindings.

In many systems, there is exactly one binder per process, however in FlexiNet we needed to support multiple binders and binding protocols, with possibly conflicting use of names. Each protocol stack therefore contains a reference to the generator and resolver to be used for generating and resolving the names of interfaces passed as arguments to invocations, or returned as results from invocations.

Typically, binders are arranged into a hierarchy, in order to factor out common functionality (such as the caching of previous bindings), and to allow a dynamic selection of the binder to perform a particular binding. An example binder graph is illustrated in Figure 3. This illustrates two 'basic binders', Green, as described above, and Red, which generates bindings using IIOP over TCP. There are three additional binders. Two are 'Cache' binders that store tables of previously resolved bindings. The third is a 'Choice' binder which dynamically chooses whether to use Green or Red based on the type of the interface being named, or the type of the name being resolved. For example, imagine that the choice binder has been initialised to always use Green when generating names unless explicit QoS parameters are specified requesting that Red should be used (perhaps indicating that the connected client is a CORBA interface). When resolving names, Green or Red will be used as is appropriate.

Figure 3 (a-d) illustrates a possible execution path. In (a), the process has a single reference to a remote object, resolved using Green. Invocations may be made on this object, and in the process of this, stubs to additional local objects may be generated, and additional local objects may be named. By default Cache One and the Green binder will be used for this (b). If during one of these calls, a red (IOR) name needs to be resolved, Choice will select the Red binder to perform the resolution (c). When using this newly resolved interface, any local interfaces referenced will be named using the Red binder (d). This is essential, as Red uses the CORBA IOR name format, and the remote CORBA interface may not understand FlexiNet Green names.

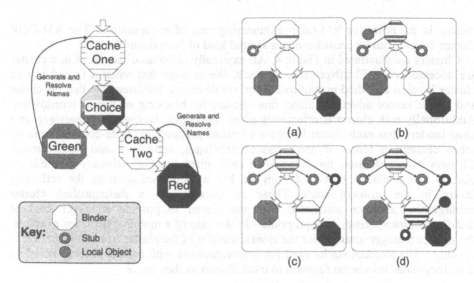

Fig. 3. A hierarchy of binders

An alternative arrangement of binders could lead to all interfaces being named by a tuple of a Green name and an Red name, allowing another process to choose which protocol to use. It is even possible to dynamically decide on the protocol to be used to name a particular interface. To illustrate this feature we have constructed a 'negotiation binder' that generates placeholder names for remote interfaces. When these are bound, a complex negotiation process is entered into, at the end of which, a binder is chosen to perform the actual binding. This approach is invaluable if different protocols have to be used depending upon the location of the client and the server. For example, to choose a specific security protocol based on the legalities of specific encryption technology or key lengths in the client's domain.

To take this approach to an extreme, we could dynamically augment the binder graph whenever a previously unknown protocol was encountered. This is perfectly feasible given Java's class loading mechanisms. The real problem is one of controlling the number of different binders that might be required if such a scheme were to be adopted.

Distribution Transparencies

The RM-ODP standard identifies nine distribution transparencies. Of these, only two, *Access* and *Location* relate directly to remote invocation. In addition to these, other FlexiNet protocols may provide varying degrees of *Failure*, *Replication* and *Security* transparency as meta-objects in the protocol stack. The remaining RM-ODP transparencies, namely, *Migration*, *Relocation*, *Persistence* and *Transaction,* cannot be tackled in this way. Instead, they require some notion of *encapsulation*, whereby all interactions with an object, or group of objects can be monitored and controlled. We achieve this in FlexiNet by implementing the RM-ODP notion of a *cluster*. A cluster is the primitive RM-ODP engineering unit of encapsulation The RM-ODP cluster concept can be considered as a special kind of Java Bean [9].

Clusters are illustrated in Figure 4. All externally referenced interfaces in a cluster are accessed via a FlexiNet protocol stack. We arrange that when a thread in one cluster invokes a method in another cluster, we de-couple the threads so that the callee and caller cannot adversely affect one another by blocking or thread termination. Additionally each cluster is effectively given a separate Java security manager, and class loader. Thus each cluster becomes a 'virtual process' that is de-coupled from all other clusters in terms of name spaces privileges, code base and management. Clusters cannot examine the internals of each other, nor may arbitrary methods on objects in one cluster be called from another without mediation by the reflective layers in the protocol stack. These co-operate with a distinguished cluster management interface associated with the cluster to provide whatever kind of distribution transparency is appropriate. In the case of a mobile object, for example, the cluster manager arranges for the atomic transfer of the cluster from one location to another. The protocol stacks used for communication with mobile objects include a directory-based relocation function to track objects as they move.

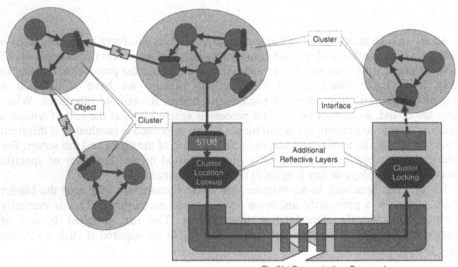

Fig. 4. Encapsulation in FlexiNet

We have experimented heavily with mobile, persistent and secure clusters in FlexiNet to support a Mobile Object Workbench [4] in an European ESPRIT project related to the investigation of Agent based programming [12,13]. Alongside this, we are exploring integration of these features and an atomic transactions infrastructure based on the CORBA Object Transaction Service. The intent is to support the interfaces associated with Enterprise Java Beans to integrate FlexiNet with Enterprise Java visual development tools.

Performance

FlexiNet is a component based framework, and the protocols and abstractions that currently populate this framework were designed for modularity and reuse, rather than performance. For example, all the layers in a typical remote method invocation stack could be implemented as one module, in order to increase performance.

However, FlexiNet is fully resource controlled, and uses pools for resources such as buffers and threads, drawing on our earlier experience in C++ with DIMMA [10]. The modularity is an advantage here, as different pool management policies may be 'slotted in' in order to trade off performance against resource usage. We benchmarked an early version of FlexiNet with UDP based communication against Sun's RMI and IONA's OrbixWeb[11] and found that over a range of computers, Java interpreters and JIT compilers, FlexiNet performs as efficiently as either of these offerings.

Recently, we have expanded FlexiNet's repertoire of protocols, and anticipate a significant performance increase. Unlike RMI, which relies on native methods in order to function, or OrbixWeb, which utilises additional stub compilation tools, FlexiNet remains 100% pure Java, with no external tools required. This makes it highly portable across Java releases and JVM implementations. Future JIT or JVM performance increases should be fully reflected in FlexiNet's performance.

Performance is notoriously difficult to measure. Many factors, such as a protocol's support for failure and simultaneous access, in addition to the actual reliability of the connection, and number of simultaneous clients will all effect the achieved performance. By tuning the combination of layers that make up a protocol, in addition the size and nature of thread and buffer pools, the performance tradeoffs can be tuned to suit the intended environment. Further work is investigating how at least some of the tradeoffs can be made automatically – by monitoring and estimating load and reliability factors. The structure of FlexiNet makes it particularly easy to add orchestration layers to collect this information.

Summary

FlexiNet was designed to provide a platform which to perform code deployment and binding related experiments. As such, the emphasis was on modularity and flexible configuration. FlexiNet has made considerable use of language level introspection and has embraced reflective techniques. Not only does the resulting system highly modular, but it also performs as efficiently as other Java middleware offerings. The ability to support all of the ODP distribution transparencies has been a goal of many distributed system platforms, and the ability to construct these using FlexiNet serves as a powerful example of its extensibility.

References

1.   Object Management Group (1997) CORBA/IIOP 2.1 Specification
      http://www.omg.org/corba/corbiiop.htm

2.   Iona Technologies, Orbix Programmers Guide (Chapter 16,22) (1997)
     http://www.iona.com/
3.   Blair G.S., Stefani, J.B. Open Distributed Processing and Multimedia. Published by
     Perseus Press; ISBN: 0201177943 (1997)
4.   Hayton R.J, Bursell M.H., Donaldson D., Herbert A.J. Mobile Java Objects, Middleware
     '98
5.   International Standards Organisation (1995): Open Distributed Processing –
     Reference Model - Architecture, ISO/IEC 10746-3
     http://www.iso.ch:8000/RM-ODP/
6.   Sun Microsystems (1996)   Java Remote Method Invocation (RMI)" Specification
     http://www.sun.com/products/jdk/1.1/docs/guide/rmi/
7.   O'Connell, J. Edwards, N. and Cole, R. A review of four distribution infrastructures.
     Distributed Systems Engineering Journal 1 (1994) 202-211
8.   Sun Microsystems: Java Core Reflection
     http://java.sun.com/products/jdk/1.1/docs/guide/reflection/index.html
9.   Sun Microsystems: Java Beans http://java.sun.com/beans/
10. Herbert et.al (1998). DIMMA – A Multi-Media ORB, Middleware'98
11. Iona Technologies: OrbixWeb http://www-usa.iona.com/products/internet/orbixweb/
12. FAST (1997) FollowMe project overview
     http://hyperwav.fast.de/generalprojectinformation
13. Bursell, M.H., Hayton R.J., Donaldson, D., Herbert A.J,. A Mobile Object Workbench.
     Mobile Agents '98.

Author Index

Lecture Notes in Computer Science

For information about Vols. 1–1697
please contact your bookseller or Springer-Verlag

Vol. 1733: H. Nakashima, C. Zhang (Eds.), Approaches to Intelligent Agents. Proceedings, 1999. XII, 241 pages. 1999. (Subseries LNAI).

Vol. 1734: H. Hellwagner, A. Reinefeld (Eds.), SCI: Scalable Coherent Interface. XXI, 490 pages. 1999.

Vol. 1564: M. Vazirgiannis, Interactive Multimedia Documents. XIII, 161 pages. 1999.

Vol. 1591: D.J. Duke, I. Herman, M.S. Marshall, PREMO: A Framework for Multimedia Middleware. XII, 254 pages. 1999.

Vol. 1624: J. A. Padget (Ed.), Collaboration between Human and Artificial Societies. XIV, 301 pages. 1999. (Subseries LNAI).

Vol. 1635: X. Tu, Artificial Animals for Computer Animation. XIV, 172 pages. 1999.

Vol. 1646: B. Westfechtel, Models and Tools for Managing Development Processes. XIV, 418 pages. 1999.

Vol. 1735: J.W. Amtrup, Incremental Speech Translation. XV, 200 pages. 1999. (Subseries LNAI).

Vol. 1736: L. Rizzo, S. Fdida (Eds.): Networked Group Communication. Proceedings, 1999. XIII, 339 pages. 1999.

Vol. 1737: P. Agouris, A. Stefanidis (Eds.), Integrated Spatial Databases. Proceedings, 1999. X, 317 pages. 1999.

Vol. 1738: C. Pandu Rangan, V. Raman, R. Ramanujam (Eds.), Foundations of Software Technology and Theoretical Computer Science. Proceedings, 1999. XII, 452 pages. 1999.

Vol. 1739: A. Braffort, R. Gherbi, S. Gibet, J. Richardson, D. Teil (Eds.), Gesture-Based Communication in Human-Computer Interaction. Proceedings, 1999. XI, 333 pages. 1999. (Subseries LNAI).

Vol. 1740: R. Baumgart (Ed.): Secure Networking – CQRE [Secure] '99. Proceedings, 1999. IX, 261 pages. 1999.

Vol. 1741: A. Aggarwal, C. Pandu Rangan (Eds.), Algorithms and Computation. Proceedings, 1999. XIII, 448 pages. 1999.

Vol. 1742: P.S. Thiagarajan, R. Yap (Eds.), Advances in Computing Science – ASIAN'99. Proceedings, 1999. XI, 397 pages. 1999.

Vol. 1743: A. Moreira, S. Demeyer (Eds.), Object-Oriented Technology. Proceedings, 1999. XVII, 389 pages. 1999.

Vol. 1744: S. Staab, Extracting Degree Information from Texts. X; 187 pages. 1999. (Subseries LNAI).

Vol. 1745: P. Banerjee, V.K. Prasanna, B.P. Sinha (Eds.), High Performance Computing – HiPC'99. Proceedings, 1999. XXII, 412 pages. 1999.

Vol. 1746: M. Walker (Ed.), Cryptography and Coding. Proceedings, 1999. IX, 313 pages. 1999.

Vol. 1747: N. Foo (Ed.), Adavanced Topics in Artificial Intelligence. Proceedings, 1999. XV, 500 pages. 1999. (Subseries LNAI).

Vol. 1748: H.V. Leong, W.-C. Lee, B. Li, L. Yin (Eds.), Mobile Data Access. Proceedings, 1999. X, 245 pages. 1999.

Vol. 1749: L. C.-K. Hui, D.L. Lee (Eds.), Internet Applications. Proceedings, 1999. XX, 518 pages. 1999.

Vol. 1750: D.E. Knuth, MMIXware. VIII, 550 pages. 1999.

Vol. 1751: H. Imai, Y. Zheng (Eds.), Public Key Cryptography. Proceedings, 2000. XI, 485 pages. 2000.

Vol. 1752: S. Krakowiak, S. Shrivastava (Eds.), Advances in Distributed Systems. VIII, 509 pages. 2000.

Vol. 1753: E. Pontelli, V. Santos Costa (Eds.), Practical Aspects of Declarative Languages. Proceedings, 2000. X, 327 pages. 2000.

Vol. 1754: J. Väänänen (Ed.), Generalized Quantifiers and Computation. Proceedings, 1997. VII, 139 pages. 1999.

Vol. 1755: D. Bjørner, M. Broy, A.V. Zamulin (Eds.), Perspectives of System Informatics. Proceedings, 1999. XII, 540 pages. 2000.

Vol. 1757: N.R. Jennings, Y. Lespérance (Eds.), Intelligent Agents VI. Proceedings, 1999. XII, 380 pages. 2000. (Subseries LNAI).

Vol. 1758: H. Heys, C. Adams (Eds.), Selected Areas in Cryptography. Proceedings, 1999. VIII, 243 pages. 2000.

Vol. 1759: M.J. Zaki, C.-T. Ho (Eds.), Large-Scale Parallel Data Mining. VIII, 261 pages. 2000. (Subseries LNAI).

Vol. 1760: J.-J. Ch. Meyer, P.-Y. Schobbens (Eds.), Formal Models of Agents. Poceedings. VIII, 253 pages. 1999. (Subseries LNAI).

Vol. 1761: R. Caferra, G. Salzer (Eds.), Automated Deduction in Classical and Non-Classical Logics. Proceedings. VIII, 299 pages. 2000. (Subseries LNAI).

Vol. 1762: K.-D. Schewe, B. Thalheim (Eds.), Foundations of Information and Knowledge Systems. Proceedings, 2000. X, 305 pages. 2000.

Vol. 1763: J. Akiyama, M. Kano, M. Urabe (Eds.), Discrete and Computational Geometry. Proceedings, 1998. VIII, 333 pages. 2000.

Vol. 1764: H. Ehrig, G. Engels, H.-J. Kreowski, G. Rozenberg (Eds.), Graph Grammars and Their Application to Computer Science. Proceedings, 1998. IX, 490 pages. 2000.

Vol. 1767: G. Bongiovanni, G. Gambosi, R. Petreschi (Eds.), Algorithms and Complexity. Proceedings, 2000. VIII, 317 pages. 2000.

Vol. 1768: A. Pfitzmann (Ed.), Information Hiding. Proceedings, 1999. IX, 492 pages. 2000.

Vol. 1769: G. Haring, C. Lindemann, M. Reiser (Eds.), Performance Evaluation: Origins and Directions. X, 529 pages. 2000.

Vol. 1770: H. Reichel, S. Tison (Eds.), STACS 2000. Proceedings, 2000. XIV, 662 pages. 2000.

Vol. 1771: P. Lambrix, Part-Whole Reasoning in an Object-Centered Framework. XII, 195 pages. 2000. (Subseries LNAI).

Vol. 1773: G. Saake, K. Schwarz, C. Türker (Eds.), Transactions and Database Dynamics. Proceedings, 1999. VIII, 247 pages. 2000.

Vol. 1774: J. Delgado, G.D. Stamoulis, A. Mullery, D. Prevedourou, K. Start (Eds.), Telecommunications and IT Convergence Towards Service E-volution. Proceedings, 2000. XIII, 350 pages. 2000.

Vol. 1780: R. Conradi (Ed.), Software Process Technology. Proceedings, 2000. IX, 249 pages. 2000.

membership, or a stylistic or content cue that connotes some personality characteristic, may be magnified in terms of its impression-forming value [2]. Second, as message senders, CMC users selective self-present by choosing self-revealing content and style with a level of deliberation and discretion greater than that which face-to-face communication provides [3]. Third, channel characteristics such as editability and timing further enhance the creation of intentionally crafted messages that may enhance person perceptions and relational communication. Fourth, feedback processes—reciprocation of desirable messaging—further enhances unusually positive or negative dynamics that originate in the aforementioned processes, through behavioral confirmation and disconfirmation processes (see for review [4]).

3   The Hyperreality of Perceptions of Others

Although we quite commonly apprehend others online with no visual cues, or few visual cues, our initial impressions of others in CMC appear to establish unexpectedly robust first impressions. This phenomenon is seen in arbitrary instances of social identification where ingroup/outgroup impressions bias perceptions, in the effects of icons and avatars, and when individuals are offered non-diagnostic photos of others.

In addition to the potent effect of arbitrary first impressions, whether social, graphical, or photographic, the social goals that interactants bring to CMC episodes lead communicators to enact patterns of interaction by which they inadvertently cause themselves to form exaggerated positive or negative perceptions of partners, through communication processes that differ substantially from the manifestation of relational communication in offline interaction.

The foundational set of discoveries that individuals create their partners online was developed by exploring the basic processes of affection exchange in CMC. Previous theoretical work argued that the CMC medium does not suppress the expression of affinity, rather, it transforms the expression of affinity from reliance on nonverbal behaviors to its expression through language, primarily. One study that substantiated this proposition [5] conducted an experiment in which dyads conversed either in a face-to-face setting or through real-time CMC chat. In each dyad, one of the members was recruited by the researchers to be an ad hoc confederate in the study. This individual was instructed to express affinity or disaffinity during the conversation. Instructions for affinity asked the individual to behave in a way that communicated that he or she liked the partner as much as possible, without making it obvious that this person had been instructed to do so. No specific behaviors were suggested to this confederate. The disaffinity confederates, likewise, were asked to get their partners not to like them as much as possible without making it obvious that the interaction was staged. Conversations were audio-video recorded for the face-to-face sessions and transcripts were collected from CMC dyads. The analysis of these conversations provided the data with which to learn how affinity was expressed in face-to-face and CMC.

Confederates in the face-to-face conditions expressed affinity primarily through variations in vocal and kinesic behavior. These included vocal pleasantness, sharpness, condescension, pause rates, and timbre; as well as smiling, body relaxation, gaze direct-ness, facial orientation, random head movements, and looking around the room. No verbal behaviors significantly connoted affinity/disaffinity in a multiple regression of all relevant cues. In CMC, however, an equivalent amount of variance in affinity was attri-buted to different forms of disagreement, changing the conversational subject, and ex-plicit positive statements of affection.

The basic conclusions of this research extend beyond the benchmarking of the ca-pability of the CMC medium and its users to express affinity through verbal rather than nonverbal cues. It suggests a different manner of affective exchange online than the manner in which it is done off-line. Off-line, nonverbal cues that convey affinity and disaffinity are predominantly interpersonal in orientation. That is, they indicate the sender's affective state or the sender's interpersonal regard, interest, involvement, and emotion toward the partner. In the CMC condition where these nonverbal beha-viors are unavailable, the majority of cues to affinity appear to focus on externalities. That is, the way that individuals manage the conversation and the way they signal congruent or incongruent affective alignment with their partner is done through by addressing a co-referential topic of conversation. This is a significant shift in the manner of affective exchange between CMC and traditional face-to-face interaction.

These findings suggest that the process of affinity expression does not provide a simple translation of the transmission of meaning from one set of cues to another set of cues, without incurring additional effects. Although the effect of these changes in focus are intrapersonal in origin and have interpersonal effects, they are conducted through conversational orientations to an object that is the focus of common ground. A byproduct of this translation, that became apparent in further research, is that our own interpersonally-effective statements of position trigger self-induced social per-ceptions of others, which often result in our own behaviors toward a partner playing a very strong role in the impressions those partners make upon us.

An experiment examined how individuals in dyads pursued affinity and disaffinity in the context of a web-supported discussion about restaurants [6]. Two participants at a time completed forms rating five local hamburger restaurants; researchers ex-changed these forms among dyad partners, and told them they would discuss their preferences via CMC after a 10-minute delay. One participant was asked to enact an affinity or disaffinity goal with respect to the other partner when the conversation ensued. Researchers predicted that opinion congruence about the restaurants would be the means by which the ad hoc confederate would enhance or reduce affinity. One of the research objectives was to see whether this participant would avail himself of information on the web in order to craft arguments and support statements of agree-ment or disagreement with his partner during the chat.

Observation and analyses showed that the confederate did look up online informa-tion moreso than did naïve participants, particularly when instructed to encourage disaffinity from his partner in the upcoming chat. Analysis of the online conversation more clearly showed that the confederates employed statements of agreement and disagreement about the restaurant preferences during their conversations, and that their arguments supporting or negating their partners positions led to changes in affect. At the end of the chat, not only did the partners' impressions of the ad hoc confederate correspond to the confederates' level of disagreement and argumentation; more dramatically, the confederates themselves changed their positions regarding the restaurants in conjunction with their disagreements and arguments.

The most striking finding, however, was the correlations between the confederates' conversational behaviors and those same confederates' impressions of their (naïve) partners at the end of the conversations. Significant correlations indicated that the more disagreements the confederate expressed, the less physically attractive they thought their partners were. Disagreements also correlated inversely with social attractiveness, i.e., the degree to which confederates thought their partners could be friends with them. Overall, the conversational strategies that focused on the object of the conversation (the neutral topic of restaurants) enacted for the purpose of asserting a relational goal, affected not only the receiver of the messages but the senders of those messages as well. In this case, fairly clearly, the CMC interactant's behavior toward his partner influenced his own perceptions of that partner's physical and social characteristics. Because those partners were randomly selected, there is no rational basis for the confederates' assessments of those partners' characteristics other than the confederates' own cognitions and behaviors towards those target individuals. This appears to be a fascinating case in which the CMC interactants invented his partner, in a sense, despite the innocent and naïve involvement that partner brought to the situation.

4   The Merger of Initial Perceptions and Relational Communication: Behavioral Confirmation and Disconfirmation Effects

The least tested aspects of the hyperpersonal model include the potential of feedback—that is, reciprocal exchanges between online partners—to further extend and exaggerate reciprocal affective messages and interpersonal perceptions. The original hyperpersonal model suggested that, in this respect, the dynamics known as behavioral confirmation may pertain. Recent research has confirmed that CMC provides sufficient interpersonal resources for the conveyance of behavioral confirmation effects; moreover, examination of behavioral disconfirmation provides even more dramatic inroads for understanding how expectancies lead to behaviors, perceptions, and unusual attributions in CMC.

Interpersonal expectancies are known to cause both confirmation and disconfirmation effects, which are both dependent upon the mutual feedback exchanged between partners who are involved in dyadic interaction. Often tested using "getting acquainted" episodes between male and female dyads, the confirmation process begins when the male partner receives information from an experimenter about a (naïve) female partner that prompts him to develop specific impressions or expectations about her [7]. When he treats her in ways that reflect his initial expectations, she responds by reciprocating his behavioral overtures, thus creating behavioral confirmation of his original expectations. Perceptual confirmation is completed when the male partner interprets her behaviors as verification of his original, pre-interaction impressions.

These perceptual effects are usually tested by analyzing males' post-interaction ratings of female partners. Behavioral disconfirmation processes also occur through dyadic interaction, but with one important difference: After developing pre-interaction partner expectations, male interactants are motivated to behave in ways that are inconsistent with their initial expectations during the subsequent interaction. When female partners reciprocate, behavioral disconfirmation occurs.

Although behaviorally, female partners may be influenced by their partners to act in ways that are inconsistent with pre-interaction expectations, how their behaviors affect males' post-interaction perceptions of them is less clear. One early experiment [8] documenting behavioral disconfirmation involved dyads using audio-voice communication. Male interactants were given expectations that their partners were "unfriendly" which prompted men to compensate for their partner's expected negativity with overt friendliness. Although this chain of events elicited disconfirming positive behaviors by the naïve partners, it did not provoke male interactants' to change initial expectations of negativity in their post-discussion partner ratings. Instead, post-discussion ratings reflected perceptual confirmation when males' maintained their negative opinions of their partners, despite the positive behavior they displayed during the interaction.

However, in a more recent study [4], evidence of a perceptual disconfirmation effect did occur. Similar to research by Ickes et al. [8], male interactants were told their partners were "in a bad mood," in order to instill a negative pre-interaction expectation. This expectancy then prompted those interactants to compensate for the (ostensible) negativity by eliciting disconfirming behaviors from their partners, much like the processes observed in Ickes et al. However, in this study, the men changed their perceptions of their partners after the interaction; in fact, male partners believed that female partners' (unexpected) positive behaviors provided evidence that original expectations were incorrect, and changed their post-interaction ratings to be in line with their partners' displayed positivity. Indeed, when the "bad mood" induction was compared to post-discussion partner ratings from oppositely-valenced experimental conditions, results indicated a perceptual disconfirmation effect.

What might account for this pattern? How could the same behavioral disconfirmation processes occur in Ickes et al. [8] and Tong and Walther [4] but result in different perceptual effects? The most obvious difference between the two studies is the communication channel dyads used. Ickes et al.'s dyads used an audio-voice system (similar to a phone) whereas Tong and Walther's dyads used text-based CMC chat. The unique perceptual disconfirmation outcomes in Tong and Walther's results may point to the ways in which CMC actually facilitates the exchange of dyadic disconfirming feedback within its reduced-cue environment.

Although these results indicate how CMC's features may contribute to the transmission and enactment of these self-fulfilling prophecies, a related question is whether interactants attribute such changes to their own ability to influence their partner, or their partner's own volition. Do communicators believe that they are responsible for behavioral and perceptual changes in their partner or do they believe their partners changed themselves? It became apparent that one's belief that he is capable of changing another person's demeanor may be an important characteristic in mediating whether that individual thinks that a partner actually changed, and just as importantly, why that partner behaved as she did. The extent to which someone believes he can change another person's demeanor can be considered an individual's level of *partner influence self-efficacy.*

Partner influence self-efficacy (PISE) can affect both confirmation and disconfirmation processes that are set into motion by the male perceiver's initial behavioral overtures to the partner during dyadic interaction. To the extent that male partners believe they are responsible for eliciting their partner's disconfirming behavior, they may "take credit" for positive changes in her negative demeanor, attributing her behavioral changes to themselves and not to their partners' real change. Such a view should result in perceptual confirmation. On the other hand, it is possible that if perceivers believe they are truly effective at changing their partner's negativity—that they were actually capable of changing her bad mood into a good one. In this case, high levels of males' PISE should result in perceptual disconfirmation.

However, the issue of self-efficacy is complicated by communication channel. It is well known that many communicators report more favorable attitudes toward channels with a greater capacity for nonverbal cues than to those with a lesser capacity [9], reflecting the widely-held assumption that "more cues is better." Such attitudes toward audio-voice and CMC interaction may produce differences in PISE that may account for why perceptual confirmation was observed in Ickes et al. [8] and perceptual disconfirmation was seen in Tong and Walther [4]. Given that communicators may feel more confident in their ability to interact with and influence their partner in audio-voice, male partners in Ickes et al. may have made different attributions about their role in their partner's behavioral positivity, when compared to males who may feel comparably lower levels of PISE in CMC chat. Therefore, knowing how channel affects self-reported feelings of PISE becomes essential to understanding how male partners make attributions at the end of the interaction.

An additional experiment tested the effect of communication channel on the patterns of expectancy effects described above, along with the additional moderating variable of PISE to see how perceivers' confidence in their own ability to influence their partners affected behavioral and perceptual outcomes [10]. As with the previous studies, it employed male-female dyads randomly assigned to use either audio-voice communication or CMC chat, and the same expectancy inductions as in the prior studies. The results indicated that self-reported PISE levels were significantly higher in audio-voice than in CMC chat, echoing people's belief that media offering more nonverbal cues are superior to media with fewer cues (particularly for interpersonal communication tasks). This also suggests that the judgments interactants make about themselves and their partners may differ across modalities.

When testing the effect of males' self-reported PISE and communication channel, an interesting interaction arose. In audio-voice, males who felt low self-efficacy maintained their negative partner ratings after the discussion. But in CMC, males' low self-efficacy was associated with a positive perceptual shift, i.e., a change from negative pre-interaction expectations, creating a disconfirmation effect. This effect was reversed in the audio-voice condition: In audio-voice, perceptual disconfirmation was more likely when males' felt confident in their own PISE.

This pattern may be accounted for by differences in PISE levels across channels: In audio-voice, the more confident males were in their ability to influence their partners, the more positivity was reflected in their post-discussion ratings. This suggests that in audio-voice the men believed they truly changed their partner's demeanor from negative to positive through their own high PISE. However, in CMC perceptual disconfirmation occurred at lower levels of PISE where the male partner attributed the female's demeanor shift to her, and not to himself. In essence, in comparison to his average audio-voice counterpart, the average male CMC interactant had relatively lower levels of PISE, which may have caused him to ignore the impact of his own influence when rating his partner after the discussion. Thus he may have attributed his partner's unexpected positive behavior to her own ability to change, rather than to his ability to induce it.

Such patterns revealed that the belief in the partner's openness to influence and belief in one's own communication self-efficacy are important to the process of confirmation and disconfirmation. Furthermore, these studies also show that CMC's unique affordances may facilitate both of these processes by allowing for selective self-presentation, behavior, and perception through dyadic feedback exchanged between partners.

5   Disconfirmation and Attribution: The Self-sealing Factor in Creating One's Partner

The last study we review in this exploration of the role of the perceiver in shaping perceptions of CMC partners sought to answer certain questions left open by the previous behavioral disconfirmation research. That line of inquiry established that CMC perceivers did not equate changes in their partners' demeanor interaction with the perceivers' own ability to change their partners' mood, although the behavioral data indicate that this was, in fact, the causal basis for partners' demeanor changes. The question therefore remained: if CMC perceivers find that their partners are behaving more socially than they expected, but they do not think that they themselves induced this change in sociability, then what do they believe is the cause of their partners' sociable demeanor?

Because the question asks whether, in a sense, different attributions may be made in CMC than in other media, we reviewed recent research on attributional differences in CMC and face-to-face interaction. Research [11] has documented that attributions for partners' self-disclosures differ in CMC than face-to-face interaction. When disclosures are made in CMC partners perceive significantly greater intimacy. Additionally, CMC participants tend to explain the causal basis for partners' disclosures differently as well.

In addition to classical attribution-theoretic dispositional and situational attributions, we make attributions representing the conclusion that one's partner behaved as she did due to some relationship-based motivation [11] or what is known as a personalistic attribution [12]. Personalistic attributions occur when an interactant believes that his partner acted as she did because of her specific feelings about him. Therefore, personalistic attributions seemed to offer a means by which CMC interactants could understand why their sociable partners appeared to act positively toward them despite their own failure to take credit for influencing their partners' sociable behavior. A personalistic attribution would be tantamount to the conclusion that the partner behaved as though she liked him because she simply liked him, rather than because he induced her to behave in any particular way. Alternatively, the attribution that a partner behaved as she did because one individual tried to get her to do so can be classified as a self attribution.

An experiment replicated several of the procedures in the second Tong and Walther study reported above [13]. That is, male-female dyads conversed via CMC chat or by phone with a partner whom the male was led to believe was either in a bad mood or had a negative personality. This induction was expected to prompt the male partner to make efforts to be more sociable in order to lead his partner to be more sociable as well, in line with the findings of the previous study. After the conversations concluded, participants completed measures assessing their partners' demeanor as well as items identifying the attributions that they made for why their partners behaved as they did. These measures allowed orthogonal scoring on the four attributional dimensions of dispositional, situational, self-induced deliberate influence on a partner's behavior, or a personalistic attribution indicating that the partner behaved the way she did because of her own genuine affection toward the male interactant.

Analyses showed very similar effects on the males' behaviors as were seen in the previous studies. Men were more sociable toward their partners when they believed that their partners were in a bad mood compared to those who believed their partners had a negative personality. Correlations between the males' and their female partners' behaviors showed that partners did respond to males' overt sociability. Men in the CMC condition detected more of a change in their partners' moods as a result of the online conversation then did men who used the telephone system.

Supporting the study's hypotheses, there were also significant differences in the attributional patterns by males depending on whether their conversations took place by phone or via CMC chat. The CMC interactants attributed their partners' chat behavior more strongly to personalistic causes. That is, they believed that their partners' liking for them was the basis for their partners' behavior. Although CMC participants registered some degree of self attributions as well, self attribution was significantly more prominent in the telephone condition.

It is worth repeating that the female partners were naïve; they were neither in a bad mood nor had a negative personality. Their behavior may have shifted slightly toward sociability, but the only cause for change above baseline would be because the males instigated this change via their own overtures toward their partners. And yet, more so in CMC than by phone, these male interactants believed that when their partners acted nicely, it was because they simply liked them. There is no real basis for their conclusion aside from their perceptions of what they could or could not do via the medium in which they operated. The evidence shows that the perceivers themselves caused their partners' responses to come into being. Yet the communication channel fostered the illusion that the females' responses originated within themselves, and not from the males' influence. This is probably due in part to the stereotype about CMC that it is too weak a channel effectively to change another person's demeanor, a stereotype which, although still popularly held, is shown by the evidence to be false. Because of this stereotype, however, and in particular because of its falsity, the illusion of liking replaces the self attribution of influence when interactants try to interpret the cause of their partner's affiliative behavior in CMC.

6   Conclusion

As a whole, the studies reviewed above showcase the potentially transformative nature of CMC in dyadic interaction. The formation of idealized pre-interaction partner expectations, the ability to influence partners' behaviors during communication, and the subsequent post-interaction attributions that individuals make about their partners reference the unique ability of CMC to facilitate the development and instantiation of self-fulfilling prophecies. Oddly much of this process takes place outside of the individuals' conscious awareness, which allows them to believe what they want to about their partners. In the end, the opportunity to create, produce, and sustain an ideal partner who may be too good to be true, is perhaps too good an opportunity to pass up.

References

1. Walther, J.B.: Computer-Mediated Communication: Impersonal, Interpersonal, and Hyperpersonal Interaction. Communication Research 23, 3–43 (1996)
2. Hancock, J., Dunham, P.: Impression Formation in Computer-Mediated Communication Revisited - An Analysis of the Breadth and Intensity of Impressions. Communication Research 28, 325–347 (2001)
3. Walther, J.B.: Selective Self-Presentation in Computer-Mediated Communication: Hyperpersonal Dimensions of Technology, Language, and Cognition. Computers in Human Behavior 23, 2538–2557 (2007)
4. Tong, S.T., Walther, J.B.: The Confirmation and Disconfirmation of Expectancies in Computer-Mediated Communication. Communication Research (to be published)
5. Walther, J.B., Loh, T., Granka, L.: Let Me Count The Ways - The Interchange of Verbal and Nonverbal Cues in Computer-Mediated and Face-to-Face Affinity. Journal of Language and Social Psychology 24, 36–65 (2005)
6. Walther, J., Van Der Heide, B., Tong, S., Carr, C., Atkin, C.: Effects of Interpersonal Goals on Inadvertent Intrapersonal Influence in Computer-Mediated Communication. Human Communication Research 36 (July 2010)
7. Snyder, M., Tanke, E.D., Berscheid, E.: Social-Perception and Interpersonal-Behavior-on Self-Fulfilling Nature of Social Stereotypes. Journal of Personality and Social Psychology 35, 656–666 (1977)
8. Ickes, W., Patterson, M.L., Rajecki, D.W., Tanford, S.: Behavioral and Cognitive Consequences of Reciprocal Versus Compensatory Responses to Preinteraction Expectancies. Social Cognition 1, 160–190 (1982)
9. Nowak, K., Watt, J.H., Walther, J.B.: Computer Mediated Teamwork and the Efficiency Framework: Exploring the Influence of Synchrony and Cues on Media Satisfaction and Outcome Success. Computers in Human Behavior 25, 1108–1119 (2009)

10. Tong, S.T., Walther, J.B.: How individuals cause hyperpersonal effects in CMC: Expectations, malleability, efficacy, and channel interactions. Presented at the Annual Meeting of the International Communication Association, London, England (2013)
11. Jiang, L., Bazarova, N., Hancock, J.: The Disclosure-Intimacy Link in Computer-Mediated Communication: An Attributional Extension of the Hyperpersonal Model. Human Communication Research 37, 58–77 (2011)
12. Newman, H.: Communication Within Ongoing Intimate-Relationships - An Attributional Perspective. Personality and Social Psychology Bulletin 7, 59–70 (1981)
13. Walther, J.B., Jang, J.-W., Kashian, N.C., Falin, J., Shin, S.Y., Paul, A., et al.: Intimacy in computer-mediated communication: The underestimation of affective influence leads to the illusion of liking online. Presented at the Annual Meeting of the International Communication Association, London, England (2013)

Image Choice to Represent the Self in Different Online Environments

Monica Whitty[1], James Doodson[1], Sadie Creese[2], and Duncan Hodges[2]

[1]Department of Media and Communications, University of Leicester, UK
{mw229,j.t.doodson}@le.ac.uk
[2]Cyber Security Centre, Department of Computer Science, University of Oxford, UK
{sadie.creese,duncan.hodges}@cs.ox.ac.uk

Abstract. This paper draws from *'impression management theory'* to examine the choices individuals make to visually represent themselves on Facebook and Twitter. We interviewed 20 participants about their image choice and the sorts of inferences others make about their identity. Participants were asked whether they believed their image influenced the types of people who connect with them, and whether their pictorial representation affected the topics and type of communication they have with other people. Contrary to previous research on online impression management, we found that few individuals were motivated to create a specific impression by playing with different images and instead individuals were motivated to appear genuine and authentic. Only a few desired hiding behind an avatar in order to feel freer to self-disclose. We found that Facebook and Twitter were perceived as very different spaces with different affordances and that these perceived affordances influenced participants' choice in image.

Keywords: social identity and presence, computer mediated communication, avatars, impression management, online pictorial representations, online identity.

1 Introduction

Ever since the beginnings of the Internet, scholars have been interested in how the self is constructed in cyberspace. They have questioned whether we are the same person online, whether we can escape our 'real identity' or whether we can 'experiment' with new identities (e.g., [1-2]). Some scholars argued that the anonymity of the Internet afforded individuals with opportunities to self-disclose more intimate information about themselves (e.g., [3-4]). These questions were asked when people were 'visually anonymous' – but are the same questions relevant to ask about online spaces where individuals are able to pictorially represent themselves (e.g., Facebook, online dating sites)? Do individuals 'play' with constructions of their identities through their choice of images and does their choice of pictorial representation allow them to feel freer to express themselves? In contrast, does the presentation of visual information about someone restrict the amount of information individuals feel comfortable disclosing? Moreover, given the degree of disclosure about self online, there are concerns around

G. Meiselwitz (Ed.): SCSM 2014, LNCS 8531, pp. 528–537, 2014.
© Springer International Publishing Switzerland 2014

whether the use of online media can result in exposure to risks of identity and online persona theft [5].

With many online sites (e.g., chat rooms, social networking sites, online dating profiles, and so forth), the initial information individuals are presented with is a visual image chosen to represent the person behind the profile. This paper draws from 'impression management theory' (e.g., [6-7]) to examine the choices individuals make to visually represent themselves on a variety of online sites. In particular, we focus on two different types of social networking sites: Facebook and Twitter.

Goffman [6] developed his impression management theory by examining verbal and non-verbal communication. According to Goffman, individuals over-communicate gestures that reinforce the desired self and under-communicate gestures that detract from the desired self. Impressions of self are therefore understood to be managed. Goffman described the self as both a 'performer' and a 'character', and contended that the 'self-as-performer' is not merely a social product, but also has a basic motivational core. In contrast, the 'self-as-character' represents an individual's unique humanity. It is this part of the self which is a social product; that is, preformed outwardly in social life. The 'self-as-character' is one's inner self. Goffman believed that individuals need to present themselves as an acceptable person to others. He stated that "the impressions that the others give tend to be treated as claims and promises they have implicitly made, and claims and promises tend to have a moral character" [6, p. 21]. He argued that individuals can be strategic in their impression formation.

Researchers have applied Goffman's theory to online presentations of self. Miller [8] claims that although depth and richness of self-presentation might not seem immediately apparent online, nonetheless "the problem of establishing and maintaining an acceptable self-remains, and there is a range of expressive resources available for this end". Whitty [9] has applied Goffman's theory to online dating profiles, and has examined the types of profiles which lead to more success.

Leary and Kowalski [7] have extended and modified Goffman's work on impression management. According to these theorists, impression management involves two components: impression motivation (i.e., being motivated to control how others see them) and impression construction (i.e., deciding how they will go about creating the desired impression). Leary and Kowalski argue that people often monitor how they impact on others and attempt to gauge the sorts of impressions they make. Often individuals do not attempt to create a particular impression but instead attempt to maintain their 'public' persona. At other times, however, individuals are highly motivated to create a particular impression. When individuals are motivated to create a certain impression they may alter their behaviours in order to manipulate how others see them. Leary and Kowalski [6] state that their "model accounts not only for why people are concerned with others' impressions of them in a particular social setting, but also for why people adopt one impression management tactic rather than another" (p.36).

The Internet is especially interesting to examine with regards to the topic of impression management given that it has been argued that the Internet affords individuals greater opportunities to create and manage impressions (e.g., [10-11]). This affordance, according to some, promotes greater self-disclosures compared with face-to-face environments [4]. It has been argued that this has been made possible because people are visually anonymous online [4]. In addition, others, such as Walther, have argued that the Internet affords greater opportunities for impression management given that many spaces are asynchronous and individuals are able to allocate more cognitive resources to the message composition than they would in face-to-face environments.

The above theories were developed to explain individuals who are visually anonymous and so we know little about impression formation when people are visually present online. Individuals can still be strategic in how they elect to represent themselves visually and so impression management theory may still be very relevant in its application to understanding how people choose to present themselves online. More recently, Nowak [12] has found that the icons individuals select to represent themselves when they use Instant Messaging reflected either physical or psychological characteristics or both.

In this study, we were interested in the choices people make with the initial image they choose for others to view when they encounter their online profile. We focused on Facebook and Twitter images. We choose these two social networking sites given that they serve different social purposes. Specifically, Facebook is more privately oriented with a focus on maintaining connections with existing friendship group [13-14]. Conversely, Twitter is more publically oriented with the potential for a different type of audience [15-17]. In particular, we were interested in whether participants chose a photograph of themselves or an avatar and what impression they hoped to achieve from their selection (if any). Drawing from impression management theory, we sought to understand whether individuals were motivated to create a certain impression and how they went about doing this with visual images. Furthermore, we asked participants whether they believed their image choice afforded them opportunities for different types of self-disclosures (e.g., feeling more free to disclose more intimate aspects about themselves) or whether, in fact, these choices inhibited or restricted their self-disclosures.

2   Method

The study employed a grounded theory approach [18] which was chosen because the research on this topic area is scant and there is little available theory to draw upon or develop. Grounded theory is an inductive, theory discovery methodology that allows the researcher to develop theory, while at the same time, grounding the theory in data collected in empirical research. It allows a researcher to listen to the data without necessarily imposing preconceived ideas on the data; however, it does not mean that previous theories cannot be brought to light in the analysis [18].

2.1   Materials

Given the exploratory nature of our study we created a semi-structured interview schedule for this study. While the basic structure of the interview was adhered to for each participant, because of the unique experience each participant had with the online plat-forms, each participant did not receive the exact same interview schedule. Participants were asked to describe their Facebook and Twitter visual representations (e.g., photo-graph or avatar) as well as any of their other pictorial representations used on other on-line applications (e.g., dating and gaming sites, instant messenger, and VoIP).

For each visual representation, participants were asked how they came about choosing their image and whether they felt their choice was in line with the norms of that particular online environment. Participants were then asked whether their image choice expressed anything about themselves or their personality, and the sorts of infe-rences others might make about their identity given their choice of image. They were then asked whether they believed their avatar influenced the types of people who connect with them in an online environment, and whether their avatar affected the topics and type of communication they have with other people.

2.2   Procedure

Prior to commencement of the study, ethical clearance was gained from the University's Ethics Committee. During January 2014, we commissioned Qualtrics to recruit partici-pants from their online panel. Participants were required to have both a Facebook and a Twitter account to allow comparisons of the avatars across the two different spaces. Facebook and Twitter were chosen due to their popularity and the differences between how the two social networks are used (as discussed earlier) Participants were also re-quired to reside in the UK to facilitate the organisation of interviews.

Participants were first required to complete an online survey and from this set of individuals, 20 participants were interviewed for the study reported in this paper. Overall, 1,223 individuals began our initial online survey which asked questions about Internet usage, image choice across a number of online platforms and psycho-logical characteristics. Of these, 209 individuals completed the survey in full and indicated their data could be used for analysis.

Participants for this interview study were recruited from the pool of participants who completed the original questionnaire. In the earlier study, 185 individuals indi-cated a willingness to take part in the follow-up interview. Each of these participants was contacted about their availability for an interview, and seventy-seven participants responded (41.6% response rate). Of these 20 were interviewed for this study.

Interviews were conducted over VoIP (Skype in this instance, using the video op-tion), which took approximately 20-40 minutes. Video was chosen given that it af-forded a closer face-to-face experience, which is considered more effective at devel-oping a rapport and trust between the interviewer and interviewee than other types of online interviews [19].

2.3   Participants

Twenty participants were recruited (10 male, 10 female), each residing in the UK. Participants were aged from 23 to 56 years, with a mean of 36 years (SD = 10.8 years). Male participants were aged from 23 to 52 years with a mean of 39 years (SD

= 8.8 years). Female participants were aged from 23 to 56 years with a mean of 33 years (SD = 12.3 years).

Table 1. Break down of demographics and types of image

	Age	Sex	Facebook profile image	Twitter profile image
1	32	F	Photograph of themselves alone	Photograph of an animal (dog)
2	45	M	Photograph of a male-female couple, including participant	Photograph of themselves alone
3	47	M	Photograph of themselves alone	Photograph of themselves alone (did not match FB)
4	23	M	Photograph with a male-female couple, including participant	Cartoon figure (anime figure)
5	50	M	Photograph of natural scene (trees and river)	Photograph of themselves alone
6	26	F	Photograph of themselves alone	Photograph of themselves alone (did not match FB).
7	36	M	Photograph of themselves alone	Photograph of themselves alone, with a text caption (did not match FB).
8	56	M	Photograph of themselves alone	Identical to FB
9	23	F	Photograph of themselves alone	Identical to FB
10	52	F	Themselves alone	Photograph of themselves alone (did not match FB).
11	36	F	Photograph of their legs	Identical to FB photograph
12	24	M	Photograph of themselves alone overlaid with text and logo	Identical to FB photograph
13	27	F	Photograph of themselves alone	Cartoon figure (anime figure)
14	26	M	Photograph of themselves alone	Default image (Twitter egg)
15	51	M	Photograph of rugby ball	Photograph of rugby player
16	34	F	Photograph of themselves alone	Photograph of art work
17	39	F	Default image (human silhouette)	Default image (Twitter egg)
18	24	F	Photograph of themselves alone with an animal (cat)	Photograph of themselves alone
19	32	M	Cartoon of two animals from a television show	Photograph of themselves alone
20	37	F	Image of a cat overlaid with text and equals sign logo (a common Internet meme)	Identical to FB

Participants tended to use Facebook regularly. Most participants used Facebook more than once a day (n=14), three used Facebook daily, two used it 2 to 3 times per week and one used it once a month. Four participants updated their profile picture 2-3 times a day, six updated daily, four more than once a day, four 2 to 3 times a week, two once a week, two 2-3 times a month and two several times a year. Participants used Twitter less often that Facebook. Most participants tended to use Twitter once a year or less (n=9) or several times a year (n=8) and three use Twitter 2-3 times a month. One participant updated their profile picture once a month, five several times a year, thirteen once a year or less, and one had never changed their Twitter image from the default option.

3   Results and Discussion

The following section outlines some of the more interesting results that emerged from our analysis. We first draw from Leary and Kowalski's [6] theory of impression management to consider whether individuals were motivated to 'impression manage', and if so how they went about constructing this impression.

3.1   Managing an Impression

A few of our participants were highly motivated to create a certain impression for their perceived audiences. If it was a profile photograph of themselves they thought carefully about the impression they were trying to convey (e.g., via the clothes they were wearing, the expressions on their face or who was in the photograph with them). For example, the following participant expressed how he thought carefully about what he was wearing in his profile photographs and the meaning these clothes conveyed:

> *I think probably that's the thing I like to show is, I don't know, smart dressing or peculiar dressing, like special things. Not bizarre but in a way different from usual. I think the other one I had before I'm just remembering, I was smoking a Churchill cigar and I had Che Guevara so that sort of image looked absolutely different from any other picture that usually I'd see or I was bored about my previous one. So even if I don't smoke the cigar, usually I smoke it twice a year, it's still the picture I want, so the image I wanted to pass to those looking at me...*
>
> *I think there are differences in the way you dress ... well at least in Italy there is a huge difference between people in the way they dress if they have a socialist background rather than a right wing background and so on. So in a way by showing these particular aspects, I am anyway showing being sympathetic with some sort of line... and so on. So yes, probably if I was open to anyone yes, they would probably get an idea what's my political point of view.* (Participant 7)

In preference to a profile photograph, others choose an image to create a certain impression. For example, some choose a cartoon, others pictures of their favourite sports team. In the following example, the participant explains how she choose to take a photograph of her feet in high heels rather than a profile photograph that would have clearly given away her identity. She used this image on both her Facebook and Twitter profiles:

> I have two names, I am Jenny April [pseudonym], and the in-joke is that Jenny wears ridiculous heels and April does very logical things, and the in-joke is that Jenny wears these amazing heels and does all these outrageous things. Which is why when I set up the online profiles for Jenny Lawrence, she wears these outrageous heels and does things that involve hanging up-side-down in apple trees in hammocks, whereas in reality April has two children and has to go and do all of those things. So it was very much an on-line persona that we set up, that's why it's slightly off the wall and it's very much an in-joke…
>
> It was a well chosen image, I didn't just grab one off of ... To be fair what I have is thousands of images on my computer, this one was very personal to me and said a lot about me. (Participant 11)

Managing Audiences and Conversations. In some cases the images were chosen in order to generate a specific type of conversation or draw in a specific audience. For example, one participant talked about pet lovers approaching her on twitter because she had used a photograph of a dog, whilst another participant talked about attracting rugby players as he had an interest in rugby in preference to football.

3.2   Authenticity

As mentioned in our Introduction, Leary and Kowalski [6] argue that often individuals do not attempt to create a specific impression but rather aim to maintain their public persona. This appeared to be more the case with our particular sample. Rather than attempting to create an impression by playing with different images, most participants felt it was important to appear genuine and authentic. Many stated that in order to do this a photograph of themselves (often a very recent photograph) was necessary. Moreover, this served a second purpose, which was to help people they knew find them to connect with their profile. This is clearly expressed by the following participant:

> To me I think it's a simple photo, it shows you as the person. I think if it's in a profile picture you're the profile. People know your face but they're not really interested in looking at a picture of a house or your dog or your car, I think they like to see what you like to look like at present or the past. Because I know some people seem to use old photos 20 years ago, which is great because obviously if you've got an old friend on Facebook you remember them, but if the person knows it's you by the name, why are you trying to be in the past when you're now in the present? It's a nice little picture, I like that that one, the white shirt. That was round the kids' house. (Participant 8)

3.3   Anonymity

Earlier research found that many online users enjoyed the anonymity the Internet afforded given that it provided a space for them to feel free to self-disclose. Very few of our participants choose or wished to hide behind an image, although there were a couple who enjoyed using an avatar to disguise their true identity in order to express themselves in ways they would not have done had they used a photograph of themselves. This is explained by the following participant:

> *But just though a conscious sort of thing of "ah, but then they'll know what my face is". If they saw me down the street and they didn't like what I said they could just "oi you're a prick" for something you did on Twitter a long time ago that no one would really remember. Whereas if it wasn't a picture of me then they wouldn't know what I look like so I can just tweet someone and just say oh, you know a celebrity, that "I really enjoyed this show you were on bla bla bla" or "I really dislike the show you were on bla bla bla". The fact that not having a picture of me makes it easier to communicate with people on Twitter...*

> *Well, like I said celebrities mainly. I see something on TV, er, one of the ones that's been getting to me recently is Dancing on Ice...*

> *Watch Dancing on Ice and in the first week, a celebrity pair that I thought did really well went out due to public vote. And I feel that...if I a picture of me...on my Twitter profile, I wouldn't have sent a message that I did. And I sent a message that was...just a little bit rude.* (P4).

3.4 Affordances of the Space

Participants often perceived Facebook and Twitter as very different spaces, each attracting different audiences to their profile. Facebook was more likely to be perceived as a place to connect with people they knew, including family members (most seemed to use privacy settings to restrict their audience), whilst Twitter was seen as a more public space. This perception appeared to influence the choices of images participants opted to present. Many felt that a recent photograph on Facebook was imperative, while the need for a photograph or authentic image was not as important for many on Twitter. Consistency of images across sites often appeared to be a decision dependent on the perceived audience as well as how the individual decided to use the site. Interestingly, not all individuals used these sites in the same way. For example, one participant pointed out that he believed that Twitter users can be either 'broadcasters' (someone who wishes to write many messages for others to read) or 'receivers' (someone who prefers to read others tweets) or both. Again, this type of perception may well influence users' image choice.

4 Conclusions

We began this paper by pointing out that scholars had noted that the Internet has afforded individuals with more freedom to play with identity and hide behind presentations of self in order to enable greater self-disclosures. The model we are developing here suggests this is not the case. Some individuals in our sample appeared to be very strategic in their choice of image, in the hope of creating a certain impression or to generate specific conversations. However, in the main, participants choose recent photographs to represent themselves and expressed a wish to be authentic and genuine towards others. This was stronger for Facebook than it was for Twitter and so the type of online space and the affordances this space is perceived to provide needs to be taken into account in any model developed to explain profile image choice.

Our future work will extend this analysis to: identify habits and motivations behind the choices that people make when selecting an avatar, and whether those motivations and habits are influenced by the type of online environment; examine links between personality and choices that people make when selecting an avatar; examine whether the type of online environment influences the extent to which an avatar represents the users physical body and personality; and identify the degree to which any of these choices are influenced by perceptions of online risk. Profile pictures and avatars are both ubiquitous (meaning most online environments include some form of pictorial representation) and easily obtainable by anyone which makes the choice of avatar an interesting security vulnerability. Of course, the vulnerability of identity and personas is something that is well understood in the security community but much less in the non-expert community. Therefore, as concerns around vulnerability begin to gain strength across society we might expect this to impact upon choices surrounding self-disclosure including graphical representations. The relationship between personality, perceptions of risk, and self-disclosures is a topic that we must return to in the longer-term if we are to better understand how best to support individuals in their own personal management of such risks.

References

1. Haraway, D.: Simians, cyborgs and women: The reinvention of nature. Free Association Books, London (1991)
2. Turkle, S.: Life on the screen: Identity in the age of the Internet. Weidenfeld & Nicolson, London (1995)
3. Bargh, J.A., McKenna, K.Y.A., Fitzsimons, G.M.: Can you see the real me? Activation and expression of the "true self" on the Internet. Journal of Social Issues 58, 33–48 (2002)
4. Joinson, A.N.: Knowing me, Knowing you: Reciprocal self-disclosure on the Internet. Cyberpsychology and Behavior 4, 587–591 (2001)
5. Creese, S., Goldsmith, M., Nurse, J.R.C., Phillips, E.: A data-reachability model for elucidating privacy and security risks related to the use of online social networks. In: Proceedings of Trust, Security and Privacy in Computing and Communications (TrustCom), pp. 1124–1131. IEEE, New York (2012)
6. Goffman, E.: The presentation of self in everyday life. Penguin, London (1963)
7. Leary, M.R., Kowalski, R.M.: Impression management: A literature review and two-component model. Psychological Bulletin 107, 34–47 (1990)
8. Miller, H.: The presentation of self in electronic life: Goffman on the internet. Embodied Knowledge and Virtual Space (1995),
   http://ess.ntu.ac.uk/miller/cyberpsych/goffman.htm
9. Whitty, M.T.: Revealing the 'real' me, searching for the 'actual' you: Presentations of self on an Internet dating site. Computers in Human Behavior 24, 1707–1723 (2008)

10. Walther, J.B.: Selective self-presentation in computer-mediated communication: Hyper-personal dimensions of technology, language, and cognition. Computers in Human Behavior 23, 2538–2557 (2007)
11. Walther, J.B., Slovacek, C., Tidwell, L.: Is a picture worth a thousand words? Photographic images in long-term and short-term computer-mediated communication. Communication Research 28, 105–134 (2001)
12. Nowak, K.L.: Choosing Buddy Icons that look like me or represent my personality: Using Buddy Icons for social presence. Computers in Human Behavior 29, 1456–1464 (2013)
13. Joinson, A.N.: Looking at, looking up or keeping up with people?: Motives and use of Facebook. In: Proceedings of the SIGCHI Conference on Human Factors in Computing Systems, pp. 1027–1036. ACM, New York (2008)
14. Raacke, J., Bonds-Raacke, J.: MySpace and Facebook: Applying the uses and gratifications theory to exploring friend-networking sites. Cyberpsychology & Behavior 11, 169–174 (2008)
15. Huberman, B., Romero, D., Wu, F.: Social networks that matter: Twitter under the microscope. First Monday 14 (2008),
    http://firstmonday.org/article/view/2317/2063
16. Hughes, D.J., Rowe, M., Batey, M., Lee, A.: A tale of two sites: Twitter vs. Facebook and the personality predictors of social media usage. Computers in Human Behavior 28, 561–569 (2012)
17. Marwick, A.E.: I tweet honestly, I tweet passionately: Twitter users, context collapse, and the imagined audience. New Media & Society 13, 114–133 (2011)
18. Glaser, B., Strauss, A.: The discovery of grounded theory: Strategies for Qualitative Research. Aldine De Gruyther, Chicago (1967)
19. O'Connor, H., Madge, C., Shaw, R., Wellens, J.: Internet-based interviewing. In: Fielding, N.G., Lee, R.M. (eds.) The SAGE Handbook of Online Research Methods, pp. 271–289. SAGE Publications Inc., Los Angeles (2008)

Games, Gamification, and Entertainment in Social Media

Using Serious Games to Train Adaptive Emotional Regulation Strategies

Mariano Alcañiz[1,2], Alejandro Rodríguez[1], Beatriz Rey[1,2], and Elena Parra[1]

[1] Instituto Interuniversitario de Investigación en Bioingeniería y Tecnología Orientada al Ser Humano, Universitat Politècnica de València, I3BH/LabHuman, Camino de Vera s/n, 46022 Valencia, España
[2] Ciber, Fisiopatología de Obesidad y Nutrición, CB06/03 Instituto de Salud Carlos III, Spain
{arodriguez,brey,malcañiz}@labhuman.i3bh.es

Abstract. Emotional Regulation (ER) strategies allow people to influence the emotions they feel, when they feel them, how they experience them, and how they express them in any situation. Deficiencies or deficits in ER strategies during the adolescence may become mental health problems in the future. The aim of this paper is to describe a virtual multiplatform system based on serious games that allows adolescents to train and evaluate their ER strategies. The system includes an ecological momentary assessment (EMA) tool, which allows the therapist to monitor the emotional status of teenagers every day in real time. Results obtained from a usability and effectiveness study about the EMA tool showed that adolescents preferred using the EMA tool than other classical instruments.

Keywords: Serious Games, Emotional Regulation, Ecological Momentary Assessment, Virtual Reality.

1 Introduction

Emotional Regulation (ER) strategies allow people to influence the emotions they feel, when they feel them, how they experience them, and how they express them in any situation. These strategies may be automatic or controlled, voluntary or involuntary. ER strategies should be differentiated depending on when they have their first impact on the emotion generation process. Despite the fact that there are diverse emotional regulation strategies, most research has been conducted into cognitive reevaluation (assigning a non-emotional meaning to an event) and expressive suppression (controlling the somatic response to an emotion). Both the physical and psychological implications will be different depending on the strategy used.

Numerous studies indicate the role that these regulation strategies play in the development and maintenance of adaptive and healthy behavior. Previous research [1] has concurred in finding diverse emotional regulation dysfunctions in the clinical population with depressive disorders. Deficiencies or deficits in ER are related to the occurrence of numerous mental and physical health problems, including borderline

G. Meiselwitz (Ed.): SCSM 2014, LNCS 8531, pp. 541–549, 2014.

personality disorder, depression, anxiety, problems of social interaction, problems of adaptations, violent behavior and other disruptive behaviors.

These deficits become especially evident during the adolescence and may become a psychosocial problem. Actually, schools and high-schools denounce a worrying increase in indiscipline and episodes of physical and psychological violence in the classroom. Proof of this concern is the Study of Violence report by the Centro Reina Sofía or Cisneros X [2-3] which showed that high percentage values of children had suffered bullying or school-based violence.

Many of these disruptive behaviors by the adolescents are built upon deficiencies in situation selection, situation modification, attention deployment, cognitive change or response modulation [4]. On the other hand, an adaptive ER involves choosing and implementing ER strategies that are adapted to the context, adapted to how controllable the internal and external events are, and in harmony with long term goals [1]. Berking believes that the effectiveness of behavior change therapies could be improved by identifying general emotional regulation abilities, developing interventions that could improve these abilities and including these interventions in the therapies [5].

The current tools used to evaluate possible deficits in ER strategies are based on subjective questionnaires, such as the Emotion Regulation Checklist [6] or the Emotion Regulation Questionnaire [7]. These questionnaires ask subjects about how they feel and manipulate their emotions in controlled environments or in common situations in real life. Another way of evaluating the ER strategies used is through tests in laboratory, where the subjects ought to do emotion generating tasks with the aim to analyze the strategies that have to be used [8]. Even though these tools are very useful for therapist (distinguishing between clinical and normal populations), they present some limitations; specifically, they are unattractive for the evaluation in adolescents' population, who are particularly reluctant to be assessed.

These limitations can be overcome with the development of instruments based on new technologies. Specifically, virtual reality (VR) systems and Information and Communication Technologies (ICT) are a technology that are very attractive and very common to young people and adolescents, who are accustomed to the simulated environments of videogames.

The development of new interactive technologies based on VR has already had some influence on certain aspects of the teaching/learning environment. VR and its application to youth education is a relatively young field but interest is growing due to its strong motivational impact [9] and the critical reasons for why and how graphic-based VR can greatly enhance the quality of education provided [10]. The devices and techniques allow navigating and interacting through VR environments in more intuitive and more natural ways. In addition, immersive and persuasive capacities of VR make it a highly appropriate technology for assessment and intervention task.

Recently, several works have used new techniques based on ICT for training of ER strategies. Playmancer project [11] is a system that uses multimodal recognition of emotions, in combination of serious games for the training of ER strategies, with the purpose of treating psychological and behavioural disorders [12]. In other project, Replay [13], a system based on a VR environment with avatars and tracking technologies was developed with the aim of improving the emotional implication of participants (students with behaviour disorders) and training ER strategies.

In this work, we describe GameTeen, a virtual multiplatform system based on serious games that allows teenagers to train and evaluate their ER strategies. Furthermore, the system includes an ecological momentary assessment (EMA) tool, which allows the therapist to monitor the emotional status of adolescent every day in real time. Finally, the results obtained of a usability and effectiveness study about the EMA tool will be presented.

2   Methods

The GameTeen system is a virtual multiplatform system based on serious games designed for teenagers, which allows training, evaluating and monitoring their emotions and the ER strategies that they apply everyday. GameTeen was developed according to recommendations of intervention program principles, which claim that a way of training and assessing how ER strategies have been applied by subjects involves the use of mood induction procedures. In the context of these procedures, subjects can learn to analyze the emotion felt and the ER strategies that they employed to regulate themselves [14].

Following this recommendation, GameTeen system was designed in three blocks. A first block would be a system where a positive or a negative emotion is induced in the subjects; it consists of two Mood Induction Games. A second block would consist of two mini-games where the participants may train two ER strategies (ER Strategies Training). Finally, in the third block, an ecological momentary assessment (EMA) would allow the therapist to monitor the emotional status of adolescent every day in real time.

2.1   Induction Games

The aim of the Mood Induction Games is to induce two different emotions in the participants. The emotions induced were joy and frustration. To achieve the desirable mood induction, several tools of positive and negative reinforcement were used respectively, such as music, sounds, emotional messages, etc. The monitoring of emotional levels in the two games was performed through periodic interruptions where the game asked participants to indicate their emotional level on a scale of 0 to 10 represented as thermometer.

Joy Induction Game. In the joy game (Figure1) the action took place in an attraction park. In this game the participants had to exploit as many balloons as possible of a shower of balloons. For this, the participants had several weapons and ammunitions that they were getting through the performance of the different ER strategies. The game had ten levels of difficulty that affected to the number of balloons and the velocity of appearance.

Fig. 1. Joy Induction Game. The game is located in an attraction park scene. In this scene, many balloons appear in continuous way while playing the game.

Frustration Induction Game. In the frustration game (Figure 2), a version of the "whack a mole" game was developed. The game is located in a rural land scene where there are several holes. In these holes, several moles can appear in a continuous way while playing the game. In this game, the participant has to whack all moles, at the same time that they are appearing, with a virtual mace. The game had three levels of difficulty that are related with the velocity and frequency of appearance of the moles. To achieve the frustration induction, the game was programmed so that some hits are not accurate and the participants are penalized.

Fig. 2. Frustration Induction Game. The game is located in a rural land scene where there are several holes. In these holes, several moles can appear in a continuous way while playing the game.

2.2 ER Strategies Training (Mini-Games)

Apart from these mood induction games, two mini-games were developed for training ER strategies. One of them consists of a respiration task where the subjects have to breathe at the same rate as indicated in the mini-game. This respiration strategy consists of a feather (Figure 3a), which goes up and down in the screen. In the other one, subjects have to click on all the numbers that appear sequentially on screen except one number, which is indicated within the mini-game (Figure 3b).

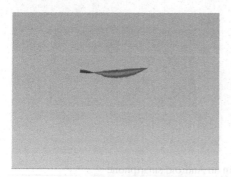
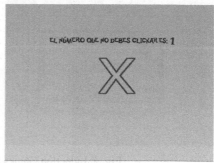

Fig. 3. Emotional Regulation Strategies Training. In the respiration strategy (a) consist in a feather that goes up and down in the screen to velocity moderate; and the distraction strategy (b) consist an sequence of number and one cross that are appearing sequentially.

2.3 Ecological Momentary Assessment (EMA)

To evaluate continuous changes in the emotions of subjects in their daily life we also developed an EMA system (Figure 4). The purpose of this system is to have a diary record of the emotions felt by the subjects by means of an android device, which can be configured and monitored from a webpage. This system includes a custom avatar who asks a set of questions about the feeling of the teenagers in predefined moments during the day. Moreover, the system has a web page where the therapist can authenticate himself/herself with the purpose of monitoring the emotional activity of all subjects in his/her study.

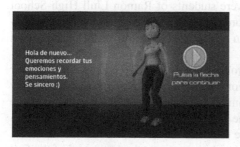

Fig. 4. EMA. Capture an example avatar and the example a question.

2.4   Technological Aspects

The Mood Induction Games and the Mini-Games were developed with the purpose of being used both on PC and on Android platforms (Figure 5). For this reason, we used the Unity3d as the development environment. It was programmed in C-Sharp. C-Sharp is a friendly programming language that has many communication devices libraries and web services libraries.

Fig. 5. Induction Games in an Android smartphone

Mainly, the PC platform was thought to be used with keyboard and mouse in the participants' home but in addition this system has the option to be used in laboratory under therapeutic supervision. For this, GameTeen has the option of registering the ECG signal of participants synchronized with game events, allowing therapists to monitor changes in the heart rate in real time in laboratory conditions.

2.5   Design Usability Study

The GameTeen platform has been evaluated with students of a high school. In this work, we present the preliminary results obtained of a usability study performed with teenagers.

Twenty one participants, 10 men and 11 women, were evaluated in this study, all of them with ages between 12-14 years old (mean 13.20 years old) with normal o corrected-to-normal vision. The subjects were students of Ramón Llull High-School of València without any psychological disorder and none of them was under psychological supervision. Their parents signed an informed consent for allowing their data to be used in this study.

The adolescents were divided in two groups. The first group had to express their emotions daily through the EMA system. For that, we lent several smartphones (Sony Xperia Neo V), whose functions were banned to except the EMA system. On the other hand, the second group had to do the same task; however they used questionnaires in paper. The questions in paper were the same that the EMA system requested. All participants had to do this task twice a day during one week. At the end of the first week, groups were exchanged, and the participants had to do the same task during other week.

When all participants were in the two groups, we asked to them that they completed the usability questionnaire, which registered information about the usability of the paper questionnaire, EMA system and the comparative between the two procedures to daily register of emotions.

3   Results

In this work, we present preliminary results obtained in the usability of EMA system when this is compared with the usability of classical tools used to measured emotions, questionnaires in paper.

Results showed that teenagers perceived more discomfort while they did the paper questionnaires than with the EMA system (p=0.001). The 50% of subjects confirmed that the EMA system was very comfortable and its alarms were useful to remember the teenagers to complete the questions. This was reflected in the fact that the 100% of subjects perceived as negative quality that the paper questionnaire did not have any alarm. Against, the 19% of adolescents liked having freedom of schedule to answer the paper questionnaire.

On the other hand, the participants appreciated that the EMA system was more useful than paper questionnaire (p=0.004). The 42% participants indicated that the EMA system was easier to use than paper questionnaires, and the 100% participants showed their disagreement by having to move so many papers from one place to another.

4   Discussion

This paper describes the GameTeen project, a psychotherapeutic multiplatform based on serious games to train and evaluate the ER strategies in teenagers. This multiplatform was developed using news technologies in VR and ICTs with the aim to improve the classical tools used in the field of ER, to improve the motivation and to help to catch the attention of teenagers that can hardly be attracted by other instruments, such as questionnaires.

GameTeen allows the adolescents to train two ER strategies when a positive or negative emotion has been induced them. These ER strategies are based on two minigames, a slowly respiration task and an attention task. In addition, GameTeen helps the therapist to evaluate the ER strategies used by the subjects and it also enables to follow the emotion felt during the evaluation. For this reason, GameTeen system has been developed for being used as much in a controllable situation through a PC, as day-to-day through an EMA system.

In this paper, we have showed preliminary results obtained of a usability study, which was carried for the EMA system. The obtained results suggest that the EMA system can be used to monitor emotions in the adolescent population.

The participants appreciated the comfortably of EMA above the paper questionnaire. In addition, they emphasized that the EMA system was very useful. This can be caused by different factors: the ease of transportation; the fact that the paper questionnaire was a huge number of pieces of paper; and the usefulness of the reminders through the alarms. These qualities were not presented in paper format.

However, we are aware that the population used for this analysis was a non-clinical population. This will require, in the future, to validate the system with a clinical population of teenagers, i.e. with adolescents who have been diagnosed an ER disorder. Nevertheless, because of these results, we are optimistic and we believe that the system might be used to help therapists to monitor the emotions with a clinical population.

In future works, we will evaluate the reliability of GameTeen as therapeutic tool for the early detection of ER patterns with a high risk of leading to health or behavioral problems. In addition, we will analyze how their use as training tool would enable their integration into psychoeducational programs for prevention of emotional disorders. Finally, we will also use physiological measurement tools, such as electroencephalogram, to study the influence of the ER strategies in the human physiologic behavior with the aim of measuring and quantifying this effect.

Acknowledgments. This study was funded by Vicerrectorado de Investigación de la Universitat Politècnica de València, Spain, PAID-06-2011, R.N. 1984; by Ministerio de Educación y Ciencia, Spain, Project Game Teen (TIN2010-20187) and partially by projects Consolider-C (SEJ2006-14301/PSIC), "CIBER of Physiopathology of Obesity and Nutrition, an initiative of ISCIII" and Excellence Research Program PROMETEO (Generalitat Valenciana. Consellería de Educación, 2008-157).

The work of Alejandro Rodríguez was supported by the Spanish MEC under an FPI Grant BES-2011-043316.

References

1. Mennin, D., Farach, F.: Emotion and evolving treatments for adult psychopathology. Clinical Psychology: Science and Practice 14, 329–352 (2007)
2. Serrano, A., Iborra, I.: Informe violencia entre compañeros en la escuela. Spanish Version (2005), http://www.centroreinasofia.es
3. Informe Cisneros X.: Acoso y Violencia Escolar en España, por Iñaki Piñuel y Araceli Oñate. Editorial IIEDDI, Spanish Version (2007)
4. Werner, K., Gross, J.J.: Emotion Regulation and Psychopathology. In: Emotion Regulation and Psychopathology: A Transdiagnostic Approach to Etiology and Treatment. Guildford Press (2010)
5. Berking, M., Wupperman, P., Reichardt, A., Pejic, T., Dippel, A., Znoj, H.: Emotion-regulation skills as a treatment target in psychotherapy. Behaviour Research and Therapy 46, 1230–1237 (2008)
6. Shields, A., Cicchetti, D.: Emotion regulation among school-age children: The development and validation of a new criterion Q-sort scale. Developmental Psychology 33(6), 906–916 (1997)
7. Gross, J.J., John, O.P.: Individual differences in two emotion regulation processes: Implications for affect, relationships, and well-being. Journal of Personality and Social Psychology 85(2), 348–362 (2003)

8. Gross, J.J., Levenson, R.W.: Hiding feelings: The acute effects of inhibiting negative and positive emotion. Journal of Abnormal Psychology 106, 95–103 (1997)
9. Winn, et al.: The Effect of Student Construction of Virtual Environments on the Performance of High- and Low-Ability Students. Annual Meeting of the American Educational Research Association (2003)
10. Pantelidis, V.: Reasons to use virtual reality in education. VR in the Schools 1(1) (1995)
11. Playmancer, http://www.playmancer.eu
12. Ben Moussa, M., Magnenat-Thalmann, N.: Applying affect recognition in serious games: The playMancer project. In: Egges, A., Geraerts, R., Overmars, M. (eds.) MIG 2009. LNCS, vol. 5884, pp. 53–62. Springer, Heidelberg (2009)
13. Replay, http://www.replayproject.eu
14. Feldman, L.B., Gross, J.J., Conner, T., Benvenuto, M.: Knowing what you're feeling and knowing what to do about it: mapping the relation between emotion differentiation and emotion regulation. Cognition and Emotion 15, 713–724 (2001)

Version Control System Gamification:
A Proposal to Encourage the Engagement
of Developers to Collaborate in Software Projects

Alexandre Altair de Melo, Mauro Hinz, Glaucio Scheibel,
Carla Diacui Medeiros Berkenbrock, Isabela Gasparini, and Fabiano Baldo

Santa Catarina State University, Brazil (UDESC)
Computer Science Department
Graduate Program in Applied Computing
Joinville, SC – Brazil
{alexandremelo.br,mmhinz,gscheibel}@gmail.com,
{diacui,isabela,baldo}@joinville.udesc.br

Abstract. This paper proposes to use gamification for recognition of software developers' collaboration and commitment. In order to improve productivity, the paper also evaluates the users' engagement in a software development project. The idea is to use the information extracted from source repositories where developers realize their commits. A tool proposes ranking via news feed that will extract information from the source repository by using software engineering metrics, such as McCabe's cyclomatic complexity, in order to build a ranking system, which highlights and rewards the most active developers. The ultimate goal is to determine whether the use of gamification encourages collaboration and commitment of all involved in software development projects.

keywords: gamification, collaboration, version control, software engineering, interface.

1 Introduction

Over the past years, the term gamification has been calling attention to be applied beyond gaming environments and carry the approach to other collaborative tasks, such as software development. The classic concept of a game can be used to verify if developers and others involved in the projects promote engagement, reach their goals and even collaborate, resulting in increased productivity. The term gamification was coined by Nick Pelling in 2002 [12] and is conceptualized as the use of design techniques, thoughts and game elements to improve the experience in non-gaming situations.

Gamification is the application of game metaphors in not-ludic contexts to influence behavior and increase motivation and engagement. According to Zichermann *et al* [23], gamification is 75% psychology and 25% technology

G. Meiselwitz (Ed.): SCSM 2014, LNCS 8531, pp. 550–558, 2014.

related, and bears a strong incentive for greater engagement of developers. The process of using gaming techniques, when used properly, has the power to engage users by stimulating communication and learning [15].

Companies in the software industry, such as SAP, began applying gamification internally with their development teams, as well as with external partners. However, this approach is also used in other types of applications and solutions, such as Linkedin, opinions from customers on Amazon, Nike+ and Foursquare, which all use gamification to motivate users to perform tasks that require collaboration and providing feedback [8].

If used in software development, feedback can be extracted directly from a version control database tool and the most active developers get rewarded [9]. The use of software allowing the users to connect, interact and be aware of what their colleagues are doing has been successful in building systems and applications, as approached by Treude and Storey [20].

This paper proposes an extension to the work of Singer and Schneider [18], in order to calculate and rank participants involved in software development projects.

This paper is organized as follows: Section [2] presents related works; Section [3] presents key points about the basic mechanisms of games and the concept behind McCabe's metric; Section [5] presents the role of a version control system for the proposed model; Section [6] introduces the proposed model which is an equation that uses the McCabe's cyclomatic complexity to reward developers who modify sources of higher complexity; Section [7] illustrates our prototype to support the proposed model; and Section [8] concludes this paper and presents future works.

2   Related Works

The concept of gamification was initially applied by Website managers as a tool that maximizes customer engagement. Among these initiatives are the examples of Yahoo Answers and StackOverflow. In the first example, anyone can respond to various questions be ranked and rewarded for that. The second one focuses on developers' interaction, rewarding and ranking users according to their responses. Due to the effectiveness of using gamification in non-academic environments, this concept has begun to be studied by scholars [6].

In another study about gamification applied to software development, by Ahmad and Jaafar [1], the behavior of users that apply gamification is analyzed and guidelines for developing gamified applications are proposed in order to assist the area of human-computer interaction. The result of this experiment led to a more participatory experience among users of the study.

In Singer and Schneider's study [18], a preliminary result of an experiment, with encouraged computer science students to make more frequent updates in version control sources, shows that by using a web-based, social networking application software, a newsfeed of commits is provided in a ranking format. Some students were motivated to participate with their bug fixes to earn scores for better ranking; however, other students made superficial commits and it was necessary that the assessment be made by an engineer to check the quality of the commits, which hasn't been completed [18].

The above-mentioned initiatives are recent studies of gamification, since the topic is still new; however, the literature in this area is already well established. When applying the concept of gamification in an activity that does not have the characteristic of being playful, it is necessary to emphasize that the concept of playing is present; therefore, the authors Crawford [4], Deterding *et al* [5] and Salen [17] discussed some standards for the design and development of games. Within these patterns, some features leading to successful games are remarkable and involve challenges, interactions, rankings, points, even social approaches and collaborative actions. The social aspect of games has been well studied in the field of health care and well-being. For example, Velazquez *et al* [21] shows social interaction promoted by games to help the elderly adhere to healthier habits.

Regarding the use of gamification for building collaborative software, Singer and Schneider [18] quote that using metrics based only on commits is simplistic and worthless because it doesn't take into consideration the effort spent on the tasks. Therefore, this work intends to extend Singer and Schneider's proposal for the use of gamification and ranking for building software, through a different form of measurement, which is not only based on the number of commits from developers, but also on lines of source code according to the complexity of its code.

3   Game Engines

Turning an everyday activity into a gaming experience, while making it challenging and fun at the same time, requires a lot of effort. There are several approaches describing the gaming mechanisms. According to Cook [3], a game's mechanisms are based on a system of rules and simulations, which facilitate and encourage the user to explore and learn within many possibilities through the use of feedback mechanisms.

According to Marczewski [12], many real-world tasks can be broken into smaller tasks. In some cases, these tasks can be converted into real games. Koster [10] also comments that games are like puzzles to be solved, like everything else in life, for example, like learning how to drive a car, playing a mandolin or multiplying seven times seven. By adding rules, challenges, opponents and rewards, these activities can turn a task into a much more pleasant and enjoyable experience. In the following sections, we will list concepts inherent in games that can be used to apply gamification in real activities.

3.1   Rewards

According to Groh [7], rewards are used to elevate the reputation of a player within the gaming community, receive a level that releases exclusive access to collected badges and are highlighted in the community. In this process, gamification expands collaboration through competition and boosts the degree of motivation and interest.

3.2 Leaderboard

Leaderboards allow users to monitor their performance in relation to others and can be divided into several subcategories, such as: Global, Friends, Relative, Remote, etc. As pointed out by Deterding *et al* [5], leaderboards represent one of the most common techniques used to create gamification.

3.3 Rules

Rules must be used by players to understand the requirements for reaching each achievement. The set of rules must be clear and acknowledged by the players; however, it must be reminded that a change of rules impacts the players negatively. Therefore, it is important to combine targets and well-define rules.

According to Marczewski [12], a game's rules are vital. When a game is being constructed, a framework and set of rules must be defined. For example, a certain action is worth one point, but a more complex action is worth five points; when reaching one hundred points, the player receives a badge. The goals of a determined game only become clear once the rules are established.

3.4 Feedback

According to Marczewski [12], obtaining feedback is vital in any gamification system. This helps users to check their progress and, periodically, what other participants are doing within the same context. Some forms of feedback are more noticeable than others. Progress bars, points and badges, for example, are some of the fastest ways to provide the status to a user.

4 Metrics

The simplest metric to evaluate the evolution of a computer program is the number of lines of source code produced in it. However, this metric is only useful when used in conjunction with another one, such as measuring the number of errors (bugs) per line of the source code [16]. Furthermore, according to O'Grady [14], it is not successful to measure productivity by using as the only basis the number of lines of codes.

McCabe [13] establishes a framework for measuring the complexity of the source code. This metric is called cyclomatic complexity. Like the idea of Rosenberg [16], this paper considers that the number of code lines changed or added is only relevant when combined with other metrics. Thus, the number of code lines is scored based on the McCabe's cyclomatic complexity of the developed code.

Watson *et al* [22] also shows that high complexity leads to code that is more difficult to test; therefore, it is important to consider that the higher the complexity is, the lower the quality that the software may have.

4.1 McCabe's Cyclomatic Complexity

McCabe's metric is calculated by [13]:

$$M = E - N + X \qquad (1)$$

where M is the metric of McCabe's cyclomatic complexity (MCC), E is the number of edges in the graph of the program, N is the number of nodes or decision points in the program's graph and X is the number of the program's outputs.

In terms of programming, the code edges that are executed as a result of a decision are the decision points. Outputs are the explicit return statements in a program. Typically, there is an explicit exchange of functions without explicit return to subroutines.

A simpler method of calculating the MCC is shown in the equation below. If D is the number of decision points in the program, then

$$M = D + 1 \qquad (2)$$

In this case, decision points can be conditional statements. Each decision point typically has two possible paths.

5 Version Control System

Version control systems (VCS) are used during the development of most information system projects. While these tools have different features, the main idea is the same; in other words, the VCS are all able to track and store changes to the software from the beginning of its development. Once the software source code is organized into files and folders, VCS can store the changes of the files [19].

According to a survey conducted by Koc *et al* [9], in a version control system, each change is associated with answers to the following questions: who, when and why. As shown in this paper, when we combine VCS with a system of gamification, new questions could arise: Was the developer's contribution relevant to the project? How much has he or she contributed in a period of time? Last, but not least, how can he or she be recognized in the group, in an explicit way because it is clear that his or her contributions and collaborations are relevant?

6 Proposed Model of Gamification

As mentioned in the Metrics section of this paper, the number of modified code lines is only relevant when combined with another metric. In the proposed score model, the number of code lines will be scored according to the cyclomatic complexity of the committed code. For example, using a hundred lines of code added to a simple program have less value than the same hundred lines added to a program of high complexity. Thus, developers who work in critical points of a project receive more points and, therefore, more rewards than developers who modify simple programs.

Following the McCabe's cyclomatic complexity metric, it is possible to evaluate the relationship between complexity and the amount of lines of code modified by a particular developer.

1. The developer commits his modification;
2. A SVN hook is triggered to verify how many lines are modified;
3. The total complexity is evaluated by the hook;
4. The proposed equation is applied and the score is added to the developer's score.

$$Score = (MLoC \times TCC) + ((BCC - TCC) \times (MLoC \times 2)) \qquad (3)$$

where MLoC are the modified lines of code made by the developer, TCC is the program's total cyclomatic complexity and BCC is the program's cyclomatic complexity before the developer's modifications.

As mentioned above, measuring the amount of modified lines is only relevant when combined with another metric. The proposal to combine it with cyclomatic complexity differentiates the value of a change in source code, which also follows the Pareto's principle, where 20% of the source code has 80% of the system's total complexity. Joining the amount of modified lines of code with complexity balances the score between simple and complex codes [11], [2].

A commit must be rated according to the overall complexity and the value of the contributions of changes in a more complex source code, not only by the number of committed lines and number of commits made by the developer.

Challenges arise with high complexities. It is known that a high complexity of source code negatively impacts the maintenance process and can induce defects by considerably making more difficulty the executions test; therefore, it is not desirable that developers receive a higher score when using increased complexity, but the score must also be influenced by changes/improvements in complexity.

The equation can be split in two parts: the score by the number of modified code lines, depending on the complexity, plus a positive or negative bonus for improving or worsening the overall complexity. This method helps avoiding that developers are benefited by a high score when increasing complexity; the positive or negative change in complexity will inversely affect the received score.

For example, if a developer modifies 10 lines of code in a source code with a complexity of 15 units, he or she will receive 150 points, but if the previous complexity was 13 units, he or she will lose 40 points for increasing the complexity. However, if the previous complexity was 17 units, he or she will earn 40 points for having reduced the complexity and thus improved the code's quality of testability.

7   Prototype of the Gamification Tool

Figure 1 shows the screen with details of the developer's individual evolution for follow-up, including a small developer profile and the list of source codes that have been modified in conjunction with scores received by such modifications.

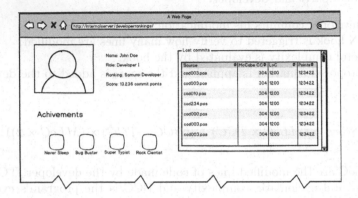

Fig. 1. Developer's profile

Figure 2 shows the screen with details of the developer group's evolution, according to each one's classification (ranking) and their total points. In this screen, developers can also compare their performances at predefined intervals. Thanks to this comparison, developers gain a sense of competition and will seek to expand their collaboration in the project to reach a higher score.

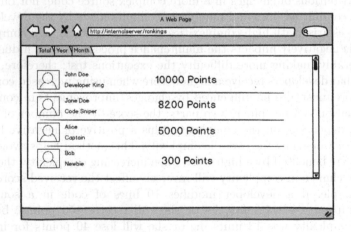

Fig. 2. Developer's Ranking

With gamification of the commit process, a plug-in (VCS hook) of the version control system calculates the complexity of source code and extracts the number of contributed or modified lines of code. The number of modifications multiplied by the value of cyclomatic complexity of the source code in question, plus the positive or negative impact in the overall complexity, results in the score reached by the developer.

After collecting the score, it is transferred to the gamification server, which will include a record of activity and scores in the developer's profile. Developers then gain access to a web system that will display the leaderboard, displaying their performance.

Furthermore, a number of rules can also be included in the server with specific scores to improve the developer's motivation; for example, an additional 100 points every 25 commits or additional 10 points every time are given he or she reduces the overall complexity.

It is up to the administrator to set up the leaderboard to identify the developers or to keep them anonymous, since the effects of anxiety due to are competition yet to be studied. In software development, it is common for developers to work individually and in isolation, which can lead to dissatisfaction, boredom and eventually decreased productivity and even quality. A source management server can create a perception of collaboration in software development.

8   Conclusion

Measuring developers' collaboration or their engagement in a software development project by measuring only the number of produced lines has already proven to have limited effectiveness, as concluded in previous researches.

Calculating the engagement of a developer using a metric that tends to be more assertive than those presented in previous studies, is the goal of this paper. Therefore, we presented the equation that combines the McCabe's cyclomatic complexity with the number of lines of code changed by the developer to obtain a balanced score between simple and complex codes.

This also prevents situations caused by a developer who wishes to rise in his or her position, by starting to make changes in several lines of simple code to receive a higher score than someone who is working on a complex code.

With McCabe's metric, we counterbalanced the effect generated by Pareto's principle, preventing developers that work in 80% of code, which possesses 20% of all the complexity, to gain an additional advantage in the ranking proposed by gamification. The development process is thus more collaborative because it balaces the accomplished work and the scores achieved tend to be more balanced.

To give sequence to this research, the implementation of the proposed equation and the prototype tool are still necessary. The proposed model must, therefore, be applied to an actual development project to validate the proposed theory and measure any gains of productivity and engagement in the project.

References

1. Ahmad, I., Jaafar, A.: Games design and integration with user's emotion. In: 2011 International Conference on User Science and Engineering (i-USEr), pp. 69–72 (2011)

2. Chidamber, S.R., Darcy, D.P., Kemerer, C.F.: Managerial use of metrics for object-oriented software: An exploratory analysis. IEEE Transactions on Software Engineering 24(8), 629–639 (1998)
3. Cook, D.: What are game mechanics. Lost Garden (2006), http://www.lostgarden.com/2006_10_01_archive.html
4. Crawford, C.: Chris Crawford on game design. New Riders (2003)
5. Deterding, S., Dixon, D., Khaled, R., Nacke, L.: From game design elements to gamefulness: defining gamification. In: Proceedings of the 15th International Academic MindTrek Conference: Envisioning Future Media Environments, pp. 9–15. ACM (2011)
6. Dubois, D.J., Tamburrelli, G.: Understanding gamification mechanisms for software development. In: Proceedings of the 2013 9th Joint Meeting on Foundations of Software Engineering, pp. 659–662. ACM (2013)
7. Groh, F.: Gamification: State of the art definition and utilization, pp. 39–47. Institute of Media Informatics Ulm University (2012)
8. Hugos, M.: Enterprise Games: Using Game Mechanics to Build a Better Business. O'Reilly (2012)
9. Koc, A., Tansel, A.: A survey of version control systems. In: ICEME 2011 (2011)
10. Koster, R.: Theory of fun for game design. O'Reilly Media, Inc. (2010)
11. Louridas, P., Spinellis, D., Vlachos, V.: Power laws in software. ACM Transactions on Software Engineering and Methodology (TOSEM) 18(1), 2 (2008)
12. Marczewski, A.: Gamification: A Simple Introduction. Andrzej Marczewski (2012)
13. McCabe, T.J.: A complexity measure. IEEE Transactions on Software Engineering (4), 308–320 (1976)
14. O'Grady, S.: The New Kingmakers. O'Reilly Media (2013)
15. Romero, M., Usart, M., Ott, M., Earp, J.: Learning through playing for or against each other? Promoting collaborative learning in digital game based learning. Learning 5, 15–2012 (2012)
16. Rosenberg, J.: Some misconceptions about lines of code. In: Proceedings of the Fourth International Software Metrics Symposium, pp. 137–142. IEEE (1997)
17. Salen, K.: Rules of play: Game design fundamentals. The MIT Press (2004)
18. Singer, L., Schneider, K.: It was a bit of a race: Gamification of version control. In: 2012 2nd International Workshop on Games and Software Engineering (GAS), pp. 5–8. IEEE (2012)
19. Toth, Z., Novak, G., Ferenc, R., Siket, I.: Using version control history to follow the changes of source code elements. In: 2013 17th European Conference on Software Maintenance and Reengineering (CSMR), pp. 319–322. IEEE (2013)
20. Treude, C., Storey, M.: Awareness 2.0: staying aware of projects, developers and tasks using dashboards and feeds. In: 2010 ACM/IEEE 32nd International Conference on Software Engineering, vol. 1, pp. 365–374. IEEE (2010)
21. Velazquez, A., Martinez-Garcia, A.I., Favela, J., Hernandez, A., Ochoa, S.F.: Design of exergames with the collaborative participation of older adults. In: 2013 IEEE 17th International Conference on Computer Supported Cooperative Work in Design (CSCWD), pp. 521–526. IEEE (2013)
22. Watson, A.H., McCabe, T.J., Wallace, D.R.: Structured testing: A testing methodology using the cyclomatic complexity metric. NIST special Publication 500(235), 1–114 (1996)
23. Zichermann, G., Cunningham, C.: Gamification by Design: Implementing game mechanics in web and mobile apps. O'Reilly Media, Inc. (2011)

Guidelines for the Gamification
in Mobile Social Networks

Fábio Pereira Alves[1,2], Cristiano Maciel[1,2], and Júnia Coutinho Anacleto[3]

[1] Universidade Federal de Mato Grosso, Instituto de Educação-PPGE, Cuiabá, Brazil
[2] Universidade Federal de Mato Grosso, Instituto de Computação-LAVI, Cuiabá, Brazil
[3] Universidade Federal de São Carlos, Centro de Ciências Exatas e de Tecnologia,
Departamento de Computação, São Carlos, Brazil
{fabioalves,cmaciel}@ufmt.br, junia@dc.ufscar.br

Abstract. Among those responsible for the large amount of content on the internet are the social networks. With the popularization of the mobile devices there has been the emergence of the so-called mobile social networking, which has changed the way the users relate to applications. In the quest for improving the user experience in mobile social networking, the gamification (the use of game design elements in non-related games) has played an important role. This article presents an analysis of data from two case studies and, from the results, suggests guidelines for the use of gamification in mobile social networks.

Keywords: Gamification; Mobile Social Networks; Foursquare; GetGlue; Design Guidelines.

1 Introduction

Among the major contributors to the flow of content on the internet are the Social Networks (SN). Along with the SN, mobile devices have changed the way users relate to applications, since mobility introduces a number of technologies specific of such devices. From the concepts of SN and mobile networks emerged the Mobile Social Networks (MSN).

Thus, according to [11], the user's concept has changed from a cog in an organizational machine to a partner in an interactive system, a final consumer and, more recently, a producer of content. Due to this change, a strong and new focus is the user engagement in using the system [11].

On the other hand, the popularity of videogames has grown dramatically in recent years and the videogame industry has become the fastest growing entertainment. To [2], the digital games occupy leading role as an element of culture, especially in places like the United States, Europe and parts of Asia.

According to [11], the use of techniques from other areas that support the design of interaction between user and application has a rich tradition in Human-Computer Interaction (HCI), and design-based games, despite having originated in the early 1980s [12], is a strong trend in HCI, especially when the goal is to create engagement and improved user experience.

G. Meiselwitz (Ed.): SCSM 2014, LNCS 8531, pp. 559–570, 2014.

In the search for techniques that increase user engagement with the application, gamification techniques, have been proven to be a viable alternative.

Gamification is the use of game-design elements in non- game contexts [7]. This concept rapidly called the attention from the fields of interaction design and digital marketing. Several applications have been launched in areas such as finance, health, education, sustainability, news and entertainment [7]. However, according to [7], little academic attention has been given to the way these game-like applications are built. Most of the systems considered "game-like" only repeats the formula of points system and rewards used in Foursquare [7].

To better understand, not only the gamification concepts, but also the best way to develop new game-like applications, it is necessary to understand the features derived from the games that the current applications use, as well as the users' behavior in face of these elements.

In this sense, this article seeks to identify the users' perception of the game elements on MSNs, and from the results obtained, it proposes guidelines for the use of gamification in this context. As examples of MSN, we use the applications Foursquare and GetGlue.

Foursquare is a MSN based on geolocation. The application has four main elements of user interaction: Check-ins (action that the user performs to post their locations at a venue, using the GPS of the mobile device); Mayorships (given to the user with the highest number of check-ins into a venue); Badges (virtual rewards won according to the accomplishment of certain challenges); Scores (rewards for each check-in performed). The scores are listed in a ranking and are compared with the friends' scores in the social network. The user who has the highest number of check-ins becomes the "mayor" of the place and his profile is shown to all other users who performed the check-in in that place. The system also has some methods to prevent misuse of the tool. In order to perform the check-in contextual elements are performed, such as the GPS, cellular antenna triangulation and the network location where the user is.

The GetGlue is a social network-based entertainment content, such as films, books, video games and television programs. The focus of the application are mobile devices, but the system has a web version with all the features. On GetGlue, the main elements of interaction with the user are Check-ins (action performed by the user to post what entertainment is being consumed); Scores (won in every check-in); and Stickers (virtual rewards won for fulfilling certain challenges).

In order to reach this goal, two case studies are performed initially, the first using the Foursquare application and the second using the GetGlue and Foursquare applications. The first case study seeks to diagnose if there is a relationship of interest in the score by users, especially when related to sharing in the social networks. The second case study investigates how the elements of games influence the motivation for the use of the applications and which of these elements may be relevant to design interaction.

2   Related Work

Most of the current research on gamification has been focused on the user's perception in relation to the elements of games. [18] removed the game elements from a social software, aiming to analyze behavior of users who were already accustomed to the gamification. The authors obtained a significant negative impact of user activity on the system, achieving a significant drop in the amount of collaborative content placed on the software. [1] studied the social and psychological effects triggered by the use of badges in applications. Among the effects listed are the setting goals, capacity for instruction, creation of status and self-assertion, building reputation and identification with the group.

On the other hand, more recently, researches started to emerge with proposed guidelines and frameworks for the implementation of gamification in various software. [17] proposes a framework of gamification for virtual learning environments, applying the framework presented in an existing tool whereas [9] proposes a generic architecture, based on gamification for corporate application. [15] seeks to identify good practice examples of successful applications by using gamification, however concluded that such standards and best practices are not well established in the industry.

However, besides having only initial results, such studies are based only on the existing literature, without regard to case studies with users of existing applications. Furthermore, these studies have not produced guidelines and do not address mobile applications or the MSN.

3   Initial Case Study

To analyze the behavior of users in applications that use gamification, a questionnaire was carried out using a MSN, Foursquare, which was selected as one of the most popular applications using gamification [19] and is considered one of the main contributors to the use of gamification [7].

The questions were elaborated based on previous works on the subject, especially the researches by [13] and by [19]. [13] investigates the experiences gained by users of a system for sharing images using a system of points and achievements, focusing on the analysis of the system as a whole and not only the perception of the game elements. Whereas [19] relates the elements of games to the user's status in relation to social group, regardless of the kind of application of game elements.

The data analysis was performed through a qualitative approach and the participants of the research were identified with the letter "P". Twenty-three users were analyzed and three users of MSN with ages from 16 to 40 years. From the users analyzed, seventeen were male and six female, and divided between occasional users of the Foursquare (eight) and frequent users (thirteen), and ten users accessing the system more than twice a day.

Among the users who answered the questionnaire, the majority (fourteen) do not believe that the points system on Foursquare is something relevant as shown in Picture 5. Among the reasons raised P5 said that "There is no impact outside Foursquare", citing the fact that the score is not shared on other social networks, unlike Badges and Mayorships. P19 said "I do my check-ins aiming to share my location with my friends", reinforcing even more the importance that users give to the social aspect of the tool.

Among the users that believe that the Foursquare score system is something relevant, more than a half (twelve) of the users attributed the relevance of the points system to the competitive aspect of the tool on Foursquare. P20 said that "The points create a health competition among users, encouraging me to use Foursquare more". P14 said that "Points are important to me because they show how popular I can become (not only among the friends added) in environments/places that I go more often".

Although the majority of users do not believe the scores of application as something relevant, 70% (sixteen) of the users describe a positive feeling, like a sensation of victory and enthusiasm, when they are given a Badge. The same is true for Mayorships, where 78% (eighteen) of the users describe the same positive feelings.

The initial case study showed that the score, despite being a major game mechanics applied to Foursquare, is not as significant for this group of users. According to some users analyzed, this is due to the fact on Foursquare, there is no score sharing functionality in other social networks. This result may be related to the work carried out by [13], in which it was observed that part of the users of systems that use gamification are indifferent to the elements of games, but not opposed to them.

Badges and the Mayorships, which can be shared with external tools, showed that there was a relationship of interest in the score when the information is shared in the users' social networks. These results can be related to the status that the individual has in relation to the social group that, according to [19], is the most important reward for the user in an application which uses gamification.

4   Final Case Study

For the final case study two questionnaires were designed and applied to the users of the Foursquare and GetGlue MSN. Both tools were selected because they are two of the MSNs with the largest community of Brazilian users.

The form applied had similar characteristics, just adapting questions to the specific features of each application. The forms had five questions about the user's profile, three questions on the frequency and how the application is used, seven on the users' perception of the game elements and one question about privacy concerns when using the applications. The questionnaire was designed based on issues raised in previous works and researches. Particularly, it took into account researches by [4] on how gamification can disrupt other ways to instill motivation in applications. As in the previous case study, researches by [13] and [19] were considered when designing the questionnaire.

Thirty-one users in total, ten from GetGlue and twenty-one Foursquare users. Of the thirty-one users who responded to the questionnaire, 5 had high school and 22 had at least higher education, 9 had specialization, 2 had masters and 3 had doctorates. The average age of participants is 27,6 years, and the fashion for 24 years. The youngest user was 19 and the oldest 57. Participants were divided into the areas of Information Technology, Education, Social Communication, Civil Engineering, Management and Veterinary, where 17 users are from areas related to information technology.

Of the thirty-one users participating in the research, twenty-nine use the applications on smartphones or tablets. Of these, nine also use the browser features of the applications and just two users only access the applications through a web browser. The majority of users uses smartphones and tablets with Android operating system (eighteen users), followed by the operational system iOS (nine users). Only one user uses BlackBerry and one uses Windows Phone. This characteristic is common to the MSNs, since when they are used in mobile devices; these applications come with a series of contextual information.

In the question "What motivates you to use the application?" the answers "Share location with friends" and "get to know interesting places" were cited by fourteen Foursquare users, while the answer "Share the film, TV program I am watching, books I am reading or songs I am listening" was mentioned by ten GetGlue users. The great majority of users responded with more than two answers, indicating that motivation to use the system is not unique. These answers, especially in this order, confirm the result obtained in the initial case study, which, in turn makes reference to the study by [19].

Despite the motivation for the use of the application, according to most other participants, divided in several aspects, sixteen users indicate the game elements, as points, badges, stickers and mayorships as a frequent motivation to use the applications. Ten users informed that only sometimes the game elements motivate them to use the applications. Five users answered that the elements of games never or almost never motivate them.

In the question "How do you see the Application?", fourteen users classify the applications such as social networks, while nine classify as application to make real time information. Five users see the applications as games and three classify them as tools to receive tips from friends.

Among the users who participated in the research, twenty-four believe that the elements of games are an essential part of the applications, and nine believe that the application would not be interesting without these aspects, while fifteen believe that the game elements complement other features. Six of the users answered that they would use the applications even without the game elements.

From the total of participants, fourteen know other applications that use the gamification. As an example, the applications Alvanista, Raptr, GoWalla and Linkedin were cited. Most of the users never cheated in the use of Foursquare to win more points or badges, whereas the users of the GetGlue analyzed have opposite behavior, being more likely to cheat an application usage. This may be explained due to the implementations by Foursquare systems against cheating, inhibiting such behavior. These security measures give more justice to the "game" created among the users, guaranteeing that the rules will be respected.

Thus, it is observed that the game elements have influence on the user's motivation, being an essential part of the applications used in the case study. Some users classified the applications as games, which emphasizes even more the need for developing mechanisms which will guarantee that the defined rules are respected.

5   Guidelines

In this session seven guidelines for the implementation of the game elements in applications having characteristics of MSNs are described. These guidelines were built based on the information collected both in the theoretical approach, mainly in the engagement profiles listed by [2], and in the results of the case studies performed. The game elements described by [11] as a basis for the description of the guidelines were taken into account, as well as the adaptation of the model   to describe the guidelines used by [4], having in each one the objective, the properties, the description of the operation, the objects of interaction and the textual identification. Also, a medium-fidelity prototype to represent each of the guidelines, allowing for a better understanding of their use was built.

5.1   Guideline 1: Score

The score is one of the game elements pointed by users in the study of initial case, as responsible for creating a "healthy competition" among the users, stimulating the use of the application

Objective: to increase the engagement and foster the use of the system when rewards the users for desired behaviors within the system.

Properties: Competition, instantaneous feedback, status in relation to the social group.

Description of the Operation:.

1. The system awards the user to perform a certain action within the system with scores.
2. The system shows the total score that the user has and the quantity of points obtained in the last activity.
3. The system allows for the sharing total points of the user in other social networks.

Objects of interaction: Self-explanatory icons: Self-explanatory icons which explain the need of blocks of texts.

Textual identification: The users' score must have large fonts, enabling the reading of the mobile devices, without the need of zoom. The score must have a recreational aspect, referencing existing structures in games. The texts must be short, favoring the keywords related to the engagement profile "Predators", such as "Win", "Gain", "Compare", "Provoke".

5.2   Guideline 2: Rankings

The ranking is pointed by the users as a "popularity measure" in relation to the users of the applications.

Objective: To increase the engagement and the time of use through competition created among the users, besides providing status to the user in relation to the other members of the social network.

Properties: Competition, status in relation to the social group.

Description of the Operation:

1. The system calculates the user's position according to the score won or objectives accomplished.
2. The system shows a list of users ordered by scores.
3. The system allows for the sharing of the user's position in ranking in other social networks.
4. The system should maintain a history of the users' positions.

Objects of interaction: Self-explanatory: Self-explanatory icons which avoid the need of blocks of text.

Textual identification: The users' names must be in large fonts, enabling the reading in mobile devices. The calculate score must have recreational aspect, referencing the existing structures in games. The texts must be short, favoring the keywords related to the engagement profile "Predators", such as "Win", "Gain", "Compare", "Provoke".

5.3   Guideline 3: Progress Bar

The progress bar seeks to give the users constant feedback, meeting the need identified by [13] with users of mobile applications that use gamification.

Objective: make the progression clear for the user when performing a certain activity, providing constant feedback and stimulating to complete the tasks.

Properties: Constant feedback, feeling of progress, incentive to fulfill tasks

Description of the Operation:

1. The system calculates the progress the user had in a certain activity.
2. In case the activity is finished the system restarts or provides another level of progress, depending on the characteristic of the challenge proposed.

Objects of interaction: Progression: symbols which indicate progression in the fulfillment of the objective must be used; Visibility: the symbols of progression must be visible in all the activities, objectives and challenges that influence the user's progression.

Textual identification: The texts should inform in a short and fast way the level in which the user is and the activity that is being monitored by the progress bar.

5.4   Guideline 4: Challenges and Missions

The challenges serve as a path to guide the user, providing instruction about what types of activity are possible within a given system [1] [13].

Objective: To guide the user towards the best possible experience in the application, optimizing the use of the developed features.

Properties: Objective, Sporadic Feedback, Optimization of the experience of use

Description of the Operation:

1. The system proposes challenges to the users. The challenges must be presented in a structure of dependences, with prerequisites.
2. The system shows the user's progression.
3. The user finishes the accomplishment of an objective.
4. The system presents the next challenges available to the user.

Objects of interaction: Self-explanatory icons which avoid the need for blocks of texts; Progression: symbols which indicate progression in the accomplishment of the objectives should be used; Compact: The icons must be compact, using in an optimized way the networks of mobile internet; Non-ambiguity: the visual information must be associated to only one concept; Familiarity: symbols and/or images which are part of the users' repertoire must be used;

Textual identification: the texts must be in large fonts, enabling the reading in mobile devices. The texts must be short, favoring the keywords related to the engagement profile "Explorer", such as "Discover", "Challenge", "Know", "Visualize", "Explore".

5.5   Guideline 5: Badges

The case studies showed the importance that the sharing of the users' badges in the social networks has about the engagement in the system.

Objective: To increase the engagement through the reward in the fulfillment of small objectives, providing sporadic feedback to the user and building the status of the user in relation to the group.

Properties: Objective, Sporadic Feedback, Status in relation to the group.

Description of the Operation:

1. The system presents the objectives to be fulfilled in order to gain a badge.
2. The user performs the objectives presented by the system.
3. The system gives to the user's profile a badge indicating the fulfillment of the objective.
4. The system offers to the user the possibility to share the information related to the badge of the other social networks.

Objects of interaction: Self-explanatory icons which avoid the need of blocks of texts; Compact: The icons must be compact, using in an optimized way the networks of mobile internet; Non ambiguity: the visual information must be associated to only one concept; Familiarity: symbols and/or images that are part of the users' repertoire;

Textual identification: The texts must be short, favoring the keywords related to the engagement profile "Competitor", such as "Gain", "Win", "Conquer", "Challenge". The texts should be large fonts, enabling the reading in mobile devices, without the need of the zoom.

5.6   Guideline 6: Gifting

The game element "Gifting" searches, through the sharing of virtual items, to create and expand the users' community. The Gifting element is an important mechanism to create an application with sustainable engagement [10].

Objective: To conquer new users and engage those already existent through the sharing of items and information in the MSN.

Properties: Sharing of items and information, Increase the scope of the application, Collaborative users

Description of the operation:

1. The system makes available virtual items and information to the users according to the fulfillment   of challenges or objectives
2. The user shares the items gained with other users of the application or form other social networks, inviting other users to use the application

Objects of interaction: Self-explanatory icons: Self-explanatory icons which avoid the need for text blocks; Compact: The icons must be compact, using in an optimized way the networks of mobile internet; Non ambiguity: a visual information must be associated to only one concept; Familiarity: symbols and/or images that are part of the repertory of the users of the applicative and easily identifiable by users of other social networks.

Textual Identification: The texts should be short, favoring the keywords related to the profile of engagement "Socializing", such as "Sharing", "Gifting", "Inviting". The texts should be in large fonts, enabling the reading in mobile devices, without the need of zoom.

5.7   Guideline 7: Preventing cheating

To ensure the adequate use of the system with game elements, it is necessary to have mechanism in place to avoid cheating. The case studies showed that when these mechanisms are weak or non-existent, the users use to "trick".

Objective: To inhibit non desired behaviors and cheating.

Properties: Checking of the information, Guarantee of the application of rules in an equalitarian way to all the users, Reliable system.

Description of the Operation:

1. The system verifies if the rules are being obeyed every time an action which influences to get the score or reward is performed.
2. If the irregularity is identified, the application performs the action, yet does not add the points or expected rewards.
3. The system informs the user about the break of the rules.
4. The system allows for the user to justify the breaking in the rules.

Objects of interaction: Self-explanatory: Self-explanatory icons which avoid the need for blocks of text; non- ambiguity: the visual information must be associated to only one concept; Familiarity: symbols and/or images which are part of the users' repertoire of the application and easily identifiable by users of other social networks must be used.

Textual identification: The texts must have large fonts, enabling the reading in mobile devices without the need for zoom. The texts should highlight the importance of the respect to the rules in game-like applications.

Then, as shown in Figure 1, two prototypes was elaborated to show the implementation of the guidelines "Ranking" and "Challenges and Missions", as example of use.

Fig. 1. Prototype of features showing the use of the guidelines Ranking and Challenges and Missions

6   Conclusions

The relationships between the people were extended to the cyberspace with the emergence of the social software [5]. With the appearance and broad use of the RSM these relationships have been deeper.

Thus, the initiatives to enhance the experience of the users in these environments play an important role in the current scenario. In this context, the integration between social software and game elements has been highlighted. To [14], while 2001s-2010s was responsible for the creation of the social framework, the 2011s-2020s will be responsible for the creation of the social framework of games.

The gamification, as this trend has been called, has been conquering space in the development of applications in several areas of knowledge, as well as academic attention in the areas of Human-Computer Interaction, Game Studies, Social Communication, Psychology and Education [7]. Yet, interdisciplinary approaches are required.

In this work information was collected about the perception of the users of the game elements in current applications with characteristics of MSNs. Besides, from the information collected guidelines were suggested for the implementation of gamification in new applications.

The guidelines described in this work reflect the results obtained in preliminary researches with the users, as well as related works, mainly of the area of human-computer interaction, game studies and psychology. The result obtained intends to guide the use of game elements in new MSNs, seeking the best use of these elements in the users' engagement process.

It is worth highlighting that the simple implementation of the guidelines described in this work is not guarantee of engagement creation with the user. To [4] gamification is more efficient when combined with new forms of motivation. On the other hand, [13] identified that the use of game elements, despite being indifferent for some of the users, does not hinder the use of symptoms. Thus, it is important to develop functionalities which meet the users' expectations that are not attracted by the game elements.

As subject that, from the results obtained in this work, may be explored is the application of the guidelines described in a real application, the analysis of other applications out of the spectrum of the MSNs, as corporative systems and virtual learning environments, and the comparison of the effects of other forms of motivation with the gamification, for instance socio-affective issues.

Acknowledgements: The authors would like to thank Pró-reitoria de Pós-Graduação - UFMT for partial supporting the development of this research.

References

1. Antin, J., Churchill, E.F.: Badges in social media: A social psychological perspective. In: CHI 2011 Gamification Workshop Proceedings, Vancouver, BC, Canada (2011)
2. Arruda, E., Arruda, D.: E se a escola virar brinquedo? Perspectivas do lazer e dos jogos digitais na aprendizagem. Paulus, São Paulo (2013) (in Portuguese)
3. Bartle, R.: Hearts, clubs, diamonds, spades: Players who suit MUDs. Journal of MUD Research 1(1), 19 (1996)
4. Batista, C.R.: Modelo e diretrizes para o processo de design de interface web adaptativa, 144 p. Tese (Doutorado em Engenharia e Gestão do Conheimento) – Programa de Pós Graduação em Engenharia e Gestão do Conhecimento. UFSC, Florianópolis (SC) (2008) (in Portuguese)
5. Castells, M., Gerhardt, K.B.: A sociedade em rede, vol. 3. Paz e Terra, São Paulo (2000) (in Portuguese)
6. Zeynep, A., Cramer, H., Holmquist, L.E., Rost, M.: Gamification and location-sharing: Some emerging social conflicts. In: CHI 2011. ACM Press (2011)

7. Deterding, S., Dixon, D., Khaled, R., Nacke, L.: From game design elements to gameful-ness: defining gamification. In: Proceedings of the 15th International Academic MindTrek Conference: Envisioning Future Media Environments, pp. 9–15. ACM (2011)

8. Van Grove, J.: FourSquare and Starbucks Team Up To Offer Customer Rewards, 1 (March 14, 2010), http://mashable.com/2010/03/11/foursquare-starbucks (retrieved)

9. Herzig, P., Ameling, M., Schill, A.: A Generic Platform for Enterprise Gamification. In: 2012 Joint Working IEEE/IFIP Conference on Software Architecture (WICSA) and Euro-pean Conference on Software Architecture (ECSA), pp. 219–223. IEEE (August 2012)

10. Kim, A.J.: Gamification Workshop 2010, Presentation (2010), http://www.slideshare.net/amyjokim/gamification-workshop-2010/

11. Liu, Y., Alexandrova, T., Nakajima, T.: Gamifying intelligent environments. In: Proceed-ings of the 2011 International ACM Workshop on Ubiquitous Meta User Interfaces, pp. 7–12. ACM (2011)

12. Malone, T.W.: Heuristics for designing enjoyable user interfaces: Lessons from computer games. In: Proceedings of the 1982 Conference on Human Factors in Computing Systems, pp. 63–68. ACM (March 1982)

13. Montola, M., Nummenmaa, T., Lucero, A., Boberg, M., Korhonen, H.: Applying game achievement systems to enhance user experience in a photo sharing service. In: Proceed-ings of the 13th International MindTrek Conference: Everyday Life in the Ubiquitous Era, pp. 94–97. ACM (September 2009)

14. Priebatsch, S.: The Game Layer on Top of the World. SxSWi, Austin (2011), http://goo.gl/oOV7j

15. Rauch, M.: Best Practices for Using Enterprise Gamification to Engage Employees and Customers. In: Kurosu, M. (ed.) Human-Computer Interaction, Part II, HCII 2013. LNCS, vol. 8005, pp. 276–283. Springer, Heidelberg (2013)

16. Branco, M., Malfatti, S., Lamar, M.V.: Jogos eletrônicos na prática: livro de tutoriais do SBGames 2012-rev. e ampl. Editora Feevale (in Portuguese)

17. Simões, J., Redondo, R.D., Vilas, A.F.: A social gamification framework for a K-6 learn-ing platform. Computers in Human Behavior (2012)

18. Thom, J., Millen, D., DiMicco, J.: Removing gamification from an enterprise sns. In: Pro-ceedings of the ACM 2012 Conference on Computer Supported Cooperative Work, pp. 1067–1070. ACM (February 2012)

19. Zichermann, G., Cunningham, C.: Gamification by Design: Implementing game mechan-ics in web and mobile apps. O'Reilly Media, Inc. (2011)

A Proposal of a Support System for Motivation Improvement Using Gamification

Kohei Otake[1,*], Ryosuke Sumita[2], Makoto Oka[3], Yoshihisa Shinozawa[1],
Tomofumi Uetake[4], and Akito Sakurai[1]

[1] Graduate School of Science and Technology, Keio University, 3-14-1 Hiyoshi, Kohoku-ku,
Yokohama-shi, Kanagawa-ken 223-8522, Japan
otake_kohei@a8.keio.jp, {shino,sakurai}@ae.keio.ac.jp
[2] Hitachi Solutions. Ltd, Japan, 4-12-7, Higashishinagawa,
Shinagawa-ku, Tokyo 140-0002, Japan
va.poccuri@gmail.com
[3] Faculty of Knowledge Engineering, Tokyo City University, 1-28-1 Tamazutsumi,
Setagaya-ku,Tokyo, 158-8557, Japan
moka@tcu.ac.jp
[4] School of Business Administration, Senshu University, 2-1-1 Higashimita Tama-ku,
Kawasaki, 214-8580, Japan
uetake@isc.senshu-u.ac.jp

Abstract. In this research, we built a support system for improving motivation by utilizing gamification, targeting one university circle, the Senshu University Philharmonic Orchestra, as an example of voluntary communities. The purpose of this research was to maintain and improve the motives of each individual orchestra member for practice. Analysis of the current conditions clarified the following two factors as obstacles for improving the motivation of section members: "It is difficult to realize one's own practice achievements" and "Achievement level of practice of other members are unknown". In order to solve these problems, we built a system that visualized practice achievements and enabled sharing of the information among section members, with applying the concept of gamification in order to reinforce these functions. Through the experimental result, we consider that the effectiveness of this system was successfully verified.

Keywords: Gamification, Voluntary Community, Motivation Management.

1 Introduction

Social networking services (SNSs) such as Twitter and Facebook have attracted much attention and become widely popular recently. SNSs enable easy information sharing from remote areas in an asynchronous manner. These services not only serve to complement communication in real-world communities, but also promote work, tasks, and

---

* Corresponding author.

G. Meiselwitz (Ed.): SCSM 2014, LNCS 8531, pp. 571–580, 2014.

management work within such communities. Therefore, companies, schools, and municipalities are quite actively using SNSs with the aim of revitalizing communication within communities formed in the real world, along with maintenance and improvement of motives among members. However, application of SNSs in non-profit and voluntarily-formed organizations (local communities, university circles, etc.) has found it difficult to care for the amount of website traffic and also retain active users continuously. Under present circumstances, still, potential capacity of SNSs is not fully utilized or fulfilled. These findings show that the purpose of belonging to voluntary organizations is ascribed as not for financial profit, but for a sense of satisfaction and amusement. In addition, most of the SNSs run by voluntary organizations do not have compelling force, where each individual user has different motivation. Therefore, if any of the existing SNSs targeting organizations with financial profits and some compelling force, like ordinary companies, is then used in such organizations, it would be difficult for users to maintain and improve their motivation. In order to manage users' motives effectively in voluntary organizations, users probably need to have motivation by means of certain methods that are substituted for some compelling force.

Gamification has attracted much attention recently as a method to help users to maintain and improve their motives. Gamification is defined as "to use gaming elements, such as concept, design, and mechanics of a game, for social activities or services other than the game itself." This idea became widespread after 2010, which has empirically been applied to course design in university education [2], rehabilitation activities in the medical field [3], and e-learning [4] with the aim of maintaining and improving users' motives. This application has produced beneficial effects. At the same time, however, this field is still in the sprouting stage. Only a few attempts have been made so far at verifying the effectiveness of implementing and running an SNS system.

Targeting voluntary organizations, in this research we built a system that supports users so as to maintain and improve their motives by utilizing gamification. Through the actual operation of this system, we verified the effectiveness of gamification as a motivation maintenance and improvement method. The subject of the evaluation experiment we conducted was within one of the circles approved by Senshu University, the Senshu University Philharmonic Orchestra. During a one-month experimental period, we verified the effectiveness of this proposed method.

2   Analysis of the Current Conditions

2.1   Existing Support Systems for Profit-Oriented Organizations

Use of SNSs in profit-oriented organizations with the purposes of information sharing [5], knowledge management [6], and communication support has achieved certain positive results and contributed to profit-earning activities, still leaving issues for each purpose.

In non-profit organizations, however, although SNSs are used with the purposes similar to those of profit-oriented organizations, similar achievements are not always guaranteed due to the differences in responsibilities and the compelling force for belonging to a community. Through this research, we focused on gamification that has attracted much attention recently as a method to support users so as to maintain and improve their motives through an SNS or groupware.

2.2   What is Gamification?

Gamification is defined as "to use gaming elements, such as concept, design, and mechanics of a game, for social activities or services other than the game itself." The following seven methods are included as the gamification.

1. Honorific badges or titles are given according to achievements.
2. Names and scores of competitors are displayed on a real-time basis
3. The graphic interface shows the progress of each task
4. Virtual currency is introduced to promote purchases of virtual goods.
5. Rewards such as coupons or gifts are provided
6. Assignments that encourage users to collaborate together are presented
7. Simple games are prepared between activities in order to keep users from being bored

In voluntary organizations, community members do not always maintain and improve their motives simply by financial rewards. For example, they do so by confirming their growth. As a motive that aims toward personal growth, humans have a need for esteem to be approved or commended by others [7][8], in addition to the convenience that can be acquired after growth. Incorporation of gamification in SNSs is likely to meet the need for esteem of each individual user, maintain and improve the individual motivation, and enhance the entire organizational performance.

3   The Purpose of Our Research

While focusing on a voluntary organization, the Senshu University Philharmonic Orchestra, the experimental subject, in this research we built and evaluated a support system for users to maintain and improve their motives based on gamification. The purpose was for each member to maintain and improve their motivation for practice. In other words, the purpose of this paper is to affirm that the introduction of this proposed system fosters an environment where community members can participate in the community ever before, which revitalizes the entire community. Our ultimate purpose of this research is to build a motivational support and improvement system that fosters a better environment for community members to participate in the community more actively than ever before, and the community itself is also revitalized, by introducing this proposed system.

4   Experimental Subjects

The experimental subject, the Senshu University Philharmonic Orchestra (SUPO), is an amateur orchestra consisting of volunteer students. All the members are not the same position in this orchestra. For example, a section leader exists in each musical instrument section. As for analysis of the current conditions, in this research we conducted a questionnaire survey regarding motives of the members of SUPO in order to clarify the motivational problems that this orchestra had.

In order to analyze the current conditions, we conducted questionnaire and interview surveys regarding "Problems associated with maintenance and improvement of motives" for 31 male and female members of SUPO. As a result of the survey, the following two problems became clear.

- It is difficult to realize the benefits of self practice
- Achievement level of practice of other members are unknown

With respect to the problem of difficulty in realizing the benefits of self practice, we considered the visualization of the amount of practice. Performing technique of musical instruments is evaluated depending significantly on feelings. In other words, it is impossible to measure the performing skills of each individual player on a quantitative scale. For this reason, each individual cannot realize his/her own growth that much, and this makes it difficult for him/her to maintain and improve motivation for practice. Humans are motivated when they realize their own growth, and their motives are improved [9]. Based on this reason, we thought that the visualization of the amount of practice can probably solve this problem.

With respect to the problem of not being able to know the achievement level of practice of other members, we examined methods for sharing information regarding the achievement level of practice which could be effective and understood intuitively. During the weekdays, each individual member of SUPO practices voluntarily. This makes it difficult each of them to know the achievement level of practice of the other members. Specifically, the section leaders devote their practice time to observe each member to understand their achievement level of practice. Therefore, we thought that these problems could be solved if an SNS could show the achievement level of practice of other members in a form by which all members can obviously understand it. This means that the section members can understand the achievement level of practice of each other, and, since information sharing produces a competition,   this encourages members to improve their motivation for practice. As a result, the amount of practice increases.

We here propose a system that incorporates the gamification elements into these factors, the visualization of achievement level of one's own practice and a method for the sharing of information regarding the achievement level of practice of other members, in order to maintain and improve users' motivation effectively.

5   Proposal of the Support System for Motivation Maintenance and Improvement

With the analytical results of the current conditions, we propose a new system called f-simo (fortissimo) that supports users to maintain and improve their motivation for practice by visualizing the practice achievements and understanding the achievement level of practice of each section member. In order to make motivation improvement measure effective, we proposed and introduced methods incorporating gamification in f-simo.

5.1   The Outline of Our Proposed System

This f-simo system provides the following four functions.

1. Increase in the avatar level along with an increase in experience points
2. Graphic representation and sharing of practice time
3. Presentation of practice time rankings
4. A character (Shimosuke) grows up by all section members together

As for these functions, 1, 2, and 6 of gamification methods (Section 2.2) were incorporated. Next section will describe each of the above functions. The figure below shows the system image of f-simo.

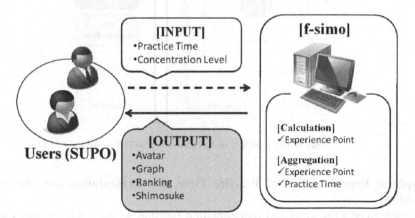

Fig. 1. System image of f-simo

After practice, on the corresponding form, the users enter their practice time and concentration level as input items regarding practice based on a self-evaluation scale of one to five. The concentration level is required to be entered because the practice achievements could depend on the concentration level even though each member spent the same period of time practicing. The experience point is calculated from these two numerical values. These items, the practice time, the concentration level, and the experience point, are also used for improvement of the avatar's level and the character (Shimosuke) that grows up based on the cooperation of all orchestra members. Avatars referred to by this research indicate characters of users used in the system. Levels serve as the indicator within the system. When the level is improved, the numerical value written on the level, the title, and the background color of the avatar changes. "Shimosuke" is the character that grows up by collaborative assignments of users. The section below describes each function.

Improvement of the Avatar Using the Experience Points
We set this function so that the user's avatar level increases by accumulating experience points and the avatar's title changes accordingly (Fig.2). The purpose of this function was to visualize the practice achievements not only with numerical values, but also with the title and change of color so that the user can realize his/her growth. This function was inspired by the first gamification method mentioned in 2.2, "honorific badges or titles given according to achievements."

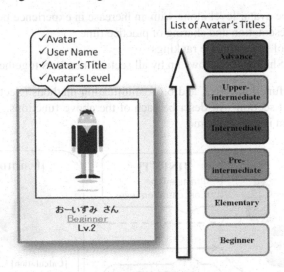

Fig. 2. The example of use and list of avatar's titles

Graphical Representation of Practice Time, and Presentation and Sharing of Rankings
We implemented the graphical representation function so that each member can understand the transition of their practice time intuitively. This function also enables users to compare their own practice time with their average practice time and the practice time of other members within the same section (Fig.3 and Fig.4). This function aims toward improving the users' motivation based on a sense of competition.

There are two rankings, the practice time of the previous day and the accumulated practice time. These two different rankings were introduced in order to avoid a decline in the motivation for practice of those who cannot come to practice on weekdays. This function was inspired by the second gamification method mentioned in 2.2, "Display of the names and scores of competitors on a real-time basis."

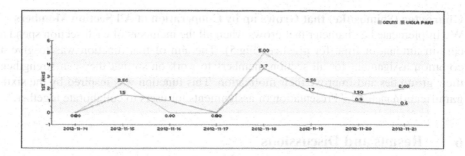

Fig. 3. A user's average practice time and the practice time of other members within "viola" section

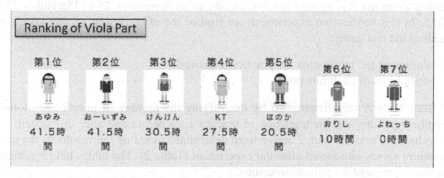

Fig. 4. The example of a graphical representation of Ranking

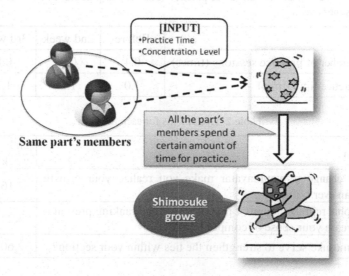

Fig. 5. The image of the cooperation which uses Shimosuke

Character (Shimosuke) that Grows up by Cooperation of All Section Members
We implemented a character that grows when all the members of each section spend a certain amount of time for practice (Fig.5). The aim of this function was to give a common assignment for all section members to work on so that they can strengthen their group ties and improve their motivation. This function was inspired by the sixth gamification method, "Presentation of assignments for users to collaborate together."

6   Results and Discussions

In order to verify the effectiveness of this system, we conducted an experimental evaluation with 25 male and female SUPO members as the experimental subjects by having them use this system for one month, from November 25 to December 15 of 2012. In this verification experiment, we studied the effectiveness of this system regarding the two items:

1. Was members' motivation for practice improved?
2. Evaluations of each function

Item 1 above was determined by quantifying the number of practice sessions of members per day and the transition of practice time before and after this system was introduced (Table 1). Item 2 above were determined based on the results of the questionnaire survey conducted after the experiment (Table 2). The tables below summarize the experiment's verification results.

Table 1. Comparison of the number of practice sessions and practice time before and after the system was introduced

	Before	2nd week	3rd week
Number of practice sessions (times)	0.4	0.6	0.8
Practice time (time)	1.0	1.2	1.7

Table 2. Evaluations for each function

Question	2nd week	3rd week
Did the change in your avatar make you realize your growth more than ever before?	3.16	3.36
Did graphic representation of practice time and ranking presentation increase your sense of competition?	3.24	3.36
Did Shimosuke serve to strengthen the ties within your section?	2.60	2.80

Table 1 shows that the number of practices and practice hours increased each week. With respect to the point as to whether all section members could improve their motivation for practice, as shown by Table 2, the average number of practice sessions and time per day increased as the weeks went by. Since the average value before this system was introduced was exceeded, we were able to verify the effectiveness of this system. With respect to the evaluations for each function, in all functions, the value of the 3rd week was higher than that of the 2nd week. Moreover, we interviewed part reader after the verification experiment and we got opinion that management of the part member became easy using visualization systems.

On the other hand, a low average value was confirmed with respect as to whether Shimosuke could serve to strength the section ties. This is likely due to the short experimental period, just one month, so that the change of the character based on the collaborated assignment could slightly be confirmed. Actually at the end of the experiment, the character brought up by the members of only one of four sections was confirmed to have grown from the initial stage. The characters of the other three sections remained the same as the initial status. This point shows that the parameters related to the character growth need adjustment. When compared to the value of the 2nd week, however, the value of the 3rd week did increase. This shows that continuous use of this function could strengthen the ties within the section.

Analysis of the access log reveals that in the third week, page views per one login increased. Analysis of the access log and the record of practice hours made it clear that the number of times of access and the practice hours are in proportion. When a user's access frequency to the site was high, the practice hours tended to increase. This tendency was notably clear in the violin part (Fig.6). We considered that competition worked strongly in the violin part, because the violin part of SUPO has many members compared with other parts.

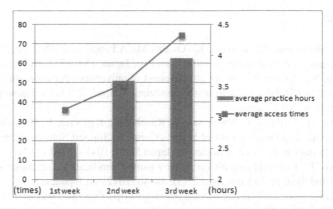

Fig. 6. Comparison of practice hours and access times in violin part

Through these experimental results, we consider that the effectiveness of this system was successfully verified. These results clarify that the following gamification methods are effective for voluntary organizations: 1. Badges obtained according to the achievement level, or level determination, and 2. Presentation of the names and scores of the current competitors on a real-time basis. When it comes to method 6, "Assignments that promote collaborative work", the continuous use of this system could increase the effectiveness of this system to a greater extent.

7   Conclusion

In this research, we built a support system for improving motivation by utilizing gamification, targeting one university circle, the Senshu University Philharmonic Orchestra, as an example of voluntary communities. The purpose of this research was to maintain and improve the motives of each individual orchestra member for practice. Analysis of the current conditions clarified the following two factors as obstacles for improving the motivation of section members: "It is difficult to realize one's own practice achievements," and "The achievement level of practice of other members are unknown." In order to solve these problems, we built a system that visualized practice achievements and enabled the sharing of information among section members, while applying the concept of gamification in order to reinforce these functions. The effectiveness verification experiment conducted for one month verified the effectiveness of this system with respect to the following functions: "1. Honorific badges or titles are given according to achievements." and "2. Names and scores of competitors are displayed on a real-time basis ". With respect to function 3, "6. Assignments that encourage users to collaborate together are presented" continuous use of this system will probably strengthen the ties between members.

We would like to put this system into continuous operation and to add another function that enhances the system loyalty. Additionally, through the use of access log obtained during this research, we are also planning to conduct further analysis focusing on user attributes.

References

1. Yano, Y., Muramoto, Y., Kitahara, K., Okubo, M.: A Proposal of SNS for activation Physical Community. Information Processing Society of Japan, 153–155 (2013) (in Japanese)
2. Kishimoto, Y., Mikami, K.: About effectiveness of university education utilizing Gamification. Journal of Digital Games Research Association Japan (2013) (in Japanese), An annual general meeting 2012, Japan
3. Matsuguma, H., Fujioka, S., Nakajima, A., Kaneko, K., Kajiwara, J., Hayashida, K., Hattori, F.: Research and Development of Serious Games to Support Stand-up Rehabilitation Exercises. Information Processing Society of Japan 53(3), 1041–1049 (2012) (in Japanese)
4. Matsumoto, T.: Possibility of e-Learning by using Gamification. Japanese Society for Information and Systems in Education 27(3), 34–40 (2012) (in Japanese)
5. Chisokukan, http://jp.fujitsu.com/group/fst/services/chisokukan/ (January 28, 2014 author checked)
6. Sabetto, T., Kotani, M.: Utilizing the enterprise social network for knowledge management. The Journal of Information Science and Technology Association 62(7), 296–301 (2012)
7. Ota, H.: Recognition and motivation [the proved effect]. Dhobun sha shuppan (2011)
8. Harvard Business Review Anthology: Power to motivate - Theory of motivation, and practice (2009)
9. Frederick, H.: Motivation to Work. John Wiley & Sons Inc. (1959)

Gamifying Social Media to Encourage Social Activities with Digital-Physical Hybrid Role-Playing

Mizuki Sakamoto and Tatsuo Nakajima

Department of Computer Science and Engineering, Waseda University, Japan
{mizuki,tatsuo}@dcl.cs.waseda.ac.jp

Abstract. This paper proposes a new way to gamify the *micro-crowdfunding* service. *Micro-crowdfunding* is a crowdsourcing service to achieve a sustainable society based on a crowdfunding concept and an aging money concept. In this type of service, each activity to achieve a sustainable society is called a mission, and performing a mission is encouraged through social and economic incentives. A new approach described in this paper enhances the original strategies by using a game concept. The approach consists of two techniques. The first technique adopts several concepts from dramaturgy. The technique coordinates multiple missions and encourages people to complete them by providing a fictional goal that most people want to achieve. The second technique incorporates persuasive ambient mirrors that reflect people's current situation with visual and fictional expressions. The technique emotionally increases people's incentives by using operant conditioning. We also conduct a user study to validate the approach proposed in this paper.

Keywords: Social Media, Crowdfunding, Crowdsourcing, Fictional Expressions, Sustainability, Dramaturgy, Digital-Physical Hybrid Role-Playing, Gamification.

1 Introduction

Sustainability is one of the most important issues in modern society. Information technologies are considered useful tools that reduce energy and recycle resources to achieve a sustainable society. However, technical advances alone cannot solve many essential problems. People need to be aware of the importance of their contribution to solving these problems. Human-computer interaction can help people become aware of this importance and alter their behavior toward a more sustainable society [2]. Psychological techniques to alter people's attitude and behavior have become popular, and findings in social psychology have been widely adopted to shape behavior through public policies [5]. If these design patterns can be immersively incorporated into our daily environments by using information technologies, they will increase the opportunity to improve a sustainable lifestyle.

In this paper, we first present a new social media service named *micro-crowdfunding*, in which each community manages the sustainability of its shared resources by using a micro-level crowdfunding method, as shown in Fig. 1 [11]. One

G. Meiselwitz (Ed.): SCSM 2014, LNCS 8531, pp. 581–591, 2014.

member of a community proposes a small mission to contribute the sustainability of its shared resources to the community. Usually, the mission is trivial and easily completed, such as clearing a shared garbage box. In our approach, a crowdfunding concept is adopted to increase each community member's awareness about which activities are effective for increasing social sustainability. The community member owns some amount of virtual money, and the money is used to invest in supporting the proposed mission. Through the investment, community members can understand why the mission is important.

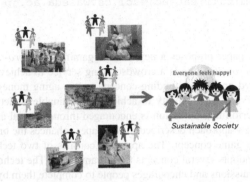

Fig. 1. Achieving a Sustainable Society with Micro-Crowdfunding

In the evaluation of the previous version of *micro-crowdfunding,* we found that an additional mechanism is necessary to encourage participants [11]. This paper proposes to add two game-based concepts to increase the emotional stimulus. The first concept is called *incentive Web* and is proposed as a tool in dramaturgy [3]. Incentive Web coordinates multiple missions to create a drama for participants that encourage them to complete these missions. The second concept is a *persuasive ambient* mirror, which offers visual and fictional expressions that reflect people's current attitudes and behavior to encourage them to complete the missions with operant conditioning. These enhancements are a promising way to gamify human activities in *micro-crowdfunding.*

The paper is organized as follows. Section 2 presents an overview of micro-crowdfunding. In Section 3, we show how incentive Web is integrated with micro-crowdfunding. Section 4 shows how a persuasive ambient mirror is added to micro-crowdfunding. Section 5 shows the evaluation of the current approach, and we discuss the current design in Section 6. Finally, we conclude the paper and describe future directions in Section 7.

2   Micro-crowdfunding: A Community-Based Crowdsourcing Service for Achieving a Sustainable Society

Crowdfunding is an emerging new way of funding new ideas or projects by borrowing funding from crowds. In this concept, a person proposes a new project, explains the importance and the target amount of money, and shows what people who fund the project will receive when the mission is successfully completed. When the total amount of funds from contributors exceeds the target amount, the project begins. After successful completion of the project, each contributor receives the benefits according to his or her funding level. If the benefit offers high scarcity value, it has a high incentive for contributors. However, existing crowdfunding platforms such as *Kickstarter* require participants to contribute real money; thus, only people who have extra money can participate.

Micro-crowdfunding adopts a crowdfunding concept to increase people's awareness of the importance of sustaining our society. It helps to motivate people in urban areas to participate in achieving a sustainable society. In *UbiAsk* [7], which is a typical crowdsourcing service based on social incentives, the completion of micro tasks is motivated through the use of social incentives, and individuals complete the tasks through their own spirit of reciprocity for strangers. This incentive is not strong enough to complete the more complex micro tasks referenced in *micro-crowdfunding*. In *micro-crowdfunding*, the completion of micro tasks is motivated within a community whose members are known to each other. An economic incentive is also used to motivate the community members to complete the tasks, but the incentive is not in the form of a monetary reward. Instead, *micro-crowdfunding* increases people's awareness of the meaning behind the completion of micro tasks, thereby increasing their intrinsic motivation to complete the tasks. Using mobile phones is a key factor in reducing the barriers to contributing to the community. The community's members increase their activities in the face of smaller incentives because activities can be performed anytime and anywhere by accessing the services through mobile phones.

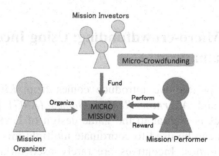

Fig. 2. An Overview of Micro-crowdfunding Activities

The main characteristics of the approach are as follows:

- The *crowdfunding* concept is adopted to allow people to choose among the small, common resources to which they would like to contribute to maintain sustainability;
- The currency used in the proposed approach is based on the *aging-money* concept, which encourages people to participate in *micro-crowdfunding* before the money's value is gradually degraded;
- The interaction in *micro-crowdfunding* is lightweight. People in a community can easily propose new micro tasks, called missions, in *micro-crowdfunding* and fund them from their smart phones through a simple interaction; and
- The participants can share information and details about a mission and receive appropriate feedback for the activities that they perform.

Fig. 2 shows an overview of *micro-crowdfunding*. In *micro-crowdfunding*, a member of a community related to a small common resource, called a *mission organizer*, proposes a new mission when he or she is aware that an activity must be completed to maintain the sustainability of a resource. Typical examples of such common resources are a public sink on a floor of a building or a public shelf used by a university laboratory. The proposal includes the mission's summary, which specifies the necessary activities and the total amount of money required to achieve the mission. The mission proposal is accomplished by touching the common resource with the mission organizer's smart phone and sending a photo showing the resource's current status. In the next step, when other members, called *mission investors*, receive requests to fund the mission, they decide whether they want to fund the mission based on the delivered photo. If some members would like to fund the mission, they simply click on the requests on their phones to notify the mission organizer that they want to fund the mission. When the total submitted funds exceed the target amount, the mission can be executed by any member who can access the resource in his or her spare time. Such a member is called a *mission performer*. The mission is usually a very simple task, such as cleaning up a public sink or putting a shelf in order. After completion, the mission performer takes a photo of the resource to show the mission's completed status and sends it to the *mission organizer*. Finally, the *mission organizer* verifies the quality of the achievement, and a completion notification of the mission containing a photo of the resource is delivered to all members who have funded the mission. More details about the design, implementation, and evaluation of *micro-crowdfunding* can be found in [11].

3   Gamifying Micro-crowdfunding: Using Incentive Web As a Tool for Dramaturgy

The first game concept that we introduce comes from *Live Action Role-Playing (LARP) games* [19] and *Alternate Reality Games (ARG)* [8]. Gamifying *micro-crowdfunding* activities is similar to the game design of LARP and ARG, and their design methodologies can be used to coordinate multiple missions for gamifying *micro-crowdfunding* activities. Incentives are rarely used alone to encourage human activities. They often require other incentives to yield meaning, and one incentive may trigger another. *Eirik Fatland* proposed a concept called *incentive Web* [3]. In the current design of *micro-crowdfunding*, we also adopt a concept called the *puppet master*[1] from ARG to define *incentive Web* to coordinate multiple missions. The *puppet master* in *micro-crowdfunding* is a game designer in each community who can gamify *micro-crowdfunding* activities. The *puppet master* proposes new missions as a *mission organizer* to achieve a goal that he or she defines as a game designer. Additionally, a *puppet master* helps users to play roles that enhance their abilities in the real world.

---

[1] A *puppet master* is hidden from a user so that the user is not aware of the existence of a magic circle. In contrast, a game master in a role-playing game is noticed by a game player. Thus, the player is always aware that he is playing a game.

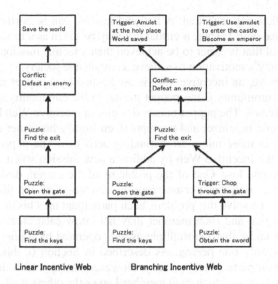

Fig. 3. Incentive Web

In [3], several types of incentives are defined and shown.

Conflict: typical dramaturgies establish some form of *conflict* between characters.

Trigger: If a certain thing happens, then another thing will also happen.

Puzzles: When the conditions of *triggers* become sufficiently complex, they represent a distinct source of challenge to the players/characters, and it makes sense to talk of them as a *puzzle*.

Instructions: *Conflicts, triggered events,* and *puzzles* all give a *puppet master* some measure of control over *micro-crowdfunding* activities. *Instructions* are a group of incentives (*meta instructions, fates,* and *suggestions*) that give a *puppet master* a great deal of control over *micro-crowdfunding* activities, particularly their chronology. *Meta-instructions* are a form of *instruction* that borders on an incentive. Unlike *fates* and *suggestions, meta-instructions* clearly have a non-diegetic purpose. *Fates* are absolute *instructions* given as a part of the character text. They are, by definition, unavoidable, although human error might make it impossible to carry them out. *Suggestions* are a less rigid version of the fateplay technique. A *fate* is something the player must do or something the character inevitably will do no matter how much he or she resists.

Tasks and scheduling: Tasks and scheduling are two types of incentives that are reminiscent of instructions but that double as purely diegetic information. A task is the job of a character or group, as defined from the onset of micro-crowdfunding activities. Schedules establish daily rhythms and/or schedules for specific events during micro-crowdfunding activities.

Fig. 3 shows two types of incentive Web. The first one is a linear incentive Web, in which performing each mission that offers its own incentive allows people to perform the next mission. The second one is a branching incentive Web, in which a participant has choices in performing missions based on his or her incentives, and multiple missions may need to be performed before performing the next mission. In micro-crowdfunding, a mission is either fictional or factual. A fictional mission can be performed as a mission defined in a fictional world. Thus, a virtual gift may be given as a reward of the mission, or a virtual sub-goal that is easier to be achieved than a factual mission can be offered to increase a community's motivation to achieve a sustainable society.

As described above, an incentive Web is established by a puppet master. One of the members in each community is the puppet master in the community to promote micro-crowdfunding activities. The puppet master designs an incentive Web by proposing new missions as a mission organizer and attempts to encourage his or her community members to participate in more micro-crowdfunding activities. The puppet master can dynamically change the incentive Web by adding a new mission when community members' activities become low. One of the problems of the current design is that participants may notice that only one person proposes new missions and that the person may be a puppet master. To solve this problem, each participant uses his or her own avatar. If a community is virtual and each member may not know each other in the real world, members may not know that the multiple avatars operated by a puppet master are actually operated by only one person. As described in Section 6, this approach is also desirable to maintain participants' privacy. However, the approach may be difficult to use in a real community in which each member knows the others well.

As discussed in Section 6, in the future design of *micro-crowdfunding*, we need to allow any community members to become *mission organizers* without losing a consistent drama defined by an *incentive Web* designed by a *puppet master*.

4   Reflecting Participants' Behavior in Virtual Forms

The basic approach of *micro-crowdfunding* to offer social and economic incentives is promising to encourage people to complete missions that are related to the sustainability of their communities [11]. However, the current strategy does not return proper feedback that stimulates people's emotions to alter their lifestyle. Our solution is to adopt *virtual forms* [10, 12, 16] to increase a psychological incentive. In this case, we choose a *persuasive ambient mirror* proposed in [9] as a *virtual form* for *micro-crowdfunding*. A *persuasive ambient mirror* monitors people's current attitudes and behavior by using sensors and presents visual and fictional expressions reflecting their current attitude and behavior. The fictional expression offers more emotionally effective feedback than factual feedback. For example, the *Virtual Aquarium* reflects people's daily toothbrushing behavior in the condition of the *Virtual Aquarium*. Similarly, in the *Mona Lisa Bookshelf,* people's housekeeping of their public bookshelf is reflected on a *Mona Lisa* picture. To increase the persuasiveness of ambient feedback, we also consider the adoption of an approach used in *documentary games* [4] to incorporate ideological messages represented as *procedural rhetoric* [1]. As shown in [13, 16], ideological messages can be incorporated into the real world by representing goods or characters that become metaphors for the ideological concept.

In the current *micro-crowdfunding* prototype system, three types of *persuasive ambient mirrors* to return ambient feedback have been added to the original *micro-crowdfunding* design, as shown in Fig. 4. The first type of *persuasive ambient mirrors* is installed as a public display in various places for community members. It shows a

Fig. 4. Persuasive Ambient Mirrors in Current Micro-Crowdfunding Prototype

scene of a natural landscape, and the fictional scene reflects the accumulated contribution of all members in a community. If their efforts are not sufficient, the landscape becomes polluted, but the landscape becomes clean if the community members complete a sufficient number of missions. The polluted state shows that the surrounding environment cannot maintain sustainability without the efforts of many members. This provides a strong incentive to encourage other members to contribute to missions. The second type of *persuasive ambient mirrors* is shown on a community member's mobile phone. It shows a fictional flower garden with a large number of flowers blooming in the garden if the member's contribution is good. The flower garden reflects each member's individual efforts and offers him or her a psychological incentive to increase his or her individual contribution. The third type of *persuasive ambient mirrors* shows an ideological message stating that the government likes to steal the people's money for useless projects that increase the government's reputation but that do not benefit the people. The *procedural rhetoric* contains an ideological message pointing out the current problems in our environmental tax system.

5   Evaluation and Discussion

In this section, we present several evaluations to validate our current design. In our experiment, we set up two configurations: the first one with *persuasive ambient mirrors* and the second without them. The mission used in the experiment was to clean the participants' public table. Additionally, we evaluated two cases using *persuasive ambient mirrors*. In the first case, a *mission performer* cleaned the public table to make the landscape more beautiful. In the second case, the first *persuasive ambient mirror* showed a monster that attempted to destroy the natural landscape. When the public desk was cleaned, the monster disappeared.

In the experiment, we surveyed acceptance of the enhancements on a 5-point Likert scale (5 = strongly agree, 4 = agree, 3 = don't know, 2= disagree, 1= strongly disagree). After Y persons attempted to use the *persuasive ambient mirrors*, they answered the survey regarding the respective *persuasive ambient mirrors*. The participants were between the ages of 21 and 52 and included 22 males and 4 females. The acceptability of the first *persuasive ambient mirror* was 3.73, the second was 3.65, and the third was 2.38. We also interviewed five participants to understand the reasons for their acceptance in detail. Most of them were familiar with computer science technologies. One of the participants said, "*The first and second persuasive ambient mirrors easily delivered the meanings, but just changing colors is not enough. Inserting textual messages on the pictures would also be effective to make the messages clear. However, returning appropriate feedback is effective to encourage a community to help each member contribute to achieving a sustainable society*". Another participant said, "*It is hard to deliver ideological messages with only a picture, but I understood that the picture meant that the current situation of something was not good*".

The results show that *persuasive ambient mirrors* containing fictional stories are promising because the destruction of nature by a monster can be easily understood and can motivate participants to protect nature. However, the current approach to expressing the ideological concept was not clearly understandable by participants in the experiment..

In the next step, it is necessary to redesign the current *persuasive ambient mirrors* using a *value-based design framework* [10, 13]. The current design adopts only the *aesthetic value* to design the first and second *persuasive ambient mirrors*. As described in [14], the personality of each person affects his or her perceived value. For example, one person may perceive value in jewelry, but another person may not perceive this value. The *persuasive ambient mirror* for each person's mobile phone can be customized according to his or her personality, but the *persuasive ambient mirrors* for a community need to use public displays that multiple persons can watch simultaneously. Because each person perceives a different value for his or her most important item, the *persuasive ambient mirrors* for public displays must offer multiple values to satisfy all of them. As described in [17], a participatory design helps to incorporate multiple values into one *persuasive ambient mirror*. When multiple people with different personalities incorporate their values in one *persuasive ambient mirror*, the potential for more people to prefer this mirror increases. For example, incorporating a pretty character increases the *empathetic value* for a person, and rarity increases the *economic value* for another person. If a *persuasive ambient mirror* contains both values, the possibility of satisfying both persons increases.

Using the *ideological value* is not easy, as shown in the results of the experiment. Delivering an ideological message is difficult because it is not easy to understand the meanings of this type of message. A lengthy explanation is usually needed to deliver an ideological message with *informative value*. However, a metaphor is an effective tool to deliver complex information without a lengthy explanation. As shown in [12, 16], virtual characters or goods appearing in some popular animation movies can be used to remind members of the importance of the ideological message embodied in the movies.

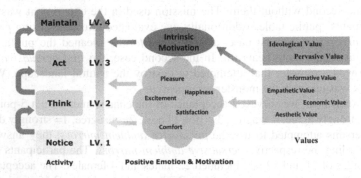

Fig. 5. A Framework for Human Attitude and Behavior Navigation

To design persuasive virtual forms that can change people's attitudes and behavior, Fig. 4. shows a framework to help with the design of the *virtual forms* based on the *value-based design framework*. First, values to increase *extrinsic motivation* are used to *inform* people of why they need to change their attitude and behavior. Next, more information is provided to make people *think* about the reasons for their changes. *Extrinsic motivation* increases people's *pleasure, happiness, excitement, satisfaction,* and *comfort* and stimulates positive emotion. However, to make people into real activists who *act* to make changes, *intrinsic motivation* should be taken into account. In this case, the *ideological value* and the *persuasive value* play more important roles. These values increase people's *intrinsic motivation,* and their self-efficacy to change their attitude and behavior helps them to *maintain* their changes. This framework becomes a guideline to design various urban and city services to shape people's attitudes and behavior [17].

6   Experiences with the Current M*icro-crowdfunding* Design

One of the questions in the current design is how participants in *micro-crowdfunding* determine the proper price for missions. In the current design, we use virtual currency that does not have a strict relationship with real money. One solution is to use real money, but these transactions are complex. An *activity-based billing system* makes a real money payment easier, but this approach is not realized in the real world [20]. In our current approach, each participant receives some amount of virtual money from the money they paid as an environmental tax [11]. The aged money is used for the sustainability of public infrastructure, but the participants' money can be used to maintain their own common resources in their community if they join *micro-crowdfunding* activities. Additionally, employing a drama to coordinate multiple missions in *micro-crowdfunding* activities allows us to determine the proper price for missions based on a good game design, specifically the level design [6]. The level design is an aspect of game development involving the creation of video game levels - locales, stages, or missions. Currently, a *puppet master* who designs an *incentive Web* determines the prices for missions, but in the future, we will reconsider this design to determine the mission's price in the community autonomously without involving the *puppet master*'s supervision.

In the current design of *micro-crowdfunding,* we did not extensively consider security issues. Of course, an authentication mechanism is needed to identify the community to which a participant belongs. *Micro-crowdfunding* uses participants' mobile phones, and we have already integrated with various social media sites such as *Facebook*. *Micro-crowdfunding* may use the existing mechanism to authenticate participants. We also need to consider privacy issues in the future. Each participant looks at the currently proposed missions and the current amount of funds for the missions on his or her mobile phone. In the current design, the real names of the mission organizer, investors, and performers are shown. This approach increases the trust relationship among participants, but their privacy is disclosed, which may increase social pressure. Another approach is to use an avatar for each participant. The participants can decorate their avatars to increase their agency, but other participants will not know the real person behind the avatar. This approach can maintain each participant's privacy, but we need to investigate how this approach affects the trust relationship among participants. If *micro-crowdfunding* ensures that participants will not cheat in *micro-crowdfunding* activities, avatars can be used without losing the trust relationship.

In the next step, we will redesign the current *micro-crowdfunding* design based on the *GamiMedia* model. The *GamiMedia* model allows us to define the meanings of video games based on a *persuasive and ambient transmedia storytelling* concept [15]. In recent video games, the background stories for each characters and scenes are defined in a complex manner. A story of a video game may have a complex relationship with other stories in animations, comics, or novels. The *GamiMedia* model can analyze the meanings of the video games. When gamifying *micro-crowdfunding* a *puppet master* considers that the current situation can offer meanings that allow each participant to understand the situation correctly. Of course, there is the ability to offer open interpretation intentionally [18]. As described in [13, 16], a *puppet master* may use a virtual character from some stories as a metaphor to add an ideological message to the stories through a transmedia storytelling concept.

A *puppet master* defines an *incentive Web* in the current design. However, if a community can create a new story based on existing stories and if each participant's story can be integrated into one story without losing the reality of each story [12, 16], most participants are satisfied to participate in *micro-crowdfunding* activities because a drama defined by a *puppet master* may not be favorable for them. We need to investigate how a community defines its own drama to encourage *micro-crowdfunding* activities.

7   Conclusion and Future Directions

In this paper, we presented two enhancements to the original design of *micro-crowdfunding*, which is social media based on a crowdfunding concept to encourage sustainable behavior. The first enhancement is to use *incentive Web* to coordinate missions to create dramas. The approach emotionally encourages people to perform more missions. The second enhancement is to add a *persuasive ambient mirror* to reflect people's current attitude and behavior. The evaluation showed that the enhancements are effective to encourage participants.

We believe that the proposed approach described in this paper is effective to gamify daily activities to create more desirable lifestyles. Daily activities can be considered missions. Missions in the real world are often boring and trivial for most people. If these missions are coordinated as a drama to increase their emotional stimulus, the potential for people to perform these missions increases because drama has desirable effects to enhance positive thinking and self-efficacy and to establish intrinsic motivation to allow people to complete missions autonomously.

References

1. Bogost, I.: Persuasive Games: The Expressive Power of Video Games. MIT Press (2007)
2. DiSalvo, C., Sengers, P., Brynjarsdóttir, H.: Mapping the Landscape of Sustainable HCI. In: Proceedings of the 28th International Conference on Human Factors in Computing Systems (2010)

3. Fatland, E.: Incentives as Tools of Larp Dramaturgy. In: Bockman, P., Hutchison, R. (eds.) Dissecting Larp, Collected Papers for Knutepunkt 2005 (2005)
4. Frasca, G.: Play the Message: Play, Game and Videogame Rhetoric. Ph.D. Dissertation. IT University of Copenhagen, Denmark (2007)
5. Institute of Government, "MINDSPACE: Influencing Behaviour through Public Policy", CabinetOffice (2010)
6. Kayali, F., Schuh, J.: Retro Evolved: Level Design Practice exemplified by the Contemporary Retro Game. In: Proceedings of DiGRA 2011 Conference: Think Design Play (2011)
7. Liu, Y., Lehdonvirta, V., Alexandrova, T., Nakajima, T.: Drawing on Mobile Crowds via Social Media. ACM/Springer Multimedia Systems Journal 18(1), 53–67 (2012)
8. McGonigal, J.: Reality Is Broken: Why Games Make Us Better and How They Can Change the World. Penguin Press (2011)
9. Nakajima, T., Lehdonvirta, V.: Designing Motivation using Persuasive Ambient Mirrors. Personal and Ubiquitous Computing 17(1), 107–126 (2013)
10. Sakamoto, M., Nakajima, T., Alexandrova, T.: Digital-Physical Hybrid Design: Harmonizing the Real World and the Virtual World. In: Proceedings of the 7th International Conference on the Design & Semantics of Form & Movement (2012)
11. Sakamoto, M., Nakajima, T.: Micro-Crowdfunding: Achieving a Sustainable Society through Economic and Social Incentives in Micro-Level Crowdfunding. In: Proceedings of International Conference on Mobile and Ubiquitous Multimedia (2013)
12. Sakamoto, M., Nakajima, T., Akioka, S.: Designing Enhanced Daily Digital Artifacts Based on the Analysis of Product Promotions Using Fictional Animation Stories. In: Yoshida, T., Kou, G., Skowron, A., Cao, J., Hacid, H., Zhong, N. (eds.) AMT 2013. LNCS, vol. 8210, pp. 266–277. Springer, Heidelberg (2013)
13. Sakamoto, M., Alexandrova, T., Nakajima, T.: Augmenting Remote Trading Card Play with Virtual Characters used in Animation and Game Stories - Towards Persuasive and Ambient Transmedia Storytelling. In: Proceedings of the 6th International Conference on Advances in Computer-Human Interactions (2013)
14. Sakamoto, M., Alexandrova, T., Nakajima, T.: Analyzing the Effects of Virtualizing and Augmenting Trading Card Game based on the Player's Personality. In: Proceedings of the Sixth International Conference on Advances in Computer-Human Interactions (2013)
15. Sakamoto, M., Nakajima, T.: The GamiMedia Model: Gamifying Content Culture. In: Rau, P.L.P. (ed.) CCD/HCII 2014. LNCS, vol. 8528, pp. 786–797. Springer, Heidelberg (2014)
16. Sakamoto, M., Nakajima, T.: A Better Integration of Fictional Stories into the Real World for Gamifying Intelligent Daily Life. In: Proceedings of the First International Symposium on Simulation and Serious Games (2014)
17. Sakamoto, M., Nakajima, T., Akioka, S.: A Methodology for Gamifying Smart Cities: Navigating Human Behavior and Attitude. In: Streitz, N., Markopoulos, P. (eds.) DAPI/HCII 2014. LNCS, vol. 8530, pp. 598–609. Springer, Heidelberg (2014)
18. Sengers, P., Gaver, B.: Staying Open to Interpretation: Engaging Multiple Meanings in Design and Evaluation. In: Proceedings of the 6th Conference on Designing Interactive Systems (2006)
19. Stenros, J.: Between Game Facilitation and Performance: Interactive Actors and Non-Player Characters in Larps. International Journal of Role-Playing (4) (2013)
20. Yamabe, T., Lehdonvirta, V., Ito, H., Soma, H., Kimura, H., Nakajima, T.: Applying Pervasive Technologies to Create Economic Incentives that Alter Consumer Behavior. In: Proceedings of the 11th International Conference on Ubiquitous Computing, pp. 175–184. ACM, New York (2009)

Co-pulse: Light Based Emotional Design
in Musical Performances

Junjie Yu[1], Ke Fang[2], and Zhiyong Fu[3]

[1,2] Interdisciplinary Program of Information Art & Design, Tsinghua University, Beijing, China
{yujunjie.thu,fkonlyone}@gmail.com
[3] Department of Information Art & Design, Tsinghua University, Beijing, China
fudesign@263.net

Abstract. The main research areas of emotional design have been divided into three parts, which are product form, function and culture. However, culture-related emotional experience has less research results to date. In this paper, we combine a unique approach with three levels of emotional design. Co-pulse is an optical media service system for musical performances. It consists of two main parts, one part is the programmable spotlight with its coding system, and the other part is the intelligent illuminated wristband worn by the audience. The entire system uses light as both the media and the signal transmission method. It can show wonderful scenes rendering visual effects followed by the music features, and also achieve the WYSIWYG communication effect. Encoding the visible light actualizes all this.

Keywords: Emotional design, pleasing design, multi-media system.

1 Introduction

The development of science, technology and social economy and culture establish the material foundation of the age. With the increasingly fast pace of life, people's living pressure is also growing, the abundance on materials makes people pay more attentions to their emotional needs.

Listening to music is a good way to express their emotions and to relax. People listen to the music through a variety of devices, such as mp3, mobile phones, laptops or even televisions in daily life. However, many people want to enjoy a live music performance as long as they have conditions. That is because a live show can mobilize more human's senses and the audience can devote themselves to relaxing.

Nevertheless, most of the time, the performers and the audience rarely interact with each other. In addition to the yelling, there isn't an efficient mechanism to communicate.

If there is a mechanism/product enable to increase the proper interaction between the performers and the audience, to enhance the full range of audio-visual experience of concerts, which would be very meaningful. This conforms to a design trend which is emotional design is no longer limited to the tangible product innovation, but also contains service, experience and the other intangible products.

G. Meiselwitz (Ed.): SCSM 2014, LNCS 8531, pp. 592–601, 2014.

In this paper, we introduce an emotional design method for service. As a case, a light-emitting wristband and its supporting system named Co-Pulse, which can be used in musical performances to enhance the interaction experience is also introduced.

2   Background

2.1   Emotion

One of the definitions of emotion is "a positive or negative experience that is associated with a particular pattern of physiological activity." [1] In Scherer's components processing model of emotion, five crucial elements of emotion are said to exist, which are cognitive appraisal, bodily symptoms, action tendencies, expression and feelings. [2]

Currently, the emotional psychology classified split into two perspectives: the first is a view that emotions can be divided into several categories completely fragmented, the second view is that most of the emotions just varying degrees, essentially the same.

Scholars who support emotion classification generally believe that human beings have a dozen "basic emotions". These emotions contain physiological factors common to all mankind. On this basis, the basic emotions of different cultures have different interpretations. There are some emotions generated under certain social conditions called "complex emotions". [3] Paul Ekman's research led him to classify six emotions as basic: anger, disgust, fear, happiness, sadness and surprise.

2.2   Emotional Design

Donald A. Norman clearly divided design and design goals into three levels in his book, namely visceral level, behavior level and reflective level. [4] The so-called visceral level is live flesh, which can bring sensory stimulation, mainly in product form results. In fact, human beings have five senses, namely sight, hearing, smell, taste and touch. We can mobilize more sensory dimension together with the full use of human instinctive reaction to create. This creates a rich sensory stimulation impressing users.

The behavior level refers to the user who through learning and using skills to solve problems gets a sense of accomplishment from this dynamic process. At this level, we are looking for theoretical support from both sociology and psychology perspectives. Therefore, you can get behavior pattern from the existing theory, and reduce the users learning costs.

The highest level is the reflective level. This level actually refers to the role of the first two levels. The user it generates deeper inner emotions: awareness, understanding, personal experiences, cultural backgrounds and various aspects intertwine. At this stage, we firstly research the user's habits, hobbies etc. These all need long-term development.

His understanding and induction of these three levels will guide our research for emotional product design. Emotional design that is putting full attention on human emotional needs into the design to enhance products' additional value. Designing a pleasurable product for people to bring them more fun and colorful life.

When we talk about consumer demands, we must mention the humanistic psychology. Maslow's five conative hierarchies of needs are: Physiological need, safety need, belongingness and love need, esteem need, self-actualization need.

The last three levels react emotional needs in product design of varying degrees. In other words, it responds the different emotional levels in emotional design.

Maslow holds that if these demands are not met, people will lose physical and mental balance. This will lead to some driving force. The driving force makes people pursue to some kind of demands. There are great possibilities for human to change their behaviors, such as purchase behavior. This research provides theoretical supports to product emotional design from psychology perspective. Therefore, designers should attach great importance and concern for the development of human needs level.

2.3   Designing for Pleasant Emotion

Emotional product design is a design concept focusing on human's inner emotional and spiritual needs, and ultimately creates a very pleasant and sensation product. It makes a pleasant aesthetic experience and makes life fun and moving.

Which behaviors will produce a pleasant feeling? From the point of view of design psychology, emotion is the core of the personality. The real value of a product is to meet the emotional needs of people.

The human factors expert and designer Patrick Jordan first proposed the design research concept about pleasing design in product design in 1996.   He visited 18 subjects and summarized feelings, special senses of pleasure or non-pleasant feelings while they are in contact with the test design products. This study pointed that, when products cause people pleasant feelings, there are "safe, self-confidence, pride, satisfaction, excitement, entertainment, nostalgia, freedom", while people feel a sense of unpleasant, there are "feeling cheated, aggression, frustration, yield, contempt, anger, anxiety" and so on.

Most of the current study to pleasant emotion is quantified Kansei engineering-based. It advocates the use of quantitative research methods to present the audience feeling. However, non-quantified study in this area is not too much.

According to the previous researches, positive emotion plays an important role in decision-making, motivation and social interaction. Alice M. Isen's study found that pleasure allows people to broaden the idea, full of creativity and imagination. Therefore, Training pleasure and other positive emotions in design, is the main direction of emotional design.

No matter how different emotions classified by many psychologists, it is undeniable that they regard pleasure as the most basic and primitive human emotion. It is a major positive emotion. The famous psychologist Donald A. Norman said in his Design Psychology, "Beautiful, fun and happy common action will produce feeling of pleasant feeling, it is a positive emotional state."

About the pleasurable emotion classification, Patrick Jordan in "Designing Pleasurable Products" proposed four kinds of pleasure. It has a representative and reference value.

Physical Pleasure
The physical pleasure includes sight, sound, smell, taste and touch these five senses. It is the most primitive response on instinct level, which is before consciousness and thinking.

Social Pleasure
Social Pleasure is derived from the interaction of objects and other people. It affected the role of product design in the relationship between people and the performance status of design products. Sometimes, social pleasure is used as a byproduct obtained.

Psychological Pleasure
Psychological pleasure is a pleasant feeling, which produced by the reactions or psychological conditions when people in contact with the design process. For products, usability and additional properties while using it play a decisive role.

Thought Pleasure
Thought Pleasure is due to people's values coincide with the design, this pleasant experience exists for thinking. For an example, if one product's target users are the young mothers, the design should present a feeling of warm and motherly to meet their expectations.

Instinctive Demand of Emotion Conversion . The 21st century civilization causes increasingly fast pace of life to people. In order to release the tension and maintain emotional balance and stability, people will produce extremely concerned about the negative situations, meanwhile worship of positive emotions such as pleasure.

Visual Pleasure
Vision is one of the most important senses, more than 80% of the information is acquired through the vision. Many facts show that, those design products, which bring users vision pleasure, are more accessible, and more likely to have a lasting emotional dependence. Many people even can work better and produce better results. For design, the visual information it conveys including design patterns, colors and materials. Designers combine these elements together and make them harmonious to achieve visual pleasure.

Color is the most direct method for transferring design information, rapidly and emotionally. Contemporary visual art psychologist Bloomer said: "Color evoke emotions, express their feelings, and even affect our normal physical feelings." [5] Kandinsky said: "Color is the most direct way to impact on the mind." [6]

Auditory Pleasure
Human auditory perception system is another main system to receive information. Auditory habits directly affect the acceptance of aesthetic judgment of human behavior. Thus, designers meditate their artwork just like composing a song. She/he must consider the overall design positioning, the sense of harmony and rhythm. This is the only way to impress the audience through people-oriented spirit, to bring the audience a pleasant emotional experience.

In addition, there are tactile pleasure, the gustatory pleasure and the olfactory pleasure. In short, it is a great way to study the expression of pleasing design from the perspective of human senses.

Spiritual Pleasure of Design
People will get a variety of information, intuitive feelings, emotions and other physiological and psychological reactions when contact with pleasing design, which is usually designed to reflect the spiritual level. Here, we will discuss four aspects of the expression of designing a spiritual pleasure, which are creating artistic conception, enriching meanings, happy memories and pleasant experience.

Memories
The process of recall involves the audience's senses, emotions and other emotional factors that can cause memories is one of the methods to express pleasant feelings. Many people are fond of a singer, a band even a piece of music for many years. When they are involved in a Co-pulse music performance, in will produce more long-term memories because of a special light effects with a particular song. What's more, the wristband with artist logo will be a reminder, which arouses sweet memories.

As one of the major positive emotions, the pleasure attracts many attentions and thinking in a wide field. Currently, how to design the product so that the audience can fully experience the pleasure is an important topic on design.

3   User Research

The purpose of this study is to enhance the experience of live concert through emotional interactive product design. We first conducted a literature survey on the basis of target users.

Concert consumers are concentrated in the age group of 18-35. These young people's consumption for concerts also has its specific features, which include:

- Visual and auditory consumption: Audio equipment, the actors' clothing, optical performances, stage design, atmosphere (such as cannons and light sticks) play an important role of a successful concert.
- Group consumption

These audiences also have some personal psychological features:

Consumer motivation
Concert consumption is a kind of highly emotional consumption type. People choose to pay money on a concert is usually because the worship of a star, or just curious about this consumption pattern. However, this is not endless. Audience may not go to a concert without hesitation, that's because they also measure the cost and the benefit.

Consumer awareness
Most of the concert audience are focused on 18-35 years old. They like to be a personalized and innovative consumer. These people have highly awareness of relevant

concert information, especially those favorite singers they love. They are very concerned about their movement. Once the concert will be held near their residence, it will produce a great attraction immediately. What's more, this information always spreads in friends and families, which for-matting the assembled consumption easily.

Learning consumption

Concert consumption is a kind of learning consumption. Experience has a great impact on consumer motivation. This experience has two sources, one is the visual experience in the past, and the other is the experience from the surrounding community. If the last concert left a deep impression to someone, he is likely to continue paying on same concerts.

Then we conducted a user investigation through questionnaires and random interviews. We posted a user study questionnaire on the network, finally collected 76 valid answers.

45 (59.2%) males and 31 (40.8%) females, a total of 76 people finished this questionnaire validly. Most (52, 68.4%) people are undergraduate degree; others are master degree 16 (21.0%), PhD 6 (7.9%) and senior middle school 2 (2.6%). All of the respondents' age distributed from 19 to 30. They came from very diverse backgrounds, 21 (27.6%) people are major in art or related fields, while others are from education, computer science etc.. 54 (71.0%) people thought that they have an outgoing personality. Only 5 (6.6%) people said they usually went to a concert alone.

In the early stage of design, in order to minimize the user's learning cost, we want to make a re-design on some familiar items. Therefore, we investigated what kind of items the audience will use during the concert. Almost all (97.4%) of the users will take their mobile phone(s) and a lot of (84.2%) people will bring a camera. Of course, the audience usually used sticks, colorful plates and other props which provided by the organizers.

In addition, we also did a literature research on the reactions when people listening to music, both on psychological and physiological aspects.

Music cognition is a complex process of people that requires a comprehensive mobilization of auditory attention, perception, sound model analysis, memory, emotional experience and other capabilities to complete (Koelsch & Siebel, 2005), which covers almost cognitive activities all aspects.

Rhythm is the most important element for music. Without rhythm, it won't be the music. Beat is an important part of the rhythm. The beat refers to the combination of the strong one and the weak one. The beat in music is the significance of the relationship between the strength to organize music (Cooper & Meyer, 1960).

There are also some scholars conducted researches carried out for the relationship between music beat and the movement. It proved that the tempo and the motion perception have neural basis. In musical performances, hearing has been one step ahead, occupying the dominant position of these five senses. The human body's natural rhythm and the music rhythm follow each other: fast tempo for percussion or a forward, slow pace for walking or swaying. This innate instinctive reaction is on visceral level.

This explains why people will swing their body with the rhythm while they are listening to music, especially those strong senses of rhythm music. Some people gently beat the desk, while others use feet hit the ground, what's more, somebody even dances excitedly. Based on the above, the conversion of human emotional needs, we use lighting effects to enhance this rhythm, so that the audience will feel more pleasant.

4   Prototype

We made a prototype to simulate the concert situation. The prototype consists of two parts: the spot light control system and the audience wristbands. (As illustrated in Fig. 1.)

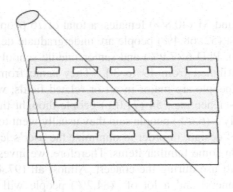

Fig. 1. A simulation of the stage

Each wristband consists of three modules: an information receiving module, a visualization and information-delivering module, and a processor. In our prototype, a visible-light-sensitive photodiode is used to receive information. The photodiode generates a high level digital pulse when a direct spot light turns on, and vice versa. Immediately it receives the high-low digital pulses, the processor interprets them into corresponding directions, which directs the visualization module to light accordingly. We use full-color LED as the visualization module. Since it also generates visible light, the LED can deliver information as well. So not only the information can be transmit-ted from spotlight, but also between wristbands. (As illustrated in Fig. 2)

The spotlight system delivers information by frequently turns on and off the light. When the frequency exceeds 30Hz, there is no visible flicker effect for human eyes. However the photodiode module has a response time little as 10 microseconds, therefore the spot light system can flicker at nearly 100 kHz. Encoded information between a start and end code is transmitted through the spot light, which directs the wristbands to light. Different spotlights transmitted different codes, so the wristband can distinguish them regardless of their identity to human eyes.

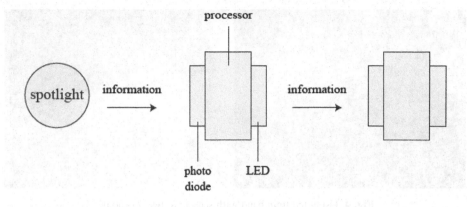

Fig. 2.

Since LED is a visible light source, it can deliver information as well. So the LED works both as the visualization module and the information-delivering module, but at different frequency bands. The visualization module uses the frequency band from 0 to 30 Hz, which can be perceived by human eyes at comfort. And information-delivering module occupies the frequency band from 10 to 100 kHz, which is adequate for communication. The two frequency bands do not overlap, so the LED can visualize and deliver information at the same time. The direction conveyed in the high frequency light includes how the next wristband should visualize, and also how it should deliver information to the next wristband. So if the direction demands the next wristband to deliver an identical direction as itself, the visualization will spread. But if the direction demands a little change of the next direction, the visualization will evolve when spread. This very flexible mechanism enables a huge possibility of visualization of the crowd. (As illustrated in Fig. 3)

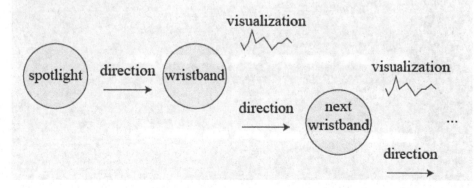

Fig. 3.

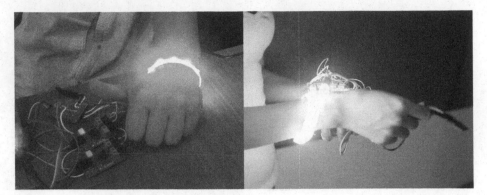

Fig. 4. Using led light band with sensors to test prototype

Due to the special context of this research, we can only used the prototype to simulate scenarios. Images (Fig.4) below presents the design process of prototype.

When the audience hear their favorite songs and wave their arms with regular rhythm, the smart wristband can identify his movement and change the luminance accordingly. In addition, the performers can adjust the direction of the spotlight and its code, and then, send color information to the audience towards a specify location. The wristbands receive information and show the color effect immediately. Performers and the audience can demonstrate a stunning color brush effect on the auditorium.

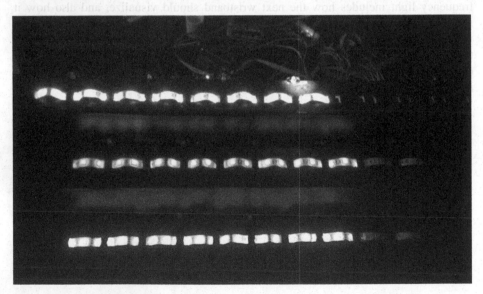

Fig. 5. Use prototype to simulate the audience wearing wristbands on the stage

Fig. 6. A 3d model effect of Co-Pulse wristband

5   Conclusion and Discussion

An outstanding art work not only carries the artist's own emotions, but also causes the emotional experience of the participants. Co-pulse as a light medium, makes the audience convert from the passive enjoyment to participating in the process of creation. This will promote long-term relationships between the user and the music. This paper can also provide some guidance and reference for culture-related emotional design in the future.

Reference

1. Schacter, D.L.: Psychology, 2nd edn., p. 310. Worth Publishers, New York (2011) ISBN 978-1-4292-3719-2
2. Scherer, K.R.: What are emotions? And how can they be measured? Social Science Information 44, 693–727 (2005)
3. Solomon, R.L.: The opponent-process theory of motivation: The costs of pleasure and the benefits of pain. American Psychologist 35, 691–712 (1980)
4. Norman, D.A.: Emotional design: Why we love (or hate) everyday things. Basic books (2007)
5. Bloomer, C.M.: Principles of visual perception, p. 129. Design Press, New York (1990)
6. Kandinsky, W.: Concerning the spiritual in art. Courier Dover Publications (2012)

Fig. 6. A 3d model effect of UC, Future wristband.

5   Conclusion and Discussion

An outstanding artwork not only carries the artist's own emotions, but also causes the emotional experience of the participants. Co-paint as a light medium, makes the artwork investigate the paint's enjoyment to participating in the process of creation. This will promote long-term relationships between the user and the music. This paper can also provide some guidance and reference for culture-related emotional design in the future.

Reference

1. Schacter, D.L.: Psychology, 2nd edn., p. 310. Worth Publishers, New York (2011) ISBN 9781429237192

2. Scherer, K.R.: What are emotions? And how can they be measured? Social Science Information 44(4), 695 (2005)

3. Sullivan, P.R.: The experience-sense theory of imagination. The logic of pleasure and the function. American Psychologist 35, 6–312 (1980)

4. Norman, D.A.: Emotional design: Why we love (or hate) everyday things. Basic books (2005)

5. Klanten, R.M.: Data flow: visualising information, p. 126. Design Press, New York (1990)

6. Kandinsky, W.: Concerning the spiritual in art. Courier Dover Publications (2012)

Author Index